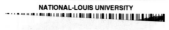

Case Incidents in Counseling for International Transitions

Edited by
Nancy Arthur and Paul Pedersen

AMERICAN COUNSELING ASSOCIATION
5999 Stevenson Avenue
Alexandria, VA 22304
www.counseling.org

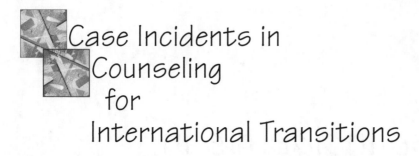

Case Incidents in Counseling for International Transitions

10 9 8 7 6 5 4 3 2 1

American Counseling Association
5999 Stevenson Avenue
Alexandria, VA 22304

Director of Publications • Carolyn C. Baker

Production Manager • Bonny E. Gaston

Copy Editor • Judith O. Johnson

Editorial Assistant • Catherine A. Brumley

Cover and text design by Bonny E. Gaston.

Library of Congress Cataloging-in-Publication Data
Case incidents in counseling for international transitions / edited by Nancy Arthur and Paul Pedersen.
   p.   cm.
  ISBN 978-1-55620-269-8 (alk. paper)
1. Cross-cultural counseling—Case studies.   I. Arthur, Nancy, 1957–   II. Pedersen, Paul, 1936--

BF636.7.C76C37 2008
158'.3—dc22   2007040996

Dedication

This book is dedicated to my father, Frederick Arthur, who passed away in November 2005, during the time of preparing this book. He was a father who showed keen interest in the world around him, past and present, and he never tired of hearing my stories about travel and work with people from many countries.

—*Nancy Arthur*

This book is dedicated to my 5½ grandchildren, Emily, Mandy, Jacob, Jack, Sammy, and (???). May we provide for their future as our grandparents provided for ours.

—*Paul Pedersen*

Acknowledgment

This edited collection was supported in part by a research grant awarded to Dr. Nancy Arthur from the Social Sciences and Humanities Research Council of Canada, Standard Grants Program, Award No. 410-200S-0530.

Table of Contents

Foreword   ix
   Allen E. Ivey
Introduction   xi
   Nancy Arthur and Paul Pedersen
About the Editors   xv
Contributors   xvii

Part 1
International Work Transitions

Case Incident 1
   Dual-Career Transitions   3
     Incident: *Roberta Neault*
     Responses: *Mary J. Heppner, P. Paul Heppner, Margaret (Peggy) Pusch*

Case Incident 2
   Transition and Adaptation to Living and Working Across Cultures   17
     Incident: *Karen Moustafa-Leonard*
     Responses: *Yu-Wei Wang, Julia A. Conrath, Sauli Puukari*

Case Incident 3
   When Cultures Clash   37
     Incident: *Christine Wihak*
     Responses: *Arthur Blue, Meredith Rogers Blue, Les Couchie, Wes G. Darou,*
     Jacques Kurtness, Pam Deters, Shu-Ping Lin

Case Incident 4
   A Successful International Transition   51
     Incident: *Dale S. Furbish*
     Responses: *Roberta Neault, Christine Wihak*

Part 2
International Student Transitions

Case Incident 5
   Multiple Transition Issues in Living and Learning Across Cultures   67
     Incident: *Natalee Popadiuk*
     Responses: *Hemla D. Singaravelu, Paul Pedersen*

Case Incident 6
Establishing a Sense of Belonging   81
   Incident: *Sauli Puukari*
   Responses: *S. Alvin Leung, Ella P. O. Chan, Kenneth Cushner*

Case Incident 7
Family and Home Country Influences on Adjustment   99
   Incident: *Kenneth Cushner*
   Responses: *Frederick T. L. Leong, Huaiyu Zhang, John Pickering,*
      Jonie Chang

Case Incident 8
Identity Confusion   113
   Incident: *John Stewart*
   Responses: *Daya Singh Sandhu, Charles P. Chen*

Case Incident 9
Managing Multiple Identities   131
   Incident: *Huaiyu Zhang, Frederick T. L. Leong*
   Responses: *John Stewart, Natalee Popadiuk*

Part 3
Immigrant and Refugee Transitions

Case Incident 10
Counseling for Transition Trauma and Health Concerns   151
   Incident: *Marianne C. Kastrup, Armando Báez-Ramos*
   Responses: *Roy Moodley, Dina B. Lubin, Saadia Akram, Monica Justin*

Case Incident 11
Integration and Identity Issues   169
   Incident: *Maria Assumpta Aneas Alvarez*
   Responses: *Mary McMahon, Mark Watson, Beatriz Malik,*
      María-Fe Sánchez García

Case Incident 12
Cross-Cultural Adjustment for Professional Immigrant Families   189
   Incident: *Noorfarah Merali*
   Responses: *Caridad Sanchez-Leguelinel, Jaya T. Mathew,*
      Joseph G. Ponterotto, Adam Zagelbaum, Jon Carlson

Case Incident 13
Coping With Isolation and Family Losses   209
   Incident: *Dina B. Lubin*
   Responses: *Noorfarah Merali, Pamela M. Clayton*

Case Incident 14
Second-Generation Issues for Young Women   225
   Incident: *Monica Justin*
   Responses: *Ellen P. Cook, Elizabeth Mathew, Mary Fukuyama*

Case Incident 15

Between Hope and Despair   245
   Incident: *Rachel Erhard*
   Responses: *Marianne C. Kastrup, Armando Báez-Ramos, Juris G. Draguns*

Part 4
Military and Peacekeeping Transitions

Case Incident 16

The Complexity of Adapting Under Stress   263
   Incident: *Stefan Kammhuber, Georg F. Fuchs*
   Responses: *Patrice Keats, Nancy Bernardy*

Case Incident 17

Counseling Military Personnel Following Traumatic Events   281
   Incident: *Philip Armstrong*
   Responses: *Marvin Westwood, Timothy G. Black, Thomas W. Britt,*
      Cynthia L. S. Pury

Case Incident 18

The Transition From Veteran Life to the Civilian World   297
   Incident: *Marvin Westwood, Timothy G. Black*
   Responses: *Stefan Kammhuber, Alexander Cowell McFarlane*

Case Incident 19

Pursuing International Humanitarian Aid Assignments   313
   Incident: *Sauli Puukari*
   Responses: *Claire O'Reilly, Julia Bürger, Karen Grant*

Foreword

This is a book "with a difference." It does not just talk about culture; rather it shows culture and cultural conflict in clear and active forms. Through a careful examination, the reader will see cultural difference and cultural conflict in new ways. I see this book as useful in many settings, ranging from management to counselor education and from international student work to those seeking new and different experiences throughout the world.

All the cases are well written, readable, and about fascinating issues. Due to my experiences in the Central Artic (Cambridge Bay, Coppermine, Inuvik), I was drawn to the story of Rebecca, an idealistic young social worker, who spent 2 years in Nunavut. Rebecca chose to focus on two example problems she faced. The most dramatic was when she saw Inuit children poking and teasing a caged polar bear cub. Her subsequent protection of the bear led her to be called "Rebecca Greenpeace" and thus set up a chain of events that made it extremely difficult for her to be helpful to the community. The interesting case is followed by expert cultural analysis that promotes thought and discussion as to culturally appropriate responses when one is not prepared.

As I worked through the book, I found consistently interesting and challenging scenarios, ranging from moving permanently to a new setting halfway around the world, the experiences of international students, and the challenge of "coming home" after a successful international experience. Particularly touching and important are the discussions of refugee and immigrant populations—each one different, but full of learning for all of us as educators, counselors, managers, and others. I think the section on refugees contains enough material for a course in itself.

The last section of the book focuses on military and peacekeeping personnel, particularly relevant during this time of the Iraq War and continued conflict and challenges faced around the world in countries such as Afghanistan. The importance of adequate preparation and sufficient debriefing after war experiences is stressed. Again, this is a section that all counselors and therapists need to read and understand.

Full of human experience, rich with detail, this book can make a difference in your practice, your teaching, and your business. I recommend it highly and know that you will enjoy the stories and analysis as much as I have.

—*Allen E. Ivey*, EdD, ABPP
Distinguished University Professor (Emeritus)
University of Massachusetts, Amherst
and
Courtesy Professor
University of South Florida, Tampa

Introduction

Multiculturalism has had a profound impact on the field of counseling in recent years, especially with regard to nondominant groups and providing services to culturally and linguistically diverse people. We believe the next big step for multicultural counseling will be to include internationalism along with domestic perspectives of multiculturalism in the preparation and training of counselors. A number of exciting initiatives in the field of counseling psychology suggest that we are already taking this step forward. For example, Leong and Savickas (2007) edited a special issue of *Applied Psychology: An International Review* about the international perspectives of counseling psychology. This special issue was intended both to document the new interest in international perspectives for counseling and to publish a resource that contributes toward that perspective. The International Association of Applied Psychology now has a Division of Counseling Psychology that sponsored this special issue. The articles in that special issue describe the practice of counseling in a variety of international contexts and identify a range of resources for each context. Division 17 of the American Psychological Association (Counseling Psychology) also has a special interest group on international counseling. The International Section "announce-only" electronic mailing list is available to its members and affiliates. Visit the section's Web site at www.internationalcounselingpsychology.org.

This collection of case incidents is intended to provide resources for counselors and counselor educators who are providing services to clients in an international context. The project stemmed from our mutual interest in supporting people during international transitions. Both of us have worked extensively with international students and workers, and our careers have revolved around preparing people for living, working, and learning across cultures. In planning for the edited collection, we immediately agreed that it was important to provide readers with material that would help make the conceptual issues come alive through the experiences of real people. To that end, we chose the critical incident method as a way of providing an expanded view of counseling to incorporate international contexts.

There is a rich literature about critical incidents, particularly when looking at multicultural issues. The critical incident technique was first described by J. C. Flanagan (1954; Flanagan & Burns, 1955) to analyze jobs. The method involves collecting anecdotes describing effective and ineffective behaviors at a particular site or workplace. These anecdotal examples are called *critical incidents*, meaning important, essential, or valuable. Each incident describes a specific example of success or failure in which the writer describes (a) the events that led up to the incident and their context, (b) what the person did (or did not) do that was effective or ineffective, (c) the apparent consequences of this behavior, and (d) whether any of the consequences were under the person's control to change.

The critical incident technique is closely related to the case study method, which evaluates the behavior of a person or persons in a clinical or decision-making setting, examining background, behavior, and changes in behavior over a period of months or years. A critical incident is a short description of an event that took place within a 5- or 10-minute period of time. A case study, by contrast, is much more complicated and might take place over weeks, months, or even years.

A major advantage of critical incidents is the focus on observable behaviors. It could be argued, however, that critical incidents tend to emphasize the extraordinary rather than the average or typical situation, which distorts or exaggerates aspects of the experience. Yet, when critical incidents are based on real people's experiences, they are often more appealing and easier to relate to than the experiences contrived about fictitious characters.

Critical incidents are particularly popular in teaching or training about multicultural relationships. In part, it is because critical incidents are more open-ended and include the complexity of real-life situations in which persons from more than one culture come into contact. There is no substitute for actual experience; however, the critical incident technique is an attempt to bring actual experiences and events to the readers as a resource. Although it is often difficult to reach consensus about the appropriate response in a multicultural critical incident, we want to encourage our readers to consider multiple perspectives.

We used critical incidents as the basis for this edited collection to provide a focal point for constructing the essence of international transitions and for deconstructing the issues that are relevant for counseling. The critical incidents contained in this edited collection are based on real-life situations and typically involve a dilemma in which there is no easy or obvious solution. The objective of basing our book on critical incidents is to stimulate thinking about basic and important issues that occur in real-life international transitions. By analyzing the incident, readers might imagine themselves in the same situation or imagine themselves in the role of counselor and develop strategies to deal with that situation. Critical incidents do not necessarily imply a single solution or a "right way" of resolving the dilemma in a situation, but they explore alternative solutions and their implications or consequences.

Critical incidents are often formatted in brief vignettes. Given the complexities involved in international transitions, we felt that readers would benefit from additional contextual information to appreciate the critical incident examples. We invited authors to provide background information, key issues for counseling, their role (if relevant) in relation to specific critical incidents, a brief analysis, and the implications for multicultural counseling. The contributors for this edited collection gave us far more than we originally expected. Readers will see the breadth of the examples as the stage is set for each critical incident. They will find themselves inside of the example as they feel the emotions of the people, realize their insights, and take on the challenges of helping people who embark on international transitions. Given the detailed text provided by our contributing authors, we decided to recast the book as *Case Incidents in Counseling for International Transitions*.

A key theme in the book is that culture is an ever-present influence in international transitions. Many times, counselors work with a diverse range of clients whose counseling issues center on their experience of international transitions. Counselors require understanding about the nature of international transitions, knowledge about conceptual frameworks for appreciating emergent issues, and expertise for helping clients select relevant interventions. Along with expertise about international transitions, counselors are invited to consider their levels of multicultural counseling competence. Counselors need to be skilled at helping clients appreciate their personal cultural beliefs and how these may be challenged through international transitions. However, we hope that this book also challenges counselors to examine their own cultural beliefs and how their views of the case incidents may be culturally bound. To that end, the book offers multiple perspectives to help readers reflect about the events, issues, and expanded opportunities associated with counseling for international transitions.

The book is organized around specific populations. For this edited collection, the focus is placed on international workers, international students, immigrants and refugees, and military and peacekeeping personnel. What will soon become apparent in reading the book is the nice range of diversity among the case incidents. We feel that the authors have provided insightful examples of the unique issues faced by groups of people during international transition while highlighting the nuances of individual circumstances. At the same time, we hope that readers will appreciate how the boundaries between populations become blurred as the authors discuss some of the common issues that are faced when crossing countries and cultures. We also appreciated the authors' contributions to addressing the reentry transition after an international experience. The focus of many cross-cultural training programs typically is on the initial stage of engagement with a new culture. Readers will see from the collection of case incident examples targeting workers and students that returning home involves many aspects of negotiating their identity, relationships, and roles.

We organized the book to offer a plurality of perspectives on the case incidents. To this end, we are most appreciative of the work completed by our international cast of authors. The case incidents are situated in many different parts of the world, and the contributions of the authors come from their professional and personal experiences of living and working in many countries. We designed the book so that there are two responses for each case incident. We also welcomed collaboration for the case incident responses. In many instances, the lead author sought consultation with and inclusion of colleagues and graduate students who had an insider view of the cultures under examination. The diversity of authorship added immensely to the wealth of the theoretical and applied perspectives about counseling for international transitions.

We hope the book will appeal to a variety of audiences who wish to learn more about the nature of international transitions and counseling in an international context. We developed this edited collection with a focus on three audiences. First, counselor educators may use our approach for infusing multicultural counseling curriculum with relevant content found in the case incidents and analyses; second, counseling practitioners in education, business, and community settings may use the case incidents for informing their work with clients; and, third, individuals who are experiencing international transitions may gain personal insights, coping skills, and inspiration from the lives of people portrayed in the case incidents.

The book offers practical information on preparing people for embarking on an international transition, dealing with culture shock, trauma, and managing the reentry transition home. A key feature of the book is an emphasis on moving beyond detailing the problems associated with cross-cultural living to detailing many practical strategies for overcoming those issues and making international transitions a success. To that end, the content of the book emphasizes proactive counseling strategies to prepare individuals and reactive strategies to help them manage aspects of international transitions that they experience as overwhelming.

The published resources for counseling in an international context are limited in scope and availability. These case incident examples demonstrate the similarities and differences confronting counselors in an international context. The case incident examples will also demonstrate how to find human resources and resource persons to supplement written publications for teaching and training in the international context.

—*Nancy Arthur* and *Paul Pedersen*

References

Flanagan, J. C. (1954). The critical incident technique. *Psychological Bulletin, 51,* 327–358.

Flanagan J. C., & Burns, R. K. (1955). The employee performance record: A new appraisal and development tool. *Harvard Business Review, 33*(5), 95–102.

Leong, F. T. L., & Savickas, M. L. (2007). Introduction to special issue on international perspectives on counseling psychology. *Applied Psychology: An International Review, 56,* 1–6.

About the Editors

Nancy Arthur is a professor in the Division of Applied Psychology, Faculty of Education, and is a Canada Research Chair in Professional Education at the University of Calgary, Alberta, Canada. She received her master's degree in sociology from the University of Alberta before specializing in counseling psychology in master's and PhD degrees from the University of Calgary. Prior to pursuing a faculty role in 1996, she worked in postsecondary education as a counselor and as a psychologist in private practice. During her 15 years as a counselor with the Southern Alberta Institute of Technology, she worked with a diverse range of adult learners, including the coordination of services for international students. Her involvement with international projects as a consultant fostered a keen interest in the counseling and teaching implications of internationalization in higher education. Nancy is a registered psychologist and continues to work with clients through consulting and private practice.

Nancy's current research interests include professional education for cultural diversity and social justice. She has developed curriculum for both classroom and online delivery of courses on career development and multicultural counseling. In 2003, she received a Teaching Excellence Award from the Faculty of Education, University of Calgary.

She was a visiting scholar at Queensland University of Technology in Australia in 2003. She has been an active member of the Canadian Counselling Association, serving as president (2001–2002) of the Career Development Chapter. Nancy has been a consulting editor of the *Canadian Journal of Counselling* since 1995 and coedited a special issue on multicultural counseling, which was published in January 2001.

Nancy has published numerous articles and book chapters on multicultural counseling and cross-cultural career transitions, and she has extensive experience presenting in local and international forums on these topics. She authored the book, *Counseling International Students: Clients From Around the World.* Her coedited book with Sandra Collins, *Culture-Infused Counselling: Celebrating the Canadian Mosaic,* received the Canadian Counselling Association Book Award in 2006.

Paul Pedersen is a visiting professor in the Department of Psychology at the University of Hawaii. He has taught at the University of Minnesota; Syracuse University; University of Alabama at Birmingham; and for 6 years at universities in Taiwan, Malaysia, and Indonesia. He was also on the Summer School faculty at Harvard University, 1984–1988, and the University of Pittsburgh–Semester at Sea voyage around the world in spring 1992. His international experience includes numerous consulting experiences in Asia, Australia, Africa, South America, and Europe and a Senior Fulbright award teaching at National Taiwan University 1999–2000.

He has authored, coauthored, or edited 45 books, 100 articles, 82 chapters, and 22 monographs on aspects of multicultural counseling and international communication. He is a fellow in Divisions 9, 17, 45, and 52 of the American Psychological Association. Research activities include codirector of research for a 10-day intercultural communication laboratory for 60 Japanese/U.S. intercultural communication experts at Nihonmatsu, Japan, funded by the Lily Foundation; reentry research among LASPAU: Academic and Professional Programs for the Americas students from Brazil; director of Higher Education Research on Sex-Role Stereotypes in Higher Education on a Department of Health, Education, and Welfare grant; director of a 3-year National Institute of Mental Health mental health training program; a National Science Foundation 6-year grant to study the reentry adjustment of engineers returning to Taiwan after study abroad; National Institute of Education grant to develop a measure of cross-cultural counseling skill; State of New York Department of Social Services grant to develop mental health training materials on unaccompanied refugee minors; a 2-year Harvard Institute for International Development project in Indonesia to evaluate and upgrade training at Bank Rakyat Training Centers; and an Asian Foundation grant to co-organize a conference in Penang, Malaysia, on constructive conflict management in a cultural context.

Professional activities include 3 years of presidency of the 1,800-member Society for Intercultural Education Training and Research; senior editor of *Multicultural Aspects of Counseling* series; advising editor for education and psychology, Greenwood Press book series; board member of the Micronesian Institute, headquartered in Washington, DC; external examiner for Universiti Putra Malaysia, Universiti Kebangsaan, and Universiti Malaysia Sabah in psychology; senior Fulbright scholar teaching at the National Taiwan University 1999–2000; member of the Committee for International Relations in Psychology at the American Psychological Association 2001–2003; master lecturer, American Psychological Association, Los Angeles, August, 1994; and senior fellow at the East West Center, Honolulu, Hawaii, 1975–1976 and 1978–1981.

Contributors

Saadia Akram, psychotherapist and clinical member of the Ontario Society of Psychotherapists, operates her private practice in Toronto, Ontario, Canada. She has more than 15 years of experience helping individuals, couples, and families with a variety of psychosocial issues. She has a deep understanding of diversity and multicultural issues. Saadia has MA and MEd degrees in psychology as well as a post–master's degree specialization in clinical psychology. She has worked more than 15 years in the nonprofit, community-based sector and gained experience in working with diverse, newcomer, and immigrant populations. She has participated in various research projects, and her articles have also been published in professional journals. Her book *Abnormal Psychology* has been recommended for master's-degree studies. She has received special training in facilitating groups and workshops and has organized several staff development trainings and community education forums. She provides services in English, Urdu, Punjabi, and Hindi.

Maria Assumpta Aneas Alvarez is a lecturer at the Faculty of Pedagogy of the Universitat de Barcelona, Spain, where she teaches counseling for professional integration, intercultural competencies, and methods of research. Her doctoral thesis was the first doctoral research about intercultural counseling in Spain. Maria has experience as a counselor in different kinds of organizations (public and private) and collectives. She has done research on counseling, gender, youth, and immigrants. As one of the pioneers of intercultural counseling in Spain, she has presented work at the international congress of the Society for Intercultural Education and Training (SIETAR) Europa, SIETAR USA, and International Academy of Intercultural Research (IAIR) and has developed training resources for Diversophy (Working in Spain) and Cultural Detective (Spain). She is a member of the IAIR and SIETAR Europa and is currently president of SIETAR España.

Philip Armstrong has a graduate degree in counseling from the University of New England, a diploma of applied science (counseling), diploma of psychology, diploma of child psychology, and statement of attainment in professional supervision. Philip is the current chief executive officer of the Australian Counselling Association and clinical director of the Clinical Counselling Centre in Brisbane, Queensland, Australia. He is also involved in curriculum development and is editor of the peer-reviewed journal *Counselling Australia* and coeditor of *cphJournal.com,* an international professional research journal. Philip has previously authored *Establishing an Allied Health Service,* been one of three lead coauthors of *Practice of Counselling,* contributed to *Technology in Counselling and Psychotherapy Practice: A Practitioners' Guide,* and coauthored the chapter "Professional Supervision via the Phone." Philip is currently involved in several other publishing projects. He is a recipient of the Defence Force Service Medal and the Defence Medal for service in the Australian Army and is married with three children.

Armando Báez-Ramos was born in Mexico City and received MD (1988) and PhD (1998) degrees from the National University of Mexico. He completed training in psychiatry

(1988–1992) in Mexico City and moved to Denmark in 1999, where he became certified as a psychiatrist by the National Ministry of Health in 2007. His areas of interest include cognitive therapy, consulation-liason psychiatry, anxiety, depression, transcultural psychiatry, and classical psychopathology. He has been appointed to consultant psychiatrist positions both in Mexico City and in Copenhagen. He has been involved in collaborative work with different groups regarding cultural aspects in psychiatry and teaches psychiatric trainees and other professionals in the area. He currently works as a consultant psychiatrist and is head of the outpatient clinic, the University Hospital Gentofte in Copenhagen, and clinical assistant lecturer at Copenhagen University, Denmark.

Nancy Bernardy is a clinical psychologist and is the director of Army Community Services in Schinnen, the Netherlands. She worked for the past 3 years as a clinical director for the Army Substance Abuse Program. Nancy moved to Europe in 2004 after working at the National Center for Posttraumatic Stress Disorder (PTSD) in Vermont, where she held an appointment at Dartmouth College. She trained extensively in assessments and psychotherapy treatments for PTSD and was the coordinator of two clinical trials of treatments for PTSD. She received a PhD in biological psychology from the University of Oklahoma in 1995 and went to Yale University to do a postdoctoral clinical fellowship in substance abuse treatment research in the Department of Psychiatry. While there, she respecialized in clinical psychology and was licensed.

Timothy G. Black, PhD, is an assistant professor of counseling psychology at the University of Victoria in Victoria, British Columbia, Canada. Focuses of Tim's research include the transition of military members to civilian life as well as the teaching of trauma counseling to graduate students. He is a published author in the areas of military-to-civilian transition, teaching trauma to graduate counselors, integral approaches to counseling ethics, and posttraumatic stress disorder. Tim's clinical work includes a specialization in group therapy with military and civilian populations as well as individual trauma therapy, life transitions, and career counseling. He codeveloped the group-based Canadian Military and Veterans Transition Program (CMVTP) with Marvin Westwood and facilitates CMVTP groups on an ongoing basis.

Arthur Blue is professor emeritus of native studies at Brandon University, Manitoba, Canada. He was trained as a clinical psychologist and practiced at the Open Arrow Clinic in Carberry, Manitoba. He was the first president of the Native Psychologists in Canada and chairman of the Board of Editors for the *Journal of Canadian Native Studies*.

Meredith Rogers Blue, MD, is a family physician forced into retirement by disabling chronic illness. She has served as a member of the Board of the Society for the Advancement of Native Studies, Member of Native Physicians in Canada.

Thomas W. Britt received his PhD in social psychology from the University of Florida in 1994 and then entered active duty as a research psychologist in the U.S. Army. He was stationed in Heidelberg, Germany, from 1994 until 1997, and during that time he deployed to Saudi Arabia, Bosnia, Hungary, and Kazakhstan to study stress, motivation, and health among soldiers deployed in support of different types of military operations. After spending 2 years at the Walter Reed Army Institute of Research in Washington, DC, he spent a year at King College in Bristol, Tennessee. He was hired by Clemson University in the fall of 2000 and was promoted to full professor in August of 2007. He has published extensively in the areas of military psychology, self-engagement at work and other locations, and organizational stress and resiliency. He recently coedited a four-volume series titled *Military Life: The Psychology of Serving in Peace and Combat*.

Julia Bürger obtained her master's degree in psychology from the University of Regensburg, Germany, in 2002. From 2003 to 2005, she worked as a full-time academic research assistant at the University of Regensburg for the research project Intercultural Problems Related to Leadership in German-Czech Companies: Analysis and Solutions and has recently published widely on the findings of this research. She also worked as a lecturer at the University of Regensburg for the interdisciplinary study program, Intercultural Competence, for 5 years before joining University College Cork, Ireland, in March 2006. She is currently working on her doctoral dissertation titled "Bicultural Training Groups: Design and Evaluation of Training to Improve Cultural Understanding," focusing on German–Irish and German–Czech bicultural training groups.

Jon Carlson, PsyD, EdD, ABPP, is distinguished professor, psychology and counseling, at Governors State University and a psychologist at the Wellness Clinic in Lake Geneva, Wisconsin. Jon has served as editor of several periodicals, including the *Journal of Individual Psychology* and *The Family Journal.* He holds diplomates in both family psychology and Adlerian psychology. He has authored 150 journal articles and 40 books, including *Time for a Better Marriage, Adlerian Therapy, The Mummy at the Dining Room Table, Bad Therapy, The Client Who Changed Me,* and *Moved by the Spirit.* He has created more than 200 professional trade videos and DVDs with leading professional therapists and educators. In 2004, the American Counseling Association named him a "Living Legend." Recently, he syndicated the advice cartoon *On The Edge* with cartoonist Joe Martin.

Ella P. O. Chan received her formal education in Hong Kong, where she began her career as a secondary school teacher. Ella immigrated to Toronto, Ontario, Canada, with her family in 1990 and worked as a guidance counselor at the North York public school board. She also received training from the Gestalt Institute of Toronto as a gestalt therapist. She returned to Hong Kong in 1997 with her family to continue her lifelong education and career in counseling. She received her EdD degree (counseling psychology) from The Chinese University of Hong Kong in 2003. Currently, she is associate dean of the School of Continuing Education at the Hong Kong Baptist University. In addition to her full-time career, she also teaches counseling-related courses for a number of academic institutions, including The Chinese University of Hong Kong. Ella's major areas of scholarly interest include group counseling, career guidance and counseling, gestalt therapy, personal growth, and parenting.

Jonie Chang is a Chinese immigrant in New Zealand. She has a BA degree from the University of Canterbury, New Zealand, majoring in education. She worked with children and teenagers with mental and/or intellectual challenges as well as their families prior to her appointment as an international student adviser at the University of Canterbury in 2003. She is interested in the area of cross-cultural transition and family counseling and is now pursuing a master's degree at Massey University, doing research on international students and their families, which led to her receiving the 2005 University of Canterbury Vice-Chancellor's Staff Development Award.

Charles P. Chen, PhD, is an associate professor of counseling psychology and a Canada Research Chair in life career development at the University of Toronto, Ontario, Canada, where he was the inaugural recipient of the 2005 OISE/UT David E. Hunt Award for Excellence in Graduate Teaching. Charles is a visiting professor in applied psychology at the Educational Science College of Shanghai Normal University, China. He has also been a guest professor at the Faculty of Education, University of Pretoria, South Africa. He has served as an academic examiner/assessor nationally and internationally. He also serves as an editorial board member for several international journals. Charles is a regular conference presenter, a guest speaker in various professional contexts, and a featured expert in news media. He publishes extensively in refereed scholarly journals and has authored several book chapters. He is the author of the book, *Career Endeavour: Pursuing a Cross-Cultural Life Transition.*

Pamela M. Clayton received her PhD in political sociology. She is a research fellow in the Department of Adult and Continuing Education at the Faculty of Education of the University of Glasgow, Scotland U.K. She is the author of a variety of publications on vocational guidance especially targeted to those subject to risk of social exclusion. Her recent publications include "Blank Slates or Hidden Treasure? Assessing and Building on the Experiential Learning of Migrant and Refugee Women in European Countries" in the *International Journal of Lifelong Education* and "Counselling Immigrant Adults at an Educational Institution" (with I. Maunonen-Eskelinen and L. Kaikkonen) in *Multicultural Counselling—Foundations and Best Practices in Europe.*

Julia A. Conrath is a graduate student in the Counseling Psychology Program at Southern Illinois University at Carbondale. She received her BA degree in psychology from the University of the Incarnate Word in San Antonio, Texas, in 2005. Her primary research interests include stress and coping of international students, cross-cultural psychology, and substance abuse.

Ellen P. Cook is a professor in the Counseling Program at the University of Cincinnati. She received a PhD in counseling psychology from the University of Iowa in 1977 and has been a counselor educator since then. Her numerous publications and presentations are in the areas of ecological counseling, career development, and gender issues. Her fourth book, currently in progress, explores recent developments in ecological counseling theory and practice. She holds professional licenses as a clinical counselor and psychologist in the state of Ohio and is a fellow of the American Psychological Association. She is also an ordained vocational deacon in the Episcopal Church and focuses her service on individual and congregational spiritual development.

Les Couchie is director of operations of the Anishinabek Nation 7th Generations Charity at the Union of Ontario Indians in North Bay, Ontario, Canada. He has devoted 25 years of service in the Aboriginal community, ranging from alcohol counseling, police officer, economic development, career education development, Aboriginal postsecondary education, and provincial charity work both for the Aboriginal and mainstream sectors.

Kenneth Cushner is executive director of international affairs and professor of education in the College and Graduate School of Education, Health and Human Services, at Kent State University, Kent, Ohio. He is author or editor of several books and articles in the field of intercultural education and training, including *Intercultural Student Teaching, Human Diversity in Education: An Integrative Approach, Human Diversity in Action: Developing Multicultural Competencies in the Classroom, Beyond Tourism: A Practical Guide to Meaningful Educational Travel, International Perspectives on Intercultural Education,* and *Intercultural Interactions: A Practical Guide* (2nd edition; with Richard Brislin). He is a founding fellow of the International Academy for Intercultural Research and, in his spare time, enjoys music (percussion and guitar), photography, and travel.

Wes G. Darou is senior risk management analyst for the Canadian International Development Agency (CIDA). Formerly, he was an education specialist in CIDA's Africa and Middle East Branch. He holds a doctorate in education from McGill University and an MSc in environmental engineering from the University of Waterloo. Wes has 25 years' experience in training, counseling, and development. His other interests include vocational training, gender equality, and First Nations development. Recent articles concern Ibrahima Sow's African personality model, First Nations counseling, and violence against girls in southern African schools.

Pam Deters is a licensed clinical psychologist in Alaska, and her expertise is in the area of American Indian and Alaska Native mental health. Her current research includes the investigation of trauma among Native children, families, and communities, with a particular emphasis on cultural revitalization and resilience subsequent to trauma. She serves as the statewide director of Alaska Natives Into Psychology, a University of Alaska training program supporting American Indian and Alaska Native graduate and undergraduate students pursuing careers in psychology. She is also recognized as a National Center for Minority Health Disparities scholar. She is a member of the Society of Indian Psychologists and currently serves as incoming coprogram chair for the American Psychological Association's Division 45—Society for the Psychological Study of Ethnic Minority Issues.

Juris G. Draguns was born in Latvia. Displaced during World War II, he graduated from high school in Germany and completed his undergraduate and graduate studies in the United States, with a PhD in clinical psychology from the University of Rochester. In 1967, he came to The Pennsylvania State University, where he was associate and full professor of clinical psychology and is now professor emeritus. He has taught and lectured, in six languages, in Australia, Germany, Latvia, Mexico, Sweden, Switzerland, and Taiwan. He is author or coauthor of more than 160 publications and has coedited 16 books, among them six editions of *Counseling Across Cultures*. His interests are focused on the interplay of culture with psychopathology, psychotherapy, counseling, and personality and on interethnic relations. He served as president of the Society for Cross-Cultural Research, received American Psychological Association's Award for Distinguished Contributions to the International Advancement of Psychology, and was awarded an honorary doctoral degree by the University of Latvia.

Rachel Erhard is head of the Graduate Program for School Counseling, School of Education, Tel Aviv University, Israel; head of Research & Development, Psychological and Counseling Services, Israeli Ministry of Education; and vice president, International Association of Counseling. As a scientific practitioner, she strives to enhance the development of a clear identity for the counseling profession that distinguishes it from other related helping professions. The mission of developing a professional paradigm has been channeled to create a theoretical and practical basis of knowledge. On one hand, she conceptualizes the role of the school counselor through research on beliefs, perceptions, attitudes, and role behavior in various educational settings. On the other hand, she develops methodologies, models, and programs of professional interventions. Her main interests and professional activities focus on issues such as social justice, social action, advocacy, and multicultural counseling. Among a variety of subjects, Rachel concentrates on introducing counseling into traditional sectors, such as the Jewish Ultra-Orthodox sector and the Israeli Arab sector.

Georg F. Fuchs was born May 30, 1965, in Burghausen, Germany. He joined the German armed forces as an officer in 1986 and holds the rank of lieutenant colonel. He has held different positions with the Mountain Infantry and in the Special Forces. During the last decade, he took part in operations in the Balkans (Bosnia-Herzegovina in 1999 and Macedonia in 2001) as well as being deployed to Afghanistan four times as an intelligence officer. For his service, he was decorated with the highest German military medal, two North Atlantic Treaty Organization medals, and the U.S. Combat Infantry Badge. His work in military concept development and intelligence, as well as his operational experience, makes him an expert on counterinsurgency operations and asymmetric warfare. He has written articles and conceptual documents and developed and conducted courses and briefings for the military and civilian institutions on these subjects. He has also worked as an expert on these subjects in a great many experiments and training exercises.

Mary A. Fukuyama received her PhD from Washington State University and has worked at the University of Florida Counseling Center for the past 25 years as a counseling psychologist, supervisor, and trainer. She is a clinical professor and teaches courses on multicultural counseling and spiritual issues for the Department of Counselor Education and the Counseling Psychology Program. She is an active member of the University of Florida's Center for Spirituality and Health, and her research interests include a qualitative study on multicultural expressions of spirituality. She coauthored, with Todd Sevig, a book titled *Integrating Spirituality Into Multicultural Counseling* and recently published a book with Woodrow M. Parker titled *Consciousness Raising: A Primer for Multicultural Counseling* (3rd edition). She is a fellow in Division 17 (Counseling Psychology) of the American Psychological Association.

Dale S. Furbish, EdD, is a senior lecturer and program leader for the Master of Career Development and the Graduate Diploma in Career at Auckland University of Technology,

Auckland, New Zealand. He is a native of the United States. He worked in U.S. higher education counseling centers for 20 years before immigrating to New Zealand with his wife Joan in 1996. Lifestyle, professional opportunities, and incomparable natural beauty were major influences on his decision to relocate to New Zealand. Dale is active in the Career Practitioner Association of New Zealand and has served as its president for two terms. He received the 2007 International Leadership Award from the National Career Development Association. Dale is interested in professional issues for New Zealand career counseling and has written a number of articles on this topic. He is also interested in international standards for career counseling and the impact of sabbaticals on career development.

María-Fe Sánchez García, PhD, is associate professor in career guidance at the Spanish University of Distance Education (Faculty of Education; UNED). She is currently head of the Careers Service at UNED. Her research has focused mainly on career guidance and development, guidance in higher education, cultural diversity in educational contexts, and gender equity. She coordinates a research group on career development and guidance at the university. Her publications include several articles in scientific journals, contributions to books (as sole author and as coauthor), and book chapters. Among others are *Necesidades y Servicios de Orientación Universitaria en la Comunidad de Madrid, Diversidad Cultural e Igualdad Escolar, Educar y Orientar Para laIgualdad en Razón del Género, Orientación Profesional: Un Proceso a lo Largo de la Vida,* **y** *Orientación Laboral Para la Diversidad y el Cambio.*

Karen Grant is a therapist, consultant, and trainer in the area of diversity and social justice in psychological practice. Her PhD research is in cross-linguistic counseling. For several years, Karen provided counseling, with the aid of translators, for immigrants and refugees from 20 different cultural groups and nine languages. She has taught and developed diversity counseling curricula for master's-degree and undergraduate counseling programs and has developed and delivered training in diversity for social service agencies and community programs. She has also provided therapy to veteran peacekeepers who served in Bosnia-Herzegovina, and she is actively interested in cultural transition and traumatic experience.

Mary J. Heppner, PhD, is currently a full professor of educational, school, and counseling psychology at the University of Missouri–Columbia. She is also an associate director of the Career Center, which is a national model and one of the most programmatically diverse centers in the United States. She has been the author of more than 100 articles, book chapters, conference papers, and books, including the textbook, *Career Counseling: Process Issues and Techniques; The Handbook of Career Counseling for Women;* and *Writing and Publishing Your Thesis, Dissertation, and Research.* She is the creator of the Career Transitions Inventory as well as of the Career Counseling Self-Efficacy Scale. Her research interests include adults in career transition, career counseling process and outcome, assessment issues in career psychology, and cross-cultural and multicultural issues. She also has a 6-year grant from the Centers for Disease Control and Prevention to examine sexual violence interventions in middle and high schools.

P. Paul Heppner, PhD, is a professor at the University of Missouri–Columbia. He has published more than 130 articles and book chapters and five books. He has made hundreds of presentations at national conferences and delivered more than 40 invited presentations in 14 countries. In addition, he has served on several national/international editorial boards, including being editor of *The Counseling Psychologist.* He is a fellow in the American Psychological Association and the American Psychological Society. In 2005–2006, he served as president of the Society of Counseling Psychology. He has been honored to receive a named professorship and several awards for his leadership, research, teaching, mentoring, international work, and promotion of diversity issues; he has been the recipient of three Fulbright awards.

Monica Justin's life experiences as a child of immigrant parents and woman of color growing up in an ethnic and racially diverse city like Montreal, Quebec, Canada, have been significant factors in contributing to her interest and passion in diversity and multicultural issues. She lives in Montreal and holds a faculty position at Concordia University. As a licensed psychologist, she maintains a private practice. Monica completed her doctoral studies at McGill University and has worked as a practitioner in a variety of counseling contexts with adolescents, adults, and newly arrived immigrants. She has also taught at various academic institutions throughout her career. Her key interests for teaching, training, research, and counseling lie in the areas of biculturalism, second-generation ethnic women, acculturation-related issues, and multicultural counseling and competency/training.

Stefan Kammhuber is professor for intercultural learning and organizational communication at the RheinAhrCampus, University of Applied Sciences, Koblenz, Germany. He graduated in psychology and speech communication from the University of Regensburg, Germany. Now, he is also codirector of the Institute for Cooperational Management at the University of Regensburg, where he offers consulting, training, and coaching in the realm of international organizational development. His research topics are intercultural learning and intercultural training, intercultural rhetoric, migration and integration, organizational communication, and rhetoric. Among his research partners and clients are international companies, public institutions, social organizations, and military institutions.

Marianne C. Kastrup, MD, PhD, has worked since 1987 as a consultant in psychiatry. From 1997 to 2001, she served as medical director of the Rehabilitation and Research Centre for Torture Victims, Copenhagen, Denmark, and has since 2002 been head of the Centre for Transcultural Psychiatry, Copenhagen. Marianne has also been an assistant professor in psychiatry, Copenhagen University, and is now an external examiner at all the universities in Denmark. For the last 20 years, she has been a member of the World Health Organization Expert Advisory Panel on Mental Health. She has extensive international organizational experiences as a member of the World Psychiatric Association Executive Committee (1996–2002); vice president, International Federation, Psychiatric Epidemiology (1990–1999); and secretary general, European Psychiatric Association from 2003. Marianne has been an expert adviser to the European Council Committee for the Prevention of Torture, Inhuman or Degrading Treatment and Punishment. She is presently a member of the board of the Danish Psychiatric Association. Marianne is the author or coauthor of more than 90 peer-reviewed articles, editor or author of more than 10 books, and author of more than 60 book chapters.

Patrice Keats is an assistant professor in the Faculty of Education, Counselling Psychology Program, at Simon Fraser University, British Columbia, Canada. Her primary program of research is in the field of traumatic stress studies. She has conducted research for, written, and presented scholarly papers on the constructs of vicarious witnessing and secondary traumatic stress in a variety of populations. This research has been recognized both nationally and internationally through publications and conference proceedings. Currently, she is conducting a national project that focuses on the experiences of photojournalists and journalists who photograph and report on trauma and disaster events. Secondarily, she conducts research in the area of counselor education. Her current project includes looking at student responses to expert videotapes used for counselor education. Finally, she is a registered clinical counselor in British Columbia and has a part-time private practice working with trauma survivors from civilian and military populations in both group and individual therapy.

Jacques Kurtness received his doctorate from Université Laval, Quebec, Canada, in 1984. He taught at l'Université du Québec à Chicoutimi and was a director in the Canadian Department of Indian and Northern Affairs. He has trained Amerindian police and is involved in negotiations and interventions with a wide range of Native communities. Since his retirement from public service, Jacques has developed his talent as an accomplished artist and painter. He has several paintings in private and corporate collections. He is the grandnephew of Kakwa, the celebrated Naskapi-Montagnais elder and informant for Frank G. Speck.

Frederick T. L. Leong is professor of psychology at Michigan State University in the Industrial/ Organizational and Clinical Psychology programs. He has authored or coauthored more than 100 articles in various counseling and psychology journals and 60 book chapters and has also edited or coedited 10 books. He is editor-in-chief of the *Encyclopedia of Counseling*. He is a fellow of the American Psychological Association (APA), Association for Psychological Science, Asian American Psychological Association, and the International Academy for Intercultural Research. His major research interests center around culture and mental health, cross-cultural psychotherapy (especially with Asians and Asian Americans), and cultural and personality factors related to career choice and work adjustment. He is the current president of APA's Division 45 (Society for the Psychological Study of Ethnic Minority Issues) and also serves on its Board of Scientific Affairs; the Minority Fellowship Program Advisory Committee; and the Commission on Ethnic Minority Recruitment, Retention, and Training Task Force.

S. Alvin Leung began his international journey in 1977 as an international student in the United States. He received his PhD in counseling psychology from the University of Illinois at Urbana–Champaign in 1988 and served as a faculty member in the counseling psychology programs at the University of Nebraska–Lincoln (1988–1991) and the University of Houston (1991–1996). He crossed borders again in 1996 and returned to Hong Kong, where he is now professor in the Department of Educational Psychology, The Chinese University of Hong Kong. He is a fellow of the American Psychological Association and the Hong Kong Professional Counselling Association. His major areas of research and teaching are career development and assessment across the life span; school counseling; multicultural, cross-cultural, and international issues in counseling; and counselor training and supervision.

Shu-Ping Lin is a psychologist, Department of Behavioral Health, Gouveneur Healthcare Services, New York City Health and Hospitals Corporation. She was formerly an assistant professor in the Department of Psychology at the University of Alaska, Fairbanks. She received her undergraduate and master's degrees in Taiwan. In 2006, she earned her PhD from The Ohio State University after her internship at the University of Maryland. Shu-Ping is interested in and passionate about the issues related to cross-cultural encounters, especially in an international context. Being proud of her international background, Shu-Ping dedicates herself to advocating for the well-being of minority groups, especially international students and immigrant families.

Dina B. Lubin is a therapist in the Department of Family and Community Medicine of St. Michael's Hospital in Toronto, Ontario, Canada, and has worked in the addictions field for the past 15 years. She has worked with a diverse clientele, including lesbians, gay men, bisexual individuals, transgender individuals, and queers (LGBTQ); homeless individuals; individuals with HIV/AIDS; and those with a variety of mental health issues. She also participates as an instructor in the University of Toronto Faculty of Medicine's Determinants of Community Health course and provides consultation to physicians, nurses, medical residents, and various allied health staff around their patients' addiction-related issues. She has extensive experience working with narcotic-dependent clients on methadone maintenance programs in Toronto and Boston, Massachusetts. An Internationally Certified Alcohol and Drug Counselor, she holds a master's degree in counseling psychology from Boston College and a bachelor of arts degree in psychology from McGill University.

Beatriz Malik is associate professor in educational guidance at the Spanish University of Distance Education (Faculty of Education), teaching guidance theories and intervention models. Main lines of research include cultural diversity and guidance, intercultural communication competencies, and inclusive education. She is coeditor, with B. Irving, of the book *Critical Reflections on Career Education and Guidance: Promoting Social Justice Within a Global Economy*. She has authored articles and book chapters and coauthored books on guidance and intercultural education. She has taken part in several European and international cooperation projects. Among others are the Leonardo Programme *New Skills for New Futures* (1998); the Counsellor Qualifications Standards project (1999–2003) leading to the International Competencies for Educational and Vocational Guidance Practitioners; and Socrates INTER Project in Intercultural Education. She currently coordinates a 2-year project under the Programma ALFA (Latin American Academic Training) to design a Euro-Latinamerican Postgraduate Progamme in Intercultural Education.

Elizabeth Mathew is a licensed psychologist in Dallas, Texas. She completed her PhD in counseling psychology from Texas Woman's University, Denton, Texas, in August of 2005. She completed her predoctoral internship at the University of Florida Counseling Center. She is currently completing a postdoctoral fellowship in pediatric psychology at the Texas Scottish Rite Hospital for Children. Elizabeth is the U.S.-born daughter of immigrants from India. Her practice interests are women's issues, acculturation, religious/spiritual identity development, and the relationship between culture and disability.

Jaya T. Mathew, LMSW, is a doctoral student in counseling psychology at Fordham University. She received her bachelor's and master's degrees in social work from the University of Texas at Austin. She has had clinical experience with inner-city urban youth in the school system and young adults in the college counseling setting. Internationally, she has worked with the foster care system in the United Kingdom. As an assistant administrator of a home health care agency, she has had experience with program management. In addition, she has served as an adjunct lecturer at City University of New York, and at Fordham University, Lincoln Center. During her graduate training, she has also been a research assistant on projects concerning multicultural competence, immigration experiences, and inner-city urban youth. Her primary research interests are in multicultural competence and diversity training.

Alexander Cowell McFarlane is currently the head of the University of Adelaide Node of the Centre of Military and Veterans Health, Adelaide, Australia. He is an international expert in the field of the impact of disasters and posttraumatic stress disorder. He is a past president of both the International Society for Traumatic Stress Studies and the Australasian Society for Traumatic Stress Studies. He is the recipient of the Robert Laufer Award for outstanding scientific achievement in the study of the effects of traumatic stress. He is currently the senior adviser in psychiatry to the Australian Defence Force and the Australian Centre for Posttraumatic Mental Health. He holds the rank of group captain in the Royal Australian Air Force specialist reserve. He has acted as an adviser to many groups in postdisaster situations, including the Kuwait government and the United Nations. He has lectured and run workshops in Europe, the United States, Japan, Asia, and South Africa.

Mary McMahon is a lecturer in the School of Education at The University of Queensland, Australia. She publishes extensively in the field of career development and has presented at national and international conferences. She is particularly interested in the career development of children and constructivist approaches to the theory, practice, and research of career development. A focus of her recent work has been on practical applications of the Systems Theory Framework of career development to counseling, assessment, and research.

Noorfarah Merali is an associate professor in the Canadian Psychological Association Accredited Counselling Psychology Graduate Program at the University of Alberta, Edmonton, Alberta, Canada. A specialist in cross-cultural adjustment and immigrant and refugee mental health, her research and practice interests focus on the acculturation process, family adaptation and resettlement, cultural differences in expressions of mental health problems, and counselor cultural competence. She has been involved in the training of mental health service providers for culturally competent practice in various health care and community settings. She has also taken a leadership role in conducting ethnic community needs assessments and in developing and evaluating mental-health related programming for immigration and settlement agencies and cultural community associations. She is a member of the College of Alberta Psychologists, Canadian Psychological Association, American Psychological Association, and Society for the Psychological Study of Social Issues (International).

Roy Moodley, PhD, is associate professor in counseling psychology at the Ontario Institute for Studies in Education at the University of Toronto, Ontario, Canada. Research and publication interests include traditional and cultural healing; multicultural and diversity counseling; race, culture, and ethnicity in psychotherapy; and masculinities. Roy coedited *Transforming Managers: Gendering Change in the Public Sector; Carl Rogers Counsels a Black Client: Race and Culture in Person-Centered Counseling; Integrating Traditional Healing Practices Into Counseling and Psychotherapy;* and *Race, Culture and Psychotherapy: Critical Perspectives in Multicultural Practice.*

Karen Moustafa-Leonard joined Indiana University–Purdue University Fort Wayne in August 2004 as assistant professor of management in the School of Business and Management Sciences. She earned a BS degree from Arkansas State University, an MA in commerce from the University of Auckland, New Zealand, and a PhD in 2004 from the University of Memphis. She has worked in management, human resources, and matériel management for various organizations, including the Auckland Area Hospital Board and Tenet Healthcare System. Her current research interests are centered on organizational behavior, including such things as media choice, accountability, and time orientation in organizations. She has published journal articles as well as chapters in research volumes and has presented her work at national and international conferences.

Roberta Neault, PhD, is a career counselor, corporate consultant, counselor educator, and coexecutive coordinator of ENET, a professional association for career practitioners in British Columbia, Canada. Author of *Beyond the Basics: Real World Skills for Career Practitioners,* a resource book of practical tips for working with diverse clients, and president and founder of Life Strategies Ltd., Roberta codeveloped the internationally recognized Career Management Professional Program, which has recently launched a Multicultural Specialist certificate stream. Recipient of the Stu Conger Award for Leadership in Career Counselling and Career Development in Canada, Roberta served, in 2006, on the Canadian team at the International Symposium on Career Development and Public Policy in Sydney, Australia. Her professional and research interests include career transitions and international/global careers, and, for 4 years, Roberta served as the career management specialist in the McRae Institute at Capilano College, British Columbia, supporting managers and professionals as they embarked on international careers.

Claire O'Reilly joined the Department of German, University College Cork, Ireland, as senior lecturer in September 2005. She graduated with an honors BA degree (in law and European studies) in 1995 from the University of Limerick, Ireland. Further studies in intercultural communication and cross-cultural psychology took her to the University of Regensburg and Friedrich Schiller University Jena in Germany. She graduated with a PhD from the University of Limerick in 2001 and completed a research postdoctorate under Alexander Thomas, Department of Organizational and Social Psychology, Regensburg, in 2002. From 2002 to 2005, she was assistant professor at the Chemnitz University of Technology, Germany, specializing in the research and teaching of intercultural training and intercultural communication. Her research interests are interdisciplinary and include theoretical contributions to the understanding of intercultural communication; aspects of international human resource management; and, more recently, the academic response to multiculturalism in German and Irish society. She has taught English in Vienna (Department of Education Scholarship) and German at the University of Limerick and given seminars and lectures in English and German at the Chemnitz University of Technology in intercultural management and intercultural communication.

John Pickering has spent 10 years working with international students and international student professionals. He headed the pastoral care team at the University of Canterbury, New Zealand, as student numbers quintupled in 5 years. Formerly a physicist, he turned his research attention to the educational and social needs of international students. Lately, he has run professional development programs for international education professionals and undertaken research on cultural aspects of plagiarism and the pastoral needs of Chinese students, in particular. He was the inaugural president of the New Zealand branch of ISANA: International Education Association and is an associate of the Centre for Advanced Cross-Cultural Research at Victoria University, New Zealand. Most recently he is experimenting with a blog in Japan as a means of helping students prepare for overseas study (http://drjohn.blog104.fc2.com/).

Joseph G. Ponterotto, PhD, is a professor of education and coordinator of the Mental Health Counseling Program at Fordham University, Lincoln Center Campus, New York. His primary teaching and research interests are in the area of multicultural counseling and both quantitative and qualitative research designs. A frequent contributor to the multicultural psychology literature, his most recent books include *Preventing Prejudice: A Guide for Counselors, Educators, and Parents* (2nd edition, coauthored with S. Utsey and P. Pedersen) and the *Handbook of Multicultural Assessment* (3rd edition, coedited with L. Suzuki).

Natalee Popadiuk is an assistant professor and registered psychologist in the Counselling Psychology Program at Simon Fraser University in Vancouver, British Columbia. With over 15 years of experience in the fields of education and counseling, she brings a wealth of knowledge and skills to her position. She has provided psychological services to diverse clinical populations in a wide variety of settings, including a suicide-prevention counseling agency, university counseling center, and in the public school system. As part of her program of research, she has explored international student issues using qualitative methodologies, focusing on women's experiences of difficult intimate relationships, high school student adjustment, and the relational aspects of cross-cultural transition. In addition to private consulting and training, she provides service to the university as a Simon Fraser University senator and to the larger community in her role as a board member for a nonprofit crisis center.

Cynthia L. S. Pury is an associate professor of psychology at Clemson University. She holds a PhD in clinical psychology from Northwestern University and interned at the North Chicago Veteran's Administration hospital, with a specialty in combat-related posttraumatic stress disorder. Her research interests include the psychology of courage and cognitive models of emotion, particularly fear and anxiety.

Margaret (Peggy) Pusch is the associate director of the Intercultural Communication Institute, Portland, Oregon; executive director of the Society for Intercultural Education, Training and Research (SIETAR) USA; and an intercultural trainer and international consultant working frequently in Europe and Japan. She cofounded and was president of the Intercultural Press, Inc., for more than 15 years. She is an exceptional writer and editor with vast experience in producing both printed and media materials relating to intercultural topics. She served as president of NAFSA: Association of International Educators (1995–1996) and of the Society for International Education, Training, and Research–United States of America (2000–2003) and is currently chair of the Board of Trustees of International Partnership for Service-Learning and Leadership. She recently received two prestigious awards: the Lifetime Achievement Award from SIETAR Europa and the Optime Merens de Collegis award from SIETAR USA and is widely regarded as one of the top administrators, editors, and trainers in the intercultural field.

Sauli Puukari works as senior lecturer in guidance and counseling in the Department of Teacher Education at the University of Jyväskylä, Finland. His teaching covers a wide range of topics related to school counseling and other topics in guidance and counseling. During the past years, he has participated in European Union–funded Leonardo projects and national activities dealing with multicultural guidance and counseling and higher education guidance services. Multicultural guidance and counseling has been his special interest since the 1990s. He is a coeditor and author of the book *Multicultural Guidance and Counselling—Theoretical Foundations and Best Practices in Europe.* He has actively developed training in multicultural counseling, participated in research studies dealing with this area, and published articles and run workshops on multicultural counseling in Finland and in a number of other countries. He is currently participating in projects involving perspectives on the role of multiculturalism in working life.

Caridad Sanchez-Leguelinel, PhD, is an associate professor at John Jay College of Criminal Justice, City University of New York. She is currently serving as the associate director for the Department of Counseling, where she also functions as the faculty supervisor for the Sophomore Peer Counseling Program and the coordinator for the Peer Counseling Training Program. She is the author of numerous articles and book chapters focusing on a wide range of topics, including multicultural counseling competency assessment, vocational counseling in criminal justice, sophomore student retention, peer counseling and mentoring programs, and general college adjustment issues. She has facilitated several professional workshops and presentations on issues of crisis management, critical stress debriefing, and trauma intervention.

Daya Singh Sandhu, EdD, NCC, NCCC, NCSC, LPCC, is a distinguished professor of research and former chairperson (1996–2004) in the Department of Educational and Counseling Psychology at the University of Louisville. He received his doctor of counselor education degree from Mississippi State University and has taught graduate courses in counseling and counseling psychology for more than 20 years. He has an interest in school counseling, multicultural counseling, issues relating to international students, and the role of spirituality in counseling and psychotherapy. In addition to more than 50 refereed journal articles and 60 book chapters, he has authored or edited 12 books, including *Counseling for Prejudice Prevention and Reduction, Empowering Women for Equity: A Counseling Approach, Asian and Pacific Islander Americans: Issues and Concerns for Counseling and Psychotherapy, Violence in American Schools: A Practical Guide for Counselors,* and *Multicultural Competencies: A Guidebook of Practices,* to name a few. He has received several distinguished awards, including a Fulbright Senior Research Scholar Award; Fulbright Senior Specialist Award; Association for Multicultural Counseling and Development Research Award; President's Distinguished Faculty Award for Outstanding Scholarship, Research and Creativity at the University of Louisville; Alumnus of the Year Award; and Kentucky Counselor Educator of the Year Award. He has also made more than 150 professional presentations at the state, national, and international levels. He is currently serving on the editorial boards of the *Journal of Counseling & Development* and the *Journal of Counseling and Values.*

Hemla D. Singaravelu, PhD, is a licensed professional counselor and associate professor in the Department of Counseling and Family Therapy at Saint Louis University. She was the cochair and director of the master's program. Prior to teaching at St. Louis University, she served as an assistant professor at Southwest Missouri State University and coordinator of Career and Mentor Programs at Fitchburg State College in Massachusetts. She received her doctorate in educational psychology–counselor education from Southern Illinois University at Carbondale, specializing in career development and multicultural/diversity counseling. She has published and presented in the area of multicultural counseling issues, career development of diverse populations, and international students. She is currently on the editorial boards of the *Journal of Counseling & Development* and *The Career Development Quarterly.* She was born and raised in Malaysia and came to the United States as an international student.

John Stewart is a professor of counseling psychology in the University of New Brunswick, Canada. He holds a doctorate degree in counseling psychology from the University of Toronto. His teaching interests include career psychology and counseling theory, and his research interests focus on the application of psychological principles to vocational development and choice and the cultural factors that influence immigrants' adaptation to the Canadian workforce. He has authored or coauthored 39 publications, including journal manuscripts, books, book chapters, and reports. He is a consulting editor for the *Canadian Journal of Counselling* and is a member of the Canadian Counselling Association. He has international experience in Asia helping emerging countries develop and implement a school counseling program. Presently, he directs the Strengthening Supports to Education in Bhutan project sponsored by the Canadian International Development Agency for the University of New Brunswick.

Yu-Wei Wang, who earned a PhD in counseling psychology from the University of Missouri–Columbia in 2004, is assistant professor of psychology at Southern Illinois University at Carbondale. She was born and raised in Kaohsiung City, Taiwan. Her research and professional interests include stress, trauma, and coping/problem solving; sexual abuse/assault recovery; college campus suicide; and multicultural counseling and training issues. Her research articles have appeared in the *Journal of Counseling Psychology, Journal of College Student Development, The Career Development Quarterly,* and *Journal of Multilingual & Multicultural Development.* She has published several book chapters on international students and qualitative research methodology. In addition, she has served on multiple local and national committees involved with issues of international students and multicultural training.

Mark Watson is a professor and head of the Psychology Department of the Nelson Mandela Metropolitan University in South Africa. His research focuses on the career development and career assessment of primary, secondary, and tertiary students from all South African population groups. He has published extensively in international journals, is the coeditor of two career books, has contributed book chapters to several international career textbooks, and is a codeveloper of an international qualitative career assessment tool. He is presently on the editorial advisory board of several national and international career journals.

Marvin Westwood, PhD, R.Psych, is a professor in the Counselling Psychology Program at the University of British Columbia, Canada, and associate member of the University of British Columbia Faculty of Medicine. He taught previously at St. Francis University and McGill University. His teaching and research areas focus on group counseling and psychotherapy, trauma repair, and therapeutic applications of the guided autobiographical life review method to the counseling process. His most recent work includes development and evaluation of a group-based approach to trauma repair—therapeutic enactment. He has developed several personal development programs for professionals across a wide range of groups (counselors/psychologists, nurses, physicians, soldiers, clergy, and so on) using guided autobiography and group-based therapeutic enactment methods. His research and teaching focus areas have been included in many invited presentations at numerous national and international conferences.

Christine Wihak, PhD, is director, Prior Learning Assessment & Recognition at Thompson Rivers University—Open Learning, Canada. A registered psychologist, her interest in cross-cultural experience and its effect on professional practice developed during the more than 10 years she spent in Nunavut. In that unusual cultural context, she worked in a variety of roles, including providing educational counseling to adult Inuit students and instructing in a counselor education program. To ease her own transition back to the Canadian mainstream, she undertook doctoral studies in educational psychology at the University of Alberta. Her research interests center on experiential learning and blending of alternative knowledge traditions.

Adam Zagelbaum is an assistant professor in the Department of Psychology and Counseling's School Counseling track at Governors State University. He obtained his doctorate from Ball State University's Counseling Psychology Program, along with certification as a school counselor. He has experience as both a school and community counselor in several different settings, including the school system of Trinidad and Tobago, the correctional facilities and alternative schools of Wisconsin, children's centers in the southern Mississippi region, and various university counseling centers. He has worked with underserved and English-as-second-language clients. His experience with immigrant populations has been particularly significant, with clients from Africa, Central America, Mexico, and Japan. His research interests center around conflict management, career development, and identity issues. He also specializes in child and adolescent counseling, family counseling, and group counseling and has presented at international conferences in addition to ones at state and national levels.

Huaiyu Zhang is a PhD student in the Clinical Psychology Program at Emory University. She obtained a bachelor's degree in bioscience from the University of Science and Technology of China and a master's degree in neuroscience from the University of Southern California. Her main research interests are maternal psychopathology, early development, and cultural issues.

Part 1
International Work Transitions

Dual-Career Transitions

Roberta Neault

In a global economy, international experience can be a valuable addition to a career portfolio. To improve their opportunities for an international placement, Todd and Naomi (pseudonyms) enrolled in a graduate cooperative program focused on preparing students for management careers in Asia.

Setting the Scene

Todd and Naomi were single when they entered the program. Both had studied and worked abroad and were now focused on returning to Asia in management-level positions. Todd's undergraduate studies (in Canada and Japan) had focused on Asia, and he spoke some Japanese and Thai. Naomi, a third-generation Japanese Canadian, spent 2 years in Japan as an assistant language teacher before beginning her graduate studies.

Several months into the program, Todd and Naomi began dating. As time progressed, it became clear to them both that they wanted to continue their relationship after the end of the on-campus year of the program.

International Relocation:
The Dual-Career-Couple Experience

Todd and Naomi narrowed their options to Thailand, Vietnam, and Malaysia—confident that any of these countries would provide good opportunities for them both at this stage of their careers. Todd and Naomi agreed to make their final choice based on who received the better offer, as long as they both felt comfortable living in that city and were confident that the other person could find suitable employment after relocation. Naomi received a job offer in Thailand. Because both Todd and Naomi had traveled previously within Thailand, they were familiar with the people, culture, food, and environment. Because Todd had previously studied the Thai language and had an extensive network in Thailand, the decision for Naomi to accept the job offer was a relatively easy one to make.

This move placed Todd in a new role—that of a "trailing spouse" (Harvey, 1998; Shahnasarian, 1991). Unlike many trailing spouses, however, Todd was also committed to an international career. In Naomi's words,

> We knew the transition would not be easy but it was the best opportunity and we were up for the challenge. . . . We were also aware of a strong network of alumni that could make the adjustment easier and less daunting.

Todd and Naomi used the alumni network and their other Thai contacts to find a wonderful apartment and settle into their new life in Bangkok. During his first year in Thailand, Todd took on several volunteer projects and short-term employment contracts to demonstrate his management skills. Eventually, his perseverance paid off, and he landed a position as marketing manager for one of Thailand's leading food exporters, where he remained for the next 2 years. Todd took on a leadership role within a Thai-Canadian organization and continued to extend his professional network. During the 3 years that they lived in Bangkok, Naomi's career was also very successful. However, both eventually reached the point where they were looking for new challenges. Their dilemma involved choosing where to look next for work. Once again, Todd and Naomi found themselves juggling two international careers in transition.

The Dilemma

In the Asian business setting, relationships are very important. Although both Todd and Naomi realized that opportunities in their current organizations were limited (both were locally owned Thai companies, not multinational corporations), they were careful not to offend their employers. To preserve the relationships (i.e., allow their employers to "save face"), Todd and Naomi explained that it was important for them to return to Canada to spend time with family and friends.

Coordinating Career Moves

Despite their stated reasons for quitting their jobs in Thailand, Todd and Naomi were actually considering several career possibilities. Each had been offered attractive positions—but in countries where it seemed unlikely that the other would find work. Once again, they created a short list of potential locations and agreed to relocate as soon as one of them was offered a suitable job, in a location where there also seemed to be a good potential for the other to find a job.

One possibility Todd and Naomi considered was to continue their careers in Thailand, and they narrowed their focus to international organizations where their local experience, well-established network, and language skills would be an asset. A second possibility was to relocate to Hong Kong. In Naomi's words, "Our general passion for Hong Kong's culture, lifestyle, proximity to China, and its booming economy led us to consider this as a potential destination." A third possibility was to repatriate—just as they had told their Thai employers they intended to do. Naomi said,

> With family, friends, and a strong network of alumni, we were interested in the possibility of returning home. The thought of not needing work authorization was attractive as we felt that the chance of finding a job quickly was a real possibility.

Repatriation: The Myths and Realities

Not all repatriations are successful. Typically, expatriates assume that returning home will be relatively easy. With friends and family nearby, no challenges with language or work visas, a local education, and an impressive résumé, it never crosses their minds that they may experience culture shock or career challenges. Unfortunately, however, many expatriates find repatriating more of a challenge than their original transition abroad (MacDonald & Arthur, 2003; Neault, 2003, 2005). Todd and Naomi had watched many friends and colleagues struggle with repatriation; they were well aware that they might encounter challenges.

When Todd and Naomi returned home, they decided to stay (separately) with their own parents for awhile; that in itself was a transition after living together for more than 3 years.

Although in the same metropolitan area, their families lived at opposite ends of the region (about an hour's drive during nonpeak time). Todd and Naomi used this opportunity to save some money as well as to reconnect with family and friends.

Todd and Naomi quickly reestablished their professional networks and actively began applying for jobs in their city. Unfortunately, many Canadian employers do not value international experience; in many ways, Canadian repatriates face similar job search challenges as immigrants do (Neault, 2005). Within a surprisingly short amount of time, however, Todd and Naomi's active job-search efforts paid off. Todd found a job (within his industry and with an Asian focus) only 2 weeks after returning to Canada. Almost immediately afterward, Naomi was also offered a job in her field, in a large international firm. During this time, each was also presented with an attractive opportunity in Asia.

In both of the Canadian offers, although the positions were junior to Todd and Naomi's management roles in Thailand, their new employers indicated potential for growth within a short period of time and expressed a respect for their international experience. After 1 month of living with his parents, Todd relocated to a small basement suite, closer to Naomi's parents' home and to his workplace.

To Stay or to Go? A Critical Decision

Four months later, Todd and Naomi began the next stage of their transition. Once again, they found themselves at a crossroads. They had structured their return to Canada as a vacation, with the potential of staying longer if they were both able to secure work. However, after several months in Canada, with each working at jobs that were not as challenging as those they had held in Asia, Todd and Naomi had to make a difficult decision. They were tired of living as transients—Naomi in her parents' home and Todd in a rented basement room. They wanted their own things around them, personal treasures that were in storage in Asia until they decided which continent to call home. Todd and Naomi talked to family, friends, and mentors, but the decision just did not seem obvious. One day, they made an appointment with a banker, just to see if they would qualify for a mortgage. They did! With a preapproved mortgage in hand, the next step suddenly seemed clear to them. They spent several weeks looking at a variety of homes in their price range, settled on a specific neighborhood, and made an offer on a condominium. The offer was accepted, Todd and Naomi contacted their storage company in Asia, and arrangements were made to bring their belongings "home."

Transition Outcomes

Todd and Naomi have chosen, for the short term at least, to repatriate. Although they both still feel very connected to Asia and expect to return there some day, for now their focus is on building their lives and careers in Canada. Both have, however, made career compromises— accepting jobs that do not fully use their skills or knowledge. Csikszentmihalyi (1997) warned of the danger of boredom and decreased productivity when individuals with high skills are not sufficiently challenged at work; underemployment could, therefore, continue to be a significant career challenge for Todd and Naomi. However, if one of them were to be offered a more challenging job that required relocation, their living arrangements would once again be in turmoil. Juggling dual careers can be very challenging. To simplify career decision making, many dual-career couples make a conscious decision to put one career first (Neault & Pickerell, 2005). Todd and Naomi have already done this several times.

Compared with hundreds of other international students, expatriates, and repatriates with whom I have worked, Todd and Naomi have been very focused and proactive about managing their careers. This has likely contributed to their ongoing positive attitudes, their career success abroad, and their relatively problem-free repatriation. Optimism has been linked to career success and job satisfaction (Neault, 2002). Todd and Naomi were openly optimistic about their opportunities in Asia and also upon returning home. They have also consistently demonstrated a willingness to prove themselves and demonstrate their skills (either through volunteering or accepting positions that they knew would underutilize their talents). This flexibility and openness have also likely contributed to their numerous successful transitions.

An alumni study in Todd and Naomi's program identified several factors that contribute to international career success: "global contacts and relationships, patience and persistence, work/life balance, language skills, flexibility and open-mindedness, cultural sensitivity, humility, watching and listening, goal-setting and action-planning, and comfort with ambiguity" (Neault, 2003, p. 6). Todd and Naomi's story exemplifies each of these characteristics. It is, therefore, not surprising that they have experienced significant career success despite compromises that each has made.

Key Issues

In Todd and Naomi's story, the key issues from a counseling perspective were managing careers, money, and interpersonal relationships (both personal and professional) and focusing on such developmental tasks as establishing a committed relationship and purchasing a home together. Within each of these major issues were several components. For example, career management challenges included juggling dual careers (and making career compromises), building professional credibility in a new country (and upon repatriation), generating job leads, making career decisions, and negotiating contracts.

Money management challenges included being paid a good salary in Thailand (compared with locals in similar positions) yet having bills to pay in Canadian dollars (e.g., student loans), having no access to financial support while in transition between jobs (e.g., employment insurance), and trying to qualify for a preapproved mortgage based on relatively new jobs in Canada and low salaries (by Canadian standards) for the past few years in Thailand.

Relationship challenges included strengthening their own relationship as a couple, staying connected with Canadian family and friends (especially aging grandparents), and maintaining personal and professional connections in Thailand and other parts of Asia.

A final challenge was deciding when and where to purchase a home, especially when their jobs, at least in the short term, were at a junior level with potential for growth but no guarantees. Todd and Naomi, like many expatriate and repatriate couples, faced numerous career–life changes within a relatively short period of time. This unrelenting change can, on its own, be stressful (Hobson, Delunas, & Kesic, 2001; Holmes & Rahe, 1967).

Reader Reflection Questions

1. Todd and Naomi entered their graduate diploma program as young single adults. How did becoming a couple affect their career plans and decisions, especially as they were embarking on international careers?
2. From a relationship counseling perspective, how might you help Todd and Naomi navigate the transitions in their lives as they moved internationally, repatriated, returned to their parents' homes, and then bought their first home together?
3. From a cross-cultural counseling perspective, how might you help Todd and Naomi adjust to the culture shock of relocating to Thailand and, later, returning home? Given their different family backgrounds, how might you help them explore the impact of culture on their own relationship?
4. From a career counseling perspective, how might you support Todd and Naomi in effectively managing their separate careers while considering the impact of each of their career decisions on their partner?

5. For Todd and Naomi, like many young professional couples, financial issues are intertwined with careers and relationships. As a counselor, how might you help them to work through some of the financial considerations as they made decisions to work abroad, repatriate, and purchase a home?

References

Csikszentmihalyi, M. (1997). *Finding flow: The psychology of engagement with everyday life.* New York: HarperCollins.

Harvey, M. (1998). Dual-career couples during international relocation: The trailing spouse. *International Journal of Human Resource Management, 9,* 309–331.

Hobson, C. J., Delunas, L., & Kesic, D. (2001). Compelling evidence of the need for corporate work/life balance initiatives: Results from a national survey of stressful life events. *Journal of Employment Counseling, 38,* 38–44.

Holmes, T. H., & Rahe, R. H. (1967). The Social Readjustment Rating Scale. *Journal of Psychosomatic Research, 11,* 213–218.

MacDonald, S., & Arthur, N. (2003). Employees' perceptions of repatriation. *Canadian Journal of Career Development, 2,* 3–11.

Neault, R. A. (2002). Thriving in the new millennium: Career management in the changing world of work. *Canadian Journal of Career Development, 1*(1), 11–21.

Neault, R. A. (2003). Managing global careers: Changes and challenges for the 21st century. *NATCON Papers.* Retrieved April 9, 2007, from www.contactpoint.ca/natcon-conat/2003/pdf/pdf-03-11.pdf

Neault, R. (2005). Managing global careers: Challenges for the 21st century. *International Journal for Educational and Vocational Guidance, 5,* 149–161.

Neault, R. A., & Pickerell, D. A. (2005). Professional women in dual career families: The juggling act. *Canadian Journal of Counselling, 39,* 187–198.

Shahnasarian, M. (1991). Job relocation and the trailing spouse. *Journal of Career Development, 17,* 179–184.

Response 1

Mary J. Heppner and P. Paul Heppner

The role of a career counselor has been a complex one since its inception. It has been a role that required competencies in a host of diverse skill sets. These skills have ranged from helping individuals assess their interests, abilities, and values; building a strong working alliance; working with the increasingly diverse labor market in an individual's home country; and working in turn with the increasingly diverse demographic of individuals seeking to enter that market (Gysbers, Heppner, & Johnston, 2003). Now, as the case of Todd and Naomi so aptly depicts, another skill set is needed: cross-national career counseling competencies that underscore the necessity of cultural sensitivity. Specifically, in this case, a career counselor's role is helping individuals attend to the myriad of issues in thinking about and finding international work experiences in an increasingly global economy. The context of the critical incidents described in this case is literally the world stage as a potential workplace and how the career counselor can assist in the transitions presented by couples seeking international employment.

The case of Todd and Naomi is data rich and provides many potential avenues for reflection and comment. We are choosing three to explore more fully in this reaction: the role of personality, the role of culture, and the importance of integrating both of these constructs within an ecological approach to career counseling.

The Role of Personality

We are struck by the role of Naomi's and Todd's personalities, as presented in this case, and how their personalities have influenced their career development. The case is an excellent example of the impact of personality on behavior. Naomi and Todd clearly reflect an approach that is taught, with many times limited success, by many career counselors—that of *taking ownership of your career*. The case presents a powerful depiction of human agency in action. In their short career narrative, there are many excellent models of proactive problem solving (Heppner, Witty, & Dixon, 2004), resilience (Masten & Reed, 2002), optimism (Scheier & Carver, 1985), and self-efficacy (Bandura, 1986) in their abilities.

It is striking how important these personality characteristics seem to be to Naomi and Todd's success thus far in their lives. They had been open to early experiences of studying and working abroad; Todd had graduated with an Asian-focused honors degree and then completed an Asian Studies diploma in Japan where he learned intermediate-level Japanese. Naomi had spent 2 years in Japan as an assistant language teacher. When Naomi initially took employment in Thailand, Todd had the strength of character to be the nontraditional "trailing spouse." They returned to their homeland of Canada. In making these moves, they networked with alumni, developed local experiences through volunteerism, and developed powerful networks for themselves. They lived, worked, and seemingly thrived in international arenas. All of these career-related activities took strength of character. Naomi and Todd proactively approached (Heppner et al., 2004), as opposed to avoiding, the career-related tasks in their lives. They clearly depict a style that is opposite that of the college student waiting to be *placed* by a career center or placement firm. It is very important for helping professionals to learn more about individual difference variables and critical life events that are related to one student passively approaching his or her career—waiting to be placed somewhere by a career center or placement firm—versus highly active, forward-oriented, engaged, and approach-oriented students like Naomi and Todd. Learning more about the early experiences, personality traits, and critical life experiences of people like Naomi and Todd can help career counselors target interventions for many other students whose lives could be changed in positive and meaningful ways by international experiences.

The Role of Culture

An implicitly important variable in this case is *culture*—although the word is mentioned infrequently in the case itself. Like personality variables, cultural variables may also be playing a critical role in influencing behavior. When it is mentioned, it relates to Naomi and Todd liking the culture of Thailand, having a passion for Hong Kong's culture, or perhaps having culture shock when they return to Canada. The construct of culture, however, has a much deeper and more profound impact on this case than is explicitly discussed. We would like to highlight some of the ways culture may be influencing every aspect of Naomi and Todd's career choices, as well as the career counselor's choices in working with them.

We know that the counselor's beliefs about the issues presented are dramatically influenced by her worldview: For example, the counselor's worldview affects how she conceptualizes the issues that Naomi and Todd are consulting with her about, how she perceives them and their concerns and how she chooses to intervene, and how she evaluates the success of the intervention. In essence, the counselor's worldview, and more specifically her view of work, gender roles, globalization, the role of family, the importance of "building a career portfolio," the importance of individualism versus collectivism, to name just a few, significantly affect every aspect of the work she does with Naomi and Todd. Because of this powerful influence, it is critically important that counselors be aware of their own worldview and how this may influence every aspect of the work they do. It is important to remember that many of these processes are so ingrained that they have become almost automatic and unconscious in the way people interact, and, thus, it takes considerable reflection and awareness to analyze how these processes affect our own work as counselors.

Similarly, we also know that Todd and Naomi's cultural background are shaping their choices, what dreams they have, how their career narrative unfolds in their lives, and how they problem solve the process of seeking employment. We know that Naomi is a third-generation Japanese American. We do not know Todd's ethnicity, because nothing is mentioned about it. We might assume he is White, because Whiteness tends not to be mentioned but rather assumed as the norm and, thus, unnecessary to comment on. We know little more about either of them as cultural beings. We find ourselves yearning to know more about their culture and the cultural context for how they perceive their employment and how that perception affects their career development. If we had the chance, the following questions come to mind.

We wonder about Naomi's cultural heritage and how this affects her career decision. For example, how have the circumstances under which her grandparents came to Canada—and how their risk taking in leaving their own country and immigrating to Canada—influenced Naomi's own interest and conceptualizations about living and working internationally? We wonder about her level of assimilation, and after these three generations in Canada, to what extent does Naomi still feel her Japanese values and heritage such as filial piety and interpersonal harmony? Most important, we wonder how this heritage might be influencing her choices in her own life. How might this heritage be having an impact on her now? Where does she see herself on the individualism–collectivism continuum, and how does this affect her choices of living close to family or moving thousands of miles away?

We also wonder about Todd's culture and background. Even though the world is getting smaller and more students are studying and working abroad, Todd is still very much in the minority in doing so. Only a small percentage of all American college students study abroad, and even fewer than that go on to work abroad during their educational experience. We wonder what critical events have occurred in Todd's life and subsequent worldview that promoted this openness to the world. We wonder if Todd views international experience as the author mentions in her lead sentence as "a valuable addition to a career portfolio" or is it something more central or deeper in his worldview and life journey. We wonder how his cultural background influences his values and to what extent he is aware of these cultural influences.

These are a few of the cultural issues that we would like to explore with Todd and Naomi and their career counselor in helping us obtain a deeper and richer picture of the role culture has played and now plays in the personal and career life choices presented in this case description.

An Ecological Approach

Examining both individual personality characteristics and culture in understanding and intervening in cases like this one is critical and emphasizes the importance of using an ecological perspective in providing career counseling. Career choice has been described as an act-in-context (Cook, Heppner, & O'Brien, 2004, 2005; Ladrine 1995). So often in career-related research and practice, the career is conceptualized as an individual choice, and the context in which that choice has been made is often ignored. The ecological model developed by Bronfenbrenner (1977), and more recently applied to the area of career planning by Cook et al. (2005), provides a model for the career counselor to help frame the individual choices within the broader life context of embedded systems and subsystems. The Ecological Model underscores that career behavior, like the career behavior evidenced in the case of Naomi and Todd, results from the dialectic between the person and the environment. Kurt Lewin's classic formulation regarding behavior being a function of people interacting in their environment is the heart of the ecological approach. Thus, in essence, vocational behavior is seen as determined by the interrelations between systems and subsystems within the larger ecosystem. The Ecological Model can be depicted as an individual operating within a microsystem, mesosystem, ecosystem, and macrosystem. These systems are nested within one another and are useful in conceptualizing the complexity of career cases such as those of Naomi and Todd. Viewing a career situation through the ecological lens helps career counselors understand the unique dynamics of the person within his or her larger environmental context, which, of course, includes the cultural context. As we have highlighted, both individual personality variables, such as Naomi's and Todd's degree of active approach behaviors and human agency, and the more macro influences, such as their culture, have an array of interrelated influences on their career choice and development. It is clear that such interrelationships occur simultaneously at multiple levels so that a focus on any one level of interaction is by definition a limited picture of the dynamics shaping observable behavior at any one time (Cook et al., 2005).

Thus, we can use the Ecological Model to help conceptualize the case of Naomi and Todd and to help them understand the multifaceted influences, some conscious, some unconscious or out of their awareness, that have an impact on their career development. For example, at the individual level, we can help them think about their interests, values, abilities, personality variables, and worldviews and how these have influenced both of them individually. As we have already mentioned, both Todd and Naomi seem to be confident and have a strong problem-solving confidence that keeps them moving ahead and proactively approaching career-development tasks in their lives. At the microsystem level are systems that have had direct influence on them, such as the innovative graduate program in management in which they were enrolled. It would be particularly interesting to help them explore what values and messages are promoted and reinforced in that unique microsystem that has helped shape their views about international work. At the mesosystem, we are really examining interactions between two or more microsystems. In Todd and Naomi's case, it would seem prudent to explore the mesosystem that is created between their home life and plans for home and family and their school and work lives to see how these microsystems both reinforce each other and also, potentially, provide areas of conflict. In exploring exosystem variables, it is important to consider the policies that influence these variables, even such things as the sheer availability of programs like the one in which they were involved in Canada and the many ways that work, study, and living abroad have been reinforced through these policies. The macrosystem is particularly interesting to explore in this case, because of the ideological components of both Asia and America in which broad issues such as culture, class, gender, and structure of opportunity all influence the many nested systems and subsystems within the scope of the macrosystem and ultimately influence Naomi and Todd's career development.

Thus, as we reflect on this case and think about the complex role of the career counselor, we are struck by the importance of both personality and culture and also with the potential usefulness of the broad view of vocational behavior that the Ecological Model provides.

References

Bandura, A. (1986). *Social foundations of thought and action.* New York: Prentice Hall.

Bronfenbrenner, U. (1977). Toward an experimental ecology of human development. *American Psychologist, 32,* 513–531.

Cook E. P., Heppner, M. J., & O'Brien, K. M. (2004). Career counseling from an ecological perspective. In R. K. Conyne & E. P. Cook (Eds.), *Ecological counseling: An innovative approach to conceptualizing person–environment interaction* (pp. 219–242). Alexandria, VA: American Counseling Association.

Cook, E. P., Heppner, M. J., & O'Brien, K. (2005). Multicultural and gender influences in women's career development: An ecological perspective. *Journal of Multicultural Counseling and Development, 33,* 165–179.

Gysbers, N. C., Heppner, M. J., & Johnston, J. A. (2003). *Career counseling: Process, issues, and techniques* (2nd ed.). Boston: Allyn & Bacon.

Heppner, P. P., Witty, T. E., & Dixon, W. A. (2004). Problem-solving appraisal and human adjustment: A review of 20 years of research utilizing the Problem Solving Inventory. *The Counseling Psychologist, 32,* 344–428.

Ladrine, H. (1995). Introduction: Cultural diversity, contextualism, and feminist psychology. In H. Ladrine (Ed.), *Bridging cultural diversity to feminist psychology: Theory, research and practice* (pp. 1–20). Washington, DC: American Psychological Association.

Masten, A. S., & Reed, M. G. J. (2002). Resilience in development. In C. R. Snyder & S. J. Lopez (Eds.), *The handbook of positive psychology* (pp. 74–88). New York: Oxford University Press.

Scheier, M. E., & Carver, C. S. (1985). Optimism, coping, and health: Assessment and implications of generalized outcome expectancies. *Health Psychology, 4,* 219–247.

Response 2

Margaret (Peggy) Pusch

Todd and Naomi, dedicated to an international career path, began by moving to Thailand. Naomi had a job, and Todd carved out a career and eventually found a job with locally owned Thai companies, effectively working there for 3 years. They anticipated problems with the transition and planned for Todd's initial situation of being the equivalent of a "trailing spouse," used established contacts in Thailand, and managed to establish themselves personally and professionally with remarkable success. They demonstrated considerable intercultural skill, using their knowledge of the culture to fit in during their stay but also to plan their departure. Convinced that they needed to leave locally owned companies to advance their international careers, they developed a strategy to leave Thailand that would avoid offending their employers and that would, in fact, allow them to maintain relationships that might be useful in the future.

Strategies for International Transitions

The first step in their strategy was to return home to Canada to, as they told their employers, "spend time with family and friends." They expected to find jobs quickly in Canada and to have a relatively easy return even though their Thai experience was not greatly valued. Aware that reentry can be more challenging than going abroad in the first place, they anticipated some difficulty, and problems did occur, but reentry was not nearly as stressful as might have been anticipated. Given their careful planning and the commitment to living in the present in a way that would contribute to a future they both desired, their return home was challenging but achieved the goals they had set for themselves.

There are several reasons why they managed this transition well, albeit with some strain due to living separately with their respective parents for a period of time and accepting jobs that held promise but had less status and salary than the positions they had held in Thailand.

- The couple had a clear picture of what to expect both in going to Thailand and returning to Canada—their expectations were appropriately realistic.
- They treated their return to Canada in the same manner they managed their transition abroad—as if they were entering a new culture but using the resources and contacts developed before their departure.

- They focused on building a life in Canada even though they expected to eventually return to Asia.
- They made conscious decisions on career moves and had clear goals in mind. They made their own decisions in a focused manner and were not being drawn to different places by assignments or other outside forces. They had some level of control over their situation.
- They sought assistance in making the decisions that are necessary in any transition, but especially challenging when those transitions are international and involve considerable financial stress.

The focused and proactive approach this couple exhibited does not eliminate all the challenges associated with cross-cultural transitions, but it allows them to maintain their ability to move on with their plans optimistically.

Suggestions for Counseling

With colleague Bruce LaBrack, I have developed and used the R2A4 system in workshop materials. Counselors may find this system useful for working with this couple. The main components of the R2A4 system follow.

- Reviewing the present by exploring how individuals are functioning at the moment and how what they are experiencing is related to prior experiences.
- Recollecting the past, identifying the factors, people, places, and events that have positively shaped those past experiences.
- Analyzing how the past and present relate to each other. What influences from the past have become irrelevant but still seem to influence and, perhaps, overwhelm an individual's ability to move on? What influences are useful and are contributing to an ability to move on?

These first three steps provide an opportunity to explore how Todd and Naomi have changed as a couple and individually. It is useful to introduce them to others who have made this step and survived. It is important to help them develop realistic expectations because this is the one factor that can make a difference in adapting to going home.

- Adjust attitudes, depending on what emotions are most prevalent, what can be used productively, and what is necessary to let go.
- Anticipate what individuals want to change or deal with more effectively. What can be or might be altered that will make life more satisfying and allow a foundation for the future to be constructed? How manageable are the challenges of the return? How can the experience be structured so that individuals are dealing with one thing at a time or, at least, be structured to keep the stress load to a reasonable size?
- Take action involving the development of a plausible plan of action, taking into account the cognitive recognition of past patterns and current desires or needs and the emotions that accompany the current transition. This is a time to take charge of the future. (Pusch & LaBrack, 1998)

Enhancing Transition Success

Todd and Naomi adapted well to Thailand, and this experience with adapting honed the skills they would need for repatriation. Sussman (1986) suggested that those who adapted well overseas could have a smoother reentry than those who did not. This requires that the return home be negotiated by applying the skills used in going abroad, having a clear picture of what to expect, and having a sense of how to fit in at home. Clearly, Todd and Naomi had a useful strategy for the return similar to the one used when going to Thailand.

The 10 top reentry challenges identified by LaBrack (2000) did not seem to be serious problems but even if some were, it did not deter Tod and Naomi from their plan. Those challenges are the following.

- Boredom with life at home
- No one wanting to hear your stories or about your stay abroad
- Difficulty explaining your experience in ways that can be comprehended by the people at home
- Homesickness for the place you left behind
- Changed relationships with the people at home
- People seeing and responding to the "wrong" changes, such as small alterations in your eating or behavioral habits, but ignoring the significant changes in your sense of who you have become
- People misunderstanding or misinterpreting your words and actions in ways that make communication difficult
- Feelings of alienation from the home culture
- An inability to apply new knowledge and skills that have been acquired abroad
- Loss or compartmentalization of the experience

This couple was considering the decisions they had to make, the jobs they were able to find, and the planning for the future and how these choices would influence an international business career. They remained focused on that and were not deterred by the difficulties that they may have experienced. They may have had especially receptive family members and friends who were interested in their stories and did not hold them accountable for unexpected patterns of behavior. It is clear that they knew people who had been through this experience, and this not only provided a warning of what to expect but a "peer group" with whom to relate. No doubt, they encountered some of the challenges LaBrack listed, but they managed to deal with them and stay with their plan.

Todd and Naomi considered change part of the process of realizing their dreams of living and working internationally. Change, however, is situational; it involves, in this case, the actual move from one place to another. Whether they consciously realized it or not, they were also navigating the transition of psychological adaptation or readaptation to encounters with the unfamiliar and a subsequent encounter with the familiar. It is more than shifting countries, homes, and furniture, it is a process of considering what is important, how to create a new emotional environment in which to function, and ways of being who you want to be and have become.

Transitions for Dual-Career Couples

Transitions, according to Bridges (2004), have three stages:

- endings
- the neutral zone
- the new beginning

Every beginning starts with an ending, and this couple completed their stay in Thailand with attention to saying good-bye, to being sure that relationships were honored, and to preparing for the physical and psychological move in a way that would keep the Thailand experience part of their continuing life plan,

Todd and Naomi had met in graduate school and became a couple just as they were starting out in their careers. This meant making choices that took both of their aspirations into account. This, alone, was a big transition. They did not have the freedom that being single allows, but they did have the support and assistance that being a couple provides. Thus, they had an instant, though small, support system that would bolster them as the transitions occurred. Relationships are often structured on unspoken agreements, but this couple discussed how they would approach employment, given both their career aspirations. They ended their single status and entered a relationship with some clarity about how it would affect their careers and how they would deal with that challenge. Todd was the "trailing spouse" first, unusual in the world of international business. Having made transitions from single to couple and from their home country to a new location, they were well on their way to acquiring practice in the skills for the next step in their transition experience. They physically returned to their home country and also separately to their childhood homes. Having been a couple for several years, they decided, again consciously, to live with their respective families as a way of saving money and of intensely reconnecting with family and friends. This may well have been a way of reassessing their relationship and its durability in the home environment as they searched for employment. This period appears to be the "neutral zone" in Bridges's (2004) model. They had to determine if their relationship would continue and if they would find work that allowed them to put down roots in their home community. Obviously, they decided to continue the relationship and even to purchase a home and live together again. This led to the new beginning for their relationship as a couple, creating a new home and settling into jobs that might not be perfect but provided reasonable satisfaction. They do not appear to have abandoned their dream of living abroad again and expanding their international careers. Every decision they have made so far has been thoroughly examined and the execution planned in a way that points to the ultimate achievement of their clearly stated goals. If they decide to go abroad again, many of these decisions will have to be made again, but Todd and Naomi have the resources, garnered from past successful experience, to do so constructively.

Styles of Reentry

The dream of having international careers and their interest in living in foreign cultures are probably sustaining factors in their ability to manage repatriation. As shown in Table 1.1, four styles of reentry are identified.

Naomi and Todd have, apparently, returned home as integrators, connecting their experience abroad with the new beginning at home and being clear about their goals for the future. They may be expatriates again. This is not a failure of coming home but a choice that is consciously made when career and life choices point in the direction of living away from home in several sequential stays or for an extended period. It is a necessary style if they wish to have international careers in business.

The free spirit style is characterized by being detached from the home culture and from the life they lived before going abroad; there is a disinterest in rekindling old relationships on the old terms and possibly an inability to renegotiate those relationships on new terms. The focus is a desire to continue, to any degree possible, the experience of being abroad. Although this may not be totally possible, every attempt is made to remain in the overseas mode. In this style is a range of responses to reentry that, at its most benign, is manifested as mild discontent and, at its most severe, almost total alienation. Clearly, this style does not fit the return of Todd and Naomi.

The detached repatriate is concerned largely with creating a comfortable environment for him- or herself and the immediate family. Having determined that the kind of life he or she lived before departure is no longer satisfying, ways will be found to maintain an adequate income and a comfortable home and to engage in activities that are enjoyable.

Table 1.1
Four Styles of Reentry

Measure	Free Spirit	Detached	Reassimilator	Integrator
Reactions to home culture	Detachment (ranging from discontent to alienation)	Reluctance to go back to old patterns and home culture	Reassimilation; delighted to be back	Positive integration
Main concern	Continue experience of being different	Survival, comfort	Easy reentry; fitting into home culture	Finding best fit with the home culture
Internal commitment	Being "unique"	Creating comfortable environment for self (and perhaps family)	Home culture; life as it has always been	Continuing to change and develop
Role one seems (or tries) to play	Eccentric	Detached but tolerant participant	Total participant	Leader or mediator; contented believer, advocate, expatriate

There is no effort, however, to continue on the expected career path or engage in the kind of community activities that he or she no longer judges to be important. He or she may also appear to fit back in fairly well and not display any signs of discontent. This style emphasizes finding a way to live at home that does not irritate the natives, although there is little pleasure, at least initially, in returning home. Naomi and Todd made every effort to connect with people at home and to move on with their original career choices. This style does not fit them.

Reassimilators rarely seek help with their return home. Frequently, they are focused on settling back into the home culture. They treat their international experience as an interesting interlude. Those anxious to reassimilate to the home culture are concerned with having an easy reentry and are committed to their primary culture. They are a total participant in the home culture because they are anxious to plug back into the position, both social and professional, that they had vacated only temporarily. The employee may want a promotion or some other tangible recognition of his or her work abroad (it *is* a well-deserved reward) but is not anxious to apply what was learned in the host environment to the job at home unless it is functionally relevant. Naomi and Todd may have appeared, at first, to be in this reentry mode, but their focus on the future tends to repudiate that possibility.

Integration is a category with many permutations. The concern for all those in this category, no matter how they act it out, is finding the best fit with their home culture in a way that uses the overseas experience and integrates it with the rest of their lives. This may mean leaving home again. Their commitments are a mix of several options or a selection of one, depending on the individuals, the circumstances in which they live, and the context in which they work or pursue professional interests.

Personal Change and Adaptation

A major challenge in this process is adapting to the home culture while maintaining one's changed self. It is necessary to develop strategies to deal with the following:

- Maintaining professional status
- Experiencing professional growth
- Continuing contacts with professional colleagues abroad

- Maintaining contact with friends abroad
- Building a new lifestyle based on a changed self-image, interests, and a broader worldview
- Renegotiating old relationships while building new relationships, often with people who do not fit well with anyone in the group, family, and/or friends to whom they are returning

They must become productive members of the home culture and society in a way that effectively uses the experience and results of being in another culture. This may require letting go of some of what has been acquired and calls for identifying what it is best to hold on to and what is not so important. The repatriate learns to use the transition experience as a basis and reference point for future personal growth.

Making an international transition involves all the stressors listed in the Social Readjustment Rating Scale (Holmes & Rahe, 1967) plus some additional considerations. People making transitions across cultures are literally off the scale on the changes they must accommodate, the process they must go through, and the formerly familiar things they must learn or relearn. One of the greatest problems in reentry is denial that it will be a problem, and this denial adds considerably to the stress that is felt and the level of decision making that must be done. This couple seemed to manage so well that they are a caution to others: Do not expect it to be this easy. I suspect, however, that their story has a back story of much more stress, many more ambiguous feelings, and far more difficulty than appear on the surface.

Most people who are trying to affirm their overseas experience are well aware of how they have changed and feel good about those changes. They anticipate more change, knowing they will continue to develop and grow in the future. It appears, as noted above, that Naomi and Todd fit this category and will continue to explore many options for the future. They have grown roots in the home community, but they can be uprooted again. If that is the case, they are not immune to the trials of adaptation in the next culture they enter, and if they return to Thailand, not immune to the impact of reentry to that country. It will be as if they returned home again.

References

Bridges, W. (2004). *Transitions: Making sense of life's changes* (2nd ed.). Cambridge, MA: Perseus Books.

Holmes, T. H., & Rahe, R. H. (1967). The Social Readjustment Rating Scale. *Journal of Psychosomatic Research, 11,* 213–218.

LaBrack, B. (2000). Top ten immediate reentry challenges. In B. LaBrack & M. D. Pusch, *Training for international transitions* [Packet for Summer Institute for Intercultural Communication]. Unpublished.

Pusch, M. D., & LaBrack. B. (1998). Reentry orientations. In *The overseas advisors handbook.* Washington, DC: The College Board.

Sussman, N. M. (1986). Re-entry research and training: Methods and implications. *International Journal of Intercultural Relations, 10,* 235–254.

Transition and Adaptation to Living and Working Across Cultures

Karen Moustafa-Leonard

Karen moved from the southern part of the United States to New Zealand to marry Dr. Esam Moustafa, a professor at the University of Auckland Medical School, who had immigrated 26 years before. It was her first trip outside of the United States and, at 28, she saw it as an adventure. After all, New Zealand was like America, wasn't it? It was English speaking, like the United States. It could not be all that different. She believed that her English/Irish/Scottish background would allow her to fit in well, with little adaptation. It would merely be a transition. She was more worried about the differences in the seasons, with New Zealand being in the southern hemisphere.

When she arrived, Esam was there to greet her and take her to their new home. She found that New Zealanders drove on the other side of the road (for her, the wrong side). This was initially very frightening, particularly at night, when the car lights were coming from the "wrong" side of the road and she was sitting on the U.S. driver's—but the New Zealand passenger's—side of the car!

A few days after the wedding, she was taken to a friend's home for dinner. The dinner consisted totally of food that had been oven boiled in one pot, somewhat like pot roast, but not exactly. The meat was lamb, which she had never eaten; potatoes; carrots; and, to her surprise, pumpkin and squash. It was not unpleasant, but it had very little taste. On the way home, they passed a "panelbeater" shop. Esam told her it was a shop where they repaired damage to car bodies (a body shop in the United States). As time went on, she noticed more and more differences in terminology and in pronunciation of words. These differences were compounded by the use of Polynesian (Maori) words such as Papatoetoe (a suburb of Auckland) and Ruapehu (a volcanic mountain of extreme climate). In addition, there was a whole new history to learn of the Polynesian and English cultures.

Shopping was a challenge. Nothing she used in cooking in the United States was available in New Zealand. There was no mayonnaise or mustard or other condiments, except something called tomato sauce, which looked and tasted like watered-down ketchup. There was no cornmeal, no crackers, no hot dogs. There were, however, milk, cheese, and ice cream—but the fat content was twice that in the United States. The chocolate was heavenly, but it was the only thing Karen found that was along the lines of the food in the United States, particularly the southern part.

Although her husband was a professor at the medical school, his salary was not large because he was a scientist, not a medical doctor. Living in New Zealand was expensive, because most items were imported. His salary covered their needs, but money for travel back to the United States for visits had to be saved.

Not wanting to complain, because she loved her husband, Karen looked forward to obtaining her permanent residency and getting a job in the health care industry. Upon attaining a job with the public health service in New Zealand, she found she had to belong to the union for her job type, the Clerical Union. In the southern part of the United States, there was little unionism. Karen did not want to join a union and asked how to decline. She was told that the only reason for declining was for religious reasons, so she joined the union.

At her job, Karen's colleagues made fun of her speech patterns, saying she talked too slowly. They thought that her enjoyment of work was silly and excluded her from their social activities, such as teatime and lunch, isolating her within the hospital. Her bosses liked her attitude, however, and she progressed rapidly through the health care services, becoming an executive officer of human resources in the Auckland Area health care service, which employed 15,000 people. At that level, she was able to fit in with her colleagues, after living in the country 4 years.

One day, Esam suggested that they plan a visit to the United States, as they had saved sufficient funds to travel. When they arrived in Honolulu for an overnight stay, Karen had her first hamburger in 4 years. She was surprised to find tears in her eyes—she did not realize she had missed hamburgers that much. Upon landing in Memphis, Tennessee, her parents wanted to know all about New Zealand and her life there, but they found her speech patterns very different. Her father commented on the change often. Karen found herself getting in the car on the driver's side, when she was not driving!

The most frightening experience of the visit for her was finding herself on the left side of a two-lane road one evening, instead of on the correct right side. Luckily, no one was coming in either lane, and she was able to correct quickly. She realized that she had not merely transitioned but had adapted to the New Zealand way of life.

When Karen and Esam moved permanently to the United States after her 8-year stay in New Zealand, returning was difficult in some ways. They had made good friends in New Zealand, and it was hard to leave. When they sold the house, the dollar had just changed from being an equivalent of $0.70 to the US$1.00 to a floating exchange. The New Zealand dollar dropped to $0.30 to the US$1.00; they lost more than half of the value of their house in this way.

When she returned to the United States, it was difficult to know which side of the road to drive on—she had to be constantly alert. It was hard becoming reaccustomed to American English. Her family and friends teased her when she used the wrong word, like *spanner* instead of *wrench*. Her sister began the family practice of using the English pronunciation for *tomato* instead of the U.S. one.

They coped by using the techniques Karen used to adapt to New Zealand: trying to find interesting features of difference rather than moaning over the things that were in New Zealand and not in the United States. Having the family support in the United States that was not available in New Zealand was very useful, and the family used teasing and encouragement to ease Karen and Esam's move to the States. The enjoyment of the experience of living in New Zealand was overtaken by their new life in the United States as they began to transition and adapt to their new life.

Key Issues

Organizations contemplating using expatriate workers should select them with care for more than technical or managerial ability. "Openness to experience" is a personality trait that has been found to be essential in successful expatriate experiences.

In transitions and adaptations, culture shock is a major component of the failures of expatriates to adjust. Training and preliminary exposures to the culture help insulate most individuals from the worst parts of the shock, but most psychologists believe it cannot be entirely overcome. The factors of culture shock include the shock of language differences, both overt and subtle, and the shock of being in cultures where not everything is written down or orally expressed. Behaviors in many cultures are predetermined by context, and people from more individualistic and lower context cultures have difficulties in fitting in because they do not know what to do—it is not written or openly told to them.

Another major problem for expatriates is returning to their home countries, surprisingly enough. Expatriates are different when they return. They have learned some parts of a new culture and have managed to understand how a different group of people interact. Often when they return to a corporation, their experience is devalued or ignored entirely. This is valuable global knowledge, which companies are generally wasting. Eventually, Karen was going to have to return home. How would she readapt into the home culture? Would it work in the same way? How long would it take to adapt back? Would it depend upon how long she lived in New Zealand before returning?

Relationships are also important counseling considerations. Although it is usual to think of individual transitions, family and social relationships influence individual adjustment to cross-cultural transitions. In this instance, the individual was in a married relationship with her husband, and she had several colleagues in New Zealand. These relationships appeared to ease the cross-cultural transition; however, the absence of family and friends who were in the United States needs to be taken into account when reviewing relationship considerations.

Transition Outcomes

Because of the need to stay in New Zealand, where her husband was employed, Karen found a way to adapt to the life. Because they were able to visit the United States only twice in 8 years, she found she had to adapt, rather than transition. Perhaps this would be a good place to discuss the personality profile of an individual who is open to experience. Karen would not have given up the experience in New Zealand, even though it took her away from her family and friends in the United States. Living in New Zealand allowed her to think of differences as acceptable and challenging, rather than as forces to fight.

This case incident illustrates that positive adaptation might not be a solution that would appeal or be available to every individual. In New Zealand, for example, some expatriates liked the country for its intense freedom and democracy, the very thing that other expatriates criticized. Karen sought new opportunities. She saw new ways of working and was able to institute changes in the organizations where she worked, primarily because of the differences in the educational system in the two countries. In New Zealand, as in most British-based educational systems, individuals were extremely specialized. In the United States, most undergraduate education is generalized, allowing less depth but more breadth of opportunities.

Writer's Role: Choosing the Side of the Road

In this case incident, Karen is the author. Esam was my husband. In my case, where neither of us had family in New Zealand, it was more difficult, although friends did help fill the gap to some extent. When we returned permanently to the United States after I had lived in New Zealand for 8 years, there were adjustment problems. On occasion, I still walk to the wrong side of the car.

Conclusion

In the long run, people who are open to experience will make the best transitions and adaptations to the change in culture. With proper training and assistance, however, most individuals will learn to at least cope with moves to another culture. Much depends on the support of the organization that is sending them overseas or the family support in both the home and adoptive cultures.

Reader Reflection Questions

1. If you were to move to New Zealand or a similar English-heritage country, what do you think you would find most difficult?
2. Could Esam have assisted Karen in adjusting better before she came to New Zealand, because he had experience of both the United States and New Zealand?
3. If you were to work in another country, what would you be most apprehensive about?
4. What assurances would you need to take a job in New Zealand?
5. How could you help someone adjust to returning to the United States after he or she had lived in another country for a while?

Response 1

Yu-Wei Wang and Julia A. Conrath

In this response, various theories are briefly described to illustrate the cross-cultural transition experiences among international workers and to sensitize counselors to various issues about which they should be aware when working with this population. The case incident will be used as an example to elaborate the applications of the theories and possible adjustment issues facing international workers. A summary with specific suggestions for counseling is provided at the end of this response.

Culture Shock and Reverse Culture Shock

Culture shock has been commonly used to describe the stress reactions associated with cross-cultural transition. The term *culture shock* was defined by two anthropologists, Kalervo Oberg and George Foster, as "a medical condition describing feelings of disorientation following entry into a new culture, feelings often so strong as to degenerate into physical symptoms" (Anderson, 1994, p. 294). Recuperation models (the U-curve and W-curve hypotheses) were developed to explain how expatriates recover from culture shock (Gullahorn & Gullahorn, 1963; Lysgaard, 1955; Oberg, 1960). These models assert that international sojourners may experience initial excitement as they enter a new culture; however, they also may feel confused by unfamiliar environmental cues (e.g., customs, facial or verbal expressions, role ambiguity), overwhelmed by cultural fatigue (i.e., fatigue from being overloaded with new information) and homesickness, and frustrated by the need to fit in and reestablish a new social network in the host country. The demands of surviving in a new country may overwhelm sojourners and lead to maladaptive outcomes (e.g., anxiety and depression). The U-curve hypothesis also suggests that expatriates may gradually recuperate from culture shock as they adapt to the new culture and environment. The W-curve hypothesis extends the U-curve hypothesis and purports that expatriates, upon returning to their home country, may experience reverse culture shock and an adaptation process (a second U-curve) similar to the first adjustment process during sojourns.

Applying the recuperation models to the case in point, Karen appeared to go through varying phases of cultural transitions as she entered and adjusted to the host culture. Due to a lack of experience living or traveling abroad and the limited exposure to the host culture prior to her move, Karen experienced culture shock upon her arrival in New Zealand.

For example, she had to adjust to driving on the other side of the road, which initially frightened her, and to learn about the different lifestyles, customs, and relevant history of the host nationals. She had to adapt to different pronunciations and terminologies, even though her mother tongue, English, is also the official language of New Zealand. Karen was surprised that she encountered culture shock, which partly stemmed from her assumption that she would not encounter many cultural difficulties because of the shared language and similar ethnic heritage. As she acquired knowledge and understanding about the host culture, however, she gradually recuperated from the culture shock and adapted to the new lifestyle and customs. During the sojourn, Karen missed family and the food, climate, and culture in her home country but was able to visit the United States only twice due to financial restraints. However, after living and working in New Zealand 8 years, Karen eventually became accustomed to the host culture and lifestyle and experienced reverse culture shock when she returned to her country of origin. Her family in the United States was surprised about how much Karen had adapted to the New Zealand culture.

In sum, in addition to the initial culture shock at the point of entering the host country, international workers may not be fully aware of the impact of the cultural transition process on them and thus unprepared for reverse culture shock when they return to their home country. Their family and friends may be surprised about the extent to which the sojourn experiences transformed the expatriates, which can add to the stress associated with reentry transitions.

Adaptation to Cross-Cultural Transition

Although the recuperation models suggest that all expatriates are confronted with stress related to cross-cultural transition, the level of stress related to the transition and the adaptation processes appears to vary among international workers. The model postulated by Schlossberg (1981) is used below to organize the factors that affect the transition experienced by sojourners. A number of other theories are presented to illustrate the impact of various factors on adaptation outcomes and sensitize counselors to possible presenting concerns of this population in counseling.

Schlossberg (1981) stated that "a transition can be said to occur if an event or nonevent results in a change in assumptions about oneself and the world and thus requires a corresponding change in one's behavior and relationships" (p. 5) and defined adaptation to transition as "a process during which an individual moves from being totally preoccupied with the transition to integrating the transition into his or her life" (p. 7). A life transition can have both a positive and negative impact on individual well-being. Overall, her model highlights three factors that affect transition processes and adaptation outcomes—namely, characteristics of transition, pretransition and posttransition environments, and individuals. Working abroad often constitutes a significant life transition for international workers and entails changes in the work itself, environment, and sojourners (Furnham & Bochner, 1986; Ward, Bochner, & Furnham, 2001). The nature of the transition, environmental differences, and individual characteristics all account for individual adjustment process and adaptation outcomes.

Characteristics of the Transition

The reasons, timing, onset, and duration of the cross-cultural transition, as well as concurrent role change, can affect international workers' perceptions of the transition and result in different stress reactions (Schlossberg, 1981). Compared with expatriates who initiate the move to the host country, those who move mostly for external reasons (e.g., job assignments or market demands) may perceive and experience more stress in the transition process. International workers may face different consequences if they choose not to move; some may be "dismissed or demoted if not agreeing to the transfer" (Furnham & Bochner, 1986, p. 150), and others may have more freedom in making this decision Also, when workers are transferred overseas, the type and level of the jobs in the host country may be similar to or different from the original positions in the home countries. Individuals who are assigned to take on positions that require them to develop new skills and knowledge face more stress in the transition process compared with their counterparts.

The timing (e.g., move during early adulthood vs. mid-life) and onset (e.g., sudden vs. gradual) of the transition may make a difference in the preparedness of the workers for the cross-cultural adaptation process. For example, Karen moved to New Zealand when she was 28 years old; she had accumulated considerable education and life experiences that could help her cope with the change. Her transition can be considered "gradual" because she anticipated her move and was able to plan ahead. Furthermore, expatriates may approach the cross-cultural transition differently, depending on whether they expect their move to be permanent or temporary. Those whose move is temporary and brief may not face as much pressure to adapt to the new culture. Some may not know exactly how long they will stay in the host country; this feeling of uncertainty and ambiguity can compromise their ability to make other life decisions. Finally, transition is usually accompanied by role change, which in turn may have various effects on expatriates. In Karen's case, she gained a new role through marriage at the same time that she moved to another country. The circumstance of marrying and leaving her home country probably generated both positive and negative affective reactions.

To sum up, counselors should be aware that the meanings of cross-cultural transition may differ for individuals, partly depending on the characteristics of transition. When working with international workers, it is critical to clarify the context and nature of the transition and explore how expatriates' perceptions of the transition affect the level of stress associated with the transition experiences.

Characteristics of Pretransition and Posttransition Environments

In addition to the characteristics of transition, the physical setting, support system, and institutional support of the pretransition and posttransition environments, and in particular the degree of differences between these two environments, may affect the amount of resources available to expatriates and their ability to cope (Schlossberg, 1981). Individuals who relocate to a host country that is notably different from their home cultures are required to make more adjustments and, thus, may experience more difficulties than their counterparts (Furnham & Bochner, 1986; Ward et al., 2001).

Regarding the change in physical environment, sojourners may be prone to physical illness while adjusting to different food, climate, and life arrangement. It may be difficult to access the support system in the home country, potentially leading to feelings of homesickness and loneliness while living in the host country. Some international workers may have none or limited social support available in the new environment. Some may not have opportunities to socialize with co-nationals who share similar cultural values and practices or find it difficult to develop new and meaningful relationships with host nationals. Finally, the transition itself may affect family dynamics; for those who move with their families, their adaptation and work efficiency may be affected by their significant others' satisfaction with the sojourn experiences. For dual-career couples, both partners' career development issues should be attended to in counseling. International workers who have children with them in the host country may also face additional stress, depending on how well their children adjust to the new environment.

Furthermore, international workers may not have the same level of institutional support in the host country, experience "a clash between company and personal interests and values" (Furnham & Bockner, 1986, p. 154), or face discrimination against foreigners. For example, a sojourner's religious beliefs and practices may differ from those of the mainstream culture in the host country. Some international workers may struggle with identifying a religious community where they can find a sense of belongingness. In addition, international workers may experience difficulties in learning about and adapting to the cultural expectations of the workplace in the host country. Also, the political and historical relations between the international workers' country of origin and the host country can affect local people's perceptions of and interactions with the expatriates. Discrimination and negative stereotypes against foreign workers may lead to feelings of strain, low self-esteem, or low self-efficacy, which subsequently may have an adverse effect on expatriates' career plans and performance. Finally, the career trajectories of international workers may be complicated by immigration regulations about employment and job markets in the host and home countries.

Because of the drastic change in the physical setting, Karen was initially worried about adjusting to the difference in seasons. She was deprived of her old support system (i.e., her family and friends in the United States), yet her husband, who already had years of adjustment experiences to the host culture, could serve as a source of support and as a cultural informant for her. Karen also encountered institutional barriers when she obtained her first position in New Zealand. Even though she did not want to join a union, union membership was essential for the type of jobs that she held. She felt excluded by her coworkers, who did not identify with her work attitude and ethics. Karen later was able to establish herself at work and build a new support system in the host country, which had a positive influence on her cultural adjustment process. Social support was crucial when she returned to the United States. Her family used encouragement to help Karen readjust to the U.S. culture.

In summary, the differences in physical settings between the home and host countries may have considerable impact on the perceived stress and well-being of international workers. Negative (or a lack of) support from others or institutions in the host culture may escalate the distress level and lead to maladjustment outcomes, whereas a healthy environment and supportive relationships may serve as a buffer against stress.

Individual Characteristics

The third factor that Schlossberg (1981) identified as an important factor in affecting the transition process is the difference in individual characteristics. It is critical for counselors to be aware of the heterogeneity of the international worker population. Variations in state of health, demographic backgrounds (e.g., sex, socioeconomic status, and race/ethnicity), value orientation, psychosocial competence, as well as prior experience with similar transitions, all affect the cultural adjustment experiences of international workers.

Specifically, the state of health can cushion stress or become another source of stress. The physical and mental health status of the international workers prior to and during the sojourn may influence their coping ability. Expatriates who are physically and psychologically adjusted in the new environment are better equipped to deal with other types of stress in the transition process. In terms of demographic backgrounds, sex role differences may play a role in the expatriates' adjustment process. International workers may face drastically different gender role expectations in a new culture and have to negotiate with the novel cultural norms in the workplace. Financial strain may be another source of stress, depending on individual preentry socioeconomic status, currency exchange rates, and job markets and economy in the host and home countries. People who move to another country as a result of a promotion may be offered strong financial sponsorship with political and social benefits and, thus, may feel that their quality of life improves after the move (Furnham & Bochner, 1986; Ward et al., 2001). In contrast, some international workers may lose financially as a result of the move.

In addition, the process of negotiating the different value orientations and worldviews in the host culture can be challenging for international workers. Expatriates often have to reexamine both their ethnic identity and their value system once they start their sojourn in a novel culture, both of which have an impact on individual career development and choices (Gysbers, Heppner, & Johnston, 2003). Sometimes, expatriates and host nationals do not share the same language or communication styles, which may create further barriers in the cross-cultural adjustment process. Those who are less confident about their communication skills, compared with their counterparts, may perceive their sojourn experience as more stressful. International workers who come from an individualist culture may have to adjust to the cultural norm of a collectivist society, and vice versa. They also need to learn to identify implicit and contextually dependent behaviors in high-context cultures or learn how to communicate explicitly in low-context cultures. Individuals may also encounter different perceptions of time in monochromic and polychromic societies, to which they will need to adjust when working with others in the host culture.

Some international workers eventually adapt to the cultural norms, and this adaptation transforms their value orientation, whereas others may change very little. According to Berry (1997), expatriates may experience acculturation stress when they are confronted with a clash between their indigenous cultural beliefs and the mainstream cultural values of host nationals. Sojourners may use different strategies (i.e., assimilation, separation, integration, and marginalization) to cope with the acculturation stress in order to maintain their cultural heritage or adopt new cultural values. Their coping patterns and abilities vary depending on their psychosocial competency, which includes self-perceptions, personality traits (e.g., optimism, openness), and self-efficacy. Specifically, the Social Cognitive Career Theory suggests that a person's personality and previous work experiences may affect her or his self-efficacy and outcome expectations, which in turn may affect her or his career development, choices, and performances (Brown & Lent, 2005). Therefore, individuals who are open to change and have high self-esteem and good coping efficacy, as well as those who can transfer pretransition work experiences and skills to the job in the host country, may perceive and experience less stress in the transition process. In contrast, if the usual problem-solving and coping mechanisms do not work in the new setting, international workers may face more immediate pressure to adjust to the new environment, become less efficient at work, and develop a myriad of maladaptive outcomes (e.g., psychosomatic symptoms, depression, and feelings of shame).

To conclude, it is important for counselors to bear in mind that international workers come from diverse backgrounds, which may have a significant impact on individual adaptation process. In Karen's case, her personal backgrounds (e.g., as someone from the southern part of the United States) affected her preentry beliefs and perceived cultural differences. Even though her native language was the same as the official language of New Zealand, she was teased by her colleagues for her different speech pattern. Karen eventually became adapted to the New Zealand culture and lifestyles. It was difficult for her to move back to the United States, because she had already established her friendship network in the host country, and she also lost financially (due to unfavorable currency exchange rate) when she and Esam sold their house in New Zealand. She chose to cope by learning about the "interesting features of difference" rather than "moaning over" losses. This coping style and experience helped her successfully manage culture shock and reverse culture shock. In a word, Karen's individual characteristics played an essential role in her transition experiences.

Conclusion and Implications for Counseling

On the basis of the Multicultural Counseling Competencies model (Sue, Arredondo, & McDavis, 1992), a number of recommendations are listed below for counselors who work with international workers. Specifically, counselors need to develop culture-specific awareness, knowledge, and skills in order to provide culturally appropriate counseling for this special population. The theories presented earlier can serve as a framework to increase counselors' awareness and knowledge about presenting issues that are relevant to cross-cultural transitions and adjustments. Possible counseling interventions are suggested as well.

In working with international workers, counselors should attend to culture entry and reentry issues, as well as to a wide range of factors—characteristics of transition, pretransition and posttransition environments, and individuals—that affect individuals' perception of the transition. The unique interplay of various circumstances accounts for variations in international workers' ability to cope successfully with cross-cultural transition. It is important to note not only that the effect of stress associated with the sojourn experience may be additive but also that these stressors interact synergistically to affect individual well-being (Wang, Lin, Pang, & Shen, 2006). Common stress associated with job change (e.g., learning about new workplace culture) may be exacerbated by culture shock and other personal and environmental factors, such as communication barriers and the lack of available social support in the host culture. Also, much attention is often given to the culture shock that sojourners experience upon entering the host culture, whereas relatively less attention is directed to the reverse culture shock that expatriates encounter when returning to their home countries. The latter can also be challenging processes because international workers may become acculturated to the host culture and subsequently have to readjust to their own culture. In addition, expatriates might miss the host culture as well as miss the relationships left behind. Often, family and friends who have not shared similar experiences cannot relate to the unique situation of the expatriates; therefore, when appropriate, family members or significant others should be included in counseling. Furthermore, sometimes workers' overseas experiences are not highly valued upon return, and some workers may encounter obstacles when attempting to obtain a job equivalent to the prior position held in the host country. These entry and reentry issues deserve special considerations in counseling workers who experience cross-cultural career transitions.

In addition, counselors should pay attention to possible stressors related to the transition itself, environmental change, and the nature and functions of the individual support system, all of which may have an impact on the well-being of expatriates. It is important for counselors to validate expatriates' unique life experiences and normalize their feelings around difficulties with transitions. Counselors can help expatriates identify sources of stress associated with the cross-cultural transition, establish support networks in the host country, and connect with host nationals who can serve as culture informants or mediators. In addition, counselors who work with sojourners should consider systemic interventions (Arthur, 2004). For companies that hire international workers, counselors can provide formal training on cross-cultural communications and adaptations. Companies can also provide host nationals with cultural sensitivity training in order to establish a culturally inclusive work environment for workers from different countries (Furnham & Bochner, 1986; Ward et al., 2001). Finally, it is essential for counselors to consider the heterogeneity of the international worker population. In dealing with common stressors associated with cross-cultural transition, some expatriates may be able to cope with cultural differences, whereas others may suffer from maladjustment. Pedersen (1991) suggested that counselors help sojourners develop appropriate skills in effectively dealing with cross-cultural differences. Helping international workers examine their psychosocial competency or learn adaptive coping strategies may facilitate the adjustment process. Counselors should be reminded that expatriates from different countries may have different perceptions about what counseling is or may have different preferences for helping styles (e.g., directive vs. nondirective). Counselors need to clarify counseling expectations with international workers and explore their preferences for helping styles. Assessments used in counseling need to be subject to cross-cultural validations, and the results should be interpreted in a manner that is culturally sensitive.

In conclusion, international workers may face a myriad of stressors associated with the cross-cultural transition, and the adaptation processes and outcomes may vary depending on a variety of factors. Counselors should attend to the interplay of these factors and the effects of this interplay on expatriates' well-being. With sufficient support and through active coping efforts, international workers, like Karen, can have a rewarding and fulfilling sojourn experience.

References

Anderson, L. E. (1994). A new look at an old construct: Cross-cultural adaptation. *International Journal of Intercultural Relations, 18,* 293–328.

Arthur, N. (2004). *Counseling international students: Clients from around the world.* New York: Kluwer Academic.

Berry, J. W. (1997). Immigration, acculturation, and adaptation. *Applied Psychology: An International Review, 46,* 5–68.

Brown, S. D., & Lent, R. W. (2005). *Career development and counseling: Putting theory and research to work.* Hoboken, NJ: Wiley.

Furnham, A., & Bochner, S. (1986). *Culture shock: Psychological reactions to unfamiliar environments.* New York: Methuen.

Gullahorn, J. T., & Gullahorn, J. E. (1963). An extension of the U-curve hypothesis. *Social Issues, 19,* 33–47.

Gysbers, N. C., Heppner, M. J., & Johnston, J. A. (2003). *Career counseling: Process, issues, and techniques* (2nd ed.). Boston: Allyn & Bacon.

Lysgaard, S. (1955). Adjustment in a foreign society: Norwegian Fulbright grantees visiting the United States. *International Social Science Bulletin, 10,* 45–51.

Oberg, K. (1960). Culture shock: Adjustment to new cultural environments. *Practical Anthropology, 7,* 177–182.

Pedersen, P. B. (1991). Counseling international students. *The Counseling Psychologist, 19,* 10–58.

Schlossberg, N. (1981). A model for analyzing human adaptation to transition. *The Counseling Psychologist, 9*(2), 2–18.

Sue, D. W., Arredondo, P., & McDavis, R. J. (1992). Multicultural competencies/standards: A call to the profession. *Journal of Counseling & Development, 70,* 477–486.

Wang, Y.-W., Lin, J. G., Pang, L.-S., & Shen, F. C. (2006). International students from Asia. In F. Leong et al. (Eds.), *Handbook of Asian American psychology* (2nd ed., pp. 245–261). Thousand Oaks, CA: Sage.

Ward, C., Bochner, S., & Furnham, A. (2001). *The psychology of culture shock* (2nd ed.). East Sussex, United Kingdom: Routledge.

Response 2

Sauli Puukari

Moving to another country poses challenges to all involved. It is a challenge not only to those who move but also to their friends, relatives, and colleagues and to the management of the organization employing the newcomers. Therefore, I approach the issues related to adaptation from multiple perspectives, pointing out challenges to different parties. One key aspect in dealing with the adaptation is openness to learn, again not just for the ones who are moving but also for the organizations and colleagues involved.

Learning from experience is vital in adapting to a new culture. In their article on experiential approach to cross-cultural learning, Yamazaki and Kayes (2004) noted that a number of studies suggest that adapting well during international assignments requires learning from experience (Porter & Tansky, 1999; Spreitzer, McCall, & Mahoney, 1997). They developed a systematic description of competencies for successful expatriate adaptation.

Learning Skill Dimension: Interpersonal

1. *Building Relationships*: Interacts with others regularly, particularly members of the host culture. Has the ability to gain access to and maintain relationships with members of host culture. Recognizes and deals effectively with misunderstandings, has a willingness to maintain contact with people even when communication is difficult.
2. *Valuing People of Different Cultures*: Expresses interest and respect for host culture, including its history, customs, beliefs, and politics. Has empathy for difference, sensitivity to diversity. Initiates and engages in open conversation with friends and colleagues about host culture.

Learning Skill Dimension: Information

3. *Listing and Observation*: Spends time observing, reading about, and studying host culture, particularly with locals. Knows cultural history and reasons for certain cultural actions and customs. Asks questions, when possible, and takes careful account of situations before taking action.
4. *Coping With Ambiguity*: Maintains work habits in the face of unexpected events, new experiences, or unfamiliar situations. Recognizes and interprets implicit behavior, especially nonverbal cues. Changes communication in response to nonverbal cues from others.

Learning Skill Dimension: Analytic

5. *Translating Complex Information*: Translates personal thoughts into language of host culture. Has knowledge of local language, symbols, or other forms of verbal language and written language. Demonstrates fluency in language of host country.

Learning Skill Dimension: Action

6. *Taking Action and Initiative*: Takes action when appropriate, even when outcome is uncertain. Understands intended and potentially unintended consequences of actions. Easily approaches and interacts with strangers.
7. *Managing Others*: Takes responsibility for accomplishing tasks related to the organizational goals. Has the ability to manage details of a job, including maintaining cohesion in a group. Communicates implications of individual actions to others in the organizations.

Learning Skill Dimension: Adaptive

8. *Adaptability and Flexibility:* Demonstrates acceptance of change, setbacks, and challenges. Views change from multiple perspectives. Can explain perspectives on a single issue.

9. *Managing Stress*: Maintains work habits during times of personal and environmental crisis or in the face of heavy emotional demands. Understands own and others' mood, emotions, and personality. Expresses personal feelings in an appropriate and nonthreatening way.

Regarding Karen's story, it seems that she had these competencies and that she was able to develop them further during her time in New Zealand. Karen's story indicated that she had true motivation and good competencies to adapt to a new culture and develop her work skills there. In her case, the difficulties of adaptation were not as great as they are for many, although she was challenged in many ways, particularly by some concrete aspects of the new country such as left-lane driving and differences in food. Her concrete experience of driving on the "wrong side of the road" became a metaphor that is a reminder about the meaning of cultural differences. Even though English is spoken both in New Zealand and the United States, Karen realized that there are differences rooted in cultural history, which made the adaptation to the new country more challenging than she had expected.

Homesickness was quite apparent, given for example her strong response to the first hamburger "after years of separation" when she visited the United States. Homesickness can be regarded as a normal feeling to be worked through rather than something to be avoided or prevented (Hannigan, 2005). Intercultural marriage might have been a topic to discuss as well, but given that Karen was not analyzing this aspect, I will focus on expatriation and repatriation processes from the perspective of work, with some attention to other aspects of the adaptation processes. I will use Karen's case as a starting point to discuss selected general issues and some specific comments related to it.

Expatriation and Repatriation Challenges

According to Chen and Starosta (1996), intercultural competency is a three-part process that leads to cultural awareness, cultural sensitivity, and cultural adroitness.

1. Cultural awareness is a cognitive process that consists of self-awareness and cultural awareness. As people become more self-aware, they also become better at understanding the effects of their behavior on others. After they learn something about the new culture and begin to understand the cultural "map," they are able to modify their behavior according to the expectations of the new country.
2. Cultural sensitivity is another process of international competency. It is important for a sojourner to be capable of incorporating values (e.g., open-mindedness, high self-concept, nonjudgmental attitudes) to understand the values of different cultures and to become sensitive to the verbal and nonverbal cues of people living in other cultures.
3. Cultural adroitness is the intercultural competency process that sojourners use to learn how to act effectively when encountering people in a new culture. When they understand what is expected from them (dos and don'ts), they learn to communicate effectively without offending people. Karen's story shows that she had developed her intercultural competency and had become culturally aware, sensitive, and adroit.

Bennett, Aston, and Colquhoun (2000) noted that building positive, mutually respectful, and trusting relationships is a key factor in successful international assignments. Trust is the most important element in good relationships; therefore it is important that people who work internationally be able to do the following.

- Develop trust relationships with people of different backgrounds and values
- Communicate well
- Collaborate in their approach
- Act as team players
- Negotiate skillfully
- Exhibit cultural competence

Given that Karen was very successful in working life in New Zealand, it seems obvious that she has done well in all the components listed above.

Black and Mendenhall (1990) discussed cross-cultural learning needed in adjusting to a new culture. The more novel the new culture, the more demanding it is to learn the new behaviors required in that culture. On this basis, Herrera and Herrera (2005) concluded that "repatriation adjustment is also made more difficult when environmental novelty is greater" (p. 67). They suggested that the following are some key variables that increase environmental novelty for some repatriates: differences in compensation; expatriate cultural differences; differences in power, autonomy, and control; and expatriate community differences.

Herrera and Herrera (2005) discussed these four variables. The variation in expatriate compensation packages is great. The compensation may affect the repatriates "negatively" when they are returning to their home countries if they have become accustomed to some forms of compensations that are not available there (e.g., driver or nanny). When cultural differences are great, it typically creates more difficult adaptation challenges during both the expatriation and repatriation (Feldman & Tompson, 1993). It is interesting that the better expatriates have adapted to a new culture, the more they may experience difficulties upon repatriation, because, as part of adjustment to the new culture, they may become less identified with their home country (Sussman, 2001).

In addition, changes in power, autonomy, and control during repatriation may cause difficulties in readapting to the home country. According to Sanchez, Spector, and Cooper (2000), the primary sources of stress during repatriation include disappointment with unfulfilled expectations, a sense of isolation, and loss of autonomy. Herrera and Herrera (2005) noted that, according to their experiences of repatriation training, repatriates who return from Asia are challenged by greater differences in power, autonomy, and control than are repatriates who return from Europe. According to them, this can be explained by repatriates having adjusted to the higher *power distance* (Hofstede, 1980) existing in Asia compared with Europe. Furthermore, Storti (1997) has noted that many repatriates feel that they have less responsibility and authority after taking their new positions in their home country. Many expatriates have become accustomed to having a good expatriate community that has become an important source of social support for them (Copeland & Norell, 2002); therefore, it may be very difficult for repatriates to leave this community and readapt to their home country.

In Karen's case, the expatriate compensation package is not relevant, but there were cultural differences, although the differences were not overwhelming for her. She was very active and open in adjusting to New Zealand, which helps to understand her challenges in reentering the United States (Sussman, 2001). Changes in power, autonomy, and control were not significant in Karen's case. Neither was the expatriate community, but relationships developed during the time in New Zealand clearly made it more difficult to move back to United States. When Karen entered New Zealand, she did not anticipate many differences, given the shared language and her little knowledge of the culture and history of New Zealand. This lack of knowledge, in her case, increased her surprise about the differences that did exist.

When Karen moved to New Zealand, she did not have a job so she had to work to find one and "plough through" her career path in New Zealand. When people have an international assignment from their employer, the process can be different. According to a study by Bonache

(2005), expatriates, when compared with local employees and repatriates, are in general more satisfied with a number of job characteristics. Expatriates see their jobs as having a greater variety of tasks and more autonomy, feel that their jobs provide opportunities for learning and applying their knowledge, and also find that their jobs give them sufficient responsibility. Bonache pointed out that these results support researchers such as Suutari (2003), according to whom the best parts of international assignments are the new work experiences and opportunities to learn. Bonache also found that the expatriates' satisfaction with career prospects was higher than that of the local employees and repatriates. Furthermore, it was found that expatriates tended to be less satisfied with the company's internal communication. On the basis of the above notions, it is clear that Karen was very eager to learn and that she took the opportunities presented to develop herself both in her jobs and in her intercultural competence. She was also able to use her educational background and work experiences to make some innovations as she achieved her new position as an executive officer of human resources in the Auckland area health care service.

During international assignments, it is very important that the families accompanying the expatriate also receive support. As Bennett et al. (2000) noted, "for any international assignment to be successful, it is critical that the family unit be regarded as a mutually supportive team" (p. 242). Existing research, however, suggests that many organizations fail to provide enough counseling and other forms of support to the families. Many studies have shown that problems with families are one of the most common difficulties for expatriates and a frequent reason for premature return (Adler, 1997; Black, Gregersen, & Mendenhall, 1992a). Especially for dual-career families in which both spouses have a job, it is important that their career and other needs are properly taken care of during international assignments (Selmer & Leung, 2003); therefore, it is very important that the spouse be regarded as a participating partner and that children's educational and social adaptation be given proper attention (Bennett et al., 2000). With regard to Karen's case, she moved to a new country to be with her husband, who had a job there. She could have benefited from predeparture training and some counseling on cultural differences, although she was very successful in her adaptation and was even able to establish her own career in New Zealand.

Given the increasing number of international careers, it is worrying that many companies still do not pay attention to supporting their expatriates and repatriates better. According to a survey in the United States, as many as 77% of expatriates felt that their international assignment had a negative impact on their careers (Black, Gregersen, Mendenhall, & Stroh, 1999). Also, studies in Germany have indicated that for the majority of returning expatriates, international assignments have been either neutral or even negative (Adler, 2001). A considerable number of repatriates change their employer upon their return or are dissatisfied because their companies did not use their international experiences (Caligiuri & Lazarova, 2001). In spite of these negative aspects associated with international assignments, people are willing to go. According to Stahl, Miller, and Tung's (2002) survey among German company expatriates, the three most common motives for accepting an international assignment were personal challenge, professional development, and importance of the job itself. Many of them felt that their companies had not paid enough attention to international human resources management, and only one third of the expatriates who responded felt that their companies appreciated their international experience.

In their discussion on expatriate adaptation, Black et al. (1999) listed the following key aspects needed in successful expatriation: (a) adjustment to the job, (b) adjustment with interacting with host-country nationals, and (c) adjustment to the general nonwork environment.

For Karen, adjustment to the job was somewhat challenging because of the negative responses of her fellow workers in the hospital, which was her first experience of working life in New Zealand. She succeeded, however, in overcoming those difficulties and obtained a more challenging job where she was respected. Interaction with host-country nationals was natural for her because she is open-minded and willing to learn from and with others. Adjustment to the general nonwork environment posed the greatest challenge for Karen. The cultural differences were greater than she had been prepared for. Her frightening experience of driving on the wrong side of the road symbolized her confusion in the midst of differences that had to do with food, language in terms of terminology, and pronunciation and its links to local culture, which all differed from what she had been accustomed to in the United States. All this resulted in homesickness and a challenge to work actively to build a relationship with the new cultural environment.

Herrera and Herrera (2005) proposed that the above three aspects related to expatriation are equally important to repatriation adjustment, which is supported by research carried out by Black and Gregersen (1991). Drawing from past research, Herrera and Herrera pointed out the following points.

1. Repatriates often return to a less desirable job than the one they had previously and must relocate to another city or they will not have a job at all.
2. Repatriates must get along with compatriots who are either strangers or have changed during the expatriation.
3. Repatriates must adapt to the changes in their home society.

Given these challenges upon repatriation, one would expect support from sending organizations for repatriates. However, according to Shepard (1998), only 25% of repatriates are given some form of repatriation counseling to help them in their reentry process.

Black, Gregersen, and Mendenhall (1992b) have pointed out that repatriation adjustment should be given proper attention and should not be regarded as only being a similar process to expatriate and domestic relocations. They noted that for expatriates the initial relationship to the new country is often based on vicarious experience, such as training, or on simple stereotypes, which may "lead them to form more flexible expectations because they know they do not have personal experience upon which to base expectations" (Black et al., 1992b, p. 741). Repatriates do have their past experience of their home country, and, therefore, they may form more rigid expectations of that country. There is also some evidence available that shows that repatriation requires different types of cognitive processes than does expatriation, which makes these processes psychologically somewhat different (Sussman, 2001).

On the basis of a number of studies on domestic relocation adjustment (Brett 1980; Nicholson, 1984), expatriation adjustment (Black, Mendenhall, & Oddou, 1991), and individual control theorists (Greenberger & Strasser, 1986), Black et al. (1992b) made the following synthesis regarding repatriation.

- Individuals establish behavioral routines based on their perceptions of expectations, reward and punishment contingencies, and preferences for certain outcomes.
- Once confronted with new and unfamiliar situations, established routines are broken and the individual's sense of control is reduced.
- Individuals attempt to reestablish a sense of control by reducing the uncertainty in the new situation through predictive and/or behavioral control.
- Therefore, those factors that influence uncertainty and loss of control would be expected to be most relevant in the adjustment process. In general, those factors that reduce uncertainty would facilitate adjustment, while those factors that increase uncertainty would inhibit adjustment. (p. 743)

In Karen's case, it seems justifiable to emphasize the meaning of her deep motivation to learn and to treat cultural differences as learning challenges and not as difficulties. In many respects, Karen was able to succeed because of her openness to learn; yet she confronted cultural differences both during her expatriation and repatriation. During her repatriation, she had to readapt to the English used in United States in her region, clearly showing how language is always linked with the cultural environment and how people change the longer they live abroad. In a sense, Karen first felt as if she were driving "on the wrong side of the road" in New Zealand and had a somewhat similar experience upon her return to the United States. Perhaps it is now justifiable to say that she is more capable of driving on "both sides of the road."

Intercultural Training to Support Expatriation and Repatriation

In Karen's case—given her intercultural competency and eagerness to learn and openness to developing herself—it seems that there was not a pressing need for intensive counseling. It is quite clear, however, that she could have benefited from intercultural training to prepare her for both expatriation and repatriation, with some additional personal or group counseling if needed. In the following, I discuss the role of intercultural training.

According to Shen (2005), there are three broad types of international training in multinational enterprises (MNEs).

1. *Preparatory training for expatriates:* Predeparture training is used for providing the employee adequate skills and knowledge that are necessary for effective working during an international assignment.
2. *Postarrival training for expatriates:* Further in-country training is used to familiarize the expatriate with the local working environment and procedures.
3. *Training for host-country nationals (HCNs) and third-country nationals (TCNs):* Training should be provided to HCNs and TCNs to facilitate understanding of corporate strategy, corporate culture, and socialization.

Shen (2005) noted that

> while there is growing recognition of the significance of international training and management development, the majority of MNEs do not pay adequate attention to training and developing international managers. It is customary for MNEs not to provide adequate pre-departure or post-arrival training for expatriates, spouses, partners or families, or training for HCNs and TCNs. (p. 663)

Shen (2005) listed the major components of predeparture training as follows: (a) cultural awareness training, (b) language training, (c) orientation (briefing on host environments, job roles), and (d) sensitivity training. Other components include formal training courses, such as management and technical skills.

A cross-cultural program should be customized on the basis of a good needs assessment. Bennett et al. (2000) have made a list of the topics that at minimum should be included in cross-cultural training.

- General and country-specific cultural awareness
- Area studies, history, geography, politics, economics
- Frameworks for understanding and valuing cultural differences
- Planning for a successful international assignment
- Intercultural business skills for working effectively in the local environment
- Understanding cultural variations for those with regional responsibilities
- Business and social customs in the host country

- International transition and stress management
- Practical approaches to culture-shock management and lifestyle adjustment
- Information on daily living issues
- Special issues: partners and families abroad
- Repatriation as a predeparture issue

Training can be an important component in facilitating success in international assignments, but companies must see that they also provide their employees other needed support, such as destination services, language training, educational counseling for children, corporate repatriation planning, and mentor programs. Training should not be regarded as a substitute for these and other important interventions (Bennet et al., 2000).

Mendenhall and Stahl (2000) have identified three emerging areas in the field of expatriate training and development: (a) in-country, real-time training, (b) global mind-set training, and (c) CD-ROM-/Internet-based training. In-country training has been regarded as an important element by researchers, who have noted that it is important to continue cross-cultural training during the early stages of international assignments (Gudykunst, Guzley, & Hammer, 1996), and, according to some researchers, in-country training can be even more effective than predeparture training (Black et al., 1999; Mendenhall, 1999). Global mind-set training has become more and more important as companies are increasingly working globally. Managers and other employees need to understand the new nature of their companies as they become more international. Among the approaches used for training global mind-set are short-term field experiences within an individual's own country where there is a possibility to be exposed to subcultures. Some companies use "reverse expatriates," who are people from foreign subsidiaries assigned to work in corporate headquarters for an extensive period of time, thus enabling multiculturalism among the managers and providing opportunities for cross-cultural encounters and training. A number of companies use assessment centers to assess their potential international assignees in order to provide them the needed training based on the detailed feedback from the assessments. Repatriates are still often an underused resource in many companies. They have developed skills and have experiences that are very valuable for international companies, and their potential should be used more systematically in developing the global mind-set. Self-training via software and the Internet provides new opportunities to support people who will be traveling or living abroad. There are a number of software packages and Internet Web sites that are available for expatriates (Mendenhall & Stahl, 2000).

Mitchell (2006) summarized some of the coping skills useful in reentry processes in the following list.

- Staying in contact with friends and colleagues abroad
- Finding forums in which to talk about the overseas experience, such as predeparture programs for those planning to study abroad
- Associating with other alumni of study abroad programs who can understand and share the difficulties the returnee is facing
- Finding comfort in reminders of the overseas experience, such as certain music or special foods
- Maintaining good health, particularly keeping healthy eating, sleeping, and exercise routines that may help to ease the stress of readjustment
- Developing self-analytical skills, which can be of help in evaluating changes, both personal and professional. This self-awareness can ease reentry transitions significantly

Looking at Karen's story as a whole, and especially her notions on her reentry process, it seems that the following summary fits her well:

The literature is very clear about the person who emerges successfully from the reentry process—this is a person who has developed his/her own meld of the two cultures with a decidedly broadened perspective on the world. In an increasingly fractious world, individuals with this experience-based cross-cultural understanding become a vital resource for effective communication among peoples and nations. (Mitchell, 2006, p. 6)

Although "driving on the wrong side of the road" symbolized her experiences related to the cultural differences that she did not expect to confront in New Zealand, Karen, together with her husband, friends, and relatives, succeeded in overcoming the difficulties during both her expatriation and repatriation and is now even more capable of confronting cultural differences with her basic orientation: openness to learn.

References

Adler, N. J. (1997). *International dimensions of organizational behavior* (3rd ed.). Cincinnati, OH: Southwestern College.

Adler, N. J. (2001). *International dimensions of organizational behavior* (4th ed.). Cincinnati, OH: Southwestern College.

Bennett, R., Aston, A., & Colquhoun, T. (2000). Cross-cultural training: A critical step in ensuring the success of international assignments. *Human Resource Management, 39,* 239–250.

Black, J. S., Gregersen, H. B. (1991). When Yankee comes home: Factors related to expatriate and spouse repatriation adjustment. *Journal of International Business Studies, 22,* 671–694.

Black, J. S., Gregersen, H. B., & Mendenhall, M. (1992a). *Global assignments: Successfully expatriating and repatriating international managers.* San Francisco: Jossey-Bass.

Black, J. S., Gregersen, H. B., & Mendenhall, M. E. (1992b). Toward a theoretical framework of repatriation adjustment. *Journal of International Business Studies, 23,* 737–760.

Black, J. S., Gregersen, H. B., Mendenhall, M. E., & Stroh, L. K. (1999). *Globalizing people through international assignments.* New York: Addison-Wesley Longman.

Black, J. S., & Mendenhall, M. (1990). Cross-cultural training effectiveness: A review and a theoretical framework for future research. *Academy of Management Review, 15,* 113–136.

Black, J. S., Mendenhall, M., & Oddou, G. (1991). Toward a comprehensive model of international adjustment: An integration of multiple theoretical perspectives. *Academy of Management Review, 16,* 291–317.

Bonache, J. (2005). Job satisfaction among expatriates, repatriates and domestic employees: The perceived impact of international assignments on work-related variables. *Personnel Review, 34,* 110–124.

Brett, J. M. (1980). The effect of job transfers on employees and their families. In C. L. Cooper & L. Payne (Eds.), *Current concerns in occupational stress* (pp. 99–136). New York: Wiley.

Caligiuri, P. M., & Lazarova, M. (2001). Strategic repatriation policies to enhance global leadership development. In M. E. Mendenhall, T. M. Kühlmann, & G. D. Stahl (Eds.), *Developing global business leaders* (pp. 243–256). Westport, CT: Quorum.

Chen, G. M., & Starosta, W. J. (1996). Intercultural communication competence: A synthesis. In B. R. Burleson & A. W. Kunkel (Eds.), *Communication yearbook* (Vol. 19, pp. 353–383). Thousand Oaks, CA: Sage.

Copeland, A. P., & Norell, S. K. (2002). Spousal adjustment on international assignments: The role of social support. *International Journal of Intercultural Relations, 26,* 255–272.

Feldman, C. F., & Tompson, H. B. (1993). Expatriation, repatriation, and domestic geographical relocation: An empirical investigation of adjustment to new job assignments. *Journal of International Business Studies, 24,* 507–529.

Greenberger, D., & Strasser, S. (1986). Development and application of a model of personal control in organizations. *Academy of Management Review, 11,* 164–177.

Gudykunst, W. B., Guzley, R. M., & Hammer, R. M. (1996). Designing intercultural training. In D. Landis & R. S. Bhagat (Eds.), *Handbook of intercultural training* (pp. 61–80).
Thousand Oaks, CA: Sage.

Hannigan, T. (2005). Homesickness and acculturation stress in the international student. In
M. A. L. van Tilburg & A. J. J. M. Vingerhoets (Eds.), *Psychological aspects of geographical
moves: Homesickness and acculturation stress* (pp. 71–82). Tilburg, the Netherlands: Tilburg
University Press.

Herrera, J. M., & Herrera, S. W. (2005). Why long-term repatriates from Asia to the U.S.
face greater challenges than long-term repatriates from Europe to the U.S. *Journal of Pro-
Change International, 1*(2), 64–72.

Hofstede, G. (1980). *Culture's consequences: International differences in work-related values.*
London: Sage.

Mendenhall, M. E. (1999). On the need for pragmatic integration in international human
resource management. *Management International Review, 39*(3), 65–87.

Mendenhall, M. E., & Stahl, G. K. (2000). Expatriate training and development: Where do
we go from here? *Human Resource Management, 39,* 251–265.

Mitchell, P. (2006). *Revisiting effective re-entry programs for returnees from US academic programs*
(LID Occasional Papers No. 1/2006). Washington, DC: AED Center for International
Training, Academy for International Development.

Nicholson, N. (1984). A theory of work role transitions. *Administrative Science Quarterly,
29,* 172–191.

Porter, G., & Tansky, J. W. (1999). Expatriate success may depend on a learning orientation:
Considerations for selection and training. *Human Resource Management, 38,* 47–60.

Sanchez, J. J., Spector, P. E., & Cooper, C. L. (2000). Adapting to a boundaryless world: A
developmental expatriate model. *The Academy of Management Executive, 14*(2), 96–106.

Selmer, J., & Leung, A. S. M. (2003). Provision and adequacy of corporate support to male
expatriate spouses: An exploratory study. *Personnel Review, 32,* 9–21.

Shen, J. (2005). International training and management development: Theory and reality.
Journal of Management Development, 24, 656–666.

Shepard, S. (1998). *Managing cross-cultural transition: A handbook for corporations, employees,
and their families.* Bayside, NY: Aletheia.

Spreitzer, G. M., McCall, M. W., Jr., & Mahoney, J. D. (1997). Early identification of international executive potential. *Journal of Applied Psychology, 82,* 6–29.

Stahl, G. K., Miller, E., & Tung, R. (2002). Toward the boundaryless career: A closer look at
the expatriate career concept and the perceived implications of an international assignment. *Journal of World Business, 37,* 216–27.

Storti, C. (1997). *The art of coming home.* Yarmouth, ME: Intercultural Press.

Sussman, N. M. (2001). Repatriation transitions: Psychological preparedness, cultural
identity, and attributions among American managers. *International Journal of Intercultural
Relations, 25,* 109–123.

Suutari, V. (2003). Global managers: Career orientation, career tracks, life-style implications,
and career commitment. *Journal of Managerial Psychology, 18,* 185–207.

Yamazaki, Y., & Kayes, D. C. (2004). An experiential approach to cross-cultural learning: A
review and integration of competencies for successful expatriate adaptation. *Academy
of Management Learning and Education, 3,* 362–379.

When Cultures Clash

Christine Wihak

Rebecca (name used with permission), an athletic, vivacious, and articulate young woman in her late 20s, was raised and educated in a large Canadian prairie city. After completing an undergraduate degree, she traveled and taught English for 6 months in South America. During a 2-year bachelor of social work program with multicultural course work, she had placement and practicum experiences that involved her with families from a variety of backgrounds, but she wanted something more, and the idea of going to the North struck a romantic chord. "It just seemed like such an unreal place." Throughout the 2nd year of her program, she brought a northern angle into her assignments and papers whenever possible.

On graduating, Rebecca was hired to work in a small Nunavut community in the Canadian Arctic. Nunavut is a very different physical and social environment than southern North America. Twenty-six isolated communities are home to 26,000 people spread across a fifth of Canada's land mass—a vast, treeless expanse. Inuktitut is the first language of the predominantly (85%) Inuit population (Government of Nunavut, 2004). Rapid social change in the postwar period has left Nunavut with a legacy of social problems, such as family violence, substance abuse, and suicide. Inuit employment and adult literacy rates are low. Many Inuit families continue to rely on subsistence hunting (Korhonen, 2002). Dramatic cultural differences create unusual challenges for a non-Inuit counselor in adapting professional practice and ethics (Wihak & Merali, 2003). The Inuit hold a worldview described as both sociocentric and ecocentric (Arnakak, 2002; Wenzel, 1991), in contrast to the egocentric Euro-Canadian worldview.

With little job-specific training, Rebecca was flown into an isolated Nunavut settlement to be a generalist social worker in a one-person office, responsible for child protection, probation, family violence, and community development. Rebecca remembered her arrival in Nunavut: "Flying in at night . . . and seeing this nothing, nothing, nothing, and then this tiny little cluster of lights that was the extent of . . . my existence for a couple of years." She thought, "What have I done?" The community was so tiny, and to someone who had grown up in a big city, the experience at first was really shocking. She spent a whole year without leaving the North, camping on the Nunavut Land a few times with families and staying at an outpost camp during her vacation. Rebecca worked in the community for 2 years, returning to southern Canada to earn a master's degree in social work.

Two years after leaving her social work job in Nunavut, Rebecca said, "I'm very, very ambivalent about the whole thing." She elaborated, "I'll always have very fond memories and I'll always have very terrible memories of living and working in that community. But I feel very, very fortunate to have had the experience, and I think overall it's been really enriching." She volunteered two stories to illustrate this mixture of feelings: one of her worst experience in the community and the other of her best experience.

In her worst experience, some hunters had found an orphaned polar bear cub and brought it back to the community. The cub was in a cage in the open, screaming and shaking. The children were poking at it through the cage, "which was not safe for them, either because it was little but . . . pretty fierce," Rebecca explained. Rebecca asked the local authorities and received what she thought was permission to move the cub into the community garage. After the bear was given some milk, "It was looking a bit more comfortable but still very agitated." The next day, she received a call saying that the proper authorities had not been consulted after all about moving the cub, and it would have to go back outside. It stayed outside for about 3 more days, until the community wildlife officials had it killed. "That was one of the hardest, the hardest things . . . watching it suffer," Rebecca remembered.

This incident created difficulties in the community, earning her the nickname "Greenpeace." This nickname affected Rebecca's work with clients, identifying her with an organization that the Inuit loathe because its international anti-sealing campaign had such a devastating effect on the economy of Inuit communities (Wenzel, 1991). Rebecca had demonstrated a great deal of anger, which is not something seen in Inuit communities (Briggs, 1970). The fact that her display of open anger was "about a stupid animal that doesn't have feelings" came back to haunt her. The episode was particularly difficult, because in her personal hierarchy of things that are important, "cultural sensitivity is way up there." However, in this case, the principle of cultural sensitivity was pitted against compassionate treatment of animals, a principle she held with equal strength.

Rebecca's best experience was working with a group of women in a cooking group. Being a big fan of collective kitchens, Rebecca was very excited about this opportunity. The 1st week, a small group of women made caribou stew, char, and a salad. The 2nd week, more women came and they had caribou stew, char, and a salad. The 3rd week, even more women came, and the group again made caribou stew, char, and a salad. "We made the same thing every week," Rebecca laughed. When she was reviewing the experience with the group at the end, Rebecca suggested, "Something for the future would be to vary it a bit, rather than having the caribou stew and the char and the salad"; however, the group leaders told her, "Well. We could have done that." Most of the Inuit women, however, only knew how to cook by using a microwave oven to heat packaged food. By repeating something over and over again, they now knew how to make one dish. If the group had made a different dish every time, the leaders told Rebecca, "They wouldn't know and cooking would still be overwhelming. They learned how to make something that has traditional food in it, it's healthy, and they've learned how to make it from scratch." Suddenly, Rebecca recognized her own faulty assumptions about effective teaching and learning strategies for Inuit. "Oh! Oh, yes. Yes, that makes sense!" She recollected, "Moments like that were just so meaningful to me. . . . Just having your whole world—broadened!" Rebecca's insight into traditional Inuit instruction deepened her ability to do effective community development work.

Writer's Role

Rebecca's two stories were given to me during an interview for my doctoral research (Wihak, 2004). They spoke immediately to my experience of encountering cultural conflicts during my own sojourn in Nunavut. At times, such conflicts can lead to an enlightening experience that uncovers one's own cultural assumptions and allows a situation to be seen from the other culture's perspective. The sojourner can then develop the capacity to hold multiple perspectives and make a conscious choice about which one would be most appropriate and effective in a given context (Bennett, 1986). This type of cognitive and affective flexibility has clear advantages for a cross-cultural counselor.

Key Issues

In Rebecca's story of the cooking class, she realized she was carrying assumptions derived from her Euro-Canadian background. For example, she may have been assuming that most adult women in cooking class like to learn to make a variety of novel dishes, will have a repertoire of basic cooking skills acquired from many experiences with seeing cooking and participating in cooking over the course of their lives, and will be able to look up a recipe in a cookbook if they have forgotten some details about how to make a new dish. In the Inuit context, however, these assumptions do not hold. Many Inuit women have had relatively little opportunity to observe or participate in cooking, or indeed in eating, many dishes that are commonplace in Euro-Canadian culture. Nor are most Inuit women literate in English (and Inuktitut cook books are scarce!). Furthermore, in Inuit tradition, learning occurs through repeated practice of observed skills (Arnakak, 2002). In addition, Rebecca may not have been aware of the significance and importance of sharing country food (caribou and char) to the Inuit (Wenzel, 1991), which is not just about cooking and eating but about reinforcing deep bonds of community and kinship. In Rebecca's "moment of meaning," her hidden assumptions were suddenly replaced with a deep insight into why the cooking teachers had been correct in their choice of method.

Not all cultural conflicts, however, can be easily resolved, but instead they leave mixed feelings. In the polar bear cub incident, Rebecca could see no way to resolve the conflict without compromising one of two valued principles. Perhaps if Rebecca had focused more intently on cultural sensitivity rather than on prevention of cruelty, she would have seen that in a culture still reliant on subsistence hunting, being indifferent to animal suffering is a necessary survival skill. Even today, Inuit hunters frequently must defend themselves and their families from bear attacks. For Inuit children, the opportunity to face the bear cub under safe conditions could be an invaluable learning opportunity, one that might save lives in the future. Awareness of such underlying cultural imperatives might have mitigated Rebecca's anger and resulted in a more effective intervention. Training in relational ethics (Wihak & Merali, 2005) might assist cross-cultural counselors in resolving such an impasse of principles, but often they must be prepared to live with prolonged, perplexing, and profound ambiguity, as Rebecca continues to do.

Reader Reflection Questions

1. How does participating in community events, such as Rebecca's involvement with the cooking class, benefit a cross-cultural counselor, and how might Rebecca bring what she learned through the cooking class into her counseling practice?
2. What strategies might Rebecca have adopted to resolve her feelings about the polar bear cub incident?
3. In the future, how might Rebecca bring what she learned from these two incidents involving Inuit culture into counseling work with a different culture?
4. What aspects of the multicultural competence model (Arredondo et al., 1996) do Rebecca's stories illustrate?
5. In relation to Bennett's (1986) model of intercultural sensitivity, where would you place Rebecca's development, based on the evidence in the two stories?

References

Arnakak, J. (2002). Incorporation of Inuit Qaujimituqangit, or Inuit traditional knowledge into the Government of Nunavut. *Journal of Aboriginal Economic Development, 3*, 33–39.

Arredondo, P., Toporek, R., Brown, S. B., Jones, J., Locke, D. C., Sanchez, J., et al. (1996). Operationalization of the Multicultural Counseling Competencies. *Journal of Multicultural Counseling and Development, 24,* 42–78.

Bennett, M. J. (1986). Towards ethnorelativism: A developmental model of intercultural sensitivity. In R. M. Paige (Ed.), *Cross-cultural orientation: New conceptualizations and applications* (pp. 27–70). Lanham, MD: University Press of America.

Briggs, J. (1970). *Never in anger: Portrait of an Eskimo family.* Cambridge, MA: Harvard University Press.

Government of Nunavut. (2004). *Our land.* Retrieved June 4, 2004, from http://www.gov.nu.ca/Nunavut/English/about/ourland.pdf

Korhonen, M. (2002). *Inuit clients and the effective helper: An investigation of culturally sensitive counseling.* Unpublished dissertation, Durham University, England.

Wenzel, G. (1991). *Animal rights, human rights: Ecology, economy and ideology in the Canadian Arctic.* Toronto, Ontario, Canada: University of Toronto Press.

Wihak, C. (2004). *Counsellors' experiences of cross-cultural sojourning.* Unpublished doctoral dissertation, University of Alberta, Edmonton, Canada.

Wihak, C., & Merali, N. (2003). Culturally sensitive counselling in Nunavut: Implications of Inuit traditional knowledge. *Canadian Journal of Counselling, 37,* 243–255.

Wihak, C., & Merali, N. (2005). *Adaptations of professional ethics among counselors living and working in a remote Native Canadian community.* Unpublished manuscript.

Response 1

Arthur Blue, Meredith Rogers Blue, Les Couchie, Wes G. Darou, and Jacques Kurtness

It is a sad truth that we see so many cases like this. To quote Arthur Blue, the first author of this response, "As I read the story of Rebecca, I marvel at the lack of empathy that exists in the education of our social workers and teachers who wander into the North." They appear to have very little understanding of working in an aboriginal environment, much less of the developmental process that takes place in Native children.

June Hearn, an anthropologist from the University of Iowa, spent several years studying and documenting the development of Athabascan children in the Northwest Territories (personal communication, 2006). The essence of her work was the difference between sexes. The process of development in the Indian population in the Northwest Territories is that boys are taught to be independent and take care of themselves. As a hunter or trapper on the land in the winter, the ability to make a decision and living with it are matters of life and death. Girls, on the other hand, are subsumed into the social life of the female group. They survive by the social contacts they have with other women in the community. It is bad practice to go around telling others what to do if one is to develop and maintain the social contact/contract. Rebecca, in this particular situation, seems to be very directive.

Local Control and Rebecca's Role

As a generalist social worker responsible for child protection, parole, and family violence, Rebecca may have held a government-mandated job. Some communities, such as the Cree of James Bay, Quebec, have the power and authority to get rid of a professional who is being inappropriate (James Bay and Northern Quebec Agreement, 1976; Prince, 1993). This village may not have had that power. In any event, it often takes time for the community to figure out the sojourner's agenda. Rebecca seems to have gone North simply on a lark;

she had little or no preparation, no understanding of these people, and little sympathy for them.

Thoughts, Just Thoughts, About "Rebecca Greenpeace"

She must have done something right, however. The fact that they gave her a nickname, even if it was disparaging, is a good sign. Teasing is used to teach children or to otherwise gently move someone's position (Blue, Darou, & Ruano, 2000). The community must have thought that she was trainable. It is generally helpful to be young, athletic, articulate, and vivacious; there is substantial research on the advantage it gives a person in a wide variety of situations to be physically attractive. She camped with some families. She would not have been invited to camp with families if they did not like her. In addition, she spent her vacation at an outpost camp, instead of flying home as Southerners generally do; the community surely noticed.

Key Issues

In terms of strategy, instead of being so directive, she should have tried to sensitize the young people to her discomfort about the treatment of animals. From that, she could perhaps have built some type of agreement with the community.

In the book, *You're So Fat: Exploring Ojibwe Discourse*, Roger Spielmann (1998) described several of these intercultural communications problems from a linguist's point of view. In the title story, a sojourner must return to the South because of her mother's death. When she comes back 6 months later, her friend's first reaction to her is "You're so fat!" The sojourner was a bit taken aback, but the friend meant it as a positive statement. Translating directly from the Ojibwe, it meant that she had finished her bereavement and was starting to eat again. Be sure to read the story about shooting the fur trader.

Hunter/gatherer peoples are generally not especially cruel the way Rebecca probably assumed. According to one of the authors of this response, Jacques Kurtness, when the Innu kill an animal, they make a prayer to the animal's spirit to thank it for allowing itself to be killed to nurture the people. After the animal is butchered, the bones are attached in a tree, and the dogs are not allowed to feed on them. Similarly, on the gathering side, there are rites and prayers around the harvesting of plants, fruits, and vegetables, and a certain proportion is left behind out of respect for the plant (Tanner, 1979).

Someone who has hunted to eat must find Rebecca's reaction to the polar bear cub incident completely bizarre. They could ask what kind of repressed memories, what pathological family background did the incident stir up in her. Is compensation for these things the reason she has gone into child protection? Her objectives seemed to be good, but her way of doing things was a problem. She likes to think for people.

Did she have some kind of difficulties in her own home? What is her awareness of her own culture? What is her relationship with men? Inuit society tends to be fairly open sexually. Was she able to express herself sexually there? How did the community react? This could work in her favor or not in her favor.

Regarding the cooking classes, why does she think it necessary to challenge the women? Is there a deeper challenge that is taking place? Do her control concerns become a problem with other older women? What was her relationship with her own mother?

According to Scott Momaday (1997), "Such ignorance and unpreparedness breeds prejudice and intolerance. . . . Fundamental differences in looking at the world . . . seem to me to constitute the most important issue in Indian [Inuit] White relations in the past 500 years" (p. 56).

Training

Perhaps instead of blaming the individual, we should assault the educational establishment, because it certainly has not produced a person who understands the culture in which she is working. Perhaps we should examine the government that hires a person who is so poorly prepared for the position.

Rebecca had received some cross-cultural training in school, and she had lived in a cultural environment presumably different from her own (in South America). In moving her theory and experience into action, something did not take. We are not asking that she become completely subsumed by the culture and live out some sort of "wannabe" pseudo-assimilation. She was hired to work in the areas of child protection, criminality, and family violence. She would be of no use to the community if she simply gave up all objectivity and made the reverse racism error of blindly accepting every part of the community members' behaviors as culturally good. We have often seen small communities, even communities made up of the majority population, hire outsiders to do this work because outsiders are not enmeshed in the sociocultural fabric.

Typically, the part of the cross-cultural training that is missing is the self-awareness aspect. In a successful training experience, Rebecca would explore her own (majority?) cultural identity, understand her power position, understand this position's effect on her theories of practice, and recognize her professional and personal impact. From a basis of understanding her own worldview, she would be in a position to effectively develop competencies in working through her community's worldview (Arthur & Collins, 2005).

Self-awareness is also the way to sort out the values conflict that a sojourner may experience between the employer and the community. The only way to negotiate the terrain between the two camps is to have a very clear idea of what one's own values are. This, however, may not be learnable; Gérard Artaud (1985) believed that this level of consciousness about one's values is a developmental stage. If one misses the window, the learning becomes much more difficult.

Examples From Professional Practice

At one time in Ontario, I (Arthur) was asked to help select teachers for the North. My conclusion was that there were no teachers produced by Southern educational institutions adequately prepared to teach in the North. Selections are made from four basic types: (a) religious zealots and other (not necessarily religious) missionary types; (b) do-gooders, the ones who are going to take care of the poor ignorant Natives; (c) tourists, those who see working in the North as a way to have some adventure and see the rest of Canada; and (d) "get-rich-quickers," people who squirrel away their money and run South at the first chance.

I (Wes) had a neighbor called Janet. She was a well-off urban White person with a master's degree in psychology, and she had a little trouble in adapting to the First Nations environment. One day Eli, an elder, took her aside and said, "Thank you Janet, for all the hard work you have done for the people in our community over the last three years." Janet thanked him profoundly; it is rare to receive a direct compliment like that from an elder. "You have really added a lot to our community," Eli continued, "and we appreciate it very much." Janet thanked him even more profusely. Eli continued, "Now, however, it is time for you to go home and help your own people."

The message was very clear. Janet was no dummy. She got a new job.

Conclusion

Rebecca's attitude seemed about right, but her behavior was disrespectful. At the risk of seeming dated, she could benefit from some training in empathy and self-disclosure. It is important to note that learning to repeat what someone has just said does not necessarily make one empathetic. Constructivist approaches get at the same material from a different direction. Essentially, although it may be a cliché, Rebecca needs to see the community through the eyes of its people, not through her eyes.

Negotiating entry into a community is fairly straightforward: ask permission, wait patiently, and then respect the conditions. When a person is imposed on a community, this becomes more complicated. The situation is a little like getting informed consent from a client in an authoritarian culture: The counselor asks for permission, but does not use it for the longest time until he or she has checked out all the nonverbals.

In the end, a person in Rebecca's position needs to listen and observe more than act. When a person makes the inevitable cultural gaffe, he or she should try to learn from it and move forward in an iterative way, trying to do the job in the most human and professional ways possible.

Note: The opinions expressed here are those of the authors and do not necessarily reflect policy of the Canadian International Development Agency.

References

Artaud, G. (1985). Une approche holistique du développement moral de l'adolescent [A holistic approach to the moral development of the adolescent]. *Revue des Sciences de l'Education, 11*, 403–419.

Arthur, N., & Collins, S. (2005). *Culture-infused counselling: Celebrating the Canadian mosaic.* Calgary, Alberta, Canada: Counselling Concepts.

Blue, A., Darou, W., & Ruano, C. (2000). *Through silence we speak: Approaches to counselling and psychotherapy with Canadian First Nation clients.* Retrieved October 23, 2007, from Western Washington University, Center for Cross-Cultural Research Web site: http://www.wwu.edu/~culture/blue-darou-ruano.htm

James Bay and Northern Quebec Agreement (JBNQA), Government of Quebec, S.Q. C46, Éditeur officiel du Québec. (1976).

Momaday, N. S. (1997). *A man made of words: Essays, stories, passages.* New York: St. Martin's Press.

Prince, R. H. (1993). Psychiatry among the James Bay Cree. *Transcultural Psychiatric Research Review, 30*, 4–23.

Spielmann, R. (1998). *You're so fat: Exploring Ojibwe discourse.* Toronto, Ontario, Canada: University of Toronto Press.

Tanner, A. (1979). *Bringing home animals.* London: Hurst.

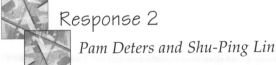

Response 2

Pam Deters and Shu-Ping Lin

Rebecca, a young female counselor who recently graduated with a bachelor's degree in social work, agreed to work in a small Inuit community in the Canadian Arctic. The counselor was raised and educated in a large urban Canadian city and, thus, was indoctrinated in an egocentric Euro-Canadian worldview. Although she has traveled to and worked in other cultures, such as teaching English for 6 months in South America, she apparently had no previous contact with the Inuit people when she was hired to work in the Nunavut region of northern Canada. Similar to other itinerate mental health providers, Rebecca held a romanticized and idealized notion of North American indigenous life ways. This unrealistic mind-set, more often than not, leads to a failure of cultural encounters between indigenous people and counselors. Thus, with romanticized ideas and little training, the counselor was flown into the community and expected to work unassisted as a generalist social worker, responsible for a wide variety of community issues ranging from child protection to community development. Rebecca's unrealistic expectations and romantic ideals appear to have interfered with her work with the Inuit community. Because of this fixed cognitive schema, she was unable to be flexible and, therefore, failed to listen actively and understand the true life experiences of these Native people.

The Inuit people stem from the Thule whale-hunting culture, and archeologists have found evidence that people lived in the region more than 4,000 years ago (Kral et al., 2000). This indigenous cultural group is 85% of the population of the Nunavut region, and Inuktitut is their primary language. There are 26 isolated communities across the vast and treeless landscape of this region. Travel between communities is difficult, and isolation and boredom are constant concerns described by the Inuit inhabitants of this region, particularly the youth. As with many other indigenous groups across North America, encroachment by Euro-Americans has led to rapid social change and significant psychosocial struggles, such as substance abuse, domestic violence, child abuse, and suicide, to name just a few (Kral et al., 2000). Despite the harsh reality of these difficulties, the Inuit people enjoy a rich, beautiful, and full spiritual life, encompassing subsistence life ways and a deep appreciation for art and the natural world. Indeed, the Inuit people continue to demonstrate cultural resiliency and strength, including long-held beliefs in a sociocentric and ecocentric worldview (Arnakak, 2002; Wenzel, 1991).

The Nature of Cross-Cultural Transitions

The differing worldviews between the counselor—Rebecca—and her Inuit clients are of primary importance when attempting to understand the cross-cultural transitions in this critical incident. The distinction between sociocentric and egocentric worldviews are often referred to as collectivism versus individualism in cross-cultural psychology (Castillo, 1997; Matsumoto, 1997). A sociocentric or collective worldview implies that the person's identity is centered within the society or the group. Typically, the individual is viewed as part of a larger, more important social group, such as the extended family or the community, with the individual dependent upon the group for his or her sense of self and well-being. Castillo noted that the commonality among sociocentric cultures is that "individual interests are subordinated to the good of the collectivity" (p. 40).

In contrast, people within a culture or society holding an egocentric or individualistic worldview are encouraged to function as unique individuals (Matsumoto, 1997). In these societies, power and status structures are taken for granted, and the emphasis is placed on equality among individual group members. Individuals typically belong to multiple social groups and tend to move more easily from group to group, not necessarily relying on a specific group to define their sense of self and well-being (Triandis, 1995). Individuals are encouraged to focus on and express their own unique perspectives, rather than focusing on and respecting diverse and collective perspectives.

Thus, the differing worldviews between counselor and client are of utmost importance when attempting to understand the issues that arose during this case incident. Clearly, the cross-cultural transition in Rebecca's case can be conceptualized by applying these theories of cultural understanding. Although the community recognized the importance of hunting and cooking to benefit the collective good, Rebecca viewed these activities through her individualistic lens, which led her to question and judge the inherent values of these people. Other theoretical issues such as ethnocentrism and colonization should be considered when conceptualizing this case incident. These issues are further elaborated in the section titled Considerations for Multicultural Counseling.

Presenting Issues

Rebecca described two presenting issues that occurred during this case incident. The first involved an orphaned polar bear cub that was captured by Inuit hunters and brought to the community. According to Rebecca, the cub was placed in a cage in the open and taunted by young children in the village. Because of her concerns for the compassionate treatment of animals, the counselor asked if she could care for the cub. This request was initially granted, and then, later, the cub was removed from her care and subsequently killed. Rebecca described this incident as very disturbing to her and indicated that it had an impact on her work with community members because of her stated sympathy for the animal and her display of open anger regarding the situation. The counselor described this issue as a conflict between cultural sensitivity and the compassionate treatment of animals.

In this situation of cultural conflict, Rebecca clearly would have benefited from the cognitive and affective flexibility described by Bennett (1986). That is, it appears advisable for Rebecca to more fully develop the capacity to view a situation from multiple perspectives and to select the perspective that seems most appropriate and effective within the given cultural context.

The other presenting issue involved the counselor's participation in an Inuit women's cooking group. Rebecca described how she met with this group once per week, and they cooked the same foods each time. When reviewing the situation with the group leaders at the end of the experience, Rebecca recommended that the group vary the dishes that were cooked each week. The women explained to her that this cooking group was conducted using a traditional Inuit instructional method, that is, learning through the observed repetition of important skills. This issue was described by the counselor as a valuable experience to correct "her own faulty assumptions about effective teaching and learning strategies for Inuit." It is probable that many of the counselor's perceived concerns and assumptions about life among the Inuit people would have been explained and understood in this same manner had she chosen to remain as a member of the community for an extended period of time. However, living for 2 years in this indigenous community was not a sufficient amount of time to fully understand and appreciate the deep complexities and richness of the worldview and belief systems of the Inuit people.

Unique Influences on the Client

A deeper understanding of the ecocentric worldview of the Inuit (Arnakak, 2002; Wenzel, 1991) may have also enhanced the counseling experience for Rebecca. Scholars indicate that many indigenous North American groups hold a belief system that includes a deep respect for the land and animals upon which they depend for survival (e.g., Berkes, 1999; LaDuke, 2005). That is, although these groups understand that animals must be killed in order for the group to survive when living a subsistence lifestyle, animals are taken only as needed, and all parts of the animal are used whenever possible. In addition, Mother Earth is respected and valued as the provider of plants and animals necessary for survival, and among those Inuit who continue to practice a traditional lifestyle, these life ways are continually reinforced through ritual and ceremony. Regarding traditional worldviews of nature and ecology, Berkes (1999) suggested that many indigenous groups believe there is a sacred and personal relationship between human beings and all other living things.

Given this information, it seems that Rebecca's strongly held beliefs in animal rights are very closely aligned to the belief systems of the Inuit people. By focusing on certain negative aspects of the polar bear incident, Rebecca may have inhibited her ability to comprehensively enrich her understanding of indigenous ecological perspectives.

Cultural Assumptions

It is important not to make an assumption that all Inuit people practice traditional life ways, living a subsistence lifestyle or participating in ceremonies and rituals. The literature on North American indigenous groups has in the past included an assumption of the "pan-Indian," or a homogeneous cultural group with all members holding similar belief systems and ways of being in the world. There are, however, currently more than 500 federally recognized indigenous tribal groups in the United States and Canada, with varying belief systems and life ways (Range et al., 1999). Thus, there is much variability among Native American indigenous groups, and a counselor working in these settings must ensure that he or she explores the cultural beliefs and practices of individual clients and communities before proceeding with counseling or any other psychosocial intervention.

Diversity of Clients

The Inuit community where Rebecca lived and worked probably represented a diverse array of clients, varying with regard to age, gender, culture (Inuit and non-Inuit), and degree of acculturation. Elders in Inuit culture have traditionally held the role of providing guidance and wisdom in their communities and continue to pass on the knowledge of traditional beliefs and life ways to community members (Kral et al., 2000). In contrast, many young people today, even those living in remote Inuit communities such as the one in which Rebecca worked, are exposed to different cultures and life ways from around the world via television, the Internet, and other media. Travel to and from the community also contributes to exposure to outside cultures and belief systems. Non-Inuit community members further contribute to this community diversity, participating in their own cultural belief systems and sharing that knowledge with others. The counselor should strive for continuous awareness of this variability among clients in the community and remain flexible and open to working with multiple perspectives, particularly when attempting to address issues of community-wide interest or development.

Possible Common Considerations for Working With This Population

Kral and colleagues (2000) described several important considerations when working with Inuit populations. They noted that relationships among the Inuit consist of three basic components related to mutual interdependence: "collaborative partnerships, extended family kinship patterns, and dyadic relations within the nuclear family" (p. 35). Other values and practices include the role of elders, the importance of healing and wellness concepts, respect for silence, and the importance of seeking advice when change is desired. Additional considerations may include an initial distrust of outsiders, particularly itinerant health workers who have a history of arriving in North American indigenous communities, working for a short period of time, and then leaving the community just as community members are beginning to develop a trusting relationship with the provider. An understanding of nonverbal behaviors, such as lack of eye contact as a sign of respect for the perceived authority figure, in indigenous groups is another important consideration. Finally, a thorough understanding of the intricate interconnectedness of community members and how to navigate dual roles within a small, rural, indigenous community are of utmost importance, given the cultural context of this critical incident.

Making Counseling Appropriate

Both individual counseling and group counseling are encouraged in order to recover Rebecca's individual well-being and that of the Inuit people. Obviously, Rebecca is struggling with the polar bear incident and might have formed the wrong perception of Inuit culture. It would be helpful for everyone involved, and particularly beneficial to Rebecca, to address her struggles around this specific incident. Furthermore, individual counseling may help Rebecca develop a positive attitude in approaching future cross-cultural conflicts and in understanding cultural differences. After all, it is essential for practitioners to have a positive attitude and open mind when working with culturally different populations.

Also, it is very important for the Inuit people to have the chance to process their understanding of the incident and feelings through further interactions with Rebecca. Frustrations stemming from Rebecca's attitude of judgment toward Inuit culture regarding the polar bear incident may result in a cynical attitude and withdrawal among village people when interacting with outsiders, particularly mental health providers. Thus, it appears essential for the Inuit people to view the incident as an opportunity for cultural understanding, as well as an opportunity to educate outsiders about Inuit culture. Ideally, the Inuit community members would be infused with empowerment through participation in a group intervention, by altering the meanings of these incidents, and, further, by developing a sense of power useful for future cultural encounters.

Theoretical Frameworks

In our view, multiculturalism is the overarching theoretical framework in conceptualizing this cross-cultural case incident (Pedersen, 2000; Sue & Sue, 2002). In the context of multiculturalism, an individual is understood and respected as a multicultural being. The inclusive definition of the term *culture* (including factors such as ethnicity, race, gender, sexual identity, age, sociopolitical status, and disability) is used when referring to multiculturalism. In that regard, a client is deemed as a unique individual who has various cultural identities. These identifying characteristics have varying influences on an individual, depending on the context. Mental health providers are encouraged to understand the individual as possessing multiple cultural identities. The complexity of individuals and cultures, as well as that of the individual in a cultural context, should be explored with enthusiasm and compassion.

Intervention Strategies

If possible, an intervention at both the individual and systemic levels should be planned to further facilitate cultural understanding and promote the concept of multiculturalism. Ideally, Inuit elders, academics or practitioners who have knowledge and understanding of North American indigenous cultures, Rebecca, and Inuit community members should be involved in this cultural intervention. The practitioner or academic who has both mainstream Western counseling knowledge and a multicultural understanding of Inuit culture should meet with Rebecca first to address her concerns and conflicts stemming from value differences. Rebecca should also be encouraged to meet with the Inuit elders and an academic or practitioner to mediate and encourage cultural understanding.

A group intervention involving the Inuit community members and Rebecca, with facilitation from elders and an academic/practitioner, is recommended to take place in a series of discussions, with the ultimate goal of mutual cultural understanding. It is important for Rebecca to respect and understand Inuit culture just as it is important for the Inuit people to understand and respect cultural values different from their own.

Considerations for Multicultural Counseling

There are two important theoretical considerations in working with North American indigenous people. It is essential to consider the following in examining this case incident.

1. Be aware of one's own ethnocentricity, especially when coming from a mainstream culture. Ethnocentricity refers to an individual's belief that his or her own cultural tradition or racial group is superior to all others (Lonner & Malpass, 1994). It is very easy for an individual to fall into a "judgment" mentality when encountering a culture for the first time, especially when that particular culture is distinctly different from his or her own. In this case incident, dramatic cultural differences surprised Rebecca, and her innate response helped her to make sense of her experience at the time; that is, comparing her culture to Inuit culture and making judgments. Rebecca's struggles appear to stem from her ethnocentric judgments. These judgments include power differentials that play out very subtly in the judger's mind. Often, minority groups, such as North American indigenous groups, are very sensitive to power differentials in cross-cultural situations. Ethnocentricity may be viewed as the foremost obstacle for cultural understanding and true acceptance among different cultures; thus, it is critical for counselors to be aware of their own ethnocentricity and be willing to challenge it.

2. Another consideration when working with North American indigenous people is the impact of colonization. Indigenous people are pervasively and persuasively under the shadow of colonization, something that sets them apart from many other ethnic groups. Because of the history of colonization worldwide, indigenous cultural groups are normally cautious when interacting with outsiders, protecting themselves from judgment and ignorance (Weaver, 1998). In this cross-cultural case incident, it is very important to determine to what extent the interactions between Rebecca and the Inuit people were cultural differences and to what extent the interactions stemmed from the Inuit people's residual conflicted feelings as a result of colonization. Also, it is critical for counselors to understand the soul wounds of colonization (Duran, 2006) and be careful not to exacerbate the problem with unintentional racism (Ridley, 2005). Counselors need to understand that building trusting relationships with indigenous communities takes time and compassion. Once trust has been built, the counselor may be rewarded with the great honor of acceptance into the indigenous culture group

Reader Reflection Questions

1. When working in a harsh arctic environment, how can Rebecca's experiences in the physical environment (e.g., weather, lodging, food, and clothing) aid in the comprehension of the Inuit way of life?
2. What can the community members do to educate and enhance Rebecca's understanding of the full spectrum of cultural diversity in this community? Furthermore, what can Rebecca do to share her own cultural beliefs with the community?
3. How can Rebecca make this cross-cultural conflict meaningful and beneficial to the Inuit people, as well as to herself?
4. How can a counselor translate one cross-cultural interaction with a specific cultural group into broader multicultural competency for use in working with diverse populations?

5. If you were asked to work in a novel cultural environment, what would you do to prepare, including arming yourself with knowledge of the people, the sociopolitical environment, and cultural expectations and beliefs?

References

Arnakak, J. (2002). Incorporation of Inuit Qaujimituqangit, or Inuit traditional knowledge into the Government of Nunavut. *Journal of Aboriginal Economic Development, 3*, 33–39.

Bennett, M. J. (1986). Towards ethnorelativism: A developmental model of intercultural sensitivity. In R. M. Paige (Ed.), *Cross-cultural orientation: New conceptualizations and applications* (pp. 27–70). Lanham, MD: University Press of America.

Berkes, F. (1999). *Sacred ecology: Traditional ecological knowledge and resource management.* Philadelphia: Taylor & Francis.

Castillo, R. J. (1997). *Culture & mental illness: A client-centered approach.* Pacific Grove, CA: Brooks/Cole.

Duran, E. (2006). *Healing the soul wound: Counseling with American Indians and other Native peoples.* New York: Teachers College Press.

Kral, M., Arnakaq, M., Ekho, N., Kunuk, O., Ootoova, E., Papatsie, M., et al. (2000). Suicide in Nunavut: Stories from Inuit elders. In J. Oakes, R. Riewe, S. Koolage, L. Simpson, & N. Schuster (Eds.), *Aboriginal health, identity, and resources* (pp. 34–44), Winnipeg, Canada: University of Manitoba Press.

LaDuke, W. (2005). *Recovering the sacred: The power of naming and claiming.* Cambridge, MA: South End Press.

Lonner, W. J., & Malpass, R. S. (1994). *Psychology and culture.* Needham Heights, MA: Allyn & Bacon.

Matsumoto, D. (1997). *Culture and modern life.* Pacific Grove, CA: Brooks/Cole.

Pedersen, P. (2000). *Handbook for developing multicultural awareness* (3rd ed.). Alexandria, VA: American Counseling Association.

Range, L. M., Leach, M. M., McIntyre, D., Posey-Deters, P. B., Marion, M., Kovac, S. H., et al. (1999). Multicultural perspectives on suicide. *Aggression and Violent Behavior, 4*, 413–430.

Ridley, C. R. (2005). *Overcoming unintentional racism in counseling and therapy: A practitioner's guide to intentional intervention.* Thousand Oaks, CA: Sage.

Sue, D. W., & Sue, D. (2002). *Counseling the culturally different: Theory and practice* (4th ed.). New York: Wiley.

Triandis, H. C. (1995). *Individualism and collectivism.* Boulder, CO: Westview Press.

Weaver, H. N. (1998). Indigenous people in a multicultural society: Unique issues for human services. *Social Work, 43*, 203–211.

Wenzel, G. (1991). *Animal rights, human rights: Ecology, economy, and ideology in the Canadian Arctic.* Toronto, Ontario, Canada: University of Toronto Press.

A Successful International Transition

Dale S. Furbish

The triggering event for my international transition was a holiday trip that my wife and I took to New Zealand in 1995. During our travel, my wife made the observation that New Zealand was a place where she could live. At various times in our lives, we had considered living in a country other than the United States, but factors such as language, climate, or sociopolitical environment had always dissuaded us from making a move. However, we found New Zealand so appealing that we decided to investigate it further as a place to reside.

Key Issues

Upon our return to Virginia (where we had lived for 20 years), we evaluated the issues that would be involved if we pursued the idea of immigrating to New Zealand. We concluded that the time was right for such an "adventure" and that there were not overwhelming impediments to our considering the transition realistically. We thus began with a sense of personal control and optimism about the situation.

We recognized that good information about what it would be like actually to live in New Zealand was essential before we could proceed. Although we were living in a relatively small city, we quickly found at least four people who had either lived in New Zealand or who were native New Zealanders. These people were very willing to share their knowledge of New Zealand and describe the living conditions. The effort we made to locate these resources was well worth it because we gained many facts and insights about day-to-day life in New Zealand. We were all the more excited about further investigating immigration after these conversations.

We also recognized that information about employment opportunities was essential for us if we were to consider living in New Zealand further. We decided that unless we could both continue to work in our respective fields, we would not make the transition. Because my wife is a qualified accountant and her employment potential in New Zealand would likely be good, we focused on my employment prospects. My professional experience was career counseling with tertiary students. Discovering that there were only six universities in New Zealand (at that time), we were apprehensive about the likelihood of employment for me.

Although in 1995, e-mail was not fully implemented at New Zealand universities, I was able to locate the e-mail addresses for all of them and wrote inquiring about employment in my field. I was pleasantly surprised to receive replies from almost all. Although none of the replies indicated that there were current job vacancies, a few suggested opportunities in other noneducational organizations. Realizing the value of "networking," I followed up on these leads. The result was an invitation to return to New Zealand for an interview with a corporate career consulting company. Although I did not have an interest in working in the private business sector, I recognized the advantages for further exploration and for making contacts afforded by a return visit to New Zealand.

During this trip, I made personal contacts with additional employment leads that others had given to me. One of the contacts was at a polytechnic that was planning to create a career center in the near future. I asked to be informed when staff hiring began.

Two months later, I received an announcement of job vacancies for the new career center and was invited to submit my application. A few weeks after that, a conference telephone interview was set up, which resulted in a job being offered to me. Eight months after we first considered the idea of moving from the United States to New Zealand, we had the opportunity to make that idea a reality.

A key issue for immigrating was, of course, qualifying for immigration to the desired country. Anticipating that we would immigrate to New Zealand if I had a job offer, we contacted the New Zealand embassy in Washington, DC, to learn about immigration requirements long before the job offer was made. Government departments are by nature bureaucracies, and allowing significant time to pass when interacting with governmental departments avoids temporal crisis. We applied for immigration with the philosophy that if we decided to immigrate, all the paperwork would be in place, but if we chose not to immigrate, the only cost would be the loss of the application fee. When approval for permanent residence in New Zealand was granted, we felt that another potential obstacle to any decision we wanted to make was removed.

The practicalities involved with moving half way around the world created another significant challenge. Although we were not sure that the move would be permanent, we decided that we would benefit financially by selling our house in Virginia in order to have adequate funds to support our immigration. We realized that many of our possessions would not be usable in New Zealand (e.g., electrical appliances use a different voltage, automobiles in New Zealand are right-hand drive). We decided to sell these also. Rather than pay for remaining household goods to be shipped from Virginia to New Zealand (which is quite costly), we held a massive household sale and liquidated everything except for two boxes of clothes and some personal items.

We sought assistance from my new employer in New Zealand in locating accommodation for us before we arrived. We rented a furnished house for 6 months. This gave us time to adjust to the new environment and explore the geographic region. This arrangement also allowed us the flexibility to evaluate our decision without making commitments of a long-term lease or house purchase. It was comfortable for us to know that if we were not satisfied with our transition, we could return to the United States without devastating consequences.

When we first arrived in New Zealand, we tried to immerse ourselves as much as possible in New Zealand culture. We consciously chose to interact with New Zealanders, even though we received a number of social invitations from Americans living in New Zealand. The time we spent with New Zealanders allowed us to develop an informed impression of life there. This socialization process was important and afforded us a sense of fitting in. We also agreed that we would make a minimum commitment to stay in New Zealand for at least 2 years in order to have time to evaluate our international transition adequately.

Adapting to work in my profession was challenging but not overwhelming. I had much to learn (and am continuing to learn) about higher education in New Zealand. Fortunately, my academic qualifications and experience were relevant for work in the New Zealand tertiary sector, and they were sufficient to allow me to join professional associations; however, my wife's American Certified Public Accountant credential did not automatically transfer to New Zealand. Nonetheless, she was easily able to find employment based on her experience, but a public accounting credential greatly expands employment opportunities and levels.

She contacted the Institute of Chartered Accountants New Zealand (ICANZ) in order to determine what was required for membership and which requirements could be transferred from her education and experience in the United States. This information was not quickly forthcoming, and personal visits to the ICANZ office were required before an answer was supplied. Persistence and personal contact proved useful for dealing with this regulatory body; such strategies can make the difference between receiving good information or not. Once the requirements were determined, she enrolled in the prescribed classes on a part-time evening basis and then took the required Chartered Accountant examination. Although her American professional credential did not automatically transfer, liaising with the parallel New Zealand professional body was important for providing career continuity.

Transition Outcomes

Nine years on, this international transition is still successful. Both my career and my wife's career have flourished. We have had career opportunities that would not have been likely had we stayed in the United States. We have also personally gained broader perspectives and attitudes from living in another culture. Perhaps we had fortunate circumstances that contributed to the success of our transition. Nonetheless, I believe the steps of gathering good information, making good decisions, being flexible, and approaching the transition with a sense of adventure greatly enhanced the likelihood of a positive outcome for us. These are strategies that are also likely to increase the probability of successful outcomes for most any international transition.

Relationship Considerations

My wife and I entered our transition with a strong relationship. We had long discussions about the pros and cons of the transition. We sought good information on which to base our decision and were mutually supportive of each other. We recognized the risks, but living overseas seemed like an adventure that appealed to us.

Neither of us has large families of origin, nor do we have children; therefore, we were not concerned about family ties and commitments. Friends and colleagues were supportive of our decision and encouraged us about our move overseas. Support from others and the absence of family commitments contributed to the ease of making our decision.

Writer's Role and Comments

The account of this international transition is autobiographical. International transitions are by nature complex undertakings, and the potential for difficulties is large; however, not all international transitions are problematic. Some, such as my own, have been exciting and rewarding experiences, both professionally and personally. Although my wife and I benefited from a number of fortunate circumstances, we proactively used transition strategies that I believe contributed to a positive outcome.

I therefore suggest to counselors working with clients who are about to undertake or who have recently undertaken an international transition to focus on client actions and attitudes that can ease the transition. Although each transition is unique, Schlossberg, Waters, and Goodman (1995) suggested that transitions can be characterized by the 4S system: situation (the specific context for the transition), self (personal coping skills), supports (social, physical, psychological, and material resources), and strategies (coping activities). Helping clients to understand their international transitions and to develop effective coping strategies are key goals when working with clients in transition. When these goals are met, the transition is likely to be eased.

Reader Reflection Questions

1. What were the key actions and attitudes that helped ease this transition?
2. In what ways was Dale's international transition different from other international transitions described in this book? In what ways was his transition similar?
3. What resources (personal, social, and physical) did Dale use in this transition? How did each contribute to the success of the transition?
4. What could have gone wrong with this transition? What remedies could have been considered if the transition was not positive?
5. What did you learn about international transitions from reading Dale's case incident? How could you apply the lessons from this transition to your clients who are making international transitions?

Reference

Schlossberg, N. K., Waters, E. B., & Goodman, J. (1995). *Counseling adults in transition: Linking practice with theory* (2nd ed.). New York: Springer.

Response 1

Roberta Neault

As I reflect on Dale's successful international career transition, I am looking at it through the eyes of a career counselor. In my response to Dale's story, I examine his experience using several career counseling theories and models, including those particularly relevant to global or international careers.

Dale's story focused on his relocation from the United States to New Zealand. Ironically, I was traveling in New Zealand as I began to draft my response. Although his transition was completed several years ago, I reflect on some of the challenges that a professional might face making a similar transition today on the basis of my recent experience of seeing his adopted country through the eyes of a foreigner. My response is organized according to issues that Dale described, and others have encountered, at three different points in time during his transition: contemplating a career change, relocating internationally, and settling in to a new country. It was during the contemplation stage of Dale's transition that he and his wife worked together to make a decision that could result in significant career and life changes.

Contemplating a Career Change

Similar to many couples in midcareer, Dale and his wife were ready for a change. They had periodically reflected about whether or not another country had the potential to become their new home. Prior to their visit to New Zealand in 1995, nowhere they had considered seemed quite right. Dale's comment that they had been previously dissuaded by language barriers, climate, and sociopolitical factors provides some clues about what they were looking for. New Zealand immediately appealed to them.

The Influence of Happenstance

It is unlikely that Dale and his wife would have considered relocating to New Zealand, however, had they not first visited it on a holiday. Krumboltz and Levin (2004) in *Luck Is*

No Accident emphasized the intersection of happenstance with success. They wrote, "Each and every person plays a key role in creating his or her own unexpected career- and life-enhancing events and transforming them into real opportunities" (p. 1). Throughout his story, Dale's proactive approach to creating luck and capitalizing on chance events shines through.

Upon returning to their Virginia home, Dale and his wife met several people who were from New Zealand and happy to share their knowledge and experiences. This good fortune also fits with happenstance theory; Krumboltz and Levin (2004) emphasized the importance of being aware of surroundings, taking risks, and being adaptable and open-minded. Considering a move to New Zealand, Dale and his wife were more aware of the New Zealanders in their community or people who had lived there, took some risks in approaching them, and were open-minded about the information provided by their contacts. Later in their story, there is much additional evidence of the couple's adaptability.

Dual-Career Couples

Their decision to consider an international move was further affected by the fact that both of their careers were relatively well established and appeared to be quite portable. Some couples' careers are not so perfectly matched, nor are they so suited to moving abroad. As a counselor, I would want to explore the readiness of each member of a dual-career couple to make a big career move.

Dale clearly stated that unless they could both continue to work within their professions, they would not relocate. As do many dual-career couples contemplating career changes that may result in relocation, they decided to focus on one career first (Neault & Pickerell, 2005). In this case, it appeared that the employment potential for Dale's wife was more certain than his own, so their immediate focus was on finding appropriate opportunities for Dale. This placed Dale's wife, temporarily at least, in the role of "trailing spouse" (Harvey, 1998; Shahnasarian, 1991). Although she fully intended to resume her career in their new location, to initiate their explorations they put Dale's career first. It is interesting that this is a strategy used by many dual-career couples, not just those in the midst of international transitions (Neault & Pickerell, 2005).

Networking and Researching Career Possibilities

It is well documented that networking is the single most effective job-search strategy, both for local and international career transitions (Moses, 2003; Neault, 2005). As a career counselor, Dale knew this well. He was creative in generating potential contacts and was delighted that almost everyone responded to him. He knew that follow-up was important and was rewarded with the offer of an interview in New Zealand. Although the job was not exactly what Dale was looking for, he recognized that it would be easier to uncover more employment opportunities if he was "on the ground" in New Zealand. Because he knew from his preliminary research that there were limited postsecondary institutions in New Zealand, he recognized the wisdom of considering related possibilities, such as the one he was being interviewed for in a corporate consulting firm.

While in New Zealand, happenstance once again had an impact on Dale's career transition. He learned of an institution that was planning to open a career center within the next few months. Proactively, he asked to be informed when hiring was to begin. Once again, this fits with Krumboltz and Levin's (2004) advice to be preparing for future opportunities. In fact, this was the very job that Dale was offered a few months later.

Although individuals and families may contemplate a career change for months or even years, very often the decision to accept an offer has to be made within days. Such was the case for Dale and his wife.

Making the Decision—A Critical Turning Point

Dale was given only a week to make the decision about whether or not to accept this job offer and relocate to New Zealand. What had once been a dream had suddenly become an immediate reality. He described recognizing that there were pros and cons to both staying in the United States and relocating to New Zealand. From a cognitive-behavioral perspective, I might have worked with Dale (and, if possible, his wife) at this point to identify some of those pros and cons for each alternative, weighed them, and prioritized items that would have the greatest influence on decision making (Amundson, 1998; Amundson, Harris-Bowlsbey, & Niles, 2005; Bolles, 2006).

Sometimes it is helpful to list all those ideas and "what ifs" that are floating through one's head and examine them somewhat dispassionately. In my experience, often what seems, at first glance, to be the most important decision-making criteria become relegated to last place when all criteria are systematically compared with each other. For example, although in the beginning of his story Dale mentioned that they had previously ruled out countries based on climate, it could be that the climate was less important to Dale and his wife than were other conditions.

Another approach is to create space to reflect on important decisions. In a counseling session, I might have asked Dale (and his wife, if I were seeing them as a couple) to visualize an ideal future or to tell me stories about some high and low career points. Amundson (1998) and his colleagues (Amundson et al., 2005) presented numerous strategies to help individuals and couples articulate their envisioned future careers.

Happenstance once again played an important role in Dale's story because he and his wife ventured on a holiday to New Zealand. Dale and his wife seem quite action oriented. Krumboltz and Levin (2004) spoke to the importance of activity in creating lucky breaks. The couple was able to reframe this holiday experience as an adventure in which they had been successful; as Dale knew from his work as a career counselor, adaptability is an important employability skill (Conference Board of Canada, n.d.). Research specific to global careers has revealed that flexibility, open-mindedness, and comfort with ambiguity were all important contributors to success (Neault, 2003).

Dale and his wife had limited family ties, which made their choice to move across the world somewhat easier. Amundson (1998) acknowledged the impact of "significant others" on career plans. Many of our clients have chosen not to pursue an international career (or to repatriate) because of such family issues as aging parents, children's educational opportunities (and costs), limited opportunities for spouse's career, and becoming grandparents. As a counselor, I would want to explore carefully the potential impact of an international career move on extended family.

Relocating Internationally

Practicalities and Paperwork

Anticipating the likelihood of an international move, Dale and his wife chose to apply for immigration before receiving a job offer. Again, Krumboltz and Levin (2004) would applaud this proactive approach to preparing for the unknown. Others might consider Dale "lucky" to have approved permanent resident status already in place when he was given only a week to make a decision about accepting a job offer. According to happenstance theory, however, "luck is no accident" (Krumboltz & Levin, 2004, p. 161).

An international move is significantly more complicated than a local one, in a number of very practical ways (Neault, 2005). As Dale pointed out in his story, it is very costly to move household items abroad—and many of them would not be useful anyway, with different electrical requirements, climate, and technology. Even something as apparently universal as a favorite movie in DVD format from North America will not work on equipment purchased in New Zealand. In some countries, there are tax implications to maintaining a home and financial ties to one's own country when living abroad. Dale and his wife chose to sell their home and car; others may decide to keep them temporarily while tentatively trying out life in the new location. Counselors supporting individuals and families through international transitions could benefit from access to up-to-date information and resources to support their clients with these very practical aspects of preparing for an international move (Kruempelmann, 2002).

The Stress of Change

Research on stress confirms that multiple life and career changes have a cumulative effect (Hobson, Delunas, & Kesic, 2001; Holmes & Rahe, 1967). Dale and his wife experienced multiple changes in a relatively short period of time (i.e., leaving their jobs, selling their home and possessions, saying good-bye to family and friends, experiencing a change in financial status, moving into a new home, beginning new jobs). As a counselor supporting individuals or families who are just settling into their new country, I would want to explore such potential stressors, their impacts, and the clients' coping strategies.

Transitions

Bridges (2001) emphasized the importance of "endings" to any successful transition. In Dale's story, he and his wife may have achieved some necessary endings by selling many of their possessions before relocating. It is interesting, however, that they chose not to acquire new belongings immediately upon arrival (which, in Bridges's model, might signify the "new beginning" stage). Instead, they chose to rent a furnished home while they adjusted and took time to consider their decision from the perspective of their adopted country. This may have prolonged their stay in the "neutral zone" that Bridges described—but also provided comfort that they had an exit strategy in place to return home if necessary.

Schlossberg and her colleagues (Schlossberg, Waters, & Goodman, 1995) identified the 4S model of transitions, acknowledging the impact of the *situation*, *supports*, *self* (i.e., the individual him- or herself), and *strategies* on successful transitions. Dale described his strong marriage as a source of strength in this transition. He also mentioned confidence that their transferable skills would keep both their careers thriving. The timing appeared to be right. Dale described some of the strategies they used to settle in (e.g., avoiding the expatriate community and focusing on building supportive relationships with locals). Dale and his wife soon decided to commit to 2 years in New Zealand; this may have been the first indication of their new beginning (Bridges, 2001) and could be interpreted, using the 4S model, as a strategy facilitating their transition success.

Foreign-Trained Professionals

Dale's wife experienced a challenge commonly reported by professional immigrants: Unfortunately her American credential as a Certified Public Accountant did not automatically transfer to New Zealand. Many developed countries, seeking the same skilled professionals, have begun to realize that the recognition of foreign credentials is an important component in attracting and retaining immigrants (Neault, 2006). In this case, Dale's wife was able to access suitable employment while going through the research, negotiation, and reeducation process necessary to earn a comparable credential in her new country. Not all professional immigrants are so fortunate; many immigrant professionals are unable to complete the transition into their former profession (Judd, 2004).

Culture Shock

Although Dale's story did not specifically mention culture shock (Neault, 2005), this is another area that I would explore with a client preparing for, or in the early stages of, an international transition. Sometimes culture shock can hit the hardest when it is least expected. One of my clients who was herself an expert on culture shock (i.e., she had written training materials, facilitated workshops, and previously lived abroad several times) became so overwhelmed by culture shock on one move that she almost repatriated.

As a Canadian traveling in New Zealand while composing this response, I reflected on the various cultural differences that, while fascinating on a short vacation, could be more difficult to adjust to in the long run. In so many ways, New Zealand and North America share a common culture; however, different accents and word usage, even when English is the primary language spoken in both regions, inevitably lead to some miscommunication. New Zealand's bicultural traditions are unlike America's "melting pot" approach to diversity, political and social systems operate differently in the two countries, standards of dress are subtly different, and even ordering a familiar cup of coffee can be a challenge. In the workplace, it would take time to understand the educational systems within which Dale was employed and the accounting systems that had an impact on his wife's work. Counselors supporting clients through international transitions would benefit from understanding the process of culture shock and effective strategies to navigate through it (Arthur & Collins, 2005).

Conclusion

Dale concluded his story by reflecting on the successful transition that he and his wife were able to achieve. Although he acknowledged their good fortune, he also identified specific strategies that contributed to their success: persistence, solid research, informed decision making, flexibility, and a spirit of adventure. These fit with the global career success factors identified in previous research (Neault, 2003). Counselors can help to facilitate successful international transitions by providing support during the decision-making phase and the relocation phase and after the move, when their clients are beginning to settle into their new cultures. Creative and ethical use of emerging technologies (e.g., secure e-mail, e-counseling groups, and tele-coaching using the Internet) could even allow the same counselor to support a client through each of these important phases.

References

Amundson, N. (1998). *Active engagement: Enhancing the career counselling process*. Richmond, British Columbia, Canada: Ergon.

Amundson, N. E., Harris-Bowlsbey, J. H., & Niles, S. G. (2005). *Essential elements of career counseling: Processes and techniques*. Upper Saddle River, NJ: Pearson Education.

Arthur, N., & Collins, S. (Eds.). (2005). *Culture-infused counselling: Celebrating the Canadian mosaic*. Calgary, Alberta, Canada: Counselling Concepts.

Bolles, R. N. (2006). *What color is your parachute: A practical manual for job-hunters and career changers*. Berkeley, CA: Ten Speed Press.

Bridges, W. (2001). *The way of transition*. Cambridge, MA: Perseus.

Conference Board of Canada. (n.d.). *Employability skills 2000+*. Retrieved May 14, 2006, from www.conferenceboard.ca/education/learning-tools/pdfs/esp2000.pdf

Harvey, M. (1998). Dual-career couples during international relocation: The trailing spouse. *International Journal of Human Resource Management, 9*, 309–331.

Hobson, C. J., Delunas, L., & Kesic, D. (2001). Compelling evidence of the need for corporate work/life balance initiatives: Results from a national survey of stressful life events. *Journal of Employment Counseling, 38*, 38–44.

Holmes, T. H., & Rahe, R. H. (1967). The Social Readjustment Rating Scale. *Journal of Psychosomatic Research, 11*, 213–218.

Judd, N. (2004). *Impact of immigration on careers of professional women.* Unpublished master's thesis, Royal Roads University, British Columbia, Canada.

Kruempelmann, E. (2002). *The global citizen: A guide to creating an international life and career for students, professionals, retirees, and families.* Berkeley, CA: Ten Speed Press.

Krumboltz, J. D., & Levin, A. S. (2004). *Luck is no accident: Making the most of happenstance in your life and career.* Atascadero, CA: Impact.

Moses, B. (2003). *What next?: The complete guide to taking control of your working life.* New York: DK Publishing.

Neault, R. A. (2003). *Managing global careers: Changes and challenges for the 21st century.* Retrieved May 15, 2006, from http://www.contactpoint.ca/natcon-conat/2003/pdf/pdf-03-11.pdf

Neault, R. (2005). Managing global careers: Challenges for the 21st century. *International Journal for Educational and Vocational Guidance, 5*, 149–161.

Neault, R. (2006). *Ring roads and roundabouts: Navigating careers in the 21st century.* Retrieved April 9, 2007, from http://www.natcon.org/natcon/papers/natcon_papers_2006_e4.pdf

Neault, R. A., & Pickerell, D. A. (2005). Professional women in dual career families: The juggling act. *Canadian Journal of Counselling, 39*, 187–198.

Schlossberg, N. K., Waters, E. B., & Goodman, J. (1995). *Counseling adults in transition: Linking practice with theory* (2nd ed.). New York: Springer.

Shahnasarian, M. (1991). Job relocation and the trailing spouse. *Journal of Career Development, 17*, 179–184.

Response 2

Christine Wihak

The nature or quality of Dale's international transition is revealed in his chosen title: "A Successful International Transition." This narrative concerns a transition that the author of the case incident and his wife made in 1996 to New Zealand from the United States. Reflecting on the transition 9 years later, Dale remembers the transition as smooth, with very positive outcomes in terms of personal and career growth for himself and his wife.

Although the transition was easy, Dale's story nevertheless illustrates three points relevant to counselors assisting clients with international transitions. The first point concerns preparation for transition and motivation to make the move. The second point relates to the issue of international credential recognition. The third point is how Dale's transition illustrates factors that facilitate or hinder adaptation to a new culture.

Preparing for the Transition

An interesting feature of Dale's story is the almost leisurely lead-up to the transition. Dale and his wife engaged in an extended decision-making process before they were ready to go. Both professionals, they started with a vague notion that they might like to go somewhere different, but the general comfort level of their life in the United States compared with possible destinations deterred them from making any definitive move. Then, while on a holiday trip to New Zealand, they felt that this country might suit them as a destination for an "adventure."

Dale and his wife next thoroughly investigated all aspects of life in New Zealand before beginning to look seriously for employment. Using the Internet and e-mail to locate likely opportunities, Dale's search for a job in career counseling resulted in a return trip to New Zealand, which allowed him to check out other employment possibilities firsthand. He and his wife also initiated an immigration application in anticipation of finding work. After several months, his search was rewarded with a suitable job offer.

At this point, Dale and his wife were faced with the actuality of making a decision. Stay or go? In Dale's description, the decision to go came suddenly. They had confidence in their own resourcefulness. They knew they had the ability to adapt to life in a new country.

The idea of an adventure or quest is a common feature found in narrative studies of professional people making international transitions (Osland, 1995; Schild-Jones, 1999; Wihak, 2004). Because of this mythic quality, Osland used the metaphor of the *Hero's Journey* (Campbell, 1968) to describe the international transition process. Dale's description of his wife and himself being in search of adventure thus fits this pattern.

The preparation process that Dale and his wife went through is also similar to that described in literature. Osland (1995), referring to the initial preparation phase, used the term *the call to adventure*. Unlike economic immigrants or refugees who may feel driven by necessity to make a move, Dale and those in similar circumstance have the luxury of choice and the time to gather enough information to make an assessment of whether the transition is likely to succeed. Although the adventure will still involve risk, it is a calculated one.

Although pointing out that "many heroes refuse the call" (p. 8), Osland (1995) described the second stage as crossing of the first threshold and entering of the belly of the whale. This is the point when expatriates decide to leave their own culture behind. Thus, the definitive turning point in Dale's story is typical of this process.

People with great personal resources, such as Dale and his wife had, may be unlikely to seek counseling with regard to a transition decision. If they do seek it, the counselor may be able to assist them in identifying important factors to consider and evidence to collect to inform their decision. This preparation process will strengthen clients' confidence in their decision, whether it be to cross the threshold or refuse the call to adventure.

The Dilemma of International Credential Recognition

The only significant difficulty in the actual transition that Dale reports is the problem his wife had in having her professional accounting designation recognized by New Zealand authorities. Dale makes relatively light of this obstacle, which his wife clearly had the resources to overcome. Nevertheless, the nonrecognition of foreign credentials is a major issue facing internationally trained immigrants (ITIs) to Canada and other countries.

Recruitment of highly skilled immigrants has been identified as one of the ways that Canada can address looming labor force shortages (Conference Board of Canada, 2004), yet paradoxically many highly educated ITIs in Canada are underemployed (Statistics Canada, 2006). The Canadian government has recognized the seriousness of this issue, leading Human Resources and Skills Development Canada (HRSDC) to undertake a number of initiatives aimed at assisting professionally trained immigrants to have their credentials recognized by licensing bodies. HRSDC (Kennedy, Cotton, & Burke, 2004) recently completed a project to develop the conceptual framework for an e-portfolio for potential immigrants to Canada, which recommended adoption of a facilitated on-line e-portfolio model embedded within the larger immigration process. Learning Innovations Forum has recently received HRSDC funding to design an e-portfolio system for skilled immigrants (http://www.futured.com/documents/LIfIAProjectAnnouncementAugust05.pdf). This e-portfolio approach is also being used in other countries, such as the Netherlands, for assessing credentials and the experience of foreign-trained professionals (Divis, Scholten,

& Mak, 2005). Such initiatives will support immigrants in using the Internet to search for employment and employment-related information, in the same way that Dale did.

HRSDC is exploring gap training (Godfrey, 2006) to ameliorate the difference between immigrants' existing skill level and the skill level required for occupational entry in Canada. For example, the federal government is funding Mount Royal College in Calgary, Alberta, to carry out a pilot project on fast-tracking internationally trained nurses and licensed practical nurses into the nursing profession in Canada (Fletcher, 2003). Professional associations and professional schools in Canada are also much involved in efforts to facilitate recognition of the credentials of ITIs and offer gap training. For example, Austin, Galli, and Diamantouros (2003) and Austin and Dean (2004) reported on university-based efforts to accelerate licensing for foreign-trained pharmacists in Canada. Nielsen (2005) reported on work that the Canadian Society for Medical Laboratory Science is doing to increase acceptance of foreign credentials. Such efforts may ultimately make it easier for ITIs to make transitions without losing professional status, as Dale's wife did.

Counselors working with ITIs need to be able to offer support and information on the issue of the recognition of foreign credentials, with referrals to appropriate services and organizations. Ideally, this support needs to be provided before the transition occurs, but few immigrants seem to receive the information that they need before departure. Even Dale and his wife, resourceful people who researched their intended destination and made extensive preparations for their transition, were unprepared on this point. Given that many ITIs may arrive in a new country unprepared for the difficulties they will have obtaining recognition for their training and experience and obtaining suitable employment, what kind of counseling support would be useful?

It seems that some type of group intervention aimed at framing the problem as a larger, systemic issue and providing peer support for building self-confidence would be useful. Peters (2000) described an educational program offered for highly skilled immigrants at the University of North London in England. Aimed at development of a professional portfolio, it included courses on the educational system, the labor market, and equal opportunities, as well as personal development and communication; completion resulted in the award of a university credential in the form of a Certificate of Professional Development. Completion rates have been high, and participants reported an increase in self-confidence about their future employability. Similar programs are starting to appear in nonprofit agencies and community colleges in Canada. Referral to such a program would be beneficial for clients who are ITIs facing the credential recognitions barrier.

Counselors also need to address the loss of identity that some immigrants experience when they are barred from pursuing their previous professional careers. Although identity change is generally an issue in international transitions (Kim, 2001), lack of professional employment may exacerbate the dilemma, particularly if it is associated with significant economic consequences. In Schild-Jones's (1999) study of professional women who made an international transition because of their husband's employment, participants "wrestled with the loss of self-identity associated with the loss of a professional life" (p. 111). Counselors working with clients faced with such an identity loss because of problems with recognition of their foreign credentials will need to support them in establishing a new framework for their lives.

Factors Supporting or Hindering Adaptation

Dale's transition experience highlights key points of Kim's (2001) comprehensive theory of intercultural adaptation, designed to encompass the experiences of immigrants, refugees, and sojourners, collectively termed *strangers*. As Kim has pointed out, cross-cultural adaptation occurs to a greater or lesser degree. The important issue is "how individuals can help themselves to accomplish their own adaptive ends" (p. 222).

In her theory, Kim (2001) identified *host communication competence,* as she termed it, as "the engine that pushes a given stranger along the adaptation process" (p. 206). This competence involves not only a knowledge of the host language but also other cognitive, affective, and operational factors that affect the individual's ability to communicate inter- personally and make use of the mass communication system of the host nation. The ease with which an individual makes an international transition will largely depend on his or her competence in this regard. Other important factors are the individuals' involvement in their own expatriate ethnic community, including interpersonal relationships and the use of ethnic mass media, the receptivity of the host environment toward newcomers, pressures the host environment exerts in terms of conformity, and the strength and prestige of the expatriate newcomers' ethnic community in the host country.

In the case of Dale and his wife, who made the transition from one English-speaking country to another, their host communication competence was high. Without the language barrier, they could readily engage in interpersonal relationships and access information through the mass media, which eased their adaptation. In addition, Dale described deliber- ately seeking social interactions with New Zealanders rather than the American expatriate community, which Kim's (2001) theory predicts would also accelerate a transition process. In addition, the generally high prestige of the United States on the world stage would contribute to the acceptance of Dale and his wife in New Zealand society.

For counselors working with transitioning clients, the adaptation theory that Kim (2001) proposed is a helpful resource for identifying both possible hindrances to adaptation and possible remedies. For example, Kim's theory suggests that clients who lack host com- munication competence will have a need for language training and for encouragement to expose themselves to the host country's mass media. The counselor could also assist such clients to develop a relationship with a *magical friend* (Osland, 1995), a term describing a cultural mentor who helps the newcomer interpret puzzling cultural differences (Wihak, 2006). The counselor could encourage clients to reduce their social interactions with their own expatriate community or at least to balance interactions with that community with interactions with the host community.

Considerations for Multicultural Counseling

Dale's story is an example of a smooth and successful transition. Nevertheless, the story illustrates a number of points where counseling intervention would be helpful. For less resourceful clients or clients making a transition to a host culture that differs markedly in language and customs from their home culture, the issues apparent in Dale's story would be magnified.

Counselors need to be prepared to intervene to ameliorate emotional difficulties that can result from encountering barriers to professional employment and intercultural adaptation that occur during a transition. In doing so, they need to recognize and assess to what extent the clients' responses are a natural consequence of the transition process as described in the literature (Kim, 2001; Osland, 1995; Schild-Jones, 1999; Wihak, 2004) and to what extent such responses represent an individual issue (Arthur & Collins, 2004; Sue & Sue, 2003). Involvement with clients making an international transition, however, takes intervention beyond the individual level.

Multicultural counselors serving such clients need to work at a systemic level on their behalf, both to remove barriers such as the nonrecognition of foreign credentials and to ensure that necessary supports such as language training and cultural mentoring are pro- vided to newcomers. Although such systemic interventions may not have traditionally been a counselor's role, the ability to act effectively in this way is considered an important part of multicultural competence (Arredondo et al., 1996).

References

Arredondo, P., Toporek, R., Brown, S. B., Jones, J., Locke, D. C., Sanchez, J., et al. (1996). Operationalization of the Multicultural Counseling Competencies. *Journal of Multicultural Counseling and Development, 24,* 42–78.

Arthur, N., & Collins, S. (Eds.). (2004). *Culture-infused counselling: Celebrating the Canadian mosaic.* Calgary, Alberta, Canada: Counselling Concepts.

Austin, Z., & Dean, M. R. (2004). Development of a curriculum for foreign-trained pharmacists seeking licensure in Canada. *Pharmacy Education, 4,* 143–151.

Austin, Z., Galli, M., & Diamantouros, A. (2003). Development of a prior learning assessment for pharmacists seeking licensure in Canada. *Pharmacy Education, 3,* 87–97.

Campbell, J. (1968). *The masks of God: Vol. 4. Creative mythology.* New York: Viking.

Conference Board of Canada. (2004). *Performance and potential 2004–5: How can Canada prosper in tomorrow's world?* Retrieved April 7, 2006, from http://www.conferenceboard.ca/boardwiseii/temp/BoardWise2LDFJAGKAPJGNJNLOLMAHPKEC200647123813/PandPReport2004-05.pdf

Divis, J., Scholten, A., & Mak, A. M. (2005). Promoting cross-border recognition and mobility developments in the Netherlands. In C. McIntosh & Z. Varoglu (Eds.), *Perspectives on distance education: Lifelong learning & distance higher education* (pp. 121–132). Paris: UNESCO.

Fletcher, M. (2003). Project looks at prior learning assessment. *The Canadian Nurse (Infirmiere Canadienne), 99*(5), 13.

Godfrey, E. (2006). *Gap analysis of First Nation technology training: Closing the gap between technology training and remote community capacity.* Retrieved October 24, 2007, from Simon Fraser University, School of Communication, Web site: http://arago.cprost.sfu.ca/smith/research/fncr/godfrey/view

Kennedy, B., Cotton, C., & Burke, R. (2004). *An on-line portfolio development model for the Going to Canada Portal: Final report for the Learning and Literacy Directorate.* Retrieved October 24, 2007, from http://capla.ca/going_to_canada.php

Kim, Y. Y. (2001). *Becoming intercultural: An integrative theory of communication and cross-cultural adaptation.* Thousand Oaks, CA: Sage.

Nielsen, C. (2005, November). *Prior learning assessment for medical laboratory technologists.* Paper presented at the CAPLA Fall Focus Workshop & Annual General Meeting, Toronto, Ontario, Canada.

Osland, J. S. (1995). *The adventure of working abroad: Hero tales from the global frontier.* San Francisco: Jossey-Bass.

Peters, H. (2000). Working towards AP(E)L with refugees and asylum seekers. In S. Bailie, C. O'Hagan, & A. Mason (Eds.), *APEL and lifelong learning* (pp. 68–71). Belfast, United Kingdom: University of Ulster.

Schild-Jones, L. (1999). *The transcultural process: Creative expression in a chaotic world.* Unpublished doctoral dissertation, Fielding Institute, Santa Barbara, CA.

Statistics Canada. (2006). The dynamics of overqualification, 1993–2001. *The Daily* (April 6, 2006). Retrieved April 7, 2006, from http://www.statcan.ca/Daily/English/060406/d060406.pdf

Sue, D. W., & Sue. D. (2003). *Counseling the culturally diverse: Theory and practice* (4th ed.). New York: Wiley.

Wihak, C. (2004). *Counsellors' experience of cross-cultural sojourning.* Unpublished doctoral dissertation, University of Alberta, Edmonton, Canada.

Wihak, C. (2006). Learning to learn culture: The experiences of sojourners in Nunavut. *Canadian and International Education Journal, 35*(1), 46–62.

Part 2
International Student Transitions

Multiple Transition Issues in Living and Learning Across Cultures

Natalee Popadiuk

Vivian (a pseudonym), a 19-year-old Chinese woman from Hong Kong, came to Canada to attend a 1-year study abroad program in business management as an undergraduate international student. Her dream of studying overseas began 4 years earlier after her parents told her that they were saving money to send her to a Canadian university for at least 1 year. They believed that the overseas experience would increase Vivian's chances of securing a high-paying management position in a Hong Kong firm upon graduation. Vivian was especially excited at the prospect of living away from home for the first time and experiencing a new adventure. In addition, Vivian's interest in becoming an international student had been fueled by listening to stories of classmates about their international studies in Canada, Australia, and the United States.

Family Background

Vivian grew up in a one-bedroom apartment with her parents and younger brother, who was 8 years her junior. Her parents have had a stable relationship for 22 years and have based their marriage on a traditional power structure of "breadwinner" and "housewife." Vivian was aware that she did not want to emulate her parents' traditional marriage, even though she respected how they have managed their relationship through the years. She agreed with them about her need to obtain a university education, which she saw as her ticket to financial independence and equal partnership with her future spouse. Vivian's father currently works as a security guard, although in the past he owned a small printing shop. Because of living in a culture that highly values education and the fact that her parents' lack of education hindered their career opportunities, Vivian's parents hold high expectations for her to excel in school, especially at university. Fortunately, she has been a strong student with an A average throughout her academic career.

Relationship Difficulties

In Grade 10, Vivian began dating David, whom she had met in her science class. From the start, they had significant difficulties in their relationship. Vivian attributed these problems to their lack of mutual interests, his preference for spending time with friends, and his inability to express love to others. Vivian regularly felt emotionally neglected and was aware of a significant power imbalance in the relationship. She believed that David was incapable of loving others because he was spoiled as the only male child in a Chinese family. Despite the difficulties in the relationship, Vivian saw potential in David and hoped that he would start to mature in the next few years.

Vivian's parents typically remained uninvolved in their daughter's relationships, but this time, they stated that she needed to break up with David while studying in Canada. She reluctantly agreed and ended the relationship 3 weeks before her departure date. David became frantic, begging her not to break up with him, and made promises to change his attitude toward her. A few days before she left for Canada, she felt so anxious about leaving him that she secretly agreed to a long-distance relationship. This decision, in turn, made her feel guilty about being a "bad daughter," because she was betraying her parents' trust.

Living and Studying in Canada

Vivian was excited when she finally arrived in Canada at the beginning of the school year. She enjoyed her classes, liked her dorm roommate, and found the international student orientations interesting and helpful. By the end of the first month, however, her relationship with David began to deteriorate when he started ignoring Vivian's e-mail messages. During a social event at the International Student Centre, she met an older male student, Shao, from China who was working on his doctorate. They spent considerable time together talking, ice skating, and sightseeing. Mostly, Vivian felt excited about the affection she received from her new friend, but she also felt guilty about betraying her boyfriend in Hong Kong. After a few months, Shao disclosed that he was engaged to a woman in China, but that he was not sure whether he wanted to marry her. He disclosed that he found Vivian extremely attractive and hoped that they might start a more intimate relationship. Shao promised to break up with his fiancée, but Vivian no longer wanted to see him, refusing his persistent invitations. Because of her desire to avoid him, she stopped attending the International Student Centre's activities.

By December, 4 months after arriving in Canada, Vivian became increasingly homesick, especially at night or during periods of inclement weather. She attempted to talk with David about his withdrawal from her, which he denied, claiming that she was the one who was ignoring him. They began arguing on a daily basis as he continued to blame Vivian for not providing him with enough attention. She missed her parents and younger brother terribly, and she wanted to return home for good. When she spoke to her parents, however, she only revealed things that she knew would make them proud of her, like doing well on a test or talking to one of her professors. Sometimes, Vivian would speak to her friends in Hong Kong about how angry she was at David or about her feelings of loneliness and homesickness. They supported her anger at her boyfriend but told her that she should not complain about living in Canada, stating that she was lucky that her parents had sent her. This had the effect of making Vivian feel even more alone and guilty for selfishly thinking of her own needs when she should be thankful for the opportunity presented to her.

Other Issues

Despite Vivian's desire for Canadian friends, she found it difficult to develop meaningful friendships with other students. The few people she talked to were friendly, but most people were too busy to get together. Vivian enjoyed spending time with her Canadian roommate, Janet, who would tell her interesting stories about her life, but Janet was usually out with her boyfriend or drinking at the student pub when she was not studying. Although invited to the pub, Vivian did not drink alcohol and found the atmosphere unpleasant. She was shocked to see how Canadian students had sex with multiple partners, even people they had just met at the bar. Another international student from Hong Kong regularly phoned Vivian to see if she wanted to go out, but Vivian did not like her, finding her to be immature and self-centered.

Another issue that affected Vivian's psychological state was how she became tired of speaking and listening to English all the time. Although relatively fluent, she struggled with pronunciation and finding the right words to express her thoughts. She wondered how much her level of English affected her ability to make friends with Canadian students, because she noticed how people would often ask her to repeat what she had just said, which made her feel self-conscious and anxious. She was also receiving lower marks on her essay assignments with accompanying comments about the lack of clarity in her writing. One of her professors called her aside after class to encourage her to have an English speaker proofread her assignments before handing them in. Vivian felt embarrassed to ask for help and ashamed that her English was not as good as she had thought.

A Downward Turn

In the short time that Vivian had been studying in Canada, she had gone from an idealistic young woman with high expectations of adventure and academic promise to a person who was feeling homesick, lonely, and overwhelmed. She continually wished that she was home with her family and David, but she did not want to disappoint or shame her parents by telling them how she felt. Vivian eventually dealt with David at the urging of her friends in Hong Kong by angrily confronting him on the phone about his lack of support. After scolding him for over 3 hours, he admitted to his faults and asked for forgiveness. She felt tremendous relief and hoped that this time David would be able to keep his promises to her. He agreed to be more loving, but she really was not sure if he was capable of following through. Vivian felt more trapped and hopeless about her situation in Canada as the weeks dragged on. Part of her was grateful to have this opportunity to fulfill her dream of studying abroad, but, mostly, her experiences did not match her expectations, and feelings of homesickness engulfed her.

Vivian began experiencing numerous physical problems, including headaches, insomnia, and a loss of appetite. She went to see doctors at the student health services, who ran tests, treated the symptoms, and told her that nothing was wrong. After the fifth trip in a month, she was surprised when a doctor asked if she had been thinking of hurting or killing herself. Vivian denied any intent to take her own life but admitted that she had recently started wishing that she would not wake up one morning or that she could be hit by a car on the way to classes. When the doctor suggested she talk to a counselor at the Student Counseling Centre, Vivian became worried that the doctor thought she was going crazy, because in Hong Kong only people who had very serious mental problems went to see a counselor. Vivian returned to her dorm room and lay on the bed feeling nauseated for the rest of the day. When Vivian phoned David later that evening, she felt especially vulnerable. As she cried telling him how lonely and terrible she felt, she heard him playing computer games instead of listening to her. Vivian became furious at his lack of attention, broke up with him, and slammed the phone down.

Later, her roommate Janet found Vivian sitting on the floor crying in the corner of her room. They talked for many hours about what had been going on with Vivian over the past few months. Janet recognized that she was not going to be able to help Vivian very much, so she suggested that she see a counselor at the Student Counseling Centre. At first Vivian was reluctant, but when Janet explained that she had gone to a counselor last year and that it had been like talking to a good friend who actually knew how to help people get through problems, Vivian felt better about trying it. Janet offered to take Vivian to the counseling offices the next day, which made her feel less anxious.

Key Issues

Vivian, a 19-year-old international student, has experienced a significant decline in psychological functioning as a result of a number of intersecting issues. At one level, she struggles with transition issues, including culture shock, language difficulties, isolation, and homesickness. These aspects have an impact on her academic work: lower marks, longer study time, and fear of participating in class. She reports feeling hopeless, overwhelmed, lonely, anxious, angry, guilty, ashamed, and passively suicidal, all without adequate support systems to mitigate the distress. In addition, Vivian's relationships are few and tenuous both at home and in Canada. The difficulties with her boyfriend have intensified during their long-distance relationship, and she is afraid of disappointing her parents by telling them how she is feeling. Although she has a positive relationship with her roommate, she finds it difficult to connect with Canadian students. She also felt sexually vulnerable in her budding romantic relationship with Shao, which then led her to disconnect from the developing friendships at the International Student Centre. Overall, Vivian is feeling overwhelmed and trapped in a seemingly no-win situation.

Reader Reflection Questions

1. It could be argued that Vivian is experiencing two major transitions. One is the cultural transition of living and studying in Canada as an international student, whereas the second is the developmental transition of a 19-year-old woman who has left her family for the first time to study at university. What specific aspects of Vivian's issues might be attributable to these two separate transition experiences, and how might a counselor approach each of these pieces when working with this client? In what ways might cultural norms and values be embedded in the two transitions?

2. Vivian discloses passive suicidal thinking when she tells the doctor that she thinks of "not wanting to wake up" and "wishing she would be hit by a car," in addition to her ongoing sense of hopelessness about the situation. What specific kinds of information would a counselor need to know in order to conduct a thorough suicide risk assessment to ascertain the full extent of her suicide risk (e.g., current and historical risk factors; protective factors)? What kind of safety planning would be appropriate if she is currently at low or moderate risk for suicide?

3. Expectations seem to play a significant role in this case study. Discuss the levels of expectations that may be affecting Vivian's psychological well-being and how cultural and socioeconomic values are implicated in these expectations (e.g., her parents' expectations of her, her expectations of herself, her expectations of her boyfriend David, his expectations of her, societal expectations). How would a counselor work with these expectations from a culturally sensitive perspective in order to help Vivian shift from distress to improved coping?

4. Vivian's issues can be seen to be clustering at three levels: intrapersonal, interpersonal, and societal. As a counselor interested in attending to a holistic perspective of people, discuss how Vivian's difficulties can be conceptualized from this framework. Where would you start working in order to make the most significant impact on her psychological functioning? In what ways might your training and the values you have learned as a counselor assist in this process and in what ways might they become barriers?

5. The relationship difficulties with David are subjectively experienced by Vivian as the most significant ongoing source of stress. In order to work with this client from a culturally sensitive feminist perspective, conceptualize Vivian's relational difficulties in terms of traditional and contemporary gender roles of women in Hong Kong; differential valuing of men and women in Asian countries; and issues of power, control, oppression, and sexual politics of women around the world.

Response 1
Hemla D. Singaravelu

Vivian's dream of studying abroad is not unlike other international students' dreams or aspirations. There are, however, several variables impinging on Vivian's academic and psychological well-being that are unique to her situation. The following paragraphs address the different layers associated with these variables by first providing a culturally sensitive conceptualization of this case incident along with some intervention strategies.

Conceptualization

Cross-Cultural Considerations

Vivian's culture and upbringing are typical of most Asians and can be explained using the collective identity, which, in the case of Hong Kong, has been influenced by Confucian and Buddhist values. The collective identity is characterized by emotional interdependence, as well as obligations to the group and concern about the welfare of the group. Other values, such as respect and reverence for elders; family loyalty and obligation; a high value on education, self-discipline, and morality; shame; order; and familial and gender hierarchy (Ho, 1987; Triandis, 1995), are prominent. For example, Confucian philosophy and ethics strongly emphasize "specific roles and proper relationships among the people in those roles" (Ho, 1987, p. 25). Here, three prominent familial relationship roles are father–child, husband–wife, and elder–younger siblings. The family structure is customarily hierarchical and patriarchal, with the father assuming leadership over the household. Respect and power are afforded to Asian parents and increase as they age. Parents usually live with their children, or they may retain their own residence as they get older, because nursing homes are a foreign concept for Asians. Buddhist values of harmonious living, compassion, respect for life, moderation of behavior, self-discipline, patience, modesty, and friendliness prevail. Deviating from these traditional values can mean that the whole family loses face (Sheu & Fukuyama, 2007). However, modern-day Asians, for example in Hong Kong, may see changes in traditional male–female roles and the weakening of parental authority (London & Devore, 1992), thus creating a larger generational gap between parents and their children.

It appears that the values and beliefs of Vivian's parents are similar to the above characterization of the East Asian culture. They seem to have high hopes for Vivian having better education and career opportunities than they were able to have in Hong Kong. Her parents have made financial sacrifices to send their daughter to Canada, with the expectation that Vivian will return home and attain a high-paying job. Hence, studying abroad is not only Vivian's dream but also her parents' dream.

Regarding relationships, her parents appear to adhere to traditional gender roles, with the father being the breadwinner and the mother the housewife. Vivian, on the other hand, does not want to hold similar relational views as do her parents and values egalitarian partnerships and financial independence. This stance may be a source of conflict in Vivian's relationship with David, who appears to have been raised in a traditional Asian hierarchical household in which the male members of the family assume a role of authority. Clearly, David and Vivian's expectations of the relationship are not the same, and, in fact, David's expectations seem to clash with Vivian's egalitarian view. However, juxtaposed to this view is Vivian's need to maintain harmony and loyalty not only to her parent–daughter role but also to her boyfriend–girlfriend role. This is evidenced by Vivian keeping secrets from her parents about her continued relationship with David, her adjustment difficulties in Canada, and her repeated hopeful attempts to work things out with David.

An International Student in Canada

The experience of studying abroad can be fulfilling and at the same time fraught with challenges. International students, like Vivian, usually must navigate through an unfamiliar cultural terrain in the new country. Common cross-cultural adjustment issues are feelings of isolation and homesickness, lack of a support system, a new educational system, and language barriers (Lin, 2000; Mori, 2000; Pedersen, 1991; Popadiuk & Arthur, 2004; Sandhu & Asrabadi, 1994). Customary ways of addressing or resolving problems may unexpectedly become unavailable to international students in their new environment. Navigating through this process of acculturation can lead to acculturative stress (Arthur, 2004; Berry, Kim, Minde, & Mok, 1987), which affects the daily life and socioemotional functioning of international students (Johnson & Sandhu, 2007). Some symptoms of acculturative stress include depression, anxiety, physical complaints, and identity confusion. The process of acculturation involves learning about the differences between international students' culture and their host culture. In an attempt to integrate the two cultures, international students are placed in situations of extreme cultural conflict and identity confusion. Eventually, students develop the ability to retain their cultural heritage but adapt to the host culture by learning necessary skills and values and living biculturally.

Considerations for Counseling

It is important to note that international students' conceptualization of mental health, help-seeking behaviors, and expectations for treatment may differ from the conceptualization in the host country. Although occasional bouts of sadness or melancholy are viewed as normal, psychological struggles like depression are seen as negative, and such expressions are often stigmatized in many Asian countries. Instead, emotional problems are often expressed somatically because of the emphasis on the mind and body interconnectedness in the Asian culture (Ho, 1987; Hughes, 1993; Sue & Sue, 2003). Students will also restrict any discussion of personal problems with counselors for fear of dishonoring or bringing shame to the family name. Typically, international students will not self-refer because of the association of shame and fear of "losing face" (Sheu & Fukuyama, 2007) and their general discomfort about counseling. Their struggles may even be kept from family members to avoid creating problems and as a way of fulfilling family obligations. Violation of this duty may cause a loss of support from the family and may lead to further shame and sense of guilt. If counselors fail to take into account the above cultural subtleties of the international client, they may misclassify the presenting problem or recommend unfamiliar treatments that could be rejected.

Presenting Problem and Intervention

Overview

In Vivian's case, her feelings of depression and anxiety manifested through physical symptoms such as headaches, insomnia, and loss of appetite. She is engulfed by homesickness, loneliness, feelings of being overwhelmed, and the lack of support and understanding from friends in Hong Kong and Canada. She realizes her fluency in the English language is not up to Canadian standards. She struggles with being the bad daughter–good daughter. Her romantic relationships have failed because the men in her life (David and Shao) hold patriarchal views about male–female relationships, and the power differential has frustrated

Vivian. Her attempts to be loyal and to maintain proper relationships and harmony have exhausted her. Her usual avenue of seeking help from family and friends in Hong Kong is unavailable to her. She is not comfortable with the social activities of her Canadian friends and their comparatively liberal sexual relationships. Vivian presents a sense of hopelessness associated with acculturative stress and has made statements about harming herself. Even though the roommate she likes may have convinced her to seek counseling services, Vivian is probably still skeptical and fears the implications of seeking counseling services. With this in mind, the following strategies are recommended in working with Vivian.

Intervention

The issues of most concern currently are Vivian's depression and the lethality of suicidal thoughts that need to be addressed in the first session. All suicidal statements must be taken seriously and responded to with empathy and sensitivity to the client's distress while thoroughly assessing for the hierarchy of risk factors. These factors are her intent to kill herself, if she has a concrete plan, and if she has the means to carry out the plan. Clients who have suicidal ideation along with intent to kill themselves, a definite plan, and means to execute this plan present the highest risk (Faiver, Eisengart, & Colonna, 2000). The counselor must address her state of crisis with sensitivity and be cognizant of its possible cultural implications.

In addition to addressing her suicidal ideation, the initial counseling session with Vivian must include education regarding the role of professional counselors, interpersonal dynamics in the therapeutic process, intake and assessment procedures, time boundaries, and course of treatment. The goal here is to demystify the counseling process and provide an accurate portrayal of it. It is important that the counselor give the impression that a solution to Vivian's problem is possible and to allow time for Vivian to express her somatic complaints and for the counselor to be affirming of her expressions. The counselor must show (verbally and nonverbally) that he or she is willing to wait until Vivian is ready to talk about her family. Sharing information about her family with a stranger, particularly anything negative, can be viewed as "washing dirty laundry in public," hence dishonoring the family name. The counselor can convey cultural understanding by protecting the dignity and self-respect of all members of her family, and even close friends, by avoiding any negative statements about them.

Because of her culture and lack of exposure to counseling services, Vivian may prefer the counselor to be more directive and take on the role of the expert by providing concrete answers, similar to her experience with medical doctors. If so, the counselor should avoid ambiguous speech and be concrete. It is recommended that directive approaches like cognitive and behavioral or solution-oriented/focused approaches be used with Vivian. However, the counselor may find Vivian to be more expressive about her emotions and problems than expected, particularly once rapport has been established. In this case, the counselor should take the opportunity to explore the subtleties of Vivian's cultural heritage through understanding her family dynamics, values, beliefs, gender and familial role expectations, and ideas about relationships. Working with international students does require that the counselor be flexible with his or her modality, making it applicable to the client, and to realize that some techniques will not be as successful as others.

In order to alleviate Vivian's depressive state, adjustment and relationship issues need to be addressed in counseling. The following interventions are recommended to address Vivian's immediate needs and the issues that might take longer to resolve.

After addressing her risk for suicide, it would be prudent to help Vivian address her loneliness and isolation by recreating or redefining her social support system. This can involve membership in new on-campus organizations and eventually reconnecting with the International Centre. Connecting with old and new friends would be ideal, but doing so requires discussing the differences in cultural values, identifying and experimenting with new behaviors, and developing new interest areas. It is hoped that these actions will allow Vivian to meet Canadian friends and classmates and enjoy their company. Friendship with co-nationals has served as a protective factor for most international students. Here, the counselor needs to learn from Vivian the unique difficulties she may have with co-nationals in order for her to reestablish her relationship with them.

It would be advisable for Vivian to be mentored by a faculty member from her department. Through the mentoring process, Vivian will learn more about the academic and linguistic expectations of her department. This process will also allow the faculty to "get to know" Vivian and the needs of international students. Seeking out opportunities to improve her English language in speech and writing will help Vivian feel more confident in the classroom and other social settings. The International Centre may have programs to facilitate this process for Vivian, and the university may also have English-as-a-second-language classes to improve her English proficiency level. The act of socializing with Canadians, either on campus or off campus, will improve Vivian's communication skills and facilitate acculturation into the Canadian culture.

An ongoing problem for Vivian is her tumultuous relationship with David. For as long as she has known David, Vivian has felt neglected in the relationship. What does she want in a relationship and will David be able to meet her expectations? How can Vivian navigate through the sexual power structure inherent in traditional male–female Asian relationships? Central to addressing this problem is exploring her conflicting values of wanting equality and independence in her relationships versus the need to please or be loyal to significant others. She experiences similar conflict with her parents and struggles with wanting to be the consummate "good daughter." There is a noticeable generational gap between Vivian's parents and Vivian with regard to traditional Asian values and gender role expectations that needs to be brought to the surface. A major question to be answered is related to her identity confusion: Who is Vivian and how can she maintain her evolving identity and at the same time be respectful of her parents and embracing of her cultural heritage?

In light of the complexities involved in this case, it is imperative that counselors be aware of their own values and biases and how these can impinge on collectivistic, hierarchical, and patriarchal orientations of the culturally different. Counselors need to understand the process of acculturation and stress encountered by international students and to focus on their clients' accomplishments and strengths.

Reader Reflection Questions

1. What are some components of Vivian's culture that might be in conflict with your own values and beliefs?
2. What forms of discrimination (conscious and unconscious) could international students face in their host country?
3. How have post–September 11, 2001, experiences affected international education and students?
4. How should possible discrimination and harassment toward international students be handled?

References

Arthur, N. (2004). *Counseling international students: Clients from around the world*. New York: Kluwer/Plenum Press.

Berry, J. W., Kim, U., Minde, T., & Mok, D. (1987). Comparative studies of acculturative stress. *International Migration Review, 21*, 490–511.

Faiver, C., Eisengart, S., & Colonna, R. (2000). *The counselor intern's handbook*. Stamford, CT: Wadsworth/Brooks & Cole.

Ho, M. K. (1987). *Family therapy with ethnic minorities*. Newbury Park, CA: Sage.

Ho, M. K. (1992). *Minority children and adolescents in therapy*. Newbury Park: CA: Sage.

Hughes, C. C. (1993). Culture in clinical psychiatry. In A. C. Gaw (Ed.), *Culture, ethnicity, and mental illness* (pp. 3–41). Washington, DC: American Psychiatric Press.

Johnson, L. R., & Sandhu, D. S. (2007). Isolation, adjustment, and acculturation issues of international students: Intervention strategies for counselors. In H. Singaravelu & M. Pope (Eds.), *A handbook for counseling international students in the United States* (pp. 13–35). Alexandria, VA: American Counseling Association.

Lin, J.-C. G. (2000). College counseling and international students. In D. C. Davis & K. M. Humphrey (Eds.), *College counseling: Issues and strategies for a new millennium* (pp. 169–183). Alexandria, VA: American Counseling Association.

London, H., & Devore, W. (1992). Layers of understanding: Counseling ethnic minority families. In R. L. Smith & P. Stevens-Smith (Eds.), *Family counseling and therapy* (pp. 358–371). Ann Arbor, MI: ERIC/CAPS.

Mori, S. (2000). Addressing the mental health concerns of international students. *Journal of Counseling & Development, 78*, 137–144.

Pedersen, P. B. (1991). Counseling international students. *The Counseling Psychologist, 19*, 10–58.

Popadiuk, N., & Arthur, N. (2004). Counseling international students in Canadian schools. *International Journal for the Advancement of Counselling, 26*(2), 125–145.

Sandhu, D. S., & Asrabadi, B. R. (1994). Development of an acculturative stress scale for international students: Preliminary findings. *Psychological Reports, 75*, 435–448.

Sheu, H. B., & Fukuyama, M. A. (2007). Counseling international students from East Asia. In H. Singaravelu & M. Pope (Eds.), *A handbook for counseling international students in the United States* (pp. 173–193). Alexandria, VA: American Counseling Association.

Sue, D. W., & Sue, D. (2003). *Counseling the culturally diverse: Theory and practice* (4th ed.). New York: Wiley.

Triandis, H. C. (1995). *Individualism & collectivism*. Boulder, CO: Westview Press.

Response 2

Paul Pedersen

Vivian has many dreams to fulfill, and some of them conflict with others. To understand Vivian's situation best and build an empathic relationship, it is important to take an "inclusive" perspective. Most of the research on empathy is defined as the shared understanding of emotions, thoughts, and actions of one person by another. In Western, "low-context" cultures, this is typically done by focusing on the individual, whereas in traditional Asian cultures, empathy more typically involves an inclusive perspective of the individuals and significant others in their complex societal contexts (Pedersen, Crethar, & Carlson, 2008). In the more collectivist and "high-context" non-Western cultures, relationships are defined inclusively to address not only the individual but the many "culture-teachers" surrounding that individual in a network of significant others. Being empathic in that indigenous cultural context requires a more inclusive perspective than in the typically more individualistic Western cultures. From the inclusive perspective, culture is broadly defined to include Vivian's ethnographic (nationality, ethnicity, language), demographic (age, gender, place of residence), status (social, educational, economic), and affiliation (formal and informal) background in both the back-home-China context and the new Canadian context. Vivian has many different competing identities, each identity has its own dream, and each dream has its own culturally learned assumptions.

Lewis-Fernandez and Kleinman (1994) have identified three culture-bound assumptions about mental health and illness that are based on North American values. The first assumption is the egocentricity of the self, in which individuals are seen as self-contained and autonomous units whose behavior is determined by a unique configuration of internal attributes. The second assumption is the mind–body dualism, which divides psychopathology into organic disorders and psychological problems. The third assumption is the view of culture as an arbitrary superimposition on the otherwise knowable biological reality. Until psychology discovered multiculturalism, it was known as the science of dissonance reduction, in which complex data were made simple and understandable. With multiculturalism, psychology has come to emphasize tolerance of ambiguity and acceptance of complexity in a culture-centered perspective.

All three assumptions apply to Vivian's situation. First, the collectivistic rules that apply to her parents' home in Hong Kong are quite different from the individualistic rules that apply to her Canadian campus. Vivian's dilemma is how to live according to both conflicting sets of rules at the same time. Second, psychological stress contributes to physiological symptoms affecting her health in a unified perspective. Third, the cultural context is necessarily complex, and any simple solution that ignores cultural complexity is certain to fail in her search to fulfill her dream—or dreams. To help Vivian achieve her dreams, we need to build a relationship of "inclusive cultural empathy" with her.

Empathy is constructed over a period of time during counseling as the foundation of a strong and positive working relationship. The conventional description of empathy moves from a broadly defined context to the individual person convergently, like a pyramid with the pointed end down (see Figure 5.1). The revised version of inclusive cultural empathy moves from the individual person toward inclusion of the broadly defined cultural context

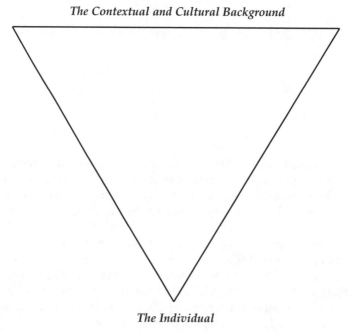

The Contextual and Cultural Background

The Individual

Figure 5.1
Conventional and Western-Based "Convergent" Empathy

in which that individual lives, like a pyramid with the pointed end up (see Figure 5.2). Inclusive cultural empathy can be illustrated in two figures contrasting (a) conventional and convergent empathy focused on the individual with (b) inclusive and divergent cultural empathy focused on the context.

Inclusive Cultural Empathy (ICE) has two defining features: (a) Culture is defined broadly to include culture teachers from the client's ethnographic (ethnicity and nationality), demographic (age, gender, lifestyle, residence), status (social, educational, economic), and affiliation (formal or informal) backgrounds and (b) the empathic counseling relationship values the full range of differences and similarities or positive and negative features as contributing to the quality of that relationship in a dynamic balance. ICE goes beyond the exclusive interaction of a counselor with a client to include the comprehensive network of interrelationships with culture teachers in the client's cultural context. Her Chinese middle-class background, Chinese traditions, and the full range of her past experiences, as well as her expectations and her family's expectations for her future, are all contemporaneous in Vivian's personal–cultural orientation, like a collection of the many different "Vivians" competing for attention and salience. Some of these identities might include

- Vivian as a 19-year-old Chinese woman from Hong Kong
- Vivian as a foreign student in a Canadian university
- Vivian as an eldest child of a middle-class family
- Vivian as an older sister to her younger brother
- Vivian as member of a stable family with traditional values
- Vivian as a "good student getting high grades"
- Vivian aspiring to a high-paying management position
- Vivian living away from home for the first time on her own
- Vivian as a member of her classmate peer group discussing their plans

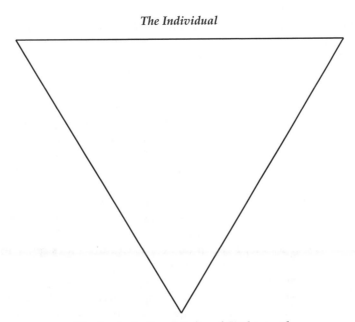

The Individual

The Contextual and Cultural Background

Figure 5.2
Inclusive and Asian-Based "Divergent" Cultural Empathy

- Vivian as David's girlfriend back in China
- Vivian as Shao's girlfriend at the Canadian university
- Vivian as a homesick lonely person in Canada
- Vivian as an English-language speaker
- Vivian as a sexually mature woman
- Vivian as a person with headaches, insomnia, and physical problems
- Vivian as a person considering suicide
- Vivian as a client receiving counseling.

ICE goes beyond accommodating cultural differences to achieve an empathic relationship of a complex and dynamic network of similarities and differences among the client's many different culture teachers who assume that every counseling context is multicultural, if culture is broadly defined. ICE is a generic counseling perspective that requires the counselor to manage both similarities and differences at the same time. This "inclusive" approach is in sharp contrast to the conventional "exclusive" perspective of dissonance reduction in conventional empathy. By reframing the counseling relationship into orthogonal multicultural categories, it becomes possible for the counselor and the client to accept the counseling relationship as it is—ambiguous and complex—without first having to change it toward the counselor's self-reference, individualistic and exclusionary cultural perspective.

Defining ICE as described in this reaction involves increased awareness to prevent false assumptions, knowledge to protect against incomplete comprehension, and skill to promote right actions. The first task is to become aware of culturally learned assumptions on which all the rest of understanding is based. If counselors are making wrong assumptions, then they will fail regardless of their other abilities. Explore Vivian's background in China to understand better the importance of her past experiences. Explore Vivian's expectations—and her family's expectations—for her future to establish priorities and goals. Explore Vivian's choices in the Canadian university to see how the past and future fit into the present.

The second task is to identify knowledge gaps, which need to be addressed to describe the cultural context of counseling. Which culturally learned values and culture teachers from her past continue to be important? What resources (financial, emotional, societal, relational) are available to Vivian in her present situation? Which expectation for the future is strongest in her thinking? Although counselors cannot hope to accumulate all relevant knowledge, they should still aspire to accomplish the complex task as best they can.

The third task is to construct or respect a complex and dynamic balance of tendencies that a competent counselor can manage. Construct a balance sheet of positive and negative features or consequences for each of Vivian's many choices. Identify common ground among her alternative futures to see what "fits" together best. The skills required for ICE include managing a comprehensive balance of essential similarities and differences at the same time.

It would be tempting for the counselor to treat Vivian as a classic example of "a foreign student with culture shock," in which all the background information of cultural differences might be considered "distracters" that prevent the counselor from diagnosing her according to the universal standard of mental health. Culture shock refers to the stress and confusion an individual might experience when visiting an unfamiliar culture (Pedersen, 1995). The research assumes an individual goes through a series of five stages from entering the new culture as a stranger toward adjusting to both the old and new culture. The counselor might want to focus on which stage of culture shock Vivian is experiencing: the honeymoon stage, depression, anger, reconciliation, or the ultimate bicultural adjustment. In fact, Vivian is experiencing all five stages at the same time, depending on which of her many identities is most salient.

The cross-cultural part might not even be the most important. Vivian is experiencing both the transition between cultures and the developmental transitions of growing up. Part of Vivian's thinking is ready to consider suicide. It will be important for Vivian to establish priorities in her many choices and opportunities through clarification and discussion. The problem of reentry to Hong Kong after graduation is not even mentioned, but this might well be the underlying crisis, whether to choose a "lonely heaven" in Canada or a "happy hell" back in Hong Kong (Pedersen, 2000b).

To be empathic, it is important to hear Vivian's "hidden messages," which she is thinking but not saying, especially not to an outside counselor (Pedersen, 2000c). The more cultural differences between Vivian and her counselor, the more difficult it will be for that counselor to hear her hidden messages. However, the counselor can assume that some of what the client is thinking is positive and some is negative. As the counselor becomes more familiar with Vivian and her many dreams, it will become easier to perceive those implicit internal dialogues and to bring them into the counseling relationship.

ICE links Vivian's specific behaviors, with her explanation of why she did it, with the cultural teachers who taught her to do it that way. Cultural teachers might come from family relationships such as relatives or from business associates, fellow countrypersons, ancestors, or those with shared beliefs. Power relationships based on social friendships, sponsors and mentors, subordinates, and supervisors or superiors may provide cultural teachers. Memberships shared with coworkers or in organizations, gender or age groups, and workplace colleagues may contribute cultural teachers. A wide range of nonfamily relationships, friendships, classmates, neighbors, or even ordinary people may also have contributed teachers without knowingly having done so (Pedersen, 2000a). Figure 5.3 illustrates a framework for identifying a client's cultural grid.

The counselor might sort out the many decisions Vivian has made or needs to make and explore each decision using the cultural grid. Decisions might include her family's decision to send Vivian abroad, Vivian's decision to go abroad, her parents modeling a breadwinner and housewife role, valuing Chinese traditions, her relationship with David, her relationship with Shao, returning to China after graduation, becoming Canadian, and many other

	Personal Variables		
	Where You Learned to Do It	*Why You Did It*	*What You Did*
Cultural Teachers			

Family relations
  Relatives
  Fellow country people
  Ancestors
  Shared beliefs			

Power relationships
  Social friends
  Sponsors and mentors
  Subordinates
  Supervisors
  Superiors			

Memberships
  Coworkers
  Organizations
  Gender and age groups
  Workplace colleagues			

Figure 5.3
A Within-Person Cultural Grid

decisions. As Vivian clarifies her own expectations for what she has done and continues to do, the importance of culture teachers will emerge. Vivian will be better able to prioritize her choices and understand their consequences in her comprehensive cultural context.

Offering simple solutions to complex problems is dangerous, especially in counseling. We are in danger of not seeing the proverbial forest for the trees. Working with the complexities of a client's many different cultural contexts is difficult and perhaps even impossible, but we continue to aspire in our counseling toward culture-centered counseling to construct a truly accurate picture of the client in context.

References

Lewis-Fernandez, R., & Kleinman, A. (1994) Culture, personality, and psychopathology. *Journal of Abnormal Psychology 103*, 67–71.

Pedersen, P. (1995). *Five stages of culture shock: Critical incidents around the world*. Westport, CT: Greenwood Press.

Pedersen, P. (2000a). *A handbook for developing multicultural awareness* (3rd. ed.). Alexandria, VA: American Counseling Association.

Pedersen, P. (2000b). "Happy hell or lonely heaven": Quality-of-life factors in the reentry of Taiwan graduates after study abroad. *Asia Journal of Counselling, 7*(2), 61–84.

Pedersen, P. (2000c) *Hidden messages in culture-centered counseling: The triad training model*. Thousand Oaks, CA: Sage.

Pedersen, P., Crethar, H., & Carlson, J. (2008). *Inclusive cultural empathy*. Washington, DC: American Psychological Association.

Case Incident 6

Establishing a Sense of Belonging

Sauli Puukari

Timo (a pseudonym) was born in 1959 to a middle-class family. His father was a civil servant who was also active in local politics. Timo's mother had an academic degree in pharmacy, but instead of a working life, she chose to take care of the family at home. They were an ordinary family living in a flat in a town in eastern Finland. Timo remembers that during his childhood his parents and grandparents often talked about the painful memories of being forced to move from Karelia (located in the eastern part of Finland, part of which was demanded by the Soviet Union as part of the peace treaty after World War II) because of the war between Finland and the Soviet Union. In retrospect, he recalls how both generations did not feel at home but continued to miss Karelia. He felt the same type of "restlessness" himself.

Timo did not have difficulties studying at school. In the beginning, he was "an excellent student," but later on, at the age of 14 to 15, he lost his motivation to strive for the highest grades, which he recalls his mother expected. During these years, he recalls often having been bored at school because it was not challenging enough for him. Since then, he has been looking for "more meaningful things" instead of grades. Timo's mother was the dominant figure at home, and his father was the breadwinner of the family.

At school he enjoyed studying history, and languages were rather easy for him. He had also developed an interest in psychology and philosophy before taking these subjects but was disappointed in the way they were taught at school. He fulfilled his responsibilities as a student but was not emotionally involved in studying. His true love during the adolescent years was music. He had taken piano lessons in classical music for 8 years, but he was really into pop music.

Timo's father was seriously ill during all the 1970s, which had a significant impact on the whole family. Due to these experiences, he felt his childhood was quite demanding. Timo also felt the 1970s were "not so positive [a] time" for him in other respects.

Recent Events Before the First Transition

After senior high school, he did his military service in the Finnish army from 1978 to 1979, which naturally loosened his connection to his family. During 1979, he was also beginning to develop a closer relationship with his future wife, Marijke, who was from the Netherlands, and he "developed this relationship over the phone lines." Before then, they had been pen pals for a number of years. During an Inter-Rail (an affordable railway pass for young people traveling in Europe) trip in Europe, he met her, and after their meeting, they gradually started developing a more serious relationship.

Peter's father died just 2 weeks before Peter went to Germany to start his university studies there. He chose Germany partly because he had studied German at school and did well in it and, thus, felt confident he could master it well enough to study there. Also, he recalls that quite a number of other Finnish students had also selected Germany as a place to study. At first, he started studying medicine for reasons he cannot remember, perhaps it had something to do with his father being sick, but he is not sure about this. He also considered going to the Netherlands, but not knowing the language there, he felt Germany was an easier alternative. In addition, he obtained information about studying in Germany from another Finnish student, an acquaintance of his, who had started her studies in medicine 2 years earlier, so he "sort of followed her paths."

In retrospect, Timo sees how he did not actually plan his international studies; instead, it was more "an urge to see something else." At those times, he felt as he "was drowning in somewhere if he would have stayed in his native country and he had to struggle free and go as far as he could." It seems his decision to go to Germany was a combination of strong intuition, a need to go somewhere abroad to broaden his life, and rational thinking behind the decision to go to Germany because of language and information obtained from people he knew. According to his experiences, the decision to go abroad had more to do with intuition, a "carpe diem" experience: "If I want to do something, I need to do it now."

First Transition—Living and Studying in Germany

Timo traveled to Germany 1979 with three projects in mind: becoming independent, learning to live in Germany and studying there, and developing a deeper relationship with Marijke. Living alone in Germany and enjoying the fresh new perspective for his life were interesting challenges for him. He also often visited Marijke in the Netherlands.

After starting his studies in medicine, Timo realized that he had not developed proper study skills during his time in senior high school in spite of high grades in the National Matriculation Examination. In addition, his skills in chemistry and physics were not strong enough to succeed in medicine. He was admitted to university because of his overall success in the National Matriculation Examination in Finland; no attention was paid to success in specific subject areas. Studies in natural sciences in a foreign language and in a foreign environment were just too much to cope with, and soon he started to consider changing his field of studies. Learning to use German in an academic setting and to live independently in Germany was itself a big challenge. His Finnish acquaintance in the same medical school had urged him to start studying medicine immediately. Reflecting later, he feels he should have perhaps spent a year studying German before starting the actual medical studies.

After Timo had been in Germany 2 years, Timo's future wife Marijke completed her studies in physiotherapy in the Netherlands and came to Germany to start her language studies at the same university where Timo was studying. She invited Timo to attend lectures given by a very enthusiastic teacher in English language. Timo was impressed by the free and intellectual style that the teacher used in his lectures connected to British studies, and after the 2-hour talk, Timo had found a new field of studies, a decision that was "made by the heart," according to him. This is a very good example of how one invitation to take part in a new lecture at a right time can make a huge difference in a person's life, as can be seen from all that followed. The path of his life changed quite dramatically, and he found deeper motivation and inner satisfaction in his studies. Marijke and Timo being together must also have had a positive effect on Timo—after all, she was also the one who invited him to attend the lectures.

After this impressive lecture series, Timo took some language courses in German—and to the disappointment of his mother—left medicine to start British studies. During this minitransition, he seriously questioned his capacity as student, and he had doubts about his potential in academic studies. He realized that he needed a new approach to strengthen his study skills. He took this second chance very seriously, studying hard—yet enjoying all of it. Retrospectively, he believes that he was perhaps a bit too serious, for example, not using all the opportunities available to travel and learn more about European cultures. The failure in medicine made him push hard toward the new goal and to prove himself capable of achieving it.

As part of his new academic program, he started British studies as his major together with history and linguistics, a program that was largely predetermined. Had he had the chance, he might have also selected psychology or sociology. Timo enjoyed analyzing novels and working on writing assignments in history and linguistics. He felt he could put his feelings into this work. According to his experiences, these types of studies were not questionable in Germany, unlike in Finland where they were questioned because they were not considered useful in the world-of-work. As part of his optional British studies, he joined a theater group, and the members produced plays at least once each academic term.

These activities were very rewarding to Timo, and his studies became "an enjoyable way of life" for him. He recalls that he "never wanted to think of returning to Finland," and sometimes he even had "forgotten he was a Finn." He did well in his studies; married Marijke in Germany; made close friends with quite a number of people, German and non-German alike; and completed his master's degree in 5½ years, which was a good achievement, particularly for an international student. During the final year of studies, he also became a father. That year was "the year of his life," when he felt he was living life at its fullest: He was studying hard for the exams and yet enjoying the friends and people around him and learning to be a father, a parent, to a baby without the support of the child's grandparents who were abroad. All of it was demanding, yet rewarding to note that he was capable of managing it all.

Work Experiences in Germany and a Difficult Transition to Finland

As part of the early study in medicine, Timo had done internships in mental hospitals in Finland during the summer. He enjoyed working there as a nurse and believed this time gave him a deeper perspective on life. He was not really interested in becoming a medical doctor, easily recognized in retrospect, but he liked challenges and was interested in learning new things. During his time at the university in Germany, he had also started working in a car factory assembling Volkswagens in the 2-month periods during summer holidays.

First Critical Incident

After the first baby was born and Timo had earned his master's degree, it was time to think about getting a permanent job in the midst of the big changes that were occurring with the reunification of Germany at the end of the 1980s. At that time, it was hard to find a decent job quickly. He could have continued working in the car factory, but after graduating, he thought, "he could not do this forever, could he!" Later, he saw this period as a time when he really needed "counseling with capital letters": His career decisions were made more in panic than based on informed choices. The guidance he received from a local employment office suggested that as a Finn in Germany, it was hard to get a job, and the personnel in the office recommended going back to Finland. At that time, Finland was not a member of the European Union, and permits to work in Germany were very difficult to obtain. Foreign students were supposed to return to their homeland after graduation. With no help from the employment office or their extended families about how Timo and Marijke could manage financially with their new child, after 11 years in Germany, during which time Timo visited Finland only seldom, he finally decided to return to Finland with his family.

The final reason for returning to Finland was that they were expecting a second child. In making the decision, Timo considered the financial situation, the information he was given from the employment office, and the fact that they had no relatives in Germany. The whole situation culminated with the news of Marijke's pregnancy with their second child, which led Timo to make the decision, together with his wife, to return to Finland. The following is an imaginary dialogue to illustrate the themes involved in the process.

Marijke: So have I, what do you think we should do.

Timo: They did not give any hope of getting a job in Germany. . . . I think it means we must move.

Marijke: I know what you mean.

Timo: Yes . . . well, knowing that we are going to have a new child, there is not much choice here, is there. . . . We must get money for our family.

Marijke: I agree.

Timo: What do you think about Finland?

Marijke: I do not know much about it, but it is your home country. I guess it would be easier for you to get a job there. I will take care of our children.

Timo: And I think we could perhaps get some help from people I know there.

Marijke: Do you mean Ari?

Timo: Yes. He might be able to give some updated info and help in finding a place to live . . . and perhaps also some help in finding a job.

Marijke: That sounds good!

Timo: I can't promise anything for sure, but what else can we do? I can't get a job here after I get my degree.

Marijke: Timo, I also think we must do something now.

Timo: OK, I will call Ari, and start planning the next steps.

In Finland, Timo's best friend from high school lived in a town where Timo and Marijke had decided to move in 1990. He received a great deal of good information from his friend about the prospects in Finland, and this information helped him and Marijke make a good plan for returning to Finland. In spite of the good plan, the first years in Finland were in many respects a painful time for Timo and Marijke. Emotionally, it was almost like being a refugee, that is, being forced to move to another country with no other options. The culture shock was huge, and Timo was not prepared for it—did not even know that such a thing existed. Part of the problem was that he was unemployed. Timo lacked the networks that are so essential in Finland when looking for a first job. Also, the non-Finnish academic degree was at that time a real handicap. If all that was not hard enough, the major recession in the beginning of the 1990s was hitting the labor market for academics especially hard. Timo recalls how their friends were really trying to help and support them, but he still felt sad. He and his wife missed the close emotional support from their friends and her parents, especially from her mother. They both felt lost. In addition, they had to struggle with financial matters. All this was also a serious challenge to their marriage.

As time went by, they slowly started adapting to the new situation and found good day care for the children, and Marijke began studying and became acquainted with another woman in their apartment building, a young mother like Marijke. Having a friend who was in the same situation made Marijke feel better. As part of her studies, she learned about intercultural theories, and this knowledge was significant for both her and Timo because it gave them words, patterns, and explanations for their experiences as they tried to adapt to the Finnish culture. Reflecting on the first years after returning to Finland, Timo thinks it was the strong relationship between him and Marijke and their ability to set priorities in the middle of difficult times that helped them go through this painful adaptation process. Also, he finally got a temporary job at the end of the 1st year of their move to Finland, and this provided regularity and security to the whole family.

Timo's first jobs were administrative jobs in higher education. Later on, he was involved in developing business services for a higher education institution, and after 10 years of temporary posts, he got a permanent job there. For him, all the jobs were more or less "happenstance choices"—opportunities that opened doors for him to enter the working life, opportunities he felt he had to use because there were not many job openings because of the recession. He found the first years of working life rather positive in the sense that the atmosphere was good and the job was not too demanding, making it possible for him to devote time to his family. The development of business services was a big challenge for him, both positive and demanding.

It took at least 10 years before Timo and his wife felt at home in Finland and could say they felt they were more adapted to life there. During those years, Timo often thought about going back to Germany, and he still misses their friends in Germany and in the Netherlands because he feels they have not built relationships that are as close with their few new friends in Finland. The experience of having close friends in Germany was very significant to him: "If I would have never had this experience I would think there's something wrong with me." This shows how important people, especially close friends, are.

Reflecting on his close relatives, Timo notes how difficult it was, particularly for his mother, to realize that her returning son was "a different person than he used to be when he left home," was married to a wife who spoke a language he did not speak, and had children. This indicates clearly how multicultural marriages also pose an adaptation challenge for relatives. Furthermore, Timo learned that he and his wife had adopted many aspects of German and Dutch culture. For example, they had learned to be more argumentative, and it was their perception that people in Finland were not accustomed to this type of thinking and behavior, which made it more difficult to build close relationships with Finns, led to misunderstandings, and made Timo and Marijke feel unsure.

Second Critical Incident

During the 1st month back in Finland, Timo went to see a career counselor. His experience, however, was that it made him feel even more uncertain, because he was encouraged to take another direction in his career path—to start a totally new study program when he was 30 years old and had a wife and children. This suggested new path was one that he did not see had any connection to his previous studies and work experiences. He especially had the feeling that the career counselor was not able to understand the multicultural perspectives of his case but was assuming too much based on the fact that they spoke the same language, Finnish. She could not realize Timo's knowledge about the Finnish labor market and other conditions in Finland was almost zero and outdated. It is possible to imagine the following type of dialogue between Timo and the career counselor.

Counselor: Given the situation in Finland, I think you could think about starting new studies here in order to broaden your prospects in the labor market.
Timo: I don't know, I am getting older and have the family.
Counselor: Lifelong learning is supported by the government and there are means to get some financial support for studying.
Timo: I did enjoy studying, but this does not feel like the kind of thing that would work well. . . . I studied in Germany.
Counselor: That's not a problem, you know, you speak Finnish fluently. I think you could easily start new studies and get better job opportunities.
Timo: Given that I have my family, it makes me feel that I am more needed to support my family by earning money . . . and my wife being from another country.
Counselor: But you know the labor markets in Finland, the new studies could bring you better opportunities and we do have a rather good system to support lifelong learning, also in learning new fields.

Timo: I am not so familiar with the situation in Finland. I studied in Germany and had a job there.

Counselor: That should not be a big problem. You speak fluent Finnish and being a Finn you can quickly adapt and get better opportunities to enter the working life.

Timo: Well, . . . I will consider this.

In spite of the many difficulties, Timo also recognizes personal strengths he has gained by going through the transitions. He particularly mentions competence in intercultural communication and his ability to understand people in similar situations. He also notes that his experiences between cultures have helped him to see things from multiple perspectives and to have broader horizons.

Key Issues

In retrospect, there are many important issues in Timo's case that are related to multicultural counseling. The most obvious and important one is that he never received any! Going back to the start in Germany, medicine was not an informed choice for him. He himself noted he would have needed counseling in order to understand what it takes to study medicine abroad, using a foreign language and studying topics that required physics and chemistry, which were not his strong points. He also noted that there are differences in academic traditions, beginning in high school, between different countries and that these difference should be taken into account.

One very important need in cases such as Timo's is for holistic guidance and counseling that address the various needs related to multicultural marriage, transition periods including culture shock, language issues, career concerns including information about working life, taking care of children, establishing new relationships, and so on in order to identify strengths. As Timo put it, he would have needed long-term, holistic, personal career counseling that would have included his whole life space in relation to his career options. Counselors both in Germany and in Finland were unable to recognize the holistic needs he had, and, thus, he did not benefit from the services. The counselors did not understand how challenging the situation was for Timo.

One obvious shortcoming was that he and Marijke received no training on how to prepare for culture shock upon their move to Finland. Fortunately, during the past years, more attention has been paid to supporting international students during their transition periods, but in those days, Timo and Marijke had to cope by themselves. Given the complexity of the challenges Timo and his wife had when they went to Finland in 1990, they would have benefited from multicultural counseling to identify and cope with the culture shock experiences related to the adaptation process. Timo himself indicated that they would have needed long-term counseling to support their integration into Finnish society because of their "foreigner-perspective," lack of extensive networks, identity crises related to their transition paths, and so on.

Writer's Role

After I interviewed Timo and carefully listened to the recording, I was reminded again how extremely important are the relationships in people's lives. They are particularly important during transitions periods, and counselors should remember to really address these relationship aspects in their clients' lives. At many points during the interview, Timo described the events from the perspective of relationships with other people. People really make a big difference.

Another important notion is that, according to my understanding, Timo would have benefited and still would benefit from confronting the painful memories around the "second" transition (time before and after returning to Finland). He himself noted that both he and Marijke have avoided discussing those times because of the strong negative emotions related to those experiences. Telling that story again and renarrating it, perhaps partly together with a counselor, would give Timo and his wife an opportunity to become freer from the emotional load related to those times and to gain new self-knowledge and learn more about the inner strengths they have—some of which are attributed to their difficult experiences. This might also help Timo to discover even new strengths he could use in his working life and in building new relationships in Finland.

Reader Reflection Questions

1. Relationships are in many ways important in Timo's case. How could you briefly describe the relationships in Timo's life (perhaps by using visual presentations) and the dynamics of them?
2. What kind of questions would have been useful for Timo in Germany to plan his future after he completed his studies there? How about when he returned to Finland?
3. Questions related to Timo's identity in relation to other people and various challenges in his life are important. Based on the above description, can you point out concrete aspects that are relevant from the point of view of identity?
4. Circumstances related to the larger societal context (e.g., recession) and to events in Timo's personal life had an impact on his career decisions. How could a counselor properly and meaningfully address these circumstances as part of a counseling process?
5. On the basis of Timo's story, he seems to be a sensitive, intelligent person who values his family, friends, and other relationships. Being sensitive can also make a person vulnerable. How could Timo use his sensitivity and intelligence in his job dealing with business services when he meets his clients?
6. How could Timo use his own transition experiences (both positive and negative) in developing himself as an employee and in growing as a human being in general?

Response 1

S. Alvin Leung and Ella P. O. Chan

It is important to understand and interpret Timo's experience and his developmental transitions in light of the interwoven circumstances, events, and significant individuals that were parts of Timo's context (Young, Valach, & Collin, 2002). First, there was a social and family context shaping Timo's self-identity. Timo's parents and grandparents were forced to move from their home city to another city because of a war, and they never developed a strong sense of belonging to their adopted home city. Their feelings of alienation were transmitted to Timo, who in growing up, did not feel he belonged and had a shaky identity as a Finn. When Timo was a young teenager, he felt restless and there was an urge to "struggle free and go as far as he could," and he looked for opportunities to study abroad in Germany. Timo's Finnish ethnic identity was almost "buried" during his years in Germany, and he, at times, had "forgotten he was a Finn." It was natural that after he completed his study in Germany, he sought to stay there permanently with the family that he formed away from his Finnish homeland. Another instance of how social and family context influenced Timo was his initial choice to study medicine in college. It was not clear how Timo arrived at this choice, but there were traces of influence from his parents (e.g., Timo's mother was disappointed that he decided not to choose medicine, Timo wanted to be a doctor to save his ailing father) and from his peers because several of his Finnish acquaintances had chosen to study medicine in Germany.

Second, there was also an economic and political context shaping the availability of choices. Timo was quite determined to stay in Germany after he completed his program in British studies; however, his choice and options were limited by the characteristics of the economic and political context that Timo was a part of (that is, the political and economic realities in Europe, Germany, and Finland at that time). As a foreign student, Timo needed to obtain a work permit so he could work legally, yet because of economic (e.g., job availability in Germany) and political circumstances (e.g., immigration policy in Germany at a time when the reunification of Germany was happening and Finland was not a part of the European Union at that time), such a permit was almost impossible to obtain. Timo had to return to Finland, even though he was reluctant to make this move. Incidentally, Finland in the 1990s was in the midst of an economic recession, and Timo had difficulties landing his first job there. Making major life transitions in an adverse economic and labor context was extremely difficult for Timo and his family.

The Nature of Cross-Cultural Transitions

Theories of cross-cultural transition suggest that cultural adaptation often involves contrasting yet predictable reactions that could be formulated into stages (e.g., Adler, 1975; Pedersen, 1995). The typical stages are an initial stage of excitement, a stage of confusion, and then a stage of reintegration. It was almost a dream come true when Timo moved to Germany to study medicine. However, Timo's initial excitements were soon dampened by his academic difficulties with studying scientific subjects in a foreign environment. There were frustrations and doubts about his ability and potential, and Timo had to find new ways to cope with the emerging demands and challenges. A turning point arose when Timo chose British studies as his new academic major, and very soon he found this to be an exciting area of study. Discovery of new meaning and purposes was an important sign of transition into the reintegration stage. Timo started to embark on a stable life structure revolving around his academic pursuit and his newly formed family, along with his wife Marijke.

Sojourners often have to go through a stressful process of reverse culture shock when they return to their home country after an extended stay in a host country (Gaw, 2000; Leung 2007; Ward, Bochner, & Furnham, 2001). The reentry transition for Timo and his family was extremely difficult and stressful, particularly because it was not their preference to return to Finland. There was no initial excitement, and the situation was confusing and challenging from the outset. Even though Timo and Marijke had made deliberate plans to relocate to a city where support from a close friend was available, they felt lonely and alienated in a place that Timo once called home, at times like "being a refugee" who was forced to relocate. They grieved for the comfortable life structure and support system they left behind in Germany. To make matters worse, they experienced financial difficulties because it was difficult for Timo to get a job in a depressed economy. The aggregation of all the psychological, social, and financial turmoil resulted in a high dose of reverse culture shock for Timo (a culture shock for Timo's wife, Marijke, because Finland was a new culture to her).

Timo and his wife were resourceful and resilient individuals who refused to become victims in times of transition. After a lengthy process, Timo obtained successive positions in administration and business service in the higher education sector, which eventually became permanent positions after 10 years of service. Marijke also became acclimated to the Finnish culture through forming new social ties and making use of the intercultural knowledge and skills she learned while studying. A new life structure emerged as Timo and his family settled down in their homeland and career.

Social adjustment seemed most difficult in the reentry process. Long after their return to Finland, Timo and Marijke still encountered communication and interpersonal difficulties within the Finnish culture. It was unfortunate but typical that it took a long time to adapt in cultural transitions (especially in the case of reverse culture shock), and as Wang (1997) pointed out, many returnees have little anticipation that reverse culture shock "is measured in years, not days" (p. 119). In Timo's case, 10 years after he returned to Finland, he was still struggling to adapt socially and psychologically.

Another useful concept instrumental to understanding the nature of cultural transition is acculturation. According to a model of acculturation by Berry (1980), acculturation is a process in which a person adopts attitudes, values, and behavior of a host culture in order to effectively cope with the demands from the new cultural environment. An individual who is in cultural transitions has to struggle between being affiliated with the culture of the host or the culture of his or her ethnic origin. Timo went to Germany to study with a shaky cultural identity as a Finn, and soon a "German" identity became more dominant, and Timo clearly embraced the values, attitudes, and behavior of the host culture. The acculturation model by Berry would consider Timo an assimilationist who preferred the cultural values and practices of the host culture over those of his home culture. At the end of Timo's study in Germany, his identification with the German culture was so strong that he had almost forgotten his Finnish identity, and that was why the return to Finland was so difficult and painful and was far more intense than he experienced when transitioning from Finland to Germany when he was younger. According to Berry's model, an adaptive option was for Timo to become an integrationist, a position of adaptation in which he must accommodate the multiple cultural identities within his ethnic identity system. Timo had to rekindle his Finnish cultural identity, to integrate that identity with other identities he had picked up along his developmental journey, and to develop competence in using diverse strategies to cope with challenges arising in his immediate environment.

Presenting Issues

In reading the life story of Timo, three core issues/themes emerged that deserved the attention of counseling intervention. The first is a career-and-life planning issue, closely connected to an individual's sense of direction, meaning, and purposes (Bolles, 2000). Timo had dreams, but there were moments that he was unsure of his direction and how to implement his dreams. It was in those moments of indecision that a helping hand would have been desirable. For example, someone could have helped Timo to make decisions regarding his choice of academic major, to decide on his career direction after graduation, and to feel more confident about how his education had equipped him for career and life (Carney & Wells, 1999). The limited career guidance that Timo received after his return to Finland was more a process of test and advice giving, with little attention devoted to exploring Timo's diverse cultural, social, and career self. It took Timo a number of years to settle down in a career in higher education administration and business service, leaving him with a taste that the jobs he had were more "happenstance choices" than informed career choices that he made with an awareness of alternatives. Timo was able to overcome most of the obstacles, yet with proper counseling his transitions might not be as consuming and stressful.

The second presenting issue was Timo's difficulties with cultural transitions and adaptation. An underlying factor closely linked to the difficulties experienced was Timo's cultural identity (Phinney, 1989). Timo developed a strong identification with the German culture soon after he started studying there, and his Finnish identity had receded into the background. It was less of an issue when he lived in Germany, yet when Timo returned to Finland as an adult, his cultural identity status caused him to respond unfavorably to the surroundings, triggering frustration and shock reaction. Hence, the surface issue presented was adaptation and adjustment, and the underlying issue was one of cultural identity. It would be necessary for counseling interventions to deal with the surface and underlying issues simultaneously, through identifying practical adaptation strategies and strengthening Timo's multicultural identities.

The third presenting issue was related more globally to the adaptation of Marijke and Timo's and Marijke's children to Finland. It is important to note that the transition to Finland could be more difficult for Marijke than for Timo because she was from the Netherlands. Marijke could have become very isolated, lonely, and resentful of the move. Marijke would need much emotional support from her husband and peers, and she also needed help and support to cope with many practical issues and demands, including child care, household management, and career planning.

Common Considerations for Working With This Population

The case of Timo illustrates several issues that are common to international students who return to their homeland after completing their education overseas.

1. Many international students encounter difficulties in their chosen area of study because of reasons such as a language barrier and a mismatch in interest and ability (Arthur, 2004). They need help to sort out different academic options, including how various academic options would equip them for a different career direction in the future. Some international students would benefit from language preparation courses so that they have the language competence before they engage in their chosen area of study.
2. Some international students have their sights set on staying in the host country after graduation. This might not be a realistic goal because of various economic, labor, and immigration restrictions, as illustrated in the case of Timo. It is important to encourage international students to develop alternative plans of action so that when their plans to stay in the host country do not materialize, they are prepared to follow an alternative course of action.
3. Many international students underestimate the intensity of reverse culture shock that they will experience (Leung, 2007; Wang, 1997). International graduates returning home should be encouraged to enroll in reentry training to prepare them for the psychological, social, and cultural transitions. Reentry training is especially important for students whose preference was to stay in the host country and for students who have been away from home for a long while.
4. We agree with the case incident description that relationships are very important to international students in times of transition. When international students return to their home country, they always miss the relationships that they formed during their formative years on campus. When they are still grieving over the loss of these relationships, they become more careful or passive in developing new relationships, to avoid being hurt again. Developing a new support system at home is especially vital to returning students (Leung, 2007).
5. International students might not be aware of channels to obtain counseling when they need help (Leong & Chou, 2002). Timo was a case in point because he never sought formal counseling when dealing with all the difficulties as a student in Germany. When he returned to Finland, the counselor was not aware of the multicultural issues behind Timo's struggle, and so the outcome was not

successful. Success in forming counseling alliances with international students depends on the counselor's ability to empathize with their multicultural experience and identities.

Unique Influences on the Client/Diversity of Clients

There are three aspects of Timo's experience that are relatively unusual. First, international students bring with them to the host country a variety of family backgrounds. Timo grew up in a rather typical family, but at the surface he was not attached to his parents. There was not a strong desire to return home to be with his family of origin. A unique experience was that Timo's father passed away 2 weeks prior to Timo's departure to Germany. It was an incident that would have devastated some international students, but he seemed to have contained his grief in a relatively short period of time.

Second, many international students are involved in cross-cultural romantic relationships, yet the issues involved in each relationship are unique. Timo's wife Marijke was from the Netherlands, and so Timo had to learn about Marijke's culture as well as Germany's culture where they both studied. The German culture was the common culture that tied Timo and Marijke together, and if they had stayed in Germany permanently, there would have been little cultural stress. However, when they decided to return to Finland, the transition was complicated by the diverse cultural backgrounds involved in the lives of Timo and Marijke.

Third, international students return home with diverse academic backgrounds and training. Some international students return home with academic training that is of great demand in their home countries. There are others, like Timo, whose field of academic study does not translate easily into career opportunities. It is important for counselors to understand the unique academic experiences that international students bring home and assist them to locate the right career opportunities.

Appropriate Counseling Intervention for Timo

It is disheartening to know that Timo never received the multicultural counseling he needed. Holistic guidance and counseling could have helped Timo deal with the many developmental issues that arose in his life journey, including the presenting concerns discussed in the previous section. Below, we discuss counseling strategies that could be used to assist Timo. Our view is that the integration among the different aspects of self-identity (e.g., ethnic identities, vocational identities) was a core developmental task for Timo, and so we propose the use of a gestalt approach (e.g., Ivey, Ivey, & Simek-Morgan, 2002; Korb, Gorrell, & Van De Riet, 1989) as the underlying framework to structure counseling interventions.

The phenomenological emphasis in gestalt therapy suggests that the counselor should not make interpretations of or assumptions about Timo's unique experiences. The counselor should respect Timo's way of perceiving and his interpretation of his experience. The overall goal is to enhance Timo's self-awareness, to immerse in those experiences more fully, and to expand his scope of perception such that he becomes more aware of the choices available to him in the present and future. The counselor would begin by inviting Timo to decide on a priority list of things that he would like to address in counseling. It is hoped that the process would enable Timo to experience how it would be to "take charge" of his life and to make decisions according to his readiness and level of comfort.

To illustrate the above process, if Timo decided to explore the issue of his childhood, the counselor would invite him to "relive" some of these incidents (he could choose which ones). Timo would be guided to take the role of a narrator and director with the help of the counselor. Gestalt interventions such as the use of imagery (Korb et al., 1989) might be used to bring Timo back to full awareness of what actually happened in some of the childhood scenes about which he normally only had blurred memories. Timo would be encouraged to visualize and "see" how he was bored in his studies and to fully experience the boredom and loneliness in his childhood, which was described as "demanding." Actual incidents and dialogues would be experimented with in the counseling session with an aim to enhance Timo's awareness of those experiences. According to the gestalt approach, a safe and secure environment in which the client can make his or her own choice of action is instrumental to awareness and integration. Through reliving "old" decisions and choices selected by Timo, the counselor could help him to accept his own responsibility and encourage him to make "new" decisions with full recognition of his choices.

Gestalt therapy also emphasizes the importance of drawing closure to events that were not fully experienced and resolved. For example, if Timo were to revisit the weeks before he departed for Germany, at a time when his ailing father was dying, he could go through a fantasy trip in which he decided to postpone his departure to stay with his family to process his "grieving" needs for his father's death. Timo's need of catharsis can also be met in the process of these gestalt experiments. Once this unfinished business and these painful feelings of remorse and regret are processed, Timo would move on with more positive energy to face the here-and-now situations in his present life before projecting to the future. The gestalt approach is considered appropriate in meeting Timo's need for "clearances" of these unfinished life issues and emotions that have caused him to feel "stuck."

Incidents like intercultural marriage, cultural shocks and disappointments, and coping issues with career and family roles after marriage could also be explored in similar ways, with an aim to expand Timo's self-awareness and encourage him to take responsibility. The sense of drifting along could be resolved gradually as Timo regained a sense of control in his own life. Once Timo's growth energies were unleashed, counseling could move on to more action-oriented stages in which practical issues could be addressed (e.g., career and life planning issues).

Once individual issues were dealt with and unfinished blockages were cleared, Timo's wife Marijke could also be involved in the counseling process. Marital counseling would be a context in which mutual concerns and feelings could be shared and discussed. Enhancing communication, strengthening marital relationships and intimacy, parenting, and practical day-to-day household tasks are issues that can be dealt with in the context of marital counseling.

We also believe that therapeutic growth groups could have been helpful to Timo, especially to deal with his social and cultural adaptation. A group with carefully selected members who were experiencing cultural adjustment issues would be most appropriate. Once trust and security were established in the group, Timo could examine his social needs and experiment using various social skills in the group microcosm. For example, Timo could share his culture shock experience and his ambivalence toward his culture of origin and his disappointment about not being able to stay in Germany, and members of the group could provide him with feedback, understanding, and support. The group could become an "experimental" context in which Timo could test his interpersonal assumptions and practice his social skills. The assertive skills required in the interpersonal exchange within the group would also serve to prepare Timo for real-life encounters. In the comfort of a supportive group, Timo could gain more confidence and be ready to face his "risks" in real life.

Overall, the gestalt method is "the therapy of the obvious" (Korb et al., 1989). The counselor is observant of the client's nonverbal cues such as hand gestures, breathing, and facial expressions. It is important, however, that the counselor be informed of the cultural meanings behind these nonverbal behaviors and be cautious in interpreting their underlying meanings based on the counselor's own cultural norm (Pedersen, Draguns, Lonner, & Trimble, 2002). In engaging clients in various role-playing, dialogue, or imagery trips, it is vital for the counselor to understand that clients from diverse cultures might engage in these "experiments" with varying degrees of comfort and articulation. It is also important to note that there are multiple, culture-specific ways to experience the here and now and to arrive at a closure to life events. Meanwhile, counselors must be aware that perceptions of choices are culture and situation specific, and in reality, clients might not feel that there was a choice (e.g., Timo had to return to Finland). Counselors, however, should invite their multicultural clients to realize that there are multiple ways to respond and react to adversities.

References

Adler, P. S. (1975). The transitional experience: An alternative view of culture shock. *Journal of Humanistic Psychology, 15,* 13–23.

Arthur, N. (2004). *Counseling international students: Clients from around the world.* New York: Kluwer Academic/Plenum.

Berry, J. W. (1980). Acculturation as varieties of adaptation. In A. M. Padilla (Ed.), *Acculturation: Theory, models, and some new findings* (pp. 9–25). Boulder, CO: Westview Press.

Bolles, R. N. (2000). *How to find your mission in life.* Berkeley, CA: Ten Speed Press.

Carney, G., & Wells, C. F. (1999). *Working well, living well.* Pacific Grove, CA: Brooks/ Cole.

Gaw, K. F. (2000). Reverse culture shock in students returning from overseas. *International Journal of Intercultural Relations, 24,* 83–104.

Ivey, A. E., Ivey, M. B., & Simek-Morgan, L. (2002). *Counseling and psychotherapy: A multicultural approach* (5th ed.). Boston: Allyn & Bacon.

Korb, M. P., Gorrell, J., & Van De Riet, V. (1989). *Gestalt theory: Practice and theory* (2nd ed.). New York: Pergamon Press.

Leong, F. T. L., & Chou, E. L. (2002). Counseling international students and sojourners. In P. B. Pedersen, J. G. Draguns, W. J. Lonner, & J. E. Trimble (Eds.), *Counseling across cultures* (5th ed., pp. 185–207). Thousand Oaks, CA: Sage.

Leung, S. A. (2007). Returning home and issues related to reverse culture shock. In H. Singaravelu & M. Pope (Eds.), *A handbook for counseling international students in the United States* (pp. 137–151). Alexandria, VA: American Counseling Association.

Pedersen, P. (1995). *The five stages of culture shock: Critical incidents around the world.* Westport, CT: Greenwood Press.

Pedersen, P. B., Draguns, J. G., Lonner, W. J., & Trimble, J. E. (2002). (Eds.). *Counseling across cultures* (5th ed.). Thousand Oaks, CA: Sage.

Phinney, J. (1989). Stages of identity development in minority adolescence. *Journal of Early Adolescence, 9*(1/2), 34–49.

Wang, M. M. (1997). Re-entry and reverse culture shock. In K. C. Cushner & R. W. Brislin (Eds.), *Improving intercultural interactions: Modules for cross-cultural training programs* (Vol. 2, pp. 109–128). Thousand Oaks, CA: Sage.

Ward, C., Bochner, S., & Furnham, A. (2001). *The psychology of culture shock.* Philadelphia: Taylor & Francis.

Young, R. A., Valach, L., & Collin, A. (2002). A contextual exploration of career. In D. Brown & Associates, *Career choice and development* (4th ed., pp. 206–252). San Francisco: Jossey-Bass.

Response 2

Kenneth Cushner

The combined and often conflicting issues that Timo encountered in his life reflect situations and issues that are shared by an increasing number of young people around the world today. Timo and Marijke found it relatively easy to make a rather permanent move to a third country, Germany. The recent relaxation of cross-border restrictions and the opening of national borders across the European Union, coupled with the encouragement for students to pursue study in universities across the continent through such relationships as Erasmus and the establishment of the Bologna Process, mean an increasing number of students will do what Timo and Marijke did. This coincides with recent worldwide trends of students seeking tertiary education outside their home country. Today, approximately 2 million students study outside their own nation, about half a million in the United States alone. This number is anticipated to increase to about 8 million worldwide by the year 2025 (American Council on Education, 2001). Timo's experiences in Finland and Germany, thus, are increasingly a global phenomenon, mirrored across Eastern Europe, with the increasing number of African and Asian students studying abroad and with the myriad of students flocking to such countries as Australia, New Zealand, Britain, and Canada. This raises issues not only for the individuals themselves but, increasingly, for institutions of higher education in a number of areas.

Issues Facing Newly Arriving International Students

Timo and his wife Marijke experienced numerous transitions that had not been anticipated, it seems, either by them or the institutions in which they studied and worked. This raises questions regarding whose responsibility it is to anticipate and address such concerns. On the one hand, Timo can be forgiven for not anticipating the transitions he encountered when first going off to Germany to study. He did not, after all, as stated in the case incident, "actually plan his international studies; instead it was more an 'urge to see something else.'" This is not uncommon, but should be recognized by those receiving young, adventurous, and impressionable young students. In addition, it is not uncommon for people who are experiencing alienation from their family and immediate surroundings to seek out, and ultimately find, that an international experience satisfies that void in their lives.

It is especially at this time, in welcoming new students to a university environment (or for anyone making a transition into a new culture for that matter), that astute counselors, perhaps working in conjunction with international student advisers, should provide orientation sessions that begin to introduce people to issues they are likely to encounter during their cross-cultural transition. Such orientation should focus on key elements such as people's emotional responses to change and strategies that an individual might adopt to ease or better prepare for such eventualities, language and communication differences, and the need for support groups and strategies for developing them in a new setting.

It is also here that the concept of reentry, a critical but often overlooked dimension of the cross-cultural experience reflecting the subsequent adjustments people are likely to encounter when they think about returning home, can be introduced (Martin & Harrell, 2004; Wang, 1997). Many sojourners do not anticipate that they will encounter difficulty upon returning home. After all, what could be easier than returning to the place they presumably know best, but one consequence of an intensive international experience, such as Timo and other international students experience, is that although they may have changed in significant ways, people whom they have left at home have not and may not be able to identify with the experiences of the returnee. Although in Timo's case this would have been a moot point because he fully intended to remain in Germany, once the process is understood at the institutional level and integrated into the student experience, it is more likely that when it is encountered, students will find others with whom they can discuss their impending concerns and reentry. For Timo, had he been aware of the process, he and his wife might have sought professional counseling once they began to consider their return to Finland, as well as once they had returned and were settling in.

Timo's experiences present the following additional issues to consider.

Belonging

There is a recurring issue of disconnectedness, or lack of belonging, reflected in his life. This is evident from his early years onward (Cushner & Brislin, 1996). Timo grew up in a family whose parents, themselves, frequently talked about the pain of having been forced to leave a homeland. Thus, he was to some degree socialized in a family unit that perceived itself as part of an outgroup, never really feeling a sense of belonging. Later, given his father's illness, his lack of emotional connection with school, his inability to pursue his passion for music, a perceived lack of family support, and a dominant mother who had career expectations to which he did not aspire, it is not surprising that Timo sought to find a niche elsewhere. Finding Marijke at this time helped bring some stability to his life and badly needed interpersonal connectivity.

Emotional Engagement

Early in cross-cultural transitions, people are often surprised at the degree to which their own emotions will be engaged. Although they may anticipate and expect certain things to be different and they anticipate a certain degree of excitement, as did Timo, most do not anticipate how this excitement may have a difficult and sometimes negative side. People do have a need to belong, to fill a niche in any context. This sense of belonging appears to have been missing, not only during Timo's childhood but when he first went to Germany as well as on his return to his homeland, Finland.

In addition, there is an element of disconfirmed expectation. People have a tendency to have certain expectations when beginning a new chapter in their lives, when embarking on an international venture, when making transitions. It is not uncommon, for instance, for people undergoing an international transition to be extremely excited, anticipating a new life, new adventures, meeting new people, and so forth. What people often fail to recognize is that making major transitions is also highly stressful and that many things will not be encountered as anticipated. Others do not share the same degree of excitement in meeting them and making them friends, for instance, and it takes time to develop a new in-group. Perhaps language skills are not as good as anticipated, and communicating across cultures or accomplishing tasks is more difficult than expected, or it just takes more time than expected to get things done. These are all relatively common experiences encountered early in a transition that may be unanticipated and that lead to strong emotional reactions.

Timo encountered these situations on a number of occasions. Early in his experience in Germany, for instance, he was faced with the reality that he was not as strong a student as he had thought and was thus not able to succeed in his initial chosen field of medicine. He was also surprised that his facility in the German language was more challenged in an academic setting than he had anticipated.

The issue of disconfirmed expectations presents itself once again upon return to an individual's home culture and lies at the foundation of the reentry experience. Typical of people returning home after a lengthy sojourn, or in Timo's situation returning to Finland, is the belief that there will be little, if any, adjustment shock. However, as Timo experienced, not only has the individual changed as a result of the time away, but the home situation may be significantly different as well. Returnees typically expect smooth transitions home—after all, they grew up in that society and know it quite well. Reconciling this unanticipated adjustment need is fundamental to a successful reentry.

Acculturation

Individuals in such transitions also face an array of issues related to acculturation (Berry, 1990), defined as the changes that occur in two cultures as a result of continual interaction. There is often a tug of forces operating between maintenance of an individual's home culture and a desire to integrate fully into a new cultural context. Berry's work suggests that there are four acculturation strategies that individuals adopt—integration, assimilation, separation, or marginalization—and it is important when counseling individuals in cultural transition that this be fully considered.

Timo's desire to move toward assimilation after being in Germany for a few years is evident in comments that he makes, such as "not wanting to think of returning to Finland" and occasionally "forgetting he was a Finn." This is not uncommon and presents an area that a counselor might wish to explore with Timo or similar clients. When this occurs with young students, for instance, it may be more of a developmental stage, in which students try on new identities before finally settling on who they are in a new context. An astute counselor, therefore, may wish to explore the "all or nothing" position exhibited by Timo and help him to consider the consequences of rejecting his home culture at this stage in his life.

Reentry

Timo decided to return home to Finland once he completed his studies in Germany and he was not able to secure an appropriate career. This brings up a few additional themes from the culture-general framework (Cushner & Brislin, 1996). He was unable to fill an appropriate and satisfying niche in Germany and felt unwanted, while at the same time disconnected from Finland. As stated in the case incident, when he returned, he felt like a refugee, his culture shock was "huge," and it was unexpected. In addition, his academic degree from a foreign university was not fully accepted, and he once again was cast in the out-group. All of this placed tremendous strain on his marriage. Issues of belonging, role expectations, and a need to have a supportive in-group are all critical to an individual's satisfactory adjustment in any setting.

Career counselors, too, must be aware of issues related to cross-cultural adjustment and intercultural interaction if they are to be of service to clients, and Timo's visit to the career counselor upon his return to Finland was not satisfactory. This particular counselor neglected some very critical issues Timo presented that could have become assets in his situation. Although Timo may not have had up-to-the-minute knowledge of the current employment context, he did return to Finland with an array of skills and experiences that, undoubtedly, could be built upon. He is multilingual, for instance. He is familiar with the educational systems in Germany. He has skills and knowledge in the particular areas in which he studied. Such talents should not be minimized or ignored, as they appear to have been. Suggesting new career pursuits at this time in his life was not productive.

Considering the Extended Social Network

Counselors, too, are wise to consider the unique conditions that are at play in mixed international or intercultural marriages. Stressors unique to Timo's immediate family, such as language and cultural disparities, differences in expectations regarding child rearing, and the reception of such a marriage by extended family members, are all important to consider. Too often, discussion in the professional literature focuses on the individual student, giving scant attention to others in the support system, such as partners and other family members (Fontaine, 1996). In counseling international students, a counselor might consider exploring such concerns as decision making (who makes decisions that affect a family unit and what are the potential consequences), how to deal with a possible sense of isolation or marginalization experienced by a spouse or child, how an individual's career direction might be affected by another's decision, and so forth.

Counselors and other support staff in campus settings can support internationalization efforts by considering these, as well as other, issues in advance and including them in various ongoing orientation activities. Internationalization is complex and comprehensive and extends well beyond the issues discussed above. It takes a comprehensive, integrated student services team to work in support of the many issues that international students encounter. In addition, it takes a special sensitivity and awareness on the part of a professional counseling staff to bring many of these issues to the awareness of others across the university community.

References

American Council on Education. (2001). *Internationalizing the campus: Words, dreams and realities*. Washington, DC: Author.

Berry, J. (1990). Psychology of acculturation: Understanding individuals moving between cultures. In R. Brislin (Ed.), *Applied cross-cultural psychology* (pp. 232–253). Newbury Park, CA: Sage.

Cushner, K., & Brislin, R. (1996). *Intercultural interactions: A practical guide* (2nd ed.). Thousand Oaks, CA: Sage.

Fontaine, G. (1996). Social support and the challenges of international assignments: Implications for training. In D. Landis & R. Bhagat (Eds.), *Handbook of intercultural training* (2nd ed., pp. 264–281). Thousand Oaks, CA: Sage.

Martin, J. N., & Harrell, T. (2004). Intercultural reentry of students and professionals: Theory and practice. In D. Landis, M. Bennett, & J. Bennett (Eds.), *Handbook of intercultural training* (3rd. ed., pp. 309–336). Thousand Oaks, CA: Sage.

Wang, M. M. (1997). Re-entry and reverse culture shock. In K. Cushner & R. Brislin (Eds.), *Improving intercultural interactions: Modules for cross-cultural training programs* (Vol. 2, pp. 109–128). Thousand Oaks, CA: Sage.

Family and Home Country Influences on Adjustment

Kenneth Cushner

Fangyi Chen (a pseudonym) was 1 of more than 40 Taiwanese students interested in obtaining admission into the College of Education's doctoral program. She spent a day meeting with local Taiwanese recruitment personnel, learning about the American university, and interviewing with two campus representatives who traveled to Taiwan. Fangyi was sure that if she was offered a place to study, she would take a leave of absence promised from her current position and spend the 3 to 4 years required to pursue her degree. Her dream was realized, she was accepted for study, and 3 months later she left home for the United States.

Arriving on campus toward the end of summer with others from Taiwan, Fangyi was excited about her new opportunity, her new university, and the new friends and professors she would meet. She was, nevertheless, a bit anxious that her spoken English might not be adequate. The first weeks of classes seemed packed with orientation activities and requests from others in her college to attend a number of functions both on and off campus, along with the classes that she found, surprisingly, quite demanding. Fangyi was exhausted at the end of each day and increasingly concerned that she would not be able to keep up with the workload that was expected of her. Add to this the expectation that she contribute in meaningful ways during classroom discussions, and Fangyi was worried that she might have made a mistake by coming to study in the United States.

Fangyi's anxiety and worry only seemed to intensify as the weeks went on. By the second semester, faculty identified Fangyi as the one Taiwanese student about whom they were most concerned. In their eyes, she seemed overly anxious, requesting guidance from each instructor almost weekly. Most of the faculty members were concerned that she did not really comprehend what was expected of her. At the same time, American students were beginning to complain to faculty that Fangyi was demanding and seemed to be lost and confused most of the time, repeatedly asking for clarification and assistance with assignments as well as validation that her work was up to standard. Although her interactions in class were marginal, her grades, nevertheless, were adequate. Although there was no academic reason to keep her from continuing in the program, there was great concern that she would not succeed with her comprehensive exams or her dissertation.

Dr. Wilson (a pseudonym), her adviser, met with her toward the middle of her 2nd year, relating the concern of others and suggesting that she consider changing her degree from the PhD to educational specialist, an advanced degree offered by the institution between the master's degree and the doctorate that comprised additional professional course work without requiring a comprehensive exam or final research project.

After a week of thinking this through, Fangyi met with her adviser to say that she was against this option and could not really return home without the PhD in hand. She would continue through the program as originally planned. In the same conversation, however, Fangyi reported that she had been under regular medical care from a campus physician who could not seem to determine the cause of some severe abdominal cramping she had been experiencing over the course of the past 6 months. She would withdraw from classes for the current semester and return home to see if her family physician could resolve her medical problems. She was sure that once this was settled she would be able to focus more intently on her academic work. Dr. Wilson was secretly hoping that Fangyi would remain at home.

However, Fangyi Chen was persistent, and this alone seemed enough to keep her on top of things. She returned to campus the following semester, reportedly pain free and feeling better, but now with a new concern. During a private meeting with Dr. Wilson, and after presenting her with a gift of green tea, she proceeded to say that her daughter might be joining her in the next month. A daughter? This was news! A child had never been spoken of before. What next?

Fangyi discussed a concern that had been developing over the years with her 15-year-old daughter at home. It seems that her daughter had been having terrible nightmares; had had recurring suicidal thoughts; and was, at times, hitting her head against walls out of frustration. The doctors in Taiwan were concerned that she only seemed to be getting worse during her extended stay with her grandmother. Fangyi could not see leaving her daughter at home any longer and wanted to bring her to the United States for medical treatment and to have her closer. She would enroll her daughter in the local high school. Perhaps it was the distance from her mother that was causing her daughter's, as well as her own, problems.

In talking with Fangyi, Dr. Wilson suggested that, given her daughter's mental health concerns and the fact that she did not speak English, bringing her to the United States for school might not be the best course of action. Worried that the adjustment demands of entering an American high school while speaking no English would only exacerbate a severe mental health condition, coupled with everyone's concerns that Fangyi was not performing as required, Dr. Wilson thought this an opportune time and legitimate reason to suggest withdrawal from the demanding doctoral program. Her daughter's health, along with that of her own, was presented as of most concern. Fangyi Chen would consider this.

Returning a week later, Fangyi reported that she had decided that the best thing for all would be to bring her daughter to the United States where she could be with her mother who would help her through her problems and enroll her in school. They, in turn, would remain as a family. This she did, and for the first 6 months, Fangyi reported a series of difficulties encountered by her daughter, but she also reported fewer incidents of mental health concerns as well as fewer problems with her own abdominal cramps.

After a return home to Taiwan the subsequent summer, Fangyi and her daughter returned to the United States refreshed and renewed. Fangyi subsequently completed her comprehensive exams to everyone's satisfaction. Surprisingly, her major professor reported that her written and oral defense far surpassed that of any of the other Taiwanese students from that special cohort. She was now encouraged to tackle the most abstract of all dissertation topics, making special reference to how new forms of curriculum decision making might both meet with obstacles but also be integrated into Taiwanese society.

Key Issues

It goes without say that there is usually much more going on in many students' lives than simply the pursuit of a degree. Understanding and addressing the needs of international students can be especially difficult when issues related to face-saving and differences in the expression of public and private information are operating. This particular situation was complicated by the fact that no one on campus, not even other students in the Taiwanese cohort, knew that Fangyi had a daughter in Taiwan, let alone one who was facing severe mental health issues.

The adviser spoke of wanting the problem to go away. That is, Dr. Wilson was initially convinced that Fangyi was not capable of pursuing the degree that she sought, attributing her lack of focus and anxiety to language or cultural concerns or simply lack of ability, and spoke of regretting she had ever gotten involved with international students. To the contrary, the interaction between Fangyi's personal commitment to complete the degree that she had begun and her reluctance to share a difficult and painful situation at home made it difficult for her academic adviser, or anyone for that matter, to work with her to gain a deeper understanding of all aspects of her situation. In retrospect, it is understandable that Fangyi's attention was often diverted due to the problems her daughter was facing at home and that these difficulties were expressed in her own medical concerns and her inability to focus on her work. Once she faced these issues and decided to reunite her family, she was able to focus on her own task, take an active role in her daughter's recovery, and complete her degree.

Reader Reflection Questions

1. As you first read about Fangyi, what are some of your initial reactions to her as an individual? As a student? As a mother? How might these initial reactions affect your counseling relationship with her?
2. What responsibility do each of the following have in this situation: Dr. Wilson? Her fellow Taiwanese students? Her American student peers?
3. If Fangyi approached you asking if she should bring her daughter to the United States, how would you respond?
4. What cultural conflicts are evident to you for Fangyi? For Dr. Wilson?
5. What kinds of orientation and/or other campus supports would help to alleviate situations such as this one?

Response 1

Frederick T. L. Leong and Huaiyu Zhang

Fangyi's story is a very striking and thought-provoking case incident that reflects the hardships she experienced during her transition period and the effort that she took to overcome her problems. In this section, we will use Leong's (1996) multidimensional and integrative model to interpret Fangyi's case.

Leong's Integrative Model

Concerned with the innate limitations of unidimensional approaches of cross-cultural counseling, Leong (1996) proposed an integrative model of multicultural counseling that is sequential and dynamic and that encompasses elements of (a) outgroup homogeneity theory, (b) cultural schema theory, (c) complimentarity theory, (d) science of complexity, and (e) mindfulness.

The fundamental component of Leong's (1996) model is inspired by Kluckhohn and Murray's (1950) seminal article "The Determinants of Personality Formation," in which they stated, "Every man is in certain respects: (a) like all other men, (b) like some other men, and (c) like no other men" (p. 35). It indicates three levels of personality formation that need to be studied: universal, group, and individual. In the universal level, each person shares common biological features in the physical and sociocultural surroundings where they grow up. The universal level reflects the training model in medical and biological sciences. In the group level, each person belongs to certain social groups and owns some characteristics of his or her groups. This level is particularly significant for multicultural counseling because it includes cultural elements such as race, gender, and socioeconomic class. The individual level emphasizes the uniqueness of a person in the ways of perceiving, understanding, and behaving that differentiate him or her from other people. Social learning theories underscore the importance of such a level as determinants of personality.

Outgroup homogeneity effect is defined as the tendency of human beings to view greater homogeneity in people of other groups than in people of their own groups. It likely results from inadequacy of contact with people from a different group, which leads to a simplistic or even biased perception of a client from that group. When outgroup homogeneity heavily influences the counselor, he or she will pay an inappropriately high degree of attention to the group level of the client instead of accurately viewing the client as an individual who is experiencing unique stresses. Hence, outgroup homogeneity effect is an obstacle in the counseling relationship because it impedes efficient shifting among the three levels of client personality. Counselors need to be aware of the potential impact of outgroup homogeneity effect and need to assess the three levels of clients and of themselves correctly.

Leong (1996) also emphasized the significance of cultural schema in affecting the counselor's apprehension and interpretation of the client's culture-related stories. In order to obtain multicultural competence, a counselor needs to develop elaborate cultural schema and gain an advanced level of cognitive complexity. Possession of cultural schema, however, does not necessarily make the counselor a culturally competent professional. For instance, racism is the result of biased and stereotyped cultural schema; therefore, it is not only the enrichment of cultural schema that is worth attention but also the elements in the schema. Cultural schema is proposed to develop along the dimension of complexity. Leong believed that a counselor with a more mature cultural schema and a higher level of cognitive complexity is more culturally competent than a counselor with a less developed cultural schema and a lower level of cognitive complexity.

A complex adaptive system is composed of a large number of agents that are independent or semi-independent elements of the system. The characteristics of a complex adaptive system include nonlinear, multivariate, nonequilibrium, open, multiple equilibria, pattern-forming, information-processing, adapting, evolving, co-evolving, self-organizing, and exhibiting emergence. Hence, a complex adaptive system has macroscopic features that exceed the sum of the individual agents. Leong maintained that each person is himself or herself a component of a complex adaptive system that consists of the universal, group, and individual levels; therefore, the complex system operates within and between the client and the counselor dynamically in the three levels.

Leong also stated the importance of complimentarity as a component of his integrative model. Based on complimentarity theory, complimentarity between the counselor and the client predicts a good therapeutic relationship, which helps to achieve favorable outcomes in counseling and psychotherapy. High complimentarity is supposed to lead to more positive relationships and, consequently, better outcomes, whereas low complimentarity is likely to cause more negative relationships and worse outcomes.

Finally, the significance of mindfulness is emphasized in Leong's model. A good sense of mindfulness is recommended to counselors to rid themselves of the outgroup homogeneity effect, obtain culturally appropriate schemas, and improve the level of cultural complementarity in counseling and psychotherapy. Langer (1989) argued that mindful individuals are open to new information and pay more attention to the context when they are interacting with other people. If a counselor works with the client with mindfulness, he or she is not likely to be restricted by simplistic cultural schema or to operate in an automatic, habitual manner. Rather, the mindful counselor will be sensitive to the client's changes in the three levels, which will facilitate a positive therapeutic outcome.

Fangyi's Three Levels of Personality

The universal level of personality states that all human beings share some common characteristics that are consistent across different physical and cultural environments. First, Fangyi is one member of the human race. She has the biological endowments that label her as a person and exert functions to sustain her daily life and to procreate. She thinks and behaves according to the operation of the nervous system. She has universal feelings, such as excitement and happiness. In this particular case scenario, she experienced stressors during her transition period in the United States and reacted to the hardships with common feelings of anxiety.

The group level is focused on the aspect of the individual as one member of a group. Fangyi is female, thus she shares some features with other women. As a doctoral student studying in the United States, she had likely been in the lower socioeconomic group. Mostly notable to a culturally sensitive counselor are Fangyi's specific cultural belongings. She is a member of the Taiwanese, who are predominantly inheritors of Chinese culture and who have been influenced by Japanese customs, which are also closely related to Chinese culture.

Wu and Tseng (1985) summarized some common features of traditional Chinese culture and contended that the value of the family as a basic unit in the society is likely to be most crucial for Chinese people. They also listed four other characteristics: (a) highlighting the parent–child bond, (b) art of personal interaction and importance of social networks, (c) restricted emotions and emphasis on morality, and (d) value of education and performance.

It seems that the level of Chinese culture significantly influenced Fangyi. The fact that she has a 15-year-old daughter indicates that Fangyi was at least in the late 30s when she came from overseas to the United States. She had to take a leave of absence from her job in Taiwan, leave her family members, and undertake an adventure to a country with a different language and culture. It appeared to be a big sacrifice for her to pursue a doctoral degree in the States, and her choice implied to what extent the value of education is embedded in a Chinese person's mind. Fangyi worried a great deal about her daughter when they were apart. Her anxiety and worry even undermined her academic performance, which led Dr. Wilson to doubt her capabilities. Eventually, Fangyi brought her daughter to the United States, and she successfully passed the comprehensive exams to everyone's satisfaction. Fangyi's relationship with her daughter underscored the cultural value of family function and the importance of the parent–child bond to her. However, she did not disclose her daughter's mental health problems to Dr. Wilson until she had decided to bring her to the States. The issues that had concerned Fangyi most were probably the culturally oriented value of emotion controlling and, more important, the fear of loss of face.

Loss of face is defined by Ho (1994) to be a "damaging social event, in which one's action is publicly given notice and negatively judged by others, resulting in a loss of moral or social standing." It is shameful in Chinese communities to lose face. Studies have indicated that Chinese people experience negative emotions in face-losing situations (Ho, Fu, & Ng, 2004). Loss of face seems to cause severe consequences to an individual's social role (Ho, 1974). It tends to break the congenial interpersonal network that is highly valued in East Asian culture (Ho, 1991). In addition, concerns about losing face and issues of shame may pose particular barriers for Asian clients in seeking mental health services because it is stigmatizing to their families (Uba, 1994).

Dr. Wilson probably did not think of the Chinese concept of face when she noticed Fangyi performing marginally in her academic work. Dr. Wilson basically attributed her problems to the hardship in the acculturation process and her ability. Instead, her problems were largely caused by worries about her 15-year-old daughter who had mental health issues. However, the concerns about losing face hampered her from telling Dr. Wilson the reasons that she felt stressed. At first, the cultural clash between these two individuals resulted in misunderstandings, which were fortunately resolved later after she openly talked about her daughter, brought her to the United States, and improved her academic performance.

Finally, the individual level emphasizes the characteristics of the person that differentiate him or her from others. Fangyi has her own learning experiences. She has made a large number of choices on her own. She chose to come to the United States, she chose not to reveal her personal hardships, she chose to bring her daughter and take an active role in helping her, she chose to focus on study when her major problem was solved. Each of her steps probably contains certain universal and group elements, but also elements of her uniqueness.

An Emphasis on Fangyi's Group Level: Multicultural Competence

If Fangyi comes to the counseling center for help with her problems, the question to the counselor is what he or she can do to counsel her. This section is aimed at discussing the culturally competent intervention with Fangyi that is at the group level.

In 1982, D. W. Sue published the influential American Psychological Association Division 17 paper titled "Cross-Cultural Counseling Competencies." In this report, he listed 11 specific competencies for multicultural counseling practice. These competencies were grouped into three broad areas: awareness, knowledge, and skills. Since then, the field of multicultural counseling has gained increased attention and has been named the "fourth force" of psychology by some scholars (Gelso & Fretz, 2001).

In 2000, Hansen and colleagues (Hansen, Pepitone-Arreola-Rockwell, & Greene, 2000) reviewed the literature, and extracted 12 practice-related multicultural competencies.

1. Awareness of how one's own cultural heritage, gender, class, ethnic-racial identity, sexual orientation, disability, and age cohort help shape personal values, assumptions, and biases related to identified groups,
2. Knowledge of how psychological theory, methods of inquiry, and professional practices are historically and culturally embedded and how they have changed over time as societal values and political priorities shift,
3. Knowledge of the history and manifestation of oppression, prejudice, and discrimination in the United States and their psychological sequelae,
4. Knowledge of sociopolitical influences that impinge on the lives of identified groups,
5. Knowledge of culture-specific diagnostic categories,
6. Knowledge of such issues as normative values about illness, help-seeking behavior, interactional styles, and worldview of the main groups that the clinician is likely to encounter professionally,
7. Knowledge of culture-specific assessment procedures and tools and their empirical support,
8. Knowledge of family structures, gender roles, values, beliefs, and worldviews and how they differ across identified groups in the United States, along with their impact on personality formation, developmental outcomes, and manifestations of mental and physical illness,
9. Ability to accurately evaluate emic and etic hypotheses related to clients from identified groups and to develop accurate clinical conceptualizations, including awareness of when clinical issues involve cultural dimensions and when theoretical orientation needs to be adapted for more effective work with members of identified groups,

10. Ability to accurately self-assess one's multicultural competence, including knowing when circumstances are negatively influencing professional activities and adapting accordingly,

11. Ability to modify assessment tools and qualify conclusions appropriately (including empirical support, where available) for use with identified groups, and

12. Ability to design and implement nonbiased, effective treatment plans and interventions for clients from identified groups, including the following: a. Ability to assess such issues as clients' level of acculturation, acculturative stress, and stage of gay or lesbian identity development. b. Ability to ascertain effects of therapist–client language difference on psychological assessment and intervention. c. Ability to establish rapport and convey empathy in culturally sensitive ways. d. Ability to initiate and explore issues of difference between the therapist and the client, when appropriate, and to incorporate these considerations into effective treatment planning. (p. 654)

Using Hansen et al.'s (2000) article, we analyzed Fangyi's situation, and concluded that the items that are most pertinent to Fangyi are Items 1, 6, 8, 9, 10, and 12c. Because the majority of the U.S. counselors are White Americans, the counselor who sees Fangyi would presumably be from this population and would be someone who is probably an inheritor of a different cultural background than Fangyi's. It is a foundation of the interaction with Fangyi for the counselor to be aware of his or her own cultural heritage, gender, class, ethnic/racial identity, and age cohort and to discern how these facts about himself or herself would influence his or her personal bias. When the counselor meets with Fangyi, there is a need for him or her to understand the normative values of people with Asian ancestors (e.g., how the family bond is valued, how much emphasis is put on education, how modesty and controlled emotions are encouraged by this group of people). By knowing the cultural norms of the people to whom Fangyi belongs, the counselor would have a better chance to understand her opportunities, decisions, and hardships. The other component of cultural context—also part of the norms but important enough to be listed separately—is the attitude toward mental disorders. The significance of loss of face cannot be overaddressed with Chinese people. Although the feeling of shame about mental illness is likely to be a universal phenomenon, it is particularly face-threatening to a Chinese person. Asian Americans, including a large portion of Chinese Americans, have been found, like other minority groups, to underutilize psychological interventions and to have a higher premature termination rate than does the majority group. Fangyi dreaded the risk of loss of face to her and her family, which held her back from telling Dr. Wilson what was really bothering her. It is also likely that when she does have the courage to talk to a counselor, her concerns of saving face may make it hard for her to reveal her real problems. Being knowledgeable about this concept would probably help the counselor better understand Fangyi's possible barriers and to be more patient in facilitating her self-disclosure. In addition to the knowledge of Fangyi's culture, the counselor also needs to be able to assess his or her own capability to help her. For example, if the counselor considers his or her own ethnic identity, personal bias, and skill level and concludes that he or she is not a good match for Fangyi, he or she needs to consult other professionals or to refer Fangyi to other counselors who are more competent for her. When applying theories to treat Fangyi, the counselor will have to be alert to the etic and emic aspects of theories and pick the ones that fit her situation the best. When it comes to the treatment plans and interventions, the counselor ought to establish rapport with Fangyi and be able to convey empathy in a way that is acceptable to her.

Model Integrations

Multicultural competence is one imperative element for a counselor to possess in order to be effective in counseling clients like Fangyi; however, a counselor should not want to stay just at this level. This last section is aimed at reaching an integrative view of the help that a counselor can offer to address Fangyi's problems.

In conceptualizing Fangyi's issues and the counselor's role in helping, we have applied both Leong's (1996) integrative model and Hansen et al.'s (2000) multicultural competence criteria in practice. Both are compatible to a large extent. The goals are to enhance the multicultural competence of counselors so that they will be more effective and efficient in helping clients from a different cultural background as well as clients from a similar cultural heritage. Both of these two reports offer insightful guidelines for counseling clients like Fangyi.

Leong's (1996) model generally recommends that counselors form rich and nonbiased cultural schema about clients. With the addition of mindfulness, the formation of cultural schema is facilitated, the outgroup homogeneity effect is likely to be avoided, and the complimentarity is reached that predicts positive outcomes. Hansen et al.'s (2000) criteria specify the contents of multicultural competencies for practitioners. By listing the 12 minimal elements, they elaborated on the guidelines that can give practicing counselors enriched ideas for counseling Fangyi.

Leong's (1996) model emphasizes the delineation of three levels of personality (i.e., universal, group, and individual), which are also embedded in Hansen et al.'s (2000) criteria but in an implicit way. For example, in Number 9 of the competencies, the authors encouraged a comparison between the universal component and the individual component. The other emphases that Leong stated in his model are the sequential, dynamic structure of the counselor's and client's personality and the trait of complexity. All the characteristics addressed in this paragraph suggest the importance of the counseling process being at an appropriate level and timing. Fangyi is an inheritor of Chinese culture, but this is only a part of her. She also experiences universal feelings and makes her own decisions. The counselor ought to be sensitive and responsible to meet the requirements of multicultural competence and be cautious about Fangyi's and his or her own dynamic swing among the three levels. Overdiagnosis or underdiagnosis at any of the three levels needs to be avoided for satisfactory treatment effects.

References

Gelso, C., & Fretz, B. (2001). *Counseling psychology* (2nd ed.). Orlando, FL: Harcourt.

Hansen, N. D., Pepitone-Arreola-Rockwell, F., & Greene, A. F. (2000). Multicultural competence: Criteria and case examples. *Professional Psychology: Research and Practice, 31,* 652–660.

Ho, D. Y. F. (1974). Face, social expectations, and conflict avoidance. In J. L. M. Dawson & W. J. Lonner (Eds.), *Readings in cross-cultural psychology: Proceedings of the inaugural meeting of the International Association for Cross-Cultural Psychology held in Hong Kong, August, 1972* (pp. 240–251). Hong Kong: University Press.

Ho, D. Y. F. (1991). The concept of "face" in Chinese-American interaction. In W. C. Hu & C. L. Grove (Eds.), *Encountering the Chinese: A guide for Americans* (pp. 111–124). Yamouth, ME: Intercultural Press.

Ho, D. Y. F. (1994). Face dynamics: From conceptualization to measurement. In S. Ting-Toomey (Ed.), *The challenge of facework: Cross-cultural and interpersonal issues* (pp. 269–286). Albany: State University of New York Press.

Ho, D. Y. F., Fu, W., & Ng, S. M. (2004). Guilt, shame and embarrassment: Revelations of face and self. *Culture and Psychology, 10*(1), 64–84.

Kluckhohn, C., & Murray, H. A. (1950). The determinants of personality formation. In C. Kluckhohn & H. A. Murray (Eds.), *Personality in nature, society and culture* (pp. 35–48). New York: Knopf.

Langer. E. J. (1989). *Mindfulness*. Reading, MA: Addison-Wesley.

Leong, F. T. L. (1996). Toward an integrative model for cross-cultural counseling and psychotherapy. *Applied & Preventive Psychology, 5,* 189–209.

Sue, D. W. (1982). Position paper: Cross-cultural counseling competencies. *The Counseling Psychologist, 10*(2), 45–52.

Uba, L. (1994). *Asian Americans: Personality patterns, identity, and mental health*: New York: Guilford Press.

Wu, D. Y. H., & Tseng, W. (1985). Introduction: The characteristics of Chinese culture. In W. Tseng & D. Y. H. Wu (Eds.), *Chinese culture and mental health* (pp. 3–13). Orlando, FL: Academic Press.

Response 2

John Pickering and Jonie Chang

Fangyi's situation is a common one for international student advisers (ISAs).[1] Her actions and reactions are reasonably common, as is the scenario of problems "back home" that continue to be the responsibility of the student studying overseas. From our perspective, the scenario at no point constituted a situation that required the *immediate* implementation of an emergency plan, which might have included the gathering of a critical incident response team; informing college senior management of the situation; possibly liaising with police, family, media; and the like. However, there was certainly a great deal of potential for the situation to develop into such a serious incident—for example, the student may have left the college and returned home without anyone knowing or the daughter may have committed suicide (in Taiwan or in the United States).

In our response, we look at the pattern of Fangyi's behavior, which is reasonably typical of a student undergoing adjustment and which reveals certain character traits that are reasonably typical of Taiwanese and many other students from Asia. As we do this, please be aware that no matter how useful it is to characterize behavior in terms of ethnic groups or countries of origin, such characterization is always only a generalization and never can be applied in total to an individual.

Next, we consider the paradigm in which Dr. Wilson was acting and how that influenced her response. As advisers to international students, it is important to periodically reflect on "where we come from" just as we seek to understand "where the student comes from." This is key to effective cross-cultural communication.

Having looked at the paradigms under which the two main players operate, we then consider an alternative response that is based on the premise of advisers as guides and is centered on the student in his or her own social and ethnic context.

Fangyi's Paradigm: Pattern of Behavior

First Year

Fangyi's initial behavior is typical of many international students—she is realizing a dream and arrives onshore excited. She brings with her many expectations based on past experience: She has been successful in her studies in Taiwan, therefore she knows how to

---

[1] ISAs in New Zealand are specialist support staff who in tertiary institutions are dedicated to the support of international students. They are generally responsible for monitoring student welfare, orientations, helping solve immigration issues, some personal problems, and dealing with critical incidents. They are not normally involved in giving academic advice, but they may mediate for students or support them through, for example, a discipline process.

study, therefore she will be successful in the United States. Similarly, she has demonstrated competence in learning English and gaining entry to the program, therefore she should not have communication problems in the States. She quickly finds the course demanding and displays anxiety over her ability to cope with the language and workload. Physically, she becomes exhausted. As is common with those coming out of an Asian education system, she is very uncertain about contributing in class. This is based on an embedded premise that it is the teacher's role to impart knowledge and the student's to absorb it. The Western concept of "learning together" is very strange to her. Furthermore, to question teachers in front of others is seen to bring shame on the teachers by suggesting they have failed to communicate knowledge properly.

Typically, her response is to fall back on "tried and true" methods, which for someone of her background is to sort it out for herself, look for "right" answers to all questions posed from the faculty, speak to faculty in private rather than embarrass them in class, and take a communal rather than individual approach to learning with her classmates. It is important to realize that she was a very successful student in Taiwan because of her ability to use these methods.

Second Year

Her response to Dr. Wilson's suggestion to change course was also typical of her culture. She would have seen a change in course as failure and as letting her family down. Not unusually, she and her family made great sacrifices for her to study, and the expectation is that she will return armed with a PhD, not for her direct benefit but for the benefit of her extended family.

She did acknowledge some difficulty in her study. She identified one problem, in her case her physical health, and she believed that if she could overcome this problem, then everything would be all right. We have noted that the identification of one issue, be it health, housing, or a particular class, is a common response of students and others when learning to live and work in new cultures. In implementing the solution of returning home for a short time, she was acting well within her Taiwanese paradigm rather than a Western one. Furthermore, she was solving the problem within a family and communal context rather than just an individual one. Also, seeking outside "expert" help is considered a last resort and evidence of the failure of a family, not just of an individual, to solve a problem.

Trust Building

An important aspect of Fangyi's behavior is that it took time to build trust with an "outsider," that is, with someone outside her family and culture. It was not until the 2nd year that Dr. Wilson learned of her medical problem and not until Fangyi returned from Taiwan that she learned of a family problem. To some extent, this slow building of trust is because of her paradigm of solving problems "in house" and not exposing her family to shame, which is an issue in regards to her daughter's behavior. It is may also be because Dr. Wilson apparently showed little interest in her family, something Fangyi may have found strange. Evidently, she was a mature woman and would have assumed that Dr. Wilson would have realized she was likely to have children. She may have assumed that Dr. Wilson may even have realized that other family members would be looking after her children—as is normal in such cultures. She, herself, may not have brought this up in discussion because she did not see it as relevant to her study until she acknowledged that a particular issue with her daughter was affecting her study.

Dr. Wilson's Paradigm

Dr. Wilson's response to Fangyi exhibited many typical characteristics of what we might label the Western academic paradigm. Dr. Wilson appears to deal with Fangyi on the intellectual and individual levels and not as a whole person whose identity is first and foremost in her relationships, first with her family and then her broader community. We see this in the way that Dr. Wilson and other faculty members responded to Fangyi's behavior.

Meaning of Signals

During her 1st year, the faculty saw her learning style as flawed and evidence of confusion and potential inadequacy; this was despite her grades, which appeared adequate. This interpretation of the signals seems to be because faculty members saw her approaching them and students outside of class as a sign of dependency and, therefore, a lack of ability. Such an interpretation may be valid for a Western student of a Western education system, but it is not necessarily so for someone from a culture in which learning is a cooperative experience.

Dr. Wilson's solutions were at the intellectual and educational level and followed a typical Western academic pattern. Having assumed some inadequacy, she prescribed a change of course that she thought would better suit Fangyi's abilities. Apart from not recognizing that Fangyi's learning style was not wholly inadequate, she also did not take into account that Fangyi sees herself as a person in relationship with family, friends, and colleagues and, therefore, to change to a course of study that awards a lower degree is to affect those relationships. Potentially, it would be to disappoint some and possibly bring shame to her family.

Dr. Wilson had an expectation of herself, and that expectation was to solve what she saw as an academic problem in an academic manner; hence, she talked first about Fangyi switching to another program. She also exhibited behavior that seemed to indicate that the option of minimizing a problem by making it go away was acceptable. This was her hope when Fangyi returned home. In other words, Dr. Wilson's expectations were to solve the problem by educational means in consultation with the individual student. This contrasts to Fangyi, who saw difficulties in terms of character and as a family problem, not merely in terms of an educational technique that needed mastering.

Mental Health

If Dr. Wilson had been faced with the issue concerning the health of her child, she probably would have quit and returned home, seeing no shame or sense of failure in that. Thus, she was surprised at and concerned about Fangyi's response. She saw the combination of mental illness, plus dislocation from home, plus language problems as a recipe for disaster and the combination of mental illness, plus mother, plus home country as best for the child, the mother, herself, and the college. This is in contrast to Fangyi, who saw her daughter's problem in terms of relationships: Misbehaving ill daughter plus distance from mother equals disaster. Her solution for her misbehaving ill daughter is daughter, plus mother, plus medical care equals a happy family and successful study.

Dr. Wilson's reaction, while typical, was also inadequate. As an academic adviser, the question must be raised, "Was she out of her depth?" Was it ethically right for her, an academic, to advise a student on a course of action related to the student's physical state and to the mental state of a family member? At what point should she have sought expert help who was able to approach the situation from a Taiwanese perspective?

Alternative Response

The Foundation for Working With Asian Students

The family is the primary social group and system for the socializing and shaping of individuals. It is where most people learn about and become exposed to the concepts of rules, boundaries, roles, and structure. Once the family system is established, it will tend to maintain its functioning in a stable state. Various rules and roles will be set up in order to maintain the stable and self-perpetuating functioning of the family system (Barker, 1998; McLeod, 1998; Worden, 2003). The family as a whole progresses through its life cycle as predictable transitions (e.g., work, marriage, childbirth, retirement) and unpredictable disruptions (e.g., illness, war) take place (Barker, 1998; McLeod, 1998), and one of the major tasks for the family as a whole is to adjust and adapt itself to these transitional stages/situations in order to uphold the functioning of the family (Barker, 1998; McLeod, 1998). In other words, the family system will go through gradual but constant change. At the same time, it will try to preserve its usual functioning, be it functional or dysfunctional. Together with the intrapersonal, psychological, interpersonal, and environmental influences that affect each individual family member, these evolving circumstances create potential situations and stresses under which individuals may require counseling intervention. In Fangyi's case, her academic pursuit disrupts the normal family life cycle, and it certainly puts pressure not only on Fangyi but also on other members of the family. As a result, it is important to conceptualize Fangyi's adjustment issues within the family system context.

Two Counseling Models

Individual counseling places its focus on individual clients. The focus is to recognize how an individual's past experience affects his or her present life, as well as to understand unconscious mental functioning (Ivey, D'Andrea, Ivey, & Simek-Morgan, 2002). The underlying assumption of individual counseling is that problems, issues, or disorders reside in the individual. Counselors aim at achieving growth and empowerment of an individual. Therefore, the individual becomes the client within the counseling relationship, forming a counselor–client dyad relationship.

Family counseling, on the other hand, constructs and understands problems and issues within a family context. It recognizes the interdependence of family members' behavioral, emotional, and psychological patterns (Walrond-Skinner, 1977). The core assumption of family counseling/therapy is that the "misbehavior" of individual family members is, in fact, a reflection of stress and dysfunction at a family system level (Barker, 1998; McLeod, 1998; Worden, 2003). Instead of pathologizing a particular family member, the individual who demonstrates problematic behavior is seen as the family symptom carrier, and his or her behavior is understood within the context of family patterns (McLeod, 1998; Worden, 2003). Family counseling/therapy focuses on the interrelatedness of members within a system. In this system, the whole is more than merely the sum of the parts. Therefore, the counseling relationship becomes a system between the counselor/therapist and the whole family, which is also the principal unit of analysis (Ivey et al., 2002).

The relational understanding that underpins family counseling approaches is compatible with Asian personality theory (Foley, 1979). Asian cultures are relatively more collectivistic, and the concepts of self and individual are understood in relation to members of the group (e.g., family, work, social; Duan & Wang, 2000). It can be argued that family counseling approaches have the potential to be used in helping these clients because of this self-in-relation cultural value.

Fangyi—A Case for Family Counseling

Dr. Wilson, although not a counselor in the sense of a mental health practitioner, exhibited an individual counseling approach by dealing only with issues brought forward by Fangyi and by responding only to interactions and exchanges that took place between herself and Fangyi, with a little input from other faculty. A family counseling approach would have had Dr. Wilson (and others) dealing with the whole family in context. This would have captured a great deal more information and addressed issues that arise from interactions among multiple participants. At the very least, Dr. Wilson would have learned of Fangyi's daughter and the daughter's issues at an earlier stage.

Although, ideally, the family members and counselor are colocated, this is not always practical when dealing with individual students. Furthermore, there may be language difficulties in trying to converse with family members. Nevertheless, the principle of dealing with the whole family and the individual as one in relation to others remains, and practical solutions about how such counseling may take place need to be addressed.

The Case for a Campuswide Approach

Dr. Wilson's approach, as we have shown, appears to have come out of a Western academic paradigm. Our experience is that most faculty in Western institutions take a similar approach. With the rise in transnational education, there is a case for all faculty, and not just specialist services on a campus, to undergo some broad cross-cultural training. Cross-cultural competencies are understood along three major dimensions: cognitive, affective, and behavioral (Graf, 2004). The implication is that if a person is to interact with culturally different people effectively and appropriately, he or she needs to have some understanding of other cultures (cognitive dimension), skills in managing contact situations (behavioral dimension) with cultural sensitivity, and respect (affective dimension; Graf, 2004). In our experience, many people in academic institutions lack the skills, although they may believe they show respect and have some understanding of other cultures. Often this understanding is only superficial, in that through exposure to another culture there is some understanding of basic political, economic, or religious systems; perhaps a little history; and a few words of the language. However, until learning that provides insight into behavior and recognizes the value of some kinds of behavior takes place, the level of understanding, on which effective skills in managing contact situations are built, remains low.

Reader Reflection Questions

Fangyi's case raises a range of questions and issues that the scenario does not answer. These questions need asking of all campuses and programs so that students are provided with culturally responsive guidance and support to assist their transition and adjustment to the host culture/community.

1. What information was given to Fangyi during the interview with the campus representatives? In other words, was there any predeparture preparation offered to Fangyi by the university? Did it prepare her for dislocation from her family? Did it prepare her for the different learning styles and academic challenges she would face?
2. What information about Fangyi was gathered (e.g., marital status, work history, family responsibilities)? Was the information reported to relevant staff at the university (e.g., pastoral care adviser)?

3. Were the orientation activities and functions organized in a way that caters for the needs of and shows respect for international students (in this case, Fangyi)? Did they acknowledge her as an adult, as a successful learner, as a family member?

4. How well prepared are the teaching and general staff on campus regarding multicultural competencies? Is there a designated unit or an individual who is responsible to assist staff members in developing their cross-cultural communication competency?

5. What are the support services/specialist advice (e.g., academic, pastoral, counseling, medical) available for international students on campus? How do those services function? For example, do they work closely together?

6. Do academic faculty know with whom they should consult and to whom they should refer students? Are they aware of their own limitations and the importance of referring students?

7. How is the guidance responsibility of an institution divided? Should an academic counselor be advising on family issues? When is it appropriate for a mental health counselor to be involved, and should he or she be counseling independently of an academic counselor? Is counseling the only way to meet Fangyi's needs and ensure her well-being?

These issues must be addressed at systemic as well as individual levels.

References

Barker, P. (1998). *Basic family therapy.* New York: Oxford University Press.

Duan, C., & Wang, L. (2000). Counseling in the Chinese cultural context: Accommodating both individualistic and collectivistic values. *Asian Journal of Counselling, 7,* 1–21.

Foley, V. (1979). Family therapy. In R. Corsini (Ed.), *Current psychotherapies* (2nd ed., pp. 460–499). Itasca, IL: Peacock.

Graf, A. (2004). Assessing intercultural training designs. *Journal of European Industrial Training, 28,* 199–214.

Ivey, A. E., D'Andrea, M., Ivey, M. B., & Simek-Morgan, L. (2002). *Theories of counseling and psychotherapy: A multicultural perspective* (5th ed.). Boston: Allyn & Bacon.

McLeod, J. (1998). *An introduction to counselling.* Buckingham, United Kingdom: Open University Press.

Walrond-Skinner, S. (1977). *Family therapy: The treatment of natural systems.* London: Routledge and Kegan Paul.

Worden, M. (2003). *Family therapy basics.* Boston: Thomson Learning.

Identity Confusion

John Stewart

Bekele (a pseudonym) was born in a country in East Africa. When I first met him, he had been studying in Canada for 5 years. The first 4 years were spent in a large urban area doing undergraduate studies. He was now doing a master's of education degree in critical studies. In his country of origin, he was a licensed elementary school teacher and had taught 5 years at the Grade 6 level. He left Africa after he had received a scholarship to study in Canada.

He was raised in a family context in which his biological father had a wife and a mistress. Bekele's mother was the mistress, and when Bekele was 12 years old he learned of his other brothers and sisters. In his immediate family, Bekele has two siblings younger than he and four siblings in his other family. His family was financially supported by his father, and so his mother did not work outside the home. His father financially supported him through teacher's college, but it was apparent to Bekele that the sons in the other family were more favored than he. The financial help provided for his basic needs only while he was studying.

Bekele applied for and received a scholarship to study in Canada. He was very appreciative of this opportunity and was anxious to complete additional studies that would prepare him to be a more competent teacher and would allow for a wider range of employment possibilities. Although he knew that he would miss the familiarity of his family and country, he considered this scholarship a great opportunity to improve his educational achievement. Overall, he was excited to come to Canada. After he was here 6 months, he began to miss his family intensely. He found that he was preoccupied with thinking about them, particularly his younger brothers whom he supported while he was teaching in Africa. In addition, he did not eat much and lost so much weight that several of his Canadian teachers asked him if he was healthy. He responded that he was healthy but that he was very busy with his studies. He said that he often lost track of time while working at the library. He added that he often forgot to buy groceries, and when he returned to his apartment, he was not able to prepare full meals. Bekele indicated that after these incidents, he was more conscious of what he ate and generally said he felt more comfortable living in Canada.

Bekele did well in his undergraduate studies and was offered another scholarship to study for a master's of education degree in critical studies. Now, Bekele was in his 2nd year of this graduate program and was working on a thesis.

Critical Incident

I met Bekele through another student who introduced us. From that point on, I saw him frequently but informally around the university. However, on one occasion, he came to my office without any apparent reason or appointment. He knew that I was a counselor, and when he did not indicate a concern, I asked him questions about such issues as the social expectations of people in his birth country, his family situation, childhood and adolescent experiences, his likes and dislikes, and his educational progress. He readily responded to these questions in some detail. He told me that he appreciated the interest I had in him and his country.

During a second interview, one question I asked Bekele concerned whether his Canadian experiences and studies had an influence on how he viewed himself. He indicated that he was not certain about his self-image anymore. He did not see himself as being exactly like his African peers, nor did he see himself as being like his Canadian peers. He said he felt that he was on the "sidelines of both cultures." He was concerned that he had been away from his home for so long, and he realized that he was changing his personal outlook about himself and others. He indicated that the focus of his thesis was on the treatment of women in his birth country. I asked him how he was dealing with the way women were treated, and he reported that he did not agree with the discrimination and that he wanted to change these attitudes and practices so that women would have more say in their personal decision making. Furthermore, he reported that he felt closer to Canadians on this issue than to his African peers. I wanted to determine if he perceived himself differently on other dimensions, so I asked him if there were any other differences between him and his African peers. He responded that he did not experience adolescent circumcision in the traditional way of his peers. Typically, adolescents in his country experience circumcision at the hands of their tribal elders. Bekele's father did not want this so Bekele went to the hospital for circumcision along with his next younger brother. In the other socialization experiences, he felt quite similar to his African peers.

He reported another change in his perspective, that of personal decision making. In his birth country, he was expected to support his siblings financially as well as support his aging parents if they needed such support. Also, he knew that he was expected to discuss major decisions with his parents and respect their wishes, for example, decisions about marriage or staying in Canada to pursue doctoral studies.

I invited Bekele to return to see me as often as he would like to continue these discussions. He was, however, reluctant to make an appointment, and I did not see him again in my office.

Bekele knew that he would be returning to Africa in the near future. He anticipated that he would be expected to follow the norms and practices of his family and culture. On one hand, he was excited about seeing his family and parents and being home, but he was not sure that he would be able to meet some of the cultural expectations relative to the dominant view within his country. He did not express much emotion about this dilemma, nor did his concerns appear to interfere with his academic work. He felt he was progressing well on his thesis.

Key Issues

Although I saw Bekele after the second interview, I did not see him in a context in which we could continue the discussion on how he was dealing with his self-image. To my knowledge, this issue may still be unresolved. He had almost finished his thesis and would have defended it within the next several months. After that, I suspect that he relocated to Africa.

This critical incident highlighted a number of issues for me. One issue was the role and function of a counselor, and, related to this, how international students may perceive and deal with their concerns. In this situation, my role as counselor was to pursue the process goals of making him feel comfortable and listened to and to reflect his thoughts and feelings. I recognized that he was not able to articulate his problem directly but only in response to my questions. I sensed that he felt somewhat uncomfortable talking about such personal issues. It seemed that his concept of counseling centered around a series of discussions with someone who was interested and listened to his discourse and who was his senior.

Another issue in this incident concerns acculturation stress and identity formation and how these phenomena are experienced in cross-cultural sojourns. Bekele had been in Canada 6 years, and as a consequence of his graduate program in critical studies and his growing awareness and sensitivity to patriarchy in his birth country, he was becoming disenchanted with the practices of discrimination against women. In addition, on this issue, he was aware that his personal perspective was different from the dominant view of his African peers. He rejected these forms of discrimination in favor of women having more control over their personal decision making and circumstances. This change appeared to be primarily psychological for him, but there was the desire on his part to change the cultural practices at the group level within his birth country. His personal identity was changing by rejecting some aspects of his culture and ethnicity in favor of some aspects of the dominant Canadian culture. I did not, however, sense that his identity formation was around only this issue of discrimination. He articulated his concern over personal decision making and his view of how such things as social issues should be addressed in his country. He had come to believe that all people should have a voice in such issues.

It was apparent, however, from the conversation that he affirmed other aspects of his ethnicity and culture. For example, he indicated that he agreed with some of the cultural practices unique to his tribe, particularly the festivals. Also, he wanted to continue to teach and speak his tribal language. However, he liked living in Canada. The standard of living was much higher, and he was concerned about adjusting to living without the availability of the varieties of food and access to constant electricity, as well as being concerned about the professional resources for teachers in his country.

Reader Reflection Questions

1. In the context of the encounter with Bekele, what are the parameters that constitute a counseling relationship? When ethnically diverse clients have different ideas of what constitutes counseling, what is the role of the counselor to change those perspectives such that they fall within the dominant perspective in Canada? Is it incumbent on the counselor to change his or her behavior to meet the expectations of the client?

2. What is acculturation and how does it influence a client's adjustment within a host country? Some models appear to indicate that it is a linear phase. Is acculturation experienced the same by immigrants and sojourners? How is personal identity related to issues of acculturation? To what degree can a client have a bicultural identity?

3. How should the issue of stress be viewed within this context? Is the stress being experienced existential anxiety or it is an adaptation to a context that produces dissonance for a client? What are the indicators of stress, and how do they vary across cultures?

4. What are the factors that influence personal identity development beyond adolescence? What are the affective, behavioral, and cognitive variables that may influence this developmental process during adulthood? What are the similarities and differences in personal identity formation across cultures? Given that change takes considerable time, should counselors address such issues when clients may not be able to continue?

5. What is the counselor's role as an advocate for change where cultural practices are different from those within the Canadian context? Is culture to be considered neutral? Given that changing cultural practices may be a long and arduous process, how do you help a client prepare for such a venture?

Response 1

Daya Singh Sandhu

Bekele's case incident is quite intriguing and interesting to me for both personal and professional reasons. From a personal perspective, it is reminiscent of my own acculturative experiences that threatened my internal and external identities when I migrated to the United States for higher education in 1969. Professionally, this case incident demonstrates that it is important for mental health professionals, especially college student personnel and college counselors, to recognize a silent minority of their clients who suffer miserably, sometimes to the extent of nervous breakdown, but who are unaware of the professional help available or hesitant to seek it. Taking this incident as an example of an international transition in the shrinking modern world and at a time of global mass migration, multicultural counselors can learn from Bekele's case how to deal effectively with culturally different clients.

In my preparation to respond properly to Bekele's case incident, I considered it imperative to discuss this case incident from three major perspectives. First, some salient multicultural themes are highlighted that are so obvious and that abruptly jump out at a culturally sensitive reader that it is hard to dismiss or ignore them. For this reason, I took the liberty to refer extensively to Bekele's original case incident as presented by the author. Second, at the end of this case incident, the author provided some very thought-provoking reflection questions for the readers. I felt compelled to add some of my comments to facilitate readers' responses. However, I did not answer these questions in their entirety because I did not wish to undermine the challenge the author has intended for his readers. Last, but not least, I attempted to address the concerns of the editors to respond to some significant questions that are the very heart and soul of counseling clients for international transitions.

Salient Multicultural Themes: Suggestions for Counselors

Beginning with the title, I believe that the author has captured the very essence or the core multicultural theme of this case incident as *identity confusion*, one of the root causes of psychological afflictions. In understanding Bekele's dilemma of identity confusion, it is important to note that his personal identity is deeply rooted in the East African culture. Because culture is considered a very powerful organizer of clients' lives (Thomas & Schwarzbaum, 2006), counselors must become aware of threats to both the external and internal identity of their clients when cultural contexts change after emigration. It is almost always inevitable that every time ethnoculturally different people are translocated, they will experience serious disturbances in their ethnocultural identities (Comas-Diaz, 2005).

Bekele's cultural identity was transformed after his migration from East Africa to Canada. He no longer has an African identity or a Canadian identity. The interaction of his ancestral cultural identity with the new and unfamiliar Canadian culture chiseled Bekele's new identity, which can be described as a hyphenated or hybrid identity (Sandhu, Kaur, & Tewari, 1999). He is now neither an African nor a Canadian, but he has become an African Canadian.

Another multicultural theme of *marginal man* also became salient here when Bekele lamented that "He did not see himself exactly like his African peers, nor did he see himself as being like his Canadian peers." He said he felt that he was on the "sidelines of both cultures." Stonequist (1961) would have described as Bekele a person who belonged to a marginal culture and who was torn between the repulsions and attractions of two different worlds, painfully ambivalent in attitudes and loyalties to both his native and Canadian cultures.

The concept of *population intrusion,* another cross-cultural theme introduced by Stonequist (1961), has direct and very significant relevance in Bekele's life. Population intrusion is defined as a process that breaks down old cultural norms and forms of an immigrant and frees him or her to replace them with some new creative and advancing ideas and thoughts from the new assimilating culture. Bekele's concern about the treatment of women in his native culture is one such prime example of population intrusion. While living in the Canadian culture, Bekele's views about women were dramatically, drastically, and diametrically changed. Bekele's counselor reported that "he [Bekele] did not agree with the discrimination and that he wanted to change these attitudes and practices so that women would have more say in their personal decision making." In addition, Bekele changed his perspective about personal decision making as practiced in his native culture. Rather than discussing major personal decision making about marriage or staying in Canada with his parents, Bekele has changed his views and would prefer to make decisions of such great importance on his own.

Bekele's case incident highlights cultural contexts as another important multicultural theme. Cultural practices accepted as normal behaviors in one society might be unacceptable and repulsive in another. A Canadian counselor might be shocked to learn that Bekele's biological father had both a wife and a mistress. Bekele's mother was the mistress and had two other children. This seems quite a strange marriage arrangement. A counselor not familiar with such marriage practices will naturally have a negative internal dialogue about his client and his culture, as explained in the Pedersen's (2000) Triad Training Model. Counselors must see things in the culture contexts of their clients and guard themselves against ethnocentrism (Vontress, Johnson, & Epp, 1999).

Acculturative stress is another major multicultural theme that has relevance here. Bekele's critical incident as an international student could serve as a showcase to highlight the acculturation and assimilation experiences of immigrants. Immediately after the immigration process is completed, the cultural transformation is launched. Subsequently, when cultural contexts change, values change, priorities change, and thus behaviors change (Sandhu et al., 1999).

Adaptation to the dominant culture through various required changes causes unavoidable psychological distress (Arthur, 2004; Kashima & Loh, 2006). As a consequence, a sense of powerlessness; feelings of inferiority and marginality; perceived alienation and discrimination; loneliness, homesickness, and sadness; and threats to cultural identity become some of the major mental health issues (Sandhu, Portes, & McPhee, 1996). In defining alienation among foreign students, Klomegah (2006) included sense of powerlessness, meaninglessness, normlessness, isolation, and self-estrangement as its five major components. In Bekele's case, all these factors contributing to his acculturative pain are summed up in one word, *self-image.* Bekele's counselor stated,

> Although I saw Bekele after the second interview, I did not see him in a context in which we could continue the discussion on how he was dealing with his self-image. To my knowledge, this issue may still be unresolved.

The psychological pain associated with migration, whether voluntary or involuntary, is generally intense and sometimes so traumatic that Zwingman (1978) has called it as an "uprooting disorder." This uprooting disorder mostly has identifiable psychological symptoms of nostalgia, depression, and a sense of helplessness (Sandhu & Asrabadi, 1998). The multicultural theme of nostalgia and loneliness after migration to another culture is evidenced in Bekele's case when "After he was here 6 months, he began to miss his family intensely. He found that he was preoccupied with thinking about them." Apparently, Bekele experienced some level of depression when he did not eat much and lost weight, which caused his Canadian teachers to question him about his health.

Reentry shock is another important multicultural theme that has not received the attention that it deserves. Specifically, in the case of sojourners and exchange and international students, it is important to remember that they all need counseling before their departure from their native country, upon arrival in the host country, during their stay, before returning, and upon reentry into their home culture (Pedersen, 1991; Sandhu, 1994). Generally, however, international students receive more attention for their adjustment problems in the foreign land than for their reentry concerns when they are preparing to return to their homes (Arthur, 2003). International students who finally do return home almost always face a wide variety of social, cultural, political, and familial difficulties (Westwood, Lawrence, & Paul, 1986).

Last but not least, the multicultural concepts of collectivism versus individualism, as proposed by Triandis (1994), are worthy of consideration in this vignette. Collectivism, in direct contrast to individualism, refers to a system in which an individual sacrifices his or her own personal interest for the welfare of the group. As evidenced from Bekele's case example,

> Bekele knew that he would be returning to Africa in the near future. He anticipated that he will be expected to follow the norms and practices of his family and culture . . . but he was not sure that he would be able to meet some of the cultural expectations.

As expected in his culture, "family comes first" would mandate Bekele to support his family financially, especially his younger brothers.

Unique Cross-Cultural Challenges for International Students

Sandhu and Asrabadi (1994) developed the Acculturative Stress Scale for International Students through empirical investigation and identified perceived discrimination, loneliness, homesickness, fear, hate, and guilt as six major psychological distressors that international students face during their cross-cultural encounters.

In addition, I (Sandhu, 1994) examined both the intrapersonal and interpersonal factors that contribute to the psychological distress of international students. The following discussion highlights these factors and also includes comments as they apply to Bekele's acculturative experiences. As described below, intrapersonal factors are rooted within Bekele's own mind, whereas interpersonal factors relate to the cultural milieu of the Canadian society or surroundings. However, it is important to note that these factors are intertwined and that they constantly interact with one another.

Intrapersonal Factors

Profound Sense of Loss

The separation from immediate family members, relatives, and close friends causes a profound sense of personal loss. As one of my close relatives remarked upon my leaving India for the United States in 1969, as an international student, leaving home for abroad is like becoming a living dead (Sandhu, 2001). Abruptly being disconnected from loved ones and acquaintances and landing among totally unfamiliar surroundings cause quite painful cultural shocks. Bekele was quite excited to come to Canada, but according to his counselor, after he was there for 6 months, Bekele began to miss his family intensely. Naturally, Cook's (1997) assertion that every adjustment is a crisis in self-esteem also affected Bekele.

Sense of Uncertainty

It seems that international students experience more adjustment problems compared with their counterparts such as visitors and exchange students who are certain about their plans to return to their native countries and who are generally supported by host families (Sandhu, 1993). As an international student, a person is generally unsure when he or she will be able to complete all the requirements to receive his or her academic degree and return home.

Sense of Inferiority

International students suffer status loss after they arrive in a foreign culture (Alexander, Workneh, Klein, & Miller, 1976). This decrease is generally attributed to the lack of social, financial, and moral support, which causes a number of disappointments and frustrations. It is obvious that it was Bekele's sense of inferiority that caused his counselor to remark about Bekele that "He indicated that he was not certain about his self-image anymore."

A large number of important themes, such as perceived discrimination, threat to cultural identity, sense of inferiority, mistrust, and guilt and hatred either for the native or the host culture, are the recurring intrapersonal themes that afflict the international students' acculturative experiences. Bekele was, of course, no exception and not immune to such difficulties.

Interpersonal Factors

Communication Problems

Language difficulties and hesitation to speak English seem to be major problems that permeate all areas of many international students' personal and social lives. For convenience and because of deep-rooted love, Bekele would like to continue to speak and teach his tribal language. It might be due to his lack of confidence in speaking English that Bekele did not communicate with his counselor freely when his counselor pointed out that "I recognized that he was not able to articulate his problem directly but only in response to my questions."

A Culture Shock

When international students try to establish relationships with the host culture, new cultural mores, norms, and expectations cause shock for them (Ojbay, 1994). They are under considerable pressure to assimilate and must negotiate the daily demands of new systems of communication and living styles (Johnson & Sandhu, 2007). Given such an extraordinary amount of pressure, international students clearly experience severe psychological problems (Popadiuk & Arthur, 2004).

Lack of a Feeling of Connectedness

During his stay in Canada, Bekele lacked a sense of belonging. For international students, their affiliation with their own racial group provides a sense of connection; this sense of belonging serves as a great source of pride and psychological and spiritual support. If there is no connectedness with people from one's own race or ethnic group, a sense of loneliness, emptiness, and sadness looms large in a foreign land. In Bekele's case, there was no evidence that he could find any acquaintances or make friends with people of his own kind. On the contrary, "he was aware that his personal perspective was different from the dominant view of his African peers." Clearly, Bekele's sense of self was injured, causing him a sense of shame and embarrassment about the practices of discrimination against women in his native country. Maybe in search of affirmation of his changed identity and newly acquired knowledge in Canada, he would champion the cause of women in his birth country in East Africa.

Implications for Counseling and Psychotherapy

Due to an extensive range of cultural diversity, international students pose unique challenges for multicultural counselors. Popadiuk and Arthur (2004) addressed a number of limitations in effectively counseling international students. Also, in response to the reflection questions posed in the case incident, here are some suggestions for counselors and other mental health professionals to help Bekele.

Counseling Relationship

Generally speaking, foreign students do not use mental health services for fear of the stigmatization of being labeled mentally unhealthy or crazy, the taboo against sharing family matters with strangers, or simply lack of awareness that such services are available. They are also afraid that they might be sent back to their home country by the immigration services because they were not functioning successfully. For all such reasons, foreign students do not seek counseling actively on their own. A therapeutic alliance with these students is difficult to develop because they seek help indirectly. Bekele is a representative example who was introduced through another student, and his counselor met him frequently but informally without making any formal appointment. Traditionally, counseling is provided on request by clients, but in the case of foreign students, it is incumbent on counselors to meet with foreign students on a regular basis and to help them proactively (Sandhu, 1994). Confidentiality, trust, expertness, and special interest in helping international students remain major challenges.

Role of the Culture

Counselors working with Bekele must understand his cultural values and cultural worldviews because they are the most influential determinants to shape his personal and cultural identity. Ignoring the cultural significance in clients' lives is like engaging in oppressive practices, but not in therapeutic ones (Thomas & Schwarzbaum, 2006). Acculturation and enculturation are the processes to create cultural congruity. A higher level of acculturation will be a good predictor of foreign students' help-seeking behaviors. International students are a unique population because multiple cultural values and assumptions of normality become salient. To enhance counseling efficacy with this population, counselors have to follow various therapeutic procedures, adopt different parameters of the process, and set special goals to match the cultural contexts of their clients. In addition, mental health professionals must learn to see their culturally diverse clients through their clients' cultural lenses, which may be quite different from the counselors' own cultural norms and standards (Comas-Diaz & Jacobsen, 1991).

Torn Between Two Worlds

International students or newly arriving immigrants are invariably torn between two worlds. On one side, they miss the culture in which they were raised; on the other side, they would like to enjoy the superior facilities of the highly civilized society in which they would like to settle for generations to come. Clearly, Bekele is no exception. For example,

[H]e indicated that he agreed with some of the cultural practices unique to his tribe, particularly the festivals. Also, he wanted to continue to teach and speak his tribal language. However, he liked living in Canada. The standard of living was much higher, and he was concerned about adjusting to living without the availability of the varieties of food and access to constant electricity, as well as being concerned about the professional resources for teachers in his country.

Counselors must distinguish between a cultured society and a civilized society, because most of their clients (international students or immigrants) face this dilemma or dichotomy of making the correct decision. International students have mixed feelings, which might range from euphoria of reuniting with their family and friends to sadness and a deep sense of loss on leaving the host country forever (Arthur, 2004).

Counseling Strategies to Help International Students Such as Bekele

As summarized below, I (Sandhu, 1994) offer several suggestions to help international students effectively. The same suggestions also have direct implications for Bekele.

Use Proactive Approaches to Counseling

A counseling center at a college or university must have a provision to provide preplanned and well-structured counseling services for incoming international students. Immediately after the arrival of the foreign students, counselors should conduct group guidance and counseling services and make these students aware of the availability and nature of the counseling services. For instance, it is interesting to note that according to the counselor in this vignette, "I met Bekele through another student who introduced us. From that point on, I saw him frequently but informally around the university. However, on one occasion, he came to my office without any apparent reason nor an appointment." Despite the fact that Bekele had so many issues to discuss, obviously he knew very little about the counseling services available to him at the university. It is also lamentable that the officials of his university did not provide this information upon his arrival. It is important that counselors use proactive approaches to help international students.

Counseling as a Continuous and Comprehensive Approach

Continuous and comprehensive approaches are crucial for international students. Counselors must take Pedersen's (1991) assertion seriously that international students' "[o]rientation is a continuous process requiring contact with students before they arrive, during their stay, and after they have returned home, as the student experiences are a continuous process of adjustment" (p. 44). Unfortunately, in Bekele's case there is no evidence that he received any type of formal orientation from any professional counselor. It was by accident that he was informally introduced to a counselor through one of his friends.

Role and Function of Counselors Working With Foreign Students

Professional counseling poses a unique challenge for counselors who work with foreign students. Bekele's counselor speaks for many mental health professionals about foreign students when he summarized his concerns in the following words.

In this situation, my role as counselor was to pursue the process goals of making him feel comfortable and listened to and to reflect his thoughts and feelings. I recognized that he was not able to articulate his problem directly but only in response to my questions. I sensed that he felt somewhat uncomfortable talking about such personal issues. It seemed that his concept of counseling centered around a series of discussions with someone who was interested and listened to his discourse and was his senior.

Because mental illness is overly stigmatized in many non-Western countries, many foreign students never seek counseling actively for fear of being labeled mentally sick (Sandhu, 1994). For this reason, Pedersen (1991) has offered an alternative scenario to help foreign students.

Counseling international students frequently occurs in an informal setting, such as hallways, home, or street corner, and frequently depends on an informal method such as presentation, discussion, or daily encounter, which might not be perceived as counseling according to standardized models. (pp. 28–29)

It is interesting that what Pedersen (1991) recommended above is exactly what happened in Bekele's case when his counselor met him informally to discuss his concerns. Bekele seemed relatively pleased with this alternative approach, because as his counselor pointed out, "He told me that he appreciated the interest I had in him and his country."

Active Involvement Recommended

As representatives from many other cultures, foreign students have a great deal to offer to promote intercultural or cross-cultural understanding. It is important that these students be actively involved in curricular and cocurricular activities. Active involvement is also a great strategy for helping foreign students like Bekele combat alienation, loneliness, and sadness when they are away from their families and loved ones. It also promotes their positive self-image because their contributions are recognized and considered important. According to Comas-Diaz (2005), "life is a learning experience. We are either learning a lesson, teaching a lesson or doing both" (p. 976). Foreign students can make some unique contributions to the learning experiences of the host students. There is a need for a paradigm shift to one of foreign students being here not only to learn but also to teach. Bekele could have easily served as a resource person to provide information about his East African country.

Planning and Initiating a Buddy System

To help foreign students like Bekele combat loneliness and alienation, it is imperative that counselors and other mental health professionals organize some social networks in which national and international students become closely acquainted through a buddy system. This type of arrangement should help foreign students feel connected and at home in the United States. It really takes a great deal of courage to function successfully when individuals are in the minority (Cook, 1997).

Synergetic Counseling and Guidance Services

When counseling foreign students, counselors must become knowledgeable about culturally responsive strategies. They should be aware of specific cultural dynamics and intercultural differences that are crucial in maintaining and promoting optimal mental health. The counselors may have to learn ways to listen to their clients through the "third ear" (Comas-Diaz, 2005).

Issues of Ethnocultural Transference and Countertransference

When working with clients from different cultures, issues relating to ethnocultural transference and countertransference are bound to emerge. In cross-cultural counseling dyads, these issues range from friendliness and overcompliance to suspicion and hostility. These issues may also involve complete idealization or rejection of the therapist. Countertransference reactions may include overidentification, distancing, and cultural myopia (Comas-Diaz & Jacobsen, 1991). Counselors should also be cautious not to let historical hostilities interfere in their working alliance with their clients. Comas-Diaz and Jacobsen (2001) coined a new word, *allodynia*, meaning a referred pain that may make therapeutic alliance a source of repugnance and hate because of historical and political hostilities rather than a relationship of support and encouragement.

Conclusion

A case incident, such as Bekele's personal story as a foreign student, portrays his journey of growth through several cultural encounters. Of course, these encounters are a blended mixture of joys and sorrows, ecstasies and agonies, or pleasures and pains. There is, however, always a chance for nurturing, an opportunity for maturity, and a challenge for excellence embedded in culture shock. Such stories also provide the counselors a glimpse into their clients' pasts and opportunities to anticipate their future (Thomas & Schwarzbaum, 2006). As many societies, especially democratic Western societies, are increasingly becoming multicultural, the exploration and understanding of the cultural heritage of the newly arriving immigrants, sojourners, and international students are becoming of utmost importance. Counseling dyads often involve recognitions and contradictions that are frequently mediated through identifications and projections (Comas-Diaz, 2005). Any therapist working with Bekele must rise above the issues of contradictions, personal projections, and prejudices to provide him the much needed professional help.

References

Alexander, A. A., Workneh, F., Klein, M. H., & Miller, M. H. (1976). Psychotherapy and the foreign student. In P. Pedersen, W. J. Lonner, & J. G. Draguns (Eds.), *Counseling across cultures* (pp. 82–97). Honolulu: University of Hawaii Press.

Arthur, N. (2003). Preparing international students for the re-entry transitions. *Canadian Journal of Counselling, 37*, 173–185.

Arthur, N. (2004). *Counseling international students: Clients from around the world*. New York: Kluwer Academic/Plenum.

Comas-Diaz, L. (2005). Becoming a multicultural psychotherapist: The confluence of culture, ethnicity, and gender. *Journal of Clinical Psychology, 61*, 973–981.

Comas-Diaz, L., & Jacobsen, F. M. (1991). Ethnocultural tranference and countertransferance in the therapeutic dyad. *American Journal of Orthopsychiatry, 61*, 392–402.

Comas-Diaz, L., & Jacobsen, F. M. (2001). Ethnocultural allodynia. *Journal of Psychotherapy Practice and Research, 10*, 246–252.

Cook, J. (Ed.). (1997). *The book of positive quotations*. Minneapolis, MN: Fairview.

Johnson, L. R., & Sandhu, D. S. S. (2007). Isolation, adjustment, and acculturation issues of international students: Intervention strategies for counselors. In H. D. Singaravelu & M. Pope (Eds.), *A handbook for counseling international students in the United States* (pp. 13–35). Alexandria, VA: American Counseling Association.

Kashima, E. S., & Loh, E. (2006). International students' acculturation: Effects of international, conational, and local ties and need for closure. *International Journal of Intercultural Relations, 30*, 471–485.

Klomegah, R. Y. (2006). Social factors relating to alienation experienced by international students in the United States. *College Student Journal, 40,* 303–315.

Ojbay, Y. (1994). An investigation of the relationship between adaptational coping process and self-perceived negative feelings of international students. *Dissertation Abstracts International, 54,* 2958A.

Pedersen, P. B. (1991). Counseling international students. *The Counseling Psychologist, 19,* 10–58.

Pedersen, P. B. (2000). *Hidden messages in culture-centered counseling: A triad training model.* Thousand Oaks, CA: Sage.

Popadiuk, N., & Arthur, N. (2004). Counselling international students in Canadian schools. *International Journal for the Advancement of Counselling, 26,* 125–145.

Sandhu, D. S. (1993). Making the foreign familiar. *American Counselor, 2*(2), 22–25.

Sandhu, D. S. (1994). An examination of the psychological needs of the international students: Implications for counselling and psychotherapy. *International Journal for the Advancement of Counselling, 17,* 229–239.

Sandhu, D. S. (2001). An ecocultural analysis of agonies and ecstasies of my life. In J. G. Ponterotto, J. M. Casas, L. A. Suzuki, & C. M. Alexander (Eds.), *Handbook of multicultural counseling* (pp. 122–137). Thousand Oaks, CA: Sage.

Sandhu, D. S., & Asrabadi, B. R. (1994). Development of an acculturative stress scale for international students: Preliminary findings. *Psychological Reports, 75,* 435–448.

Sandhu, D. S., & Asrabadi, B. R. (1998). An acculturative stress scale for international students: A practical approach to stress measurement. In C. P. Zalaquett & R. J. Wood (Eds.), *Evaluating stress: A book of resources* (Vol. 2, pp. 1–33). London: Scarecrow Press.

Sandhu, D. S., Kaur, K. P., & Tewari, N. (1999). Acculturative experiences of Asian and Pacific Islander Americans: Considerations for counseling and psychotherapy. In D. S. Sandhu (Ed.), *Asian and Pacific Islander Americans: Issues and concerns for counseling and psychotherapy* (pp. 3–19). Commack, NY: Nova Science.

Sandhu, D. S., Portes, P. R., & McPhee, S. A. (1996). Assessing cultural adaptation: Psychometric properties of the Cultural Adaptation Pain Scale. *Journal of Multicultural Counseling and Development, 24,* 15–25.

Stonequist, E. V. (1961). *The marginal man: A study in personality and culture conflict.* New York: Russell & Russell.

Thomas, A. J., & Schwarzbaum, S. (2006). *Culture & identity: Life stories for counselors and therapists.* Thousand Oaks, CA: Sage.

Triandis, H. C. (1994). *Culture and social behavior.* New York: McGraw Hill.

Vontress, C. E., Johnson, J. A., & Epp, L. R. (1999). *Cross-cultural counseling: A casebook.* Alexandria, VA: American Counseling Association.

Westwood, M. J., Lawrence, W. S., & Paul, D. (1986). Preparing for re-entry: A program for the sojourning students. *International Journal for the Advancement of Counselling, 9,* 221–230.

Zwingman, C. A. A. (1978). *Uprooting and related phenomena: A descriptive bibliotherapy* (Doc. MNH/78.23). Geneva, Switzerland: World Health Organization.

 Response 2

Charles P. Chen

This analysis of Bekele's case intends to form an initial theoretical framework of a contextual multicultural counseling (CMC) model. The intention of proposing the CMC model is originated and stimulated by Bekele's case, which is both unique and representative, to some degree, of other international students' transitional experiences in North America. International students from countries and regions of non-Western cultures, such as Bekele, seem to encounter a range of issues that require special attention in the helping practice. Scholars and practitioners in the helping realm are therefore called on to consider and develop counseling interventions that can accommodate the special cross-cultural adjustment needs of this group of clients in Western societies (Arthur, 1997, 2004; Chen, 1999, 2004; Pedersen, 1991).

Helping Context

Bekele's encounter with the counselor did not entirely fall into the essential parameters of a counseling relationship as defined in a formal helping setting (Corey, 2001). There could be complicated social, cultural, personal, and other reasons behind Bekele's decision to drop by at the counselor's office in such an informal manner. This help-seeking behavior poses challenges to the counseling structure and relationship that normally function in the mainstream culture in North America. The challenge here is the counselor's effort to strike a balance between maintaining the professional standard and ethics of the helping service and being more flexible to meet the needs of the client. Once an initial trust is established in this relationship, the counselor can guide Bekele into the norms of a counseling process that falls within the dominant perspective of counseling services in North America (Corey, 2001). What is required on the part of the counselor is an open mind and a set of situational strategies that can combine sensitivity, knowledge, and skills in this helping context.

Central to Bekele's case is the experience of understanding his self-identity as it evolves through the cross-cultural transition. He was searching for a zone of comfort in which he could keep part of the original self that was deeply rooted in his cultural heritage while accepting the evolving and changing part of his sense of self in the host culture. As a result, he found himself having to deal with the daunting task of carrying on cultural values from two different cultures (i.e., his African culture and the newly acquired Western culture in Canada). Very often, the differences in the two cultures yield conflicting perspectives in dealing with various issues in life, and, hence, Bekele struggled to develop a bicultural identity that encompasses variables of both cultures.

International students, especially those students who are from non-Western cultures, often face the similar bicultural identity challenge that Bekele encountered. The process of adjusting to the host culture, or the acculturation process, is a daunting yet unavoidable task for these students as they try to fit themselves into the various aspects of life norms in the West (Arthur, 2004; Chen, 1999). As the acculturation proceeds, these students are constantly exposed to values, ideas, and ways of doing things that are taken for granted as normal characteristics or even necessities of social functioning in the host country's sociocultural system. However, most of these social and cultural norms are "foreign" to the students, and many of these norms could even be in conflict with the worldview and customs of the students' culture of origin, within which their self-identity has been nurtured and established (Arthur, 2004; Pedersen, 1991).

As such, Bekele's feeling of being on the "sidelines of both cultures" exemplifies a very typical dilemma that is representative of the common feelings of many other international students as they negotiate and position their identity in the new cultural environment, coping with the bicultural identity. Although the degree to which the two cultural selves will interact and coexist may vary significantly from one individual to another, international students' experience in dealing with bicultural identity is a commonly shared and essential aspect of their identity development during the process of acculturation (Arthur, 1997; Chen, 2004). Hence, drawing attention to the issue of identity negotiation pertains to a central part of counseling international students in their cross-cultural transition.

Considering a CMC Model

The consideration of forming a CMC model is informed by the contextual theory of career development and counseling proposed by Young, Valach, and Collin (2002). Based on both social constructionist and social constructivist worldviews, the contextual theory is one of the emerging theoretical models in counseling psychology that draws attention to the dynamic nature and function of individuals' subjective world in relation to human action in their life career development experiences. The central premise of the CMC model rests on the key tenets that form the original contextual theory. It attempts to illustrate that the contextual theoretical key concepts derived from the contextual career theory could be incorporated into the formation of the coping and helping practice in a multicultural counseling situation, such as the one with Bekele. In other words, the CMC framework borrows key concepts from contextual theory, with the intention of using these concepts for a multicultural counseling approach. Following this intention, this section discusses the relevant theoretical components of the CMC approach and some of their related intervention strategies for counseling Bekele and other international students in similar processes of cross-cultural transitions.

Toward a CMC Theoretical Framework

As a building block for the CMC approach, the construct of context is considered essential to theorize a helping framework. The basic rationale of paying attention to context appears to have particular relevance for multicultural counseling. Context in CMC refers to a broad and inclusive concept that encompasses all situations and variables pertaining to a client's personal background experiences, help-seeking needs, and experiences through the entire helping process. Examples of contexts in Bekele's case include factors such as personal views on issues, his relationship with his family, his acculturation experience in Canada and his perception of the pros and cons regarding this cross-cultural transition, and his informal contacts and communication with the counselor in the Canadian university where he was studying.

It is these pivotal contextual factors that are worthy of much consideration in CMC. Although microevents and situations are certainly critical contexts and/or subcontexts for the helping process, the notion of context in the CMC approach highlights the general principle of keeping an open and flexible stance in dealing with cross-cultural and multicultural issues in a helping situation. In this sense, context is a macroconstruct that guides the helping practice to become more sensitive and appropriate to each client's distinctive cultural and personal needs, in which three key aspects reflect special relevance to CMC.

First, meaning in life should be explored and understood within the client's context of cross-cultural transition and acculturation. Second, contextual meaning derived from these life experiences and events are always interweaving, and, therefore, it is of critical importance to understand the dynamic and interactive relationship when life experiences interplay in a cross-cultural transition. Third, this acculturation undergoes a multifaceted transitional experience, reflecting a multiplicity of diverse and complex variables and influences in an individual's adjustment and coping. As such, a holistic and comprehensive approach is required to include a wealth of diverse issues, factors, and considerations when examining and interpreting meanings of life in a cross-cultural and multicultural context.

To follow these key tenets that theorize the outlook of the CMC framework, it is pertinent to conceptualize that individuals' cross-cultural transition and acculturation experiences are an ever-changing and ongoing interaction of various contextual variables. From this perspective, the CMC approach draws attention to the process of human development through pathways of cross-cultural transition and acculturation. It is this process that is of essential importance to the helping interventions. The process-focused orientation, therefore, is regarded as a fundamental theoretical principle for the CMC approach. It recognizes the complexity of the interactive and multifaceted correlation between a wealth of very diverse influencing factors in the context. It then suggests that cross-cultural and multicultural counseling be conducted in an open and situational manner, during which a client's unique background and ongoing coping experiences are validated. Furthermore, the contextual variables are incorporated into the client's current effort to attain resources for constructive coping, which will lead the client to personal growth while undergoing cross-cultural transition and acculturation.

Of central importance to the CMC approach is a focus on human action in the coping and helping process. Although the client's action manifests behavior, action is cognitively and socially directed, and therefore it is a representation of human intention and meaning. Actions surrounding and derived from the cross-cultural transition and acculturation experiences are social processes in which the client is engaged. From this contextual worldview, actions in the CMC framework can be synthesized into three perspectives. First, actions demonstrate behavior, such as when Bekele went to visit the counselor. Second, actions occur with internal processes. For example, Bekele felt the need to talk to someone because he had been reflecting on various pros and cons in his ongoing experience of cross-cultural transition and acculturation. Third, actions are rooted in and reflect social meaning. For example, Bekele's interest in his thesis research illustrated his intention to address and work on the issue of gender equality in his culture of origin.

The constructionist principle of conceiving human action as a whole (Young et al., 2002) appears to have particular meaningfulness to the CMC approach. To operationalize the principles of meaning, interweaving, and multiplicity in the action of cross-cultural transition and acculturation, the client's actions are considered an action system rather than segmental acts. This is to say that the wholeness of the action system must be emphasized in the helping process. Individual actions are an important part of this action system; in the meantime, it is equally important that joint actions are noted in the client's effort of cross-cultural transition and acculturation. This means that actions of others who are associated with the client, especially those of significant others, are considered part of the action system that affects the client in adjusting to and coping with the transition. In the case of Bekele, his family members and their influences obviously exemplify the role of joint actions in his transitional experiences in Canada.

The CMC Intervention Strategies

Guided by the theoretical framework elaborated in the foregoing discussion, several intervention strategies may be considered to implement the CMC model in the helping process. It is important to note that although these strategies are directly addressed to the case of Bekele, they are also intended to be applicable to other international students from non-Western cultures who also encounter the similar challenges of cross-cultural transition. For brevity, a few points should be noted in the following discussion. The term *transition* refers only to the client's cross-cultural transition and acculturation experiences. Likewise, the terms *client(s)* and *international student(s)* mean only those students, such as Bekele, from non-Western cultures. Also, for the sake of convenience in this discussion, I am making the assumption that it would be a female counselor who worked with Bekele, so I use feminine pronouns when referring to the counselor.

Build a humanistic helping relationship. Rooted in the social constructivist school of thinking, the CMC model is a humanistic approach. This means that the counselor holds a genuine respect for Bekele and has a true interest in Bekele's psychological welfare in the transition. This caring and supportive attitude is the foundation for working with Bekele in a flexible manner. A critical point for the counselor to be aware of is that the notion of "humanistic" in this kind of helping context does not imply imposing a totally Western-oriented "humanistic approach" on the client. Rather, being humanistic should be perceived from a broad sense; that is, the counselor is willing to be more flexible to facilitate the special and very often culturally sensitive help-seeking needs of international students.

It appears that the counselor in Bekele's case did a skillful job in using a humanistic approach to build a necessary initial rapport with Bekele. Due to very dynamic and contextual reasons, international students may perceive the counseling relationship very differently than it is commonly understood in the mainstream Western culture, and this could be a common phenomenon when working with these students. It is consistent with the process orientation of the CMC model that the counselor gave particular attention to pursuing the process goals of making the client feel comfortable and listened to. This effort in building rapport, especially during the initial encounter, is of vital importance to the counselor–client work alliance.

Once a trustworthy relationship is built, it can have the potential to grow and develop into a more formal counseling relationship. As the informal helping relationship proceeds, Bekele and other clients like him would gain a better understanding of the nature and function of a professional helping context in a university setting. The counselor could help the client gradually increase the level of comfort with respect to a more formal helping relationship; that is, the client is facilitated to become more knowledgeable about the general characteristics of counseling services and to become more accepting of a counseling relationship.

In a sense, this effort of relationship building itself could be used as part of the process of a constructive transitional experience for the client. If Bekele had come back more times for counseling, this would be a reasonable and desirable direction to proceed during this helping process. This was and remains a challenge for Bekele's counselor and her colleagues who work with international students on campus. A contextual and process-oriented counseling philosophy seems to be particularly heuristic in dealing with such challenges while helping clients in a cross-cultural and multicultural context. Within the general code of helping ethics, the counselor is advised to be sensitive, open-minded, and patient, qualities that facilitate providing the client time and space in making the transitions.

Facilitate narrative meaning-making. Corresponding to a focus on the process orientation, the essence of the CMC approach is to make the helping interventions a contextual self-exploration experience that facilitates the client's personal growth via the counseling engagement. With rapport and a trustworthy work alliance in place, the counselor can help the client become more comfortable in sharing his or her views and experiences on issues of concern through narrative accounts that truly reflect how the client thinks and feels. In a few contacts with the counselor, Bekele had already presented some useful stories that formed the unique context of his cultural heritage, as well as his dilemmas in relation to his transition and acculturation in Canada. Narrative intervention has a distinct advantage and relevance in counseling international students. It provides the counselor with an opportunity to learn from the client (i.e., learn the client's culture, and how this cultural background has influenced the client's personal life and his or her transition in the sociocultural environment of the host country).

In Bekele's case, the narrative accounts had already revealed rich yet somewhat scattered information regarding his background history as well as his concerns, issues, and needs in the transition process. The counselor could sense that Bekele was not able to articulate his problem directly but only in response to the counselor's questions. What the counselor had observed here can often be a general challenge for working with international students in a counseling encounter. Variables such as personal history and style, language ability, cultural upbringing, and experiences in the current acculturation can all have an impact on international students' capacity to communicate their feelings and thoughts to the counselor. This is where the helping role and function of the counselor can substantially affect the direction of a narrative exploration. The counselor can help the client identify, clarify, and make sense of the meanings associated with or derived from these seemingly scattered episodes in the client's description of events and stories.

In Bekele case incident, the counselor had already combined the client's personal accounts into a more consistent narrative flow. The next step would be to seek Bekele's reaction and reflection on this narrative profile should the counseling proceed. Furthermore, provided that a safe and trustworthy counselor–client work alliance is formed, the counselor can be more proactive and contextual in assuming the role of a coauthor to help Bekele construct a future narrative. The construction of this future narrative is to project and design a contextual plan that is meaningful to Bekele's identity development and personal growth as he is moving forward in the cross-cultural transition and acculturation.

It is pivotal that the counselor keep a high level of cultural sensitivity so that she will not simplistically generalize the client into a certain category of culture or a cluster of sociocultural characteristics such as "African," "Asian," "Arabic," "South American," or "Caribbean." It is helpful to be more knowledgeable about the general and collective characteristics of a non-Western culture; yet, this knowledge can cause stereotyping and oversimplification if it is not used in a sensitive manner. Thus, the essential task for meaning-making in the narrative exploration is to constantly draw attention to the dynamics that interplay among various contextual constructs, such as personal, familial, cultural, and cross-cultural influences. Meaning-making only becomes relevant and meaningful to the enhancement of the international students' coping and adjustment experiences if cultural variables are considered and understood within each student's unique individual acculturation experiences.

Highlight actions. Drawing attention to the construct of action is a central task for the helping interventions and their outcomes. The counselor can incorporate the notion of action into different phases of the counseling encounter. As Bekele presents the narrative accounts and makes an effort to construct his future narrative, he can be guided to see the actions connected to his cross-cultural transition. An increased awareness of the vital function of human action in sociocultural discourse and life experiences can be developed on both levels of actions in the acculturation process, namely, individual actions and joint actions. The counselor can ask Bekele to describe and comment on his personal actions during the transitional experience. For example, Bekele's actions to study in Canada, to pursue a graduate thesis topic tackling the issue of gender equality, and to come to talk to a counselor, just to mention a few, were demonstrative of his individual actions in life.

In the meantime, the counselor can also help Bekele identify the dynamic and close interaction between the individual actions and the joint actions. In doing so, Bekele becomes more aware of the impact of joint actions on his cross-cultural transition. For example, the negotiation of his identity in transition reflects a context of joint actions. Although his family was not physically present in Canada, its influences were apparently felt in Bekele's struggle in defining his self-identity in acculturation. As such, Bekele was not sure that he would be able to meet some of the cultural expectations, especially those from his family, when he progressed further in his acculturation in the West.

Recognizing this impact of joint actions can be an important aspect in helping international students understand the complexity of their cross-cultural transition. The counseling process can stress the need to steer and direct an individual's action intention and plans in relation to others, especially significant others, in the broad context of the client's transitional experiences. In doing so, the client becomes more cognizant in mobilizing individual actions as well as joint actions with others, making a bridge between the two.

This bridging effort can accommodate the consideration of collective and communal influences and needs in individual experiences when actions are constructed, deconstructed, reconstructed, and implemented in a cross-cultural transition. Also, joint actions can include other relevant contexts and factors. For example, the need of building and using a social support system in the host culture can be incorporated into the broad domain of joint actions in the transition and acculturation process.

Conclusion

To analyze and comment on the case of an international student's cross-cultural transition in Canada, this discussion has attempted to form a CMC framework that may add to the growing need of helping international students from non-Western cultures. The CMC framework is at its preliminary stage of development, and it is only one of the possibilities that might shed some light on the complex helping practice in working with clients in a cross-cultural and multicultural counseling situation. The relevance and potential of the CMC approach remains to be studied further and developed, and the current discussion represents an initial interest and effort in building this approach.

Acknowledgment

This chapter was supported in part by a research grant from the Social Sciences and Humanities Research Council of Canada, Standard Grants Program, Award No. 410-2002-1027.

References

Arthur, N. (1997). Counseling issues with international students. *Canadian Journal of Counselling, 31*, 259–274.

Arthur, N. (2004). *Counseling international students: Clients from around the world.* New York: Kluwer Academic/Plenum.

Chen, C. P. (1999). Common stressors among international students: Research and counseling implications. *Journal of College Counseling, 2*, 49–65.

Chen, C. P. (2004). Transforming career in cross-cultural transition: The experience of non-Western culture counsellor trainees. *Counselling Psychology Quarterly, 17*, 137–154.

Corey, G. (2001). *Theory and practice of counseling and psychology* (6th ed.). Belmont, CA: Wadsworth/Thomson Learning.

Pedersen, P. (1991). Counseling international students. *The Counseling Psychologist, 19*, 10–58.

Young, R. A., Valach, L., & Collin, A. (2002). A contextualist explanation of career. In D. Brown (Ed.), *Career choice and development* (4th ed., pp. 206–252). San Francisco: Jossey-Bass.

Managing Multiple Identities

Huaiyu Zhang and Frederick T. L. Leong

Wenzhu (a pseudonym) was born and raised in a small city in the southwest of China. Her father was a high school teacher, and her mother was a primary school teacher. In addition to frequently grumbling about how Chairman Mao's era had ruined her life, Wenzhu's mother liked to draw attention to the personal sacrifice she had made for the whole family, especially for Wenzhu. In the 1960s, Wenzhu's mother was forced to quit college, and she left Shanghai to work in the countryside, which was thousands of miles away. When the chance came for her to go back to Shanghai, she had already married a local man and had given birth to Wenzhu. For the integrity of the whole family, she stayed there. Immediately after Wenzhu's birth, the Chinese government enforced a policy called the Birth Plan, which restricted each couple to only one child. Thus, Wenzhu grew up as a single child in her family and carried her mother's unfulfilled dreams of returning to Shanghai and achieving a bright future.

Ever since her childhood, Wenzhu had been exempted from the household duties. Her parents continued to peel boiled eggs for breakfast for her even during her high school years. Gone was her leisure time, too. The only emphasis in her adolescent years was study. To her mother's great satisfaction, Wenzhu excelled in school. She gained a great deal of face for her parents among relatives and neighbors by receiving an admission letter from Fudan University, which is the best educational institution in Shanghai. Everyone in her community learned that Wenzhu received remarkable scores on the national college entrance exam and greeted her by calling her "Fudan student."

Taking her mother's advice, Wenzhu majored in English at Fudan University. "Your journey is not over yet," her mother kept telling her over the telephone: "If I were you, I would dream of going abroad after graduation. If the dream were to come true, your dad and I could rest our worries." Wenzhu's feelings were mixed about living far from her parents. At first, she had a really hard time organizing her life because she had done nothing except study at home. In the meanwhile, she obtained much more freedom. She found that Shanghai residents rejected her as a countrywoman because she did not speak their dialect and she could not understand why they were so cordial to foreigners who spoke English. Wenzhu began to develop stereotypes about Shanghai people, including her mother. This great metropolitan city gradually imparted its values to her, as well as broadening her outlook.

Wenzhu had a boyfriend by the end of her 2nd year, and she brought him to meet her family during winter vacation. Comparing their backgrounds, Wenzhu's mother did not think that they would be a good match because he was from a rural area and both of his parents were peasants. She was even more disappointed to learn that he had no ambition to go abroad. Under pressure from her mother, Wenzhu ended the romantic relationship. She continued to work hard during her Fudan years. Her parents were delighted that she was admitted to the professional writing program of the University of Southern California (USC). Once again, she was in the spotlight in her community. Wenzhu thought that she should gain respite now, because she had fulfilled her mother's greatest wish, although her conclusion was premature.

Wenzhu's first impression of Los Angeles was that it was not the paradise of which she had dreamed. It was such a huge city that she found it took forever to go places by riding her bike. Upon her arrival in California, she found that many American people had a hard time pronouncing her Chinese name, so she named herself Wendy when she met people for the first time. She was assigned to a class of 10 students. She was the only Chinese in the class. Wenzhu had been proud of her English before she came; however, now she found herself having trouble communicating with her classmates. She could only understand half of the conversations with them. They talked so fast, and their slang and accents made her even more confused. They seemed to form their own small groups naturally, and she was left alone, belonging to none of them.

Wenzhu's only consolation was her association with Chinese friends. She felt a great deal more comfortable with them than with the American students. They talked to each other in Chinese, watched Chinese TV channels, ate the same kinds of food, and shared the same understandings when communicating. Her friends preferred to call her Wenzhu and she felt "at home" when with them. Wenzhu spent most of her free time shopping, eating, and having fun with her Chinese friends.

Wenzhu's mother constantly nagged her about the traditional value of filial piety and indicated how it was about time for her to pay them back. Wenzhu had a graduate assistantship in the English department, which entitled her to a tuition waiver and monthly stipend. She economized in order to save some money for her parents. They wanted her to give them a portion of her savings to subsidize the purchase of a new apartment in her home city. They also spread the word among their neighbors and relatives that Wenzhu would soon invite them to the United States. To Wenzhu, the pressure was invisible, but pervasive.

Wenzhu's lifestyle did not change much until she met a female Chinese writer from Iowa State University. The writer was invited by the USC program as a guest speaker. Wenzhu was chosen by the host to have lunch with her. During their conversation, Wenzhu expressed her concern that Iowa might not be an ideal place for a Chinese writer because there were very few Chinese people. The writer smiled at her and challenged Wenzhu's thoughts by asking why she bothered to come to the United States if she chose to stay within a Chinese community on the West Coast. "It would be a big waste of resources if you live within the Western culture and exclude yourself from it," the writer remarked.

Her words touched Wenzhu, causing a great deal of reflection. Wenzhu totally understood what the author said and aspired to change herself. She was motivated to watch English channels, attend parties and dinners involving mostly American people, and make more American friends. Wenzhu gained by becoming involved in this new way of living. She began to appreciate it and found it very interesting to sense the difference between the two cultures.

Critical Incident

One of Wenzhu's American friends, Kevin, began to date her. She found Kevin to be mature and caring and really liked him. Wenzhu consulted her parents. They were rather unhappy about this development. Although it was prestigious for their daughter to have a White boyfriend, they held stereotypes that Westerners were promiscuous and that they could not maintain stable relationships. Her parents also worried that they would have a hard time communicating with him. Wenzhu was upset about her parents' opinion, but this time she did not want to give up so easily. She had learned from her American friends that each individual, instead of his or her parent, should be responsible for his or her own life. Wenzhu not only stayed in the relationship but moved in to live with Kevin. However, she was not ready to inform her parents what was going on between Kevin and her. Whenever she considered telling them the truth, she foresaw an outburst of rage from them.

The feeling of withholding such a big secret from her parents made Wenzhu feel distressed and guilty. Her pain culminated when her parents called her to express their intention to visit her during the summer, which was 2 months away. They addressed the importance of their visiting her by reminding her how they had already boasted about the plan to others and how it would be a loss of face if they could not make it in the near future. Wenzhu went into a panic when she first heard about their visit. If her parents came, they would immediately learn the shocking fact about Kevin and her. They had not even given permission for her to date him, how would they accept the news that they were living together? Her parents would not only be angry about her defiance, but they would also be angry about the level of intimacy, which was still a taboo according to traditional Chinese values. She knew it was wrong to keep such a secret from them, but she also could imagine how mad and upset they would be if they knew the truth. It would probably ruin their trip. Wenzhu also thought about how it was difficult to turn down her mother, who was always assertive and demanding with her. Should she move out to prevent the unpleasant situation? Kevin would be very hurt if she did that. Wenzhu found herself caught in a dilemma of conflicting outcomes and finally decided to go to the university counseling center for some help.

Key Issues

This case incident is a composite description that was adopted from one coauthor's personal experiences and her observations of other Chinese immigrants' stories. Wenzhu, the main role in the case incident, grew up in a traditional city in China and moved to the United States to pursue a higher degree in her late 20s. She encountered problems in interpersonal relationships during her transition period in the United States. Most of her problems were not unusual for Chinese immigrants to face in the States. Within the past 20 years or so, a large portion of Chinese immigrants have been a very intellectual population. When interacting with other people in particular environments, they must deal with conflicts between traditional Chinese values and Western values.

Wenzhu had encountered two major interpersonal challenges in the United States. Her first problem dealt with language and cultural barriers. At first, she had trouble consorting with American people because of these barriers. When she felt deserted, she would try to make more Chinese friends. She gradually learned to appreciate the host culture and became acculturated to it. The next challenge occurred during her progress of acculturation. The fuse was her romantic relationship with an American man and how her parents objected to it. However, as she became more experienced in using her own more individualistic thoughts, she decided not to obey her parents as much as she had in China. The conflict made her very stressed, especially when her parents planned to visit her.

Reader Reflection Questions

1. What else would you want to learn about Wenzhu?
2. How do you think Wenzhu's level of acculturation affected her interpersonal problems?
3. What do you think are Wenzhu's strengths and weaknesses in her interpersonal relationships?
4. What assessment tools (inventories) might you suggest for her to use?

5. How would you deal with her challenges and, in turn, give advice to help her?
6. How would you address a balancing point between two different cultural value systems when counseling her?

Response 1

John Stewart

Wenzhu met an influential Chinese writer who challenged her to live more fully in the Western culture. Wenzhu accepted the challenge and worked diligently at learning English by watching English-language television, attending parties, and interacting with European American people. She developed a relationship with a European American man, a relationship about which her parents were cautious. For them, it was prestigious for Wenzhu to have a European American boyfriend, but they were worried about his possible promiscuous behavior and their inability to communicate with him. Wenzhu chose to resist her parents based on the idea that individuals should be able to make their personal decisions. In this case incident, it is possible to see her efforts to gain support from new relationships, including her boyfriend and her Chinese friends. Wenzhu appeared to be caught in the middle—she wanted both groups to become one but they seemed incompatible with one another. She was in the middle and unable to bring the two groups together.

Presenting Issues

In this case incident, it is not clear from Wenzhu whether or not she intends to stay in the United States. However, her parents have let it be known that Wenzhu would soon take them to the United States. For this discussion, I am making the assumption that Wenzhu intends to stay in the United States after finishing her studies.

Migrants face three issues (Roysircar, 2003) when they enter a country of their choice: decisions about the components of their personal cultural identity they want to maintain, decisions regarding the desired level of interaction with people in the dominant culture, and the stress and mental health issues that arise from these issues. Wenzhu appeared to struggle with some components of all three of these issues. The components of Wenzhu's presenting issues include the following: the cognition that individuals should be able to make their personal decisions, the decision to interact with people of the dominant culture, and the anxiety she experienced when her two groups of friends did not intermingle and communicate the way she had expected.

Assessment Issues

Personal Psychological and Personal Demographic Issues

Wenzhu's worldview can be described as a collectivist one within which she conceptualizes herself more from a sociocentric than a psychocentric perspective (Dana, 1993). That is, she viewed herself within a group context, preferring to make decisions that involve her family unit and aspiring to the values of respect for her parents and her personal responsibility to bring them honor. In addition, she valued education as a medium to bring prestige to her parents, and within this domain, she aspired to be literate in English. She valued relationships and harmony within these relationships. Furthermore, she is a woman and both vicariously and instrumentally has learned her role as a woman from her mother. She appeared to have been in the United States for at least a year and perhaps longer when the incident took place. Prior to coming to the United States, she earned an undergraduate degree from Fudan University in Shanghai. In terms of her age, she is likely between 21 and 25 years old.

Acculturation Issues

Wenzhu appeared to be struggling with her acculturation status (Kim & Abreu, 2001). Soon after arriving in Los Angeles, Wenzhu experienced a marginalization versus integration dynamic. When she arrived in the United States, she had certain expectations about life in America and was disappointed. She experienced language difficulties and a lack of group involvement and consequently resorted to forming a group of Chinese individuals. In this way, she was able to continue to study English, but her need for social affiliation was met with her new Chinese friends. She did not have to participate in American society. This position resulted in her marginalizing herself within American society. After she met the visiting professor, however, she challenged herself to fully embrace as much of American culture as possible. She watched English television, attended parties and dinners where Euro-Americans were in the majority, and made friends with Euro-Americans. As a consequence of these experiences, she began to sense the differences between the two cultures—American and Chinese. This awareness appears to be the beginning of an integrated or bicultural acculturation status.

Wenzhu demonstrated cognitive and behavioral indicators that suggest she has developed some aspects of a bicultural identity. It is important to realize that newcomers to a dominant culture different from their own often develop multiple identities; they view some aspects of their lives from one cultural perspective whereas other aspects are viewed from the other cultural perspective (Justin, 2005). In this situation, Wenzhu appeared to embrace American culture and language, but in other aspects, although she might understand the differences, she was not able to use behavior to reflect the cultural insights she had developed. For example, Wenzhu did not know how to bridge her group of new friends from different cultures. As a consequence, she experienced anxiety and awkward feelings. In this regard, she was behaving in a manner expected of traditional Chinese women—not to be assertive and not to express her feelings outside the family unit (Diller, 2004). As a consequence of her changing psychological dynamics, Wenzhu experienced acculturation stress.

This stress was a result of a number of competing cognitions and values. She appeared to have adopted the American belief that individuals should make personal decisions themselves, but she desired support by having Kevin accepted by her Chinese friends against the wishes of her mother. However, she sent money to her parents for a new apartment to please them and have them save face within their Chinese community. The interaction of these cognitions and values resulted in Wenzhu experiencing stress.

Interpersonal Relationships and Her Desire for Harmony

Wenzhu experienced sex role conflict (Porter, 2000). Social learning theory suggests that individuals learn roles and behaviors appropriate to their genders within the family and societal context during their early years (Allen, 1994). Typically, Asian females are socialized to be passive and nonexpressive of their emotions. Although these behaviors were appropriate in her birth country, they did not enable her to meet many new non-Chinese friends. Wenzhu's sex role conflict focused on her self-control versus her self-expression and spontaneity.

Counseling Goals

I conceptualize the goals of this counseling intervention under two types: process goals and outcome goals (Hackney & Cormier, 2005). There are two process goals I would endeavor to follow during counseling. I would use culturally appropriate behaviors to make Wenzhu feel as comfortable as possible. Furthermore, I would work collaboratively with her to help her take ownership of the outcome goals. By taking ownership, Wenzhu will feel more empowered to accomplish them. Collaboratively, I would work with Wenzhu to focus on two outcome goals: to learn the behaviors to express her feelings appropriate to the context and to integrate her ideas of personal decision making so that she is able to use culturally appropriate ideas within the appropriate context. I recommend working toward these goals using a combination of feminist therapy and cognitive-behavioral therapy. I think that Wenzhu demonstrates a great deal of motivation to understand and learn about the American cultural context, and I would use this motivation as a factor in collaborating with her about different types of interventions.

Interventions

Recent theorizing in cross-cultural counseling (Arthur & Merali, 2005; Bemak & Chung, 2000) suggests the use of a four-level approach to psychotherapy with recent immigrants. Level 1 concerns mental health education; Level 2 involves individual, group, and/or family psychotherapy; Level 3 focuses on cultural empowerment; and Level 4 integrates Western and indigenous healing methodologies. I like this approach because it incorporates the complexity of culture and the many and varied experiences of recent immigrants. Although I do not think all four levels may be necessary with Wenzhu, I do think this model is helpful due to its comprehensiveness, which helps to uncover issues that arise as a result of the interaction between the culture of origin, the migration experience, and the experiences within the dominant culture of the host country.

Level 1 helps to establish realistic expectations relative to the delivery of North American mental health services. In this level of intervention, the counselor educates the client about the counseling process, including issues such as the role of the counselor and client, intake procedures, assessment, time issues, payment issues, and/or the types of counseling interventions that could be used. It is helpful for counselors to distinguish the counseling relationship from that of a doctor–patient relationship. Depending on the home culture of the recent immigrant, the only helping relationship the immigrant has experienced may be the medical relationship. Sometimes there could be a tendency to see the counseling relationship within the same dynamics as the doctor–patient relationship.

In this level, there are a number of issues counselors should be sensitive to while providing professional services for Asian clients (Baruth & Manning, 2003). One issue concerns the belief that counseling may reflect badly on the family. Counselors will want to address this issue to provide clarity and perspective to the client's perceptions of the nature and purposes of counseling. Furthermore, the counselor may want to avoid the use of paraphrase, because the use of this communication technique may be perceived as a weakness by Asian clients. In addition, the counselor may want to use a gentle but firm voice, qualities that enhance Asian clients' perceptions about the counselor's credibility. As well, counselors should interpret such traits like modesty and self-depreciation as not necessarily indicative of low self-esteem in Asian clients. Through the presentation and discussion of issues like these, Asian clients will develop a realistic expectation about the counseling process.

Level 2 encompasses the use of individual, group, and/or family counseling practices but from a culturally sensitive perspective. During this phase, counselors strive to achieve credibility based on their demonstration of cultural sensitivity, understanding of their clients and their ethnic background, and overall attention to their clients' personal context.

For example, Asian clients may expect the counselor to adopt a directive and authoritative stance in counseling (Diller, 2004). Counselors must be sensitive to traditional Chinese teaching that personal and familial information is not shared outside the home and to understand that silence may be experienced that should not be interpreted as resistance (Baruth & Manning, 2003). In addition, counselors might want to incorporate aspects of the client's religion and spirituality into the counseling process. Furthermore, if possible, the counselor might want to incorporate family members and/or group approaches to interventions, particularly for clients whose worldview is collectivist.

From a multicultural perspective, group work must achieve three goals: valuing diversity, developing multicultural competence, and promoting a multicultural identity (Ling Han & Vasquez, 2000). To value diversity, clients must be willing to explore their attitudes and cognitions about their cultural background and how this background affects present functioning. Developing cultural competence focuses on helping clients develop interpersonal skills and learning how to switch from one set of culturally appropriate behaviors to another. Identity involves developing positive self-awareness and prizing a racial identity.

There are a number of advantages to using group work with recent immigrant clients. Group work can help immigrants adapt positively during acculturation (Arthur & Merali, 2005), develop a sense of interdependence with others, enhance their self-esteem levels, alleviate stress, and increase motivation for personal empowerment (Porter, 2000). Conversely, the disadvantage of group work for Asian clients involves the reluctance to share information that may bring dishonor to the immediate family or relatives, to share strong emotions in public, and to disclose personal issues to others (Baruth & Manning, 2003).

When working with Asian clients, counselors need to make a number of decisions. They need to decide whether the advantages of group work outweigh the disadvantages for their client. They need to decide whether to use heterogeneously or homogeneously constituted groups (Ling Han & Vasquez, 2000). Generally, homogeneously constituted groups promote growth in group-member trust and understanding, foster self-disclosure, and have less conflict and better attendance. However, heterogeneously constituted groups simulate a context for mainstream society, allow for the exchange of feedback from and information about diverse others, and provide a context for the development of culturally appropriate interpersonal skills. In addition, counselors must consider the issue of verbal participation by clients and the use of same or mixed-sex groups (Ling Han & Vasquez, 2000). Generally, mixed groups provide opportunities for working through sex role issues. Overall, the groups that have the most potential for positive outcomes are groups that are homogeneous in terms of gender, background, profession, and social class (Baruth & Manning, 2003).

Family participation in counseling also provides support for culturally diverse clients (Arthur & Merali, 2005; Porter, 2000). Family counseling incorporates the benefits of group work and permits the counselor to assess the family's attitudes toward understanding the presenting issue(s) in psychological terms and the family's overall willingness to support the person in difficulty. Counselors must understand how family power is recognized both formally and informally in public and in private, the role of elders, the norms for children, and gender role expectations (Porter, 2000). Overall, for Asian clients, family counseling provides a context in which the dignity of the client is protected, the honor of the family is preserved, and the client receives help (Baruth & Manning, 2003).

I suggest the use of a structured, directive, and goal-directed problem-solving approach (Zane, Morton, Chu, & Lin, 2004). It seems to me that Wenzhu's problem involved three aspects: making personal decisions by herself apart from the wishes of her family, the need for support to continue to date her boyfriend, and her interactions with friends from different cultural backgrounds. I recommend using cognitive-behavioral therapy focused on understanding the cognitive issues underlying these three issues, learning behavior strategies to cope with ways to express herself appropriate to the cultural context, and strategizing ways for Wenzhu to achieve her goal of keeping her boyfriend and her need to gain support from her friends and family. Furthermore, I suggest the use of a feminist approach, in which issues are seen as embedded in the larger sociopolitical systems that were operative during the formative years of Wenzhu's development. In this approach, I would proceed using four healing processes: validation of her experience, empowering Wenzhu to act in her relationships, developing her self-empathy, and developing a sense of mutuality in her relationships (Ling Han & Vasquez, 2000).

Level 3 focuses on the client's mastery of the new environment. The focus during this level is on helping the client develop effective coping strategies to deal with everyday challenges, including the integration of the two cultures into a positive bicultural self-identity. In this level, Wenzhu needs to understand how to access resources and services relative to health, education, finances, and employment. I would work toward helping Wenzhu enhance her ability to understand and deal with these systems and to build a network of supports. The counselor's knowledge of agencies and programs that promote positive contacts with members of the dominant culture is very helpful. Finally, social justice issues may need to be incorporated into the counseling process. Counselors may need to serve as advocates for their clients, for example, by helping them to deal with discriminatory issues related to employment. This may take the form of writing letters, phone calls, and coaching clients to deal with such barriers. In this case incident, Wenzhu does not seem to have any issues involving social justice.

Level 4 seeks to achieve the integration of Western and culturally specific healing methods. Counselors must be receptive to culturally appropriate ways of healing and display acceptance, understanding, and support of their clients' cultural beliefs. They must be willing to explore the use of ethnically traditional healing strategies with their clients. The use of such healing methods helps to build support, motivation, and credibility in the counseling process. In this case incident, I do not think there is a need to integrate Western and culturally specific healing methods with Wenzhu.

After achieving the outcome goals, I would encourage Wenzhu to make an appointment within 4 weeks of the last counseling session. The purpose of this session would be to determine how well Wenzhu is coping with her involvement with American culture and to reassure her of support should she need it in the future.

Implications for the Role of Counselors

The issues presented in this case incident have implications for counselors' roles within the larger educational institutional environment, particularly institutions that seek to diversify their student enrollment through international recruitment. There are a number of roles counselors can perform (Axelson, 1999; Ramirez, 1999; Roysircar, 2004). Overall, I advocate that counselors perform the role of multicultural ambassador (Ramirez, 1999) and function within the institution as intercultural communicators (Axelson, 1999). In this role, counselors demonstrate and share their cultural awareness, promote intergroup understanding and cross-cultural communication, and work against international student alienation. As multicultural ambassadors, counselors could have an impact on three aspects of educational institutions: students, faculty and staff, and the structures and policies of the institution itself.

First, for students, counselors could serve as student advocates by providing peer mentoring support for international students to encourage them in their negotiation of transitional issues that are primarily educational and not personal in nature. For example, international students often need help in understanding the differences in interpersonal habits between ethnic student subgroups, institutional policies, faculty teaching practices, and writing and speaking skills in the dominant language. Such services would necessitate programs directed at developing the multicultural knowledge and skills of senior students to work with international students new to the institution. Such mentoring would not only orient international students to the educational environment but provide someone with whom new students could affiliate during their first and/or second semester at the institution. In addition, counselors could serve as interpreters of the institution's bureaucratic system. International students need help in making sense of the social, political, and class factors embedded in the system. By helping international students unpack such issues, counselors meet the needs of individuals within a seemingly impersonal system.

As multicultural ambassadors, counselors perform a role as in-service consultants to the institution's employees. They could provide workshops and/or presentations to faculty and staff designed to promote understanding of the social, interpersonal, emotional, and learning styles of international students. For example, helping the instructors of Wenzhu's professional writing class to become aware of differing levels of functioning in English and asking all class members to be sensitive to the differences between expressive and receptive language rates among international students would help students like Wenzhu maintain motivation to learn the norms and interpersonal skills to integrate with the dominant group. Instead, Wenzhu sought out the comfort of a group of Chinese friends to meet her group affiliation needs. Furthermore, counselors could interpret the immediate and intermediate needs of international students to faculty and staff and suggest ways they may facilitate meeting these needs. For example, they could suggest the benefits of planning a number of group activities that include all students and promote social interaction and foster intergroup understanding. Wenzhu felt she did not belong to any of the subgroups that members of the writing class formed.

Counselors, as multicultural ambassadors, could advocate for change in the institution's structures and policies that have an impact on international students. For example, the institution needs to provide orientation for international students that goes beyond course registration and familiarizing them with the campus layout. International students need help in understanding themselves relative to the rest of the educational community. They need to understand the norms of the dominant group and how they can integrate with that group. International students who do not negotiate such transitions often feel alienated and resort to becoming involved in their individual ethnic group without attempting to learn about other groups and to learn ways to relate to them. Furthermore, counselors could function as advocates for international students, particularly when administrative needs are considered more important than student needs. Counselors are able to explain these administrative needs and class experiences to international students to further their understanding of an educational environment that appears to be unresponsive to them. For example, Asian students often expect faculty members to be directive in the progress of their studies. The focus of the dominant culture expects that students will take the initiative and act in their own self-interests. Students from collectivist cultures often get lost in such a system, and if they are not able to negotiate an understanding of the system and develop the skills to promote themselves within such a system, they often become alienated and dissatisfied with their educational experience.

Overall, there are many roles that counselors could perform in the larger educational environment. Obviously, they could not perform all the ones mentioned above. However, if counselors adopted a stance as multicultural ambassador and one or more of the roles mentioned, they could promote an awareness of and an appreciation for the needs of international students at three levels within the educational institution: the student, faculty and staff, and structures and policies of the institution.

References

Allen, B. P. (1994). *Personality theories*. Toronto, Ontario, Canada: Allyn & Bacon.

Arthur, N., & Merali, N. (2005). Counselling immigrants and refugees. In N. Arthur & S. Collins (Eds.), *Culture-infused counselling: Celebrating the Canadian mosaic* (pp. 331–360). Calgary, Alberta, Canada: Counselling Concepts.

Axelson, J. (1999). *Counseling and development in a multicultural society* (3rd ed.). Toronto, Ontario, Canada: Brooks/Cole.

Baruth, L. G., & Manning, M. L. (2003). *Multicultural counseling and psychotherapy: A lifespan perspective.* Upper Saddle River, NJ: Pearson Education.

Bemak, F. P., & Chung, R. C. (2000). Psychological intervention with immigrants and refugees. In J. F. Aponte & J. Wohl (Eds.), *Psychological interventions and cultural diversity* (2nd ed., pp. 200–213). Toronto, Ontario, Canada: Allyn & Bacon.

Dana, R. H. (1993). *Multicultural assessment perspective for professional psychology.* Toronto, Ontario, Canada: Allyn & Bacon.

Diller, J. V. (2004). *Cultural diversity: A primer for the human services* (2nd ed.). Toronto, Ontario, Canada: Thomson, Brooks/Cole.

Hackney, H., & Cormier, S. (2005). *The professional counselor: A process guide to helping* (5th ed.). Toronto, Ontario, Canada: Pearson/Allyn & Bacon.

Justin, M. (2005). Counselling members of non-dominant ethnic groups. In N. Arthur & S. Collins (Eds.), *Culture-infused counselling: Celebrating the Canadian mosaic* (pp. 361–385). Calgary, Alberta, Canada: Counselling Concepts.

Kim, B. S. K., & Abreu, J. M. (2001). Acculturation measurement: Theory, current instruments, and future directions. In J. G. Ponterotto, J. M. Casas, L. A. Suzuki, & M. Alexandra (Eds.), *Handbook of multicultural counseling* (2nd ed., pp. 394–424). Thousand Oaks, CA: Sage.

Ling Han, A., & Vasquez, M. J. T. (2000). Group interventions and treatment with ethnic minorities. In J. F. Aponte & J. Wohl (Eds.), *Psychological interventions and cultural diversity* (2nd ed., pp. 110–130). Toronto, Ontario, Canada: Allyn & Bacon.

Porter, R. Y. (2000). Clinical issues and intervention with ethnic minority women. In J. F. Aponte & J. Wohl (Eds.), *Psychological interventions and cultural diversity* (2nd ed., pp. 183–199). Toronto, Ontario, Canada: Allyn & Bacon.

Ramirez M., III. (1999). *Multicultural psychotherapy: An approach to individual and cultural differences* (2nd ed.). Toronto, Ontario, Canada: Allyn & Bacon.

Roysircar, G. (2003). Understanding immigrants: Acculturation theory and research. In F. D. Harper & J. McFadden (Eds.), *Culture and counseling: New approaches* (pp. 164–185). Toronto, Ontario, Canada: Allyn & Bacon.

Roysircar, G. (2004). Counseling and psychotherapy for acculturation and ethnic identity concerns with immigrants and international student clients. In T. B. Smith (Ed.), *Practicing multiculturalism: Affirming diversity in counseling and psychology* (pp. 255–275). Toronto, Ontario, Canada: Pearson/Allyn & Bacon.

Zane, N., Morton, T., Chu, J., & Lin, N. (2004). Counselling and psychotherapy with Asian clients. In T. B. Smith (Ed.), *Practicing multiculturalism: Affirming diversity in counseling and psychology* (pp. 190–214). Boston: Allyn & Bacon.

Response 2

Natalee Popadiuk

The case incident of Wenzhu, or Wendy, provides a vivid account of the ways in which social identities and social group membership become constructed along ethnic, gender, and class lines. These statuses are produced within a broader context of power relations that confer status and privilege on some members of society while marginalizing others (Constantine, 2002). A feminist lens provides opportunity for a critical analysis of power relations not only of gender but also of ethnicity, social class, age, sexual orientation, education, disability, religion, and the like (Reynolds & Constantine, 2004). These statuses can be conceptualized along a continuum of more highly valued (dominant) aspects to less valued and oppressed (marginalized) aspects (Freire, 2003; Prilleltensky & Fox, 1997).

In choosing the particular aspects of ethnicity, gender, and social class to discuss Wenzhu's case incident, I have made a decision to foreground things that seem most salient in this story. This selection also means that I have necessarily chosen not to explore other, potentially important, issues, largely due to space limitations. By applying a feminist lens, I am stepping outside the dominant discourse in the field of international student research, which typically examines issues from an apolitical stance (e.g., Popadiuk & Arthur, 2004; Poyrazali, Kavanaugh, Baker, & Al-Timimi, 2004). These views are important; however, my intention is to add a unique perspective to the field by exploring Wenzhu's multiple and social group statuses and how they shape her multicultural experiences (Croteau, Talbot, Lance, & Evans, 2002; Tsang, Bogo, & George, 2003).

I have organized the discussion of Wenzhu's story along two dimensions: cultural–institutional and interpersonal. Much of the literature examines international student issues from an intrapsychic perspective, that is, a focus on the individual and his or her problems. I, instead, highlight the contextual areas of inquiry. From the cultural–institutional level, I explore social and historical events in China that had an impact on Wenzhu's family members and their worldviews. In addition, I examine some of the culturally relevant discourses regarding gender, ethnicity, and social class. From the interpersonal context, I consider power relations, interpersonal relationships, and prevailing norms that had an impact on Wenzhu's transitional experiences. Considering that ethnicity, gender, and social class intersect at both the cultural–institutional and interpersonal levels, this analysis is necessarily complex and incomplete. Nonetheless, it is my hope that this work inspires other psychologists, educators, and researchers to venture into a feminist understanding of power, privilege, and oppression.

Cultural–Institutional Analysis

Arredondo's (1999) Dimensions of Personal Identity Model highlights three dimensions that interact to create an individual's personal identity. In Dimension A, salient issues are related to age, culture, ethnicity, gender, language, and social class. Dimension B includes institutional-level factors such as educational background, geographic location, religion/spirituality, work experiences, and health care practices/beliefs. Finally, in Dimension C, historical movements and eras that may have profoundly affected the person or the family are examined. Arredondo stated that therapists using this model can develop a plan about cultural group beliefs and attitudes, explore the transmission of these beliefs across generations, and determine the impact on the individual's worldview. This framework is also useful for practitioners in considering their own personal identities and social group memberships and how these may interact with, influence, and impinge on a client's personal identity.

Arredondo's (1999) model can be useful for exploring issues of social class related to education, geographic location, career, and historical eras. For example, Wenzhu and her family can be located as part of the Chinese middle-class due to their attainment of post-secondary education, professional positions, urban living, and overseas opportunities. Historically, her family's social class was affected by a significant event, China's Cultural Revolution, during the time when Wenzhu's mother was in university. Along with millions of other educated young people, her mother was forced to move away from the city to the countryside in order to be "reeducated." This political move was seen by Chairman Mao Ze Dong as a way of dealing with social class inequities, namely by sending the educated, city-dwelling elite into the hinterlands of China to mix with uneducated poor farmers and peasants. Wenzhu's mother, therefore, lost her dream to study abroad. This had an impact on her worldview and, subsequently, the hopes and dreams she held for her daughter. In addition to the impact of this era, the prevailing cultural norms in China during the 1980s changed from desiring a watch, a bicycle, and a stable job in the government to a more capitalist orientation of obtaining a foreign degree, a job in a foreign or a private company, a car, and a private apartment (Tang & Parish, 2000). Thus, Wenzhu's current social class can be seen as a combination of forces driven by significant historical events and eras through multiple generations.

A second sociopolitical aspect mentioned in this story relates to the Chinese government's enforced Birth Plan, which restricted Wenzhu's parents to one child. The Birth Plan in China further entrenched the notion of male gender preference, with often devastating consequences for female children. For example, in many rural areas, poor peasants and farmers gave up female babies for adoption, committed infanticide, or treated young girls like slaves with little or no educational opportunities (Hsiung & Wong, 1998). Although many modern families fully accept girls, a male gender preference still exists, and male children typically experience significant privilege compared with female children. In Wenzhu's story, parental gender preference is not mentioned, but the issue may nonetheless be relevant. Even if Wenzhu's parents did not subscribe to this value, these attitudes and beliefs are historically and culturally embedded in the social matrix of the culture (Popadiuk, 2002). Wenzhu would have likely experienced a significant, if unrecognized, burden of negotiating overt and covert oppression and sexism within her cultural milieu. This oppressive social location would have likely had an impact on her identity, her sense of self-worth, and her worldview; therefore, a concept such as gender can be viewed within the context of current prevailing cultural norms, familial biases and preferences, and historical policies and political agendas.

Third, Wenzhu's family subscribed to the cultural–institutional virtue of filial piety. A deeply embedded concept in Chinese culture, this virtue refers primarily to the responsibility of children to respect and obey their parents. Adult children are expected to care for aging parents in return for the parents' earlier sacrifices. Filial piety is traditionally considered a lifelong responsibility, although modern ideals have influenced and mediated this concept in China and abroad. In Wenzhu's case, there appeared to be a tension, not easily negotiated, between the traditional virtue of filial piety and a Western, individualistic orientation. As an example, Wenzhu finally believed that she had fulfilled her mother's expectation to study overseas after successfully living and studying in Los Angeles. She reacted with a feeling of "respite now, because she had fulfilled her mother's greatest wish." To her dismay, she discovered that her mother's expectations had not changed. Instead, Wenzhu's mother is described as "nagging" her to send money so they could buy a new apartment in China, and also be brought to the United States. The cultural expectation of filial piety created a unique burden on Wenzhu. Although she did not discuss the specific impact of these demands, the story stated that "the pressure was invisible, but pervasive," suggesting an oppressive experience over which she had little control.

Interpersonal Analysis

Although Arredondo's (1999) framework is useful for unpacking historical eras, group membership, and social locations, another feminist theory, relational-cultural theory (formerly self-in-relation theory), is more useful in discussing interpersonal relationships (Miller & Stiver, 1997; Walker, 2004). This theoretical orientation posits that empathic, mutually engaging connections with others become the primary psychological change agents toward growth, healing, and well-being. Alternatively, disconnections from other people significantly restrict psychological growth and lead to alienation, depression, and anxiety. Because even strong relationships are prone to periods of disconnection, the act of reconnecting through mutual understanding and empathy becomes an important part of the growth process. The relational-cultural theory moves away from traditional perspectives that pathologize women's tendency to develop strong relational ties, emphasizing this relational orientation as a valuable growth-promoting resource. The relational-cultural theory can provide a culturally sensitive feminist perspective of relationships in many collectivist and ethnically diverse populations. Three important areas of connection and disconnection are noted in Wenzhu's life: her relationship with parents, her relationship with friends and boyfriends, and her relationship with a Chinese woman writer.

First, by noticing the language of the story, specifically what is overtly stated, implied, or omitted, questions can be asked about Wenzhu's relationships with her parents. Arguably, the most important and influential person in Wenzhu's life was her mother. It is interesting that little is mentioned about her father, and so we are left wondering about his role in the family; the level of power he held; and, ultimately, the kind of relationship he had with his daughter. By omitting information about the father–daughter relationship, he becomes invisible; there is no way to adequately assess the level of connection or disconnection between them. Meanwhile, the portrayal of Wenzhu's mother indicates an ambivalent, and likely difficult, interpersonal dynamic between mother and daughter. For example, some of the ways in which the mother is described included she grumbled, she drew attention to her personal sacrifices, and she kept nagging and reminding Wenzhu that it was time to pay her parents back. This description speaks to a gender bias in how women and mothers are often ascribed negative attributes. During Wenzhu's cultural transition, her attitude toward and her relationship with her mother changed. Fulfilling the dream to study abroad, dating a European American boyfriend, and being exposed to new ideas and attitudes shifted the power dynamic between Wenzhu and her mother. From a relational-cultural theory, Wenzhu can be seen as moving in and out of connection with her mother through all of her transitional experiences. Issues related to gender, mother–daughter relationships, and growth in connection to others become salient aspects to explore in counseling.

The second area of exploration relates to Wenzhu's desire for friendships and intimate relationships. Initially, she desired to become friends with other students at Fudan University. Despite the fact that she was an excellent student, received admission to the best university, and obtained "remarkable scores," she was, at first, rejected by most other Chinese students. This disconnection from others left Wenzhu feeling isolated and unhappy. She particularly experienced this marginalization in relation to her status as a "countrywoman" and her use of a different (i.e., lesser, rural) dialect. These classist attitudes surfaced again when she dated a Chinese man who did not meet her mother's social class expectations: His parents were peasants, he was from rural China, and he lacked ambition to travel overseas. Despite finding connection through this intimate dating relationship, she was required to end the relationship at the request of her parents. Similarly, in Los Angeles, Wenzhu experienced a serious lack of connection during her transition, but this time the alienation was worse: She felt pressure to rename herself, she was the only Chinese person in her department, she struggled with English, and she was alienated from American peers. This sense of isolation fueled her need to reinvent herself as Wendy in order to connect with others, be accepted, and accommodate to the new environment. When Wenzhu discovered the difficulty in connecting with Americans, she befriended other Chinese nationals instead.

From a relational-cultural perspective, Wenzhu attempted to empower herself in the disempowering environment of both universities by finding ways in which she could connect with others. Through this lens, Wenzhu could be seen as a resourceful young woman who implicitly understood the need to be in mutually empathic, growth-enhancing relationships. In both cases, she initially experienced oppression that kept her silenced, powerless, and marginalized. She felt different from the others; in fact, she became "other." During these periods of disconnection, Wenzhu had the experience of "being on the outside" and "being from somewhere else." In Los Angeles, her alienation may have been due to overt or unintentional racism. Her statuses as a Chinese woman from China who did not speak perfect English and who embodied different social and cultural norms may not have been as highly valued. Her previous oppressive experiences at Fudan University may have also constrained her thinking about how she might be perceived or treated in her new setting or about how she might choose to interact with others. Whenever Wenzhu connected in a meaningful relationship, she appeared to experience a sense of well-being. She became a fully participating and valued member of the group. By coming into contact with people of a similar social class and social location, such as the Chinese nationals, Wenzhu's own status became equalized rather than marginalized.

The third area related to the importance of connection through relationship occurred when she entered into a discussion that became a turning point in her sojourn. A Chinese woman working at Iowa State University significantly affected Wenzhu when she challenged Wenzhu to immerse herself in American culture. This woman's social statuses yielded her considerable power and influence: She was a renowned scholar, a university professor, a writer, and an older woman (mother figure), and she had successfully negotiated a similar cultural transition at an earlier time. The discussion over lunch propelled Wenzhu to shift her thinking about her current attitudes and actions regarding her stay in America. Indeed, after their meeting, Wenzhu began to immerse herself in American culture by watching English-language television, attending dinner parties with Americans, and dating an American student of European ancestry. Despite her parents' disapproval, she decided to continue dating this man, which was a very different decision than she had made earlier. Through this relationship, she was further exposed to new relationships with other American students, and her world continued to shift.

From a relational-cultural perspective, the single event with this writer could be viewed as a growth-fostering relationship. The writer was able to share parts of herself, which had an impact on Wenzhu at a deep level. There was a strong sense of mutual empathy between the two women, highlighted by five important components of the theory: zest in emotional connection, action, knowledge, sense of worth, and greater desire for more connections (Miller & Stiver, 1997; Walker, 2004). In other words, a strong feeling of zest, energy, or vitality could be used to describe their interaction. This powerful interplay between them prompted Wenzhu to take action by immersing herself in American culture. In addition, the conversation created an opportunity for an enlarged and more accurate sense of self and other. Through the recognition and acknowledgment of their shared international and academic experiences, Wenzhu experienced a greater sense of worth. The connection had been so meaningful that by the end of it, Wenzhu left reflecting on her attitudes with a greater desire to connect with others.

Feminist Therapy

As previously discussed, feminist perspectives emphasize a politicized and systemic exploration of client issues rather than focusing solely or primarily on individual pathology and diagnostic labels. Some feminist researchers propose that "every diagnosis must be questioned regarding its origins and embedded assumptions" (Evans, Kincade, Marbley, & Seem, 2005, p. 271). This means that individual, relational, and cultural issues should all be considered in order to more fully determine the nature, extent, and contributing factors of a problem. Feminist therapy is one of the few theoretical orientations that deliberately raises and names power inequities that create oppressive racist, sexist, and classist realities. This perspective purposefully engages clients in an exploration about the sociopolitical aspects of power, privilege, and oppression and how these issues affect their experiences and shape their everyday lives.

Brown (2006) elucidated how feminist therapists conceptualize individual problems brought in by clients: "We speak of the experiences of power and powerlessness in people's lives, experiences that interact with the bodies and biologies we bring into the world to create distress, resilience, dysfunction, and competence" (p. 17). In this statement, Brown highlighted the complex interaction between an individual's state of well-being or distress and the underlying, often invisible, forces of power and powerlessness. This focus on external sources, however, does not negate the fact that biological, physiological, or psychological issues may be a primary concern. Instead, it provides a systemic theoretical framework that seeks to account for diversity and the complexity of influences of individual lives and problems (Arthur & McMahon, 2005). Contextual perspectives, therefore, seek to address the layers in a way that depathologizes individuals and expands perspectives of how cultural influences affect and influence individual functioning.

Therapist Self-Reflection

An example of how feminist therapy provides something unique to counseling is the focus on therapist self-reflection and self-knowledge. Feminist therapists are expected to understand their own social locations and group memberships and how these may interact with clients. Part of this work might entail a counselor's own personal therapy; reading and reflecting on his or her own group statuses; and engaging in meaningful, relevant dialogue with colleagues. A therapist working with Wenzhu, for example, would want to be aware of any personal negative bias, prejudice, or stereotypes associated with individuals from China, international students, or women. If a counselor experienced significant personal attitudinal barriers in working with Wenzhu, he or she would need to actively address these issues outside of the sessions, because, invariably, an individual's own perceptions and attributes will become problematic in working with the client. If the counselor is not able to overcome biases, there are ethical reasons to support referral to another counselor who could better accommodate the client's needs.

Raising Issues of Gender, Ethnicity, and Social Class

Another aspect that is of primary concern to feminist therapists is a systemic, contextual perspective that examines issues of gender, ethnicity, and social class. In practice, some counselors who do not subscribe to feminist ideology argue against raising politicized topics such as power, privilege, and oppression. A feminist therapist working with Wenzhu would want to introduce these issues sensitively when appropriate and relevant to the topic at hand. For example, a feminist therapist would likely bring up the issues of gender, social class, and ethnicity in order to contextualize Wenzhu's presenting problems. The surfacing of these issues typically leads to a greater sense of connection and understanding between the therapist and client, and the client gains a contextualized perspective that serves to normalize and depathologize the issues. Because a counselor's silence may indicate complicity with or ignorance of the oppressive and institutionalized forms of racism, sexism, and classism, it is vital that counselors be able to talk about such issues openly. Once discussions of gender, culture, socioeconomic status, and the like are sensitively broached with clients, there is almost always a sense of resonance, curiosity, and relief that there is space to openly discuss a taboo subject.

Therapist Self-Disclosure

In feminist counseling, therapists often judiciously use self-disclosure for a number of reasons, including minimizing the power differential, creating mutually empathic interactions, and normalizing a client's struggle or dilemma. In Wenzhu's case, once rapport, trust, and credibility were established, a feminist therapist might disclose something about similar experiences regarding geographic dislocation, experiences of racism or sexism, or developmental struggles. This can have the effect of minimizing the power dynamic inherent in the counseling relationship, in which the counselor or psychologist is often seen as an objective, all-knowing expert. It allows clients to experience the therapist as another human being who may better understand the situation, having already gone through a similar experience. The powerful relational dynamic inherent in this type of self-disclosure is highlighted in Wenzhu's story when she meets with the Chinese scholar.

A feminist therapist is also likely to self-disclose about the personal impact the client has had on the therapist. Providing feedback to the client allows the development of the relationship to grow as the therapist and client mutually experience and interact with the story as it unfolds. Self-disclosure may also be used to normalize the client's problems by using the therapist's own experiences or drawing on the stories of other women who have gone through a similar experience. For example, Wenzhu's therapist might share information with Wenzhu regarding other international students from China who have come for counseling and who have also experienced periods of alienation, homesickness, and feelings of sadness. This type of disclosure is a powerful way of normalizing and validating a client's experience and contextualizing it within a broader context. It often provides an opportunity to demonstrate a more specific insider understanding of issues related to diverse group memberships and social locations of clients.

Strength-Based Counseling

A third issue often associated with feminist counseling is the focus on strengths and resiliency and less emphasis on individual psychopathology and labeling. The counselor is acutely aware of and notices particular aspects of the client's story that may hide the person's strengths. For example, Wenzhu may have discussed how alienated and sad she felt during the initial transition to university. She may have spoken of depressive symptoms, including difficulty sleeping, inability to concentrate, and finding herself crying. A feminist therapist would assess for depression but may conceptualize it differently than therapies based primarily on a medical model. After ensuring that no medical condition was causing the depressive symptoms, her therapist may validate the alienation by suggesting that it is a very normal reaction to a rather unusual and unique experience. Furthermore, exploring how she has typically adjusted to and responded to change may be a helpful area of examination. Acknowledging that cultural transitions typically take considerable time and energy often provides space for clients to reflect on their own and others' expectations.

Recognition of the internal resources (e.g., courage, determination) and coping strategies (e.g., joining a Chinese club, making continued attempts to connect with others) that Wenzhu used to help herself through the difficult periods would also be an important part of the therapy. The psychologist would reflect back Wenzhu's strengths as they became evident, reframe situations from a different perspective, normalize experiences that were confusing, and provide feedback about recurring patterns.

Advocacy

Finally, many feminist psychologists engage in politically oriented action in their agencies and communities with the goal of eradicating sexism, racism, and classism. This may take the form of multiple levels of advocacy. For example, a feminist therapist might ask herself or himself, "How else can I be a helpful agent to this client?" In Wenzhu's case, the therapist might advocate with a professor on her behalf to have more time to write an exam or hand in a late assignment without penalty if she has fallen behind, or the counselor might assist her in connecting with the international student resources on campus or other cultural associations in the community. Another type of advocacy might deal with systemic issues concerning accessibility of counseling to culturally diverse students. For example, Wenzhu's therapist might have found that there were not enough support services to assist Wenzhu adequately in connecting with other students during her initial transition period. The counselor might, therefore, advocate for orientation sessions, groups, or mentoring programs that would not only meet the needs of Wenzhu but also the needs of other international students who may be experiencing a similar transitional process.

Advocacy work also raises questions about the accessibility of counseling, including the need for targeted outreach, building relationships with international students outside the counseling offices, or having diverse ethnicities and languages represented among the counseling staff. Depending on Wenzhu's language ability, she may have felt more comfortable speaking in her own language in a setting other than a traditional counseling office. In addition, advocacy may extend to the larger university community in relation to overarching policies and procedures related to international student recruitment and retention, policies on sexual and racial discrimination, and the atmosphere and attitude toward culturally diverse people throughout the university.

Conclusion

Counselors must be aware of how sociodemographic factors intersect and affect each other and of how this provides a changing constellation of privilege and oppression dependent on the broader context. Given that most traditional psychological theories are individualistic in orientation, client issues are often conceptualized as problems located inside the individual. A feminist approach, therefore, takes into account a politicized, systemic perspective that includes institutional–cultural, interpersonal, and intrapsychic levels. Although treating intrapsychic concerns is necessary and part of feminist therapy, so is effectively assessing and working with relational and cultural issues that directly and indirectly have an impact on a person's sense of well-being. An analysis of power, privilege, and oppression within and across each of these levels, therefore, becomes the foundational work for understanding how cross-cultural transitions are deeply embedded in historical, political, and social contexts.

References

Arthur, N., & McMahon, M. (2005). Multicultural career counseling: Theoretical applications of the Systems Theory Framework. *The Career Development Quarterly, 53*, 208–221.

Arredondo, P. (1999). Multicultural counseling competencies as tools to address oppression and racism. *Journal of Counseling & Development, 77*, 102–108.

Brown, L. S. (2006). Still subversive after all these years: The relevance of feminist therapy in the age of evidence-based practice. *Psychology of Women Quarterly, 30*, 15–24.

Constantine, M. G. (2002). The intersection of race, ethnicity, gender, and social class in counseling: Examining selves in cultural contexts. *Journal of Multicultural Counseling and Development, 30*, 210–215.

Croteau, J. M., Talbot, D. M., Lance, T. S., & Evans, N. J. (2002). A qualitative study of the interplay between privilege and oppression. *Journal of Multicultural Counseling and Development, 30*, 239–258.

Evans, K. M., Kincade, E. A., Marbley, A. F., & Seem, S. R. (2005). Feminism and feminist therapy: Lessons from the past and hopes for the future. *Journal of Counseling & Development, 83*, 269–277.

Freire, P. (2003). From *Pedagogy of the oppressed*. In A. Darder, M. Baltodano, & R. D. Torres (Eds.), *The critical pedagogy reader* (pp. 57–68). New York: RoutledgeFalmer.

Hsiung, P. C., & Wong, W. L. R. (1998). Jie Gui—Connecting the tracks: Chinese women's activism surrounding the 1995 World Conference on Women in Beijing. *Gender & History, 10*, 470–497.

Miller, J. B., & Stiver, I. P. (1997). *The healing connection: How women form relationships in therapy and in life*. Boston: Beacon Press.

Popadiuk, N. E. (2002). *The lives of women international students in difficult intimate relationships: Personal stories and sociocultural perspectives*. Unpublished dissertation, University of Calgary, Alberta, Canada.

Popadiuk, N. E., & Arthur, N. (2004). Counselling international students in Canadian schools. *International Journal for the Advancement of Counselling, 26,* 125–145.

Poyrazali, S., Kavanaugh, P. R., Baker, A., & Al-Timimi, N. (2004). Social support and demographic correlates of acculturative stress in international students. *Journal of College Counseling, 7,* 73–82.

Prilleltensky, I., & Fox, D. (1997). Introducing critical psychology: Values, assumptions, and the status quo. In D. Fox & I. Prilleltensky (Eds.), *Critical psychology: An introduction* (pp. 3–20). Thousand Oaks, CA: Sage.

Reynolds, A. L., & Constantine, M. G. (2004). Feminism and multiculturalism: Parallels and Intersections. *Journal of Multicultural Counseling and Development, 32,* 346–357.

Tang, W., & Parish, W. L. (2000). *Chinese urban life under reform.* New York: Cambridge University Press.

Tsang, A. K. T., Bogo, M., & George, U. (2003). Critical issues in cross-cultural counseling research: Case example of an ongoing project. *Journal of Multicultural Counseling and Development, 31,* 63–78.

Walker, M. (2004). How relationships heal. In M. Walker & W. B. Rosen (Eds.), *How connections heal: Stories from relational-cultural therapy* (pp. 3–21). New York: Guilford Press.

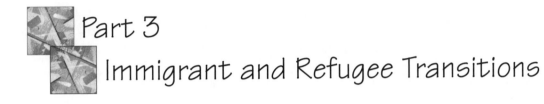

Part 3
Immigrant and Refugee Transitions

Counseling for Transition Trauma and Health Concerns

Marianne C. Kastrup and Armando Báez-Ramos

This case incident develops in the heart of the immigrant neighborhood in Copenhagen and the psychiatric department of the University Hospital in Copenhagen, Denmark. To protect the identity of our client, we call her Y.

Y. is a young woman in her 20s. Her parents moved from a Middle Eastern country to Denmark about 20 years ago, when Y. was 4 years old. They wanted better opportunities for themselves and their children. Although integration into the new country has only been partial because Y.´s parents still do not speak Danish, they have developed a good, industrious life running a company. All the children help in the little business in addition to their school obligations. The family is Muslim, and the parents follow the traditional religious rituals of their original culture.

Y.´s public education in the Danish school system has introduced her to new values, norms, and habits. She respects the family religion, although she is not very religious herself. Y.´s vision of the future is based on acquiring a higher education, earning her own money, and having the chance to travel regularly as part of her job. She experiences no conflicts in following the rules of the family and at the same time working in a Danish environment. Y. speaks her mother tongue and Danish, English, and German. On the other hand, Y.´s family hopes that Y. will marry fairly soon, have children, and dedicate her life to the care of the family, just as her mother has done.

Y.´s mother came to Denmark as part of an immigration process that accepted "guest workers" coming to Northern Europe. She was able to speak and read only her native language and was exposed, according to Y., to a series of frustrating experiences, with the result that she ended up taking care of her family in a non-European fashion, which resulted in social isolation, lack of acquisition of the Danish language, and social sedimentation.

Considering our client's case, we find that there are several common issues related to this type of international transition. First, the motivation for the migration was based on the search for better economical, social, and environmental opportunities. It was a voluntary migration with no premigration traumatic experiences.

The second issue is the adaptation process in the new environment, not only in terms of speaking the language and adapting to new social structures and social codes but also in terms of not wanting to abandon the traditions of the homeland and not showing flexibility to new cultural patterns (i.e., cultural misencounters that lead to social defeat).

Third is the issue of the intergenerational conflicts that arise as a natural process of becoming exposed, as a second-generation immigrant, to the new set of values in the host country (e.g., the conflictive split between home values and the host country's values, opportunities versus obligations).

Key Issues

Y.'s contact with the psychiatric system started while she was trying to complete her high school education. She was having problems with her performance in exams 2 years before referral to treatment. She was admitted to a general psychiatric department with suicidal intentions after an overdose of the drug paracethamol. She was diagnosed with an adaptive reaction and discharged a few days later with the recommendation to seek further help through her general practitioner. The approach was for her to take responsibility herself to seek help, but the consequences of doing so could be the loss of her family's support (Okasha, 2000).

A few days later, Y. had her first episode of self-mutilation, making incisions in her arms with tiny pieces of glass in order to relieve what she described as "psychic pain." She was again admitted to the psychiatric department, this time to a secure ward with continuous observation because of her active parasuicidal behavior.

This time, the diagnosis was described as a psychotic condition, and the client received a second-generation antipsychotic and a selective serotonin reuptake inhibitor antidepressant. The psychiatrist in charge suggested that Y. move from home in order to improve. She was shocked by this suggestion, and when discharged 2 weeks later, she decided not to follow the recommended medication, arguing later that her parents did not expect her to do so.

Y. returned home to her family, and she started working in the family business again but felt that she needed to continue her studies in order to attain some independence from her father's sphere of control.

As mentioned, Y. has been raised in a traditional Muslim family, but she also has been exposed to conventional Danish values during her schooling. Y. feels a strong attachment to her parents' religion and culture (e.g., traditional nuclear family, marriage with a person from the same culture, gender roles with the woman taking care of the family while the man is the economic provider); however, Y. has always wanted a professional career. Her father has opposed this idea strongly, and this issue leads to constant discussions that, as a rule, end with Y.'s self-destructive behavior.

We met Y. after one of these discussions, which had resulted in a new admission to the psychiatric hospital after a suicide attempt. Y. had cut her arms with fine lines in order to "punish myself because I'm not good enough for my parents. I'm stupid because I'm not finishing my high school studies." Y. believed that she did not deserve to live. While admitted to the psychiatric ward for the second time, Y. was again started on medication. Furthermore, a psychotherapeutic process oriented toward mindfulness and development of coping strategies against suicidal thoughts and impulses was begun. The admission lasted 6 weeks, with follow-up by the second author of this case incident to monitor the psychopharmacologic treatment and continue psychotherapy.

Relationship Considerations

Because Y.'s father had been resistant to Y.'s taking medication on previous occasions, the client and we decided to invite the family to an informational consultation, which was accepted by all in the family. Because of languages barriers, we used an interpreter. In this session, the consultant psychiatrist decided to open a discussion as part of a psychoeducational process in order to obtain support from the family, because Y.'s abandonment of the pharmacological treatment had previously led to relapse and suicidal behavior.

We recognized that the family had other points of view regarding the alleviation of the client's symptoms, for example, that Y. must marry and have children in order to solve her psychic problems, but we were attempting to find a "common place" in which the therapeutic process could continue.

After this session, the client knew that her family accepted our interventions, and we had demonstrated that we were open to the family's perspectives regarding her future life.

Transition Outcomes

After 2 years of continuous psychotherapy, Y. has finished her high school with satisfactory results. During a critical period, Y. was inclined to destructive behavior, in which she, for example, threw objects around her bedroom. At present, she continues in group therapy and has decided to move to another European city for a while, with the intention of improving her language skills.

Critical Incident

The turning point in the case is related to the change in approach with respect to the treatment offered to Y. When the attitude by the psychiatric personnel changed and a greater emphasis was put on integrating the values and norms of Y.'s family and including the family members in the therapeutic process, the family—and of particular importance the father—reacted positively. An opening took place, and the family accepted participating in a psychoeducational process, the result of which was reflected in the outcome of the therapeutic intervention generally.

Writers' Role

We were involved in the client's diagnostic and therapeutic process, and the second author participated in the clinical discussions of Y.´s case when she was admitted for the first time to the psychiatric department and has been the treating psychotherapist.

Comments

Cultural competence may be defined in several ways and it comprises many aspects (Tseng, 2003). We have learned that the sympathetic and seemingly empathic comment from the first psychiatrist who saw Y. was not accepted well because of a lack of intercultural sensitivity. Moving away from home as a way to solve Y.'s intrapsychic conflicts was a shock both to the client and, mainly, to her family.

We have also learned that direct communication using a psychoeducational approach with the client and the relatives who are involved in the critical incident can be carried out regardless of the underlying explanation of the pathological processes (in the present case, the family's understanding of Y.´s disorder as "a thing you can cure with having kids, getting married, and so on"). We attribute the good outcome in this case to finding the common place, in which the client's cultural background is intertwined with the medical/therapeutic approach.

This case incident also reveals how important it is not only to focus on the psychopathological aspects of the client—recognizing how essential they may be—but also to pay due respect to the cultural norms and values of the client. This is much in line with what has been emphasized by Helman (2001) and Kleinman (1988), for example. In order to increase the competence of staff working with such populations, it is recommended that practical guidelines be developed (e.g., Bhugra & Bhui, 2001; Tseng, 2003).

Reader Reflection Questions

1. How would you explore whether Y. has experienced conflicts in following the rules of the family—despite her saying that she has not?
2. Do you think that the adaptation process of the family was successful?
3. What could the first psychiatrist have done differently in the initial contact Y. had with mental health services?
4. Could the educational system have done something to anticipate the intergenerational conflicts and prevented them?
5. Was the follow-up—when Y. was discharged with the recommendation that she seek further help via her general practitioner—adequate?
6. How can psychoeducational programs for migrants be established?

References

Bhugra, D., & Bhui, K. (2001). *Cross-cultural psychiatry. A practical guide.* London: Arnold.

Helman, C. G. (2001). *Culture, health and illness.* London: Arnold.

Kleinman, A. (1988). *Rethinking psychiatry: From cultural category to personal experience.* New York: Free Press.

Okasha, A. (2000). The impact of Arab culture on psychiatric ethics. In A. Okasha, J. Arboleda-Floréz, & N. Sartorius (Eds.), *Ethics, culture and psychiatry* (pp. 15–21). Washington, DC: American Psychiatric Press.

Tseng W. S. (2003). *Clinician's guide to cultural psychiatry.* San Diego, CA: Academic Press.

Response 1

Roy Moodley, Dina B. Lubin, and Saadia Akram

The case vignette of client Y. offers clinicians an excellent example of the kinds of conflicts and tensions that second-generation immigrant clients experience. It also offers counselors an opportunity to explore critically the intersections between culture and therapy, particularly in Islamic culture. In the past, there has been a paucity of research and publication regarding Muslim clients in therapy, but since the events of September 11, 2001, there has been a growing interest in this client group (see Husain, 1998; Inayat, 2002, 2005); therefore, it is critical to explore the case study of Y., a 20-year-old Muslim woman of Middle Eastern origin living in Copenhagen, to uncover and analyze the clinical and cultural intersections.

Y.'s narrative seems to reflect the deep inner tensions and anxieties of living as a second-generation immigrant in the West. For example, as a nonpracticing Muslim, Y. was still expected to acquiesce to certain religious and cultural norms regarding dress codes, family life, marriage, and career development, while at the same time she had a great desire to be autonomous, follow an individual career path, and pursue goals in which she believed. These aspirations included higher education, earning an income, and having opportunities to travel and experience the world. This presented a paradox: She felt a strong sense of obligation and deference to her parents who held more traditional views while at the same time she wanted to be free to follow her own path. Although she respected her family's views, she struggled with accommodating them yet yearning to satisfy her desire for self-fulfillment and personal development. On the other hand, Y.'s parents believed that her aspirations were the source of her psychological problems and that the solution was for Y. to marry, settle down, and have a more "traditional" life.

In this response, we consider Y.'s narrative, which appears to be intertwined with a number of psychosocial, cultural, and religious constructs. We examine how these factors came to influence and shape Y.'s subjectivity and, consequently, her psychological difficulties. We discuss and analyze the process of therapy that Y. undertook. This is followed by a discussion on the incorporation of family and community values into counseling and psychotherapy. Finally, we attempt a broader consideration of the use of multicultural counseling competencies in working with such a client. The key to a creative, meaningful, ethical, and "human rights" process of therapy with Y. is to be aware of not forcing the client to fit into a single ethnic or gender classification, which could easily lead to stereotyping and oppression in the therapy.

Unique Influences on the Client

In considering Y.'s narrative, it is paramount to consider a number of critical variables that may have influenced and shaped Y.'s subjectivity, her sense of self, and her worldview. Among these variables are the critical role of Islamic culture, the Muslim religion, immigration and life experiences in Denmark, her relationship with her family, and the family's valuation of counseling and psychotherapy. We begin by suggesting that there is a great emphasis in traditional Muslim families on keeping their affairs and conflicts private (Ali, Liu, & Humedian, 2004), which to a large extent colors how Y. and her family will see counseling and psychotherapy.

It also seems important to understand the complex ways in which the variables of Islamic culture and religion and immigration and acculturation collectively interact to establish and reinforce particular types of values that may or may not be consistent with the client's own needs and aspirations. The interdependence and interconnectedness between culture, religion, community, and family are emphasized from childhood and throughout an individual's life in the Muslim culture. Whereas in Western society the emphasis is typically on self-autonomy, independence, and individuation (Levy-Warren, 1996), in many non-Western cultures, by contrast, self is defined in relation to others rather than independently of others (Yeh, Hunter, Madan-Bahel, Chiang, & Arora, 2004). Consequently, individuals work together toward maintaining a collective way of life (Triandis, 1995). There appears to be no direct evidence that Y.'s family maintained this traditional view in the strictest sense of the word, although authoritative parenting styles are more privileged in some Muslim cultures that emphasize obedience and adherence to behavioral patterns that advance the harmony of the collective (Dwairy & Achoui, 2006) than they are in other cultures. This sense of collectivity is reflected through people's sacrifice of their own needs in favor of the needs of family and others, such as seen in the system of Zakat and Qurbani (see The Quran).[1] In Islam, the concepts of Zakat and Qurbani, which encourage Islam's followers to make sacrifices in the name of God for the welfare and betterment of others, are highly emphasized. Zakat is one of the five main pillars of the Islamic religion. It is obligatory for every adult Muslim to give away 2.5% of his or her savings each year to poor people (as charity). It is not easy to follow this obligation and make financial sacrifices, but as Muslims, they must sacrifice and put other people's financial needs first.

The literal meaning of Qurbani is "to make a sacrifice" and, in the religious sense, to make a sacrifice in the name of God. According to history, when God sent a message to the Prophet Ibrahim (peace be upon him) to sacrifice his son in the name of God, he discussed God's message with his son, the Prophet Ismail (peace be upon him), and he became ready for this sacrifice. At the time of the sacrifice, God substituted an animal for the Prophet Ismail. It is not easy to sacrifice one's son, or to be ready to be sacrificed in the name of God. Actually, God tested them through this sacrifice/Qurbani. Muslims sacrifice an animal when they go for Haj and also for Eid-ul-Izha. Zakat and Qurbani are examples of giving God's order top priority and making sacrifices of loved ones and finances in the name of God.

---

[1]For a discussion on Zakat, see The Quran (Al-Bakra, 2: 43 & 83) and for Qurbani (Al Bakra, 2: 196; Al Hajj, 22: 34 & 36).

In many Islamic cultures, the concepts of Zakat and Qurbani place great emphasis on individual self-sacrifice for the group's collective benefit. In Y.'s case, she may not have been strictly raised to sacrifice her own needs in relation to the family, such as in the system of Zakat (The Holy Quran, Al-Bakra, 2: 43 & 83) and Qurbani (The Holy Quran, Al Bakra, 2: 196 and Al Hajj, 22: 34 & 36).

Y. had great aspirations to become not only financially independent but to find meaning in her life *beyond* meeting the expectations of her family, the community, and the collectivity. It was important for her to feel that she had attained a certain level of personal success as a professional modern woman, without having to depend on a husband to support her. She wanted to be able to identify herself as a working woman who was respected for her achievements. Her parents, however, seemed to be more allied with the traditional Muslim views that women are supposed to marry, have children, and spend their life completely devoted to the demands of their family. In many cultures, marriage is considered a reasonable solution to mental health issues (a culturally acceptable way to fulfill sexual needs; see Kakar, 1981). Gender roles appear to be clearly defined, and to stray from these roles can be seen as a sign of disrespect. It seems that Y. may have felt an enormous sense of pressure to "settle down." Her relationship and closeness with her own ethnic group (especially when living in a highly concentrated immigrant area) may have directly or indirectly influenced her current situation. This position may also have been strengthened by the challenges that the family faced in their immigration and acculturation process within Danish culture (see Berry, 1997). The degree of satisfaction they experienced from their relocation and the extent to which they may have (or may not have) felt successful in attaining their goals for migration (for example, to find better economical, social, or environmental opportunities) are both significant areas that could have influenced the way Y. experienced and understood her life in Denmark.

Therapy With Y.: Culture Infused or Culture Confused?

Therapy with Y. was conducted in a conventional Eurocentric approach and, to some extent, was focused on criteria in the *Diagnostic and Statistical Manual of Mental Disorders* (4th ed., text rev.; American Psychiatric Association, 2000), but the therapy attempted to be culturally sensitive. In this section of the response, we consider Y.'s therapy and ask the question, Was the therapy culture-infused counseling (see Arthur & Collins, 2005) or culture-confused counseling? Y. was diagnosed as having depression, accompanied by self-harm behaviors and suicidal ideations. Intergenerational conflict, accompanied by adjustment difficulties, was also a focus of the treatment. Y.'s failure to succeed academically was also noted as a significant contributor to her poor mental health. On the one hand, these features of diagnosis are clear and evident in Y.'s behaviors and responses, but seen from a multicultural and diversity perspective, this analysis could have been more inclusive of the complexities surrounding culture, ethnicity, race, and psychopathology. For example, knowing that suicide is strictly forbidden according to the Islam faith and is seen as a criminal act (Hedayat-Diba, 2000) would have offered the therapist other ways of interpreting Y.'s narrative. Also, knowing that, in Muslim communities, a strong social network of support is offered to members of the community to cope with mental health issues such as depression would have offered alternative treatment strategies. Clinicians could, for example, recognize the meaningfulness of the family and community support for these clients (Loewenthal, Cinnirella, Evdoka, & Murphy, 2001) and acknowledge this in therapy, which may bring to the surface some of the hidden dimensions of family life. For example, in Y.'s case, her parents did not believe that it was in her best interest to move out of the family home, in contrast to what was suggested to Y. by one of her clinicians (who felt that autonomy from her family would be the best solution). This set up much resistance in the family and may have led to Y.'s further depressive episodes. Understanding the role of the family, as well as migration and settlement issues, religiosity, socioeconomic status, attitude to counseling, and traditional healing methods, is key to assessment, diagnosis, and therapy outcomes.

In Y.'s case, it seems evident that the process was dependent on the Eurocentric approaches of psychotherapy, which privileges individuality over collectivity. This would have led to conscious and unconscious tensions and resistances in therapy. Although it seems important to contextualize the client in her or his family culture and ethnicity, the client's own personal and unique experience can at times become the most important aspect of counseling and psychotherapy. It is critical to contextualize clients within their cultures, while at the same time recognizing individual differences (see also Pedersen, 2001).

In Muslim societies, there is a strong emphasis placed on carrying on family traditions and upholding family and religious values. Respect for one's parents and deference to them are encouraged repeatedly in The Quran (Ali et al., 2004). This deference is typically maintained throughout the life span. According to Al-Krenawi and Graham (2000), Muslims have a collectivist identity, in which the centrality of family, extended family, and community help to define the self. They also suggested that the social structure of Muslim families is male dominant (see, also, Abudabbeh & Aseel, 1999). In the incident, we learn that Y.'s father was quite adamant that he did not believe that his daughter should consider the use of pharmacotherapy for her depressive symptoms. This did not appear to be questioned by Y. or anyone else in the family, in spite of the fact that her depression had resulted in suicidal actions in the past when she abandoned her medication regimen. This suggests the extremely powerful nature of parental influence, particularly that of the father.

Understanding Y.'s parents' migration, acculturation, and adaptation process is critical to formulating a treatment plan for Y. The sociopolitical environment and belonging to a minority group in Denmark may have also contributed to her psychological difficulties.[2] Their experiences of settling in Danish society, their perception of feeling included or excluded, and their own conflicts need to be considered. This focus also needs to take into account the role of religion in the way that Y.'s parents negotiated their integration into Danish society. The case describes Y. as being nonreligious. It is important to ask who it is that defines her level of religiosity. Is it Y. herself, or is it the mental health professionals who have been involved in her care? Although she might not practice religious rituals regularly or in any formal way, she may still hold the religion in high regard and be in agreement with the religious values associated with Islam. Being sensitive to the complex and myriad ways in which clients attend to their religious and spiritual needs is important in counseling and psychotherapy. Offering the possibility for clients to share these views is extremely important because their subjective experience of their religion and its practices and the unique way in which they connect to their religion or sense of spirituality are important to acknowledge (see Fukumaya & Sevig, 1999).

Incorporating Family and Community Values Into Therapy

Much has been written on the centrality of family in the Muslim cultures, and interventions very often need to be couched in the context of family, extended family, and community

---

[2]Denmark has been reflecting a wave of anti-Islamic sentiments surfacing in what is now known as the Cartoon incident (published drawings of the prophet Muhammed [peace be upon him] in the private newspaper, *Jyllands Posten*) that became an international incident. The prime minister of Denmark spoke in January of 2006 about his commitment to condemn any expression or action that attempts to demonize groups of people on the basis of their religion or ethnic background. In February of 2006, the prime minister and the minister of foreign affairs held a meeting with the ambassadors to Denmark. In this meeting, information was disseminated regarding international reactions to the published drawings of the prophet Muhammed (peace be upon him) in the private newspaper *Jyllands Posten* (Factsheet Denmark, 2006).

(Al-Krenawi & Graham, 2000). Within the culture, family identity takes center stage, and the individual remains embedded in the collective identity (Hofstede, 1986). An individual's life is dominated by family and family relationships (Dwairy, 1998). In Y.'s therapy, the strategy of bringing the family together was a critical part of the therapeutic outcome. This may have offered Y. an opportunity to discuss concerns, specifically regarding her conflict and the ways that the family can support her. Moreover, it is also an opportunity for Y. to communicate her needs in a safe setting, in the presence of a professional who can facilitate this exchange. When family members are brought into treatment, it should be emphasized to them that their input is integral to the success of the client's treatment.

Another issue to consider is the cross-cultural dynamics between the therapist and the family members, both in the treatment planning as well as in the therapy process. The regulation and management of cultural empathy are critical to maintain the level of compassion and connectedness to the family group. According to Ridley and Lingle (1996), this involves a clinician's ability to understand a client's unique self-experience and respond in a way that conveys this understanding of the client's experiences. At the same time, the therapist needs to be sensitive to the family and the community values that may be contradictory to his or her own views. In Y.'s case, the clinician had initially suggested that she move out of her family's home in order to improve her mental health; however, this suggestion was quickly rejected by both Y. and her parents, who did not view this as an option at the time. The clinician would have demonstrated greater cultural empathy had she or he recognized that although Y. was the identified client, the family played a pivotal role in her therapy on many levels, in a sense making them clients as well. Without family cooperation, any intervention would have been minimally effective. Because the parents' influence was so embedded in her, it would have been a mistake to ignore the weight that they carried in regard to Y.'s processing and ultimate resolution of her emotional conflicts.

It must be clear that Muslim clients—particularly when families are involved—must be assured and reassured that their disclosures will be held with the utmost respect and confidentiality. Because they tend to be very private about family matters, they may need to be reminded at various points that confidentiality remains a priority in order for them to feel safe in therapy. If the family cannot establish trust with the practitioner, then the therapeutic process is likely to suffer. It is also especially important to take the time to answer any questions that family members may have about the therapeutic process and explain it to them in such a way that it becomes somewhat demystified, because therapy is typically looked on with suspicion. This stigma around mental health treatment needs to be acknowledged and explored so that the clinician gains a better sense of the family's attitude toward accepting professional help (Al-Issa, 2000; Haque-Khan, 1997). If alternative healing practices are part of the family repertoire of healing, then that should be acknowledged and discussed. Some Muslim families consult their own cultural and traditional healing practitioners in addition to the Western therapist (Moodley & West, 2005).

Finding a "Common Place"

The meeting point between the client, the counselor, and the therapist's and client's culture can form a particular space—a "third space" or a hybrid space—that is, an overlap of the intersecting possibilities of healing in which the margins become the center and where the client can be free of her or his own origins and myths (see Moodley, 2007, for a detailed discussion). This third space acts as a transitional space within which the client and the therapist are in a dynamic relationship—a relationship of therapeutic intimacy and transformation.

This relationship is continuously being created through therapy to provide an empowering place for the client to engage in therapy nonoppressively. McWhirter (1997) developed a model for empowerment of the client in therapy that is said to be useful with Muslim clients (see Ali et al., 2004). The model integrates five elements (collaboration, context, critical consciousness, competence, and community) to facilitate empowerment of the client. Indeed, for the therapist, self-awareness, clinical competence, and culture-infused counseling skills are essential components in establishing an empathic and compassionate relationship so that the five elements can be negotiated as part of the third space. The third space also allows the multiple cultural variables of the big five or big seven sociocultural variables (gender, race, class, sexual orientations, disability, religion, and age; Moodley & Lubin, in press) to be explored. Indeed many of these cultural variables have been largely unexplored with Y., for example, the extent to which Y.'s age might have influenced the onset of her psychiatric symptoms. The 20s are a time of transition into adulthood that encompasses an expectation of greater responsibility and the ability to make decisions about dating/marriage, housing, higher education, and employment. Sexual orientation was another psychosocial variable that was not explored. Perhaps if Y. is struggling with her sexuality, she might feel unable to articulate this because it would be too shameful, therefore causing her to repress it or even punish herself for it through her self-mutilating actions. Moreover, we must wonder whether Y.'s family would accept her if she were to outwardly identify as lesbian, transgendered, or bisexual. In addition, there was no mention of Y.'s sense of her socioeconomic class. Understanding class, in particular in relation to her cohorts, may have offered some insight into whether she may have felt "different" from others or socially isolated. According to Smith (2005), "unexamined classist assumptions constitute a significant obstacle for practitioners" (p. 687). If religion was discussed more consciously as part of the counseling, it may have offered Y. an opportunity to understand that The Quran offered much guidance regarding her educational aspirations (see The Quran: Al-Alaq, 96: 1; Taha, 20:114). According to the Prophet Muhammed (peace be upon him), "whoever goes out in search of knowledge is on the path of Allah until returning" (Khan, 2000, p. 8). This passage and others would have helped Y. understand that there was less contradiction in the way she lived her life than she perhaps thought. It has long been known that many Muslims believe that reciting holy verses from The Quran can empower people and help them overcome negative impulses or help them find the answers to specific questions or crises in their lives (Armstrong, 2000).

Conclusion

Cross-cultural counseling and psychotherapy cannot be undertaken in a vacuum. As Chantler (2005) said, "Therapy cannot be extricated from social, cultural, and political practices, so engagement with context is vital to counseling minoritised and subordinated groups" (p. 253). For example, in attempting to treat Y. for depression and suicide ideation, it is critical that the social, cultural, religious, and political variables are addressed. The key to a successful therapy with Y. is an emic/etic philosophy that is embedded in the concept of culture-infused counseling. Through this process, the client's culture and ethnicity are not just reified and celebrated but critically understood in the context of the presenting issues and the solutions that are being sought. What is not expected, however, is for the therapist to become an expert on the client's culture; however, at the very least, therapists need to have a basic appreciation for, and an acceptance of, some of the important tenets of Islamic culture and Muslim religious practices, about which most Muslim clients will share information easily and readily in a trusting relationship.

References

Abudabbeh, N., & Aseel, H. (1999). Transcultural counseling and Arab Americans. In J. McFadden (Ed.), *Transcultural counseling* (2nd ed., pp. 283–296). Alexandria, VA: American Counseling Association.

Ali, S. R., Liu, W. M., & Humedian, M. (2004). Islam 101: Understanding the religion and therapy implications. *Professional Psychology: Research and Practice, 35,* 635–642.

Al-Issa, I. (2000). *Al-Junun: Mental illness in the Islamic world.* Madison, CT: International Universities Press.

Al-Krenawi, A., & Graham, J. (2000). Culturally sensitive social work practice with Arab clients in mental health settings. *Health and Social Work, 25*(5), 9–23.

American Psychiatric Association. (2000). *Diagnostic and statistical manual of mental disorders* (4th ed., text rev.). Washington, DC: Author.

Armstrong, K. (2000). *Islam: A short history.* New York: Random House.

Arthur, N., & Collins, A. (2005). *Culture-infused counselling: Celebrating the Canadian mosaic.* Calgary, Alberta, Canada: Counselling Concepts.

Berry, J. (1997). Immigration, acculturation, and adaptation. *Applied Psychology: An International Review, 46,* 5–68.

Chantler, K. (2005). From disconnection to connection: "Race," gender and the politics of therapy. *British Journal of Guidance & Counselling, 33,* 239–256.

Dwairy, M. A. (1998). *Cross-cultural counseling: The Arab Palestinian case.* New York: Haworth.

Dwairy, M. A., & Achoui, M. (2006). Introduction to three cross-regional research studies on parenting styles, individuation, and mental health in Arab societies. *Journal of Cross-Cultural Psychology, 37,* 221–229.

Factsheet Denmark. (2006) Retrieved September 28, 2006, from http://www.globalisering.dk/multimedia/Globalisering1.pdf#search=%22factsheet%20denmark%22

Fukuyama, M., & Sevig, T. D. (1999). *Integrating spirituality into multicultural counseling.* Thousand Oaks, CA: Sage.

Haque-Khan, A. (1997). Muslim women's voices: Generation, acculturation, and faith in the perceptions of mental health and psychological help. *Dissertation Abstracts International, 58*(05), 2676B.

Hedayat-Diba, Z. (2000). Psychotherapy with Muslims. In P. S. Richards & A. E. Bergin (Eds.), *Handbook of psychotherapy and religious diversity* (pp. 289–314). Washington, DC: American Psychological Association.

Hofstede, G. (1986). Cultural differences in teaching and learning. *International Journal of Intercultural Relations, 10,* 310–320.

Husain, S. A. (1998). Religion and mental health from the Muslim perspective. In H. G. Koenig (Ed.), *Handbook of religion and mental health* (pp. 279–290). London: Academic Press.

Inayat, Q. (2002). The meaning of being a Muslim: An aftermath of the Twin Towers episode. *Counselling Psychology Quarterly, 15,* 351–358.

Inayat, Q. (2005). Islam, divinity and spiritual healing. In R. Moodley & W. West (Eds.), *Integrating traditional healing practices into counseling and psychotherapy* (pp. 159–169). Thousand Oaks, CA: Sage.

Kakar, S. (1981). *The inner world: A psycho-analytic study of childhood and society in India* (2nd ed.). Delhi, India: Oxford University Press.

Khan, S. (2000). *Tell me about the Prophet Muhammad.* New Delhi, India: Goodword Books.

Levy-Warren, M. (1996). *The adolescent journey: Development, identity formation, and psychotherapy.* London: Aronson.

Loewenthal, K. M., Cinnirella, M., Evdoka, G., & Murphy, P. (2001). Faith conquers all? Beliefs about the role of religious factors in coping with depression among different cultural groups in the U.K. *British Journal of Medical Psychology, 74,* 293–303.

McWhirter, E. H. (1997). Empowerment, social activism, and counseling. *Counseling and Human Development, 29,* 1–14.

Moodley, R. (2007). (Re)placing multiculturalism in counselling and psychotherapy. *British Journal of Guidance and Counselling, 35,* 1–22.

Moodley, R., & Lubin, D. B. (in press). Developing your career to working with diversity. In S. Palmer & R. Bor (Eds.), *The practitioner's handbook.* London: Sage.

Moodley, R., & West, W. (2005). *Integrating traditional healing practices into counseling and psychotherapy*. Thousand Oaks, CA: Sage.

Pedersen, P. (2001). Multiculturalism and the paradigm shift in counselling: Controversies and alternative futures. *Canadian Journal of Counselling, 35*, 15–25.

Ridley, C. R., & Lingle, D. W. (1996). Cultural empathy in multicultural counseling: A multidimensional process model. In P. B. Pedersen, J. G. Draguns, W. J. Lonner, & J. E. Trimble (Eds.), *Counseling across cultures* (4th ed., pp. 21–46). Thousand Oaks, CA: Sage.

Smith, L. (2005), Psychotherapy, classism, and the poor: Conspicuous by the absence. *American Psychologist, 60*, 687–696.

Triandis, H. C. (1995). *Individualism and collectivism*. Boulder, CO: Westview.

Yeh, C. J., Hunter, C. D., Madan-Bahel, A., Chiang, L., & Arora, A. K. (2004). Indigenous and independent perspectives of healing: Implications for counseling and research. *Journal of Counseling & Development, 82*, 410–419.

Response 2

Monica Justin

Y.'s history presents a client's personal story of immigration. The case incident touches on several issues related to cross-cultural transitions, acculturation experiences, bicultural identity development, and emergent cultural values conflicts faced by Y. and her extended family unit. Although there are several unique elements to Y.'s case, many aspects of her story can be contextualized within a cross-cultural framework.

As outlined in her case history, Y. is a young woman currently in her 20s. She immigrated to Denmark at the age of 4 with her family, and given her young age at the time of immigration, it can be assumed that Y. has lived a bicultural experience. Y.'s family is described as having emigrated from a Middle Eastern country, and after immigration, they continued to follow traditional Muslim rituals and practices from their culture of origin. It is therefore assumed that her upbringing and family context represent a more traditional and conservative ethnic, cultural, and gendered environment in comparison with the cultural norms that may be evident in contemporary Danish society.

Y. is described as possessing a strong ethnic identity situated within her family, cultural, and religious milieus. She is simultaneously described as possessing more contemporary values, such as a wish to pursue higher education, a desire to work, financial independence, and travel. These elements lend further support to conceptualizing Y.'s case in the context of bicultural identity issues and a differential acculturation experience relative to her parents. For example, Y.'s mother is described as "taking care of the family in a non-European fashion," and neither of her parents has acquired the Danish language. The relationship between Y. and her other siblings is not explicitly mentioned in the case history, and therefore there is no picture of the acculturation experience of other children in the family.

In addition to a range of cross-cultural issues inherent in this case, the authors of the case incident also note incidents of diagnosed depression, suicide attempts via overdose, self-mutilation tendencies, and a psychotic condition beginning during her high school years. Y.'s father and "his sphere of control" also represent an important element of the case, given the correlation between Y.'s self-destructive behavior and her father's oppositional standpoint in various interactions. As a result, Y.'s case presents several multifaceted cross-cultural and diagnostic issues that intersect and come together to define her experience as a young woman and second-generation immigrant.

Cross-Cultural Transitions

Cross-cultural transitions represent a unique and complex context vis-à-vis issues related to the development of ethnic identity. With the myriad of issues represented in Y.'s case, it becomes important to first situate her story in a cross-cultural/multicultural framework. The significance of using this framework is supported by numerous authors and scholars in the discipline of multicultural counseling (Arthur & Collins, 2005; Ponterotto, Casas, Suzuki, & Alexander, 2001; Sue & Sue, 1999, 2003). The salient themes in the literature on cross-cultural transitions, acculturation, and bicultural identity development highlight the importance of understanding an individual's experience within a larger social, cultural, and environmental context. This context incorporates a range of variables related to both primary and secondary dimensions of diversity such as gender, age, race, ethnicity, religion, and cultural values orientations (Reese & Brandt, 1997). Examining how these multiple factors intersect and present challenging crossroads relative to individual identity development can be understood as a push–pull phenomenon that occurs within the individual. This internal and invisible battle fundamentally requires an individual to assume an active decision-making stance in constructing his or her personal identity, related ethnic identity, and degree of cultural maintenance and retention (Bhabha 1990, 1994; Justin 2005). The result of navigating this personal journey, the emotional challenges, and recurring reflexive self-questioning can be expressed and externalized in a variety of ways, including exercising constructive or destructive behaviors as coping mechanisms. Furthermore, acculturation brings about additional challenges for the individual as he or she adjusts to the demands and expectations of two cultural worlds and the need to create a personal balance in walking the fine line between both worlds. This personal process can be further complicated by the absence of role models and mentors to assist in offering guidance or support through the complexities of critical self-inquiry and decision making (Akhtar, 1994; Das Gupta, 1998).

Although a variety of concepts exist in the literature to define the aforementioned experiences, many of the processes are similar and interrelated. For example, in examining the experience of acculturation and adjustment for a new immigrant, it becomes imperative to also consider emergent cultural values conflicts when the new host culture and culture of origin represent vastly different social and cultural spheres (Baptiste, 1993; Das & Kemp, 1997; Das Gupta, 1998; Dhruvarajan, 1993; Justin, 2003, 2005; Sue & Sue, 1999). It is my opinion that these issues must be examined in relationship to each other rather than as separate entities. Therefore, adhering to principles of cross-cultural counseling first requires a therapist to normalize and depathologize externalized behavior, thereby situating behavior in the context of the multiple variables that may be simultaneously influencing a client's life.

Cross-Cultural Issues

As noted previously, the issues presented in the following discussion are not separate and mutually exclusive entities, but rather interrelated issues influencing the client on a variety of levels, including personal, social, and cultural levels. The multilayered and multifaceted issues at work in Y.'s life include the following: (a) acculturation and differential acculturation levels among family members, (b) cultural values and cultural values conflicts, (c) challenges of constructing and negotiating a bicultural and hybrid identity, and (d) personal coping mechanisms.

Acculturation

Acculturation is a primary factor in situating Y.'s story, given her immigration to Denmark with her family at the age of 4 years. Immigration at a young age readily allows children to adjust more rapidly and fluidly to their new environment in terms of learning and adopting cultural and social norms and acquiring language (Baptiste, 1993; Berry, 2001). This adjustment and rapid acculturation can quickly translate to solidifying their identification with the new cultural norms in comparison to the culture of origin, in which parents and older family members may be more strongly entrenched. In addition, these scholars have presented convincing arguments supporting the numerous internal and external challenges that emerge because of the differential acculturation experiences among individual family members. Individuals immigrating at a young age, such as Y. did, often tend to adopt an integration attitude in their acculturation process. Conversely, older family members may adopt more of a separation and/or maginalization attitude in their acculturative experience because they may experience challenges in learning a second language later in life and developing social connections, and they may mourn the loss of support systems from their culture of origin. Y.'s case seems to support the arguments in the literature, because her parents appear to be more entrenched in their Middle Eastern culture and Muslim religion than Y. is, as noted by their traditional cultural practices. For example, Y.'s mother is described as "taking care of her family in a non-European manner, which resulted in social isolation, lack of acquisition of the Danish language, and social sedimentation." Baptiste also argued that the acquisition of the new culture rules of a host society and the ability to function within that society place additional demands and pressures on children because they may become the cultural liaison, mediator, and buffer in facilitating communication and interactions between the older generation and the new culture. For example, after 14 years in Denmark, Y.'s parents have not acquired proficiency in speaking Danish, whereas Y. has become proficient in speaking her native tongue, English, Danish, and German. Hence, in considering these facts, Y.'s personal rate and level of acculturation, her resulting bicultural identity, and the differential acculturation rates of other family members are important elements to explore in working with this case incident.

Cultural Values and Cultural Values Conflicts

Related to the issue of differential acculturation is the accompanying fear of cultural dilution and loss of cultural values upon immigration (Das & Kemp, 1997; Das Gupta, 1998). This fear adds to the tensions and intergeneration conflicts that can emerge in immigrant families, particularly between parents and children (Baptiste, 1993). Parents attempt to maintain the same social and cultural parameters that existed in their culture of origin. However, the dilemma that presents itself is that the same family, community, and social reinforcements that previously existed in the culture of origin are no longer available in a new culture to reinforce the desired cultural or gendered behaviors. Hence, the push–pull a child feels between two opposing cultural frameworks often results in tensions and cultural values conflicts within the family as the child attempts to integrate new cultural values and attitudes into his or her personal identity. From an acculturation and cultural values standpoint, Y. appears to be negotiating an integration attitude as she is self-described as valuing her family's cultural and religious traditions yet also seeking education, a professional career, and financial independence. This apparent clash of cultural values and gender role expectations seems to be a constant source of tension between Y. and her father.

Bicultural/Hybrid Identity

Bicultural identity (Jambunathan, Burts, & Pierce, 2000), or bienculturation or multienculturation (Ho, 1995), fundamentally refers to individuals having incorporated a plurality of cultural influences through their lived experience. As a result, the individual internalizes the overt and covert cultural messages from the different cultural contexts, which allows him or her to develop a deep personal understanding of different cultural prescriptions. Over time, individuals develop the skill of effectively navigating the demands and expectations of the two opposing cultural milieus in which they live. As a young immigrant to Denmark, it can be assumed that Y. has lived a bicultural experience. Growing up in Denmark can be seen as a vastly different cultural context from her home life and family's culture of origin in the Middle East. It is important to note that the opposing cultural value systems can present very challenging situations and demands for an individual in terms of integrating into a new host culture. Contextualizing Y.'s case through the lens of biculturalism, it seems that her ability to effectively navigate gender roles, cultural expectations, and demands of her two cultural spheres has caused instances of cultural clashes and pressures that she may not have developed adequate skills to manage. These are discussed in a later section.

Hybrid identity is a newer concept in the literature that describes the crossroads and paradoxical positioning of identity (Bhabha, 1990, 1994). It extends the notion of biculturalism because individuals are seen as possessing multiple identities, given the multiple contexts they must negotiate in their lives. This is even more evident for individuals who immigrate to a new country and culture and negotiate new roles, values, and social norms. The multiple and intersecting identities that each individual possesses often give rise to paradoxical intersections. Bhabha asserted that this constant process results in creating a third space, which displaces conventional ways of understanding identity. The creation of this third space requires individuals to develop very personal meanings and definitions of identity without the help of previous models and paradigms, simply because their personal experience defies previous conceptualizations. When this standpoint is adopted, it is possible to begin to depathologize the experience of second-generation immigrants as they navigate the contradictory and opposing cultural influences they must negotiate in constructing a congruent bicultural identity (Justin, 2003, 2005). Applying this concept to Y.'s experience normalizes the ongoing challenges she has experienced in constructing and effectively living a bicultural identity in light of the cultural demands of her family, which may be contradictory to gender expectations of Danish society.

Coping Mechanisms

Finally, it is important to consider that the process of integration into a new society is different for males and females (Dion & Dion, as cited in Arthur & Merali, 2005). These authors argued that females can be more receptive to adopting and integrating values and practices from a host culture compared with their male counterparts. Simultaneously, cultural-based gender expectations and roles placed on females can be higher, more exigent, and restrictive. The consequences of adopting new behaviors can be perceived as a transgression of cultural expectations and have dramatic consequences for some women (Arthur & Merali, 2005). For example, immigrant women often experience more psychological consequences and mental health issues (i.e., depression, anxiety, and emotional disorders) as a result of these conflicts.

Y.'s story highlights the parallels between psychological symptoms and the more dramatic cutting and self-mutilation behaviors. The emergence of these behaviors appears to be linked to Y.'s father's strong opposition to her pursuing a professional career. The parallels described by Arthur and Merali (2005) lend further support to the differential integration experience and psychological consequences for women who explore and move away from culturally prescribed roles.

Counseling and Cross-Cultural Competency

As a therapist, my counseling orientation is informed by a social constructivist, feminist, and culture-infused framework. Therefore, my initial approach with clients involves contextualizing client concerns and overlaying a multicultural competency perspective. As supported by the literature (Arthur & Collins, 2005; Sue & Sue, 2003), working effectively and competently with clients from different ethnic and cultural backgrounds requires attention to a range of personal and therapeutic issues. Literature in the discipline of multicultural counseling has consistently argued that the lack or absence of cultural sensitivity and competence expressed by a counselor often results in high attrition rates when working with culturally diverse client populations (Arthur & Collins, 2005; Sue & Sue, 1999; Sue, Zane, & Young, 1994), hence strengthening the recommendation that all therapists need to acquire and implement cultural competence in a therapeutic context.

As therapists, we are also situated in our own cultural framework. It is important for us to acknowledge this subjective framework in order to work effectively with diverse clients, because we often conceptualize well-being, functional attitudes, behavior, and decision making in light of our internalized cultural standpoint (Ho, 1995). Hence, the lens through which we view ourselves and our clients and understand pathology and dysfunctional behavior is informed by our worldview and value orientation.

Therapeutic Interventions

The experiences of any client, but particularly immigrant clients, are complex, unique, and diverse. Given the multiplicity of issues at work and resulting stressors, there are common elements that have an impact on the acculturative experience and the mental health of immigrants in a new country and culture. Examining the impact of immigration, acculturation, intergenerational conflicts, cultural values conflicts, and hybrid identity development becomes critical considerations in examining Y.'s case history.

Stigma of Counseling

Seeking counseling is a well-accepted behavior in a North American context; however, when working with clients such as Y. and her family, it is imperative to keep in mind that many cultures do not value or perceive counseling in the same way. Given the cultural norm of not disclosing information to individuals outside the family, seeking counseling may not be an immediate consideration for clients or an intervention supported by the extended family. Therefore, in working with a client like Y., it would be necessary to acknowledge the challenge counseling presents from a cultural standpoint and to demonstrate cultural sensitivity and understanding about Y.'s culture of origin. Operating from this perspective would demonstrate an openness to working from a cultural perspective and minimize the risk of attrition that continues to be cited as a common reason for ethnic clients dropping out of therapy (Ponterotto et al., 2001; Sue & Sue, 2003).

Contextualizing Issues

A conceptual shift is required when working with second- and later generation clients such as Y. First, it is necessary to understand that cultural adaptation is not a one-time process but rather an ongoing process that continues to be negotiated over the course of an individual's life. Furthermore, values and behavioral acculturation are two separate phenomena at work in the lives of most immigrants. For example, assuming that because Y. has grown up in Danish society, she has been completely acculturated would be a misassumption. On a behavioral level, she may appear acculturated in terms of her social mannerisms and academic and career goals; however, on a values level, she continues to ascribe to numerous cultural values from her family's culture of origin (e.g., family, marriage, religion).

Second, understanding that individuals such as Y. face numerous and complex issues in defining their place, role, and identity in a new culture and within their families requires constant self-questioning and active decision making. The constant negotiation of cultural demands (both inside and outside the home) and the juggling act that is required to create a livable balance between two cultural spheres are demanding. Therefore, understanding Y. as an active agent in her life who is attempting to exercise personal authority normalizes her behavior and does not exclusively frame her behavior as pathological. This stance also actively contributes to creating a trusting working alliance in which a client does not feel judged.

The coping mechanisms that Y. is using may be seen as self-destructive (i.e., cutting behavior and suicidal ideation); however, they can also be understood as a lack of internal coping resources and skills in the face of high internal and external stressors (James, 1994; Levenkron, 1998). Framing her decision making and behavior in this manner offers a culturally sensitive diagnostic lens. It is important to note that a cultural framework should not be used to minimize the importance of promptly intervening with a client, nor can it be used to normalize all behaviors. Nonetheless, a cultural framework should be used to paint a broader picture of the phenomenon at hand rather than immediately imposing a clinical diagnosis.

Finally, acknowledging the multifaceted and multilayered issues Y. is negotiating in her life—acculturation, intergenerational issues, culturally prescribed gender roles, and hybrid identity—helps to situate her story in a different light. Including family as a whole, or specific family members, can be a vital resource and source of support to a client in the therapeutic process. When working with clients who come from traditional and collectivist-based value systems, engaging elders of the family (e.g., parents) can demonstrate a respect and appreciation for their role as heads of the family. It can also facilitate encouraging their support and understanding about the counseling process, thereby minimizing the stigma about seeking counseling. Working with Y. and her family from a multidisciplinary team approach and seeking to bring in therapists with various expertise (e.g., family therapy, individual approach, cross-cultural, and diagnostic expertise) can offer a broad-spectrum intervention approach versus applying a singular intervention strategy.

Finally, avoiding a "one size fits all" approach to counseling clients from diverse populations is an important consideration. Each client needs to be seen as a unique individual who represents a unique combination of cultural influences; therefore, remaining open to using new or creative ways of engaging the client, raising poignant personal issues, and demonstrating a willingness to respect and understand cultural parameters are principles that can guide interventions. Facilitating the development of internal and external coping strategies, offering support and mentoring in creating flexible solutions, and examining the paradoxes of bicultural/hybrid identity development can offer a safe space in which to examine these issues for clients who may feel isolated and alone in the process. According to the crisis literature, it is often the sense of isolation, alienation, and helplessness that is seen as a driving force for the emergence of self-destructive coping strategies in a client's life.

References

Akhtar, S. (1994). A third individuation: Immigration identity and the psychoanalytic process. *Journal of American Psychoanalytic Association, 43,* 1051–1084.

Arthur, N., & Collins, S. (Eds.). (2005). *Culture-infused counselling: Celebrating the Canadian mosaic.* Calgary, Alberta, Canada: Counselling Concepts.

Arthur, N., & Merali, N. (2005). Counselling immigrants and refugees. In N. Arthur & S. Collins (Eds.), *Culture-infused counselling: Celebrating the Canadian mosaic* (pp. 331–360). Calgary, Alberta, Canada: Counselling Concepts.

Baptiste, D. A. (1993). Immigrant families, adolescents, and acculturation: Insights for therapists. *Marriage and Family Review, 19,* 341–363.

Berry, J. W. (2001). A psychology of immigration. *Journal of Social Issues, 57,* 615–631.

Bhabha, H. K. (1990). The third space (interview with Homi Bhabha). In J. Rutherford (Ed.), *Identity, community, culture, difference* (pp. 208–210). London: Lawrence & Wishart.

Bhabha, H. K. (1994). *The location of culture*. New York: Routledge.

Das, A. K., & Kemp, S. F. (1997). Between two worlds: Counseling South Asian Americans. *Journal of Multicultural Counseling and Development, 25*, 23–33.

Das Gupta, S. (1998). Gender roles and cultural continuity in the Asian Indian immigrant community in the U.S. *Sex Roles, 38*, 953–974.

Dhruvarajan, V. (1993). Ethnic cultural retention and transmission among first generation Hindu Asian Indians in a Canadian prairie city. *Journal of Comparative Family Studies, 24*, 63–79.

Ho, D. Y. F. (1995). Internalized culture, culturocentricism, and transcendence. *The Counseling Psychologist, 23*, 4–24.

Jambunathan, S., Burts, D., & Pierce, S. (2000). Comparison of parenting attitudes among five ethnic groups in the United States. *Journal of Comparative Family Studies, 31*, 395–406.

James, B. (1994). *Handbook for treatment of attachment-trauma problems of children*. New York: Lexington Books.

Justin, M. (2003). *Walking between two worlds: The bicultural experience of second-generation East Indian Canadian women*. Unpublished doctoral dissertation, McGill University, Montreal, Quebec, Canada.

Justin, M. (2005). Counselling non-dominant ethnic groups. In N. Arthur & S. Collins (Eds.), *Culture-infused counselling: Celebrating the Canadian mosaic* (pp. 361–386). Calgary, Alberta, Canada: Counselling Concepts.

Levenkron, S. (1998). *Cutting: Understanding and overcoming self-mutilation*. New York: Norton.

Ponterotto, J. G., Casas, J. M., Suzuki, L. A., & Alexander, C. M. (Eds.). (2001). *Handbook of multicultural counseling* (2nd ed.). Thousand Oaks, CA: Sage.

Reese, B. L., & Brandt, R. (1997). Dimensions of diversity. In R. Ross (Ed.), *The fifth discipline fieldbook: Strategies and tools* (pp. 19–37). New York: Doubleday.

Sue, D. W., & Sue, D. (1999). *Counseling the culturally different: Theory and practice* (3rd ed.). New York: Wiley.

Sue, D. W., & Sue, D. (2003). *Counseling the culturally diverse: Theory and practice* (4th ed.). New York: Wiley.

Sue, S., Zane, N., & Young, K. (1994). Research on psychotherapy with culturally diverse populations. In A. E. Bergin & S. L. Garfield (Eds.), *Handbook of psychotherapy and behavior change* (pp. 783–847). New York: Wiley.

Integration and Identity Issues

Maria Assumpta Aneas Alvarez

Mohamed (a pseudonym), who is now 30 years old, comes from an upper-middle-class family in Fez, Morocco. His family lives in a big house in the center of town and very close to other relatives. Mohamed's father is a high-level civil servant, and many of his uncles are military officers. His mother's family has large farms. His father has two wives, which is an indication of his economic level, given that the Koran permits polygamy only when the man can financially support his wives. Both women live in the family home together with 7 children, while 5 other children have their own homes.

Mohamed's entire family is devoutly religious. They consider themselves good Muslims and sincerely try to follow the five pillars of Islam: statement of faith, ritual prayer, charity, fasting during the month of Ramadan, and a pilgrimage to Mecca. In fact, 2 years ago Mohamed's parents made their pilgrimage to Mecca.

Mohamed is his father's youngest son. His mother always spoiled him; they even share a resemblance: fair skin and honey-colored hair and eyes. He completed his secondary studies without any effort, receiving very high grades. He went to university and began studying chemistry.

Many years ago, one of his older brothers went to Madrid, Spain, to study economics. He finished his studies, found work, and has since lived there with his family. This gave Mohamed the idea of also finishing his studies in Spain. Five years ago, with his parents' permission, he went to Spain.

Although he went to Madrid, he now lives in Barcelona. He barely gets by with the money his family sends him. They think he is still studying, but he stopped going to classes years ago.

When Mohamed arrived at the university, he suffered a great shock. He almost could not walk holding his head up because he did not want to see his classmates dressed in such a vulgar, unseemly way. The professors did not seem anything like his professors in Morocco, who always had an air of wisdom and authority. Here they could be taken for students! Although his brother encouraged Mohamed to try to appreciate his professors, he never saw in them the qualities of a genuinely good teacher, so he began to miss classes and eventually abandoned his studies. He dedicated himself instead to getting to know the Muslim community in Madrid.

That is when he began to realize that many Spaniards feel a certain mistrust and suspicion toward Moroccans because of their skin color and religion. This distanced him even more from Spanish society. He did not feel comfortable with his brother, either; he considered him too liberal, as if he had lost his identity. Because Mohamed had already lost interest in the university, he decided to move to Barcelona, along with some friends.

Although he enrolled in a university in Barcelona, he seldom went to class and, instead, dedicated himself to exploring Moroccan and Muslim social circles, as well as studying information technology and accounting in order to find a good job.

His job search, however, left him as disappointed as had his university experience; he could not find anything that lived up to his expectations. He looked for work as a computer technician or in an entry-level management position of a small chemical company. Mohamed thought that, having the better part of his chemistry degree finished and being fluent in three languages (Arabic, French, and Spanish), he could find a job at least as good as what he could get in Fez, but all he seemed to receive were job offers to be an administrative assistant or warehouse worker, and with salaries far below his expectations.

Critical Incident

Eventually, he found work at a fairly good salary as the manager of a sales office. He was obliged, however, to carry out all of the different functions and tasks within the office, some of which he did not particularly want to do. This led to various arguments with his boss. Unable to resolve the problem, Mohamed quit. In his second job, as a warehouse worker, he also felt deceived. His boss was a rude, vulgar man who demanded what Mohamed considered an almost inhuman amount of work. He was never paid what he had been initially promised, and he thought that the job was beneath him. He quit after a few weeks. After these experiences, he worked in other places, such as a supermarket or in construction, but always left because he felt humiliated and mistreated.

His rejection of Spaniards and their lifestyle and culture grows almost daily, and he feels less and less interested in integrating or even socializing with the local people. He lives with his friends in a primarily immigrant neighborhood whose streets remind him vaguely of the Kasbah in Fez, but this vague similarity also makes him think about what he left behind in his homeland and the failure of his attempt at a transition.

Mohamed's problem is that returning to Morocco without a degree, without work, without anything would represent such an immense failure and humiliation that he would prefer to hide all of these problems from members of his family and have them believe that everything is going well for him in Spain. In the bottom of his heart, however, he feels that he has fallen and that he cannot get up.

Key Issues

- Frustration and conflict between his initial expectations that motivated his transition and the reality of the situation
- Change of social status
- Cultural differences with respect to exercising power and interpersonal communication
- Dilemma: What is Mohamed's best option—stay in Spain and be unhappy, change his attitude, or acknowledge his failure and suffer a humiliating return to Morocco?

Relationship Considerations

In Morocco, Mohamed was considered a privileged man. Accustomed to being respected and treated with great consideration because of his social position, he is not aware that he is very direct and passionate when he speaks; he only softens his proud, dominant attitude when in the presence of people whom he loves or respects, such as his parents, and in Spain he seldom meets anyone like that. As much as he thinks that he treats people politely, the truth is that he is considered haughty and at times aggressive.

Mohamed's brother has tried to get him to understand many things. He has tried to help him so that he would not have problems with his professors or at work, but Mohamed does not listen to his advice. He only talks of Islam and the horrible shortcomings of Western society and Spain. Years go by without making any progress on his degree. His older brother is very concerned about him but has said nothing to their parents because he knows that it would sadden and worry them.

Juan Pons, the chief executive officer of the company where Mohamed was sales manager, trusted him but was ultimately disappointed by his lack of commitment. Juan thought that by hiring a Moroccan he was demonstrating that in Catalonia immigrants were given opportunities. He knew perfectly well that there was a great deal to do in the office, that the job demanded hard work and long hours, but he thought that Mohamed was up to the task even though he had little experience. When Mohamed began to complain that he had to fill orders, make photocopies, and straighten up the storeroom, Juan knew that he had made an error in hiring him. When one Friday Mohamed called to quit, Juan felt very angry and also greatly disappointed.

Transition Outcomes

At the time that I met Mohamed, he was at a dead end. In Spain he could not find a job at the professional and salary level that he thought he deserved. If he returned to Morocco, he would always be the failure who spent 5 years in Spain but never managed to get his university degree.

Writer's Comments

A client of our counseling service spoke to me of a very bright friend of hers who had a great deal of trouble finding work. I offered my help, and Mohamed and I saw each other on three separate occasions. The first impression that he made on me was very good: He was well dressed, good-looking, and polite. He seemed to be very motivated and accepted the offer to participate in our program. He did not like to talk much about his family, but he had no problem talking about himself, his university days in Morocco, or his time in Madrid or Barcelona. He demonstrated a very critical attitude toward everyone and everything except when speaking of his own country and culture.

In Mohamed's international transition, the cultural dilemmas and a somewhat problematic personality combined to create an intractable personal problem. On a personal level, Mohamed was practically predestined to occupy a position of leadership and power in Morocco by virtue of being born into a rich, prestigious, and powerful family. Everything had been conceded to him rather easily, and he developed a sense of self that made him feel that he deserved all that he desired.

Now in a new context, with different rules of the game, the shock or fall was very hard on him. In Spain, job opportunities are influenced by social position almost as much as they are in Morocco; but for that very reason, the "powerful" Mohamed was just one more student in Spain and, in addition, a Moroccan immigrant. However, even with social connections, a candidate for a high-level job in Spain must have a university degree, professional experience, or an enormous capacity for hard work and sacrifice. Mohamed's mistake was to think that he would be valued and respected in Spain for the same reasons that he was in Morocco.

At the same time, Mohamed's personality impeded him from seeing and understanding, in an objective and realistic way, the dynamics that regulate professional relationships in Spain. His egocentric and ethnocentric attitude stopped him from analyzing and evaluating the achievements, strategies, and advice of his friends and acquaintances, some of whom had truly achieved many of their goals. His attitude stopped him from learning and understanding the rules of the game in Spain, rules that for him were simply "wrong." For that reason, it was impossible for him to consider that maybe he was the one who was wrong and, therefore, needed to correct his errors in judgment. The situation could be summed up as "Everyone else does things wrong, they're always wrong, and they're wrong when they don't give me what I very much deserve."

From a cultural perspective, there are not vast differences between Spain and Morocco. Moroccan culture is more hierarchical and direct than Spanish culture; this is the reason for differences in the attitude and teaching styles of his professors and why some Moroccan workers are considered irresponsible or untrustworthy if they are not closely supervised. This is also why, on so many occasions, Spaniards think that Arabs are proud and haughty. There are many similarities between the two cultures, such as the value placed on the collective, attitude toward norms, and so on, but differences do exist, and only with an open mind and flexible approach can Mohamed perceive them, understand them, and adjust his behavior adequately to the new environment.

The largest gaps between the two cultures are in the accumulation of prejudices and political and economic conflicts that for centuries have accompanied relations between Morocco and Spain and that have made both sides view the other as an unfriendly or threatening neighbor and have stopped both countries from seeing how much the two cultures have in common.

The most serious and complex issue in this case is religion. Islam is a monotheistic religion that shares many more values with Christianity and Judaism than is normally believed or accepted. As with so many religions, the fundamental beliefs have been reinterpreted and manipulated at times to make them accommodate better to religious or political purposes. Westerners and Muslims alike have used Islam in a way that has created a host of prejudices that in turn have created real cultural barriers that are difficult to overcome. However, these barriers must be overcome by people—of Muslim or any other religious belief—who live, study, and work together. It is because of these negative biases that it is easy for a Spaniard, when confronted with an Arab-looking person, a non-Christian name, or any other reminder that a person is Muslim, to put up a wall and to reject or at least suspect the person, even though the rejection or suspicion are totally unjustified because they are based on prejudices that distort intercultural relationships.

Moroccans, or any Arabs or Muslims, who cannot bring added value (e.g., economic power, social prestige) with them in their attempt at a transition to life in the West, specifically in Spain, where the sentiment is that they are only immigrants who "take jobs away from locals" or come to "take advantage of our social services and welfare system," must be capable of tolerating and overcoming dirty looks and negative attitudes. They must be capable of creating intercultural relationships and interpersonal recognition without retreating into themselves or their own subgroups, which would be the safest and most convenient thing to do but would hinder true integration and only favor social marginalization and cultural segregation.

Counseling Points

1. How would you communicate with this client? When would you analyze his successes and failures? How would you approach this client (by being direct or by approaching things slowly and indirectly)?
2. How would you get Mohamed to understand that he, too, has made mistakes and must change his attitude?
3. What would you recommend to Mohamed? Would you suggest that he stay in Spain? Would you suggest that he return to Morocco? What are the challenges and advantages of both options?

4. What sort of monitoring and follow-up by a counselor would you view as appropriate for a person like Mohamed? Would you suggest direct supervision? Would you offer him more freedom and the opportunity to take the initiative? What are some other options that would support Mohamed?
5. What does Mohamed expect from the counselor?
6. What could make Mohamed abandon the program before having finished it?

Reader Reflections Questions

1. Are the basic values of Islam as described in the five pillars so different from Christian values?
2. Do you know of any cases in which a rich and powerful Muslim is respected as a friend or in which a Muslim immigrant or refugee is treated with mistrust or even fear? When this happens, what do you think are the cultural influences involved?
3. Is there another culture that, objectively speaking, is somewhat similar to yours but because of religious prejudices or historical reasons is perceived as different and threatening, as is the case between Spanish and Moroccan cultures? What are the consequences that this situation has generated with respect to intercultural relations between the two cultures? How could this phenomenon be minimized?

Response 1

Mary McMahon and Mark Watson

In responding to this case incident in counseling for international transition, we will use the Systems Theory Framework of career development (STF; McMahon & Patton, 1995; Patton & McMahon, 1999, 2006) as a lens through which to view Mohamed's situation and the career counseling process. A prerequisite with the STF, as with any other approach to career counseling, is engagement in terms of the client's willingness to engage, the counselor's capacity to start where the client is, and the skill to facilitate the client's engagement in the process. First, the STF will be outlined at a theoretical level and applied to Mohamed. Second, the practical application of the STF to career counseling will be described and applied to counseling Mohamed. Throughout the response, issues related to international transition illustrated through the example of Mohamed will be examined from the STF perspective.

The STF of Career Development

The STF is a metatheoretical framework that provides an understanding of career development that is consistent with the emerging constructivist position on career development and career counseling. It is responsive to holistic understandings about career, the inseparability of career and life, personal meaning, subjectivity, and recursiveness between influences. A detailed description of the STF is not possible in this response, and readers are directed to previous accounts (e.g., McMahon & Patton, 1995, 2006; Patton & McMahon, 1999, 2006; Patton, McMahon, & Watson, 2006). Thus, we briefly describe the STF and illustrate its application to Mohamed's situation.

The STF illustrates both the content influences and the process influences on an individual's career development. The content influences are described as a series of interconnecting systems of influence on career development, specifically the individual system, the social system, and the environmental/societal system, whereas the process influences include recursiveness, change over time, and chance. All influences are set in the context of past, present, and future; thus, the STF is conceptualized as a dynamic open system.

The Individual System of Influences

Central to the STF is the individual system of influences within which is included a range of intrapersonal influences on career development, such as personality, ability, gender, and sexual orientation. In the case of Mohamed, his age, his devout faith in the Muslim religion, his academic ability, and his personality are examples of intrapersonal influences that are affecting his current career situation.

The Social System of Influences

Individuals do not live in isolation, and the significant others with whom they interact, such as family and peers, are known as the social system. In the case of Mohamed, his family, especially his older brother and his parents; his friends in Barcelona; and his employers are all examples of his social system of influences. More recently, the career counselor has also entered Mohamed's social system of influences.

The Environmental/Societal System of Influences

The individual system, and indeed all systems in the STF, may be viewed as systems in their own right and also as subsystems of other systems. For example, the individual is a subsystem of the social system. The individual and social systems exist within an environmental/societal system in which influences such as geographic location, globalization, and political decisions are located. In the case of Mohamed, his past geographic location in Morocco and his present geographic location in Spain, the history related to Moroccan immigrants to Spain, and his past and present socioeconomic background are examples of environmental/societal influences on Mohamed's present career situation.

The Process Influences

The STF presents career development as a dynamic process depicted through its process influences: recursiveness, change over time, and chance. Fundamental to understanding the STF is the notion that each system is an open system. An open system is subject to influence from outside and may also influence what is beyond its boundaries. Such interaction is termed *recursiveness* in the STF. Significantly, the nature of the influences on an individual and their degree of influence may change over time. The final process influence is chance, that is, unexpected events that have an influence on career development.

In the case of Mohamed, intrapersonal influences, such as his devout Muslim faith, his academic ability, and his personality, are recursively related to his social system of influences, such as his friends and parents, and also to the environmental/societal influence of his geographic location in Spain. All of Mohamed's systems of influence are recursively related to his present career situation. Although some influences, such as Mohamed's socioeconomic circumstances and geographic location, have changed over time, others, such as his devout faith and future lifestyle aspirations, have changed very little.

The Context of Past, Present, and Future

All of the systems of influence exist within the context of time—past, present, and future—all of which are inextricably linked. The past influences the present, and together past and present influence the future. In the case of Mohamed, past influences, such as the intrapersonal influence of his upbringing as a devout Muslim and the lifestyle and occupational expectations associated with the status of his past socioeconomic situation, are recursively related to his present career situation and also to his future options.

As a metatheoretical framework, the STF provides an opportunity for individual analysis of career development at a microlevel, a process through which the meaning of such influences is elaborated by the individual. Essentially, the STF provides an opportunity for individuals to construct their personal theories of career development through the narration of their career stories and the elaboration of meaning in career counseling. Thus, in terms of career development practice, systems theory lends itself to a theoretical and practical consistency.

It is also important that the STF allows the concepts of culture and transition to be considered at a metalevel. In the recursively connected systems of the STF, culture is viewed as a social construction within and by individuals (Patton & McMahon, 2006) on the basis of the meaning they ascribe to the influence of the multiple groups to which they belong and with which they interrelate. Mohamed has socially constructed his culture on the basis of intrapersonal influences such as his Moroccan and Islamic backgrounds, with which he identifies strongly, and social and environmental/societal influences such as his status as a Moroccan immigrant in Spain, through which he feels marginalized. Several authors (e.g., Arthur & Collins, 2005; Patton & McMahon, 2006; Stead, 2004; Watson, 2006) have advocated that culture should be centrally located within all career counseling relationships. Viewed in this way, the interplay of cultural influences between Mohamed and the career counselor is taken into consideration, and a new culture is created in the career counseling process whereby perspectives may be exchanged and new meanings generated about career issues (Arthur & McMahon, 2005).

Transition may be viewed as inseparable from the STF, because incremental change over time is inherent to individuals and their systems of influence. Individuals are always in a process of incremental adjustment. However, in addition to incremental change, large-scale changes, whether planned or unplanned, frequently feature in the lives of individuals, and the resultant process of adjustment and adaptation is known as transition. In Mohamed's case, the major change in his life was planned, because he chose, with the support of his family, to move from Morocco to further his studies in Spain. However, transition is a multilevel construct, in which different levels of the transition may progress at different rates. For example, although Mohamed has made a geographic transition, he is struggling with the corresponding emotional and cultural transition.

The STF and Career Counseling

At a practical level, the STF provides a map to guide career counselors as they encourage clients to relate the details and reality of their own maps through the telling of their career stories (McMahon & Patton, 2003; McMahon, Patton, & Watson, 2004). Together, counselor and client gain insight into the interconnectedness of systemic influences on the client's situation. Although the STF may serve as a map of the possible elements of clients' career stories, it may also serve as a map of the counseling relationship. Just as Mohamed exists within his own system of career influences, so too does the career counselor. Career counseling, therefore, constitutes the connection of two systems of influence, the client's and the counselor's, and consequently the formation of a new dynamic system, the therapeutic system (Patton & McMahon, 1999, 2006).

The STF has been applied to a range of cultural groups, settings, and countries (Patton & McMahon, 1997; Patton et al., 2006). For example, Arthur and McMahon (2005) proposed that the STF might be applicable to clients with either individualist or collectivist worldviews, because counseling "proceeds from the worldview represented by clients through the telling of their career stories" (p. 216). The STF suggests the possibility of expanded roles and levels of intervention for career counselors, particularly in relation to multicultural career counseling; thus, it seems that the STF has much to offer career counseling.

Conceptual Understandings

In applying the STF to career counseling, McMahon (2005) suggested a number of conceptual understandings and practical considerations that may guide the work of career counselors. Conceptual understandings related to the individual, systemic thinking, story, and recursiveness may provide a theoretical base for counselors. Importantly, career counseling is viewed as an interpersonal process in which the uniqueness of individuals is recognized (Patton & McMahon, 2006) and in which Mohamed is considered an expert on his own life who seeks to make sense of his life through the telling of stories. Indeed, his life is multistoried. Career counseling may be viewed as providing Mohamed with a space in which he may tell and coconstruct stories. Through the telling of such stories, the recursiveness and connection between the influences of Mohamed's system and the meaning he attributes to his stories may be examined, and patterns and themes in and between his stories may be uncovered.

Practical Considerations

The use of story fosters connectedness between individuals and the elements in their systems of influence, as well as connectedness between elements of the systems. At a fundamental level, a story that needs to be coconstructed between Mohamed and his career counselor is the story of the counseling relationship itself. In this regard, Cochran (1997) suggested that it is important to clarify the career issue or the gap between what is "the existing state of affairs" and what ought to be, could be, or should be "the desired state of affairs" (p. 16). Furthermore, clarification of what is desirable (what the client wants from the career counselor) and what is possible (what the career counselor can offer) is also important. Thus, Mohamed and his career counselor need to discuss Mohamed's expectations of the career counselor and of the career counseling process, the role of his career counselor, and his career counselor's expectations of Mohamed and of the career counseling process. This would help clarify Mohamed's role as an expert in his life and the career counselor's role as an expert in the career counseling process. Together they may coconstruct a story for working collaboratively that is facilitative of producing a story of a preferred future for Mohamed.

As a starting point, Mohamed may tell his frequently told story about his experiences in Spain. He could also be invited to tell stories about his career that have been told by others in his system of influences, such as those told by his older brother and by his parents about their hopes and dreams for Mohamed. Career counseling may also provide Mohamed with an opportunity to tell stories that have been long forgotten, stories he has never told, stories he has been afraid to tell, and stories he did not know he could tell. In addition, career counseling is focused on the coconstruction of future stories for Mohamed. Although these multiple stories may appear discrete and unrelated, systemic thinking encourages Mohamed and his career counselor to take a holistic view by locating him within the context of his whole system of influences and identifying themes and patterns that permeate his stories.

The nature of the career counseling relationship that facilitates the telling of stories is one in which a "mattering" climate is created (Schlossberg, Lynch, & Chickering, 1989). Such a climate could provide Mohamed with a relationship in which he feels valued, cared about, and appreciated and in which his career issues really do matter.

Practice Dimensions

In practice, Mohamed's career counselor would be encouraged to develop the key recursive dimensions of the STF approach to career counseling, specifically, connection, reflection, meaning-making, learning, and agency (McMahon, 2003). In addition, the STF offers the possibility of expanded roles and levels of intervention that the career counselor could explore with Mohamed.

Connection

Connection occurs on many levels in career counseling. First, Mohamed's career counselor needs to connect with his or her own career stories in order to understand his or her own history, values, biases, beliefs and prejudices, and the sociopolitical system in which he or she lives and works. Second, Mohamed and his career counselor connect in a recursive relationship that builds, deepens, and strengthens over time. Third, the career counseling process provides an opportunity for Mohamed to connect with his own system of influences through the telling of his career stories. Through the telling of his stories, Mohamed may increasingly recognize connections within his system of influences and identify themes and patterns that permeate his career stories. Fundamental to connecting with Mohamed and his career stories is the need for the career counselor to engage at an appropriate level or to "start where the client is." Thus, Mohamed and his career counselor need to engage in dialogue about Mohamed's present career situation and the situation he would prefer, his future story, and the process of transitioning toward it.

Reflection

Peavy (1998) suggested that career counseling may be a process that creates care, hope, encouragement, clarification, and activation. Mohamed's career counselor could encourage him to be an "explorer in his own life" and, in so doing, try to make sense of the complexities of his life, draw new insights, and formulate new strategies (Amundson, Parker, & Arthur, 2002). These processes may be enhanced if Mohamed's career counselor creates a space for reflection in which Mohamed feels safe to narrate his story, elicit meaning, and coconstruct new or alternative stories.

Meaning-Making

Meaning-making occurs through an open communication interchange in which shared meaning is generated through dialogue and negotiation (Peavy, 2000). In describing a process that possibly relates to Mohamed and his frequently told story, Morgan (2000) suggested that clients relate "thin descriptions" of their circumstances, which produce "thin conclusions" (p. 12) that necessarily limit the possibilities for the future and frequently sustain problems. Thus, Mohamed's career counselor could work with Mohamed to explore alternative stories that might assist him to break from his thin conclusions and produce new and preferred stories for his life.

Learning

Career counseling may provide Mohamed with an opportunity to recognize or learn what is required for him to move toward his preferred future. Learning is facilitated by reflection and meaning-making, and it is through learning that agency is fostered. In reflecting on his career stories, Mohamed may learn how the decisions he has made have had a part to play in the level of dissatisfaction he now feels with his life. Through a supportive career counseling relationship, the career counselor could assist Mohamed to confidently and creatively apply his learning to the coconstruction of a future story and facilitate his transition to this "desired state of affairs" (Cochran, 1997, p. 16).

Agency

Agency is people's capacity to "act for themselves and speak on their own behalf" (Monk, Winslade, Crocket, & Epston, 1997, p. 301). In the case of Mohamed, he has demonstrated active agency in his decisions to move to Spain, move to Barcelona, leave university, and leave his employment. However, despite being an active agent in his life, Mohamed's decisions have not resulted in a life that he wants or with which he feels satisfied. Indeed, in some ways his successive decisions have moved him away from the life he really wants. Thus, a challenge for both Mohamed and his career counselor is to identify how he might actively work toward a life that is more satisfying for him.

Expanded Roles and Levels of Intervention

The STF suggests expanded roles for career counselors and levels of intervention. For example, Mohamed may benefit if his career counselor engages with him in roles such as coach, advocate, nurturer, or supporter (McMahon, 2006). Similarly, it may become apparent in the counseling process that intervention at another level of Mohamed's system may be helpful. Examples of such interventions include involving members of his social system, such as the friend who made his initial referral to the career counselor or his brother, or advocating on Mohamed's behalf with a university or employer.

Conclusion

Viewing this case incident in counseling for international transition through the lens of the STF provides an opportunity to consider Mohamed's career situation both theoretically and practically. In essence, Mohamed and his career counselor would build a relationship in which Mohamed could assume more self-responsibility and control, increase meaningful participation in his life, and move toward a preferred future (Peavy, 1998). The STF approach to career counseling is not presented as a panacea for Mohamed's career situation, but rather as an option predicated on Mohamed's willingness to engage and on the capacity of Mohamed and his career counselor to negotiate a workable relationship.

References

Amundson, N. E., Parker, P., & Arthur, M. B. (2002). Merging two worlds: Linking occupational and organisational career counselling. *Australian Journal of Career Development, 11*(3), 26–35.

Arthur, N., & Collins, S. (2005). *Culture-infused counselling: Celebrating the Canadian mosaic.* Calgary, Alberta, Canada: Counselling Concepts.

Arthur, N., & McMahon, M. (2005). A Systems Theory Framework for multicultural counseling. *The Career Development Quarterly, 53,* 208–223.

Cochran, L. (1997). *Career counseling: A narrative approach.* Thousand Oaks, CA: Sage.

McMahon, M. (2003, April). *Life career journeys: Reflection, connection, meaning, learning, and agency.* Paper presented at the Australian Association of Career Counsellors' 12th National Conference, Adelaide, Australia.

McMahon, M. (2005). Career counseling: Applying the Systems Theory Framework of career development. *Journal of Employment Counseling, 42,* 29–38.

McMahon, M. (2006). Career counselling and metaphor. In K. Inkson, *Understanding careers: The metaphors of working lives* (pp. 270–297). Thousand Oaks, CA: Sage.

McMahon, M., & Patton, W. (1995). Development of a systems theory of career development. *Australian Journal of Career Development, 4*(2), 15–20.

McMahon, M., & Patton, W. (2003). Influences on career decisions. In M. McMahon & W. Patton (Eds.), *Ideas for career practitioners: Celebrating excellence in Australian career practice* (pp. 130–132). Brisbane, Queensland, Australia: Australian Academic Press.

McMahon, M., & Patton, W. (2006). The Systems Theory Framework: A conceptual and practical map for career counselling. In M. McMahon & W. Patton (Eds.), *Career counselling: Constructivist approaches* (pp. 94–109). London: Routledge.

McMahon, M., Patton, W., & Watson, M. (2004). Creating career stories through reflection: An application of the Systems Theory Framework of career development. *Australian Journal of Career Development, 13*(3), 13–16.

Monk, G., Winslade, J., Crocket, K., & Epston, D. (1997). *Narrative therapy in practice: The archaeology of hope.* San Francisco: Jossey-Bass.

Morgan, A. (2000). *What is narrative therapy?* Adelaide, South Australia, Australia: Dulwich Centre Publications.

Patton, W., & McMahon, M. (1997). *Career development in practice: A systems theory perspective.* Sydney, New South Wales, Australia: New Hobsons Press.

Patton, W., & McMahon, M. (1999). *Career development and systems theory: A new relationship.* Pacific Grove, CA: Brooks/Cole.

Patton, W., & McMahon, M. (2006). *Career development and systems theory: Connecting theory and practice* (2nd ed.). Rotterdam, The Netherlands: Sense.

Patton, W., McMahon, M., & Watson, M. (2006). The Systems Theory Framework of career development. In G. Stead & M. Watson (Eds.), *Career psychology in the South African context* (2nd ed., pp. 65–78). Pretoria, South Africa: Van Schaik.

Peavy, R. V. (1998). *Sociodynamic counselling: A constructivist perspective.* Victoria, British Columbia, Canada: Trafford.

Peavy, R. V. (2000, April). The sociodynamic perspective and the practice of counselling. In *Proceedings of international career conference, 2000* (pp. 1–15). Perth, Western Australia, Australia: Curriculum Council of Western Australia.

Schlossberg, N. K., Lynch, A. Q., & Chickering, A. W. (1989). *Improving higher education environments for adults.* San Francisco: Jossey-Bass.

Stead, G. B. (2004). Culture and career psychology: A social constructivist perspective. *Journal of Vocational Behavior, 64,* 389–406.

Watson, M. B. (2006). Career counselling theory, culture and constructivism. In M. McMahon & W. Patton (Eds.), *Career counselling: Constructivist approaches* (pp. 45–56). London: Routledge.

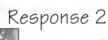

Response 2

Beatriz Malik and María-Fe Sánchez García

The case incident takes place in Spain, where the person involved, Mohamed, decides to continue his studies. The influences from his upbringing in Morocco, where he comes from, must also be taken into account. As stated in the case incident's description, there are many similarities between both countries, but there are also noteworthy differences. We focus very briefly on two settings, the university and the world of work, where most of the "action" occurs. In the other sections, we address other key issues, such as acculturation, culture shock, social relations, stereotypes, and prejudices.

The university in Spain is also hierarchical in nature, especially the relationship among the faculty. Differences among the categories of professors are well-defined, and control is still exerted in many aspects by those with the highest status, although this is gradually changing. Participation in the governing bodies is large, which allows for a higher representation of the different categories. The relationship with the students is asymmetrical (i.e., the professor evaluates and controls), but it is true that, in general, this relationship is quite informal, with the usual exceptions. There are many young (and not so young) lecturers and professors who could indeed be mistaken for students, by no means lessening their quality as teachers. For a student who is accustomed to professors with an air of authority, this may be quite shocking.

The Spanish economic context is characterized by a capitalist economy, based on neoliberal principles, in which most aspects of life are subservient to the needs of the global market. Work relations are regulated by the rules of supply and demand, in which the benefits of the companies are more important than the collective good or, even, workers' interests. The maximum efficiency of the latter is sought, at the lowest cost for the employer.

As in many other industrialized countries, training and qualifications of workers have become an increasingly important issue, "highlighting the difference" among workers. It is necessary to conform to the rules of the game in order to access a job and to maintain it, and it is very difficult to ignore these rules. Workers are compelled to keep themselves employable by engaging in continuous training and demonstrating previous experience. As Irving (2005) contended, "current government policy rhetoric places significant emphasis on lifelong learning, the importance of self-directed career management, the acquisition of employability skills, and the need to acquire appropriate training and relevant qualifications" (p. 20). There exists little questioning of labor market practices or structural inequalities in society.

Work-related values, and even other cultural values and worldviews, are influenced by these trends and are accepted and tolerated by society in general. Continuing with Irving's (2005) discourse (referring to young people's expectations regarding career advisers, but it is also applicable to this situation), we can say that continued emphasis on individual choice, opportunities for all, the importance of success, and fair competition within the context of a free and open labor market feeds into this reductive vision. Many people, especially young people, have become accustomed to the reality of employment insecurity, uncertainty, and precariousness of the working conditions, although most of them aspire to more satisfactory positions. Unemployment and underemployment are very common, as is the increasing emergence of "overqualified workers" (i.e., people who hold positions below their skills and qualifications).

Although the case incident points out that a common element between Spain and Morocco is the value placed on the collective, we must emphasize that, at present, this may be true only in small towns or villages (and not in all of them), in rural areas, or among ethnic groups such as Roma and immigrants who come from collectivist cultures. In most big cities, people have become much more individualistic, especially the younger generations, although, of course, there are always exceptions. There are, indeed, common elements and values between the Christian and the Muslim faith, many more than some people would like to admit. Our observations and perceptions of Spanish society are that it is no longer a homogeneous society. It appears that Spain is not as influenced today by the Catholic religion as it was some years ago (except for some traditions and festivities), and many people do not practice any religion.

The Nature of Cross-Cultural Transitions

People are constantly in transition, and although transitions have always existed (they are in fact inherent to human nature), they have become a major issue in today's globalized world, especially in the field of career theory and the practice of career guidance and counseling.

The question that dominates career development today is how to help individuals cope with transitions. Regarding cross-cultural transitions, they occur whenever a person moves to a context with differing cultural values from his or her own place of origin. This is the case for immigrants, refugees, sojourners, international students, and migrants within the same country with distinct regions, among others, whose cultural background differs from the predominant worldviews, values, and beliefs of the population in the host location. Sometimes these differences are very slight, whereas other times they may be considerable, leading to a greater "cultural distance."

Berry (1997) characterized cross-cultural transitions by their dimensions of voluntariness, mobility, and permanence. According to this classification, we can say that Mohamed's transition is characterized by voluntariness: It was his decision to move to Spain, motivated by his desire to continue studying there, following his brother's example. The transition was not due to economic or political reasons or other difficult life circumstances (at least not that we know of from the description in the case incident). Nevertheless, as Arthur (2000) stated,

> [T]he nature of cross-cultural transitions entails a period of dissonance in which personal meanings are challenged, and this dissonance may result in a firm grasp on original cultural beliefs and rejection of contrasting values. If this position is taken and maintained early in the transition experience, individuals may remain closed to experiencing aspects of the new culture that they might eventually appreciate. (p. 213)

This is exactly what has happened to Mohamed. He has felt challenged from the beginning and held on to the meanings and values he brought with him, without even trying to understand those contrasting values he finds or appreciating the commonalities between the two cultural contexts.

Whether voluntary or not, transitions imply leaving something familiar behind and encountering something new. As highlighted by Bridges (1991), the process of transition often entails loss as familiar ways of operating routines or settings are left behind. Moreover, exposure to norms and behavior that contrast with an individual's own culture during cross-cultural transitions poses challenges for an individual's understanding of self, assumptions about others, or the beliefs about the world (Ishiyama, 1995). People in cross-cultural transitions are immersed in situations that require learning and adjustment to new role demands. Disruptions to familiar ways of interacting can manifest in psychological or physical reactions associated with culture shock (Lysgaard, 1955; Oberg, 1960; Winkelman, quoted in Arthur, 2000). In the case of Mohamed, he has experienced a great culture shock and is not adjusting to these new demands. Regarding his process of acculturation (i.e., psychological change that results in adaptation to the new cultural context), Mohamed is striving to maintain his original cultural identity and does not actively engage in the new context, thus adopting a position of separation (Berry, 1999). He probably lacks the necessary coping strategies to do so, and the new environment is doing nothing to improve the situation. He does not encounter some of the barriers that immigrants usually face: language competency (he is fluent in Spanish) or low self-esteem (his is rather too high), but there other difficulties that we will see in the following section.

Presenting Issues

- Change of social status
- Dominant personality, little flexibility
- Ethnocentrism, reinforcement of his own cultural values—seeks support from peers
- Stereotypes and prejudiced attitudes on his part and in the host society
- Difficulties finding a job that suits him

- Problems at work, derived both from his personality and from the work situation, exploitation in the workplace

Mohamed has experienced a huge culture shock. His expectations regarding his transition have been undermined and he feels disoriented, with a total sense of failure and seeing no way out. His social position in Morocco was quite privileged, but this has changed significantly in the new context, and he has not been able to adjust to his new temporary social status. He displays a very dominant and egocentric personality, which could be derived from his upbringing in a upper-middle-class family in which he was overprotected and spoiled by his mother and where almost anything he wanted was conceded to him rather easily. He is thus accustomed to getting what he desires and becoming angry when he does not achieve it, and he has developed no resistance to frustration. He shows a certain feeling of superiority, both at university and in the workplace. These characteristics of his personality, as well as his negative attitudes toward the Spanish lifestyle, may have been intensified by culture shock (first defined by Oberg, 1960) and also by acculturation and acculturative stress (Berry, 1997; Berry & Annis, 1974; Berry, Kim, & Boski, 1988).

His rejection of the host country's customs and values leads him to reinforce his cultural identity and to seek other groups with which he identifies—the Muslim community and Moroccan social circles. He becomes aware of the mistrust that many Spaniards feel toward Moroccan immigrants but does not realize or does not want to acknowledge that not all of them feel the same. He does not appreciate any common values between his own culture and the other cultures he encounters in Spain (we cannot speak of only "one" culture; there is a great diversity within the country). When talking with the counselor, he demonstrated a critical attitude with everything except his own country and culture; he is very ethnocentric.

Mohamed became very prejudiced against Spanish society (he was not so initially), because many Spanish citizens are prejudiced against Moroccan immigrants. He is unable to accept the differences he finds in the Spanish university compared with the university in Morocco. Professors look younger, they do not seem to exert the same authority, and they lack the air of wisdom they had back home. The different dress codes also shock him, making him feel uncomfortable. By walking with his head low, he probably gives the impression of wanting to avoid contact with his classmates. He makes no effort whatsoever to relate to them, and they most likely take the cue by not approaching him either[1] to welcome him, for instance, or to make him feel a little more comfortable in class and at the university. A situation is thus created in which neither takes the initiative of establishing a relationship, and Mohamed feels completely alienated in this environment, eventually abandoning his studies.

All of the foregoing hinders his adaptation process, his openness to others (interpersonal relations), and his understanding of the context in which he is immersed. As already stated, in the nature of cross-cultural transitions, he adopts a position of separation by not engaging in his new context.

In the work area, he cannot find any job that is fit for him, in accordance with his qualifications (although he did not finish his degree, he studied information technology and accounting), and his perceived competencies. He is intolerant in work relations, considering the situation only from his point of view. He is not capable of adopting other perspectives, as shown in the case of his job with Juan Pons. Mohamed decides which tasks to carry out and which ones are not proper for him to do, otherwise he leaves. He shows a lack of negotiating skills: He could have tried to reach a consensus with his boss in order to avoid doing some of the tasks or he could have compromised with his boss to perform those tasks only for some time until someone else could be hired.

---

[1]This latter is not described explicitly in the case incident, but is inferred by the authors extrapolating from similar situations.

Obviously, in this situation, there are many issues related to the labor market that must be considered on a systemic basis and not only from an individual perspective. It is quite common in Spain to find many people whose qualifications are not in accordance with their jobs; they are overqualified. This is true not only of autochthonous people but also of many immigrants who come with university degrees or other qualifications and cannot obtain a job in their field of expertise. Sometimes it is due to the equivalence of degrees, but there are many other factors involved, as in other countries.

In the first case, Juan Pons hires Mohamed to show that in Catalonia there is no discrimination toward immigrants (this in itself is a symptom that there is discrimination; otherwise, there would be no need to demonstrate the opposite), and although he tries to trust Mohamed and wants to give him an opportunity, deep inside he feels some mistrust. Stereotypes and prejudices are so rooted in people's subconscious that even when they apparently do not have them, stereotypes and prejudices surface when things go wrong or when someone acts "according" to those stereotypes. When Mohamed quits, Pons reacts by admitting that those who told him that he should mistrust Mohamed were right. Instead of considering the situation from another standpoint, it is easier to believe the stereotype, to simplify the reality. He could have blamed Mohamed as an individual (and not as a member of a cultural group) who has not acted properly as a worker (not giving notice with enough time) according to the rules, or he could have examined the situation from a different angle. He could have considered the responsibility and the additional functions he was placing on Mohamed. He could also have considered whether he had discussed the situation with Mohamed sufficiently or had shown any sign of really meaning to hire an additional employee to help with the workload.

The second example provides a clear illustration of exploitation in the workplace, which unfortunately is too common in the case of low-skilled workers and of many immigrants who need the work. There are a considerable number of people working long hours for very low wages who do not dare report their employers, either because they have no work permit and are afraid of being deported or because what they earn is much higher than what they earned in their countries of origin and they cannot find a better job (or most jobs offer the same conditions for them).

Unique Influences on the Client

Religious influences and cultural values from Islam were reinforced after Mohamed joined the Muslim communities in Spain, which in many cases tend to reaffirm members' identity and values in a society that is sometimes hostile toward them, thereby developing strong in-group attachments.

Mohamed is also influenced by his socialization process: He has developed a haughty and arrogant personality, a strong sense of self but little critical self-awareness. Now, his personality acts as a strong obstacle in his relation to others (namely those from the dominant culture) and as a barrier to his understanding of the environment. He is also influenced by his family's social status in Morocco, because he had no financial problems and could have occupied a leadership position.

His brother was very influential at first and inspired Mohamed's decision to continue his studies in Spain, but his influence decreased considerably after some time. He has adjusted very well to his new social milieu and could act as a positive role model, but in Mohamed's eyes, he is too liberal and has given up his identity, so Mohamed does not accept his advice.

Common Considerations for Working With This Population

- Awareness of cultural background and the observance of customs and beliefs of the culture of origin: religious influences, collectivist versus individualistic values, and so on.

- Cultural distance, culture shock, and acculturation processes.
- The need to consider each person's individual characteristics and situation. We cannot assume that all people coming from the same country will face the same issues—or even share the same values. Even in the case of Islam, there are many differences among the people who profess this religion. It is necessary to assess the cultural identity of clients as well as their degree of acculturation. To what extent do they identify with their culture of origin and with other cultural groups to which they belong?
- The need for both sides to overcome stereotypes and prejudiced attitudes: the host society and the person in transition.
- The sense of failure that originates when the initial expectations have not been met. This sense of failure is very common among migrants, as is the reluctance to let their family know about it. They want their families to think everything is all right.

How Can Counseling Be Made Appropriate?

First of all, we must consider the transition process, the elements that have led to it, and its consequences. All the influences of the context on the individual, for instance the experience at the university and in the workplace and their interrelations and recursiveness, should be taken into account. The counselor must be knowledgeable about the labor market conditions. It is also necessary to assess the degree of acculturation and the coping strategies to manage culture shock and acculturative stress.

The counselor must be culturally competent; she or he must be aware of her or his own cultural values, stereotypes, and biases; she or he must be knowledgeable of the influences on this specific client; and she or he must be able to use the appropriate intervention skills. It would be desirable to promote the acquisition of intercultural communication competencies in the workplace.

Theoretical Frameworks That Inform Response

In accordance with our position that career guidance must be holistic and consider all relevant elements in the career decision-making process, both individual and contextual factors (including cultural variables), we advocate for the use of comprehensive theories that take these factors into account. Career development theories proposed by authors such as Lent, Brown, and Hackett (1994); Schlossberg, Waters, and Goodman (1995); and Cook, Heppner, and O'Brien (2001) take into account contextual factors in addition to considering decision making and other dimensions. All of these theories may be considered within the Systems Theory Framework (STF), proposed by McMahon and Patton (1995; Patton & McMahon, 1999, 2006), as an overarching or metatheoretical framework of career theory that provides a sound foundation for intervention in the career development of diverse clients. The STF examines the multiple systems that influence a person's career development and advocates that cultural influences must be incorporated into the ongoing assessment, case planning, interventions, and evaluation practices with all clients, a position that we also support.

Multicultural counseling takes into consideration the cultural background and individual experiences of diverse clients and how their psychosocial needs might be identified and met through counseling (Axelson, 1993; Lee, 1997; Pedersen, 1991). We agree with Pedersen that all counseling is multicultural in nature, because, in essence, cultural diversity is a characteristic of all counseling relationships. All individuals are diverse and incorporate the elements of their culture in personal ways,

Intercultural education promotes exchange, communication, and negotiation between different interacting cultural groups. The intercultural approach is viewed as a model for transforming school and society and is defined as follows:

An educational approach based on recognition of cultural diversity, aimed at every member of the society as a whole. It posits a formal and informal intervention model, holistic, integral and encompassing all dimensions of the educational process in order to achieve a real equality of opportunities/results, to promote intercultural communication and competency, and to overcome racism in all its expressions. (Aguado, 2003, p. 63)

This approach is essential to promote a more socially just agenda, by valuing diversity in all its dimensions and promoting intercultural understanding within school and in the wider society.

A critical recognitive perspective of social justice advocates that diverse groups must be included in all major social institutions and provided with opportunities to participate in decision-making processes, without giving up their values and beliefs (Gale & Densmore, 2000; Irving, 2005), and the critical dialogical framework (Douglas, 2005) endeavors to open communication channels through strong professional representations, seeking to influence policy and promote social justice and increasing sensitivity to the needs of those it seeks to help.

Intervention Strategies

Intervention strategies should be aimed at both individual and systemic levels. At an individual level, interviews should explore issues such as motivation to come to Spain, expectations, personal concerns, and career goals. Mohamed can be encouraged to describe his experiences of culture related to several influences (according to the STF). These accounts may be elaborated in terms of the social system, for example, levels of support and encouragement and obstacles from influences such as family, peers, and workplace (Arthur & McMahon, 2005).

A useful technique is the career portfolio *(proyecto profesional)*, which entails a process of self-analysis, that is, self-assessment of one's own potential, competencies, knowledge, values, past experiences, and so on. It can help Mohamed discover his weak and strong points and difficulties in adjusting to the university and the workplace. Furthermore, it also places an emphasis on critically analyzing the environment and the labor market (its rules, requirements, contradictions). Above all, it can help him evaluate the distance between what he wants and what is available and between what he has to offer and what he could obtain. The career portfolio involves a process of personal clarification, based on contrasting one's self with the environment (Sánchez García, 2004). That way, Mohamed could reach a better understanding of the factors that influence his career development and establish future and realistic goals.

In this sense, as Arthur (2000) stated, when people are experiencing difficulties in the acculturation process, it is easy to lose sight of progress in managing cross-cultural transitions. Alternatively, they can be encouraged to monitor specific areas of competency development, tracking critical incidents or events that are meaningful in their experience of transition.

There should also be group dynamics, with autochthonous people as well as people from other countries searching for work or planning their career with the assistance of a career development practitioner. This would help Mohamed see that his concerns and problems are quite common, and members of the group can explore and share coping strategies. At the systemic levels, interventions should focus on the social conditions that hinder the career development process and that contribute to the client's other problems. In this case, the counselor should aim at challenging the adverse conditions in the workplace and try to fight against prejudices and institutional racism. Based on the STF, Arthur and McMahon (2005) provided some interesting examples on advocacy-based interventions to address systemic influences.

Who Should Be Involved in Counseling Interventions

Career guidance or counseling services at the university should be involved. Ideally, counseling should be provided at Mohamed's university because he actually came to Spain as a student; however, not all higher education guidance centers in Spain offer holistic career development services. They usually provide information on further training, grants, work experience, and job vacancies, but little or no work is done exploring other issues related to career development, and they focus mainly on matching the person to the labor market, on his or her adjustment to it, and on the efficient use of the resources. Furthermore, they do not work from a multicultural perspective; cultural influences are not taken into account. Counseling services, addressing personal problems, are available only in a few universities, and they are usually independent from the educational and career services.

The counselor could also be part of a public employment service. These services work through collaborating with associations and nongovernmental organizations—some of which may adopt a multicultural perspective. There are many associations that work with immigrants. These associations are formed by members from their own community and by autochtonous people, for instance Moroccan associations that provide assistance in a wide range of issues.

It would also be interesting and very helpful to invite Mohamed's brother to some of the counseling sessions. Even though Mohamed might be reluctant at first, he could eventually understand his brother's position with the assistance of the counselor or find out that it is not necessary to give up one's own cultural values to adjust to a new society, although a certain level of compromise is required. At any rate, even if he is not willing to adjust, it would probably help him to adopt a different attitude and to take whatever course of action he decides, either finishing his studies or finding and maintaining a job that satisfies him, in order to go back to Morocco without the dreaded feelings of failure and humiliation.

A support group that would be very useful to engage is the Muslim community with which he relates. Some kind of collaborative relationship could be established, whereby members of the community offer their knowledge of relevant cultural issues and the availability of a peer support group, and the counselor could provide guidance in his or her areas of expertise. If at least someone from the community could take part in some activity or session, it would certainly facilitate Mohamed's engagement in career development.

If possible, potential employers should also be involved in the counseling interventions, but that is probably difficult to achieve unless they are very interested. An intercultural mediator could be engaged to help both parties reach a solution. If there had been a mediator in the case of Juan Pons, perhaps Mohamed would still be working there.

Considerations for Multicultural Counseling

According to Sue, Arredondo, and McDavis (1992), the culturally responsive counselor must have the awareness, knowledge, and skills to intervene successfully in the lives of clients from culturally diverse backgrounds, and he or she uses strategies and techniques that are consistent with the life experiences and cultural values of clients. Multicultural counseling must also consider the multiple systems of influence and multiple roles of career counselors (Arthur & McMahon, 2005). All of the issues considered in the previous sections are related to multicultural counseling.

The framework of competencies provided by Yamazaki and Kayes (2004) for successful cross-cultural adaptation can be used both in the training of counselors and in promoting intercultural competence of clients and employers. The competency clusters include building relationships, valuing people of different cultures, listening and observation, coping with ambiguity, translating complex information, taking action and initiative, managing others, possessing adaptability and flexibility, and managing stress. For each of these clusters, they proposed some behavioral indicators, knowledge or skill required, and communication ability.

References

Aguado, T. (2003). *Pedagogía intercultural* [Intercultural pedagogy]. Madrid, Spain: McGraw-Hill.

Arthur, N. (2000). Career competencies for managing cross-cultural transitions. *Canadian Journal of Counselling, 34,* 204–217.

Arthur, N., & McMahon, M. (2005). Multicultural career counseling: Theoretical applications of the Systems Theory Framework. *The Career Development Quarterly, 53,* 208–222.

Axelson, J. A. (1993). *Counseling and development in a multicultural society* (2nd ed.). Pacific Grove, CA: Brooks/Cole.

Berry, J. W. (1997). Immigration, acculturation, and adaptation. *Applied Psychology: An International Review, 46,* 5–68.

Berry, J. W. (1999). Intercultural relations in plural societies. *Canadian Psychology, 40*(1), 12–21.

Berry, J. W., & Annis, R. C. (1974). Acculturative stress: The role of ecology, culture and differentiation. *Journal of Cross-Cultural Psychology, 5,* 382–406.

Berry, J. W., Kim, U., & Boski, P. (1988). Psychological acculturation of immigration. In Y. Y. Kim & W. B. Gudykunst (Eds.), *Cross-cultural adaptation: Current approaches* (pp. 62–98). Newbury Park, CA: Sage.

Bridges, W. (1991). *Managing transitions: Making the most of change.* Reading, MA: Addison Wesley.

Cook, E. P., Heppner, M. J., & O'Brien, K. M. (2001). Career development of women of color and White women: Assumptions, conceptualization, and interventions from an ecological perspective. *The Career Development Quarterly, 50,* 291–305.

Douglas, F. (2005). Welfare to work: Economic challenges to socially just career guidance practice. In B. A. Irving & B. Malik (Eds.), *Critical reflections on career education and guidance: Promoting social justice within a global economy* (pp. 25–40). Milton Park, Abingdon, United Kingdom: RoutledgeFalmer.

Gale, T., & Densmore, K. (2000). *Just schooling: Explorations in the cultural politics of teaching.* Buckingham, United Kingdom: Open University Press.

Irving, B. A. (2005). Social justice: A context for career education and guidance. In B. A. Irving & B. Malik (Eds.), *Critical reflections on career education and guidance: Promoting social justice within a global economy* (pp. 10–24). Milton Park, Abingdon, United Kingdom: RoutledgeFalmer.

Ishiyama, F. I. (1995). Culturally dislocated clients: Self-validation and cultural conflict issues and counselling implication. *Canadian Journal of Counselling, 29,* 262–275.

Lee, C. C. (1997). The promise and pitfalls of multicultural counseling. In C. C. Lee (Ed.), *Multicultural issues in counseling: New approaches to diversity* (pp. 3–13). Alexandria, VA: American Counseling Association.

Lent, R. W., Brown, S. D., & Hackett, G. (1994). Toward a unifying social cognitive theory of career and academic interest, choice and performance. *Journal of Vocational Behavior, 45,* 79–122.

Lysgaard, S. (1955). Adjustment in foreign society: Norwegian Fulbright grantees visiting the United States. *International Social Science Bulletin, 10,* 45–51.

McMahon, M., & Patton, W. (1995). Development of a systems theory of career development. *Australian Journal of Career Development, 4*(2), 15–20.

Oberg, K. (1960). Cultural shock: Adjustment to new cultural environments. *Practical Anthropology, 7,* 177–182.

Patton, W., & McMahon, M. (1999). *Career development and systems theory: A new relationship.* Pacific Grove, CA: Brooks/Cole.

Patton, W., & McMahon, M. (2006). The Systems Theory Framework of career development and counseling: Connecting theory and practice. *International Journal for the Advancement of Counselling, 28,* 153–166.

Pedersen, P. B. (Ed.). (1991). Multiculturalism as a fourth force in counseling [Special issue]. *Journal of Counseling & Development, 70*(1).

Sánchez García, M. F. (2004). *Orientación laboral. Para la diversidad y el cambio* [Occupational guidance for diversity and change]. Madrid, Spain: Sanz y Torres.

Schlossberg, N. K., Waters, E. B., & Goodman, J. (1995). *Counseling adults in transition: Linking practice with theory* (2nd ed.). New York: Springer.

Sue, D. W., Arredondo, P., & McDavis, R. J. (1992). Multicultural counseling competencies and standards: A call to the profession. *Journal of Counseling & Development, 70,* 477–486.

Yamazaki, Y., & Kayes, D. C. (2004). *An experiential approach to cross-cultural learning: A review and integration of competencies for successful expatriate adaptation.* Retrieved May 11, 2006 from http://www.learningfromexperience.com/images/uploads/Yamazaki_and_Kayes.pdf

Cross-Cultural Adjustment for Professional Immigrant Families

Noorfarah Merali

Dalbir Kumar (all family names are pseudonyms), a 45-year-old male physician from India, immigrated 2 years ago to Canada with his wife, Gita, and their two children, Zia (10 years old) and Vivec (12 years old). Dalbir had always dreamed of living in Canada, perceiving it to be a "land of opportunity." In contrast to India's problems with overpopulation, severe gaps between the rich and poor, and tension between members of different social castes, he viewed Canada to be a developed country characterized by slower population growth, economic prosperity for all, solid educational opportunities for his children, and acceptance of diversity and multiculturalism. Although his wife and children were reluctant to leave their relatives and friends in India for an unfamiliar place, Dalbir convinced them that moving to Canada would be beneficial for the family's future.

Upon arriving in Canada, he was astonished to find that the medical training he received in India was not recognized as "adequate preparation" to practice as a physician in Canada. He was denied entry into a variety of medical practices/clinics that he had hoped to join, and his appeal to the Canadian Medical Association yielded a similar rejection of his foreign credentials. The failure to recognize education and training received outside of Canada is an ongoing problem that excludes immigrants from the Canadian job market. Seeing no immediate options in the medical field and feeling a need to obtain employment to support his family while he identified his next steps, Dalbir applied for a variety of white-collar and blue-collar jobs. For many of the jobs that required interaction with the public, such as a restaurant manager position, he received interviews but was subsequently not hired. He cited his "accented speech" and "racism" as perceived reasons for rejection, stating that he "got a negative reaction from the interviewers as soon as they saw him and heard him talk." Dalbir's perceptions of his situation are very plausible, because a number of Canadian studies have uncovered negative public attitudes toward dark-skinned immigrant groups (Berry & Kalin, 1995; Dion, 2001; Dion & Kawami, 1996; Kalin, 1996).

Dalbir ended up taking the only job he was offered: a position working on an assembly line in a meat-packaging plant. He was paid a very low wage. Given the savings he had brought to Canada, he thought he would be able to "get by" for at least a year until he found a way to enter the medical profession. Dalbir worked long hours, packing close to 100 chickens a day, with very limited breaks.

Key Issues

As time went by, Dalbir experienced more and more muscle tension and pain in his right arm from the fast-paced and repetitive nature of the work. After 8 months working at the plant, Dalbir's right arm "gave out," and he could no longer perform his tasks on the assembly line. He was referred to his family physician and then to the local Workers' Compensation Board (WCB) for an assessment of occupational injury. Dalbir was diagnosed with a severe repetitive strain injury to his right arm, which required participation in a 3-month rehabilitation program consisting of physiotherapy and occupational therapy. With treatment, it was expected that some of his pain would subside and he would be able to regain some mobility in his right arm; however, he would no longer be able to perform work tasks that would further strain it.

Dalbir was incredibly distressed by his situation. He worried about his employment prospects now that his unrecognized education and his status as a visible minority were compounded by a physical disability. He returned home from his full-day rehabilitation program each day feeling fatigued, sore, and in pain. His wife Gita cared for him by placing hot compresses on his arm, preparing his warm bath water with soothing Epson salts, and listening to all his frustrations. As he went through his rehabilitation, Dalbir and his wife decided that she should look for work even though she had always stayed home with the children. The family needed another source of income; Dalbir's WCB checks were not enough to cover the family expenses, and the family's savings were starting to become depleted. Gita quickly found a cleaning position in a nearby hotel.

The change in the family's circumstances led Dalbir to feel extreme guilt and regret about "pushing" his wife and children to move to Canada. He felt personally responsible for "ruining" his family's life and future as well as his own health. Dalbir reported feeling as if he was no longer "a real man." He could not provide for his family, he could not take care of his family but rather needed to be taken care of, and he was also a very bad decision maker. In Dalbir's view, he had failed both himself and his family. He reported experiencing severe depression, characterized by feelings of intense sadness, irritability, and hopelessness; difficulty sleeping and concentrating; reduced appetite and energy; and thoughts of ending his life.

Relationship Considerations

Dalbir also reported significant tension in his marriage and ongoing conflict. Gita's move from a stay-at-home mother to a working mother led to a great deal of resentment toward Dalbir. She expressed a great deal of frustration and anger toward him for "forcing" the family to leave their happy life in India for "a miserable life in Canada." The following interaction that transpired when Gita was placing a hot compress on Dalbir's arm illustrates the strain placed on their marriage by his injury and the reversal of their roles.

> *Gita:* I knew we should have stayed in India. We had such a happy life there—we had both of our families around us, time with the kids, lots of money, and our health. Now look what kind of life we have. You are sick, we don't have barely any money, and I have to leave the kids each day to go to work.
>
> *Dalbir:* I know I've changed everything for us. If I was okay I would still be working—I don't like you having to work. I would rather have you be at home with the kids because they need you. But what can I do? I am useless now—my hand doesn't work anymore.
>
> *Gita:* It feels like I have to wear the pants in the family now—I have to take care of you and provide for you. This is not the kind of marriage I dreamed of when I was a little girl!
>
> *Dalbir:* It's not the way I want things to be either! But do you think I can help it? Do you think I did this to myself? I didn't make my arm stop working—I was

working so hard to try and bring home some money to take care of you and the kids!

As Gita took over the breadwinner and caretaker role, Dalbir felt more and more inadequate as a man, intensifying guilt and increasing depression. He had expected Gita to console him and help him get through this difficult time, but instead the marital relationship became a stressor that compounded his sense of hopelessness and despair. From Dalbir's perspective, once Gita started working he could expect hot compresses from her, but not empathy or support.

Transition Outcomes

In Dalbir's appraisal of his situation, his move to Canada had resulted in multiple losses: (a) loss of his dream, (b) underemployment and subsequent job loss, (c) loss of health, and (d) loss of his role in the family and his sense of masculinity. These were unresolved issues at the time he presented for counseling.

Writer's Role

When I encountered Dalbir, I was working as a mental health counselor in the Repetitive Strain Injury Program at the local WCB Rehabilitation Centre. This role involved assessment and intervention. I assessed clients' psychological and interpersonal functioning, as well as their pain-coping ability. I was also responsible for providing counseling services in conjunction with clients' physical rehabilitation to assist them to cope with their work-related injuries and the impact of these injuries on their lives. I was Dalbir's counselor at the WCB Rehabilitation Centre and worked with him for 12 sessions.

Writer's Comments

Working with Dalbir sensitized me to the fact that Canada's immigration policy and its related processes often mislead immigrants. Applicants for the "independent" immigration category are admitted to Canada on the basis of a thorough assessment of their education and training to ensure that their credentials match labor market needs. This process leads highly educated and experienced immigrants like Dalbir to expect to be successful in finding employment in Canada. Immigrants are not informed of the barriers they are likely to face in having their foreign educational credentials accepted by the professional associations governing their occupations in Canada. The discrepancy between Dalbir's expectations about immigrating to Canada and the reality of his resettlement experience appeared to be no fault of his own.

Working in the role of a mental health counselor at the WCB, I encountered more immigrant clients like Dalbir than I had come across in any other counseling position. They were all people who achieved high levels of education in their countries of origin, but who, upon arriving to Canada, were unable to obtain related employment. Many ended up doing repetitive work in factory settings with limited breaks and poor working conditions. This experience highlighted the downward spiral of underemployment and the concentration of new immigrants in manual labor positions in settings with a high risk of occupational injury.

An important lesson from working with Dalbir was that when experiences of underemployment and unemployment are compounded by physical/occupational injury, men may experience a "double role reversal" in their families, which seriously challenges their sense of masculinity. Unemployment and underemployment often lead to traditional men being removed from the breadwinner or provider role that they view to be essential to their masculine identity and to previously unemployed wives entering the workforce. Physical injury may compound men's feelings of loss of masculinity by taking away some of their physical strength and leading them to require caretaking. Dalbir's case elucidated this situation. His wife replaced him in performing his two most important roles: family provider and caretaker. The loss of family status and physical health that Dalbir's situation forced him to cope with represented a major adaptation challenge during the resettlement process.

Dalbir's case also made it clear that the outcome of international transition for immigrant families may weigh heavily on the mind of the family decision maker. He had idealized life in Canadian society and had pushed his family to move abroad. In patriarchal family systems, men may have the strongest voice in making family decisions about migration, and other family members may have participated in the move with varying levels of choice or voluntariness. When migration leads to negative outcomes for the individual and the family, the person most instrumental in making the decision to move may feel the greatest sense of responsibility for the family's lost status and difficult resettlement circumstances. Other family members may also blame the family decision maker for current family problems, as did Dalbir's wife. Such family dynamics can heighten the decision maker's feelings of responsibility and contribute to family conflict after immigration.

Reader Reflection Questions

1. How do you define masculinity? How are your criteria for being masculine related to your gender socialization, culture, physical ability/disability, and employment status?
2. Are there any ways a counselor could assist Dalbir to reclaim his masculinity despite being unemployed and physically weak?
3. What counseling strategies or approaches may be useful for assisting immigrant couples to deal with the impact of role reversals on their marital relationships?
4. How do counselors instill a sense of hope among clients like Dalbir, whose negative affect stems from a realistic appraisal of their life situations (i.e., multiple barriers including a lack of recognition of foreign educational credentials, perceived racism, and physical injury)?

References

Berry, J. W., & Kalin, R. (1995). Multicultural and ethnic attitudes in Canada: Overview of the 1991 survey. *Canadian Journal of Behavioural Science, 27*, 301–320.

Dion, K. L. (2001). Immigrants' perceptions of housing discrimination in Toronto: The Housing New Canadians project. *Journal of Social Issues, 57*, 523–540.

Dion, K. L., & Kawami, K. (1996). Ethnicity and perceived discrimination in Toronto. *Canadian Journal of Behavioural Science, 28*, 203–213.

Kalin, R. (1996). Ethnic attitudes as a function of ethnic presence. *Canadian Journal of Behavioural Science, 28*, 171–179.

Response 1

Caridad Sanchez-Leguelinel, Jaya T. Mathew, and Joseph G. Ponterotto

Dalbir is a 45-year-old Indian man who is struggling with transitional and adjustment issues related to his recent decision to immigrate to Canada with his family. He has experienced much disillusionment in his self-identity during the transition, including loss of his career identity and status as a medical professional, loss of his patriarchal role in the family, loss of class status and issues of racism, and deterioration of health and physical capacity. There is also increased tension in the marriage related to the role reversal that has occurred in caretaking functions and economic provision, resulting in intense feelings of blame, guilt, and failure. As a consequence of these many losses, he is experiencing depressive symptoms exhibited in his feelings of sadness, hopelessness, and anger; decreased appetite and interest; difficulty sleeping and concentrating; and suicidal ideation.

Cultural Context: Establishing the Theoretical Framework

Building upon 4 decades of conceptual writing and research in multicultural counseling, Sue, Ivey, and Pedersen (1996) developed a comprehensive metatheory of multicultural counseling and therapy (MCT). We rely on MCT to provide the theoretical framework from which to conceptualize Dalbir's issues and establish a culturally appropriate treatment plan. We begin by briefly summarizing the six main propositions of MCT.

Proposition 1 states that MCT is a metatheory, and as such it recognizes that culture is an important component in all counseling theories. One of the main goals of MCT theory is to work with clients to develop new approaches to thinking, feeling, and acting that are consistent and respectful of their cultural framework and worldview. Proposition 2 emphasizes the importance of understanding clients as unique in their identity, as individuals, and as members of various groups. MCT theory emphasizes the importance of providing an open environment for individuals to relate to the world from their various identities.

Proposition 3 focuses on the many factors that influence counseling goals and process. Cultural identity is developed through a series of cognitive, emotional, and behavioral stages that produce different attitudes toward oneself and others. MCT theory promotes equality in the relationship (eliminating traditional counselor–client power differentials) and working together toward a common goal. Proposition 4 stresses the need to develop therapeutic interventions and goals that are consistent with an individual's life experience and cultural values. MCT theory encourages openness to new treatment alternatives from different countries and cultures that have previously been discounted in Western cultures.

In Proposition 5, MCT theory proposes to expand the traditional conceptualization of counseling. Furthermore, the theory challenges existing ethical standards that promote a narrow Western definition of the counseling relationship. In addition, community resources and outside support units, as well as informal settings and methods, are seen as vehicles to enhance the therapeutic relationship. Finally, Proposition 6 emphasizes the importance of the liberation of consciousness as a basic goal in MCT theory (Utsey, Bolden, & Brown, 2001). This implies that only in understanding the development of an individual's relationship to self, family, community, and organization can the counseling process be effective. As such, counselors draw from traditional methods of counseling from various cultures and adapt theories that are respectful of an individual's culture.

Understanding the Issues From an Indian Cultural Context

To understand fully the complexities and difficulties of the international transition for the Kumar family, it is important to examine the issues from a cultural context, specifically, the Indian culture. Although diverse, the Indian culture and community are generally grounded in three primary concepts: caste, karma, and dharma. Caste refers to a hierarchical classification of individuals regarding social position, employment, and wealth. Karma refers to an individual's destiny and the belief that a person whose works are selfless and focus on devotion to God is more likely to be at a higher status in his or her next life than a person whose actions are selfish and focused on himself or herself. Thus, one's earthly actions influence one's destiny. Dharma refers to living life in harmony with the universe. It further reflects responsibility, in that all people have duties that they must fulfill to other people, their family, and God. How well people accomplish these duties affects their status in their subsequent life. Many Indians believe that karma determines caste, which in turn determines social standing, class status, educational opportunities, wealth, respect, and life circumstances such as marriage. Inherent in these concepts are the notions of patience and harmony, most clearly exhibited in tolerance toward religion and diversity (Almeida, 1996).

Social Status

Regarding caste, Dalbir presents a multilayered and complex situation relating to status. In a hierarchical system, it can be determined that an educated and practicing medical professional, with a capacity to accumulate savings, would be close to the higher end of the caste system. The family is likely to have benefited from privileges associated with this class status, including respect and ranking within the community, economic stability that frequently includes retaining servants to perform household duties, and increased possibility for opportunities such as immigration, which would be impossible for individuals of lower class ranking. The Kumar family's transition to Canada becomes particularly traumatic when its social class standing is so significantly affected. Dalbir moves from being an economically prosperous medical professional to an unemployed and disabled individual, unable to provide for himself or his family. The high value placed on respect in the Indian cultures makes his shift from respected professional to a racially discriminated minority, who is only able to find employment on an assembly line in a meat-packing company, especially difficult. He also experiences the descent of his wife, Gita, in the social class system as she moves from family and home caretaker to hotel maid, which may be considered equivalent to a servant and a person of much lower social class standing.

Masculinity—Gender Roles

Dalbir also struggles with the loss of his traditional male role in the family and his self-identity as a man. In the Indian culture, masculinity is often defined through employment and economic status, physical strength, strong mental capacity, and respect within the community. Men are often socialized to be the provider, leader, and adviser for the entire family. Dalbir's self-esteem and male identity have been challenged, beginning with his move from caretaker of the family to needing care from his wife and family. His current unemployment status and subsequent need to depend on his wife for financial support have an especially strong impact in the Indian culture.

Beyond providing financial stability, men are often responsible for providing the physical strength and emotional support for the family. Dalbir is experiencing challenges in both areas, with his decreasing physical strength and ability resulting from his severe injury and his intense feelings of regret and self-doubt regarding his decision to move the family to Canada. Dalbir may also be experiencing shame at his use of psychological services for his depressive state, which can be perceived as a weakness. Last, his professed failures as the caretaker of the family, husband, father, and provider would all challenge his perceptions of self-esteem, worth, identity, and respect.

Indian Community

The role of community is very important in the Indian culture, because it can serve as either a great source of support or a great source of shame and embarrassment. The Indian community can be competitive, and individuals are often defined by their economic and social status. Self-identity and respect are usually experienced as an extension of an individual's role and standing within the community. Dalbir clearly retains his status as a medical professional within the Indian community, but it is now marred by his failure to establish himself in Canada and the subsequent financial difficulties that have occurred in his family. He may be questioned by the community on his judgment, decision-making capacity, and failures. These factors may serve to further promote his sense of shame and desire for isolation from the community and serve to promote his loss of respect by self, family, and the community.

Acculturation

The issues related to Dalbir's immigration have made the process of acculturation particularly challenging. Acculturation refers to the dynamic process of integrating into a new culture while maintaining one's own culture. The extent to which Indian individuals are able to acculturate depends on various factors, including class status, social standing, economic stability, family size, education level, religious beliefs, understanding of the new culture, connectedness to the previous culture, community supports in the new and previous culture, and willingness to immigrate and adapt to the new culture (Almeida, 1996). Dalbir struggles with issues of acculturation because he moved his family to Canada with the hope of finding greater economic, educational, and cultural opportunities; however, his family moved with limited willingness and little community support. He did not have sufficient information about the new culture to understand that his medical credentials would not be recognized and that issues of discrimination and racism would severely impede his opportunity to prosper and succeed. His multiple losses—of status, masculine and caretaker identities, connection and respect from the community and his family, along with his inability to establish himself within the new culture—have made successful acculturation very difficult.

Cultural Context: The Immigration Experience

The Kumar family is also dealing with natural stages of culture shock (Oberg, 1960), which Pedersen (1995) described as the internalized and personal process that occurs when individuals are faced with unexpected and unfamiliar situations in a new environment, along with their adjustment to these situations. The adjustment includes development of new perceptions of self and others that will allow the individual to better function and manage in the new environment. Culture shock is experienced in varying degrees as individuals navigate through the complexities of adjusting, depending on their ability to cope with the multifaceted challenges they encounter. The culture shock process can be identified through five stages: the honeymoon stage, disintegration stage, reintegration stage, autonomy stage, and interdependence stage (Adler, 1975).

The honeymoon stage refers to the time when the individual is excitedly exploring and experiencing a new setting with high hopes for opportunity and growth. During this initial excitement, the individual remains firmly attached to his or her own culture, identity, and experiences. The disintegration stage is characterized by an overwhelming experience of the differences between cultures and the inherent difficulties that will be encountered in the process of adjustment to and coping with the new environment. Individuals tend to internalize their inadequacies in coping, which in turn leads to feelings of blame and failure. The reintegration stage is notable by the individual's attempt to function and integrate within the new culture. There is frequently a perception of the new culture as being unacceptable and unsatisfactory compared with the previous culture, which is expressed in feelings of anger and bitterness toward the new culture that presents great adjustment difficulties. The autonomy stage continues the reintegration process, with increased bicultural identity that facilitates a balance between the two cultures and an increased sense of ability to function in the new culture. The last stage is known as the interdependence stage and is characterized by a multicultural integration in which the individual is able to embrace both cultures; appreciate positive aspects and understand negative influences of the cultures; and function, develop, and prosper through a reciprocal interdependence on both cultures.

In understanding Dalbir's process through culture shock, it is evident that he transitioned through the first stage quickly and had very little opportunity to truly feel the excitement and anticipation of a new experience. The rejection of his medical credentials, the extensive difficulty he had in finding employment, and the realization that his decision to immigrate has led to extensive hardships for himself and his family contribute to his feelings of self-blame and failure that are frequently characterized by the second stage of disintegration. Dalbir is presently struggling with the third stage of reintegration, in which he blames the new culture for the difficulties he has experienced, his feelings of inadequacy, and his failure and inability to cope. He continues to struggle with feelings of anger, blame, hopelessness, and an overwhelming sense of failure that make further progress through the culture shock stages particularly difficult.

Treatment Plan and Intervention Strategies

To integrate cultural sensitivity and awareness in the treatment plan, it is important to consider core values that transcend the worldviews of many Indian people (Ho, 1987). Generally speaking, many Indians strive to live harmoniously with the world and their environment while maintaining a strong work ethic, self-discipline, modesty, and respect for life. They identify with selfless, modest, and humble beliefs that allow them to remain stoic and uncomplaining when confronting and struggling with life's adversities and challenges. Indian men are responsible for the family's well-being and are expected to work hard and make any sacrifices necessary for the success and stability of the family. There is an inherent belief that individuals should be accepting of life's struggles in order to be rewarded and ascend to a higher caste in the next life (Almeida, 1996). Finally, many Indians believe that they should not impose on others by requiring assistance to deal with their life struggles. Many of these beliefs may present obstacles to the use of traditional Western psychological services.

Many Indians may perceive counseling as a brief and direct intervention that must deal with the present difficulties and future destiny. Therapists must maintain an awareness of the balance between the traditional cultural values and the new cultural mandates that individuals continually confront as they struggle to acculturate to a new environment. Counselors will want to validate and respect the hierarchical roles of members in the family structure, with the husband/father meriting the greatest level of respect and obedience, the wife/mother providing the nurturing care of the family, and the children feeling obligation and loyalty toward the family.

Indian immigrants to North America may prefer treatment sessions that last for extended periods of time and look for concrete advice that is respectful of their complex family and cultural issues. They may present with symptoms of depression, reflecting deeper underlying feelings and conflicts that they are experiencing. This is related to the fact that many Indians may be hesitant to speak of personal feelings because it is thought to be self-focused and disrespectful of the family (Almeida, 1996; Ho, 1987).

Individual Interventions

Atkinson, Thompson, and Grant (1993) described a three-dimensional counseling model to be used in the treatment of ethnic minorities and immigrant populations. The model assists counselors in selecting appropriate roles and interventions that are based on locus of the problem, level of acculturation, and counseling goals. Expanded roles for counselors is a theme highly consistent with MCT theory. The locus of the problem identifies the source of the problem as being an internal process, such as personality or emotionally driven, or an external process, such as factors of racism and discrimination. Level of acculturation describes the extent to which an individual has adapted to the values, beliefs, and customs of the new culture and is measured on a continuum from low to high. Counseling goals can be characterized as being in two main categories, prevention of problems and remediation of problems, with the client and his or her culture determining the focus and direction of the goals. Regarding the three-dimensional counseling model, Dalbir's presentation can be described as representing an external locus of the problems, with low acculturation and requiring remediation.

Counselors are encouraged to incorporate nontraditional roles in their treatment modality to be reflective of the client's placement on the three counseling dimensions. The counselor's roles vary greatly, beginning with adviser, advocate, facilitator of indigenous support systems, facilitator of indigenous healing systems, consultant, change agent, and counselor and ending with traditional psychotherapist. With respect to Dalbir and according to the Atkinson et al. (1993) model, the counselor's main role should be that of advocate because of the need to remediate the problems that have resulted from oppression and racial discrimination. A large part of this role would be to establish a relationship with Dalbir that would allow him to develop the goals for counseling. The counselor may also want to provide direct advocacy on behalf of Dalbir regarding the inherent discrimination and inequities of foreign medical credentialing as well as advocating with appropriate governmental agencies regarding the overt and hidden racism that occurs on varying levels in the Canadian community. In fact, the need for counseling professionals to be more proactive socially in fighting external factors such as racism, religious bigotry, and unfair employment practices is currently an important thrust in the field (see recent work by Toporek, Gerstein, Fouad, Roysircar, & Israel, 2006).

The counselor's role, however, does not need to be limited to that of advocate; it can also incorporate some aspects of adviser and facilitator of indigenous support systems. Both of these roles take a more preventative approach in promoting the counseling goals. As an adviser, the counselor can be helpful to Dalbir by informing him that his emotional reaction to his immigration and current life circumstances, including feelings of depression, failure, guilt, and blame, is consistent with the immigrant experience in which individuals struggle with racial discrimination and cultural conflicts that place them at an extreme disadvantage in the community. This is especially relevant for Dalbir, who places the blame for all his family conflicts on himself rather than on the more accurate and appropriate external sources in the new culture. The counselor can be instrumental in advising Dalbir on the strategies that can help to ease the impact of these problems and to develop an awareness to prevent the problems in the future. As a facilitator of indigenous support systems, the counselor can help Dalbir attribute his feelings of depression, insecurity, and failure to a common internal reaction that results from the transition to a new culture. The counselor can assist Dalbir in establishing support systems similar to those that existed in India. Once the support systems are in place, they can work to prevent further internalization of feelings that result from Dalbir's culture shock and stress during his continued transition to the new environment.

Marital Therapy

The process of immigration frequently results in the change of status and roles within the martial relationship (Ho, 1987). Given the negative stigma associated with divorce and separation in Indian culture, conflict between the couple may be a source of great concern and stress. Ho (1987) described four intervention strategies that can be used in the treatment of Asian/Pacific couples. The therapist will first need to assess the couple's readiness for therapy. In the case of Dalbir and Gita, the therapist will assess the extent to which they are able to express their feelings about each other openly, the role reversal that has occurred in their marriage, the impact on their sexual life, and the feelings related to the many challenges that they have encountered in their transition. Second, the therapist will want to place emphasis on the social moral explanation of marital disharmony. Dalbir and Gita will be invited to consider their adapted roles in the marriage as a vehicle to solve the family problems. Consistent with the belief that Indians must do everything within their power to preserve the family unit, the couple can reframe the importance of their new role expectations to be consistent with this belief. Next, the therapist may challenge the couple's willingness and ability to collaborate. The therapist may explore the feelings of shame, confusion, and frustration that are being expressed by Dalbir and Gita to redirect their struggle toward a focus on obligation and self-worth. Given the obligation of sacrifice for future life fulfillment, the couple may reconceptualize their self-sacrifices as a way to regain positive self-worth and appreciation from the spouse. The understanding that the sacrifice is being experienced for the benefit of the family will ease the many negative feelings currently associated with the conflicts. Last, the therapist will want to teach the couple skills for negotiation. As Dalbir and Gita develop modified roles in their relationships, they will be required to develop new negotiation skills to manage the conflicts that arise from the new roles.

Family Systems

A family-centered approach may be beneficial in the treatment, because the Indian family provides the core framework for individual identity and development (Almeida, 1996). Ho (1987) proposed a family therapy approach to be used with ethnic minorities and specified the benefits of this approach for Asian/Pacific families who have recently immigrated to America. He described the specific techniques and skills to be applied in the beginning, problem-solving, and evaluation and termination phases of counseling.

In the beginning phase, the therapist is responsible to educate the family on the use of therapy, to describe the course of treatment, and to identify the structure that will be used in the treatment. This is accomplished through various applicable skills, including engaging the family, collecting data and cultural transitional mapping, mutual goal setting, and selecting a focus for therapy. For the Kumar family, this could include engaging the family by establishing trust and rapport. A therapist can demonstrate concern for the family by expressing warmth and acceptance for all family members and by being open to questions regarding the therapist's personal background.

Next, the therapist can gather background information about the members of the Kumar family and their transition to Canada, through traditional questioning and nontraditional techniques such as encouraging the family to tell stories through family photography and music. This information is used to develop a comprehensive map to understand the transitional positioning of the family and should include personal demographic data, past problem-solving ability, family structure and role definitions, social and cultural data, and the process of migration for the family and the individual members. The therapist can then assist the Kumar family in developing goals for treatment that are culturally contextualized and realistically based on their needs for employment and rehabilitation. Focusing the treatment on external problems will allow the family to respond more positively to treatment and allow Dalbir to minimize his feelings of shame and failure regarding the family and will assist in reestablishing his position in the family.

Last, the therapist will need to make a determination about which family members or subsystems should be included in the therapy process. Before including the children in treatment, Zia, age 10, and Vivec, age 12, the therapist will need to consider that Dalbir and Gita will be hesitant to express their feelings because of fear of losing authority or control in front of their children. They will also be concerned about the expression of negative feelings by their children, which would reflect a lack of respect for them as parents and result in feelings of shame.

In the problem-solving phase of treatment, the therapist can use an indirect approach; social, moral, and organic reframing and relabeling; promotion of filial piety, obligation, and self-control; restructuring of social support systems; and employment of a therapist helper to serve as techniques for problem solving. A therapist will want to use a nonconfrontational and indirect approach when needing to challenge Dalbir's impasse regarding his personal situation and family conflicts. The therapist will also want to redefine the current family conflicts to be reflective of outside negative forces rather than as a direct result of Dalbir's failings. By reframing the family's difficulties as representative of life's general struggles and sacrifices, which can lead to rewards in future destiny, the therapist can alleviate feelings of blame, failing, and shame that interfere with the family's ability to focus on specific problem solving. The therapist is encouraged to take a very active role, representative of a teacher or coach, during this technique to facilitate the relabeling of the family's conflicts. In promoting filial piety, obligation, and self-control, the therapist can emphasize the family's obligations to remain together as a unit and can encourage parents to exercise self-control with each other and the other family members. Dalbir and Gita would be encouraged to support each other in direct and positive ways that would fulfill their duty to maintain harmony with life and within their family. It would also strengthen their parental position and serve as important modeling for their children.

The therapist is also charged with restructuring the social support system for the family. It is common for recently immigrated families to isolate themselves from the larger community and become overly self-contained, resulting in unrealistic demands on family members. The therapist will want to help the members of the Kumar family reestablish a social support system that is reflective of their cultural and transitional needs. This support network can be instrumental in helping the Kumar family navigate the many challenges that they have faced in their transition and to develop more acculturated skills that will facilitate their continued transition. Finally, the therapist may want to consider the use of a therapist helper who can more easily navigate in the family system. For the Kumar family, the helper could be an elder family member or a respected member of the community who would be an impartial mediator in the conflict resolution, with regular coaching and supervision from the therapist.

In the last phase of treatment, evaluation and termination, the therapist may want to rely on nontraditional methods to evaluate the progress of treatment. It is important to remember that the emphasis on humility and modesty may prevent the Kumar family from articulating self-promoting expressions of progress and development. Furthermore, a reduction of symptoms would not necessarily reflect improvement in the family structure or relationships. The therapist may consider visiting the Kumar family and attending social events in their community to assess progress and development. However, such action needs to be carefully considered, because, in some cases, it could bring shame and embarrassment on the family.

With respect to termination, the therapist must keep in mind the notion that some Indians may believe that they are imposing on others when they seek help outside the family and feel shame in being a burden to the therapist, resulting in a possible premature request for termination. A therapist may also want to consider some form of culturally appropriate contact with the family after termination. This would provide a model for the possibilities of good relationships for the family outside of the traditional family structure.

Conclusion

The case of Dalbir and his family as immigrants to North America is complex and requires careful conceptualization and intervention planning. Unfortunately, the struggles of the

Kumar family, while unique in their total constellation, are not uncommon, because many professional immigrant families face similar hardships, prejudice, and culture shock as they adjust to work and life in their new homeland. In our response to the Kumar family scenario, we attempted to incorporate culturally relevant conceptualizations and culturally consistent interventions. In doing so, we risked overgeneralizing core cultural values of the Indian people. It is essential to highlight that the Indian people are very diverse, with different religions, languages, acculturation levels, and worldviews represented among the many immigrants who live in North America. As such, some of our interpretations and interventions may be appropriate for some Indian immigrant families, but certainly not all. It is the ethical duty of the counselor or therapist to conduct a full multicultural assessment before reaching any conclusions about what a family's problems may be or what intervention plan is most appropriate.

References

Adler, P. S. (1975). The transitional experience: An alternative view of culture shock. *Journal of Humanistic Psychology, 15,* 13–23.

Almeida, R. (1996). Hindu, Christian, and Muslim families. In M. McGoldrick, J. Giordano, & J. K. Pearce (Eds.), *Ethnicity & family therapy* (2nd ed., pp. 395–423). New York: Guilford Press.

Atkinson, D. R., Thompson, C. E., & Grant, S. K. (1993). A three-dimensional model for counseling racial/ethnic minorities. *The Counseling Psychologist, 21,* 257–277.

Ho, M. K. (1987). *Family therapy with ethnic minorities.* Newbury Park, CA: Sage.

Oberg, K. (1960). Culture shock: Adjustment to new cultural environments. *Practical Anthropology, 7,* 177–182.

Pedersen, P. (1995). *The five stages of culture shock: Critical incidents around the world.* Westport, CT: Greenwood Press.

Sue, D. W., Ivey, A. E., & Pedersen, P. B. (1996). *A theory of multicultural counseling and therapy.* Pacific Grove, CA: Brooks/Cole.

Toporek, R. L., Gerstein, L. H., Fouad, N. A., Roysircar, G., & Israel, T. (2006). *Handbook for social justice in counseling psychology: Leadership, vision, and action.* Thousand Oaks, CA: Sage.

Utsey, S. O., Bolden, M. A., & Brown, A. L. (2001). Visions of revolution from the spirit of Franz Fanon: A psychology of liberation for counseling African Americans confronting societal racism and oppression. In J. G. Ponterotto, J. M. Casas, L. A. Suzuki, & C. A. Alexander (Eds.), *Handbook of multicultural counseling* (2nd ed., pp. 311–336). Thousand Oaks, CA: Sage.

Response 2

Adam Zagelbaum and Jon Carlson

Dalbir and his family are significantly struggling with culture clashes that affect gender roles, socioeconomic status (SES), educational level, and interpersonal issues. The initial concern that Dalbir experienced with his medical degree and license not being recognized in Canada has shattered his dream of working in his intended field and challenged his methods to provide for his family. Although the medical profession is a challenging one, the training requirements to enter it in India are not as intensive or lengthy as they are in the United States and Canada. This matter has historically been a problem for immigrants coming to North America in order to practice medicine, and the problem continues today.

The University of Alberta (2006), for example, does not accept international students into its medical program. There are likely many cases of people such as Dalbir who are either misinformed about the way in which their medical licenses are received in Canada or do not understand that the Medical Counsel of Canada has a specific testing and training protocol that must be followed. Strassman (2006) noted that this issue is also relevant to U.S. citizens who wish to practice medicine in Canada; therefore, Dalbir may be able to take comfort in the fact that he is not alone in his struggle.

Professional Practice Issues for Immigrants in Canada

Even when immigrants are approved for Canadian citizenship, they are required to pass several Canadian exams and the Test of English as a Foreign Language. Canadian medical graduates must perform these same tasks (University of Alberta, 2006). However, after these tests are passed, international medical graduates are often required to receive additional training within Canada in order to obtain the license. Such training usually is incurred as an additional expense for the license seeker and takes at minimum 1 year (Strassman, 2006). There are different amounts of training, however, required for different Canadian cities and provinces. It is not surprising, therefore, to see that Dalbir may be highly frustrated with the amount of time and financial expenses involved in obtaining a Canadian medical license.

Caste Issues

Dalbir also has a significant issue regarding his status as an educated man coming from India. In previous centuries, the caste system was more overt in India than it is now. Although undertones of the caste system and covert messages about it still exist in the society, the caste system itself does not appear to be overly salient, but there are some covert belief systems still in place, whereby people are perceived in hierarchical fashions that relate to socioeconomic status and opportunities related to said status. It is possible that Dalbir is Hindu and not Muslim. The majority Hindu population often portrays Muslims as less educated and qualified (Ali, 2002). According to Ali, since 1948 Muslims have been experiencing major downward social mobility in India. Many of these individuals have lost their positions in the government and have not been able to receive the education to become functionally literate in the national languages of Hindi and English. These social, educational, and economic factors have divided and estranged Hindus and Muslims where it appears that many Muslims are not likely to have as many educational and social opportunities as Hindus. This is why Dalbir, as an educated man with the status of a doctor, may be more likely to be Hindu. In much the same way as non-Whites in the United States often have their roles and identities defined by the dominant White culture (Ali, 2002), Dalbir may have engaged in this type of behavior in his native country. In Canada, however, Dalbir is not part of the majority White culture, which may also be contributing to his loss of esteem and identity.

White-Collar Versus Blue-Collar Work

Members of low-SES households and blue-collar workers are often viewed as low functioning and undereducated in many countries, likely because of the fundamental attribution error (Norenzayan & Nisbett, 2000). Western cultures are particularly overt about these perceptions because of their tendency to focus on individuals instead of on situational factors (Norenzayan & Nisbett, 2000). This is highly unfortunate for Dalbir, because not only is he dealing with the fact that he is not recognized as being a white-collar worker, but he is also dealing with the reality of having to actually perform blue-collar work in order to contribute financially to his family. In India, Dalbir would be ridiculed by members of his profession and SES group for engaging in such work. It is somewhat a common practice for lower SES individuals to pretend that they are Sheikhs in an attempt to avoid ostracism and embarrassment (Ali, 2002). Ali referred to the "Sheikh factor" (p. 604), that is, lower ranking Muslim caste groups attempting to raise their status over time by claiming that they are Sheikh. A white-collar worker being demoted to blue-collar status is both overtly demeaning to Dalbir and covertly demeaning because of the personal shame and feelings of failure that may be dominating his self-perception at the present time. In other words, Dalbir is likely to be extremely depressed because of the work he is unable to perform and the social perceptions others would have of him in his culture for doing such work. All of these issues are also compounded by the fact that he is male.

Gender Issues

Dalbir's masculine identity in his native country is overtly awarded by its paternalistic society. Men are largely expected to be breadwinners in Indian culture, and they are accustomed to have certain entitlements because of the caste system. Because Dalbir was able to seek education to be a doctor, he would be ascribed certain rights by the lower castes because of his demanding work. He was able to receive higher wages because of his education and employment position. He was also able to marry a woman of the same caste. It is because of these factors that Dalbir may be accustomed to having a certain sense of entitlement and control within his family, which is not uncommon for many men in his position (Krishnan, 2005). Dalbir is probably viewed in his native country as a "macho" man because of the power and prestige associated with his work, SES, and family role as breadwinner; therefore, his inability to perform these roles in Canada is a crushing blow for him.

Gita, on the other hand, would not be expected, in many cases, to provide family income and may not even be granted educational opportunities in Indian culture (Krishnan, 2005). With her husband in a highly respected profession, she might not view herself as someone who must seek education or employment. In her native country, however, she might be susceptible to marital violence if placed in an impoverished situation and with the additional stress associated with having multiple children to care for (Martin, Tsui, Maitra, & Marinshaw, 1999). In some Indian states, research has demonstrated that although physical violence against women by their husbands is often higher in low SES households, sexual violence against women by their husbands is often higher in high SES households (Duvvury, Nayak, & Allendorf, 2002). Thus, Gita's gender role status is also an issue when it comes to understanding how Dalbir's experience can affect the entire family. It is probably undesirable for her that she must take on a role as a wage earner, and it is insulting to have a husband who cannot perform work that allows for a steady income. Although the maternal role of caring for her husband may be a natural tendency for Gita, the necessity for Dalbir to be cared for by his wife because he was injured doing blue-collar work would be viewed as personal failures that have forced Gita to sacrifice her femininity.

Theoretical Frameworks That Inform the Response

Adlerian therapy (Carlson, Watts, & Maniacci, 2006) provides positive and encouraging ways to work with clients and specifically relates to Dalbir and his family. This approach frames individuals and systems within a strength-based model that does not take away from the natural powers and abilities of the participating parties. The counselor is not viewed as an expert, and the client is not viewed as a novice. This is especially important for dealing with clients who may already be feeling powerless and imposed on by others. Dalbir and his family were capable of learning, communicating, and modeling effective behaviors; however, others did not view them in terms of such strengths. Meetings with job interviewers were viewed as trials, in which Dalbir had to "prove" himself, instead of opportunities to collaborate and work toward resolution of the issues. The same is true for Gita, who had to "prove her worth" to the family by seeking employment and taking care of Dalbir's injuries. These constraints have placed labels and restraints on the resources within the family system. Thus, instead of defining the solutions, Dalbir and his family spent more time working through issues of frustration with the Canadian Medical Association because of the perceived and actual amount of disrespect. The use of certain problem-centered approaches in this particular case would target individuals like Dalbir and Gita for their shortcomings instead of recognizing systemic strengths.

How Can Counseling Be Made Appropriate?

One significant factor that should be noted is that elders are highly respected in Indian culture. It is not usually the practice for younger individuals to bestow advice on older individuals. In order to respect this cultural practice, a therapist working with Dalbir should not be younger than he is. Because Indian culture is collectivist, it is also recommended that Dalbir's family be included in the process.

The family system in Indian culture is a highly respected unit (McGoldrick, Giordano, & Pearce, 1996). Family members are not usually encouraged to seek external help in order to resolve personal matters because this can be seen as a failure of the collective unit; however, considering that Dalbir and his family do not have other members to turn to in Canada, seeking help from a therapist appears necessary. This resource may be the only way to effectively engage the system in a healing process, especially because it is clear that the stressors are at an all-time high for Dalbir and Gita. Considering how much authority parents have in the Indian family system (McGoldrick et al., 1996), it is likely that the children are experiencing stress and depression vicariously from Dalbir and Gita.

Using a family approach in this case would show respect to the communal perspective to which this family is accustomed. A positive or solution-focused approach may also help to mediate tensions that exist between Dalbir and many of the people with whom he typically has contact. Given that Dalbir is constantly feeling challenged and insulted by others regarding the emasculated roles in which he has been placed, calling attention to what his family members are doing well may allow a more collaborative working alliance to be formed. By brainstorming ways in which the family can use its strengths to work through this incident, a sense of group responsibility is established. Systemically, this also means that no one member is to blame if a solution does not immediately work. Dalbir can believe that his knowledge and expertise have relevance, Gita has the ability to see that she is not to blame, and Zia and Vivec have a chance to contribute their thoughts and feelings as well. In the larger community and school context, it will be easier to address the need for the children to have peer networks and the resources to promote these resources in this system. This also respects the family's value toward partnerships. It is important to recognize that the family consists of very intelligent members who have learned English and connected interpersonally with Canadians in order to make the move from India. By focusing on solutions, these qualities are not overlooked or disrespected.

Reclaiming Masculinity

Considering that masculinity has long been a concept significantly derived from being an active member of the family and workplace, it is not surprising that Dalbir would be struggling with this issue in both settings. Englar-Carlson and Stephens (2006) and Kiselica (2001) have advocated for counseling approaches to become more focused on *male-friendliness*, meaning that the issue of masculinity needs to be openly discussed. Recommendations for reframing the counseling approach include reexamining the formal office setting and using tactics that build on male strengths in order to establish rapport and validate the man's presence for being involved with the counseling process. Although Dalbir may not be an active member of the workforce because of his physical injury, he still has effective problem-solving skills. Using these qualities as the foundation for counseling would allow Dalbir to feel respected by the counselor and encouraged to apply his strengths in areas that would allow for him to become active in other ways.

One of these other ways would involve becoming an advocate for people like him who have their credentials denied by the Canadian Medical Board. Dalbir can take charge of the situation by networking with other people who are interested in taking up his cause and speaking to members of the government who can further advocate for his rights. In doing so, Dalbir becomes a pioneer and/or leader among community members, who may previously have been unaware of how this matter affects people like him.

Dalbir may also be able to use his talents in closely related fields such as a pharmaceutical researcher, sales representative, and/or international relations worker for a drug company. Although he would not be practicing medicine, he would still be able to put his training and knowledge of medicine to use. Because not every employee of a drug company has been formally trained in medicine, Dalbir would also be viewed as somewhat of an expert. This would allow him to regain some sense of respect and esteem that was likely devalued when he was not able to apply for licensure.

Often, men devalue themselves by believing they are not living up to their masculine ideals. It is not unusual for someone like Dalbir to feel fearful and angry and exhibit signs of depression (O'Neil & Fishman, 1986). The key to empowering Dalbir is to address the reality of his situation and to reframe his previously salient skills in a way that can be applied to his present circumstances. By showing Dalbir that he can use his skills in other ways than holding a job, he may be less inclined to devalue himself and more inclined to realign himself with the male values and characteristics that helped influence his family to move to Canada in the first place.

As far as his marriage is concerned, the same strategy applies. Gita has taken on the role of breadwinner, but this does not mean that Dalbir has relinquished his masculinity. The counselor can focus on the reality of this situation by demonstrating that Gita has not stopped her nurturing roles regarding the mother–child relationship just because she has taken on the role of a worker. Thus, the same is true for Dalbir. He has not lost his ability to advocate and network with others who can help him find resources to take up the matter of his unrecognized credentials. Pointing out to Gita that she had placed some degree of trust in Dalbir in the past to provide for his family may serve as an important source of empathy that she can use to support him during this stressful period. In addition, considering that aforementioned research has demonstrated that individuals like Dalbir may often react to stress by sexually assaulting their spouses (Duvvury et al., 2002), Gita may also feel encouraged that her husband has remained faithful and stable within their marital relationship and has not engaged in such acts. Dalbir should be respected for putting himself into the blue- and white-collar positions that he did because of the trust that he had in his family to stand by him during this unfortunate period. The systemic elements of provider, nurturer, child, and citizen are still present in the Kumar family, but circumstances have altered the specific behaviors of those who contribute these elements to the system. In other words, the system still has strengths, but they have just taken on a temporary restructuring.

Instilling Hope

The matter of instilling hope is not a simplistic issue that can be accomplished with a single act, but because Dalbir is a skilled individual who has used facts and data in his profession as a doctor, an assessment instrument may be a good way of beginning this process. The use of testimonials and bibliotherapy can be used to show Dalbir that there are immigrants in Canada who are struggling with similar predicaments, and this is an important starting point that will allow him to see that although he is not a member of a caste in Canada, he is a member of a significant group of professionals. Administration of the Masculine Gender Role Stress Scale (Eisler & Skidmore, 1987) can better inform Dalbir that what he is currently experiencing is a normal process when an individual's normal activities as breadwinner are reduced in some capacity. Showing Dalbir the data that support the normative pieces of his situation can encourage him to recognize that he is not solely responsible for the stress he has been experiencing at home and in the world-of-work. In addition, by using a scale, Dalbir can begin to operationalize ways in which he and his family can cope better with the stress. The use of a scale implies that changes in frequency and intensity will occur. The counselor would have to reassess Dalbir at certain points in order to note improvements, but in doing so, tangible steps are taken to ensure that changes are being made.

The other small step that can be made toward instilling Dalbir with hope in the counseling process is calling attention to the fact that gender is largely a social construction. Dalbir is clearly down on himself for not having a salient provider role within his family at the present time, but pointing out examples of societies in which the role of provider and caregiver are not as clearly delineated may enhance his sense of identity. He can network with other men who are not the breadwinners in their families in order to see that there are a group of people who share his struggle but who make adjustments to maintain their strengths and abilities within their family system.

Intervention Strategies

Because Dalbir was and remains particularly skilled in the area of medicine and record keeping, the idea of using his interpersonal communication skills would serve him well in terms of getting an audience with a Canadian minister of health care and finding other people who would share in his cause to have his credentials properly recognized. There are several testimonials and publications that should likely be given to Dalbir so that, at the least, he can gain an understanding of how immigrants often have difficulty obtaining medical licensure in Canada (Strassman, 2006). There may also be individuals who would be willing to sponsor him for training that could allow him to gain a temporary status as a supervised provider of medical services. Dalbir would have to pass the required tests and pay necessary fees to gain this temporary status, but such arrangements may be possible (Strassman, 2006). Dalbir could use his talents to keep weekly records of his progress in the meetings with members of his community and set up a regular meeting time when these reports could be discussed with his family. This strategy would allow Dalbir to regain much of the family time he had lost when working, while at the same time it might encourage his children to work harder at school. Systemically, Dalbir would also be able to have a way of bringing data into parent–teacher conferences, which would allow people in the school systems to understand that Dalbir and his family were willing to work with the system. Dalbir would also be able to feel valued by those who would listen to his ideas and become less defensive when working with government officials.

Another strategy that could be used in this case is having the family communicate more with members of the local community when they were feeling stressed. Attending the local Hindu temple may allow Dalbir to feel connected to some members of his faith and receive a necessary advocacy voice for those affected by his situation. There are currently 70 temples in Canada (Kukreja, n.d.). Although there are approximately 297,200 practicing Hindus in Canada, this is still a minority group (Kukreja, n.d.). Dalbir and his family may not feel comfortable seeking out this type of support or connection on their own, because they are from India and may not perceive enough of a connection to Canadian Hindus. However, because family members are likely feeling isolated and removed from their culture, encouraging them to seek this contact may aid in the mediation of stress and depression. Knowing that there are other well-respected and educated Hindus in their community may provide additional support and relief that cannot be accomplished through counseling alone.

By involving their children in local peer networks, Dalbir and Gita would also become more familiar with other parents in their community. Although it is not the same type of connection to community that they were accustomed to in their native country, it is a better transition into the local community than when Dalbir initially began his employment venture.

Who Should Be Involved in Counseling Interventions?

Because of the systemic interactions involved with this particular case, it is imperative that the whole family work together to ensure the most effective outcome. Dalbir would have a specific role in using his interpersonal skills to advocate for help from the community, the children would have a specific role in adhering to agreed-on behavioral goals to support and respect their parents' actions, and the counselor would have a specific role of collaborating with the family and advocating for its successes. This amount of participation not only mirrors a communal approach to addressing an issue but also distributes responsibilities for success throughout the counseling interventions. No one individual has the sole responsibility of making or breaking the intervention, which leads to less resistance and defensiveness on all parties' parts while the change process occurs. As long as participants are consistently committed to making the intervention work, the process can be maintained and shared. If particular errors are made along the way, the system comes together in order to address these matters. This way, the collectivistic integrity is maintained, and participants are more likely to make necessary adjustments that will aid the intervention.

Considerations for Multicultural Counseling

The most important considerations for multicultural counseling in this case incident are that collectivistic thinking should not be interpreted as resistance on the part of clients who have immigrated to an individualistic society and that even if clients are not native to the country in which the counseling is taking place, taking an expert role is not appropriate. Although there may be language barriers, socioeconomic issues, and other factors that may contribute to a client's disadvantaged circumstances, immigrant clients are not completely powerless when it comes to assessing potential solutions. Clients like Dalbir possess significant amounts of skill and insight in order to transition into Canada in the first place, and by assuming that further education or instruction is needed, counselors are reducing the chances of establishing parity in the working alliance. True collaboration with a collectivistic client reduces resistance and shows a dedication to understanding the person from a community perspective.

There may be contraindications in this approach for certain clients who have in their family systems members from several generations who have immigrated with them, because older members are not always able to engage in every intervention because of health concerns or other factors. It is important to give major consideration in such cases to the value of an older family member's perspective in order to engage all the significant members of the family system effectively in the counseling. However, requiring these family members to participate actively in all intervention processes may unfairly tax them and create new stressors for the system to address during the counseling process. It is not the job of the counselor to add stress to the system, because this may lead to resistance; however, the strengths of a multigenerational family system should still be addressed and encouraged during the counseling process so that clients feel respected and validated.

References

Ali, S. (2002). Collective and elective ethnicity: Caste among urban Muslims in India. *Sociological Forum, 17*, 593–620.

Carlson, J., Watts, R., & Maniacci, M. (2006). *Adlerian therapy: Theory and practice.* Washington, DC: American Psychological Association.

Duvvury, N., Nayak, M., & Allendorf, K. (2002). *Links between masculinity and violence: Aggregate analysis.* Washington, DC: International Center for Research on Women.

Eisler, R., & Skidmore, J. (1987). Masculine gender role stress: Implications for the assessment of men. *Clinical Psychology Review, 11*, 45–60.

Englar-Carlson, M., & Stephens, M. (2006). *In the room with men.* Washington, DC: American Psychological Association.

Kiselica, M. (2001). A male-friendly therapeutic process with school-age boys. In G. R. Brooks & G. E. Good (Eds.), *The new handbook of psychotherapy and counseling with men: Vol. 2. A comprehensive guide to settings, problems, and treatment approaches* (pp. 43–58). San Francisco: Jossey-Bass.

Krishnan, S. (2005). Gender, caste, and economic inequalities and marital violence in rural south India. *Health Care for Women International, 26*, 87–98.

Kukreja, P. (n.d.). *Group backgrounds: Hindu.* Retrieved October 31, 2007, from Ryerson University School Journalism, Diversity Watch, http://www.diversitywatch.ryerson.ca/backgrounds/hindu.htm

Martin, S., Tsui, A., Maitra, K., & Marinshaw, R. (1999). Domestic violence in northern India. *American Journal of Epidemiology, 150*, 417–426.

McGoldrick, M., Giordano, J., & Pearce, J. (Eds.). *Ethnicity and family therapy* (2nd ed.). New York: Guilford.

Norenzayan, A., & Nisbett, R. (2000). Culture and causal cognition. *Current Directions in Psychological Science, 9*, 132–135.

O'Neil, J., & Fishman, D. (1986). Adult men's career transitions and gender-role themes. In Z. Leibowitz & D. Lea (Eds.), *Adult career development: Concepts, issues, and practices* (pp. 132–162). Alexandria, VA: National Career Development Association.

Strassman, R. (2006). *Problems in Canada.* Retrieved April 23, 2006, from http://www.psych.org/pnews/98-02-06/strass.html

The University of Alberta. (2006). *Doctor of medicine admissions: Frequently asked questions.* Retrieved April 23, 2006, from http://www.med.ualberta.ca/education/ugme/admissions/dofm_faq.cfm

Coping With Isolation and Family Losses

Dina B. Lubin

Ahmed (a pseudonym), a 36-year-old Middle Eastern man, fled his war-torn home country in the mid 1980s because of the stress of political unrest and his family's belief that he could find a better, more promising life for himself in North America. At the age of 16, Ahmed, the second oldest of six children (one of whom had just been fatally shot in the war), left behind the only support system he had ever known—his close, fairly prominent Muslim family—and ventured to Canada with the hope of beginning a new life, perhaps studying abroad, and ultimately finding a successful and rewarding career for himself. Self-described as a son who made his parents proud and for whom they had much hope, Ahmed never entertained the thought of ever entering into any type of criminal lifestyle and viewed himself as someone who would make positive contributions to society and be somewhat of a role model for people at home.

Upon arrival in Canada, the situation was vastly different from what he had envisioned. He felt isolated and alone, missing his family and his roots in the Middle East. Even with all its freedom and potential for opportunity, North America was a significant change from life in a predominantly Muslim culture.

Key Issues

Within the 1st year, Ahmed befriended some individuals from the "wrong crowd" and began to use narcotics and participate in the accompanying illicit lifestyle of theft, drug trafficking, driving with a suspended license, and so on. As a result, he accumulated a fairly substantial legal history consisting of several charges and brief periods of incarceration, all of which brought him much shame. Because of his dependence on drugs, he was not able to hold a job for any significant length of time, and he received financial support primarily from a wealthy friend whom he met in Canada and occasional contributions from a relative living in the United States. As time passed and as the political climate in the Middle East became even more unstable, Ahmed was unable to contact his family abroad, and this brought him frustration, a sense of loneliness, and a state of chronic fear that something bad had happened to them. The resultant anxiety led to an escalation of his drug use, as an attempt to cope.

Over the years of being separated from his family, Ahmed did learn through the grapevine that the family experienced a great deal of trauma—the murder of his older brother in a Scandinavian country; the sudden death of his 21-year-old sister of respiratory failure; and the great loss of the family patriarch, Ahmed's beloved father who had had a fatal heart attack. Upon learning of these losses, Ahmed's emotional state became even more delicate as he struggled with feelings of intense guilt about not being able to contact his family members and not being physically present to support them. As the oldest remaining male sibling, he felt that it was his responsibility to assume the patriarchal role and take care of the family financially, emotionally, and otherwise. After the events of September 11, 2001, the sense of urgency to be with his family became more intensified because he worried about his family's safety when his home country became a target in the search for Osama bin Laden and the threat of the Taliban loomed. For Ahmed, there was a constant sense of angst and helplessness, being unable to travel to his home country and existing in a chronic state of uncertainty as to his family's well-being.

In the late 1990s, Ahmed began methadone treatment in Toronto, a process that ultimately led to the cessation of his illegal narcotic use and offered him access to supportive counseling. Although methadone helped him abstain from narcotic use, he did develop a psychological dependence on marijuana, particularly during the periods after the deaths of family members when he felt especially helpless. Consequently, Ahmed withdrew more from others, had difficulty concentrating or goal setting, and had a great deal of difficulty removing himself from the state of psychological inertia that enveloped him. Because he came from a Muslim background, where addiction is viewed as a "moral sin," his history of addiction brought him a great sense of shame and remorse.

Relationship Considerations

Ahmed was concerned about his family as a whole and about how they were managing with the loss of his father and three of the six siblings. Moreover, Ahmed's mother was quite physically weak, and because of her many ailments, he worried about her health and her ability to manage her household.

Ahmed's addiction was something that he believed would likely compromise his family relationships. He believed that disclosing it would cause tremendous disturbance and disappointment to members of his family, and they would never be able to understand or forgive him for his descent into the taboo world of drug addiction. He worried that they would reject him if there was future contact, as would his community. He struggled with the desire to contact them and reunite with them while at the same time fearing that such contact could devastate the people he loved most.

Transition Outcomes

Having made the decision to flee his home country, Ahmed removed himself from a dangerous part of the world and came to a safer, more stable country where there could potentially be many opportunities for him. In doing so, however, he became vulnerable to feeling isolated in a foreign country and in a different culture and without the opportunity to maintain contact with his family at home. This vulnerability resulted in experimentation with drugs, which subsequently led to a chronic addiction requiring the intervention of methadone treatment. Ahmed's involvement with the drug subculture led to feelings of shame, guilt, and remorse for which he would need counseling to assist him in understanding the events that took place and putting his addiction into context instead of continuing to view it as a moral sin (as is the traditional Muslim point of view).

Writer's Role

Counseling became the vehicle through which Ahmed was able to process his feelings about his losses and his anxiety around being separated from his family and to reconceptualize his beliefs and attitudes around substance abuse and the role it came to play in his life after he took refuge in Canada. As his counselor, my role was to help facilitate this process for Ahmed and provide a safe, supportive environment for him to be able to explore his internal conflicts and examine the course that his life ultimately took once he left his family behind and began a new life in Canada.

Writer's Comments

Ahmed was a young man who struggled with the belief that he could have a better life for himself in the West, although living this life would mean doing without his main frame of reference—his family and community. Because political strife prevented him from being able to maintain contact with these individuals, Ahmed felt alone and frustrated at the thought of not being able to support his family members through the many setbacks they experienced over the years since he left the Middle East. The sense of helplessness that pervaded him resulted in Ahmed's downward spiral into a world that brought much shame and guilt to him. Coming to terms with his substance dependence and identifying as an addict were daunting tasks, but ones that Ahmed was able to achieve over time in his counseling sessions, with much support from someone who did not judge him or criticize the choices he made.

As a therapist, my work with Ahmed enabled me to understand on a deeper level the significance of an individual's own community, culture, and family bonds in his or her overall sense of emotional stability and to understand that when these factors are taken away or are missing, the individual is much more vulnerable to developing mental health problems such as addiction, whose insidious nature can and often does interfere with living a satisfying, productive life. In my work with Ahmed, I became particularly aware of the importance of addressing the sense of displacement that a refugee experiences on landing in a different country and being immersed in a culture to which she or he cannot relate. This isolation, compounded by the lack of family connections, was a critical area of focus for counseling because it served as the basis for why Ahmed became involved in drug use.

Reader Reflection Questions

1. How do you feel about the approach taken by Ahmed's counselor? What other approaches could be used?
2. What are some ways to help build trust and rapport with a client with an addiction, particularly one from a different cultural background?
3. What are some preconceived ideas that people tend to hold about substance users? How could this potentially affect the counseling relationship?
4. What role do your own family values and cultural background play in the way that you "work with" clients from a different cultural background?
5. What are some ways to approach the sense of displacement that a refugee might feel upon acclimatizing to another country/culture?
6. What are some ways that you, as a counselor, can further develop your own multicultural competence for working with refugees?

Response 1

Noorfarah Merali

Understanding Ahmed's complex presenting problems requires knowledge about the context of his immigration to Canada, the Muslim cultural context shaping his life experiences, and Ahmed's unique response to international transition (individual context). Each of these three levels of context is discussed below. Common challenges in international transition encountered among refugees with similar backgrounds are identified. Ahmed's specific presenting issues are linked to his refugee status, his collectivist culture, and his religious beliefs relating to substance abuse.

Immigration Context

Ahmed's immigration to Canada was prompted by war and political uncertainty in his country of origin. The current global context is characterized by a high degree of social and political upheaval in many different nations. Civil unrest and armed conflict have led to the forced displacement of millions of refugees worldwide (Bemak, Chung, & Pedersen, 2003). Berry and Kim (1988) differentiated refugees from other migrant groups on the basis of the involuntary nature of their migration and their unspecified length of stay in the country of asylum. Some refugees permanently resettle abroad, whereas others, like Ahmed, contemplate returning to their home countries to reconnect with their families and communities (Berry & Kim, 1988).

The unique immigration experiences of refugees have been conceptualized as a life-altering process characterized by six stages: (a) predeparture, (b) flight, (c) first asylum, (d) claimant, (e) settlement, and (f) adaptation. These stages are collectively referred to as the *refugee career* (Prendes-Lintel, 2001). During the predeparture period, refugees may experience various traumatic events due to the unstable conditions in their home countries. For Ahmed, these traumas involved death of a sibling who was shot in the war and witnessing political violence. The period of flight addresses refugees' conditions of exodus from their home countries, whereas the stage of first asylum and the claimant stage encompass refugees' entry experiences in the host country. Ahmed's independent migration to Canada separated him from his family and community and led to a loss of personal coping resources. Personal coping resources include individual factors, such as spirituality and religion, as well as environmental factors, such as material assets and social support (Hiebert, 1988; Lazarus & Folkman, 1984). These resources are often disrupted or depleted during the refugee career (Prendes-Lintel, 2001).

Ahmed's experiences of social isolation, joblessness, and financial hardship during the process of settlement in Canada need to be considered in light of his migration trajectory. Ahmed's difficulty coping with family separation during the adaptation process in Canada is understandable, given the additional traumatic events in his family subsequent to Ahmed's migration and the increase in instability in the Middle East. In the settlement and adaptation stages, many refugees experience intense distress about leaving other family members behind, which further challenges their successful settlement (Prendes-Lintel, 2001).

Cultural Context

Muslim Family Values

As a self-identified Muslim, Ahmed belongs to the second largest faith community in the world (Esposito, 1998). The Muslim culture, shaped by the principles of Islam, is highly collectivistic; there is a strong emphasis on the maintenance of family bonds and responsibilities, because the religion encourages unity and brotherhood (Abu-Laban, 1991; Ali & Liu, 2004). Individuals, therefore, often define themselves through family relationships and through their contributions to their families (Abu-Laban, 1991).

In the Muslim cultural context, Ahmed's separation from his family and community through the refugee career would represent a marked life disruption. Although his family encouraged him to leave his country of origin in search of safety and prosperity, his socialization would lead him to perceive migration as an act of self-interest that subordinated his family's needs. His desire to reconnect with members of his family and to step into the family caregiver role in response to the multiple traumatic life events that have befallen them is fully consistent with Muslim cultural values. Reuniting with the family would allow Ahmed to reestablish a sense of well-being by reclaiming the role and way of life he lost through migration.

Unique Social/Political Circumstances of Muslim Refugees

Ahmed's increasing fears about his family's safety are realistic, given the escalation of political violence in the Middle East after September 11, 2001. His difficulty locating and contacting his family would only serve to exacerbate these legitimate fears. Ahmed's anxieties about the impact of events in his country of origin on his family are shared by many other Muslim refugees living in North America (Nassar-McMillan & Hakim-Larson, 2003). In addition to having an impact on the situation in the Middle East, the events of September 11 have created an adverse social and political climate in North America that poses significant challenges to Muslim refugees' integration. Paired with the increase in negative public attitudes toward Muslims, the rise in racism, discrimination, and hate crimes against members of this group has led to many Muslims feeling isolated during the resettlement process (Ali & Liu, 2004; Nassar-McMillan & Hakim-Larson, 2003). The current sociopolitical climate has also affected Muslims' employment prospects and integration in school and community settings (Ali & Liu, 2004). Thus, Ahmed's experiences of isolation and chronic joblessness need to be understood in relation to these contextual factors.

Individual Context

To cope with his distress about not being able to respond to family needs and about being isolated and jobless, Ahmed affiliated with the "wrong crowd" and resorted to illicit drug use. Despite making some progress in dealing with his drug addiction, his increasing fears about his family's safety and his inability to help members of his family appeared to trigger further substance abuse issues. The substance abuse can be viewed as a reaction to his learned helplessness. Because of experiencing multiple traumatic events, cultural disruption, and a loss of traditional coping resources, many Muslim refugees from the Middle East have struggled with depression, intense anxiety, and substance abuse issues (Nassar-McMillan & Hakim-Larson, 2003).

Ahmed's drug use has compounded his presenting problems, because he perceives it as a barrier to uniting with his family. He recognizes the drug use as a coping strategy that is incongruent with his religion. Because Ahmed identifies substance abuse as a sinful and forbidden behavior according to the Islamic faith (Ali & Liu, 2004), he expects his family to reject the person he has become. He is experiencing a great deal of shame and self-rejection as a result. Although Ahmed recognizes that situational factors have affected his presenting problems, he sees his own behavior as being a major obstacle to achieving his desired goal of rejoining his family.

Intervention: Theoretical Frameworks

Two complementary theoretical frameworks inform the counseling strategies put forth to assist Ahmed to deal with his complex presenting problems. The theory of Multicultural Counseling and Therapy (Cheatham et al., 2002) postulates that culturally sensitive counseling requires (a) responding to clients' multiple levels of experience; (b) assisting clients to see themselves and their problems in context; (c) expanding counseling to include the various helping roles of the family, community, and cultural groups; and (d) devising interventions that match clients' religious or cultural backgrounds.

The Multilevel Model of counseling and psychotherapy (Bemak, Chung, & Bornemann, 1996; Bemak et al., 2003), devised specifically for working with refugees, organizes counseling activities to respond to clients' multiple layers of experience into four levels of intervention. Level I involves providing mental health education to increase clients' understanding of mental health problems, their causes, and counseling approaches used to address them. Level II encompasses individual, group, or family-based interventions that respond to clients' unique presenting problems and respect the culture and collectivistic way of life of refugee populations. Group or family-based interventions aim to facilitate social support and active problem solving by allowing people to share similar life experiences and learn new ways of coping. Level III involves promoting clients' cultural empowerment by helping them to understand how local systems work and connecting them to relevant services and resources in various areas such as health care, education, finances, and employment. Access to services and resources in these areas is often disrupted by the refugee career (Prendes-Lintel, 2001). Level IV involves drawing on healing strategies and approaches indigenous to clients' heritage cultures to promote their well-being. Bemak et al. suggested that the order of application of these levels of intervention needs to be tailored to an individual client's unique life situation and needs.

Counseling Strategies

Level I: Mental Health Education

It is clear from the description of the case that Ahmed sees his anxiety and drug abuse as signs of personal weakness and inadequacy. Due to the lack of acceptance of substance abuse in the Islamic religion, he also perceives himself as sinful, which would further contribute to a poor self-image. A key part of mental health education for Ahmed would be normalizing the substance abuse as a response to the natural elevation in anxiety that can be expected when a person endures multiple traumatic life events and has no supports or coping resources in place to deal with them.

The fact that many other Muslim refugees who have resettled in North America have also encountered problems with substance abuse because of premigration trauma, family separation, and social isolation can be emphasized to help Ahmed recognize that he is not alone. Because they also share his religious beliefs, being aware of these other examples may serve to "liberate his consciousness" (Cheatham et al., 2002, p. 351) about how he came to use a coping strategy that is inconsistent with his faith. This educational approach could help Ahmed to see his problems in the context of the refugee career. It can then be explained to Ahmed that the purpose of counseling will be to (a) problem solve with him to help him identify other ways of dealing with his realistic worries about his family and his need to be there for them, (b) help him try to reconnect with his family through various community services and resources, and (c) come up with strategies that could help him stay "clean."

Level II: Individual, Group, or Family Counseling;
Level IV: Indigenous Healing

Ahmed expresses a strong desire to find his remaining family members, reconnect with them, and step into his father's previous caregiver role. His devotion to his family should be commended. Even though he is living abroad, his constant concerns about the welfare of the members of his family and the desire to be there for them are the hallmark of being a good son in the Muslim culture. In addition to difficulty in locating and reaching his family in the Middle East, Ahmed sees his drug abuse as a major barrier to reuniting with them successfully. His family concerns and substance abuse appear to interact in the sense that his dependence on drugs is fueled by concerns about his family and a lack of alternative coping resources.

Ahmed's belief that his drug use is sinful needs to be carefully examined. At first glance, it would seem that a counselor should try to help him overcome this belief. Although it is important to normalize Ahmed's entry into a cycle of drug abuse, his belief that abusing drugs is sinful can be considered as serving as an important motivator for overcoming the problem. It would be most useful to allow him to hang onto this belief. It may help him become invested in redirecting his coping attempts in ways that are more consistent with his faith.

Connecting Ahmed to his cultural community through a local Muslim community association and a local mosque may very helpful for three reasons. First, as a Muslim counselor writing this response to the case incident, I am aware that community associations tend to have links to other members and humanitarian workers living abroad who can provide assistance in locating missing family members. Having the backup of a coordinated community effort to help Ahmed find and reach out to his family may reduce the feelings of helplessness and powerlessness that are triggering his substance abuse.

Second, through community contact, Ahmed is likely to encounter other Muslim refugees who are struggling with similar fears, problems, and challenges. The interpersonal contact with others in similar situations could counter Ahmed's social isolation and promote support building. There may also be support groups for refugees within the community that Ahmed could become a part of to share his feelings and experiences and learn from the experiences of others. Building positive connections through a support group could lessen the need for Ahmed to affiliate with the "wrong crowd" to gain a sense of belonging.

Third, participation in mosque may help Ahmed to recover traditional coping strategies, such as congregational prayers, that were lost through his migration to North America. Park (2005) discussed the important role that religion plays as a vehicle for meaning-making when a person is confronted with loss and bereavement. Also, in discussing ways of incorporating religion and spirituality into the helping process, Pergament (1997) and Richards and Bergin (1997) highlighted the fact that many religions have specific rituals and prayers that promote healthy coping with life adversity.

In the Muslim religion, prayer is a daily source of strength and affirmation. Some prayers are performed individually, whereas others are performed congregationally (Ali & Liu, 2004). Once Ahmed is connected with a local mosque, the counselor can engage in a dialogue with him about how he is affected by this involvement. The counselor can work with Ahmed to identify religious or spiritual coping strategies that he can apply whenever his worries about his family crop up. These can serve as competing responses to substance abuse. With the counselor, Ahmed can monitor how new religious coping strategies to social support are working for him. Ahmed's significant progress in addressing his drug problem prior to the increase in political instability in the Middle East, which heightened his worries about his family, should be highlighted as evidence of his strength and ability to overcome this problem.

Level III: Cultural Empowerment

Ahmed expressed a great deal of distress about "abandoning" his family in a negative sociopolitical climate and moving abroad. Since his immigration to Canada, Ahmed has experienced chronic joblessness in addition to social isolation and substance abuse issues. To eventually achieve his goal of stepping into a caregiver role in his family, Ahmed not only needs to stay "clean" but also needs to achieve a certain level of financial independence and stability in the host society. Ahmed's successful settlement in the host society can be framed as a means of eventually being able to respond to his family's needs.

The counselor can connect Ahmed to financial services, such as social assistance, that he may be able to access at the present time. The counselor can work with Ahmed to examine his interests in terms of career options or possibly reentering the educational system. If Ahmed is unsure of his interests, he can complete vocational interest inventories to help him learn more about himself and about prospective jobs or careers he might like to pursue. Ahmed can be connected to settlement service agencies offering career counseling, job-finding clubs, and job-placement services specifically tailored for refugees who have interrupted educational and employment histories. If he is interested in going back to school or seeking vocational training, he can also be connected to the educational system and to student loan services. The counselor needs to be open to having Ahmed discuss any perceived barriers to seeking employment or integrating into the educational system because of racism or discrimination based on his Muslim background (Ali & Liu, 2004). Ways of responding to any emerging barriers can also be discussed, and the counselor may need to take on the role of client advocate (Sue & Sue, 2003).

In the process of engaging Ahmed in career and life planning, the counselor can educate Ahmed about family class immigration procedures and the criteria for sponsoring his family to come to Canada. In this discussion, Ahmed's move to the host society and the steps he begins to take toward becoming settled can be cognitively reframed as a way of eventually bringing his family to safety. This reframing process may motivate Ahmed to address his joblessness and reliance on a wealthy friend for money. It may also help him to reinterpret his move away from his family as a temporary situation and to see that he is now taking steps to change the situation and respond to his family's needs and best interests. This would be consistent with his cultural value system. Such a reinterpretation would establish an important familial role for Ahmed even though he is living apart from his family. When working with clients from collectivist cultures, counselors need to be sensitive to the fact that clients will often be reluctant to pursue self-improvement if it does not directly contribute to family or group interests (McCarthy, 2005; Sue & Sue, 2003).

Conclusion

To generate helpful counseling strategies for working with Ahmed, his presenting problems need to be understood in relation to his migration trajectory as a refugee and his collectivist Muslim cultural heritage. In the Middle East, Ahmed witnessed political violence, including the death of a sibling. Escaping from this threatening climate led Ahmed to be separated from his family and his cultural community, leaving him without any financial, social, or religious support to cope with the realities of life in Canada or with his continuing concerns about his family's well-being. Ahmed's sense of helplessness precipitated substance use, a coping strategy inconsistent with his Islamic faith. The development of his substance abuse was something he feared would alienate him from his family, despite his intense desire to reunite with them. Ahmed's family orientation led to a culturally consistent preoccupation with his family's welfare at the expense of addressing his own resettlement problems, such as chronic joblessness.

In working with Ahmed, it is extremely important to normalize his substance abuse and to make parallels between his experiences and those of other Muslim refugees with similar migration trajectories. Reconnecting Ahmed to his cultural community could restore traditional religious coping strategies and access to social support, which could act as competing responses to the substance abuse. The Muslim community may also be able to offer some assistance in locating his family, thereby reducing Ahmed's sense of helplessness. Helping Ahmed to explore career directions and to reframe the pursuit of a job and career in Canada as a way of eventually sponsoring his family and bringing family members to safety would be consistent with his collectivist values and counseling goals. Ahmed could be connected to relevant settlement services and programs to facilitate his economic and cultural integration into Canada. The Multilevel Model of counseling and psychotherapy (Bemak et al., 1996; Bemak et al., 2003) makes it clear that counselors need to incorporate individual, group, and community-based interventions in order to respond to the multiple layers of experience that frame refugees' unique presenting problems.

References

Abu-Laban, S. M. (1991). Family and religion among Muslim immigrants and their descendents. In E. Waugh, S. M. Abu-Laban, & R. B. Qureshi (Eds.), *Muslim families in North America* (pp. 6–31). Edmonton, Alberta, Canada: University of Alberta Press.

Ali, S. R., & Liu, W. M. (2004). Islam 101: Understanding the religion and therapy implications. *Professional Psychology: Research and Practice, 35,* 635–642.

Bemak, F., Chung, R. C., & Bornemann, T. H. (1996). Counseling and psychotherapy with refugees. In P. B. Pedersen, J. G. Draguns, & W. J. Trimble (Eds.), *Counseling across cultures* (4th ed., pp. 243–265). Thousand Oaks, CA: Sage.

Bemak, F., Chung, R. C., & Pedersen, P. B. (2003). *Counseling refugees: A psychosocial approach to innovative multicultural interventions.* Westport, CT: Greenwood Press.

Berry, J. W., & Kim, U. (1988). Acculturation and mental health. In P. R. Dasen, J. W. Berry, & S. N. Sartorius (Eds.), *Health and cross-cultural psychology: Toward applications* (pp. 207–238). Newbury Park, CA: Sage.

Cheatham, H., D'Andrea, M., Ivey, A. E., Ivey, M. B., Pedersen, P., Rigazio-DiGilio, S., et al. (2002). Multicultural counseling and therapy. In A. E. Ivey, M. D'Andrea, M. B. Ivey, & L. Simek-Morgan (Eds.), *Theories of counseling and psychotherapy: A multicultural perspective* (5th ed., pp. 291–362). Boston: Allyn & Bacon.

Esposito, J. L. (1998). *Islam: The straight path.* New York: Oxford University Press.

Hiebert, B. (1988). Controlling stress: A conceptual update. *Canadian Journal of Counselling, 22,* 226–241.

Lazarus, R. S., & Folkman, S. (1984). *Stress, appraisal, and coping.* New York: Springer.

McCarthy, J. (2005). Individualism and collectivism: What do they have to do with counseling? *Journal of Multicultural Counseling and Development, 33,* 108–117.

Nassar-McMillan, S. C., & Hakim-Larson, J. (2003). Counseling considerations among Arab Americans. *Journal of Counseling & Development, 81,* 150–159.

Park, C. (2005). Religion as a meaning-making system in coping with life stress. *Journal of Social Issues, 61,* 707–729.

Pergament, K. L. (1997). *The psychology of religion and coping: Theory, research, and practice.* New York: Guilford Press.

Prendes-Lintel, M. (2001). A working model in counseling recent refugees. In J. G. Ponterotto, J. M. Casas, L. A. Suzuki, & C. M. Alexander (Eds.), *Handbook of multicultural counseling* (pp. 729–752). Thousand Oaks, CA: Sage.

Richards, P. S., & Bergin, A. E. (1997). *A spiritual strategy for counseling and psychotherapy.* Washington, DC: American Psychological Association.

Sue, D. W., & Sue, D. (2003). *Counseling the culturally diverse: Theory and practice* (4th ed.). New York: Wiley.

Response 2

Pamela M. Clayton

This response comes primarily from a sociological perspective, in which individual and society and structure and agency interact in a complex way, with one having primacy at one time and another at other times. This means understanding individuals in their context but generalizing neither from the general to the particular nor from the particular to the general (Jenkins, 1996). Awareness of a range of possibilities forms a useful background, but the method best adapted for use with refugees is holistic, person-centered counseling (Keys, 2002). The differences between "mainstream" counseling and counseling for refugees arise out of what refugees, from any country, have in common. Many have lost everything. They had no time to prepare for the transition. They may know little of the new country. They may end up (whatever their intentions) in a country whose language they do not know. They are, on first arrival, in a no-man's-land and without a map. They may be so traumatized that they could not read the map if they had one. However, they are not children (except, of course, when they are!). They are human adults who in their own countries in former times had position, stability, knowledge of their surroundings, families and friends, work, and education. Like all people, they had multiple identities (Woodward, 2002). To be integrated into the new country means being at ease, knowing how it works, feeling comfortable and safe. The multicultural counselor has an important role to play in this integration (Clayton, 2007).

Summary of the Case Incident

Ahmed was a refugee who had been in Canada for 20 years. He had arrived alone as a teenager with characteristically unrealistic hopes and aspirations. He had made a cross-cultural transition in the worst of ways: as a refugee; as an immature youth; alone; unable to keep in contact with his family; with little or no knowledge of the country he was coming to; and, apparently, without preexisting support networks of co-nationals or relatives. Any one of these factors would have tested him. The combination of all six proved too much for him.

By the time Ahmed had access to counseling, he had a history of drug addiction, and although he had stopped using heroin, he was still a drug user in times of stress. His main anxiety seemed to center round his family, which had suffered traumatic events in his absence, including the death of his father. This had left Ahmed as the titular head of the family—a role he could not fulfill because he could not send money and was afraid to return to take up his duties because he would be condemned for his drug addiction. As far as the account goes, his anxieties did not concern his own present situation in Canada but were largely about a situation thousands of miles away over which he had no control.

Reflections on the Situation Presented

When I reflect on this account, I think that lack of control—over his addiction, over his life, over his responsibilities—was a key factor in his distress (Brown, 1996), but I wonder if, also, he simply did not know what to do so he focused on and agonized about issues about which he could do nothing. Although his concerns and anguish about his family were genuine, I wonder if it would have been helpful to undertake counseling that would help him, little by little, to take control of his own life? He had made a start through the methadone program, but it is clear that his life circumstances were still very fragile, and it is possible that his very hopelessness about his future—an unbearable thought—caused him not to think about it except in terms of fear and apprehension. It is unclear whether returning to his home country was in any case affordable for him.

Refugees do not lose their human condition of having multiple identities just because through, for example, loss of home and employment, they lose some of them on going into exile. The same applies to Ahmed's drug addiction: It formed only one facet, albeit an important one, of his identity. The label "drug addict" can hide this from the observer, with a resulting failure to explore other sources of identity (Goffman, 1964). For example, it is clear that his identity as a son loomed large in his troubled mind, but to recognize him as a whole person requires seeking other sources of identity. It is quite possible that some of these were trouble free and could be a source of an improved self-image.

The Counselor's Approach

Nothing here is to be taken as criticism of the counselor's approach because I do not have enough information. For example, it is not stated how long she or he had been working with Ahmed; whether he was referred for counseling or came voluntarily; whether the aim of the counseling was to move forward into action that Ahmed could take to complete the process of finding and following a path in life that seemed worthwhile to him; or whether the result of this particular therapy was to enable him to find equilibrium, self-understanding, and self-forgiveness before moving on to a more action-orientated type of counseling. I need to know how capable Ahmed was of reflection, self-awareness, and learning. Perhaps he could have benefited from a cognitive approach such as transactional analysis, which combines therapy with learning and action (Berne, 1966).

I also do not know the theoretical basis of the counseling, although it is clear that it was person-centered, nonjudgmental, and empathic. These facets are essential in any counseling relationship and particularly in one in which the client is ashamed of his or her behavior and operating under a burden of guilt and in which the building of trust and rapport is more problematic.

It is clear that the counselor went through a valuable learning process that would inform his or her work with other refugees: "I became particularly aware of the importance of addressing the sense of displacement that a refugee experiences on landing in a different country and being immersed in a culture to which she or he cannot relate." Counselors who are new to counseling refugees need to become informed through reading about the potential effects of flight and exile on their health and the reasons for a high incidence of depression and anxiety among this group. There is a great deal of research literature on this topic, and there are a number of institutions with expertise on which to draw (Burnett & Peel, 2001).

I am unclear about the extent of the counselor's knowledge of Islam. It is true that alcohol is forbidden and the use of tobacco, though widespread, is frowned on by the most rigid, but in Muslim Yemen the chewing of the narcotic *qat* is almost universal and water pipes have not been used only for tobacco (Baasher, 1981). Furthermore, a Muslim country like Afghanistan is the majority stakeholder in European heroin addiction (CBC News, 2007). I am not saying that his family would have condoned his drug addiction, but their presumed attitude would have as much to do with their disappointment in and worries about him as with the "traditional Muslim point of view" that it was a "moral sin." Furthermore, his father was dead and mothers of sons (without overgeneralizing) might be less rigid and more forgiving. I would not have stated this to Ahmed, but it would have been in my mind. Furthermore, if the issue was principally one of Islam, a skilled drugs counselor who was also a Muslim might have been more appropriate.

This, however, raises delicate issues. There are many schools of Islam and, hence, a number of translations of the Quran and the Hadith (sayings of the Prophet Mohammed) into various languages. If a counselor deals with a significant number of Muslim clients, it might be a good idea to make contact with local Muslim groups and develop a good personal and working relationship with them, while maintaining confidentiality of course. Then the counselor can seek honest advice. This would apply to any religion in which religious issues are troubling the client.

The Issue of Addiction

Preconceived ideas in general, especially negative ones, are always a danger in a counseling relationship, and there is evidence that counselors are not immune to these (Batumubwira, 2005; Højer, 2005). I would be surprised, however, if a skilled and experienced counselor felt prejudice against a substance user in a culture where this is rather common. Living as I do in a city where too many young people abuse substances, resulting in chaotic lives and even death, I find that there is both sad sympathy for users, especially the very young, and repugnance toward those who supply drugs without themselves using them. The widespread availability of highly addictive drugs such as crack cocaine, a mainstream culture that is generally complacent about the excesses of alcohol, a youth culture in which drugs such as ecstasy and cannabis are seen as harmless, and a high level of poverty and hopelessness in some areas of the city make it difficult for some impressionable young people to evade the temptations of trying drugs "for a laugh" or to keep in with the crowd. Nevertheless, despite some sympathy and understanding, there is a great deal of incomprehension about the cause of drug taking, especially because not all in the same milieu engage in it. Furthermore, where addiction leads to crime against property and people, incipient sympathy tends to diminish.

One issue that makes it difficult for reasonable people to have a rigid attitude toward drug taking is the divide between substances that can be used legally, such as tobacco and alcohol, and those that cannot, such as heroin and cocaine. There is also the gray area of substances that have a legal use but may be abused, such as glue. Another is the line between use and abuse, although it is not generally recognized that even drugs like heroin can be used in a controlled way in conjunction with a life that is generally "normal," involving a job, family, and friends.

I have focused on young people, although they are not the only substance users, because Ahmed was only 16 when he arrived in Canada. Furthermore, he lacked maturity, compounded by the naïve belief of his family that he could not only survive alone in a country so different from his own but even thrive. In initially sending only one child, they placed great burdens on him, burdens of expectation and of hope, and indirectly they bear some of the responsibility for his downfall. It would be a delicate task to allow Ahmed to see that his family had made a mistake, but doing so might redress the great fear he had of contacting them in case they judged him as harshly as he judged himself.

Multicultural Counseling

From the point of view of multicultural counseling, it is noteworthy that Ahmed had already been in Canada for 20 years and had experienced elements of Canadian culture probably alien to the counselor, such as involvement in crime and imprisonment. This demonstrates neatly the point that all counseling is multicultural in that mainstream culture is filtered through factors such as age, sex, religion, politics, ethnicity, and class (Puukari & Launikari, 2005). Again, the main focus of the multicultural element of the counseling, as described, seems to have been on Ahmed's religion, and this, of course, is an important element in culture. There are, however, many others, including language. I assume that after 20 years Ahmed spoke good English—but this may be a false assumption on my part, especially if his criminal associates were from the same country as he was.

An ever-present possibility with refugees is that they have suffered torture or trauma in their countries of origin or perhaps on the flight to exile. This is a highly specialized area of therapy, and both diagnosis and treatment are difficult. A counselor might suspect that a guidance seeker is suffering psychological distress for these reasons, but it is a delicate matter to suggest that they be referred to psychiatric help because this carries a stigma in many societies (Novoa & Dorn, 2007). There are specialist services, and good contacts should be maintained with these. The important thing to remember is that such therapy is rarely within the expertise of the counselor who, with the greatest of goodwill, can add to the harm by inappropriate attempts to "help."

A Danish guidance counselor, Vagn Særkjær, introduced me to the concept of the personality as being like an onion. The personality is both formed and protected by many layers, of which the most important are upbringing, family, religion, food, clothes, habitation, and work. A move to another country removes some of these layers, and the more that are removed, the more vulnerable the individual becomes (Særkjær, 2004). Ahmed had lost most of these layers in one fell swoop when he moved alone to Canada, leaving only upbringing and religion. It has been observed that religious observance often becomes stronger in such circumstances. It is sometimes all that remains of the old life, especially when it is difficult to start a stable new life with work and personal relationships (Modood & Werbner, 1997). An important aspect of multicultural counseling is to recognize that, potentially, the guidance seeker, especially one who has recently arrived, is in this psychological position—in a halfway house or even homeless.

The Role of Values in Multicultural Counseling

Among many things people learn as they grow up are values: What is right and what is wrong, what is desirable and what is not, how to act and how not to act. They learn from observation as well as through instruction, and everyone has values—even people castigated as having none—and having values does not necessarily mean acting on them. Even within the same society, however, people do not all have the same values, although a certain value consensus is necessary to ensure social stability. Some—many—values are universal (that is, held in all cultures though not necessarily by all individuals), such as loyalty and authenticity. Others are culturally specific, such as the values put on success or on the prime importance of leading a good life. Cultural conflict and culture shock often have at their roots a clash of values, between what one person "instinctively" feels is right and what another "knows" is wrong (Oberg, 1954).

The problem is that people's values do not constitute a checklist, but rather lie buried. Indeed, sometimes people can hold contradictory values, which appear as hypocrisy, simply because they are unaware of what makes them react and think the way they do. So they may believe, deep down, that their culture is superior and that others should adopt it. They may associate intelligence with communicative competence, so be unable to appreciate a guidance seeker struggling in a foreign tongue. So before people can avoid these unworthy and unproductive feelings, they have to raise their values from the deep, examine and evaluate them, and if necessary clean them up and keep them within sight.

This does not mean, however, that all values in other cultures should be countenanced. Cultural relativity—condoning practices just because they are common in another culture, although people's carefully considered values tell them that they are not supportable—is also to be avoided. Ritual murder, for example, is not only illegal in most countries, people are allowed to believe that it is wrong.

Learning to Be a Multicultural Counselor

In many ways, realigning people's values is the hardest part, but there is a great deal of other hard work in becoming a multicultural counselor for refugees. This involves reading research materials; keeping knowledge up-to-date on matters such as rights and entitlements; getting involved in refugee groups and networks; and liaising with a range of agencies dealing with various aspects of life, for example, housing, legal advice, social benefits, health services, schools, colleges, employment services. The list is long and the guidance counselor's time is short.

It is also important to learn about the cultures and systems from which guidance seekers come. This is not so that counselors can "read" the individual from their cultural or national context, but so that they may have an informed understanding of their background. Just as our societies are very diverse, so are the societies that refugees come from, and each—as is normal in person-centered counseling—is a unique individual with a unique personal history.

Because the case incident described involves a Muslim, let me tell the story of a young woman from the Sudan. Fatima (as I shall call her) is of Muslim origin. Because the treatment of women, in particular by the Sudanese government, in her words "can be extreme" and because her work as a social worker was threatened on the grounds that she was not doing it the way the government thought was "Islamic," she was forced to flee the country. She has rejected her religion and identifies herself as a Black African, not as a Muslim. Her values prioritized the treatment of women and disadvantaged children, and when these clashed with the values of the powerful, she rejected theirs. Life in exile has not been easy. Whereas she had a good job in the Sudan, with quite a high status and good level of education, she is now frustrated by lack of employment. She misses her work and family and suffered the pain of her mother's death while in exile (Clayton, 2005).

In other words, any stereotyped notion of a Muslim woman disintegrates when Fatima walks in, because she is a confident woman who communicates well. It is worth remembering that even quiet and timid people can be surprisingly different from what might be expected. I believe that *awareness* is the watchword: Counselors must be aware of multiple possibilities but never prejudge the issue or form preconceived ideas about the guidance seeker.

It is also necessary to put pressure on the counselor's organization to make any necessary changes. An individual may be the most wonderful counselor in the world, but guidance seekers may never meet him or her if they do not know the service exists or what it can do or if their first experience of the service is unfortunate. One of the best services I knew was one that was started by people from the same background as their target group—disadvantaged people of any background, not just refugees. They designed the building, outside and in, so that from the outside it was possible to see where to go when inside, and once inside there was a "safe" area for browsing without being disturbed, beyond which there was a receptionist who could dispense basic advice and help people who were nervous. Last, there were the guidance officers. Every member of the staff, including cleaners and, of course, the receptionist, was trained to be welcoming and nonjudgmental. There was a nursery, and tea and coffee were available. They also did extensive outreach and developed innovative ways of enhancing access to the service (Clayton, 2000).

Conclusion

To be a counselor to refugees is a hard job, involving a great deal of learning and some pain. Maintaining emotional distance in the face of tragic stories is difficult but necessary, both for the counselor's emotional well-being and for the sake of the guidance seeker, who needs advice based on reason and not on sympathy (Novoa & Dorn, 2007).

The rewards are great but rare. The unemployment rate even among highly qualified refugees is extremely high in countries like the United Kingdom. The best outcomes for some refugee women I have interviewed are that they feel safe and their children are receiving a good education. This almost—but perhaps not quite—makes up for their own disappointed hopes (Clayton, 2005).

References

Baasher, T. (1981). The use of drugs in the Islamic world. *British Journal of Addiction, 76,* 233–243.

Batumubwira, A. (2005). An immigrant's voice—Complexity of the client–counselor relation. In M. Launikari & S. Puukari (Eds.), *Multicultural guidance and counselling: Theoretical foundations and best practices in Europe* (pp. 45–52). Helsinki, Finland: Centre for International Mobility.

Berne, E. (1996). *Transactional analysis in psychotherapy: A systematic individual and social psychiatry*. New York: Grove Press.

Brown, G. W. (1996). Life events, loss and depressive disorders. In T. Heller, J. Reynolds, R. Gomm, R. Muston, & S. Pattison (Eds.), *Mental health matters: A reader* (pp. 36–45). Basingstoke, United Kingdom: Palgrave.

Burnett, A., & Peel, M. (2001, March 3). Health needs of asylum seekers and refugees. *British Medical Journal*, 544–547.

CBC News. (2007). *Afghanistan: Heroin producer to the world*. Retrieved August 10, 2007, from http://www.cbc.ca/news/background/drugs/heroin-afghanistan.html

Clayton, P. (Ed.). (2000). *Access to vocational guidance for people at risk of social exclusion*. Glasgow, United Kingdom: University of Glasgow, Department of Adult and Continuing Education. (ERIC Document Reproduction Service No. ED 442 970)

Clayton, P. (2005). Blank slates or hidden treasure? Assessing and building on the experiential learning of migrant and refugee women in European countries. *International Journal of Lifelong Education 24*, 227–242.

Clayton, P. (2007). Introduction. In S. Greco, P. M. Clayton, & A. Janko Spreizer (Eds.), *Migrants and refugees in Europe: Models of integration and new challenges for vocational guidance* (pp. 7–22). Milan: FrancoAngeli.

Goffman, I. (1964). *Stigma: Notes on the management of spoiled identity*. Englewood Cliffs, NJ: Prentice Hall.

Højer, B. (2005). *Educational and vocational guidance of refugees and immigrants—A qualitative analysis of the intercultural guidance interview*. Retrieved August 10, 2007, from http://www.gla.ac.uk/rg/fmulguen.htm

Jenkins, R. (1996). *Social identity*. London: Routledge.

Keys, S. (2002, July). Staying alive. In *Higher education section of the Carl R. Rogers symposium 2002*. Retrieved August 10, 2007, from http://www.gla.ac.uk/rg/emulti03.htm

Modood, T., & Werbner, P. (1997). *The politics of multiculturalism in the new Europe*. London: Zed Books.

Novoa, M., & Dorn, C. (2007). Traumatisation as an issue in guidance for asylum seekers and refugees. In S. Greco, P. M. Clayton, & A. Janko Spreizer (Eds.), *Migrants and refugees in Europe: Models of integration and new challenges for vocational guidance* (pp. 91–104). Milan: FrancoAngeli.

Oberg, K. (1954). *Culture shock*. Retrieved August 10, 2007, from http://www.smcm.edu/academics/internationaled/Pdf/cultureshockarticle.pdf

Puukari, S., & Launikari, M. (2005). Multicultural counseling—Starting points and perspectives. In M. Launikari & S. Puukari (Eds.), *Multicultural guidance and counselling: Theoretical foundations and best practices in Europe* (pp. 27–44). Helsinki, Finland: Centre for International Mobility.

Særkjær, V. (2004). *Multicultural competence—An introduction*. Retrieved August 10, 2007, from http://www.gla.ac.uk/rg/ats_en01.pdf

Woodward, K. (2002). *Understanding identity*. London: Arnold.

Case Incident 14

Second-Generation Issues
for Young Women

Monica Justin

As a child of immigrant parents, Sheela's (a pseudonym) story highlights several common themes and issues for many second-generation young women. I first met Sheela as a client at the university counseling center on a referral by health services. This client was diagnosed with moderate symptoms of depression and was prescribed antidepression medication.

Context of Case Incident

Sheela presented as an articulate and intelligent young woman with a quiet demeanor. She initially appeared somewhat reserved as she entered my office. As we began the session, she asked about my ethnic background, commenting that she was surprised to see a non-White counselor at the center. She reported feeling relieved and reassured by the fact that I was a woman of color. My self-disclosure about my ethnocultural background became the point of entry for our conversation. Sheela started feeling more at ease because I might understand her cultural background more readily, given that I shared a similar ethnic background. As I inquired about her referral from health services and the reason for coming to counseling, she began to describe several aspects of her personal life and recent life circumstances.

Sheela is a 24-year-old East Indian woman in her 2nd year of studying for a business degree. She first came to Canada 2½ years earlier as a young adult. She had left India 3 years earlier, after her mother's unexpected death, and lived in California for 1 year with a cousin. She eventually came to live with her uncle and aunt in Canada because they wanted to sponsor her. Sheela described feeling immediately welcomed by her extended family. Nonetheless, she mentioned that the numerous transitions she had experienced in the past 3 years had been difficult. Sheela referred to her aunt and uncle as her parents. Upon arriving in Canada, she became the eldest daughter in their family. Her uncle and aunt have two daughters of their own, both younger than Sheela. Sheela referred to her cousins as her sisters and described a loving relationship among the family members. As our sessions proceeded, Sheela described various tensions that emerged over the years between her younger sisters and herself, such as sibling rivalry, arguments, and resentments as they adjusted to living together and as she took on the role of eldest daughter in the family. As eldest female child, she assumed various responsibilities in the home, such as cooking and cleaning when her parents worked late, ensuring that her sisters did their homework, and supervising their activities. She consistently described her parents as loving and generous, because they treated her as their own daughter, making no distinction between her and their biological children. Simultaneously, she also described struggling to adjust to life in Canada, learning new cultural norms, feeling pressured to do well at university, and grieving and mourning the death of her biological mother and the familiarity of life in India. Sheela often described feeling alone with her feelings and unable to share these concerns with her aunt or uncle because she did not want them to think she was ungrateful for all they had done for her.

Although she expressed gratitude for her current living situation and comforts of being with family, she described an emotional emptiness, loneliness, and growing sense of disconnection. These emotions were coupled with feelings and guilt and frustration at herself for not feeling content and satisfied with her new life, a life that offered more personal, professional, and financial opportunities than one in India. Outwardly, Sheela appeared composed as she described the emotions with which she was struggling. She concurrently described increasing symptoms of depression, such as difficulty sleeping and the loss of energy, appetite, and ability to concentrate. Her school grades were dropping, and she found it difficult getting through her day. She was initially referred to health services by a concerned professor. This referral resulted in an evaluation by the psychiatrist who identified moderate symptoms of depression, prescribed antidepressant medication (Paxil), and agreed to follow her on a monthly basis. As we continued to discuss Sheela's diagnosis and symptoms, it became inherently significant to conduct a suicide risk assessment. Sheela revealed hesitantly at first that she did have thoughts of ending her life but ultimately had no concrete plan of action and no previous risk behavior. Furthermore, the thought of hurting her family through such actions was shameful to her, because this would express a deep lack of respect and gratitude for their care. She acknowledged, however, that her growing unhappiness was unsettling to her and that she felt powerless to change her feelings and thoughts.

As we continued to work together, further details of her life in India emerged, and she described a more complete picture of her acculturation experience in Canada. For example, as she began university, she also held a part-time job, which gave her a sense of personal authority and some measure of financial independence. She also described enjoying a level of personal freedom in Canadian society that she could not enjoy in India. Coupled with these self-described cultural advantages, Sheela also described a firm sense of connection to her East Indian ethnic and cultural value system. For example, she described a deep personal connection, adherence, and attachment to numerous elements of her ethnic and cultural heritage, such as looking forward to having her parents pursue an arranged marriage once she graduated from university. Our counseling relationship continued over several months as we progressively navigated Sheela's emotional highs and lows, adjustment issues, and strategies for creating a new sense of personal congruence and identity that was founded in her individual acculturation experience.

Key Issues

Sheela's case highlights a variety of key issues. From a traditional counseling orientation, it is possible to clearly identify classic symptoms of depression as being of primary concern. Nonetheless, the dilemmas that Sheela was experiencing cannot be simply understood within a singular context. Hence, it becomes equally important to situate Sheela's case within a multicultural framework that looks beyond diagnosis. Key issues to consider from this culturally infused counseling paradigm include (a) acculturation issues for individuals who immigrate as young adults, (b) personality dimensions (sense of self) that are inherently connected to ethnic identity and cultural values and norms, and (c) the construction of hybrid identity. The multidimensional nature of each of these constructs requires an awareness of how each dimension intersects and influences a client's presenting concerns.

Relationship Considerations

Sheela's parents and siblings represent significant individuals in her life and in her case. Her current family represents a reconstructed family in a unique way. For example, her new parents are actually her aunt and uncle, and her younger siblings are in reality her first cousins. Sheela's uncle is one of her mother's older brothers; therefore, there exists a biological link between Sheela and her new family. The fact that her uncle sponsored her and brought her into the family as one of his own children speaks to the importance of cultural values, in that extended family is the norm in the East Indian culture. The complexities of defining the family dynamics and structure represent but one complex element of this case.

Transition Outcomes

Counseling with Sheela continued over the course of 3½ months, with sessions on a weekly basis. Initially, sessions primarily focused on helping Sheela cope and negotiate the emotional and physical symptoms of depression. Simultaneously, attention was given to normalizing and contextualizing her experience by framing her recent life experiences within a cultural framework. Over the course of 3 months, Sheela slowly reduced her use of Paxil; however, initially it helped her manage her depressive symptoms until she created additional coping strategies. She progressively became more capable of normalizing the feelings and reactions she was struggling with in a variety of areas of her life (e.g., grief, acculturation, adjustment, relationships with the family). Although by the end of therapy she had not completely resolved all these issues, she presented as more competent and capable of understanding the underlying issues contributing to the emotional strain with which she had been living. After terminating her weekly sessions, we agreed to meet once a month to assess continuing progress. However, we also agreed that if she felt she was relapsing into a negative emotional spiral, she could resume more regular sessions. Sheela developed a personal action plan that included sharing her personal challenges first with her mother and then with her siblings and father. This first step presented a twofold opportunity: (a) making her family aware of the issues with which Sheela was struggling and (b) thereby expanding her system of support. Simultaneously, this allowed Sheela to feel less isolated and alone with her sense of numerous personal losses and transition experience. It is important to note the multidimensional issue with respect to Sheela's family situation. First, although her adjustment into an existing family dynamic contributed to one aspect of her personal concerns, her cultural connection and ethnic identity also made her family an asset and resource. Although her family did not actively participate in the therapy sessions, making them aware that she was seeking counseling and thereby indirectly including them in the process facilitated the creation of a meaningful change process on both internal and external levels.

The process of engaging in a deeper dialogue that highlighted and examined cultural values, expectations, and acculturation processes and the necessity of constructing a bicultural identity simultaneously represented challenges and opportunities for personal growth for this client.

Writer's Role

As a therapist, working with Sheela also represented a variety of challenges and opportunities for both personal and professional growth. Sharing a similar ethnic background with a client always requires constant attention to the multiple ways a shared ethnicity can help and hinder the working alliance and counseling dynamic. Notably, the working alliance can be influenced in both covert and overt ways. For example, an explicit advantage mentioned by the client in this case incident is the client's positive attitude about a shared ethnicity with the counselor. This resulted in immediately setting a positive tone to building an effective working alliance. The client described she felt an immediate sense of relief when meeting a non-White counselor, based on her assumption that this would somehow make it easier to express her cultural identity and be understood from a cultural perspective. A shared ethnicity between client and counselor simultaneously also requires that the counselor constantly engage in an ongoing process of reflexive evaluation. This involves examining personal assumptions, questioning and clarifying the unique issues in a client's life and thereby not assuming an implicit understanding of the client's worldview and cultural context. For both a client and counselor, the inherent danger lies in assuming that a shared ethnicity and cultural worldview are expressed in the same way between the counselor and client. Furthermore, it becomes important to continually explore and examine a client's impressions, understanding, and meaning ascribed to the counselor's ethnicity. It is important to note that a shared ethnic background does not automatically mean that the counselor and client express and live their cultural values, beliefs, and identity in the same way.

My role as counselor involved assuming different priorities and identities in the therapeutic process, such as (a) therapist/counselor, (b) a cultural sounding board that served to facilitate an exploration of cultural norms and emerging dilemmas, and (c) facilitator and collaborator in helping Sheela define and develop an action plan and brainstorming options for navigating personal challenges. Coupled with managing these multiple roles, it was equally important to engage in critical reflexivity through peer and formal supervision processes in order to continually monitor my personal process and attend to potential blind spots that might emerge in the working alliance.

Analysis

Understanding a client beyond a clinical diagnosis is an inherent requirement of culturally infused counseling practice. Sheela was initially referred for counseling on the basis of a diagnosis of depression; however, several additional issues need to be considered in conceptualizing her case. For example, issues of acculturation, acculturative stress, and hybrid identity development become critical considerations. Understanding a client's presenting issues within a cultural context leads to normalizing and situating concerns in a broader framework (Arthur & Collins, 2005). This requires a counselor to engage in a paradigm shift that moves beyond the traditional Western counseling framework to incorporate a culturally infused model of counseling. Furthermore, framing issues within the context of multicultural competencies lays the foundation for effective and ethical practice (Pettifor, 2005).

First, acknowledging that acculturation holds both short- and long-term implications for an individual is important in Sheela's case. As noted in the literature (Baptiste, 1993; Berry, 2001), the reasons for immigration and the circumstances of immigration can add numerous layers and stressors to an individual's experience and adjustment. Immediate adjustment concerns such as housing, employment, and so forth were not direct concerns for Sheela because she came to live with a family that was already established in Canada. However, longer term implications of this transition involved negotiating the existing relationships in her new family and establishing her place and role in the family.

Intergenerational conflicts are also cited in the literature as a common issue in the acculturation process. Typically, this has been conceptualized as existing between first- and second- (or later) generation individuals (Aycan & Kanungo, 1998; Pettys & Balgopal, 1998). However, as evident in Sheela's case incident, both intergenerational and intragenerational issues are involved in her adjustment and settlement (i.e., siblings, parents, and within herself). Outwardly, Sheela appears to be acculturated on a behavioral level; however, the internal and emotional dilemmas she described in sessions also highlight tensions relative to values-level acculturation. As practitioners, we need to shift our thinking to accommodate longer term implications of adjustment as represented by Sheela's story.

In conjunction with a myriad of adjustment issues, an individual begins to simultaneously embark on the process of deconstructing an old identity and reconstructing a new hybrid identity. This identity development process typically represents new and unfamiliar territory for an individual. It can create ambivalence, confusion, and disorientation vis-à-vis negotiating and integrating new values, attitudes, beliefs, and behaviors (Bhabha, 1994). As acknowledged in the literature, identity development is neither a linear nor a compartmentalized process; rather it is a fluid, dynamic, and evolving entity (Jambunathan, Burts & Pierce, 2000). It requires individuals to assume an active, conscious stance in defining and negotiating the creation of a hybrid identity and actively make decisions about values, attitudes, and behaviors that they will retain and maintain and others that they will put aside.

Finally, the working alliance plays an equally important role in the counseling process. It needs to be a negotiated process in the counseling sessions. As a counselor, engaging in an ongoing process of reflexivity, critical analysis, and supervision to identify blind spots is critical (Arthur & Collins, 2005). Conscious attention to the myriad cultural influences, sense of connection or disconnection with ethnic identity factors, and the individual's acculturation experience fundamentally allows a counselor to build a complex and multifaceted picture of the client.

Reader Reflection Questions

1. In adopting a culturally infused perspective, what additional issues can you identify as being relevant in this case?
2. Consider which theoretical counseling orientation(s) inform your work? How do these fit or clash with a culturally infused perspective?
3. Briefly describe how you would proceed to work with this client in therapy based on your counseling orientations?
4. As highlighted in the case incident, sharing the same ethnic background as your client can present both advantages and challenges to creating an effective working alliance. List and briefly explain three advantages and disadvantages your ethnic background may have in developing an effective working alliance.
5. What issues might you find personally challenging in working with a client like Sheela on the basis of cultural values and worldview?

References

Arthur, N., & Collins, S. (2005). *Culture-infused counselling: Celebrating the Canadian mosaic.* Calgary, Alberta, Canada: Counselling Concepts.

Aycan, Z., & Kanungo, R. K. (1998). Impact of acculturation and socialization beliefs and behavioral occurrences among Indo-Canadian immigrants. *Journal of Comparative Family Studies, 29,* 451–467.

Baptiste, D. A. (1993). Immigrant families, adolescents, and acculturation: Insights for therapists. *Marriage and Family Review, 19,* 341–363.

Berry, J. W. (2001). A psychology of immigration. *Journal of Social Issues, 57,* 615–631.

Bhabha, H. K. (1994). *The location of culture.* London: Routledge.

Jambunathan, S., Burts, D., & Pierce, S. (2000). Comparison of parenting attitudes among five ethnic groups in the United States. *Journal of Comparative Family Studies, 31,* 395–406.

Pettifor, J. (2005). Ethics and multicultural counselling. In N. Arthur & S. Collins (Eds.), *Culture-infused counselling: Celebrating the Canadian mosaic* (pp. 213–238). Calgary, Alberta, Canada: Counselling Concepts.

Pettys, G. L., & Balgopal, P. R. (1998). Multigenerational conflicts and new immigrants: An Indo-American experience. *Families in Society: The Journal of Contemporary Human Services, 79,* 410–423.

Response 1

Ellen P. Cook

Effective counseling requires expertise in two rhythms of thought alternating within the counseling process: to be able to discern within the minutiae of a client's life certain broad, implicit patterns that professionals agree are problematic and then to look once again for the particulars that render this client's pattern unique. Experienced practitioners can intuit the meaningfulness of the mundane and help the client see how new life paths are forged one step at a time.

The ecological perspective (EP) offers one such guide to identify both some general problem areas and then the specifics that are necessary to know in order to help Sheela in her exquisitely personal quest for a more satisfying life. In discussing Sheela from an ecological perspective, I will first provide a general overview of EP and then turn to how it can enrich the understanding of Sheela as a cultural being within her life context.

EP

EP is not a theory per se, but a way of thinking about individuals, groups, and counseling interventions with them. EP provides a template for suggesting what counselors include in conceptualizing problems and, therefore, the focus of interventions as a consequence. EP is essentially a metatheoretical perspective that attempts to embrace diverse counseling theories under a single conceptual umbrella. Many strategies, each in its own way, can effectively help clients. EP is intended to assist counselors to decide where and when to use these familiar change strategies.

Ecological principles have been widely embraced in counseling, psychology, and social work. How we (Conyne & Cook, 2004a) have synthesized these principles into a metatheory applicable to a range of populations and presenting issues is unique; the conceptual building blocks are not. Three aspects of human behavior, as understood in EP, are highlighted here: its contextual nature, its interactional nature, and the importance of meaning-making.

Behavior Is Contextual

The fundamental precept in EP is a restatement of Kurt Lewin's (1936) famous formula: All human behavior must be understood as the outcome of a human being's interaction with his or her environment. Behavior always occurs within a set of contexts whose differentiation is commonly represented as concentric or nested circles (Bronfenbrenner, 1979). Conyne and Cook (2004b) described how the individual with his or her unique biological, psychological, and social makeup functions at the center of these interpenetrating contexts, influenced most directly by interpersonal relationships in everyday life. The next level of proximity is groups of which the individual is a member, followed by neighborhoods, communities, large organizations, and broader social institutions (cf. Shinn & Toohey, 2003). Encompassing all other levels are macrolevel influences, representing the broader sociocultural mores, patterns of behavior, values, and so on, that effectively structure life implicitly or explicitly for members of the society. Counselors need to remember that the physical environment, whether natural (e.g., topography) or human made (e.g., architecture), exerts an often subtle but undeniable influence on behavior.

Although individual development is most directly shaped by proximal factors that individuals experience on an everyday level (see Bronfenbrenner, 1995), more distal, abstract factors will always play a role as well, whether directly (e.g., an economic depression results in loss of work for a family's breadwinner) or indirectly (e.g., social values representing the "good life" are mediated by a particular family's religious values). The nature of the person, interactions within social groups, and models of human action in a variety of settings all embody coherent frameworks of meaning implicit across a culture (Markus & Kitayama, 1998).

Behavior Is Interactional

Individuals are not passive placeholders within these environments but rather actively interact with them. Individuals are influenced by, and in turn influence, the contexts of their lives. Individuals do have some genetically based propensities for behavior, but whether and how these propensities are actualized within an individual life is likely to be moderated by the individual's interactions with his or her life contexts (e.g., Bussey & Bandura, 1999). Markus and Kitayama (1998) have argued that personality "is completely interdependent with the meanings and practices of particular sociocultural contexts. People develop their personalities over time through their active participation in the various social worlds in which they engage" (pp. 66–67).

How a particular individual client reacts to salient events within the immediate life context is crucial for his or her counselor to understand. Individuals with similar genetic constitutions or social histories may react to certain events similarly—or very differently. Culture is a multidimensional construct representing person–environment (P–E) interactions at myriad levels. Swartz-Kulstad and Martin (2000) described a number of "variables related to culture and context that impact the P–E fit" (p. 179): personal culture orientation, family, community environment, communication style, and language. In essence, culturally related behavior is affected by the interaction of both individual and contextual variability. This interaction may result in behavior either shared across persons or unique to the individual, depending on the nature of the factors contributing to the situation. In Sheela's case, her presenting issue concerning acculturation may be experienced by any immigrants, may be unique to people sharing her cultural heritage, or may be idiosyncratic to Sheela herself. Ecologically minded counselors routinely remind themselves to look for within-group diversity among groups of people they predict to behave similarly. For example, sequelae of cross-cultural transitions can vary according to gender or native culture (e.g., Asian women face different issues than Hispanic men) or with individual history (e.g., for Sheela, with personal bereavement).

EP, then, is essentially a perspective focused on interactions among variables. As Belsky (1995) concluded, "in ecological research, the main effects are likely to be in the interactions" (p. 550). From a counselor's perspective, the most significant interactions are connected with meaning-making.

Behavior Is Meaningful

EP, as elaborated in Conyne and Cook (2004a), draws heavily on constructivism (e.g., Sexton & Griffin, 1997) in its emphasis on meaning-making. A person always responds to events as he or she perceives and understands them. Some potent meanings are not obvious to those living within a particular culture, as in the Western idealization of self-determination. As the old adage goes, the fish is not aware of living in water.

EP elaborates how differences in meaning-making occur according to variations at each contextual level: for example, individual spiritual development, family values leading to similar career choices, organizational mission statements shaping on-the-job behavior, and cultural valuing of communal versus individual values at every level of interpersonal context. Biological sex and physical markers of race evoke complex systems of meaning that structure social roles, political rights, career opportunities, and other powerful determinants of possibilities within the fabric of social life, yet there is also incredible variability across individuals within the same category because of the interaction between person and context. Individuals may not be able to change the particulars of their lives, but they can alter how they perceive and thus react to them. A counselor and client can determine which meanings implicit within a client's life may contribute to her or his distress and which of these meanings are possible or even desirable to change.

Ecological Counseling Goals

The purpose of counseling within EP is to help individuals maximize *concordance* within their lives, defined as "mutually beneficial interaction between person and environment" involving a "harmonious balance between challenge and support" (Conyne & Cook, 2004b, p. 24). The metaphor of organisms inhabiting a physical environment illuminates how person–environment interaction is a question of survival: What environment offers the nutrients and challenges required to thrive? Human organisms certainly require water, light, and air. Unlike trees, however, they also require love, community, a sense of purpose, and hope. The need for some nutrients seems prewired in the human constitution; other needs are determined by personal experience.

The sense of *discordance* is universal at times and common among clients: Something essential in life is missing, or is present but toxic; a person does not fit in roles, relationships, life paths. Individuals experience discordance according to their meaning-making. In the case of Sheela, where many potential causes of distress are present, a counselor must attempt to discern just where Sheela may experience herself or her interpersonal/cultural/physical environment as a source of pain. The counselor considers what life resources lend strength (nutrients) to the client and what challenges from within and outside the client complicate this client's quest to make a life worth living.

A good place to start this process of exploration is the client's ecological niche, the phenomenologically defined space where daily life occurs: the specific individuals, physical environment (e.g., qualities of home or office space), interpersonal environment (e.g., family, coworkers, friends, acquaintances at a local coffee shop), and customary activities (e.g., church, hobby group, exercise club). The niche is a rich source of clues about the quality of the client's life. In effect, a person's life can be too small to allow him or her to grow or be so large that a person feels drained and fragmented.

Cultural variability within and across the multifaceted contexts is apparent in how human lives are elaborated over time. Sheela and her counselor can draw on EP to understand what it means to her to be living in her present contexts with a particular identity and history. From there, they can identify sources of discordance and possible solutions drawing on Sheela's personal and contextually derived strengths. In EP, Sheela would be encouraged to explore how she might adapt to, change, or leave some part of her environment for one that offers her more life support. Whatever Sheela chooses to do now, she can optimize her future person–environment interactions with her unique strengths and confidence.

Thinking Ecologically About Sheela's Life

Sheela's Multifaceted Life Transitions

Sheela describes a case of cross-cultural transition from an Eastern (Indian) to Western (Canadian) culture, a move that appears to be more or less permanent. She is requesting help in completing this transition culturally, emotionally, and socially, as well as physically.

She does not suggest returning to her native home as a possibility. For whatever reason, she appears determined to live in her new home successfully, without looking back.

Cultural, identity, and emotional issues seem apparent in her distress. An ecological counselor would be especially concerned about her phenomenological experience of two life events: first, the death of her mother and her subsequent loss of her whole family of origin as she suddenly moves overseas and, second, her "adoption" by her extended family, requiring her to assimilate quickly into this new family as a daughter and sibling with full status and responsibilities. Taken separately, each family life transition signifies a new set of roles and responsibilities for Sheela in the most intimate of her life contexts. Together, they signify that she has been transplanted emotionally as well as physically.

A variety of cultural factors may complicate Sheela's experiences of being transplanted. Gender and ethnic identities are central to a woman's life, but they can covary in complicated ways (Hoffman, 2006). Either or both gender or cultural socialization could predispose Sheela to experience relationships with others as central to her self-perceptions and her life decisions (Cook, Heppner, & O'Brien, 2002). When these relationships change, so can a person's grounding of self. Sheela has effectively divorced herself from a network of relationships defining her very sense of self as a human being since birth. She may be grieving the loss of not only her relationships but herself.

It is curious, then, that what Sheela feels she has gained and lost in this transition is not clear. She has gained some sense of personal authority and financial independence from her job. However, her distress may signify that she has moved from living on terra firma to quicksand and that she needs a lifeline from the counselor.

Exploring Sheela's Concerns Within EP

Sheela has already been evaluated by health services as depressed and was prescribed medication. The fact that she followed through with this referral from a concerned teacher suggests some comfort with a Western medical facility, but this trust in Western medicine should not be assumed. She may not be comfortable with this Western approach to conceptualizing distress, and she may have her own culturally based impressions concerning her symptoms that would be important to understand (Sussman, 2004). How any client views medical diagnosis is crucial in his or her cooperation with professional interventions (Kress, Eriksen, Rayle, & Ford, 2005).

It is not surprising that Sheela is depressed; the counselor needs to determine just why she, as a unique individual, is expressing this pattern of distress. Because *all* physical or psychological symptoms are expressed behaviorally in particular contexts, this diagnosis is an invitation to look deeper into Sheela's unique life circumstances. This understanding draws on the counselor's hypotheses, based on others' experiences as a starting point, but relies on Sheela's phenomenological experiences of herself interacting within challenging life circumstances. Because of the power of proximal, "up-close" contexts in people's lives (Bronfenbrenner, 1995), these particulars seem a sensible place to start exploration. Why did she leave India immediately after her mother's death? Did she have any choice in the move? Had she made plans to leave India prior to her mother's death, or did her mother's death somehow change the family's circumstances or her status within it? Did she feel herself to be a financial burden and intrusion on her father's grief? Did some unique family issues complicate her departure—for example, long-standing family conflicts? These details are not peripheral: They are crucial to understand Sheela's personal experience of *her* immigration.

Turning attention to her new life, did she have any previous relationships with her new family in Canada or California? Her immersion into the role of eldest daughter seems precipitous to an outsider, but it may or may not be so for her. Did she have a similar family role in India, so her responsibilities were familiar to her? From a cultural perspective, might she view these responsibilities as a privilege or a burden, perhaps culturally prescribed (e.g., for a "homeless" or unmarried woman)? Was her extended family behaving magnanimously, beyond what typically occurred for a woman in her situation, or were both Sheela and her family enacting a cultural script for dealing with a family crisis? Did her new parents see her as a solution to housekeeping or child-care needs? These and similar questions help to establish how Sheela views herself as a person within her present cultural/familial context.

Sheela also reported some mourning over her loss of her life in India. This sense of loss seems predictable, but it should not be assumed that her loss can be easily understood from another's perspective. Grief represents loss and disruption of an individual's life story, often complicated by internal and interpersonal cultural conflicts (Neimeyer & Levitt, 2000). It is important to know much more about what losses she is grieving, and why.

There are clues but not the whole picture. Sheela described a firm sense of connection to her "East Indian ethnic and cultural value system." However, her new family's comfort with Sheela's cultural identity should not be taken for granted. There may be differences between Sheela and her new family in religious practices, celebrations, and so on that complicate her acculturation. Thus, the degree to which her new family maintains its family heritage would influence the degree to which Sheela feels validated in holding onto her own precious roots.

The nature of Sheela's relationship with her new family would influence the mourning she is experiencing over the loss of her mother. She described her new family in terms of *parents* and *siblings*. Did broader cultural norms and her new family's unique communication patterns permit sharing of feelings about her loss? How much of her self-described depression is actually disenfranchised grief—grief that cannot be openly expressed and worked through because of lack of recognition and support for doing so?

Finally, there is little information about the cultural significance of her relationship with her cousins/siblings. How were the relationship tensions expressed? Did interpersonal communication norms permit open resolution of these issues with the knowledge and assistance of the parents? Did her cousins lose any privileges or special status upon her arrival? Did she know how to perform these "oldest daughter" roles based on her life in India, or did she need to learn as life progressed in Canada?

An ecologically oriented counselor would agree with Sheela's counselor that the identity development process involved in acculturation is a long-term, active process. The fact that Sheela has begun work outside the home, continued an education, and striven to fit into her new family by fulfilling its culturally defined expectations for her illustrates her determination to make her new life work in the face of personal tragedy. School and work roles should also be considered as contributors to her distress, however. For example, Sheela's general intelligence level, previous educational success, and facility with English as a second language would help identify school-related stresses. Whether she, as a woman with an Indian heritage, chose her major on the basis of personal interests or because of family needs, expectations, or traditions would help clarify the satisfaction she is experiencing in her studies.

The ecologically oriented counselor recognizes proximal (up-close and personal) relationships as crucial to overall life development and day-to-day life satisfaction. A counselor must ascertain whether the range and intensity of relationships appear sufficient from the person's perspective to provide the recognition, safety, support, challenge, and caring that all individuals need to thrive in their setting. Sheela mentions no friends or social activities. Is this pattern normative for women of her status in her culture, or is it indicative of something about Sheela—for example, her attractiveness, discrimination against her, her personal avoidance of contact, or her home responsibilities? How lonely is she, and why?

The broader community context is essential to consider in understanding her feelings of alienation. If there is a thriving East Indian community where she lives, there may be more opportunities for her to simultaneously maintain her familiar cultural identity and gradually become acculturated to Western aspects of her new life. If her new family's background is unique in her new city or university, her cultural background is more likely to mark her as someone "different" in others' eyes. Discussion of these possibilities can suggest interventions appropriate to Sheela's uniquely determined person–environment interactions, for example, Sheela altering her interactions with others, changing the environment (e.g., advocating for herself in the face of on-the-job discrimination), or leaving the present environment for a more compatible one (e.g., finding a job within a culturally familiar context such as an East Indian store; see discussion of types of contextual changes in Cook, Conyne, Savageau, & Tang, 2004).

Finally, counselors are likely to overlook the significance of physical space in clients' person–environment fit issues. The degree to which Sheela's new space physically resembles her home in terms of topography, interpersonal density, climate, and so on would have an impact on readiness for acculturation. The physical space of her new home would be important to consider. Does she find the space compatible with her needs and comfort levels?

Implications for Counseling Interventions

The ecologically oriented counselor and client work together to arrive at goals and interventions that they view as ecologically valid, that are meaningful to the client, that build on strengths available to the client, and that are likely to improve the client's ability to cope with challenges in his or her life context in the future. The counselor may choose to use a variety of counseling interventions, depending on the specifics of the client's life and the counselor's skills. The counselor will give considerable thought to how Sheela and he or she might conceptualize her distress in a way that is most meaningful and empowering to her. The possibilities are rooted in Sheela's personal meaning-making. For example, the guiding image might be a tree transplanted into a new forest and what it needs to grow. There might be a cultural myth that Sheela suggests as consistent with her life story thus far; in counseling, she might explore how she can write a new ending. Other clients might be more comfortable discussing what tools they need to add to their life toolbox. Alternatively, the focus may well be on the grieving process and how Sheela imagines her mother's ongoing relationship with her.

EP counselors would discuss with Sheela the construct of concordance: first, to identify her perceptions about the nature and causes of her excessively stressful interactions with her life contexts (discordance) and, second, how her fit within her world as she experiences it might change. As suggested above, EP counselors would have determined the unique configuration of Sheela's immigration process, her acculturation thus far, the interpersonal resources and stresses complicating her new life, how others accept or challenge her cultural identity, and the personal tragedies and life dreams presently coloring her sense of possibilities in her new life context. Sheela could identify the personal and interpersonal strengths and resources she already possesses and the ways that she might expand her base of support (e.g., communicating with her family in India via video cam, joining international student groups on campus). Early in counseling, the counselor could explore some mundane ways that Sheela might immediately feel less isolated. When individuals can feel more comfortable in their everyday life context, they may feel empowered to take larger steps in enriching life in general.

References

Belsky, J. (1995). Expanding the ecology of human development: An evolutionary perspective. In P. Moen, G. H. Elder, Jr., & K. Luscher (Eds.), *Examining lives in context: Perspectives on the ecology of human development* (pp. 545–561). Washington, DC: American Psychological Association.

Bronfenbrenner, U. (1979). *The ecology of human development*. Cambridge, MA: Harvard University Press.

Bronfenbrenner, U. (1995). Developmental ecology through space and time: A future perspective. In P. Moen, G. H. Elder, Jr., & K. Luscher (Eds.), *Examining lives in context: Perspectives on the ecology of human development* (pp. 619–647). Washington, DC: American Psychological Association.

Bussey, K., & Bandura, A. (1999). Social cognitive theory of gender development and differentiation. *Psychological Review, 106,* 676–713.

Conyne, R. K., & Cook, E. P. (Eds.). (2004a). *Ecological counseling: An innovative approach to conceptualizing person–environment interaction.* Alexandria, VA: American Counseling Association.

Conyne, R. K., & Cook, E. P. (2004b). Understanding persons within environments: An introduction to ecological counseling. In R. K. Conyne & E. P. Cook (Eds.), *Ecological counseling: An innovative approach to conceptualizing person–environment interaction.* (pp. 3–35). Alexandria, VA: American Counseling Association.

Cook, E. P., Conyne, R. K., Savageau, C., & Tang, M. (2004). The process of ecological counseling. In R. K. Conyne & E. P. Cook (Eds.), *Ecological counseling: An innovative approach to conceptualizing person–environment interaction* (pp. 109–140). Alexandria, VA: American Counseling Association.

Cook, E. P., Heppner, M. J., & O'Brien, K. M. (2002). Career development of women of color and White women: Assumptions, conceptualization, and interventions from an ecological perspective. *The Career Development Quarterly, 50,* 291–305.

Hoffman, R. (2006). Gender self-definition and gender self-acceptance in women: Intersections with feminist, womanist, and ethnic identities. *Journal of Counseling & Development, 84,* 358–372.

Kress, V. E. W., Eriksen, K. P., Rayle, A. D., & Ford, S. J. W. (2005). The *DSM-IV* and culture: Considerations for counselors. *Journal of Counseling & Development, 83,* 97–104.

Lewin, K. (1936). *Principles of topological psychology.* New York: McGraw Hill.

Markus, H. R., & Kitayama, S. (1998). The cultural psychology of personality. *Journal of Cross-Cultural Psychology, 29,* 63–87.

Neimeyer, R. A., & Levitt, H. M. (2000). What's narrative got to do with it? Construction and coherence in accounts of loss. In J. H. Harvey & E. D. Miller (Eds.), *Loss and trauma: General and close relationship perspectives* (pp. 401–412). Philadelphia: Brunner-Rutledge.

Sexton, T. L., & Griffin, B. L. (Eds.). (1997). *Constructivist thinking in counseling practice, research, and training.* New York: Teachers College Press.

Shinn, M., & Toohey, S. M. (2003). Community contexts of human welfare. *Annual Review of Psychology, 54,* 427–459.

Sussman, L. K. (2004). The role of culture in definitions, interpretations, and management of illness. In U. P. Gielen, J. M. Fish, & J. G. Draguns (Eds.), *Handbook of culture, therapy, and healing* (pp. 37–65). Mahwah, NJ: Erlbaum.

Swartz-Kulstad, J. L., & Martin, W. E., Jr. (2000). Culture as an essential aspect of person–environment fit. In W. E. Martin Jr. & J. L. Swartz-Kulstad (Eds.), *Person–environment psychology and mental health: Assessment and intervention* (pp. 169–195). Mahwah, NJ: Erlbaum.

Response 2

Elizabeth Mathew and Mary A. Fukuyama

The story of Sheela as a relatively new immigrant to Canada is a compelling one, especially given the complexity and intensity of her presenting issues. We discuss this case incident by applying theoretical perspectives drawn from feminist therapy and multicultural counseling competencies literature. The client's presenting concerns of multiple losses, case conceptualization, cross-cultural factors that stimulate further questions, and counselor matching and interventions are discussed. The following is a feminist multicultural perspective on the case study of Sheela.

Presenting Concerns and Conceptualization

Sheela's case illustrates a woman living within the context of multiple losses and learning to redefine herself through the process of grief. Her immigration transition can be understood as the interface between three primary losses. The counseling context can serve as a place where these losses are explored, human connection is gained, and client learning is transferred into her everyday life within the context of loss.

First, Sheela has lost relational connection. Through the words of her counselor, information is given regarding the unexpected death of her mother. It is unclear how her mother died (e.g., trauma, disease) or the impact that her mother's mode of death had on the client's life. In addition, information is given regarding a cousin in California with whom she lived for 1 year. Although the quality of this relationship, as well as descriptors of her cousin (e.g., gender, age, family status), is unknown, this brief connection was interrupted when the client migrated to Canada to stay with her aunt, uncle, and two female cousins. Each of these relational losses appeared to be characterized by abruptness, paucity of time between transitions, and lack of continuity. She seems to walk into each new phase without anyone who has truly known her past.

What is most striking about Sheela's relational loss is less about the information that is given and more about the information that is absent. There is no discussion of Sheela's life before her migration to the West. She is presented without a life story before her mother's death. It is impossible to fully conceptualize Sheela's relational loss without knowing the depth of connection she had to her mother; the role of her biological father; the presence of siblings or other extended family members, friends, and community members in India; and the impact they had on her life. According to Segal (1991), from an Asian Indian cultural perspective, the self is defined in *allocentric* terms, or defined in relation with others, primarily family members. Thus, Sheela's life can be viewed as being part of a musical ensemble, each member having an impact on the sound of the other. Yet, she is presented rather like a traveling soloist whose backup band keeps shifting. This presentation does not acknowledge that at each new stage, her song (or sense of self) is changed. Sheela has experienced significant seen and unseen relational loss.

Second, Sheela has lost personal power. It is unclear how much of her transition to the United States and then to Canada was voluntary (based on an informed choice) and how much was necessary (due to the lack of other options). Traditional Asian Indian culture is patriarchal, meaning that power and hierarchy within the family begin with the eldest living man and women are identified through their relationships with men, such as father or husband (Miltiades, 2002; Segal, 1991). Patriarchal cultural norms, independent of how they are perceived along a continuum of oppressiveness toward women, become a means of communicating a person's status within society. No mention of a father figure leaves one with the assumption that the client has experienced a loss of status within her cultural context prior to migration. This loss of status is exacerbated by the immigration experience, in which she is left alone, in unfamiliar territory, searching to create a new family life and identity.

In addition, Sheela leaves her cousin's residence to join her aunt, uncle, and younger female cousins. It is unclear if these individuals were strangers to her upon arrival to Canada or if she had previous face-to-face contact with them. Although the counselor points out that Sheela describes her new family as "loving," it is clear that she has also taken on, or been given, the role of a caregiver within the home (e.g., cooking, cleaning, supervising younger cousins). The added responsibilities mixed with the inevitable feeling of obligation toward her new family could lead to multiple role strain or psychological/physical distress when the demands of multiple roles exceed the rewards (Barnett & Baruch, 1985; Hyde, DeLamater, & Hewitt, 1998; McBride, 1990). Researchers have noted that an increase in feelings of obligation toward family members has been related to an increase in amount of time spent in caregiving activities (Dautzenberg et al., 2000). Sheela likely does not feel the liberty to say "no" to participating in any of these tasks and has the potential of being exploited due to her lack of power. Her desire for an arranged marriage may reflect a desire to renew her status (lost without any family of origin) as well as a culturally acceptable "escape" from a situation where she lacks power (life with extended family in Canada). Her pursuit of higher education also represents an opportunity to expand options and increase personal power.

Third, Sheela has lost identity. Like other immigrants, she must struggle to define her Eastern ethnicity in relation to her Western surroundings. Assimilation and acculturation affect this identity-formation process. Assimilation and acculturation refer to two distinctive cultural adaptation processes, each with its unique nuance. Assimilation describes social forces to accommodate to a new culture, but, in the process, an individual denies or loses her or his original culture and language. Acculturation, on the other hand, describes a process of learning second-culture skills in order to adapt, without sacrificing the original culture.

A growing body of ethnic literature (fiction and nonfiction) provides an insider's view of what it is like to struggle with forces of assimilation and acculturation. As described by a Pulitzer-prize winning Indian American author,

> When I was growing up in Rhode Island in the 1970s I felt neither Indian nor American. Like many immigrant off-spring I felt intense pressure to be two things, loyal to the old world and fluent in the new, approved of on either side of the hyphen. Looking back, I see that this was generally the case. But my perception as a young girl was that I fell short at both ends, shuttling between two dimensions that had nothing to do with one another. (Lahiri, 2006, p. 43)

Sheela's process of adaptation to a new country will unfold in the context of the acculturation/assimilation norms in her family and local community. Her inclination to seek education will also provide tools and support for engaging in her adopted country. Developing a bicultural identity is a long-term project, likely beyond the scope of one counselor's experiences; however, providing therapeutic support for negotiating cultural dissonance and modeling a bicultural worldview will be empowering.

Cross-Cultural Factors

There are many demographic variables missing from the text that would allow a more comprehensive look at Sheela's loss of identity and that raise more questions than can be answered in this commentary. Specifically, where she is from within the subcontinent of

India, her religious/spiritual identity, and her socioeconomic status are cross-cultural factors that strongly influence cultural adjustment. The Asian Indian ethnic group represents many diverse backgrounds and must be understood within the subethnic categories of linguistic–regional and religious statuses. Although most Asian Indian immigrants have been exposed to the English language due to British colonization until the late 1940s, there exist 16 major Indian languages (Sheth, 1995). In each of the 29 states of India, one Indian language dominates (Kurien, 1999); therefore, linguistic preferences delineate regional identity for the Asian Indian. Durvasula and Mylvaganam (1994) noted that Asian Indian immigrants to the United States from one region of India feel that they have few similarities with Asian Indian immigrants from a different region of India. This may apply to Sheela's experience in terms of how much she identifies with her mother language and how well she feels she can connect with other Asian Indian immigrants in Canada.

Religious affiliation intensifies the diversity within the Asian Indian immigrant community. India is home to individuals who identify with all of the major world religions. The majority of Asian Indians (approximately 83%) are Hindu, 11% are Muslim, 3% are Christian, and 2% are Sikhs (Ramisetty-Mikler, 1993). Hinduism is a pervasive presence in and influence on Asian Indian cultural norms. The concepts of dharma, or duty despite hardship, and karma, or belief that previous behavior dictates future outcomes, permeate society regardless of the individual's particular faith orientation (Guglani, Coleman, & Sonuga-Barke, 2000; Miltiades, 2002). Beliefs about dharma and karma may be playing a role in Sheela's grief process.

Finally, Sheela's socioeconomic level or class status is unknown. In the Asian Indian culture, class and religious identification have been intricately connected, resulting in cultural norms. Specifically, the ancient caste system, with its history of misunderstandings, controversy, and oppression, is associated with the Hindu faith and has left behind a residue of caste consciousness that has differing levels of impact throughout India and has been associated with differential access to resources (Firth, 2005; van der Gaag, 2005). An example would be skin-tone privilege, how Asian Indian culture promotes fair skin as opposed to dark skin as being the ideal image of beauty (Fernandes, 2006). When working with individuals of Asian Indian descent, it is important to explore the intersection of regional–linguistic, religious, and class identity as well as its influence on the person's sense of self.

Counselor Matching and Interventions

Effective counseling can serve as a catalyst whereby Sheela learns how to gain within the context of multiple losses. This case illustrates the opportunity for therapeutic connection. Through a collaborative relationship, a counselor can serve as someone who wants to know who Sheela was before immigration, seeks to know Sheela in the midst of her grief transition, and helps Sheela plan who she wants to be.

It is interesting to note in this case study that the counselor (as a non-White) was able to bond with the client due to a "shared ethnic background." Perhaps for reasons of confidentiality, not all of the details are provided. However, forming a therapeutic alliance between counselor and client is one of the first critical steps in counseling. In this case, it was important to share ethnicity, but what if the counselor was from a different ethnic background? Some of the counselor–client matching literature suggests that it is more important to match "consciousness" about racial identity than actual race or ethnicity itself (Helms & Cook, 1999).

Racial identity theories posit that persons in minority roles may adapt in various ways in relation to the dominant culture, progressing through "statuses or stages" of consciousness (Sue & Sue, 1999). Each identity stage is accompanied by four sets of beliefs and attitudes: (a) how one feels about self; (b) how one feels about others in same race/ethnicity group;

(c) how one feels about members of other racial/ethnic minority groups; and (d) how one feels toward Whites (or the dominant culture). Numerous racial identity theorists have described racial identity development as a five-stage or status model, and a brief summary of the commonalities follows.

Generally speaking, an individual may at first conform to the dominant culture and may have self-deprecating attitudes toward self and others in his or her ethnic or racial group. These attitudes mirror negative dominant culture attitudes and stereotypes around race or color. A second stage or status is one of dissonance, when the individual becomes aware of racism and oppression and may experience a critical incident that triggers questioning a conformist position. In the next stage or status, individuals seek affirmative experiences for their racial/ethnic identity through immersion in their racial/ethnic community and among peers. A fourth stage or status invites a period of introspection, in which the individual attempts to balance between the dichotomies of dominant and minority cultures and to incorporate individual preferences. In the fifth or final stage or status, individuals integrate self-knowledge with cultural awareness, are able to identify with culturally different others, and transcend personal cultural identities for the sake of working on the larger issues of racism and other oppressions (Helms, 1995; Tatum, 1997).

Persons in dominant cultural roles, sometimes referred to as the "majority," such as White persons, also may proceed through racial identity development statuses. Helms (1992) and others (Ponterotto, 1993) proposed that Whites move through racial identity statuses that include some of the following descriptors: preencounter, contact, disintegration, reintegration, pseudoindependence, immersion, integration, and autonomy. The racial identity of the counselor is central to understanding ways in which the therapeutic alliance may be shaped. Four possible counselor–client dyad combinations were identified: parallel, progressive, regressive, and crossed. Following is a discussion of the four combinations.

It has been suggested that some counselor–client dyad types promote harmony (parallel or progressive), whereas other dyad types do not (regressive or crossed). One way to predict the quality of the counselor–client relationship is through matching racial identity statuses.

Parallel: Counselors and clients share similar racial identity attitudes and behaviors (e.g., contact, preencounter). The saliency of racial identity is similar, and there may be similarity in worldview regarding racial consciousness.

Progressive: In this dyad, counselors and clients are similar to the parallel type, except that the counselor is slightly advanced and provides guidance for the racial identity development of the client. Counselors are secure in their racial identities and model good multicultural communication and interaction. This is a harmonious combination and lends itself to greater possibilities for growth.

Regressive: This type occurs when the client is more racially and culturally aware than the counselor; the client's racial identity status is beyond the counselor's. This combination is a disservice to the client, and referral is warranted.

Crossed: This dyad occurs when the counselor's and client's racial identity statuses are diametrically opposed to one another, for example, when a person sees race as central or core to his or her life and the other does not see race as important. In such instances, the counselor and client are not in harmony and probably cannot develop an effective relationship. In the crossed dyad, alliances are much more difficult to form because, at best, they are mutually ignorant, and, at worst, each person believes that the other is essentially wrong in his or her worldview.

In applying this matching dyad model, clients will benefit more when matching with their counselors in either the parallel or progressive combinations. Counselors who are advanced are not afraid to discuss racial issues. Progressive relationships are more likely to promote positive change in areas of racial consciousness. It seems that in this case study, the counselor and Sheela are in a progressive match.

Milton Bennett (2004) described a similar process in terms of developing intercultural sensitivity. The model is composed of six positions along a continuum that moves from ethnocentrism ("my culture defines reality") toward ethnorelativism ("my culture is one of many"). The six positions include denial, defense, minimizing differences, acceptance, adaptation, and integration of differences. The last stage is of particular relevance to this case study. People in this stage are not only adapting to new cultures, they are negotiating the state of being between cultures, which addresses what it is like to be "culturally marginal." Bennett (2005) described two features: encapsulated marginality (i.e., being stuck between cultures, marked by feelings of confusion or alienation) and constructive marginality (i.e., moving between cultures in a dynamic, fluid way). This phenomenon is common among nondominant minority groups, long-term expatriates, and global nomads. Counseling issues may include resolving cross-cultural conflicts and discussing some of these questions: "When does it matter or hurt to be marginal (feelings of inclusion or exclusion) and how does one become comfortable with being truly multicultural?" One could presume that the counselor has achieved success in adaptation to Canadian culture and can serve as a cultural broker and guide.

In addition, the counselor in a university setting can serve as campus advocate as well as bridge to community resources. Sheela might have benefited from connecting with other students on campus (e.g., South Asian Student Alliance, Hindu Student Organization) as well as participating in group therapy with other people going through grief/loss or cultural transition (e.g., bereavement therapy group, international students support group, Asian American female therapy group).

The counselor was wise to conduct a suicide risk assessment, because suicide and depression among South Asian women are significant mental health issues. In a qualitative focus group study in the United Kingdom, South Asian women indicated that suicide was seen as a logical response to distress caused by pressures from family and larger socioeconomic problems and exacerbated by lack of privacy in close-knit communities (Chew-Graham, Bashir, Chantler, Burman, & Batsleer, 2002). In another British study, factors contributing toward suicidality in a group of South Asian women included sexual and physical abuse, domestic violence, immigration issues, forced marriages, racism, issues of loss, and stress related to poverty and homelessness (Batsleer, Chantler, & Burman, 2003).

Effective counseling can be an opportunity for empowerment. Ultimately, it is Sheela who is the expert on her experience. Feminist therapy would focus on how Sheela is a unique person and highlight her strengths as an individual. There would be active movement beyond diagnostic labels (labels such as depression that likely lead to person blaming and internalization of problems) to helping the client see how multiple contexts of oppression (e.g., biological, cultural, social, political) interact with each other, thereby influencing her presenting concerns and resulting in externalizing the problem (Evans, Kincade, Marbley, & Seem, 2005; Israeli & Santor, 2000).

Sheela's counselor noted that Sheela developed a personal action plan that included informing the family about her seeking counseling. In this case, the client reached a level of empowerment that allowed her to share her emotional struggles with her family. Research has indicated that Asian Indian immigrant women are, first, not likely to seek help outside their families and, second, not likely to seek help outside their ethnic communities because of the stigma that exists in the Asian Indian American community against the mental health profession (Bottorff, Johnson, & Venables, 2001). Sheela's choice to include her family after seeking therapy is likely an exception to a pattern within the community. A word of caution: Counselors cannot assume that their clients will want to involve their families. It may well be inaccurate and/or disempowering to assume that all Asian Indian female clients will want their families to know that they are in therapy.

Finally, effective counseling can increase a client's self-awareness. Feminist therapy uses multiple interventions to help the client view him- or herself differently. For example, cognitive restructuring helps the client focus on what she or he does control (e.g., personal response) rather than what she or he does not control (e.g., death in the family, racism). Also, with a gender role analysis, clients are challenged to question how society and/or culture say they "should" be and explore how they actually want to be (Evans et al., 2005; Israeli & Santor, 2000). In the case of Sheela, the counselor can help her explore the meaning of each loss in her life as well as the weight of compound grief, help her reframe her migration to the West as an opportunity to access her fullest potential, and help her make informed choices for her future that include role flexibility.

Conclusion

The essence of multiculturally competent therapeutic intervention is the willingness of a therapist to explore her or his bias within the therapeutic relationship. Sheela's counselor modeled this well by pursuing supervision/peer consultation regarding this case. She also modeled the use of self-reflection/self-exploration when monitoring her role as a therapist. Even as an in-group member, the counselor allowed herself to be vulnerable to the exploration of her own process in the therapeutic context.

References

Barnett, R. C., & Baruch, G. K. (1985). Women's involvement in multiple roles and psychological distress. *Journal of Personality and Social Psychology, 49*, 135–145.

Batsleer, J., Chantler, K., & Burman, E. (2003). Responses of health and social care staff to South Asian women who attempt suicide and/or self-harm. *Journal of Social Work Practice, 17*, 103–125.

Bennett, M. J. (2004). Becoming interculturally competent. In J. S. Wurzel (Ed.), *Toward multiculturalism: A reader in multicultural education* (2nd ed., pp. 62–77). Newton, MA: Intercultural Resource.

Bennett, M. J. (2005, July). *The developmental model of intercultural sensitivity*. Workshop presentation at Summer Institute for Intercultural Communication, Forest Grove, OR.

Bottorff, J. L., Johnson, J. L., & Venables, L. J. (2001). Voices of immigrant South Asian women. *Journal of Healthcare for the Poor and Underserved, 12*, 392–402.

Chew-Graham, C., Bashir, C., Chantler, K., Burman, E., & Batsleer, J. (2002). South Asian women, psychological distress and self-harm: Lessons for primary care trusts. *Health and Social Care in the Community, 10*, 339–347.

Dautzenberg, M. G., Diederiks, J. P., Philipsen, H., Stevens, F. C., Tan, F. E., & Vernooij-Dassen, M. J. (2000). The competing demands of paid work and parent care. *Research on Aging, 22*, 165–187.

Durvasula, R. S., & Mylvaganam, G. A. (1994). Mental health of Asian Indians: Relevant issues and community implications. *Journal of Community Psychology, 22*, 97–106.

Evans, K. M., Kincade, E. A., Marbley, A. F., & Seem, S. R. (2005). Feminism and feminist therapy: Lessons from the past and hopes for the future. *Journal of Counseling & Development, 83*, 269–277.

Fernandes, A. (2006, March 16). Fair and lovely: Perfect radiance [International Issue]. *Femina*, p. 17.

Firth, S. (2005, August 20). End-of-life: A Hindu view. *The Lancet, 366*, 682–686.

Guglani, S., Coleman, P. G., & Sonuga-Barke, E. J. S. (2000). Mental health of elderly Asians in Britain: A comparison of Hindus from nuclear and extended families of differing cultural identities. *International Journal of Geriatric Psychiatry, 15*, 1046–1053.

Helms, J. E. (1992). *A race is a nice thing to have: A guide to being a White person or understanding the White persons in your life*. Topeka, KS: Content Communications.

Helms, J. E. (1995). An update of Helms' White and people of color racial identity models. In J. G. Ponterotto, J. M. Casas, L. A. Suzuki, & C. M. Alexander (Eds.), *Handbook of multicultural counseling* (pp. 181–198). Thousand Oaks, CA: Sage.

Helms, J. E., & Cook, D. A. (1999). *Using race and culture in counseling and psychotherapy: Theory and process*. Boston: Allyn & Bacon.

Hyde, J. S., DeLamater, J. D., & Hewitt, E. C. (1998). Sexuality and the dual-earner couple: Multiple roles and sexual functioning. *Journal of Family Psychology, 12*, 354–368.

Israeli, A. L., & Santor, D. A. (2000). Reviewing effective components of feminist therapy. *Counselling Psychology Quarterly, 13*, 233–247.

Kurien, P. (1999). Gendered ethnicity: Creating a Hindu Indian identity in the United States. *The American Behavioral Scientist, 42*, 648–670.

Lahiri, J. (2006, March 6). My two lives. *Newsweek*, 43.

McBride, A. B. (1990). Mental health effects of women's multiple roles. *American Psychologist, 45*, 381–384.

Miltiades, H. B. (2002). The social and psychological effect of an adult child's emigration on non-immigrant Asian Indian elderly parents. *Journal of Cross-Cultural Gerontology, 17*, 33–55.

Ponterotto, J. G. (1993). White racial identity and the counseling professional. *The Counseling Psychologist, 21*, 213–217.

Ramisetty-Mikler, S. (1993). Asian Indian immigrants in America and sociocultural issues in counseling. *Journal of Multicultural Counseling and Development, 21*, 36–49.

Segal, U. A. (1991). Cultural variables in Asian Indian families. *Families in Society: The Journal of Contemporary Human Services, 72*, 233–240.

Sheth, M. (1995). Asian Indian Americans. In P. G. Min (Ed.), *Asian Indians: Contemporary trends and issues* (pp. 169–198). Thousand Oaks, CA: Sage.

Sue, D. W., & Sue, D. (1999). *Counseling the culturally different: Theory and practice* (3rd ed.). New York: Wiley.

Tatum, B. D. (1997). *Why are all the Black kids sitting together in the cafeteria? And other conversations about race*. New York: Basic Books.

van der Gaag, N. (2005, July). Caste out: Blatant rather than latent, caste is still alive—and kicking—in the West. *New Internationalist, 380*, 14–16.

Between Hope and Despair

Rachel Erhard

Israel's 1948 Declaration of Independence provides a guarantee that the nation "shall be open to Jewish immigration and to the ingathering of the exiles." This "open gate" policy allows every Jew to immigrate to Israel and to receive Israeli citizenship automatically upon arrival. The Jewish population in the country is today, as a result of this immigration policy, over 6 million.

Although ideologically Israeli society has an interest in immigration and, in practice, steps are taken to ease newcomers' absorption, the transition process is difficult nevertheless for many of the large number of immigrants who have flocked to Israel since its inception. Whereas Israeli society, with its modern Western outlook, was not unfamiliar to immigrants from Europe and English-speaking countries, this was not true for newcomers from non-Western parts of the world. For North African and Asian Jews, Israel's Western-inspired cultural patterns often remain foreign well past the absorption period (Hacohen, 2001; Smooha, 1978).

Ethiopian Jewry

Most of Ethiopian Jewry comes from isolated villages in northern Ethiopia, cut off from the technological advances of the 20th century and subsisting on primitive agriculture. Jews have lived in Ethiopia for centuries and have succeeded in avoiding assimilation despite heavy external pressure to convert to Christianity. Insularism, strong religious beliefs, strict adherence to religious customs, and avoiding intermarriage have all worked to keep this community together (Ben-Ezer, 2002; Erlich, Salomon, & Kaplan, 2003; Onolmbemhew, 1998; Weill, 1997).

Immigration from Ethiopia was illegal until 1984 and had to be carried out in secret operations. During that year, civil strife and famine led to a mass exodus on foot of 8,000 Jews from their villages to Sudan. The government of Israel initiated their evacuation. The second wave of immigration was in 1991 during a revolt against the ruling Ethiopian government, when the Israeli government airlifted some 15,000 Ethiopian Jews to Israel in a dramatic period of 36 hours (Budovsky, David, Akiva, & Eran, 1994). Today, approximately 100,000 Ethiopians live in Israel, a third of whom are below age 18 (half of them are Israeli born; Central Bureau of Statistics, 2004). The majority of Ethiopian immigrants live in some 10 communities, in low socioeconomic-status neighborhoods despite Israeli government attempts at preventing the creation of "ghettos." Unemployment is more common among Ethiopians than in the general Israeli population (Offer, 2000).

Each wave of immigration to Israel encounters its own unique problems, but frequently newcomers are shocked at the hostility with which they are received by the people who are already there (Hacohen, 2001; Smooha, 1978) Ethiopians, however, are faced with an especially severe problem because they are dark-skinned. Only on arrival to Israel do they learn that their being "Black" in a world of "Whites" could cause problems. Several authors have noted strong feelings of discrimination and social inferiority related to color (Erhard, 2000; Onolmbemhew, 1998; Parfitt & Trevisan Semi, 2005).

The transition from Ethiopia to Israel caused the collapse of all traditional frameworks of affiliation, village community structure, and family alignments. A dramatic change occurred in the sources of social support—inside the families and in the community. This is expressed in a decline in the power of the traditional leadership, and no alternative leadership has appeared to replace it. In the families, difficulties arise in relations between spouses and between generations, and daily family life is deeply disrupted (Budovsky et al., 1994; Weill, 1995).

These changes in the fine fabric of the family are extremely harmful because the family is of utmost importance in the Ethiopian community, and individuals' obligation to their family is paramount. Children are raised to be humble and shy. Ethiopian culture uses shame as an educational tool for imparting social norms. A child who does not behave according to expectations disgraces both the family and the entire community. There is a strong cultural norm of keeping family secrets from strangers. As a result of the absorption crisis, traditional values like family honor and reputation crumbled, seriously damaging the social status and power of the family, and once parents' status is impaired, they lose the power and ability to support their children. One of the results is a reversal of roles within the family: children becoming the source of assistance and support for their parents (Chiswick, 2003; Weill, 1997).

The absorption of the Ethiopian children and youth in Israel's education system has been riddled with difficulties (Israeli Association for Ethiopian Jews, 2004; Shafat, 1995). Although the goal was educational integration by directing Ethiopian students to different schools throughout the system, this did not work out, instead creating very high concentrations of Ethiopian immigrants in a small number of settings. Most schools that have populations of Ethiopian students are poor in resources and are unable to meet the unique needs of these students; the level of expectations for the students is also very low. A large proportion of the Ethiopians students, in effect, study in segregated settings in the form of streaming (i.e., homogeneous graded classes or groupings in numerous subjects). The educational segregation leads to feelings of deprivation and discrimination. In addition, compared with the rest of the population, a relatively large number of Ethiopian students are educated in residential schools. Among other factors, the separation of residential school students from their families, the disconnect between parents and school, and the sense that there is nowhere to progress to as a result of consistent streaming explain the high drop-out rates of Ethiopian students from the educational system, compared with other Israeli Jewish students. A third of Ethiopian secondary school pupils do not come to school, and the dropout rates are 5 times higher than the national average. The ratio of those obtaining matriculation diplomas is significantly below average, and the quality of the diploma obtained is not high, seriously reducing these students' chances to enter higher education (Central Bureau of Statistics, 2001; Weill, 1997).

Critical Incident

One December day, when the students at a high school in the south of Israel received their semester report cards, a school custodian found Esther (a pseudonym), a 12th-grade student, unconscious in one of the classrooms late in the day. Later, it became evident that she had attempted suicide by swallowing some 50 assorted pills. She left a note at her side saying,

[N]othing went according to how I wanted. I see no future and hope. I am really miserable. I am in a situation I cannot get out of. I have no more energy. I have no more energy left for anything. I apologize to my parents and family.

After a 3-day hospitalization in intensive care and a week in the recovery ward, Esther was discharged. The hospital psychiatrist did not diagnose her as a suicidal personality but identified a minor depression in response to failures, disappointments, and crises that she experienced over the last 2 years. Her hospital discharge letter recommended that she continue supportive therapy and mental health follow-up at school and in the community.

Esther

Esther is 17 years old, pretty, and pleasant. She started high school along with all the junior high graduates who had previously studied with her. Her academic achievement in the 10th grade was above average; she was popular and the staff perceived her as a successful example of immigrant absorption. Toward the end of the 10th grade, she approached the school counselor to request assistance in transferring to a distant residential school where the academic level far surpassed that of the current school. The reason she gave for her request was her dream of studying nursing at university, and doing so would require high academic achievement and a matriculation diploma. Esther explained to the counselor that she lacked elementary study conditions at home (she shared a room with two sisters) and that the family's economic situation was so precarious that she occasionally did not have money for the bus and for buying books and school supplies.

The counselor helped her with the administrative preparations to apply for the residential school, and she started 11th grade there. There was a gap between the academic level of the school she came from and that of the residential school, and, despite her high motivation and the effort she invested in her studies, she experienced repeated failures. Her social adjustment at the residential school was not successful. The number of Ethiopian students at the school was relatively small, and they were estranged from the other students. Esther felt cut off from her family, friends, and community. Toward the end of the school year, Esther dropped out of the residential school and returned home. The school counselor, accidentally meeting Esther in the street, offered to help her find another residential school more suitable to her academic level. Esther rejected the offer and preferred to return to the neighborhood and her old school.

During the summer holiday between 11th and 12th grades, Esther began working as a waitress and continued to do so even after the beginning of the academic year. She would arrive at school tired and found it difficult to adjust to the academic pressure characteristic of the 12th-grade preparations for the matriculation examinations. She failed two tests in mathematics, a subject she had been studying at a high level, and it was suggested she transfer to a lower grouping (that did not enable admission to university). The school counselor summoned her twice: the first time to discuss the issue of the mathematics grouping and later to discuss the retrogression of her studies in most subjects, not only mathematics. During these discussions, she was introverted, sad, and quiet, and her few words mainly referred to the hardships of her family and request for financial assistance for things such as bus tickets and financing the school outing. In her report card, distributed on the day she attempted suicide, was the statement that if her academic achievement did not improve, she would not be allowed to take the matriculation examinations.

The Family

The extended family, consisting at that time of the grandparents (her father's parents); Esther's parents; Esther, the eldest daughter; and two younger sisters, came to Israel

11 years earlier. The grandfather was a respected religious-social leader in Ethiopia. The move from Ethiopia to Israel resulted in culture shock for the grandfather. After initial euphoria, he felt his familiar and dignified world slip away. The situation broke his heart, and he died 2 years after immigrating to Israel. His widowed wife lives with the family; she is housebound and provides some minimal help with the domestic chores. Esther's parents gave birth to two sons in Israel (the youngest is 6 years old). The family of eight lives in a two-bedroom apartment. The father is employed by a contracting company as a cleaner and earns a minimum wage. The mother's health is poor, and she infrequently takes odd jobs. The family maintains a traditional lifestyle. The parents have difficulty adjusting to Israeli society; their command of Hebrew is still minimal; and Esther, as the eldest daughter, occasionally acts as the family's "foreign minister" when dealing with institutional bodies. She has also adopted a central role as a mediator in the family, mainly in dealing with her parents' tense relationship and in giving academic assistance to her brothers and sisters. Her parents were ambivalent about her transfer to the residential school. On the one hand, they believed that by studying at the residential school, Esther could attain academic success, and this would pave her way to university. On the other hand, she had such a central family role that they felt her absence would weaken them and make it even more difficult to cope. Once she opted for residential school, however, her lack of success there was experienced by her family as a disgrace. Her parents reacted to her suicide attempt with impassiveness and hopelessness.

The Community

The community lives in a small and remote neighborhood on the outskirts of a medium-sized (30,000 residents) city in the south of Israel. The community's socioeconomic status is low, the unemployment rate is high, and more than 50% of the residents receive some support from the welfare office. The dilapidated housing blocks are three stories high, covered in Hebrew and Amharic graffiti, with sand yards. There are virtually no cars in the streets, there are no playgrounds, and children play football in the empty stores. The neighborhood's population is elderly. The young people leave at the first available opportunity, and they prefer to study in residential schools. The elderly residents spend most of their day sitting outside, doing nothing. In less than 2 months, the neighborhood experienced five suicide attempts by Ethiopian students, two of which succeeded. The wave of adolescent suicides generates much tension among parents and welfare services, but, given welfare services' inadequate handling of problems, including delinquency, drugs, school dropout, and loitering, the people of the neighborhood feel remote from services and lack faith in their ability to help.

The School

The school, which educates all the students in the city, is a large municipal high school (approximately 1,000 students) located in the center of town. The changes the school has gone through reflect the demographic changes. When it opened in the 1960s, this school was small and selective, accepting only students with high academic achievement. Other students were sent to a vocational school out of the city. In the 1980s, the school became comprehensive, and all the city's students studied there.

When Ethiopians settled on the city's periphery, it resulted in a relatively large influx of Ethiopian students into the school (approximately a fifth of the student population). The school staff lacks professionalism—knowledge, methods, tools, teaching strategies, and training—to cope with the unique difficulties of Ethiopian students. Due to a lack of resources, no budgetary allocations were made for helping professional staff (counselors, psychologists, and social workers) provide extra lessons, enrichment programs, and social activities to enhance the Ethiopians' absorption processes. The school takes various segregation-oriented measures that it feels are necessitated by the Ethiopian students' low academic level and the need to create settings that keep the academically "strong" population in the school. Students are segregated according to their academic achievement, and the majority of Ethiopian students are in the weak groups; they are mainly directed toward the vocational courses of study. The Ethiopian students perceive their segregation to low-level classes as an expression of discrimination and lack of faith in their academic capabilities, feelings that explain the many discipline problems among them. The proportion of Ethiopian students in the school who are eventually eligible for matriculation diplomas is relatively low.

Key Issues

Esther's suicide attempt really disturbed the counselor and intensified her feelings of low professional competence and self-efficacy in counseling Ethiopian students.

The counselor perceives Esther as shy and introverted, virtually unwilling to discuss her personal problems. She perceives Esther as internalizing a social tradition in which feelings are not to be openly discussed and verbal expression of feelings is not a way of coping with difficulty. Throughout their encounters, Esther clings to the façade that "everything is fine" and does not admit to the existence of an emotional or academic problem. She only mentions the economic problems for which she requests assistance.

The counselor is unsure if she has gained Esther's trust; in other words, she is not sure that Esther relates to her as an older sister or a family relative able to offer personal–emotional support and not just assistance with daily hassles.

The counselor has had no contact with Esther's parents, with the exception of a single encounter with the mother when she came to sign the residential school transfer documents. The counselor heard about the family's hardships from the homeroom teacher and the community's social worker. She does not perceive the parents as a source of support for Esther during the current crisis, although she knows that she must treat them with respect and exhibit faith in their ability to help their daughter. She understands that cooperating with the parents, despite their perceived weakness, is necessary, and building a rehabilitative plan without their involvement will prevent their support and the possibility of getting their cooperation and assistance.

The school counselor is not sure regarding the most effective intervention plan—one that would take into account the academic timing (4 months before the matriculation exams); the cultural uniqueness of the Ethiopian community; the specific community in this city; and, most important, Esther's and her family's available coping resources. The counselor asks herself, given her sense that she might not have the professional wherewithal to deal with Esther's case, whether she should be the one who continues working with Esther.

Reader Reflection Questions

1. Can Esther be helped in achieving her academic goals, or should she be helped, on the contrary, to let go of her current ambitions, which she obviously has very little chance of attaining?
2. How should Esther's family be involved in the counseling process even though they have so few relevant resources?
3. How can the counselor expand roles and become a social change agent and an advocate for the Ethiopian community?

References

Ben-Ezer, G. (2002). *The Ethiopian Jewish exodus: Narratives of the migration journey to Israel 1977–1985*. London: Routledge.

Budovsky, D., David, Y., Akiva, B., & Eran, Y. (1994). *Ethiopian Jews in the transition between cultures: The family and life cycle.* Jerusalem: Beitachin Center for Information and Counseling About Family Matters.

Central Bureau of Statistics. (2001). *Diligence in studying and dropping out of high-school students (9th grade to 12th grade)* [in Hebrew]. Jerusalem: Author.

Central Bureau of Statistics. (2004). *Immigration population from Ethiopia, by period of immigration, age and sex* [in Hebrew] (Statistical Abstract of Israel, No. 56, Table 2.26). Jerusalem: Author.

Chiswick, C. U. (2003). *Immigrant religious adjustment: An economic approach to Jewish migration* (Discussion Paper 863). Bonn, Germany: Institute for the Study of Labor.

Erhard, R. (2000). Immigrant youth—Ethiopians in Israel. In J. Gibson-Cline (Ed.), *Youth and coping in twelve nations: Survey of 18–20-year-old young people* (pp. 203–217). London: Routledge.

Erlich, C. H., Salomon, A., & Kaplan, H. (2003). *Ethiopia: Christianity, Islam, Jewry* [in Hebrew]. Tel-Aviv, Israel: The Open University of Israel.

Hacohen, D. (2001). Immigration and absorption. In E. Ya'ar & Z. Shavit (Eds.), *Trends in Israeli society* (pp. 365–486). Tel-Aviv, Israel: The Open University of Israel.

Israeli Association for Ethiopian Jews. (2004). *Narrow pass: Report on Ethiopian youths' integration in Israeli secondary education* [in Hebrew]. Jerusalem: Israeli Association for Ethiopian Jews.

Offer, S. (2000). *Poverty within the Ethiopian community in Israel: Characteristics and perceptions.* Unpublished master's thesis, Haifa University, Haifa, Israel.

Onolmbemhew, D. N. (1998). *The Black Jews of Ethiopia: The last exodus.* Lanham, MD: Scarecrow Press.

Parfitt, T., & Trevisan Semi, E. (2005). *Jews of Ethiopia: The birth of an elite.* London: Routledge.

Shafat, M. (1995). *Adolescent Ethiopian immigrants in a crisis of identity.* Unpublished master's thesis, Bar Ilan University, Ramat Gan, Israel.

Smooha, S. (1978). *Israel: Pluralism and conflict,* London: Routledge & Kegan Paul.

Weill, S. (1995). Collective designation and collective identity among Ethiopian Jews [in Hebrew]. *Israel Social Research, 10,* 25–40.

Weill, S. (1997). *Graduate Ethiopian Jews from the Israeli education system, 1997–1999: Past, present and the future* [in Hebrew]. Jerusalem: Hebrew University, The Institute for Innovation in Education.

Response 1

Marianne C. Kastrup and Armando Báez-Ramos

This case deals with the particular problems related to the migration of persons of Jewish origin from non-Western countries to Israel. The author of the case incident outlines the guarantee provided by the Israeli government to allow Jewish immigration as part of an "open gate" policy that automatically grants Israeli citizenship upon arrival. This very open policy can give the impression that all migrants are received with the same welcome and given similar possibilities as newcomers to the Israeli society. The present-day Israeli society is a very Western, highly developed society in which migrants coming from similar countries integrate fairly easily, in contrast to the experiences of many Jews migrating to Israel from non-Western countries like Ethiopia. The Jews originating from such areas have usually lived in traditional settings and may have had little contact with the modern Western way of life.

Because of differences in migration policies, migrants may experience discrimination in different ways. If the policy allows the maintenance of multicultural norms, the migrants, and in particular members of the younger generation, may feel less discrimination and be less insecure regarding their identity in contrast to ethnic minority young people who are growing up in a setting that is insisting on fast assimilation (Virta, Sam, & Westin, 2004). Furthermore, it is known that a high degree of cultural identity may be a protective factor against the development of mental problems (Sam, 1998). Studies have shown a relationship between lack of identification and marginalization both with respect to the country of origin and to the country of exile and the kind and degree of subsequent psychological problems. This case incident is an example of the conflicts that may arise from the marginalization and lack of identification.

General Consequences

Migrants of African origin may experience open hostility from the Israeli host population, who may refer to their different looks and habits, and the host population may behave in a condescending manner toward these migrants, thereby giving the impression that the migrant population is considered second-class citizens.

The feeling of alienation that such behavior may lead to is further strengthened by the sociocultural problems that this population frequently has experienced before coming to Israel, such as the uprooting from traditional culture, loss of family coherence, or change in child-rearing practices. The acculturation process and the often very extensive social changes that migrants go through are seen as strong risk factors for the later development of mental health problems, and it is well-known that the stress related to acculturation may manifest itself in a series of psychological and psychosomatic symptoms (Koch, Bjerregaard, & Curtis, 2004).

For the upcoming generation of such migrants, this shift in value systems may give rise to an identity crisis. Young migrants and their descendants very often experience a conflict between the values and norms of the family and the demands of society and may feel pressure to adjust to norms from both sides. This dilemma of such a double-sided adjustment may give rise to both emotional and psychological problems (Oppedal, Røysamb, & Heyerdahl, 2005).

Migrants from non-Western countries frequently come from cultures that are collectivistic rather than individualistic (Oppedal et al., 2005). These migrants must adjust to new values and norms and accept that their children have grown up with norms for personal development that are different from those demanded in the educational system of the new country, and the children may find that the behavior and performance that are rewarded in the educational system go against the behavior that is cherished by the family. Lack of parental support—even psychological—may have an impact on the building of identity in the adolescent, and the lack of a reliable identification model may increase this feeling of insecurity (Adam & van Essen, 2004).

Added to this, the author of the case incident emphasizes how traditional Ethiopian culture considers shame a useful instrument against a person who is not adhering to the prevailing social norms and values. A child reared in this setting who shows signs of maladjustment may, therefore, bring shame not just to him- or herself but also to the entire family. Furthermore, many of the children entering the Israeli educational system have little previous schooling and parents with very limited resources, both professional and economical. It is, thus, understandable that such children run an increased risk of psychological problems and unsatisfactory school performance, as well as the risk of dropping out of school.

Adam and van Essen (2004) have described the problems of adolescent refugees in exile, pointing out the many developmental aspects that are involved, including creating a new self-image and identity and dealing with ambivalence and uncertainties. Norwegian studies have found that migrant fathers report more problems in accepting their daughters' liberation than do others in the family and that fathers report more problems among their daughters than among their sons (Oppedal & Røysamb, 2004).

Furthermore, the adolescents must reshape relationships and learn to form new relationships and direct themselves toward new professional goals. Studies report that children and adolescents usually adjust faster to the new surroundings than do adults, but despite that, young people may find themselves between the wishes of the family to continue the traditional culture and the demands of the society for adjustment. These competing demands may result in intergenerational conflicts because the young person has one foot in the culture of his or her family and the other foot in the world of other young people (Browner-Elhanan, 1997; Guarnaccia & Lopez 1998). Members of the younger generation should also recognize that the family should not be seen as the only authority in life and seek other role models (Adam & van Essen, 2004).

Strategies to overcome these obstacles and facilitate the productive integrative processes of the less resourceful migrant youth should be developed, as shown in this case incident.

Critical Incident

The critical incident concerns a situation in which a 17-year-old girl, Esther, is found in a school classroom unconscious after having taken an overdose and leaving a note saying that she was in a situation without any prospects for the future. The day of her suicide attempt she had been informed that she would only be allowed to take her matriculation to university exams provided there was an improvement in her school performance.

Context

To understand this case, a brief history of her educational career and family and social background is provided.

The impression is of a community that is fairly extensively deprived, with a high unemployment rate and apparently little expectation for achieving in life. The population could be described as residual, in which the most able individuals tend to leave as soon as they have the opportunity to do so and those remaining are either too old to move or likely to be unemployed, delinquent, abusers, and so on. Signs of a society in disintegration, including delinquency, a high level of substance abuse, and a high rate of attempted suicide, are described.

The young generation will, in such settings, follow the same pattern. The able ones leave and the less able remain, with the risks that this implies. Many may feel caught in this transition because one part of their identity is with the family and local community but another part wants to break out and grasp the opportunities available. It also should be kept in mind that whereas the adults have taken the decision to migrate, members of the younger generation will usually have no say in this decision, which, so to say, has been forced on them.

Esther grew up in such a community in a family with limited economic resources. Until Grade 10, she did well and showed no psychological problems. She wanted an education and was given a opportunity to enter a better residential school. This change moved her away from her family but gave her an opportunity to develop her potential. Contrary to expectations, her performance started to decline, and so did her social competencies. She did not feel part of the school environment, but instead she felt alienated and cut off from her social background.

The result of this was that she dropped out, and despite being offered a possible transfer to another residential school, she preferred to return home to her family and continue schooling there. The problems, however, continued, and her performance further deteriorated. It became clear that she felt under pressure and, in order to help her family economically, had taken a job outside school hours. This extra work could partly explain her lower performance in the educational system.

On the other hand, the school she is attending is characterized by the frequently encountered tendency that comprehensive schools show in mixed multicultural areas. Despite good intentions, these schools may end up segregating students into groups of low academic level, and such groups often have a preponderance of certain ethnic groups that interpret this segregation as an expression of discrimination toward them. From this case incident, it appears that despite integration-oriented measures the school has not been able to achieve successful integration.

Having grown up in this deprived mixed community, Esther epitomizes the difficult choices with which a person is faced if he or she wants to escape. There are many issues of concern in such families. First of all, her own family has managed the transition from Ethiopia to Israel with difficulty, and their expectations have not been fulfilled. From the story, it appears that her grandfather felt a significant loss in status and was never able to perform in Israel. Similarly, her parents have low-paid, unskilled jobs and little command of Hebrew. They retain a very traditional way of living and seem marginalized in the country, despite being Jewish.

As do many migrant children around the world, Esther has the difficult task of acting as a "liaison officer," or a culture mediator, between the modern Israeli society and her traditional family. The case provides a good description of how this position is a strain for children who act like small adults and are frequently given tasks and responsibilities far beyond their capacity. Furthermore, they may feel like an accomplice, trying to hide the problems at home because the family fears interventions by the authorities. The children may have to live a kind of double life, showing one side at school and another at home. It is not clear whether there also are language problems apart from the social and cultural problems that may prevent the young people from properly expressing their feelings and may result in their acting out or in low self-confidence (Adam & van Essen, 2004).

Serving as an interpreter is another burden that should not be placed on children. By doing so, they may gain an insight into the problems of their families that they are too young to understand and handle properly. Having such information may result in some children not translating properly what has been said because they may try to hide unpleasant news from their parents or they may experience anxiety by listening to the fears and worries of their parents. Many parents may place all their expectations on the children, who may experience a heavy obligation to fulfill all the—frequently unrealistic—dreams of their parents in the new country.

All in all, there are ample opportunities for the first generation growing up in a new culture to be caught in this difficult situation. It is to be expected that the cultural confrontation is perceived more strongly in societies that are seen as monocultural, and it has been demonstrated that the cultural encounter between the family and society may be less problematic if an individual grows up in a family that is ethnically homogenous than if he or she grows up in a family that is more culturally heterogeneous. It also seems that the cultural confrontations are likely to be greater within the family in a monocultural society than the confrontations seen in societies that are more multicultural and that are more knowledgeable about and tolerant toward other cultures (Helweg-Larsen, Kastrup, Baez, & Flachs, 2007; Saraiva, Sundquist, Johannsson, Johannsson, & Sundquist, 2005).

Discussion

Until the suicide attempt, Esther has had a school counselor who perceived her as an introverted student adhering to a tradition in which feelings were not expressed openly. The counselor apparently has done little to overcome these obstacles, having had limited contact with Esther's parents and not gaining their trust because she sees them as a source of very limited support for Esther. Esther herself does not ease the situation by maintaining a facade and putting emphasis on the financial problems of her family and avoiding discussions about the emotional problems and conflicts she has encountered.

Implications

The critical incident represents a dilemma that Esther is facing that has no obvious correct or easy solution. In order to solve it, it is also necessary to discuss the implications of the possible paths.

According to Adam and van Essen (2004) there are three phases to consider: One phase is stabilization, in which safety and security are reestablished, and the focus is on diminishing the stress put on the young person. Another phase is integration, which involves dealing with the stresses of the past but also adapting to the new environment. The last phase is socialization, which means finding a role in both cultures rather than one that is between them.

Should the focus be on supporting Esther's academic achievement and encouraging her empowerment as an individual? Her school performance originally paralleled her aspirations. This could be seen as an indication that, given better support and obtaining a feeling of identity, she may be able to follow the curriculum and strive to attend an institution of higher learning. Choosing this solution may lead to Esther moving further away from her background and sharing fewer values with her family. On the other hand, she may fulfill some of the aspirations of her family about succeeding in her new country.

On the other hand, should the focus be on supporting the survival and integration of the entire family in the Israeli community and easing Esther's position as the family's culture mediator? This focus may, on the short term, mean that Esther cannot continue her academic career but will have to set other priorities in order to facilitate the empowerment of the family. In the long run, however, Esther may feel more settled, with fewer obligations for her family. When this happens, she may want to return to school and try to pick up some of what she missed. In choosing this solution, Esther may be in less risk of feeling alienated from her background.

A third solution could be to work on a kind of combination of the two, in which the focus might be on empowering the members of her family to enable them to see the advantage of allowing Esther to continue her academic career while still remaining with her family but having fewer obligations and more time for her studies. This solution requires that Esther accept being in a sort of limbo between her traditional culture and the Israeli community, but it has the advantage that she remains true to the values of her family and still becomes integrated into Israeli society.

There is no easy solution, and it is difficult to judge which of the three solutions outlined would have the best outcome for Esther and her family.

References

Adam, H., & van Essen, J. (2004). Adolescent refugees in exile. In J. Wilson & B. Drozdek (Eds.), *Broken spirits: The treatment of traumatized asylum seekers, refugees, war and torture victims* (pp. 521–546). New York: Brunner-Routledge.

Browner-Elhanan, K. J. (1997). Acculturation issues in adolescent immigrants: How are they related to health? *Adolescent Medicine, 8,* 397–401.

Guarnaccia, P. J., & Lopez, S. (1998). The mental health and adjustment of immigrant and refugee children. *Child and Adolescent Psychiatric Clinics of North America, 7,* 537–553.

Helweg-Larsen, K., Kastrup, M., Baez, A., & Flachs, E. (2007). *Etniske forskelle i kontaktmønstret til psykiatrisk behandling: Et registerbaseret studie* [Ethnic differences in the utilization of psychiatric treatment: A register-based study]. Copenhagen, Denmark: Videnscenter for Transkulturel Psykiatri.

Koch, M. W., Bjerregaard, P., & Curtis, C. (2004). Acculturation and mental health—Empirical verification of J. W. Berry's model of acculturative stress. *International Journal of Circumpolar Health, 63*(Suppl. 2), 371–376.

Oppedal, B., & Røysamb, E. (2004). Mental health, life stress and social support among young Norwegian adolescents with immigrant and host national background. *Scandinavian Journal of Psychology, 45,* 131–144.

Oppedal, B., Røysamb, E., & Heyerdahl, S. (2005). Ethnic group, acculturation, and psychiatric problems in young immigrants. *Journal of Child Psychology and Psychiatry, 46,* 646–660.

Sam, D. L. (1998). Predicting life satisfaction among adolescents from immigrant families in Norway. *Ethnicity & Health, 3,* 5–18.

Saraiva, L. T., Sundquist, J., Johansson, L. M., Johansson, S. E., & Sundquist, K. (2005). Incidence of mental disorders in second-generation immigrants in Sweden: A four-year cohort study. *Ethnicity & Health, 10,* 243–256.

Virta, E., Sam, D. L., & Westin, C. (2004). Adolescents with Turkish background in Norway and Sweden: A comparative study of their psychological adaptation. *Scandinavian Journal of Psychology, 45,* 15–25.

Response 2

Juris G. Draguns

Adolescent immigrants often painfully experience the disjunction between the demands and opportunities of the culture in which they currently reside and the store of experience and knowledge bequeathed to them by their parental and ancestral culture. In the foregoing case, Esther, a daughter of Ethiopian immigrants to Israel, was caught in such a conflict. In this commentary, attempts are made to propose potential solutions to the dilemmas in which Esther finds herself and to facilitate her adaptation and self-realization.

To this end, four objectives are pursued in this response. First, Esther's implicit conception of Israeli culture is reconstructed, with a focus on Israeli schools. Second, teachers' and counselors' impressions of Esther are inferred from the available information in her case incident. Third, proceeding from these glimpses, measures are proposed to help overcome Esther's distress, restore her well-being, and enable her to resume the pursuit of her goals in the modern Israeli society, In the fourth and final section, an attempt is made to embed this formulation of Esther's problems and resources within a more inclusive conceptual framework for providing counseling services to culturally distinctive individuals sensitively and efficiently.

Israeli Culture Through Esther's Eyes

How does Israeli culture look from Esther's point of view? No relevant statements are found in the case incident, but a number of plausible inferences can be made. From Esther's perspective, Israeli society is characterized by highly attractive, yet remote, goals. To attain them, Esther must traverse a maze of tremendous complexity that can be roughly equated with the Israeli educational system. Blind alleys are numerous; they can be entered with ease, but exited with utmost difficulty. Consequently, the opportunity structure of the Israeli society may well appear to Esther as monolithic, extraneous, and impersonal. Moreover, faced with goals that are difficult to attain and obstacles that are formidable and numerous, Esther finds herself essentially on her own. Right moves are rewarded by their results, but otherwise barely attract notice. In contrast, any mistakes or stumbles are immediately noted by the teachers, counselors, and administrators. Thus, Esther was summoned to the counselor's office when she experienced setbacks, at which time the consequences of academic failure were spelled out to her. In the school system, Esther is faced with stark and absolute alternatives and with inflexible deadlines. The choice is between matriculating within the 4-month period or permanently lowering her educational aspirations.

Assuming that the above conception adequately captures Esther's subjective reality, can it be modified through new, more helpful, and empathic interactions within the Israeli school system? In Esther's current situation, is there room for compromises, delays, and detours? Specifically, can the matriculation examination be postponed in light of Esther's recent crisis? Given the seriousness of Esther's presenting problems, it is readily apparent that very little can be accomplished before the matriculation examination. Within the tight time frame, Esther's current ambitions may, as stated in the case incident, indeed have "very little chance of succeeding." Would this, however, still be the case if more flexibility was allowed? Several European Union countries provide an alternative pathway to higher education that would allow students to qualify over a period of time and in a piecemeal fashion. Is a comparable provision available in Israel?

If Esther is freed from categorical choices, the benefits may extend beyond reducing her current stress and relieving pressure. In the optimal case, her perceptions may change and she may come to see Israeli institutions in a different and more favorable light, as more open and sensitive and less rigid, which may help Esther progress toward optimism and hopefulness, even if slightly.

Esther Through the Eyes of Her Counselors and Teachers

On the basis of the case incident, two impressions dominate how Esther is perceived by her teachers, counselors, and helpers. First and foremost, her recent suicide attempt and psychiatric hospitalization highlight her fragility and vulnerability as a person who has a limited capacity for dealing with stress. Second, Esther's descent from an economically precarious and socially marginal immigrant community accentuates expectation of educational problems and difficulties and the improbability of academic success.

Certainly, there is no denying the seriousness of Esther's recent difficulties, and her treatment needs continue to be urgent and pressing. Similarly, the issues faced by Esther's family and the Ethiopian community are forbidding in their complexity; they are eloquently described and amply documented in the case incident. Nonetheless, it may be useful to reverse figure and ground and look at Esther's life story for assets and achievements that may balance and indeed offset the recent disappointments she has faced and the resulting crises she has experienced.

It should not be overlooked that for the first 15 years of her life, Esther was described by the author of the case incident as "a successful example of immigrant absorption." Her grades were above average, she was perceived as attractive and popular, and her educational and occupational goals were specific and ambitious, well above those of many of her Ethiopian immigrant peers. Despite crowding, poverty, and lack of effective support from her stressed and demoralized parents, she persevered in scaling scholastic hurdles. Moreover, she effectively acted as a mediator between her family and the Israeli community at large, demonstrating that she was able to function in the traditional miniculture of her family and the modern Israeli milieu. In addition to going to school, Esther worked virtually full-time, even though this load eventually proved to be too heavy for her to bear. Her examining psychiatrist saw no justification for diagnosing major depressive disorder nor for imputing chronic suicidality and emphasized the role of major and cumulative stress in precipitating her depressive reaction. All told, Esther's biography provides a record of considerable cognitive, personal, and social resources, all of which can be mobilized for her rehabilitation. Instead of looking at her as a seriously impaired individual, Esther may more realistically be viewed as an adolescent who has coped effectively with a great many challenges before succumbing to an unusual combination of stresses coupled with a paucity of social support. On the basis of this realization, I propose a number of interventions.

From Reconceptualization to Remediation: Interventions at Four Levels

Working at the Individual Level

In the aftermath of Esther's suicide attempt, the paramount objective is to reduce her distress as expeditiously as possible. Although Esther appears to be uncommunicative, this does not constitute an insurmountable obstacle to prompt and efficient intervention. Emphasis should be placed on behavioral and simple cognitive interventions, specifically relaxation training to counteract anxiety in the form of tension and agitation. Esther's depressive cognitions and affect can be remedied by rudimentary cognitive techniques, such as antidepressive self-statements and simple cognitive restructuring of concrete events that evoke a disproportionately helpless or even catastrophic reaction. I had the opportunity to witness a rapid therapeutic reaction to such techniques in a somewhat similar situation (Draguns, 2008). The client was an elderly Ukrainian immigrant to the United States who responded to muscular relaxation and cognitive self-reassurance virtually from the moment they were introduced. His seriously debilitating symptoms disappeared over the course of 10 sessions. If these techniques prove helpful in Esther's case, their impact may extend well beyond symptomatic relief. Experience of therapeutic benefit may rekindle hope, enhance Esther's self-efficacy, and promote the development of a therapeutic relationship with the counselor.

In the optimal scenario, the second step would be to create the conditions for a counseling dialogue for which Esther appeared to be unprepared both before and after her hospitalization. However, the experience of perceptible reduction of distress is likely to promote trust, increase spontaneity, and spark self-disclosure. Once this is accomplished, counseling should proceed along expected lines, with the constant recognition, however, that the very concept of counseling is embedded in the mainstream Israeli culture and may be novel and alien to a newcomer socialized in the traditional and isolated community of Ethiopian Jews. With this realization, counseling Esther shades off into her immediate cultural milieu, that of her family.

Helping Esther Through Helping Her Family

Esther's case incident conveys a vivid picture of a family under stress. Rescued from civil war, destitution, and famine and transplanted to Israel, Esther's parents and grandparents never succeeded in reestablishing their status or reaffirming their identity. The network of community ties was disrupted, and the family's financial status remained precarious. More important, parental authority was impaired and social modeling disrupted. Esther's dreams and goals remained alien to her parents and her problems and crisis baffling. All of these circumstances would inevitably augment her family's disorientation and helplessness. Moreover, it would reduce her parents' ability to contribute support, understanding, and guidance to a minimum.

For these reasons, it is imperative to support and strengthen Esther's family, both for its own sake and to restore its role as a source of stability and acceptance at this difficult juncture in Esther's life. How can this objective be accomplished? Restoring the family's dignity and status and conveying respect for its traditional authority would be the overriding goals.

Limitations of professional and cultural experience make it unrealistic for me to translate these general recommendations into concrete measures. Fortunately, there is extensive cultural documentation on Ethiopian Jews both before and after their return to Israel. This source of information should be tapped to work out ways of establishing and developing contact with Esther's family and eventually using the family's resources for Esther's benefit. Certainly, any pressure for self-disclosure should be avoided. What would be a routine recommendation with a typical Israeli family—to institute family counseling at the first opportunity—remains in this case an important, but remote and problematic, goal. Whether or not it is ever realized, involving Esther's family in the treatment plan is an essential objective, to be realized with cultural sophistication and sensitivity.

Beyond the Family: Community Considerations

The tight fabric of Ethiopian Jewish communities did not survive their transplantation to Israel. For Esther's benefit, it would be highly desirable to restore her ties to her ethnic heritage to the maximum extent possible. In Esther's case incident, the cultural isolation of Ethiopian students in residential and day schools was decried. Modest measures to counteract this isolation may be achieved through participation in social and recreational groups, devoted, in part, to the cultivation of folklore and tradition and also including discussion of challenges and experiences in integrating into the Israeli community. In particular, negotiating the pathway toward the attainment of goals in the mainstream society while preserving and taking pride in their unique cultural heritage may help young Israelis of Ethiopian descent build a more integrative identity as an alternative to assimilation and an antidote to marginalization, within Berry's (1990) framework of accommodation. Instead of mutually exclusive orientations either to the modern Israeli society or the traditional Ethiopian diaspora, Esther and her peers would be encouraged to incorporate and fuse elements derived from both of these backgrounds. In this manner, personal conflict between these two options would be forestalled and experience of stress averted.

Strengthening Counseling Resources

It is to the credit of Esther's counselor that she explicitly sought guidance in dealing with this clinically challenging and culturally distinctive case. The foregoing sections have attempted to answer her questions. Yet an aura of vagueness limits the applicability of these recommendations. On the personal and emotional level, needs for affective support should be recognized and gratified, together with those for specific and technical, practically useful, information. Knowledgeable and experienced counselors should provide both. An additional, little used, resource can be suggested. In the multiethnic environment of Miami, Florida, Weidman (1975) pioneered working with culture brokers, knowledgeable and perceptive members of the client's culture. Culture brokers bridge the gap between modern counseling techniques; clients' culturally based expectations; and the indigenous beliefs, attitudes, and behaviors that are relevant for alleviation of distress and resolution of problems. What techniques and outlooks can be borrowed from the tradition and experience of Ethiopian Jews and blended with the best that contemporary counseling has to offer? If this question is answered, Esther will be guided toward hope, competence, and fulfillment.

Integrative Counseling: Helping Individuals in Cultural Contexts

Leong (1996) has proposed that individual, cultural, and universal elements should be fused in comprehensive counseling interventions. Thus, even in counseling a culturally different individual, the error should not be committed of intervening only on the cultural plane.

In Esther's case, the proposed behavioral and cognitive techniques are designed to reduce distress and promote coping anywhere. Similarly, activation of hope and counteracting despair are humanly universal objectives that are attained in culturally fitting and meaningful ways. On the cultural level, both obstacles and opportunities are taken into account to go beyond counseling in a uniform, universalistic way. With Esther, progress in working on both universal and cultural level may open opportunities for addressing Esther's private and unique experiences. In this manner, the panhuman, cultural, and personal threads will coalesce in enabling Esther to cope and to pursue her goals.

References

Berry, J. W. (1990). Psychology of acculturation. In J. J. Berman (Ed.), *Nebraska symposium on motivation: Cross-cultural perspectives* (pp. 201–234). Lincoln: University of Nebraska Press.

Draguns, J. G. (2008). Universal and cultural threads in counseling. In P. B. Pedersen, J. G. Draguns, W. J. Lonner, & J. E. Trimble (Eds.), *Counseling across cultures* (6th ed., pp. 21–36). Thousand Oaks, CA: Sage.

Leong, F. T. L. (1996). Toward an integrative model for cross-cultural counseling and psychotherapy. *Applied and Preventive Psychology, 5,* 189–209.

Weidman, H. (1975). Concepts as strategies of change. *Psychiatric Annals, 5,* 312–314.

Part 4
Military and Peacekeeping Transitions

The Complexity of Adapting Under Stress

Stefan Kammhuber and Georg F. Fuchs

After September 11, 2001, Afghanistan was again the focus of the world's public—this time as a gathering, retreat, and training area of Islamic terrorists. The Taliban regime was providing cover for the activities of the terrorist organization Al Qaida, which led to the United States forcing a regime change by military means. The so-called Petersberg Conference—which actually began before military operations were over—followed this military victory. At this conference, participants decided on a road map for the establishment of an elected government and the appointment of Hamid Karzai as interim president of Afghanistan.

The German Bundeswehr in Afghanistan

Since January 2002, the German armed forces have also been a part of the International Security Assistance Force, together with 35 other nations, and Germany's contribution of 2,500 men and women makes it the biggest contingent in the approximately 8,000-strong protection force. The United Nations has provided this mission with a "robust mandate," which means that the soldiers are allowed to use their weapons for protecting themselves as well as protecting anyone who does not participate in the hostilities. Provincial Reconstruction Teams will, in cooperation with civilian government and nongovernmental organizations and other departments, coordinate reconstruction efforts as well as support the national army and police and provide security to the population through the Protection Force.

Transformation of the German Bundeswehr

Germany has only been taking part in international operations since the mid-1990s because the political attitude since World War II was that no German soldier should ever again set foot on foreign soil. The Bundeswehr equipped and trained for territorial defense only, not for international operations. After the reunification of West Germany and East Germany, Germany's role in Europe and in the world has changed, and now Germany wants to play a stronger role internationally. "The freedom of Germany is also defended at Hindukush," a quotation from the former minister of defense Peter Struck is interpreted as a political–strategic decision that the Bundeswehr increasingly sees itself as an internationally deployable force.

Inside an International Military Mission

Alexander (a pseudonym) is a first lieutenant in this "new" Bundeswehr. He is 28 years old and has already taken part in foreign missions in Bosnia and Kosovo. He was married 2 years ago, and his firstborn child is now 6 months old. He has now been sent to Afghanistan for 4 months. He will be deployed in the borderland of Afghanistan and will, together with his team, gather information about the complicated, and for Germans often difficult to understand, Afghan tribal structure, among other things. There is always strain involved in such missions. Alexander found it hard to leave his wife and child, and he thinks about them very often. However, the everyday routine and, above all, the constant feeling of being under threat are so demanding that they prevent him from musing too much. The only bad times are when he has nothing to do. Then he writes a letter, something he earlier seldom did, but he has become accustomed to doing so during international service. The necessary calm for writing is hard to find because there is very little privacy during such service. Several people share one tent, and therefore there are almost always other people around.

Afghanistan in Alexander's Eyes

Alexander has bad as well as good impressions of Afghanistan. He is fascinated by the beautiful landscape and the friendliness that the Afghans show, especially to the Germans whom they see as unselfish helpers and honest brokers in the reconstruction effort. This feeling is somewhat in contrast to the way Afghans feel about the armies of other countries, with their history of colonialism in Afghanistan or other countries. At the same time, however, he is intimidated by a society that for generations has known nothing but war. For these people, death is as much of an everyday affair as the peaceful coexistence with fellow citizens in Germany is for Alexander, and life is as quickly taken here as people go to a court of law at home. He is, of course, aware of the sinister actions carried out by the warlords, who are still important actors with enormous influence. He is also aware of the problematical drug trade, which largely finances the warlords and against whom the Bundeswehr are not allowed to take action. He is for the first time in a society that is thoroughly influenced by religion. Because he was raised in the former German Democratic Republic, he has had very little to do with religion, and, thus, he has difficulty understanding why people follow religious guidelines in their everyday life to such a degree. In general, it is difficult for him, after 2 months of service, to understand the people's ways. Sometimes his impression is that he will never succeed in seeing behind outer appearances and understand the Afghans' way of acting and thinking. Often, conflicting tribes invite the German soldiers to be "neutral observers" or "independent mediators" at so-called *jirgas*. For the Bundeswehr, this is a chance to learn more about tribal structure and the connection and interaction between these vast networks. With this knowledge, the military missions can often be carried out in a more goal-oriented way. Attendance at the jirgas is one small component that contributes to the general understanding of the situation in the operational area.

The Water Problem: Alexander as a Neutral Observer

Alexander and his team of 16 soldiers, therefore, have the task of being neutral observers at a gathering of two tribes at the invitation of the local people. The agenda is the regulation of the use of a river's water, an issue about which there obviously has been conflict for a long time. For the Bundeswehr, the issue is crucial because it is interested in a lasting solution to this problem. A solution would remove the main reason for the hostilities between the tribes and, hopefully, stabilize the situation. The issue of the river's water involves the interests of a large number of tribes so that a quick and geographically limited solution probably would not be very durable.

Alexander and his Afghan interpreter, who is also a stranger to this remote part of the country, are warmly welcomed. In the tent, 40 to 50 men, all of them heavily armed, from different tribes are gathered. Alexander's team secures the surrounding area around the tent. The gathering begins in a very friendly manner by drinking tea, and the conversation is made up of general chitchat for at least half an hour. In the meantime, Alexander is puzzled. He had expected there to be a tense atmosphere between the different groups. Because the jirgas has begun in so harmonious and friendly way, he cannot now even distinguish between the different parties.

Observer, Facilitator, Referee, or Judge?

Suddenly members of one group or the other, almost as if they would assault him, begin pulling Alexander aside and continuously asking him how he sees the situation regarding the access to water. In this way, through one-sided argumentation and flattering but also by hidden threats, they try to make their position clear and convince him of the justness of their argument. He should, in their opinion, be on their side and should say this openly, but they have also now put him under pressure publicly and demand a decision in favor of one or the other party. In return, they say that they will provide him with information that will be of the greatest importance to the Bundeswehr (e.g., about relevant personnel, stockpiles of weapons). They, however, remain imprecise, and when he tries to go into detail or to ask further or find out more, they change the subject or say there will be later talks. It becomes more and more difficult for Alexander to remain neutral—not to give any quick concessions and not to yield to the pressure. The arguments of all sides seem to him to be logical and acceptable. In addition, he can only follow the content of the discussion with difficulty. Members of the tribes quarrel in detail about conflicts that originated far back in time and about which Alexander cannot really make any judgment and that also partly seem to be completely irrelevant in the context of solving the current problem. This very confusing discussion makes Alexander increasingly insecure about how to behave. Whom should he support? Perhaps, he should assure them that the Bundeswehr will take responsibility for all necessary measures and will build everything? Just do not make any mistakes! Who knows how they will react? They are all armed. In the end, Alexander uses his radio to discuss the situation with his experienced superior.

Reader Reflection Questions

1. Which stressors have an impact on Alexander's well-being regarding this mission?
2. Which of Alexander's individual prerequisites have an influence on his experiences in this particular mission in Afghanistan? Also, think about psychological resources Alexander can activate to cope with the situation.
3. Which culture-specific rules, norms, and values of both Afghan and German culture have an impact on the course of the critical incident?
4. How should Alexander act in this particular situation? Try to find several alternatives of action. Reflect on the positive and negative consequences of these alternatives on accomplishing the task, on Alexander's psychological well-being, and on maintaining the relationship to the Afghan people.
5. How would you describe the role of intercultural learning and intercultural competence in international military missions in general?

Response 1

Patrice Keats

Because physicians first recognized the devastating impact of stressful combat experiences, ideas about how the *masculine male* should manage these experiences became embedded in military culture. Hysteria, weakness, and vulnerability were juxtaposed with heroism, strength, and endurance. In early treatments, a man's moral character was attacked, because professional helpers considered those who suffered the stresses of war as malingerers, cowards, and "moral invalids" (Herman, 1992, p. 21). Although treatments now focus on understanding and compassion rather than on shaming and punishment, the stigma of psychological stress still exists in the military culture. In attempts to change this attitude, some armed forces have adopted the idea of the operational stress injury (e.g., anxiety, depression, posttraumatic stress) in order to put psychological struggles on par with physiological ones. Operational stress is also evident in noncombat missions (e.g., peacekeeping) due to exposure to casualties, threats, and restrictive rules of engagement (see Veterans Affairs Canada, 2006). Consequently, because of the combination of upholding a strong masculine identity, struggling with operational stress, and managing an international transition to a new culture, men face a complex process of adaptation.

Using the framework of military culture, I address issues related to masculinity, trauma, and cross-cultural transition by using the case incident of Alexander as an illustration that shows the complexity of adaptive transitions. In light of this understanding, I recommend focus points for counselors working with military personnel deployed to overseas missions.

Military Culture and the Bundeswehr

Military Culture

It is unusual to consider cultural adaptation when looking at the transition from civilian to military life. The military, however, is a structured organization in which members share basic assumptions, beliefs, and characteristic behaviors in pursuit of victory in combat. This being so, a military organization can be defined as a culture in and of itself. Krueger (2000) emphasized how military members and their families "participate in fostering a common 'military mind-set'" (p. 252). This affective social force controls patterns of organizational behavior by shaping members' cognitions and perceptions of meanings, realities, and senses of belonging (Winslow, 1998). Military organizations include a myriad of culturally symbolic identifications that create common bonds among members. For example, members generally live and work in the same vicinity (e.g., barracks, units), participate in ritualized customs (e.g., weddings, funerals), wear distinguishing emblems (e.g., badges, tattoos), and adhere to detailed dress codes (e.g., button designs, kit colors), all of which emphasize hierarchy and collective tradition. Through generations, this distinctiveness is shared with pride, thus creating group cohesion, shared lifestyle expectations, and identification for its members.

Especially important to military members is a high degree of group alliance (Brooks, 1999; Krueger, 2000). Strong interpersonal relationships are seen as essential to a member's initiation into the esprit de corps; training rewards group cooperation and performance, because they are essential to combat effectiveness. In the Canadian military, the greatest losses are seen in terms of the group, because the group provides safety, security, belonging, and status: "[H]e fights for something more than himself; he fights for his comrades" (Department of National Defence, as cited in Winslow, 1998, p. 358). Soldiers are highly dependent on each other. Because they are not able to leave the group, it is essential that soldiers fit in by following both explicit and implicit rules that define belonging. This process sets up unique dynamics for members as they vie for their place in the hierarchy.

Bundeswehr

Alexander is a military member (first lieutenant) of the German Bundeswehr. Three important aspects of this force need to be considered in light of Alexander's experience. First, due to the consequences of the Second World War, German citizens have an antimilitary sentiment; thus, members of the Bundeswehr are supposed to have different values than did soldiers in past German military movements. Inner leadership is emphasized so members can balance "claims of subordination against demands of conscience" (Thompson & Peltier, 1990, p. 587). Specifically, the Bundeswehr soldier is encouraged to act as an autonomous moral citizen who can decide if the actions required by a superior officer match with the values of German citizenship. The freedom to exercise these moral rights is valued over blind obedience and is believed to increase the morale of soldiers in light of current attitudes about the military forces.

Despite this attitude, military careers such as Alexander's are not as honored or respected by the general public as are other careers. This lack of recognition and societal support creates difficulties for soldiers assimilating to civilian life after service (deVries, 1996; Scaer, 2001). Second, it is only within the last 10 years that the Bundeswehr has begun to participate in humanitarian relief and peacekeeping missions outside of Germany (Kummel & Leonhard, 2005; Young, 1996). Although Alexander had previous experience with foreign missions in Bosnia and Kosovo, it is not clear whether he was exposed to any cross-cultural training before his deployment to Afghanistan. Third, it is only since 2001 that women have been able to enter all areas of German military service (Kummel, 2002). Furthermore, army recruits are predominantly Caucasian, so the Bundeswehr is currently not well prepared to deal with ethnic, cultural, gender, and religious diversity (Winslow, Kammhuber, & Soeters, 2004). This being the case, Alexander probably has little experience with, or exposure to, different cultural groups within his military peer group environment and outside of cultural experiences during deployment. Specifically, being a member of an individualist culture, Alexander is faced with an ethnically diverse and collectively conscious Afghanistan. He finds himself intimidated by a society that has a history of war, loss, and corruption. Furthermore, rules of engagement restrict his actions against the harm he witnesses toward the citizens in this regard. In addition, he struggles with understanding how the Islamic religion has so thoroughly influenced politics and everyday activities. His actions during the case incident (e.g., surprise at the preamble to the council meeting, requests for loyalty) indicate that he had little knowledge of the difference in communication and negotiating styles between German and Afghanistan cultures.

Masculinity in Military Contexts

Because participation in warfare has been traditionally viewed as a masculine role, it is essential to consider the construct of the *combat masculine warrior* (Dunivin, 1994; Krueger, 2000). According to Krueger, military organizations have a deeply entrenched "cult of masculinity" (p. 253), which includes masculine norms, values, and lifestyles. Dunivin saw military culture creating a "masculine male" through initiation traditions and other socialization activities that reward competitive, aggressive, and virile men. Also, the cult of masculinity is challenged by current models of inclusion, due to its essential exclusion of females and homosexuals (Kummel & Leonhard, 2005). Rosen, Knudson, and Fancher (2003) pointed to the idea of hypermasculinity as a characteristic that men develop due to the strong bonding between comrades in male-only peer groups. Hypermasculinity, such as "expressions of extreme, exaggerated, or stereotypic masculine attributes and behaviors"

(Rosen et al., 2003, p. 326), limits men's ability to develop and maintain a more adaptive emotional and behavioral repertoire in the face of transitions back to civilian life and into new cultures.

As a man, Alexander is required to understand the social protocol of masculinity in Afghanistan. Standing on the borderline between two cultures (German and Afghan), he needs to be identified as competent and empowered in the eyes of all the men present (Lomsky-Feder & Rapoport, 2003). Indeed, finding himself in the position of an anxious outsider during the case incident, he is caught in an ambiguous situation with no frame of reference. There is a certain threat, not only corporally but also to his identity as a man and his status as a German officer.

Stress and Adaptation

With a similar affect to hypermasculinity, operational stress injuries affect soldiers' abilities to develop adaptive emotional resilience and behavioral flexibility. To manage cultural difference, an individual needs to be open, flexible, resilient, and creative; operational stress often leaves a member experiencing a more closed, rigid, intolerant, and habitual way of being. Influencing a soldier's adaptability, operational stress impedes successful intercultural communication (Novinger, 2001). Although there is no mention of Alexander's status in terms of operational stress, he does experience a potentially dangerous and threatening situation in the critical incident and is stationed in a culture where there is constant threat of violence, including suicide bombings and other unpredictable attacks from militia forces. To understand possible reactions to the situation, I outline different types of stress that affect military members during and after deployment as well as behaviors exhibited by people from traumatized cultures (e.g., military, Afghanistan).

Operational Stress

Operational stress injury is a term used by the Canadian military to define any persistent psychological difficulty resulting from operational duties during a mission. The term describes a broad range of problems, including diagnosed psychiatric conditions such as anxiety and panic disorders, major depression, acute and posttraumatic stress, as well as problems that are less severe but that interfere with daily functioning, such as lack of concentration, anger, and emotional exhaustion. Below, I describe two types of stress within the operational stress umbrella.

Acute and posttraumatic stress. Traumatic stress occurs when people respond with intense fear, helplessness, or horror to an event where they experience or witness an actual or threatened death, serious injury, or damage to the physical integrity of themselves or others (American Psychiatric Association, 2000). If a person experiences this kind of event, as Alexander did, there are two possible consequences: (a) acute stress, which happens during the event or arises within the 4-week period after the event in which a person experiences dissociative symptoms (e.g., dazed or numbed feelings), persistently reexperiences the event (e.g., recurrent thoughts, dreams), attempts to persistently avoid any reminders of the event, and experiences increased arousal (e.g., poor concentration, restlessness) and (b) posttraumatic stress occurring 4 or more weeks after the event with similar, yet persistent, responses that interfere with normal functioning. Smith (2002), in her study on Vietnam veterans, proposed that posttraumatic stress disorder is intertwined with conceptions of masculinity, because issues related to employment, deteriorating health, or lack of social support left veterans experiencing a crisis of masculinity as they struggled to transition into civilian life.

Combat stress reaction. Combat stress reactions occur during a single combat situation, a series of events, or prolonged continuously stressful situations (Doran, Gaskin, Schumm,

& Smith, 2004). Signs of combat stress include physical reactions such as sleeplessness or trembling; emotional reactions including extreme nervousness, anger outbursts, or despair; behavioral reactions during work duties such as an inability to do a job (e.g., due to careless-ness, inability to make decisions, alcohol or drug abuse); and cognitive problems such as nightmares, memory loss, flashbacks, or a loss of a sense of what is real. Military personnel may also find that they experience bouts of depression and notice such changes as weight loss, sleep problems, lack of energy, feelings of hopelessness, and uncontrollable crying. These are all aspects that would be important for Alexander and his comrades to monitor for themselves and with each other.

There are a number of studies that address the contextual aspects of combat stress responses. Breslau (2004) pointed out that posttraumatic stress is one of the few psychiat-ric disorders that have contextual or social, rather than biological, causes. In this regard, Solomon (1993) showed that behavioral criteria for combat stress responses were subject to the level of stress that either the individual or the unit could tolerate as acceptable. The level was determined by the amount of suffering an individual could endure, the ability of the unit to serve as a holding environment, and unit morale (see also Kirmayer, 2005, for a discussion about cultural responses to trauma). This subjective measure of tolerance for stress resulted in soldiers not getting immediate care (high tolerance for stress) or normal reactions to stress labeled as pathological (low tolerance for stress).

Traumatized Cultures

McFarlane and van der Kolk (1996) stated that there appears to be a "universal tendency for people under threat to form very close attachments to other people" (p. 25). They believed that the greater the threat and horror, the stronger the alliance. This alliance is evident in both the military and Afghan cultures as they came together during the critical incident. Furthermore, when cultural societies become too focused on past trauma, people lose their flexibility to respond to the future and remain focused on revenge or compensation for past wrongs at the expense of endurance, resilience, and individual initiative. By directing their view to past trauma experiences, people become unable to identify other factors that may be responsible for the challenges they face, and they fail to use more effective strategies to address individual and collective adaptations to the problem. Difficulties are, in part, cre-ated by an inability to communicate the intensity of their emotions and perceptions with words. During the case incident, tensions rose dramatically when the Afghan groups began to speak about past wrongs suffered under the hands of the opposing tribe; this resulted in continued threat of violence and lack of productivity in the negotiation.

Cross-Cultural Transition and Communication

A transition is a period or process of moving from one state to another and is generally a time of uncertainty and disorganization. Berry and Ward (2006) saw cross-cultural transi-tions as requiring people to access adjustive resources in order to deal with the chaos of stress-provoking life changes. In a successful adaptation (i.e., coming to feel psychological well-being or satisfaction), stress management is an important element of the acculturation process. Transition is either facilitated or impeded by the characteristics of an individual or situation, such as how people view change, use coping strategies, access available social support, or understand their own cultural identity and social status. Indeed, soldiers who are already coping with high stress related to a mission or competitive interpersonal group dynamics will find added stress while transitioning to a new cultural milieu.

Porges (2004) studied how people responded neurologically to situations that they either perceived as safe (prosocial) or dangerous (defensive). He believed that this perception was triggered in neurophysiological, rather than cognitive, sequences to facilitate appropriate behavioral reactions (e.g., defensive—increased heart rate, sweating, mobilization or immobilization; prosocial—eye gaze, listening, facial expression, vocalization). To create relationships, people subdue or inhibit defensive reactions such as fighting or fleeing in order to engage, attach, and form social bonds. If people are persistently stressed or traumatized, they will often have an inability to inhibit defense mechanisms in a safe environment or an inability to activate defense mechanisms in a risky environment, or both. It appears that a persistent stress response influences an individual's ability to assess safe or dangerous situations accurately. Therefore, when faced with the unfamiliar, an overstressed person often responds defensively. This has significant implications in cross-cultural transitioning processes for military personnel who deal with dangerous situations or develop operational stress injuries.

Anxiety/Uncertainty Management Theory

Because of the understanding of how stress may affect transitioning processes discussed above, I align with Gudykunst's (1998, 2005) anxiety/uncertainty management theory as it applies to cross-cultural adjustment. Primarily, Gudykunst saw communicative interactions with strangers being influenced by anxiety, uncertainty, and mindfulness. First, uncertainty occurs when a person is unable to predict another's behavior using her or his current frame of reference (i.e., cultural, sociological, and psychological) and identity perspective (i.e., human-self in common with others, social-self as member of a group, personal-self as unique). In attempting to predict behaviors of people in a group, a person accesses knowledge about intergroup behavior; one-on-one, a person accesses knowledge about interpersonal behaviors. Second, Gudykunst (2005) defined anxiety as "the affective (emotional) equivalent of uncertainty" (p. 287). He believed that people always experience some degree of anxiety when they communicate. The level of anxiety a person experiences in an interaction determines the effectiveness of a message being received as intended (e.g., high anxiety, low effectiveness). Finally, Gudykunst advocated the use of mindfulness so that information processing can involve a combination of attention, awareness, intention, and control. Conscious awareness of communicative behavior allows such things as more alertness and openness to new information, broader categories to predict behavior, and a focus on process versus outcome. Gudykunst hypothesized that management of uncertainty and anxiety responses would facilitate both effective communication and intercultural adjustment. In an environment with a high degree of unfamiliarity, uncertainty produces high anxiety and stress on the part of communicators. Alexander found himself in this exact situation, and, indeed, communications did fail. Added to this stress was Alexander's dependence on an interpreter. It is important to note that the interpreter was a key player in Alexander's communication process. As an intermediary for Alexander, his position or status in the Afghan groups dictated the limits of his interactions (e.g., implicit or explicit rules about what can be said or asked). The interpreter's religious affiliations, lack of familiarity with intergroup behaviors (e.g., persuading, isolating, threatening), and struggle to interpret what people said as tensions rose undoubtedly increased both his and Alexander's anxiety and uncertainty and, in turn, the effectiveness of communication.

Suggestions for Counseling Interventions

Alexander experienced stress before, during, and after the critical incident. Before engaging in the incident, Alexander reported feeling lonely, homesick, and hemmed in (i.e., lack of person space). In cultural terms, beneath his impressions of the beautiful Afghanistan landscape and expressed friendliness of locals, he constantly felt threatened and confused by the religious influences and intimidated by cultural violence and death. In quiet times, he had persistently avoided thoughts about his situation. Although Alexander has been in Afghanistan for 2 months, he has remained unsettled and on guard. As he entered into the critical event as a neutral observer, he attempted to create safety because the heavily armed tribes outnumbered his troops more than two to one. Unsure of who was present (e.g., local militias are often indistinguishable from and intermixed with noncombatants; see Levinger, 2005), he was immediately confused by the Afghan style of conducting a *jirgas* (i.e., tribal council). His cultural naivety left him struggling to read and predict the behaviors of the men around him, which caused uncertainty and anxiety. Undoubtedly, during and after the incident, Alexander may have experienced stress-related responses such as trembling or emotional exhaustion. Thus, I suggest below some possible avenues of counseling intervention on personal and group levels.

Multicultural Counseling Interventions

It appears that Alexander did not have clear understanding of Afghan culture, especially in light of his mission. There was a discrepancy between him and his environment that caused stress and taxed his resources. He lacked understanding and openness to differences in communication (e.g., Afghan men beginning council with palaver in order to build relationships rather than entering immediately into direct communication) and negotiation styles (e.g., vying for loyalty, promises of information). By maintaining his own habits of communication, he was unaware of cultural expectations during the council (Zimmerman, Holman, & Sparrow, 2003). To assist Alexander before the operation with cultural transitioning, I would suggest that Alexander explore his own cultural values, beliefs, and worldviews. Consequently, he could be aware of his own perspectives and able to see the differences between his interactions and those of the Afghan tribes. Knowing that culture is not a set of unalterable categories but rather a dynamic complexity that is continuously changing and evolving may help Alexander step aside from any tendency to generalize isolated behavior of some individuals to all Afghan people. Exploring how he can shift from being the center (e.g., comparing all he sees through the filter of his own culture) and holding his concepts about Afghan people more tentatively, he may be able to create different meanings, perceive differently, and accept different perspectives as he becomes more fully informed about the cultural networks that he is charged with understanding. It may also help him to learn how to work with an interpreter, especially understanding how the interpreter is culturally situated and the influence of this cultural situation in the process of translation. In addition, Alexander may be able to tap into his cultural intelligence (Brislin, Worthley, & MacNab, 2006), using his higher level skills and abilities to gain more understanding and accept a not-knowing, versus should-know, stance while he evaluates the situation and moves toward unity and understanding.

Furthering intercultural adjustment, Alexander, along with the military group, could participate in Gudykunst's (1998) psychoeducational training model, which focuses on the concepts of uncertainty, anxiety, and mindfulness. Gudykunst's recommendations include sessions in which participants explore cultural difference through culturally based exercises, understand how anxiety and uncertainty influence adaptation to new cultures, learn and practice methods to successfully manage anxiety in new cultural environments (these sessions would have a dual purpose of exposing Alexander and his comrades to a variety of techniques to reduce anxiety and to practice those that work best), and learn and practice methods to successfully manage uncertainty so that participants can better predict both group and individual behaviors in a new culture. Specific to Alexander's situation, assistance in understanding individualist and collectivist behaviors in conflict resolution would also be helpful to increase effectiveness in dealing with conflicts between groups as well as in adjusting to cultural differences (Ting-Toomey, 1994).

Personal Intervention for Alexander

To defuse persistent stress and learn how to better manage it in the future, Alexander may need time after the event to express his thoughts and feelings, as well as to debrief his actions with his peers. Furthermore, he needs to monitor any operational stress responses that create dysfunction or overwhelm his ability to carry out future duties. Alexander finds comfort in writing letters to his wife and anticipates returning home to see his child, indicating that Alexander has strong support at home. However, transitioning from the stresses of the mission to everyday civilian life may create depression, lack of energy, or disorientation. Educating Alexander about the possibility of these responses and actions that he can take (e.g., personal coping strategies, accessing peer support, professional assistance) will ensure that his return remains a happy one.

Issues and Interventions for Military Personnel

In every military operation, personnel are subject to highly stressful and dangerous situations in which injury and death are possible. Mental health assistance is necessary for debilitating stress responses during and after operations. Interventions during an operation may include the opportunity to debrief traumatic experiences (e.g., critical incident stress management; see Mitchell, 2004); to recognize and act on operational stress reactions that become overwhelming, with self-help strategies, peers, or professional helper(s) if available on site (e.g., Combat Stress Control Unit; see Bacon & Staudenmeier, 2003; Reyes & Hicklin, 2005); and to talk about other general concerns that cause stress (e.g., worries related to family members at home) with a psychologist or counselor if available. When military personnel return home after an operation, there is often difficulty with readjustment and operational stress injuries. In recognition of this struggle, the United States army, for example, requires soldiers to remain at an intermediary base for a number of days before going home. This allows soldiers an opportunity to rest, debrief, and obtain information about available support in their communities. In addition, military members may have a peer support system that uses nonprofessional peer helpers (e.g., Operational Stress Injury Social Support in Canada). These types of peer support groups offer the opportunity for members to stay connected, because leaving the intensity of their alliance can cause depression, loneliness, and isolation at home. Finally, effective group-based therapy, such as therapeutic enactment, has significant benefits for military members (see Keats, 2003; Shaw & Westwood, 2002; Westwood, Black, & McLean, 2002).

Conclusion

For therapists without military service experience, I recommend two actions. First is taking the time to learn as much as possible about the operations with which the clients were involved. Secondary wounding can take place from a therapist's lack of knowledge, recognition, and respect for the risks of military service. As noted previously, Alexander may be subject to this type of wounding upon his return home. Second, taking the position of an outsider seeking to understand a soldier's experience is more helpful than a stance that sends a message of expertise about the military context without an insider perspective. As with all counseling, therapists are essentially limited by their own cultural constraints and need to be mindful communicators.

References

American Psychiatric Association. (2000). *Diagnostic and statistical manual of mental disorders* (4th ed., text rev.). Washington, DC: Author.

Bacon, B. L., & Staudenmeier, J. J. (2003). A historical overview of combat stress control units of the U.S. army. *Military Medicine, 168*, 689–693.

Berry, J. W., & Ward, C. (2006). Commentary on "Redefining interactions across cultures and organizations." *Group & Organization Management, 31*, 64–77.

Breslau, J. (2004). Cultures of trauma: Anthropological views of posttraumatic stress disorder in international health. *Culture, Medicine, and Psychiatry, 28*, 113–126.

Brislin, R., Worthley, R., & MacNab, B. (2006). Cultural intelligence: Understanding behaviors that serve people's goals. *Group & Organization Management, 31*, 40–55.

Brooks, G. (1999). A few good men: Military socialization and gender role strain. *Society for the Psychological Study of Men and Masculinity Bulletin, 4*(2), 9–11.

deVries, M. (1996). Trauma in cultural perspective. In B. van der Kolk, A. McFarlane, & L. Weisaeth (Eds.), *Traumatic stress: The effects of overwhelming experience on mind, body, and society* (pp. 398–413). New York: Guilford.

Doran, A., Gaskin, T., Schumm, W., & Smith, J. E. (2004). *Dealing with combat and operational stress.* Retrieved July 2, 2006, from http://www.osi.andrews.af.mil/library/deployment-stress/thedeployedspouse/dealingwithcombatandoperationalstress/index.asp

Dunivin, K. O. (1994). Military culture: Change and continuity. *Armed Forces & Society, 20*, 531–547.

Gonzalez, R., Biever, J. L., & Gardner, G. T. (1994). The multicultural perspective in therapy: A social constructionist approach. *Psychotherapy, 31*, 515–524.

Gudykunst, W. B. (1998). Applying anxiety/uncertainty management (AUM) theory to intercultural adjustment training. *International Journal of Intercultural Relations, 22*, 227–250.

Gudykunst, W. B. (2005). An anxiety/uncertainty management (AUM) theory of effective communication: Making the mesh of the net finer. In W. B. Gudykunst (Ed.), *Theorizing about intercultural communication* (pp. 281–322). Thousand Oaks, CA: Sage.

Herman, J. L. (1992). *Trauma and recovery: The aftermath of violence—From domestic abuse to political terror.* New York: Basic Books.

Keats, P. A. (2003). Soldiers healing soldiers: An overview of the group-based Transition Program for Canadian Peacekeepers. *Disaster and Trauma Times of Canada, 1*(1), 2–4.

Kirmayer L. J. (2005). Culture, context and experience in psychiatric diagnosis. *Psychopathology, 38*, 192–196.

Krueger, G. P. (2000). Military culture. In A. E. Kazdin (Ed.), *Encyclopedia of psychology* (Vol. 5, pp. 251–259), Washington, DC: American Psychological Association.

Kummel, G. (2002). Complete access: Women in the Bundeswehr and male ambivalence. *Armed Forces & Society, 28*, 555–573.

Kummel, G., & Leonhard, N. (2005). Casualties and civil-military relations: The German policy between learning and indifference. *Armed Forces & Society, 31*, 513–536.

Levinger, G. (2005). Five obstacles facing military ethics. *Peace and Conflict: Journal of Peace Psychology, 11*, 41–46.

Lomsky-Feder, E., & Rapoport, T. (2003). Juggling models of masculinity: Russian-Jewish immigrants in the Israeli army. *Sociological Inquiry, 73*, 114–137.

McFarlane, A., & van der Kolk, B. (1996). Trauma and its challenge to society. In B. van der Kolk, A. McFarlane, & L. Weisaeth (Eds.), *Traumatic stress: The effects of overwhelming experience on mind, body, and society* (pp. 24–46). New York: Guilford.

Mitchell, J. T. (2004). Characteristics of successful early intervention programs. *International Journal of Emergency Mental Health, 6*(4), 175–184.

Novinger, T. (2001). *Intercultural communication: A practical guide.* Austin: University of Texas Press.

Porges, S. W. (2004). Neuroception: A subconscious system for detecting threats and safety. *Zero to Three, 24*(5), 19–24.

Reyes, V. A., & Hicklin, T. A. (2005). Anger in the combat zone. *Military Medicine, 170*, 483–487.

Rosen, L. N., Knudson, K. H., & Fancher, P. (2003). Cohesion and the culture of hypermasculinity in U.S. army units. *Armed Forces & Society, 29,* 325–352.

Scaer, R. (2001). *The body bears the burden: Trauma, dissociation, and disease.* New York: Hawthorn Medical.

Shaw, M., & Westwood, M. (2002). Transformation in life stories: The Canadian War Veterans Life Review Project. In J. Webster & B. Haight (Eds.), *Critical advances in reminiscence work: From theory to application* (pp. 257–274). New York: Springer.

Smith, M. M. (2002). For God, country, and manhood: The social construction of post-traumatic stress disorder among Vietnam veterans. *Dissertation Abstracts International, 62*(11), 3954A.

Solomon, Z. (1993). *Combat stress reaction: The enduring toll of war.* New York: Plenum.

Thompson, W. C., & Peltier, M. D. (1990). The education of military officers in the Federal Republic of Germany. *Armed Forces & Society, 16,* 587–606.

Ting-Toomey, S. (1994). Managing intercultural conflicts effectively. In L. Samovar & R. Porter (Eds.), *Intercultural communication: A reader* (6th ed., pp. 259–261). Belmont, CA: Wadsworth.

Westwood, M., Black, T., & McLean, H. (2002). A re-entry program for peacekeeping soldiers: Promoting personal and career transition. *Canadian Journal of Counselling, 36,* 221–232.

Winslow, D. (1998). Military culture in the breakdown of discipline in peace operations. *Canadian Review of Sociology and Anthropology, 35,* 345–367.

Winslow, D., Kammhuber, S., & Soeters, J. (2004). Diversity management and training in non-American forces. In D. Landis, J. Bennett, & M. Bennett (Eds.), *Handbook of intercultural training* (3rd ed., pp. 395–415). Thousand Oaks, CA: Sage.

Veterans Affairs Canada. (2006). *What is operational stress injury?* Retrieved June 8, 2006, from http://www.vac-acc.gc.ca/clients/sub.cfm?source=mhealth/definition

Young, T. D. (1996). German national command structures after unification: A new German general staff. *Armed Forces & Society, 22,* 379–400.

Zimmerman, A., Holman, D., & Sparrow, P. (2003). Unraveling adjustment mechanisms: Adjustment of German expatriates to intercultural interactions, work, and living conditions in the People's Republic of China. *International Journal of Cross Cultural Management, 3,* 45–65.

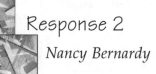

Response 2

Nancy Bernardy

The struggle in Afghanistan has become a nearly forgotten battle, with the Iraq war on center stage in many arenas, including the world's media and people's minds. It was a struggle fought against a small Taliban regime whose primary weapon was terror tactics. However, the conflict in Afghanistan is increasingly and infuriatingly heading toward anarchy, similar to the situation today in Iraq, with almost two military personnel now killed each week. The Taliban has stepped up attacks in recent months, principally targeting international soldiers. It is against this dangerous backdrop that international protection forces are attempting to carry out their United Nations–assigned "robust mandate." As part of this mandate, international soldiers work on reconstruction projects as well as provide security to the Afghan people and support to the local authorities.

An integral part of the mandate is to get a pulse of the Afghan community, and this is a particular challenge that protection forces face. Afghan support of the presence of the United Nations protection forces is high, and that fact, along with the friendly attitude of the Afghan people, makes this a desired peacekeeper assignment. Most Afghans seem frightened that the International Security Assistance Force might leave, and they appreciate the stability the United Nations forces provide. Yet allegiance on the Afghan people's part often comes down to support for those who help provide basics such as food and water and, thus, can easily change, depending on available resources.

The story of one German soldier's attempt to be a part of the diplomatic effort in Afghanistan is set against this backdrop. Alexander is a young German officer who has been deployed to Afghanistan for a few months and is currently battling a number of stressors that affect his ability to carry out his mission. He struggles with loneliness and culture shock similar to that faced by many who travel to a foreign land and cannot speak the language nor understand the local customs, only to a worse degree. He is asked to do an almost impossible job: attempt to make things normal in a country where his idea of "normalcy" has never existed. He is asked to try to provide support to a population that has been subjected to long-term severe trauma and torture. This process is complicated by problems in communication and a lack of cultural sensitivity on the part of Alexander.

Issues and Influences on Alexander to Accomplish Mission

Researchers know from studies of peacekeeping forces in previous conflicts that poorer mental health outcomes are seen in those who meet two criteria: Military members have themselves endured traumatic events in the country where they are serving and they have also experienced extreme or chronic stressors at home prior to their military service (Michel, 2005). These findings suggest that there are vulnerable individuals who have experienced previous trauma that probably should not be sent as a member of peacekeeping forces. Unfortunately, the ability to prescreen and select soldiers who should or should not go into a peacekeeping mission is typically not a choice that is available to the military command.

In service members who see relatively little combat exposure, such as in Alexander's case, there is typically a low level of chronic mental health problems overall and little risk of the development of psychiatric disorders down the road related to peacekeeping service. Chronic stress effects are frequently seen immediately after peacekeeping service but then diminish within 6 months to a year after returning home (Michel, 2005). A usual diagnosis for people experiencing some of the problems that Alexander faces is "adjustment disorder," and this is probably the most common diagnosis now given to military personnel serving downrange or on reintegration to their homes. It is a temporary diagnosis in response to time-limited stressors and can be coded according to the subtype that best characterizes predominant symptoms such as anxiety, depressed mood, or conduct disturbance. It also does not carry the weight of the implications of a diagnosis of posttraumatic stress disorder (PTSD), particularly in a military population.

Although there is little risk of chronic psychological problems from Alexander's current service, at the time cross-cultural transitions are experienced, they can be extremely uncomfortable and challenging. The challenge itself develops because different cultures can define normalcy differently from others and is complicated by an inability to communicate about seemingly normal behaviors. Attempting to compare German and Afghan cultures is more difficult than comparing apples and oranges. Germans live in a highly structured, regulated society that is governed by rules on almost every aspect of life, whereas Afghans have constantly been exposed to violent disorder and have had to attempt to figure out who and what to support to survive. Afghanistan, many soldiers like to say, is a place that time has forgotten. Germany, on the other hand, is a place where punctuality is next to godliness. For a German such as Alexander, time is precious and time is money. He may feel as if he is trying to keep time in a land without watches and clocks, and that can be very unnerving for a German.

For Alexander, the more immediate issue is how to act as a "neutral observer" in a situation that has been a long-standing conflict: the disputed regulation by various tribes of the use of water from a river. He and his interpreter attend a tribal meeting at which many of the disputing tribes are represented, and his expectations are high that he can help be part of the solution to this critical problem. Yet he is pushed and pulled from all sides, becomes confused, and is unable to maintain his neutral role. In fact, it appears that he has now moved from observing the meeting to being the person responsible for solving the problem, and he does not know what to do. He wonders how he has gotten himself into this mess, and, more important, how he will get out of it alive.

There are a number of stressors that may be making this problem worse for Alexander than it needs to be. First and foremost, he is lonely and he misses his newborn son and wife a great deal. He is bothered by his lack of privacy and finds that he is having difficulty concentrating. He appears to be exhibiting a number of symptoms of chronic stress that are commonly observed in peacekeepers in these situations. Alexander is also having difficulty understanding Afghanistan as a different culture. How can a person who has lived his life in safety begin to understand what it is like to face death as a part of everyday business? The power and influence of the warlords, the fear of the insurgency, and the proliferation of the drug business in Afghanistan are all incomprehensible to Alexander. He feels helpless in his attempts to understand the Afghans and has difficulty reconciling all of his experiences in Afghanistan to his concept of religion. The poverty in Afghanistan is much worse than he had expected to see, and reconstruction efforts have been more difficult to accomplish. All of these stressors make it more difficult for Alexander to use the best coping resources that he can.

It is commonly observed that in cases of extreme or chronic stress, such as that experienced by Alexander, one's appraisal or perception of events is crucial to the ability to cope with the situation. The appraisal, in turn, then drives the psychological and biological responses that lead either to negative consequences, such as the development of PTSD or health problems, or to positive consequences, such as a more active, problem-focused coping accompanied with good outcomes. Some have suggested that the process of coping with the trauma may be more important for positive mental health outcomes than the experience of the trauma itself (Aldwin & Yancura, 2004). If Alexander is able to use fewer defenses and less emotion-focused coping, such as wishful thinking and denial, and in turn can challenge his appraisals, when necessary, and use problem-focused coping, he will be able to develop more adaptive responses and be better able to deal with the mission at hand. He needs to seek and use social support from his supervisors and his coworkers to help him develop appropriate coping skills. He also needs to learn that flexibility in his coping responses, including a number of different styles that may use things such as palliative coping (exercise, relaxation, yoga), will help him adapt to the situation. It is important to remember that there are times when even defenses may be helpful.

So what should Alexander do regarding his mission and the dilemma in which he now finds himself? First and foremost, Alexander is doing the right thing by contacting his supervisor. It is hoped that his supervisor is a source of social support, is experienced, and will also remind Alexander what his mission is. Alexander is there to provide support, to assist, and to be a "neutral observer." Just as he cannot truly understand the Afghan culture, he also cannot know how to solve a problem regarding the regulation of water that has existed far back in time; nor is it his place as an observer to solve that problem. He needs to be a good listener, to help create an atmosphere that allows the various tribes to again be able to discuss the dispute among themselves, and perhaps to be a mediator, and he needs to remove himself from the role of decision maker. He, as an outsider and as a "peacekeeper," cannot be the judge of the solution for this problem. More important, it is essential that the solution to this problem come from negotiations among the Afghans themselves.

One alternative that would certainly make Alexander more comfortable would be to ask the tribal leaders to lay down their arms at the door of the tent before the discussions and negotiations continue. He can assure them that his team is protecting the surrounding area and that by laying down their arms, they will contribute to better communication among all groups. He needs to be very clear that he is not the solution to this problem and that it needs to come from the Afghan groups working together. They are the ones who know the background of the dispute, know their needs for the water, and have to be willing to make concessions to come to an agreement. That agreement cannot be exchanged for bribes or promises of information on enemies. Alexander needs to be certain that he does not support one tribe over another but rather thinks that it is through the process of the tribes working together on all decisions that a strong Afghanistan, together under Islamic law, will be united. Promises that the Bundeswehr will take responsibility for such measures should not be made and cannot be kept by Alexander. Such promises would only worsen his predicament.

Clinical Consideration in Working With This Population

Unfortunately, the military leadership does not have the time or the necessary training to focus on early interventions with peacekeeping populations that could help prevent chronic stress symptoms from developing. There are clinical implications for debriefing, for preventive interventions, and for introducing active coping techniques to enable the development of more adaptive responses on the part of peacekeepers. It is known that early interventions can be helpful. Research has suggested that psychological debriefing does not help prevent the development of PTSD in peacekeeping groups, but it also does no harm (Michel, 2005). It is important to note that the peacekeeping groups say that they like it. Some clinicians have turned to the use of the term *defusing* to avoid the issue of debriefing. Defusing is the process of having the platoon leader talk to the group about stressful events that have occurred, doing some psychoeducation, and encouraging cross-talk among the peacekeepers. This process of defusing allows peacekeepers to help themselves and provides an important element of social support. The broader and deeper the system of social support, the less chance a peacekeeper has to develop a chronic form of PTSD. In groups of peacekeepers assigned to previous conflicts who have used defusing and peer support, more favorable mental health outcomes postdeployment have been observed. Chronic stress symptoms can be serious for some peacekeepers. The idea of "losing face" can be a tremendous loss for peacekeepers, and eventual suicide is not untypical in extreme cases.

There are some early steps for prevention of future mental health problems that can be taken with peacekeeping troops. During the selection and recruitment process, special attention should be paid to any previous traumas or negative life events before service. The ideal solution would be to allow the individual to receive treatment for that preexisting condition before deployment. Platoon leaders can also help reduce any potentially traumatizing events that occur in country through the defusing process. Platoon leaders should receive training in the psychoeducational aspects of stress and know how to then convey that material to their troops. Leaders, however, need to remember that they need to participate in the defusing process as well. It is essential that there be a supply of adequate treatment for mental health problems in the locations of the peacekeeping service. This is one of the major lessons that has been learned in Iraq. Treatment should not be postponed until the end of a tour of service when the soldier returns home. Acute interventions may require a crisis intervention, brief cognitive-behavioral therapy, or stress debriefing. It may be something as simple as getting a few days in a rest and relaxation facility where the soldier can get a hot shower, some warm food, and rest. Motivating soldiers who are providing a protection force to seek treatment is a special challenge. It is difficult to get them to stop and ask for help. Not only are they often asked to do various jobs, including providing security, for which they have not been adequately trained but they are often asked to do these jobs with little availability of means. They do not want to leave their network of buddies who provide their social support. All of these factors suggest a model that leads to increased stresses on the peacekeeping forces and a subsequent vulnerability to developing mental health problems if interventions are not provided.

Intervention Strategies for the Case Incident

If it appears that a more thorough intervention is needed and a form of chronic PTSD is present, some peacekeepers may need to be referred to specialists for intensive psychotherapy and even adjunctive pharmacotherapy. The effects of trauma experienced by peacekeepers can show up as depression, anxiety, somatoform disorders, personality disorders, or chronic or complex PTSD. A clinician might see aspects of these various disorders as a part of posttraumatic symptomatology that fall along a continuum (Wilson, Friedman, & Lindy, 2001). They may be interrelated processes in PTSD that require skilled clinical intervention and management.

Generally speaking, current treatment is largely the domain of psychologists, and the effects from psychotherapy are greater than the effects from drugs. Numerous treatment approaches have been used to treat PTSD, including brief eclectic psychotherapy; psychodynamic therapy; "power" therapies such as Eye Movement Desensitization and Reprocessing; and, more recently, Internet-based therapies. Various forms of cognitive-behavioral therapies are recognized as the recommended treatment for PTSD to take control of traumatic memories and correct disturbed cognitions, and these include forms of exposure therapy, anxiety management, systematic desensitization, cognitive-processing therapy, and present-centered approaches (Wilson et al., 2001). Unfortunately, high dropout rates are often seen in the cognitive-behavioral therapy approaches, and residual symptoms are seen at the end of treatment with end-state functioning that is not reflective of positive life changes. This suggests that alternative treatment approaches are still needed, with more sophisticated clinical end points that can reflect things such as quality of life, ability to return to work, social reintegration, and social relationships.

A primary intervention component within this framework is the relationship between the service member and his or her health care provider. The provider must be willing to accept the service member at face value, and qualities such as genuineness, warmth, understanding, and empathy are going to be crucial for a relationship to be developed. There are some specific intervention strategies that should be followed in most cases. First and foremost, service members must feel safe and without pressure to tell their stories. It is important from the beginning that the health care provider be available for an ongoing relationship. It is not the time to have them meet with one provider for a screening and then be transferred to another one to tell again their symptoms and experiences. Consistency and support from one individual are key to the development of trust.

Important points are to listen to the service members' distress and their complaints and do not treat if you must judge. Any physical symptoms need to be treated seriously. Be patient and get a full history, particularly of previous traumas or stressors before service. Provide a psychoeducation model that helps service members understand that their symptoms do not mean that they are "going crazy" but that they symptoms are a rather typical response to pressure. Place symptoms in a normal stress-reaction framework. The primary intervention at this stage is to provide relief of symptoms. A useful approach is to list likely early treatment goals, such as an improvement in sleep, that address physical symptoms. Medication that helps provide quality sleep will be a useful adjunct and will probably contribute to a rapidly improved mood. Finally, the health care provider should listen to whatever stories the service member now wants to tell (Wilson et al., 2001). Recently, a health care provider from Walter Reed Medical Center made the following statement, "If they leave feeling like they've got you squared away about how things really were downrange [i.e., Iraq or Afghanistan], then you have succeeded."

Considerations About the Role of Intercultural Learning and Competence

After the recent natural disasters such as the earthquake in Pakistan and the tsunami in Asia, mental health providers have learned that they cannot just all travel to a country and think that they can then help the people there by imposing their norms and values on another culture to solve problems. They have to start learning about another country's culture, values, and backgrounds before they go. Some university training programs have instituted courses in cultural psychology/psychiatry that work to help bridge these barriers. The United States army has recently adopted a derivative of this approach by developing training areas that attempt to recreate the countries, including people dressed according to local customs, where the soldiers will be deployed to allow them to practice their skills in situations that are similar to ones they will face on arrival at their new duty stations. One of the best things that we, as mental health providers, can do is to work through local health care providers, religious leaders, and community leaders in the country of the mission to provide support and determine needs. Skills and any support items, including counseling and case management, can then be passed on from the leaders to the local people who need treatment. It is recognized that even something as simple as asking basic questions about a trauma or a severe stressor that has been endured needs to take into account the patient's cultural experience in order to obtain the right information and to know how to proceed with useful therapies. These techniques will, hopefully, then allow the counseling field to help increase the understanding of ethnic identity while decreasing the symptoms of chronic stress.

References

Aldwin, C. M., & Yancura, L. A. (2004). Coping and health: A comparison of the stress and trauma literatures. In P. P. Schnurr & B. L. Green (Eds.), *Trauma and health: Physical health consequences of exposure to extreme stress* (pp. 99–125). Washington, DC: American Psychological Association.

Michel, P. (2005, June). *Stress and mental health among personnel in international military operations*. Preconference workshop presented at the 9th European Conference on Traumatic Stress, Stockholm, Sweden.

Wilson, J. P., Friedman, M. J., & Lindy, J. D. (2001). Practical considerations in the treatment of PTSD: Guidelines for practitioners. In J. P. Wilson, M. J. Friedman, & J. D. Lindy (Eds.), *Treating psychological trauma & PTSD* (pp. 409–432). New York: Guilford Press.

Counseling Military Personnel Following Traumatic Events

Philip Armstrong

Ron (a pseudonym) was in the 3rd month of a 4-month rifle company deployment to Butterworth Airbase in Malaysia. At that time, telecommunications in Malaysia were very primitive outside of the major cities, with very few dependable landlines or mobile phone towers. Communication between the airbase and the rifle company while in the field was via a military mobile setup that was unreliable at best. Ron held the rank of corporal and was serving as a section commander in a rifle platoon in the Australian Army.

Ron at the time of the incident was on orderly room duty, having just returned to the airbase after suffering a minor injury in the field. Had Ron remained in the field, there is a significant likelihood he would have been a casualty of the incident described in this case incident. Several hours into his duty in the orderly room, Ron received a phone call from the company commander in the field. The reception was broken and faint; however, Ron could make out the words "accident and fatalities" before the line went dead. Ron was by himself in the orderly room and was unsure of what to make of the phone call; however, he was very concerned about the implications of what he had heard. The phone rang again, and again the reception was poor. This time the company commander was able to tell Ron there had been a field accident that had resulted in a death and some injuries when the line went dead again. This situation continued for a further 2 hours. Each time the phone rang, reception was poor, and Ron was informed of further deaths and injuries and some names. With each phone call, Ron became more and more apprehensive and did not want to answer the phone for fear of notification of further deaths and the casualties' names; most of the dead soldiers so far were Ron's close mates.

Critical Incident

Five hours into the incident, Ron finally received a phone call from the company commander that had good reception. There had been a field accident and five soldiers were dead and seven seriously injured. The company was moving back to the airbase and would be there within 8 hours. During that time, Ron had to write five fatality and seven casualty reports to be sent back to Australia. He was also required to report the incident to the battalion headquarters in Australia. By the time the company arrived back at the air base, Ron had not slept for 24 hours and had by himself completed all procedural tasks; this was equivalent to the work of three soldiers at a level that was two times above his current rank. On the company's return, Ron was immediately interviewed by the military police about his actions and the sequence of events.

It was during the interview that Ron found out that the soldier who was being held responsible for the accident was a soldier that Ron had tried to have returned to Australia several times because the soldier was unfit for overseas duty. Ron informed the military police that this soldier was significantly injured prior to deployment and should not have been deployed, per standing orders in regards to overseas duty. The company commander had covertly deployed with the soldier because he was short one soldier for overseas deployment, and another company might have been deployed had he not resolved the issue of having sufficient soldiers. The soldier should not have been in a position where he could have been responsible for an accident. The soldier was deployed against standing orders, even though Ron had formally approached the company commander regarding the situation several times. It was at this stage that Ron concluded that if he had succeeded in having the soldier returned to Australia, Ron's mates would not be dead. The company commander was in significant breach of military law and should have had charges laid against him, particularly in view of the accident. Ron inquired as to why this had not happened but received no reply.

The military police took no action against the company commander; however, a charge of theft was suddenly made against Ron 2 days later. This charge was not substantiated and was soon dropped. However, the harm was done, and Ron was ostracized by the rest of the company for the remainder of the tour. Theft was considered to be the worst offense a soldier could commit against his mates. Ron spent the rest of the tour being placed on duty with no rest while the remainder of the company was debriefed regarding the accident and was subsequently rested. Ron was neither debriefed nor rested and was ordered to correlate the investigation of the accident report and forward it to Australia. This included viewing all the forensic material, including graphic photos of the corpses and the coroner's report of the injuries sustained by the deceased. The report made no mention of the company commander's dubious actions.

On his return to Australia, Ron started having nightmares that included graphic pictures of mutilated soldiers. He became hypervigilant and nervous around phones and small rooms. Ron became disillusioned with the concept of loyalty—something that he had previously held strongly and that was the glue that held his world of the army together. Ron became depressed and tried to tell anyone who would listen his story. He ceased doing this after receiving a poor performance report, the first one in 9 years of service. Ron was not able to attend the memorial service for his fallen mates because of his sense of guilt over the accident. Meanwhile, Ron's health had deteriorated, and he found himself continually dwelling on the photos of his dead mates and his perceived failure to prevent the accident. The company commander and another officer involved in the incident took their discharges prior to the conclusion of a military investigation into the event. The ensuing investigation made no reference to their actions, and neither was called to account. In any case, at this time military law had no jurisdiction over civilians in Australia. Ron was medically discharged approximately 12 months after the incident (prior to the findings of the investigation) due to further injuries he received while training. Ron's marriage failed shortly after, and he sought psychiatric help. Ron was not able to reconcile himself regarding the incident and continued to experience flashbacks, sleep deprivation due to recurring nightmares, hypertension, depression, and intrusive thoughts. Ron became withdrawn and antisocial. He was not able to resolve his grief over the deaths of his mates because he was not able to face their family members because of his knowledge of what he saw as the truth. He simply could not face them without making issues worse for them by telling them his side of the story. To this day, Ron still feels significant guilt about the accident and feels that he did not do enough to prevent it and that he could have pursued the truth further.

Writer's Role

My role in this incident was as a friend to Ron. I believed his story and to the detriment of my own military career tried to seek justice for Ron. I was in Malaysia at the time of the incident and was involved in the following investigation, which was primarily a cover-up from my perception. This incident was the catalyst for my leaving the army and going to university to study to become a counselor.

I believe the incident was extremely traumatic for Ron and that it undermined Ron's personal integrity by undermining the deep-seated belief he had, until the incident, in the loyalty that the army had instilled in him toward his fellow soldiers and the military system within which he lived. He believed that the loyalty was mutual and that the system would look after him. Ron's belief system, which was to look after his mates and be honest, was shattered as he experienced the system turning on him to protect an officer who held a senior rank. This officer's career was more important than the truth and the life of five regular soldiers. The guilt Ron felt was irrational but real to him.

Ron's trauma was further complicated by ongoing bullying and slurring his reputation by unsubstantiated claims of theft. Ron's grief for the passing of his mates was compounded by the real perpetrators of the accident not being held accountable, as Ron saw it. Although Ron did pursue the truth by relating the facts from his perspective to the military police and the following tribunal, the dismissal of his truth by these authorities only added to his disempowerment. Rationally, Ron did all that could be reasonably done in this situation. Unfortunately, Ron has yet to come to this conclusion himself.

Ron was in dire need of personal counseling that would challenge his mistaken belief that he had any direct responsibility for the deaths and injuries of his mates. Had Ron been debriefed and received professional critical incident counseling at the time, there is a strong possibility that he would not have developed the more chronic symptoms that lead to posttraumatic stress disorder. Normalizing Ron's reactions to the incident as well as providing support while he was going through the investigation may have significantly minimized the downward spiral that Ron experienced. This normalization and support may also have given him the support and strength to deal with the ongoing issues he experienced without these issues further adding to his emotional distress. To be effective and not complicate the issues for Ron, it would possibly have been necessary for the counselor to have been a civilian. Ron's loss of faith in the military may have made him be resistant and uncooperative to counseling from a military counselor.

Key Issues

Ron's symptoms were complicated in the grieving process because the ongoing investigation took over a year and Ron was victimized by elements of his unit who were faithful to the officers. The fact that these officers remained in the same unit and were senior and had influence over Ron's career would have also complicated any recovery during this time. The emotional repercussions of the situation turned into a nonfinite grieving process for Ron because no action was taken directly after the incident. Had Ron received the support and help of an experienced critical incident counselor from the beginning, his trauma-related stress may not have developed into a more acute disorder.

This case incident is not defined or influenced by borders, culture, or religion; it is generic to any system that instills discipline and loyalty in its members as the core motivation to act as one, unified body. Most military and paramilitary organizations work from this concept and depend on the inherent loyalty of their members to each other to be effective. This loyalty is usually stronger than the loyalty of members to a political system or ideology. Many soldiers fight on regardless of the war already being lost because of loyalty to each other and not to the cause. When this loyalty is fractured, often due to political and career issues of senior members, the involved individual (who is usually junior in rank or position) usually experiences significant emotional and psychological damage as his or her world ceases to make sense. The results of such a breakdown can be catastrophic to the organization and its leaders if they cannot contain the incident. The cost of containment to the individual or individuals involved is irrelevant, because the coherence and order of the larger group are predetermined priorities if the group is to remain useful to its leaders. The challenge is for the individual to retain some semblance of self and sanity should he or she be the sacrificial lamb.

Reader Reflection Questions

1. Is counseling about the individual when a greater cause may be at hand, and how can counseling help the individual in these circumstances?
2. Is it possible for counselors not to be influenced by their loyalty to the organization in cases such as this and to remain effective and balanced as well as objective for the client?
3. How can counselors support a client in a political environment that is willing to sacrifice the client without becoming victims themselves?
4. Is it ethically acceptable to expect counselors to jeopardize their own careers by supporting a client who is obviously out of favor with the powers that be? On the other hand, if a counselor who is renowned as a renegade is used to support the individual in a case such as this one, how can he or she support the client without making things worse or influencing the situation with his or her own politics?

Response 1

Marvin Westwood and Timothy G. Black

To understand the multicultural competencies required in counseling practice in situations like this, counselors need first to understand the differing cultural worlds at play when the counselor meets the clients. Only after comprehending the client–cultural context can they begin to address how a counselor can best respond in order to assist the client. The case of Ron possesses enormous challenges to the professional counselor, and this case can serve to help prepare counselors in their professional work.

Understanding the Role of Culture and the Client–Counselor Context

The following questions were posed by the author of the case incident. "Is counseling about the individual when a greater cause may be at hand, and how can counseling help the individual in these circumstances?" "Is it possible for counselors not to be influenced by their loyalty to the organization in cases such as this and to remain effective and balanced as well as objective for the client?" "How can counselors support a client in a political environment that is willing to sacrifice the client without becoming victims themselves?" "Is it ethically acceptable to expect counselors to jeopardize their own careers by supporting a client who is obviously out of favor with the powers that be?" "On the other hand, if a counselor who is renowned as a renegade is used to support the individual in cases such as this one, how can he or she support the client without making things worse or influencing the situation with his or her own politics?" This case incident challenges counselors to consider what is their role, their ethical responsibility to the client, the community, society, and so on. Is the client Ron or is the client the military? For civilian counselors, the answer is very clear: It is Ron. But what can counselors really do to help him? To fully appreciate the barriers to helping, consider the context of the culture he came from before he was discharged.

In reviewing this critical incident, it is helpful to think about the military and civilian worlds as clearly different and distinct cultures. One of the most helpful ways to do this is to reflect on the high- and low-context culture concept as defined by Hall (1974), in which he distinguished between these two concepts. High-context cultures operate by the group defining the roles and identities of the members of the group. The primacy of the group takes precedence over the individual character in such cultures. In this case, the military culture is clearly high context. In contrast, low-context cultures deemphasize the primacy of the group as a basis of role and identity and place a higher value on the individual. The civilian world to which Ron returns is best understood in these terms. Conflict arises when counselors (from low-context cultures) work with clients from high-context cultures, because working to meet the needs/goals of the individual can be contrary to the goals the group holds for that person. It requires skillful accommodation and repositioning by the counselor to help clients who are members of groups that are highly contextualized in this way. With this in mind, Ron can be seen as someone who has been caught between two cultural worlds, resulting in extreme dissonance of thought, feeling, and behavior, as seen in the description of Ron. Examine more closely the complexity of Ron's situation as a way to understand his situation and the challenge for those in the civilian culture who want to help individuals like Ron.

The incident involving Ron contains what might be called "archetypal" issues that we have experienced in working with military veterans. Archetypal issues with this counseling population include power and rank in the military, attachment bonds with comrades, guilt and responsibility, reentry into civilian life, acculturation into the military, and honor and justice. Ron's story speaks to all of these issues and how each one carries with it culturally embedded networks of meaning, which may be "invisible" to civilian counselors who have not been exposed to or who do not understand the distinct culture of the military.

Power and Rank

The military is, first and foremost, a hierarchical and power-based organization. It is also a role-based culture, which we will deal with more explicitly in the section on acculturation into the military. Rank in the military is generally divided into officer ranks or enlisted personnel, with the officer ranks further divided into the four categories of officers, senior noncommissioned officers (senior NCOs), NCOs, and "other ranks" (Black, Westwood, & Sorsdahl, 2007). Rank and power are two sides of the same coin, and Ron's experience as a corporal (i.e., enlisted personnel) in the Australian army places him near the bottom of the hierarchy. Simply put, Ron has very little power in the organization. We see issues of power in several critical events that took place in this incident.

Ron receives a call from the company commander in the field. The company commander outranks Ron as section commander, and, as such, Ron is obliged to follow any and all orders or directives given by the company commander. In fact, as a soldier, Ron will want to do his best to follow orders and fulfill his duties to the best of his abilities, because that is how he has been trained to think and feel. Enlisted personnel are trained to think and feel as though they are doing the right thing when they follow orders unquestioningly and to the fullest extent possible. Ron is prevented from doing this because of the failure of the telecommunications equipment. However, we see Ron's desire to fulfill his duty and obligations, all the while being exposed to the traumatic incidents occurring on the other end of the line. Despite Ron's natural desire to avoid answering the continuous phone calls reporting the death and injury of his mates, Ron's rank and military identity override this inclination.

Ron finally receives a clear phone call from the company commander disclosing the death of five soldiers and serious injury to seven more. At this time, Ron is required to write up the injury and fatality reports and send them back to Australia. We cannot forget that some of Ron's friends had died or been injured, and yet his duties required him to follow orders and fill out the reports. After this, Ron is interviewed by the military police (MP) and questioned about his actions. The rank of MP carries with it a kind of ultimate authority of the larger organization of the military. Ron is unable to do anything except follow orders or suffer even more dire consequences for failing to comply with the MPs.

Ron reported to the MPs that there were standing orders not to deploy the soldier responsible for the accident because of a serious injury the individual had incurred. However, the company commander (of higher rank and more power) deployed the individual "covertly" against standing orders. We cannot overemphasize the implications, in terms of rank and power, of a corporal calling to task the illegal actions of a superior officer. After his repeated attempts to have people hear his story, he is given a poor performance report. Once again rank and power are implicated. Performance reports have implications for promotion within the military organization, and poor reports can functionally sentence an individual to a particular rank for the duration of his or her career. These reports are filled out by superior officers. Enlisted personnel are expected to follow orders (and implicitly accept the wisdom and judgment of their superiors), and questioning the actions of a senior officer would likely be construed as "breaking ranks."

The last event in which we see the rank and power in the military hierarchy is when Ron is medically discharged 12 months after the incident. Once an individual is no longer fit for military duty, he or she is medically discharged, regardless of a possible desire to stay on with the organization in another capacity. Discharge is a top-down decision in which individuals have virtually no recourse. Wrongful discharges do occur, but once the decision is made the damage has been done.

Guilt and Responsibility

Understanding the acculturation into the military, counselors can then begin to understand the ubiquitous feelings of guilt and responsibility that people like Ron feel. A military person is trained, perhaps constructed, to feel most at ease when with the unit or group and to sacrifice himself or herself for the good of the mission if necessary. This is not merely a romantic Hollywood notion of camaraderie and soldierly conduct. It is a reality that is emotionally based and grounded in the military acculturation process. When comrades die and other individuals live, this will inevitably bring up survivors' guilt and thoughts of responsibility. Military members are acculturated to believe that they are responsible for the lives of the men and women around them and that those men and women are responsible for them. Death is a fact of life for military members; however, guilt is a built-in mechanism for ensuring that people will not think first about themselves, thus jeopardizing more lives than necessary. Guilt and responsibility to comrades ensure that the military member will think about the group and hence the mission first, increasing the likelihood of the mission's success and the success of the entire operation. Military units cannot afford to have highly independent and self-centered men and women in the ranks. People are required to think of the safety of the group prior to their own safety, and when someone dies, then the people left alive have failed in their task of keeping their mates alive, knowing their mates would have done that for them. This kind of mentality is so ingrained and reinforced in the military organization that we have found it is somewhat resistant to cognitive reframing, especially by civilian counselors who will "never understand" anyway. In our experience, it is only fellow military members who can "absolve" another military member of his or her feelings of not doing enough, not doing the right thing, and not keeping his or her mates alive.

Attachment Bonds With Comrades

Because member-to-member loyalty and bonding are expected over individual aspirations and goals, there will often be a heightened sense of betrayal as the group and authorities of the group move to censure or shun a member of the group. How similar is this to "sitting shiva" for someone who has gone against the group and is still alive—a practice used in orthodox Judaism. Disownment of women who marry outside of the traditional Hindu culture is another example of this. Discharge, expulsion, exclusion, rejection are often the ways that high-context cultures maintain compliance, and unfortunately what comes with this type of sanction of the individual are feelings of failure, lowered self-esteem, powerlessness, and shame. Most often these feelings lead people to withdraw and become isolated and, in some cases, to commit suicide because of the loss of meaning and the feeling of belonging to the original group.

Acculturation Into the Military

In this section, we deal with the issue of the acculturation process into a military organization. Militaries function only as well as the abilities of their members to give and take direct orders. The chain of command is everything, and at the bottom of the chain is the enlisted member, who is most effective when obeying superiors and carrying out orders from them unquestioningly and with speed and efficiency. People are not born with this innate ability to follow the orders of superiors unquestioningly, and, therefore, military organizations have used psychological techniques, among other things, to help "create" an effective military member. Essentially, military organizations bring in new recruits and immediately work on breaking down each person's sense of autonomous individuality.

Heads shaved; civilian clothes replaced with military fatigues; and an uncompromising demand for preordained modes of communication and behaviors, including when, where, and how to eat, talk, socialize, exercise, and interact in every facet of the job, all contribute to the making of the military mind. Group allegiance and emotional bonds to fellow comrades are fostered, whereas individual autonomy and independent thinking are actively discouraged and even met with punitive actions. The result of the acculturation process is a military member who will follow orders unquestioningly and who will think about the safety and well-being of the group in the service of completing a task above all else, including individual preservation of life and limb.

The process of military acculturation is efficient and is, based on reports from the military clients we have worked with, indelible. The phrase, "once military, always military" rings true in this respect. As such, the counselor working with Ron would need to have an appreciation for the fact that despite Ron's discharge from the military organization, he will more likely identify as military rather than identify as civilian, despite his civilian status. We have found in working with the people in our groups that there is often a mixture of loyalty to their military identity, in the form of loyalty to their mates or officers who were worthy of respect, and a sense of betrayal at the organization that has, in their estimation, abandoned them, mistreated them, and left them with a "heap of baggage" to deal with in their civilian lives. Civilian counselors must understand these kinds of acculturation issues and avoid the understandable mistake of taking an antimilitary position "in support" of the veteran who feels betrayed. Such counselors may find themselves out of favor with clients, who may feel betrayed by the military but who also feel that civilians should not criticize the military, of which they still consider themselves a part.

Ensuring Compliance

Another characteristic of high-context cultural groups is the way the group applies sanctions or uses rejection or shaming as a way to punish individuals who do not conform to the dominant values or understood roles of behaving. This comes from the need for the cultural group to ensure conformism. In Ron's situation, it seems that the charge of theft was a way to distance Ron from the group and to convey to him that his voice was not credible; to ensure compliance and conformism, control of the individual by the group is required.

The Challenge for the Counselor

Counselors can, with cross-cultural understanding in mind, act to support and assist clients like Ron who have now returned to a civilian/lower-context culture. Of course, the first challenge is to establish the relationship, which may require a highly skillful approach because of the feelings of client depression and betrayal and the inability to trust another person. We offer six short-term considerations for counselors to enhance the therapeutic alliance and to help clients with presenting symptoms.

1. As with any client who has been traumatized, the counselor can assist clients to make sense of what has happened to them and to understand the feelings/ reactions they have to the betrayal experience and expulsion from the group. Normalizing their experience of the trauma by providing pertinent information about symptoms/reactions enables clients to make sense of what occurred and what the effects have been.
2. Providing effective strategies for maintaining self-regulation and coping strategies to deal with the trauma symptoms should be included early in the counseling.
3. The process of reentry into an earlier cultural context is also recommended here after the work with managing the trauma. Clients can begin to see how their reactions are normal and to be expected when crossing cultures that are extremely dissimilar, as in Ron's case.
4. After attending to the already mentioned adjustment needs of clients, the counselor can be very helpful in working to restore a sense of purpose, establish short-term goals for survival, and begin to establish an early level of a felt sense of efficacy that they can cope and find some meaning in this newer context.
5. Relationship development, support, and information on how to access support outside the sessions would also be essential. This could be the place where the counselor advocates for the client to begin entry into an ongoing support or relationship group to begin to learn to trust others, perhaps now in a different way because he or she is operating in a different culture.
6. Career goals and/or initial life planning may be possible as the next phase to assist the client to reestablish himself or herself in the world-of-work or school so that he or she can begin to receive initial self-validation.

The recommendations in the list are short-term assisting suggestions that are good starting places for the counselor, but in order to help clients who have experienced a significant trauma, we recommend a particular group-based approach for trauma repair, referred to as therapeutic enactment, which was developed by Marvin Westwood and Patricia Wilensky (2005). Through working with clients in a supportive group environment, they are able to recover from the trauma event by returning to personal action and restore "what was taken from them." Talking therapies are insufficient to restore the deep core schemas related to loss of esteem, acquisition of shame, loss of personal control, and loss of confidence in personal efficacy. This approach allows members to recreate an event in concrete terms, thus permitting a reexperiencing of a critical or significant event, complete with all of the thoughts, feelings, and actions that were associated with the original event. Relearning by returning to the action of the event is the crux of the therapeutic correction for the client. Returning to the original action requires careful planning to do it well. This planning leads to highly controlled enactments within the group that result in the restoration of the individual client's experience of self.

In the therapeutic process, new awareness, reactions, and insights are activated, all mediated by the cathartic effect that is essential to transformative change. Most striking about the therapeutic enactment model is the client's movement from a previously diminished sense of self to a heightened experience of personal control and a reclaiming of the self within the safety of a strong group container while the enactment or reenactment takes place. The moment of repair takes place when clients have the opportunity to rework and to regain control of a critical moment in their lives. This moment may have been the instant in their life experience when they experienced significant loss of trust or control. The repair occurs when they begin to incorporate and transform this moment so that they regain a lost part of themselves. This reparative moment transforms feelings of self-shame into feelings of acceptance and self-caring. In Ron's case, this is the preferred approach because the degree of shattered belief and sense of betrayal will interfere with his ability to trust and regain his own self-esteem and confidence that he lost in the shunning of him by members of his own culture. This is a form of cultural invalidation that can only be restored by reexperiencing the events that caused his injury.

Therapeutic Enactment Intervention

After the enactment, an individual follow-up with the client is essential to ensure integration and consolidation of the reorganized self-schema. In addition, clients may be referred to particular types of personal therapy as a continued support of their repair process. Specifically, therapeutic enactments take place in groups that can include anywhere from 8 to 25 participants, with an ideal group size of 20 members.

The therapeutic enactment model has five phases: (a) assessment and preparation, (b) group building, (c) enactment, (d) group processing, and (e) integration and transfer. First, the assessment and preparation phase involves a pregroup meeting with the lead (i.e., the client who is doing the enactment and is the primary focus of the enactment) in order to assess the lead's needs and develop a detailed plan for the enactment event. In the group-building phase, the group begins with the creation of an atmosphere of safety, affection, and cohesion among the group members. Feelings of inclusion, belonging, spontaneity, and support for one another are essential ingredients that encourage risk taking by members and participation in the enactment. The enactment phase is the point when leads enact their chosen scenes. These scenes represent a past, present, or anticipated future situation or event. In this phase, the leader/therapist helps the lead create the scene by involving other group members in the enactment. Group members assume various roles that are directed by the leader/therapist. Moving through the enactment facilitates catharsis and resolution for the lead, which in turn promotes repair of psychological injury. The fourth phase of the model is group processing. Here, the leader/therapist invites the lead and other group members to express their personal reactions to the enactment experience. This sharing of reactions helps consolidate the client's experience and further connects members through increased inclusion in the group process. Integration and transfer constitute the final phase of the enactment process. In this phase, there are two separate components. The first level of integration occurs when the client reflects on the enactment experience and the thoughts and reflections of other group members. The second level of integration takes place when the individual client is encouraged to make a personal commitment to transfer or apply the newly acquired learning and insight into everyday life. In this way, the lead is able to use the new meanings and felt sense of change, which is gained from the enactment, as a way of practicing new ways of being in the world. Finally, one of the major benefits from the group is helping clients to feel accepted and to belong again, which tends to move them from a place of isolation to belonging.

We have attempted to identify an analysis that clarifies what goes on for clients caught across cultures, such as Ron, and have provided several specific approaches to aiding the client to recover from the trauma or injury and better prepare him or her to begin living more fully by experiencing trauma repair. In our work, we find it is the other members of the group who provide so much of the healing processes for the client. In providing this, the members develop a sense of efficacy and community.

It is important for us, as counselors, to note the humility that comes forth when we consider the degree of personal life damage that does occur for a client like Ron, who appears to have acted from a place that was right for him in a military cultural context, only to find himself punished by this same military culture.

References

Black, T. G., Westwood, M. J., & Sorsdahl, M. N. (2007). From the front line to the front of the class: Counseling students who are military veterans. In J. A. Lippincott & R. B. Lippincott (Eds.), *Special populations in college counseling: A handbook for mental health professionals* (pp. 20–30). Alexandria, VA: American Counseling Association.

Hall, E. T. (1974). *Beyond culture: The hidden dimension.* New York: Doubleday.

Westwood, M. J., & Wilensky, P. (2005). *Therapeutic enactment: Restoring vitality through trauma repair in groups.* Vancouver, British Columbia, Canada: Group Action Press.

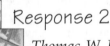

Response 2

Thomas W. Britt and Cynthia L. S. Pury

When thinking about counseling individuals who have experienced stress as a result of international transitions, military personnel represent a unique population. First of all, the military itself represents a unique culture, with its own norms, values, and expected codes of conduct (see Castro, 2006; Siebold, 2006; Soeters, Poponete, & Page, 2006). Individuals who join the military undergo a process of transformation in which they are trained to supplant the identity they formed prior to military service with an identity emphasizing a commitment to group and national goals, including the willingness to die for one's country (McGurk, Cotting, Britt, & Adler, 2006). Military personnel are exposed to stressors in basic training that are meant to prepare them for the high levels of stress they will encounter during different training and combat operations. In addition, personnel are exposed to the values (e.g., integrity, courage, selfless service, responsibility) that are expected of them as service members. They receive classes on these values, and the hope is that military personnel will come to possess these values after continued training. The end product of socialization into the military is the transition from one cultural milieu to a decidedly different one.

In addition to the military culture, service members must also frequently adapt to different cultures as a result of deploying to different locations for training or combat (Miller & Moskos, 1995). For example, peacekeeping operations are becoming more frequent for military personnel, and such operations require service members to interact with members of the local population (Soeters & Bos-Bakx, 2003). In order for military personnel to be effective, they need to understand the customs and norms of the local population(s) so they can effectively maintain peace and prevent the former warring factions from returning to combat. Part of "winning the hearts and minds" of the local population involves an adaptation to the local culture (Collins, 2006) and understanding the best way to influence the attitudes and therefore the behavior of the local population. The current combat operation in Iraq reflects the importance of military personnel understanding and using elements of Iraqi culture in order to effectively perform their mission. Failing to understand the Iraqi culture and customs results in local Iraqis distrusting the motives of outside military personnel, thereby decreasing the possibility of mission success (Collins, 2006).

Given these frequent cultural and international transitions, counseling professionals will find unique challenges in designing therapeutic approaches to treat psychological problems that military personnel develop as a result of exposure to traumatic events. Counselors working with military clients will need to understand the nature and power of the military culture on the client and also to consider the impact of other transitions (e.g., serving overseas, participating in combat and peacekeeping missions) on their presenting difficulties.

The Critical Incident and Complicating International Transitions

The critical incident under consideration deals with a soldier, Ron, who has been deployed away from his home station to a training exercise in another country. Ron has therefore had to adapt to the initial transition of becoming a member of the Australian military as well as the transition to the deployed environment of Malaysia. In general, soldiers who are deployed to training exercises in other countries are exposed to pervasive, "low-level" stressors, such as being away from home, high levels of workload, and lack of contact with familiar surroundings (Britt, Castro, & Adler, 2005). These omnipresent stressors provide a malevolent environment (King, King, Fairbank, Keane, & Adams, 1998) that can exacerbate the effects of more severe stressors.

Psychological Consequences for Ron

It is in the context of this type of environment that Ron experiences a series of traumatic events that certainly meet the criteria in the *Diagnostic and Statistical Manual for Mental Disorders* (4th ed., text rev; *DSM-IV-TR;* American Psychiatric Association [APA], 2000) for posttraumatic stress disorder (PTSD). These criteria involve exposure to an event resulting in violent death with a response of intense fear, helplessness, or horror. While he is back at base due to an injury, he learns that many of his fellow unit members have been killed or injured in a training exercise that he would have taken part in if he had not been injured. This information arrives slowly over a series of low-quality phone calls and with a great deal of confusion. Ron's job, in the immediate aftermath of the accident, was to report the deaths and injuries of his friends, which he accomplished under conditions of sleep deprivation. In addition to the deaths of his comrades, Ron also experienced two violations of trust and justice. The first occurred immediately after the accident when he found out that it was caused by someone Ron did not believe should have been deployed. In fact, it turns out that the commander of the military unit deployed the soldier so that the commander would have the needed number of military personnel for the deployment, despite Ron's repeated requests to return the soldier to Australia. The second betrayal of trust was when Ron was accused of theft 2 days later.

He then experienced retraumatization by being required to view graphic photographs of his friends' corpses as part of the investigation. Opportunities for closure were removed when he was subsequently removed from the training exercise without being able to process his complex emotional reactions to the series of events and when he felt too guilty to attend his comrades' memorial services. Therefore, Ron was faced with the psychological impact of a traumatic stressor involving death of close friends, visual images of those deaths, and a lack of closure. He was also faced with moral violations resulting from being part of an organization that violated the very ethical codes that were espoused.

He presents with many classic symptoms of PTSD as described by the *DSM-IV-TR* (APA, 2000; see also Maguen, Suvak, & Litz, 2006). The case incident highlights his persistent reexperiencing of the event with flashbacks, nightmares, intrusive thoughts, and distress at exposure to reminders of the trauma (telephone rings and small rooms). He shows avoidance and numbing symptoms of social withdrawal and, possibly, inability to make contact with his friends' families. Finally, symptoms of persistently increased arousal are reflected in his hypervigilance, sleep disturbance, and, possibly, his hypertension. Further inquiry is likely to turn up other symptoms of avoidance/numbing and increased arousal. Beyond these definitional symptoms of PTSD, he presents with excessive guilt and with depression, symptoms quite common in individuals with PTSD (APA, 2000).

The events that transpired during Ron's deployment are not unlike the experiences reported by Vietnam veterans. Shay (1994) eloquently described the reasons why many Vietnam veterans still have prolonged psychological difficulties resulting from their participation in the combat operation. A point repeatedly emphasized by Shay is that although Vietnam veterans do have difficulties with the physical aspects of the traumatic events they encountered (e.g., the smell of dead bodies, sounds, images of wounded soldiers), it is the violation of the moral contract the veterans had with commanders and the broader military that is especially difficult to resolve. Many veterans with PTSD report witnessing ethical violations by unit leaders, as well as having doubts about the moral integrity of civilian leaders. These types of doubts make it especially difficult for veterans to meaningfully integrate their combat experiences into their current worldview (see Campbell, 2006).

In addition to the failures of the military itself, Ron is experiencing a great deal of guilt over his own actions. We can think of at least four potential sources of guilt. These sources are merely working hypotheses that should be investigated more fully in the course of counseling, although we believe that each one is a likely scenario and could provide a basis for cognitive intervention. First and most obviously, Ron may be experiencing survivor guilt (APA, 2000). Had he not been injured earlier in the exercise, Ron would have been with his unit when the accident occurred. Thus, a "lucky" injury may have saved his life.

The second sources of guilt, hindsight bias and the devaluation of failed attempts, are related to Ron's unsuccessful attempt to have the responsible soldier returned from deployment. We believe it is very likely that Ron has some guilt over his own role in the solder not being returned. Hindsight bias, the reinterpretation of past beliefs after an outcome becomes known (Guilbault, Bryant, Brockway, & Posavac, 2004), may be leading Ron to mischaracterize his desire to have the solder returned home. In other words, knowing that this solder has in fact caused an accident may have altered Ron's perceived prior certainty that he was a danger. Thus, Ron may believe that he should have tried harder because he was certain an accident would occur. In reality, he may not have been so certain at the time.

The third potential source of guilt may be a devaluing of his actions because they were not successful. We would argue that Ron's repeated attempts to stand up to his commanding officer about the soldier were quite noble and perhaps even courageous. Recent research on courage shows that when people are asked to think of their own courageous actions, they overwhelmingly report successful actions rather than failed actions (Pury, Kowalski, & Spearman, 2006), and when asked to rate the courageousness of various actions, the same action is rated as less courageous if it is unsuccessful than if it is successful (Hensel & Pury, 2005).

The fourth potential source of guilt is over his lack of contact with his friends' families and missing their memorial services. This is understandable, given the common PTSD symptom of avoidance and his (most likely mistaken) belief that he did not, in fact, do everything he could have to prevent the accident. However, part of Ron's successful treatment may involve his making contact with these families and/or in some other way memorializing his dead comrades, a task that may be easier once his guilt over his actions during deployment is reduced. These four potential sources of guilt are not unique to military personnel, although solders may be especially likely to want to see themselves as courageous and, perhaps, to view the lack of courage as especially damning. In that context, to the extent that Ron could view a visit to his comrades' graves as courageous, he might be restoring his military identity as well.

The Importance of Meaning in Adjustment to Traumatic Events

An additional factor that exacerbates Ron's psychological reactions to the deaths of his comrades is that he had no opportunity to make sense of the event while still in the deployed environment. Military psychologists and psychiatrists currently agree that the best place to treat combat stress reactions is in the deployed environment. In current U.S. doctrine, Combat Stress Control (CSC) teams deploy with combat and support units in order to treat soldiers with early signs of combat stress (Lewis, 2006). The acronym PIES is used to describe the orientation to treatment, emphasizing *proximity* to the front lines, *immediate* counseling, *expectancy* that the soldier will return to the unit, and *simplicity* in terms of the nature of therapy (e.g., resting the soldier, processing the stressor, and providing coping strategies to increase efficacy).

Not only did Ron not receive any form of treatment after the traumatic event, he was also removed from the deployed environment without being given the opportunity to process his reactions with the other members of his military unit. In addition to individual therapy, many mental health professionals are recommending military personnel go through debriefings as a unit so that unit members can process traumatic events and use each other as mechanisms for social support (Valach & Young, 2002). This is especially true when personnel are deployed to foreign countries where they are separated from their traditional sources of support.

The Importance of Addressing Stigma in Treatment Seeking

A final factor worth considering in the context of Ron's difficulties is the stigma associated with seeking treatment for psychological problems in the military (Britt, 2000; Hoge et al., 2004). As mentioned earlier, the military culture emphasizes courage, bravery, and other aspects of masculinity that strongly suggest personnel should be capable of dealing with their own reactions to events. Military personnel may be experiencing symptoms of PTSD as a natural response to traumatic events they encountered during the deployment, yet interpret those symptoms as reflecting a weakness in their character for which they assume responsibility (Corrigan & Watson, 2002). This attributional processing, in addition to the fear of stigma associated with treatment, will likely lead service members not to seek help from mental health professionals when experiencing symptoms.

In a study of service members who recently returned from Iraq, Hoge et al. (2004) found that although many soldiers reported experiencing a psychological problem, only a minority had sought treatment from mental health professionals. Hoge et al. argued that stigma and other barriers to care (e.g., access to mental health resources, not having the time to seek treatment) were likely reasons for the discrepancy between those service members needing help and those actually getting treatment.

Ron's programmatic decompensation helps to illustrate the issue of stigma in seeking treatment for mental health problems. It was not until Ron had reached a desperate state that he sought psychological treatment. By this point, Ron's problems had become severe, and he found it difficult to reconcile the events surrounding the death of his fellow unit members with his current living environment. Had Ron received treatment earlier, he might have received the aid he needed in understanding that his reactions were normal reactions to a series of traumatic events, and he could have been provided with skills to successfully cope with the problems he was facing.

Current Strategies for Helping Soldiers Cope With Traumatic Events

Early treatment for psychological symptoms resulting from exposure to traumatic events during deployments is one of the major emphasis areas in current military policy. In fact, all service members returning from Iraq and Afghanistan must receive a psychological screening prior to returning to their home station (see Wright, Huffman, Adler, & Castro, 2002, for a description of this screening program). If military personnel show psychological symptoms, they are required to meet briefly with a mental health professional who, if necessary, writes a referral for the service member to receive counseling after returning to his or her home station. In addition, service members in the United States army can now receive anonymous mental health treatment for a specified number of sessions if needed. These types of programs are specifically designed to remove stigma as a barrier to seeking treatment for psychological problems. Our guess would be that had Ron gone through a psychological screening prior to returning home, the issues he was having would have been detected and he would have received treatment much sooner.

In summary, counseling military personnel requires a recognition of the multiple cultures in which they operate and the number and types of international transitions they have encountered. The story of Ron illustrates how the cultural context of the military can interact with traumatic events (both psychological and moral) to influence the development of psychological problems. Counselors need to recognize the unique culture of the military when designing treatment approaches that will help service members deal with their symptoms and return to their units.

References

American Psychiatric Association. (2000). *Diagnostic and statistical manual of mental disorders* (4th ed., text rev.). Washington, DC: American Psychiatric Association.

Britt, T. W. (2000). The stigma of psychological problems in a work environment: Evidence from the screening of service members returning from Bosnia. *Journal of Applied Social Psychology, 30,* 1599–1618.

Britt, T. W., Castro, C. A., & Adler, A. B. (2005). Self-engagement, stressors, and health: A longitudinal study. *Personality and Social Psychology Bulletin, 31,* 1475–1486.

Campbell, S. J. (2006). What has befallen me? The psychological aftermath of combat. In T. W. Britt, C. A. Castro, & A. B. Adler (Eds.), *Military life: The psychology of serving in peace and combat: Vol. 1. Military performance* (pp. 2–11). Westport, CT: Praeger Security International.

Castro, C. A. (2006). Military courage. In T. W. Britt, A. B. Adler, & C. A. Castro (Eds.), *Military life: The psychology of serving in peace and combat: Vol. 4. Military culture* (pp. 60–78). Westport, CT: Praeger Security International.

Collins, S. (2006). Psychological operations in combat, peacekeeping, and fighting terrorism: In T. W. Britt, C. A. Castro, & A. B. Adler (Eds.), *Military life: The psychology of serv-*

ing in peace and combat: Vol 1. Military performance (pp. 283–298). Westport, CT: Praeger Security International.

Corrigan, P. W., & Watson, A. C. (2002). The paradox of self-stigma and mental illness. *Clinical Psychology: Science and Practice, 9*, 35–53.

Guilbault, R. L., Bryant, F. B., Brockway, J. H., & Posavac, E. J. (2004). A meta-analysis of research on hindsight bias. *Basic and Applied Social Psychology, 26*, 103–117.

Hensel, A. D., & Pury, C. L. S. (2005, October). *Courage in retrospect: An investigation into the roles of self-presentation and hindsight.* Poster presented at the 4th International Positive Psychology Summit, Washington, DC.

Hoge, C. W., Castro, C. A., Messer, S. C., McGurk, D., Cotting, D. I., & Koffman, R. L. (2004). Combat duty in Iraq and Afghanistan, mental health problems, and barriers to care. *The New England Journal of Medicine, 351*, 13–22.

King, L. A., King, D. W., Fairbank, J., Keane, T. M., & Adams, G. A. (1998). Resilience recovery factors in post-traumatic stress disorder among female and male Vietnam veterans: Hardiness, postwar social support, and additional stressful life events. *Journal of Personality and Social Psychology, 74*, 420–434.

Lewis, S. J. (2006). Combat stress control: Putting principle into practice. In A. B. Adler, C. A. Castro, & T. W. Britt (Eds.), *Military life: The psychology of serving in peace and combat: Vol. 2. Operational stress* (pp. 121–140). Westport, CT: Praeger Security International.

Maguen, S., Suvak, M., & Litz, B. T. (2006). Predictors and prevalence of posttraumatic stress disorder among military personnel. In A. B. Adler, C. A. Castro, & T. W. Britt (Eds.), *Military life: The psychology of serving in peace and combat: Vol. 2. Operational stress* (pp. 141–169). Westport, CT: Praeger Security International.

McGurk, D., Cotting, D. I., Britt, T. W., & Adler, A. B. (2006). Joining the ranks: The role of indoctrination in transforming civilians to service members. In A. B. Adler, C. A. Castro, & T. W. Britt (Eds.), *Military life: The psychology of serving in peace and combat: Vol. 2. Operational stress* (pp. 13–31). Westport, CT: Praeger Security International.

Miller, L. L., & Moskos, C. (1995). Humanitarians or warriors?: Race, gender, and combat status in Operation Restore Hope. *Armed Forces and Society, 21*, 615–637.

Pury, C. L. S., Kowalski, R. M., & Spearman, J. (2006). *Distinctions between general and personal courage.* Manuscript submitted for publication.

Siebold, G. L. (2006). Military culture and values: A personal view. In T. W. Britt, A. B. Adler, & C. A. Castro (Eds.), *Military life: The psychology of serving in peace and combat: Vol. 4. Military culture* (pp. 2–10). Westport, CT: Praeger Security International.

Shay, J. (1994). *Achilles in Vietnam.* New York: Touchstone.

Soeters, J., & Box-Bakx, M. (2003). Cross-cultural issues in peacekeeping operations. In T. W. Britt & A. B. Adler (Eds.), *The psychology of the peacekeeper: Lessons from the field* (pp. 283–298). Westport, CT: Praeger.

Soeters, J. L., Poponete, C. R., & Page, J. T. (2006). Culture's consequence in the military. In T. W. Britt, A. B. Adler, & C. A. Castro (Eds.), *Military life: The psychology of serving in peace and combat: Vol. 4. Military culture* (pp. 13–34). Westport, CT: Praeger Security International.

Valach, L., & Young, R. A. (2002). Contextual action theory in career counseling: Some misunderstood issues. *Canadian Journal of Counselling, 36*, 97–112.

Wright, K. M., Huffman, A. H., Adler, A. B., & Castro, C. A. (2002). Psychological screening program overview. *Military Medicine, 167*, 853–861.

The Transition From Veteran Life to the Civilian World

Marvin Westwood and Timothy G. Black

Bert (a pseudonym) is 26 years old, and when he finished high school, he got a job in construction driving the rigs. He married his high school sweetheart when he was 23 years old and now has 2- and 4-year-olds of his own. Bert was not making enough money to pay their mortgage and bills as his construction work became more irregular. Bert's uncles were both in the Canadian army and, in order to support his wife and young family, he decided to do likewise. After joining an infantry unit, he completed his work-up training and 6 months later was sent overseas on a tour of duty as a United Nations peacekeeper to Bosnia. Bert served two consecutive tours of 3 months each. As the end of his second tour was approaching, Bert was injured in a land mine incident in which his mate, hung over from the night before and not as vigilant as he could have been, missed seeing the ground antennae. Bert's leg was badly wounded and his mate, his best friend, was killed in the incident. Bert was sent home to Canada where he was given a medical discharge for the injury to his leg and after having been diagnosed with posttraumatic stress disorder (PTSD). Bert's physical injuries have left him with a permanent limp, but it is the massive guilt he experiences that is most debilitating, because he believes he should have told his friend to stay back and recover from his hangover. Instead, Bert overrode his legitimate concerns, and he now feels as though he is responsible for his friend's death.

Coming home felt like a crash landing. Bert was discharged from his military duties and did not know how he could ever fit into civilian society again. He saw himself as different from everyone except his military buddies, who were no longer around. He lost interest in his life, his work, his wife, and his children, and he has begun to withdraw into a depression, using drugs and alcohol to numb the feelings of disconnectedness and immense guilt over his friend's death. Bert's children have come to fear him and stay away from him because of his angry outbursts. Bert's wife has told him she cannot continue like this much longer.

This kind of critical incident is not uncommon for Canadian Forces members who have been sent overseas on United Nations peacekeeping missions and have witnessed or experienced the realities of war. There is a bonding that takes place in military training that sets up the mentality that military-trained people and civilians are very different. This kind of mentality is strengthened when military personnel are sent on overseas duties, especially when they are sent into war zones. Upon their return to Canada and their subsequent discharge from the military "family," many people experience a sense of isolation and aloneness in their lives as civilians, often feeling misunderstood or simply out of place in the civilian world. The truth contained in the phrase "once military, always military" can be easily seen whenever former military personnel get together. There is an instant camaraderie that exists, regardless of whether or not the individuals know each other. This camaraderie is often cited as the aspect of military life that former military members miss the most in their civilian lives.

Key Issues

The transition event here has two components. First is the transition that takes place moving from a foreign war zone back to Canada. The second is the transition from the culture of the Canadian military to civilian society. The problem is that Bert has been in a foreign war zone, and he has witnessed death and has been physically and psychologically injured "on the job." Upon returning from overseas, he received a medical discharge and returned to a civilian culture that often does not understand wounded military personnel; nor does it have the capacity to support them in their transition to a life outside the military culture. The biggest problem facing Bert is not how to heal his wounds but how to heal in a civilian culture that does not understand his point of view or his combined felt sense of allegiance to and betrayal by the Canadian Forces.

Relationship Considerations

The people involved are Bert, his wife, his two children, his case worker with the Department of Veteran Affairs, his therapist, his military buddies, and his occupational therapist. The relationships within Bert's immediate family are self-explanatory. Given the fact that Bert was medically discharged, he is supported by the Department of Veterans Affairs in receiving medical and psychological treatment for his wounds. The occupational therapist works directly with Bert on his physical injury, and his therapist, working independently of the government funding agencies, seeks to assist Bert in navigating his transition into civilian life. Bert's military buddies are all in different areas of the province but come together on weekends to relive old memories, get drunk or stoned, and party. Many of them are supportive of Bert in the best way they know how, and many of them are also struggling to find their way in civilian life.

Transition Outcomes

Because of the trauma and isolation he experienced, Bert has continued to make poor career and relationship decisions. The only place he feels like himself is when he is drinking with his buddies as they reminisce over past times. However, as Bert has continued to struggle, he has become increasingly negative in his attitude and prone to angry outbursts with them, both when drunk and sober. Currently, his friends are beginning to avoid Bert because he has become so unpleasant to be around. Bert has decided to take part in the Canadian Military and Veterans Transition Program (CMVTP) that is facilitated by his therapists. He is currently working through some of these transition issues both in individual therapy and in the group.

Writers' Role

We were involved with Bert as therapists and facilitators of the CMVTP. We have worked with him individually and in the group to help him come to terms with the trauma of his experiences and the contextual factors of living in the civilian world that make it more challenging for him to heal.

Writers' Comments

Through working with Bert, we have learned a great deal about the serious challenges that former military members who have gone overseas into war zones face, if and when they are forced to return to civilian society. We have learned that the supports for understanding and contextualizing the transition issues are not readily available. We have learned that although friends and family members may be overjoyed, or at the least relieved, to have their son or daughter back at home, they may also inadvertently add to the challenges by lacking the understanding of the most basic differences between military culture and civilian culture. For example, in the military, the rule is that military personnel look out for each other and keep each other safe and alive at all costs; they do this by following orders unquestioningly and by "watching each other's backs." A soldier may not trust his buddy enough to tell him that his wife back home has filed for divorce, but he will jump into the line of fire to try and keep him alive. This kind of mentality does not exist in the civilian world, with perhaps the exception of paramilitary organizations such as the police or fire departments. It is possible to see how there are completely different cultural contexts (military & civilian) operating here, and recognition of the differences helps explain the degree of alienation confusion and conflict that follow—especially at the point of reentry. The powerful norms of all cultural groups, which shape and influence what individuals do and how they feel, are typically implicit and not explicitly made known. People who were once from the same culture become strangers and estranged from one another upon return.

We have learned that it is not necessary to have been in the military to help a former military member, but we have also learned that we are limited in our ability to help the person feel truly understood. As such, we have learned that because military training occurs in groups, group approaches to dealing with transition can be very helpful because of the instant camaraderie and understanding that can develop. Finally, we have learned about how Canadian civilian culture, while honoring World War veterans, still has a gap to bridge in terms of supporting and understanding what modern-day veterans are faced with on their return home. In other words, the responsibility for successful adjustment not only requires psychosocial support for the returnees but also requires that the dominant culture become familiar with the cultural context of the soldier.

Reader Reflection Questions

1. What are some of the challenges that counselors might face in building an effective working alliance with clients from military backgrounds? What strategies might be used to overcome such challenges?
2. How might counselors prepare military personnel for the cross-cultural transition of returning home?
3. What considerations would you make in organizing group approaches with military personnel in transition?
4. How might counselors be involved in preparing the dominant culture for returning soldiers? What are key considerations in related programming?

Response 1

Stefan Kammhuber

The story of Bert illustrates issues that are of central relevance for internationally deployed armies. The number of international military interventions is increasing and, therefore, the frequency of soldier deployment. The demands of the operational realm associated with international military interventions differ substantially from those, for instance, of international economics cooperations or of students in international exchange programs. The stressors are more frequent and of greater intensity. Military missions occur in regions that have been, or still are, ravaged by war and crises. The soldier is confronted by unimaginable human suffering, the consequences of war and destruction, death, physical injuries and psychological suffering, the brutalization of morality, cruelty, sadism, or apathy. Soldiers experience this far away from home, under the scarcely comfortable conditions of camp life, in which they are required to contend with their homesickness, lack of privacy, restrictions to their sexuality, and so forth. Bert had never experienced these conditions during his modest, yet seemingly picturesque, life before joining the military—nor are they generally experienced by soldiers on their first deployment. Although the media provide images of war and crises, these images do not convey the emotional impact that emerges in the actual situation. These media-provided images are merged with the explicitly and implicitly propagandized image of soldiers who are able to be tough and bear struggles and inconveniences without complaint and who, if possible, do not display any weaknesses. The soldier who seeks contact with an accompanying army psychologist is readily considered to be "weak/soft" or "mentally unstable" and accordingly is deemed "unfit for combat." This impression is then internalized and becomes the benchmark for all future actions.

I deem the following issues to be of importance for subsequent counseling.

Motives Underlying Participation in the Mission

In this case incident, Bert's motives to take on a career in the military seem to be of a financial nature: a secure income that allows him to care for his family. Particularly for soldiers of lower ranks in the German Federal Armed Forces, financial motives are also an important incentive to take part in overseas deployment because the associated bonuses are appealing. At the same time, on the basis of intercultural research, it is known that the motivational circumstances of departing soldiers are closely related to the culture shock phenomenon (Thomas, Kammhuber, & Layes, 1997). Soldiers who view their deployment as an opportunity to escape from their situation at home, to seek adventure, or to improve their financial situation, without assigning the actual aim of the mission a great deal of importance, are at greater risk to yield to the burdens of international deployment than are soldiers who are able to extract meaning from their deployment and commence deployment feeling intrinsically motivated. Counseling, within the context of military deployment, can commence as early as the preparation phase, during which the clarification and reflection of the motivational circumstances of soldiers prior to deployment taking place are facilitated.

In Bert's case, the question is to what extent he was able to impart deeper meaning to his activities in Bosnia prior to, during, or subsequent to his deployment. Particularly the experience of existential borderline situations, for example the death of a friend and/or personal injury and the associated traumatization, may potentially be reinforced if the suffering that is experienced is subjectively deemed to have been futile.

This is where Victor Frankl's logotherapy, which emanates from humanism, can be readily applied. Moreover, Frankl, as a survivor of the Holocaust, aimed to facilitate a systematic process of finding meaning, that is, asking his clients what constructive, positive implications could be derived from their painful experiences. In my mind, this therapeutic component is an important constituent of the counseling process in this specific case.

Role Conflicts

Bert is in a permanent conflict of roles, which can aggravate the typical stress reaction due to his deployment conditions. Bert is a husband and father. Social and financial care is expected of him. It is in this particular context, however, in which foreign/overseas deployment proves to be the basis of conflict between these expectations. On the one hand, he strives to care for his family, yet he is required to leave them repeatedly for months at a time. Moreover, foreign/overseas deployment puts every relationship to the test, which can severely impede the soldier's capacity to fulfill the occupational demands. At the same time, Bert, the soldier, is obligated to be loyal toward his country. Foreign/overseas deployment is a component of his duties and responsibilities, even though his personal situation may be contrary to his sense of duty. Bert is also a comrade to his peers in the infantry. Although the spirit of comradeship is generally strongly manifest in the army, it is even more so in the infantry. Mutual support, even when this may entail the endangerment of one's own life and body, is a given. This sense of duty is even more intense when the peer in question is also a personal friend. Hence the feeling, even when this is unsubstantiated, that one has failed to safeguard a friend or peer is difficult to bear. After returning home, the conflicting and competing loyalties to family, peers, and country become even more obvious and, thus, even more difficult to manage than during the period of deployment. During the counseling process with Bert, it is suggested that the identification and assessment of the differing role expectations and the related intrapersonal conflicts, followed by exploring possible integrative solutions, would be very valuable.

Traumatization and Its Consequences

Through the death of his friend, his own injury, and his experiences in a war zone, Bert is suffering from traumatization, with the associated psychological and physical symptoms. Because there can be differential diagnoses, assessment would be necessary at the beginning of counseling to discern whether Bert's symptomatology is consistent with (a) an acute stress disorder, (b) posttraumatic stress disorder (PTSD), or (c) an enduring personality change after extreme stress. The three diagnostic categories differ in the length and intensity of associated stress symptoms. The description of the symptomatology, in Bert's case, suggests the third category, which is also associated with the most complicated treatment. It is characterized by a hostile and suspicious disposition toward the world, social withdrawal, feelings of emptiness and hopelessness, chronic nervousness, and feelings of estrangement, which are noticeable even after several years. In addition to pharmacological management of the accompanying physical reactions, intense counseling aimed at root causes may be able to facilitate change. Interventions might include the above-mentioned approach of logotherapy but also the careful reestablishment of a social network and the relearning of trust development and social competencies, for instance. One approach would certainly be to use Bert's peer network from the army as a resource through which he might be able to restore his feelings of self-worth, but he might also use the peer group as a "safe domain" to practice social competencies. In vivo counseling is suggested; that is, the counselor accompanies Bert in these situations until his reactions have become more stable.

Preparation, Continuous Attention, and Debriefing

Counseling, in the context of international military deployment, should be embedded in a systematic process of preparation, intermittent (slight change), and debriefing measures/interventions. A model (Winslow, Kammhuber, & Soeters, 2003; see Table 18.1), which is gradually being implemented in the German Federal Armed Forces, is suggested. It is composed of sensitization to cultural differences at the commencement of a military career, deployment-specific preparation, accompanied coaching, preparations prior to departure from the foreign region, and supportive measures subsequent to return.

According to the model outlined in the table, Bert would have had the opportunity to learn which stress factors are linked with overseas deployment, particularly the opportunity to consciously consider the exposure to death and injury, during the course of a preparational seminar/measure. Courses that deal with this difficult issue with the intention of assisting

Table 18.1
Model Used by the German Federal Armed Forces

Intervention	Goals	Time of Intervention
1. Sensitization of cultural differences	• Familiarization with the intercultural demands of the German Federal Armed Forces • Fostering cultural consciousness by realizing the certainty of cultural differences between oneself and others • Experiencing, feeling, thinking, and acting • Development and management of stereotypes and prejudices • Recognizing stress factors of acculturation	• Commencement of military career, basic training
2. Cultural and deployment-specific preparation	• Familiarization with cultural, deployment, and task-specific demands • Familiarization with the psychological dynamics of overseas deployment • Familiarization with the anticipated stress factors relevant to deployment • Development of coping strategies in the management of stress factors	• Throughout the course of deployment-specific preparations of a mission
3. Support during deployment, coaching, and counseling	• Preparation, intermittent support, and reflection of deployment situations • Counseling in crises situations, PTSD (e.g., accidents, injury, and death)	• During the course of the mission; preformed by qualified psychologists
4. Preparation prior to departure from foreign country	• Familiarization with "reentry" demands • Planning of own homecoming	• Shortly before departing foreign country
5. Support subsequent to return	• Support for the soldier and his family in coming to terms with the demands of reentry	• Subsequent to arrival within the setting of individual or group counseling

Note: PTSD = posttraumatic stress disorder.

soldiers are available at the Center for Internal Management of the German Federal Forces. Although this intervention/measure cannot preempt the actual experience, it may introduce coping strategies that could work against traumatization.

In addition, a suitably trained army psychologist could work on such grievous issues with soldiers throughout the length of deployment, either in group or individual counseling. In Bert's case, it would be necessary to discern the intensity of his traumatization, followed by a procedure to assess for PTSD. The cultural trend of "the strong male" may be a barrier if Bert fears that by taking part in counseling, he will be perceived as labile and weak and having succumbed to pressure. Nevertheless, there are ways to counteract this concern. First, in the case of individual therapy, counseling would have to occur discreetly. Another option is group counseling, which would allow Bert to experience that others, like him, have similar difficulties in coming to terms with the events of the past. Although not immediately effective, the open discussion about these issues and the exemplary behavior of senior soldiers are beneficial. For example, in the German Federal Armed Forces an educational film was produced in which a senior physician openly disclosed how he sought treatment subsequent to deployment and was thus able to fulfill his occupational demands again (Thomas, Layes, & Kammhuber, 1998).

During the postdeployment period, Bert and his family should not be left unaided but should be assisted in a systematic and goal-oriented manner. This seems to be a central factor in the history of the presenting issue in this case; that is, in addition to Bert himself, his entire social circle is affected by the traumatization. Hence, family counseling would be advised in order to elucidate the symptoms associated with trauma and how the family might support Bert in coming to terms with his experiences without being aversely affected themselves. As mentioned previously, in vivo counseling would aid Bert in coping with everyday situations, allow him to develop a sense of confidence in his behavior, and support him in the establishment of a supportive social network, which he may in turn use as a psychological resource. Bert should have further social networks in addition to his peers from the squad, because a process of separation from them will inevitably occur and, hence, lead to consequences described in this case incident. Moreover, it is important for a person to aim for integration that makes life beyond the troop or squad valued.

Conclusion

A systematic approach that includes the key persons and groups in Bert's life (i.e., family, friends, and army peers) is crucial for the success of counseling. At the same time, the military is responsible for an appropriate choice of soldiers for international deployment, the correspondent preparation for stress factors that will be encountered in deployment, the endorsement of fitting motivational factors conveyed through comprehensible explanation of the mission's objective, and qualified postdeployment care. However, central to these issues is the intermediate aim to foster the development of a military culture that distances itself from the "soldier as a fighting machine" and encourages the image of the professional soldier who is not only adept at handling weapon systems but also mindful of his or her own personality and conscious of the dynamics of psychological processes in stressful situations.

References

Thomas, A., Kammhuber, S., & Layes, G. (1997). Interkulturelle kompetenz: Ein handbuch für internationale einsätze der Bundeswehr [Intercultural competence: A handbook for international Bundeswehr missions]. In *Untersuchungen des psychologischen dienstes der Bundeswehr*. Munich, Germany: Verlag für Wehrwissenschaften.

Thomas, A., Layes, G., & Kammhuber, S. (1998). Sensibilisierungs- und Orientierungstraining für die kulturallgemeine und kulturspezifische Vorbereitung von Soldaten auf internationale Einsätze [Awareness and orientation training for the culture-general and culture-specific preparation of soldiers in international missions]. In *Untersuchungen des Psychologischen Dienstes der Bundeswehr, 33*. Munich, Germany: Verlag für Wehrwissenschaften.

Winslow, D., Kammhuber, S., & Soeters, J. (2003). Diversity management and training in non-American forces. In D. Landis (Ed.), *Handbook of intercultural training* (3rd ed., pp. 395–415). Thousand Oaks, CA: Sage.

Response 2

Alexander Cowell McFarlane

The decision to pursue a military career involves complex motivations, including a desire to serve the nation and pursue a career that poses interesting challenges and excitement. Taking on these roles always involves trade-offs in an individual's personal life and a willingness to undertake direction about the nature of service. When a member of the services is injured, the individual is faced with a very different set of expectations and adaptations. In many regards, these are universal, and the challenge for a defense force and Department of Veterans Affairs is how best to manage these transitions and disrupted lives.

The Context of War-Related Trauma

Independent of the culture or the circumstances, it is almost ubiquitous for trauma victims to have a sense of isolation and disenfranchisement. Particularly when serious physical injury accompanies the psychological wounds, an individual must adjust to an unanticipated life of struggle to overcome handicap and disability. Increasingly, the modern world is one that encourages aspiration and success and is relatively intolerant of the predicament of people who are not able-bodied and capable of living freely in a rapidly changing world. A traumatic event can leave individuals with less of a sense of the future and less of a capacity to embrace the certainties ahead, because their confrontation with death, such as Bert experienced, erodes such certainties.

Although there are heroic stereotypes of the wounded soldier, the glory and recognition that come with the status of a veteran can be quickly forgotten by the community. Victims readily evoke ambivalence because they demand, collectively, a sense of social responsibility that can be rejected by the less-empathic members of the community. As a consequence, veterans who are disabled have often been seen in a somewhat ambivalent light, particularly as the memory of the war or the humanitarian mission in which they served fades into the past.

The Struggle for Language

Another critical dimension of traumatic experiences is the struggle to express these events and the experience in a language that can be understood and embraced by those close to the veteran. No matter how able the veteran, it is always a struggle to create a truly empathic understanding of the veteran's predicament if the listener is naive to the experiential world from which the veteran comes. Neuroimaging research has also demonstrated much about how the underlying neurobiology of posttraumatic stress disorder (PTSD) represents a state of speechless terror. The very nature of this disorder is to erode the capacity for expressive language (van der Kolk, 1997). An individual such as Bert further struggles with the immense desire to forget rather than constantly revisit the haunting memories of how his friend died and the sense of horror about the threat sustained to his own life. The internal battle to manage the associated affect and preoccupation mitigates against the active exploration and free discussion of these experiences.

Because of the disinclination to explore these experiences, the individual becomes trapped in his or her own silent rumination, which is very difficult for those, including family, who have not struggled with the immediacy of threat and the haunting nature of traumatic memories. These elements are what bind some aspects of the veterans' community together. Even though there is not often much verbal acknowledgment of the fear and suffering, there is a sense of camaraderie and mutual respect in these domains. The unspoken empathy can seem to create a division from or the exclusion of family members.

The novelist Jim Jones (1963), in the *The Thin Red Line*, explored these issues when describing a scene in which soldiers were watching some comrades who had been injured in the shelling of a landing craft in Guadalcanal in the Second World War:

> They had been initiated into a strange, insane, twilight fraternity where explanation would be forever impossible. Everybody understood this; as did they themselves, dimly. It did not need to be mentioned. Everyone was sorry, and so were they themselves. But there was nothing to be

done about it. Tenderness was all that could be given, and, like most of the self-labeled human emotions, it meant nothing when put alongside the intensity of the experience. (p. 46)

Motivations for Military Service

These issues arise against the background of a further complex dynamic of being a member of a military force in peacetime. Bert's motivation was partly driven by the financial instability of his construction work, and in the hope of stabilizing these uncertainties, he joined the military, partly because of his family's tradition of service. This decision to join military life was, therefore, part of a developmental dynamic of trying to bring some stability into his life and to ensure a future for his wife and children. Ironically, this desire is in some ways at odds with the notion of giving oneself to the service of one's country, often involving putting oneself in harm's way. These complex contradictory motivations, particularly in the life of an individual such as Bert, create unusual conflicts, given that the outcome was far from what he anticipated.

Rather than stabilizing his circumstances, his injuries and his changed state of mind came to erode the very reason for his military service. The complex shifts that occur in marriages across time are a further backdrop to his predicament. His absences from his family created an emerging sense of independence in his wife. On his return as an injured soldier, his incapacity to be the breadwinner and an active participant in the future of the family left him with a sense of being a burden and dependent, the very role he wished to avoid.

Returning From Deployment

From a military perspective, there are also two important contextual issues. The first one is the management of service personnel returning from deployment. One of the greatest conceptual challenges in the field of traumatic stress has been the challenge of understanding the often-delayed presentation of psychopathology. There has tended to be the presumption that if individuals have coped with the stresses of war, the relief of homecoming will, in general, lead to an improvement in their mental health. However, it is the delayed onset and the progressively increasing perturbations that frequently occur after a passage of time that repeatedly have caught health care systems wrong-footed. The recent study of Grieger et al. (2006), one that is particularly pertinent to Bert, highlights the progressive emergence of PTSD and depression in the year after combat-related injury in the Middle East. Such a study characterizes how, in the early days and weeks, the focus on survival and the very substantial support provided in medical facilities, such as Bert received, mitigate the early emergence of distress. It is once the individual begins his or her rehabilitation and attempts the transition back to family life that symptoms of distress become more prominent. It is important not to underestimate the significance of depression in this setting (Ikin et al., 2004).

A further critical step that Bert must face is the transition from service life to civilian life. The support and camaraderie in the armed forces do much to sustain injured soldiers because of the shared ethos and respect. The unspoken support of the group serves to sustain even the identity of the injured soldier. The process of a medical discharge, then, confronts the individual with the realities of civilian life, which is far less structured and where social groups are more fluid. The lack of immediate understanding of the veteran's predicament in the civilian world potentially saps any meaning that the individual has developed to sustain himself or herself. The world of persecution and turmoil that peacekeepers are attempting to contain has little resemblance to civilized civilian life, which means there is little immediate experience for friends who are not in the armed forces and relatives to draw on to empathize with the predicament faced on discharge by an individual like Bert.

The Changed World and Veterans

In countries such as Australia, Canada, and the United Kingdom, with the death of World War I and World War II veterans, the number of veterans has been declining very significantly over the last decade. Progressively, many of the designated services that previously existed for injured veterans have been mainstreamed into community services. The new generation of veterans, such as Bert, must struggle to obtain services in an environment where their special needs do not carry the same weight as they did for a previous generation of veterans. It is, therefore, critical that there be regular reviews and networks that actively manage cases and provide opportunities for connection for veterans in Bert's situation.

The Nature of Cross-Cultural Transitions

A central element of survival in a combat environment is the capacity to depend on the man or woman standing next to oneself for vigilance and protection. Unusually intense attachments form in this environment. These bonds are the essence of survival and are the keystone around which individuals sustain themselves in the face of threat and possible death. These attachments are often unspoken and have an edge of toughness, but there is also intense loyalty. The intensity of this interdependence is in many ways ritualized and symbolized in the culture of military life; therefore, there are outward ceremonies and structures that support these relationships, but the critical element is the underlying ties and sentiment within the group.

The challenge of moving away from this environment is that when an injured soldier such as Bert returns to civilian life, the quality of attachments is very different. Those who look in from the outside come to see the preoccupation of the survivors and veterans with their old friendships as being anachronistic. The veteran feels misunderstood and isolated in a world where relationships are seemingly cast off and often transitional. In the civilian world, an individual's identity becomes the dominant theme of his or her life and choices rather than the bond of group identity that plays such a critical role in sustaining individuals in military life.

Presenting Issues

Identity Issues

The challenge in a clinical setting in managing a veteran such as Bert is to see beyond the immediate injuries and possible psychiatric diagnoses such as PTSD and depression. Of critical importance is the way in which his injuries and disabilities potentially permeate his identity and interact with his characteristic ways of coping. Given that he was seriously injured in a setting where one of his best friends was killed, it is predictable that many future encounters will act as triggers to those memories, particularly when elements of trust are involved. The injury occurred and his friend's death arose because his friend had a hangover and was not as vigilant as he should have been on the day of his death. Potential mistrust and watchfulness in relationships with those on whom he depends are, therefore, likely to be permeating issues in Bert's presentation.

This self-doubt and struggle to sustain self-esteem would be most intimately manifest in his marriage. Injured veterans often struggle with believing that they are still attractive to their partner and that they have the capacity to sustain their relationship. The challenge for Bert of reestablishing his parenting role with his children is also one of particular importance. The emotional numbing associated with PTSD can often erode an individual's capacity for empathy. This erosion cannot easily be disguised in the relationship with children.

The Challenge of Physical Injury

PTSD that arises when an individual has sustained significant physical injuries presents further unusual challenges. The pain and disability from their injuries that constantly confront individuals are potent triggers that sustain the traumatic memory. From a clinical perspective, it can sometimes be extremely difficult to ascertain whether their continued preoccupation with pain is a somatic traumatic memory or whether it is truly indicative of an ongoing organic injury. These relationships are often not consciously recognized or understood by the individual.

In an individual such as Bert who is making a series of difficult transitions, anger can often be a dominant aspect of his presentation. Anger has the immediate potential of driving away those on whom he should most depend. It is important that the irritability associated with PTSD is often used as a way of keeping emotions of helplessness and fear of dependency at bay. Quite apart from his psychological symptoms, Bert faces a major struggle in redeveloping his sense of identity in the face of these substantial injuries.

Unique Factors in This Case

For Bert, his situation is not simply his own suffering and disability. There will be many complex feelings associated with his sense of grief and loss about the death of his best friend. On one hand, he may feel a sense of guilt about not being more protective and vigilant, knowing that his friend was struggling somewhat on the day that he was killed. On the other hand, he may feel angry and let down by his friend's carelessness. Such ambivalence can be an important dynamic, disrupting the normal grief process.

Traumatic bereavements also present a particularly challenging psychological state to resolve. On one hand, the normal processing of the feelings of attachment and loss requires a regular revisitation of the relationship and a holding on to the positive memories and the life of the dead individual. The way in which his friend died, however, presents a shocking reality in which the emergence of the feelings of grief will often provoke the images and feelings of how his friend was killed. The immediate instinct is to try to avoid these horrific revisitations and distract oneself from them. As a consequence, it is much more difficult to access the normal feelings of loss and sadness that go with grief. His loss will also, therefore, make Bert struggle with situations involving responsibility and care. He will tend to oscillate between being excessively vigilant and overprotective, for example when looking after his children.

Cultural Assumptions

There is a long-standing assumption, in part reflected in the more recent treatment literature, that veterans are difficult to treat. They, therefore, provoke a sense of potential therapeutic elitism in many therapists. Also, establishing a therapeutic relationship with a veteran confronts the sense of the cultural divide of "them and us" into which veterans can retreat. It is critical that a treatment service and the people who work in it identify and deal with this dynamic.

By its nature, military life embodies a willingness to tolerate physical hardship and many deprivations of comfort. To cope in such an environment, individuals need to be willing to deny and normalize their distress and physical hardship. This attitude requires inattentiveness to one's internal states. In many regards, this is the antithesis of what is required in a therapeutic engagement, in which clients need to identify their symptoms and use introspection to guide them and hold them in the treatment process. Clearly, the demand for this complete shift is very confrontational and difficult for the veteran to manage.

Common Issues in This Population

The provision of care for veterans like Bert requires clinicians to understand the special entitlements and service arrangements that are available for veterans. Particularly in a large country like Canada where many people live in remote communities that do not have specialist services in the near vicinity, there are often special arrangements for veterans. Unfortunately, there is a disconnect between veterans and access to these services because an individual clinician may have relatively infrequent contact with veteran clients. Veterans' networks play a very important role, often through the interest of their wives and husbands at accessing these services. Using information hotlines is also an important method of accessing such information. With a client such as Bert, the progressive downhill spiral of his adaptation and relationships on his return to civilian life emphasizes the importance of early access to these different services and pension entitlements.

Implicit to the systems that support veterans is a conflict between veterans' groups reinforcing adaptive and maladaptive behaviors. Advocates for veterans are important in ensuring that members receive their appropriate entitlements; however, veterans' benefit systems need to ensure that there is not an excessive emphasis on permanent disability in order to access entitlements because individuals' adaptive capacity will frequently change with time.

Diversity of Clients

As with any group, it is easy to stereotype veterans and their behavior. It is important to acknowledge that there is a range of temperaments and motivations within these groups. Although some will identify strongly with their veteran status, others will actively seek to disengage from any reminders of military service once they return to the civilian community. Conversely, there are some who will go to extraordinary lengths to deny and minimize their psychological suffering and attempt to sustain their function in the face of considerable suffering. There will be others who develop a life mission in struggling with the bureaucracy and attacking its prevailing failures.

Counseling in International Critical Incidents

Although accepting the diversity of cultures and other important factors in the manifestation of illnesses, an often minimized fact is the diversity within cultures. As a consequence, there is a set of broad principles that can be readily applied to the provision of counseling and will only require relatively minor adaptations between cultures (McFarlane, 2000).

A modern trend, which is inescapable in the modern age of management accountability, is the development of evidence-based guidelines for treatment. The plethora of clinical trials in dealing with physical and psychiatric illness has served, in many ways, to create an environment in which clinician preference carries much less weight than accumulated evidence. However, such guidelines frequently do not address the many stages and challenges that precede engaging the individual in treatment and, equally, the fact that research is often deficient in the areas of the management of chronic illness and disability.

With an individual like Bert, the real challenge is to assist him in identifying his difficulties and accessing care. There is a series of steps involved. Predeployment briefings for family and military personnel are the beginning of an educational strategy that emphasizes issues of self-care and the importance of changed patterns of communication. Again, education and anticipation of some of the possible challenges Bert will face in his reintegration into society are central. Unfortunately, the available literature does not suggest that there is a major impact from such education programs; hence, this emphasizes the importance of the physicians and surgeons who are initially responsible for Bert's care to carry out a screening assessment of his mental state and engage a mental health professional if there is significant doubt about whether he is suffering from depression or PTSD. Counseling is involved in assisting Bert to accept the importance of this process and to see the potential benefits of early intervention to prevent secondary morbidity.

The identification of PTSD and depression alone is, however, insufficient. Bert will require many other issues to be addressed in his life, such as assistance in dealing with relationship issues and reintegration into his family. He will need specific counseling about how to work with an occupational therapist to optimize his functioning in the face of his physical disabilities. There is then the central question of his fitness for work and finding out what are the potential retraining and employment opportunities for him. Optimal counseling requires a multidisciplinary team who have a variety of skills.

Given the known risk of alcohol and drug abuse in veterans' communities as a form of self-medication, it is important that treatment address this risk, and if early patterns of substance abuse begin to emerge, that early referral occurs (Jacobsen, Southwick, & Kosten, 2001).

The choice of the type of counseling also needs to take into account the individual's temperament. There is a range of temperaments regarding the willingness to tolerate distress. Some individuals predominantly use an avoidant form of coping, and with such a group, despite the evidence for the benefits of exposure-based treatments (Foa, Keane, & Friedman, 2000; National Institute for Health and Clinical Excellence, 2005), 30% of individuals will decline this approach. Eye Movement Desensitization and Reprocessing, for which significant evidence exists about its effectiveness, may represent a method of treatment that depends less on verbal exchange with a therapist and may be more readily accepted. One of the challenges in dealing with veterans' communities—and why there may be different treatment outcomes than there are with single-incident civilian trauma—is that these are often individuals who have had multiple confrontations with death, injury, and suffering.

The challenge in the treatment environment can, therefore, be to decide which traumatic event to focus on in exposure-based treatments. One way that this has been addressed, with demonstrated benefits, is the development of in-client programs that have a group of veterans with similar experience involved in a month-long treatment program (Creamer, Morris, Biddle, & Elliott, 1999). These programs have multiple dimensions, including psychoeducation, drug and alcohol counseling, cognitive-behavioral therapy, and pharmacotherapy.

In the longer term, helping individuals with the day-to-day crises that confront them in their environment and the way that their symptoms and memories intrude is an important part of supportive long-term counseling. An individual like Bert faces many future challenges in his life, and understanding the way that his reactivity will potentially sabotage his relationships is important to explore. In so doing, it is often possible to develop preventative behaviors that will allow him to walk away from situations that would otherwise become unmanageable.

Theoretical Frameworks That Inform Response

The centrality of the response to traumatic events has dominated the understanding of nonpsychotic disorders since the late 19th century (van der Kolk, McFarlane, & Weisaeth, 1996). At the core is the fact that experiences such as combat, which involve a range of emotions such as fear and horror that are often difficult to express and characterize, come to be captured as traumatic memories, which have an unusually rich somatic sensory quality. A critical process is the repeated triggering of the memories by a range of often unrecognized environmental stimuli (McFarlane, Yehuda, & Clark, 2002). Superimposed upon this are the meaning structures and interpersonal consequences of these memories. In an attempt to manage and modulate this distress, a series of secondary and reactive strategies emerge. In essence, these are individuals who come to be intolerant of affect, and their secondary attempts of coping lead not only to the exclusion of negative emotions but also to a removal from engagement with potentially rewarding experiences in their lives and relationships.

Intervention Strategies

Bert's predicament is not an isolated or unfamiliar tale. Ultimately, his struggles will be managed better only if both his individual needs are met and a number of broader and systemic issues are addressed. At a basic level, primary prevention should be the essence of any public health intervention. Primary intervention in military settings involves creating an awareness of the risks to individuals and having training capability that increases their resilience; primary prevention should also involve screening. The core principle of secondary prevention is the early diagnosis and treatment of psychological disorders before secondary maladaptive behaviors come to dominate the individual's behavior. The evidence-based treatments that are now available are outlined above. Tertiary prevention should focus on rehabilitation and dealing with the secondary morbidities, such as relationship breakdown and drug and alcohol abuse (Jacobsen et al., 2001).

The Essential Features of Counseling

Of greatest importance in counseling traumatized individuals is the willingness of the therapist to engage with their reality. Much of Bert's life is characterized by his sense of alienation and consequent embitterment. As a consequence, any therapist must engage in anticipating what is not said as much as what is said. The prevalence of dissociative symptoms in trauma victims further highlights the importance of noting unanticipated absences of emotion or memory. This requires an unusual observational set that is contrary to the normal priority of focusing on the immediately apparent rather than on what is not obvious. As a consequence, there is a series of primary skills necessary for counseling traumatized victims.

Multicultural Issues

Modern communities such as Canada, the United States, Australia, and Europe have a considerable degree of ethnic diversity. Often minority cultures are associated with significant socioeconomic disadvantage. It should be recognized that such socioeconomic disadvantage represents important risk factors for adverse outcomes from traumatic exposures. Military service may be seen as a method of escaping such adversity and identifying to a greater degree with the mainstream culture. If an individual such as Bert becomes injured and again becomes an outsider, this can only magnify the initial stresses from which he or she wanted to escape.

Conclusion

Time does not heal all wounds. Although veterans are embraced by society to a much greater degree than are most victim groups, they also stand at significant risk of being marginalized in the life of a community as the conflict in which they were injured becomes a past rather than present-day fact. The challenge of a veterans' health scheme is both to create a cultural context in which these individuals' sense of meaning can be sustained and to provide optimal motivation for positive treatment outcomes.

Reader Reflection Questions

1. How would Bert's engagement in a counseling relationship be affected by the circumstances of his physical injury, which happened in the same incident in which his best friend was killed?

2. What are the transitions in self-monitoring and awareness that are required for a soldier, such as Bert, moving from a combat environment to civilian life, where he must engage with treatment?
3. How does Bert maintain a sense of identity as a veteran who has been injured and returned to his family after losing his ideal of using military service as a way of ensuring security for his family?
4. What are methods of approaching the challenges for Bert as a parent, particularly if he is emotionally numbed?

Acknowledgments

This work was supported by the National Health and Medical Research Council Program Grant No. 300403.

References

Creamer, M., Morris, P., Biddle, D., & Elliott, P. (1999). Treatment outcome in Australian veterans with combat-related posttraumatic stress disorder: A cause for cautious optimism? *Journal of Traumatic Stress, 12,* 545–558.

Foa, E. B., Keane, T. M., & Friedman, M. J. (Eds.). (2000). *Effective treatments for PTSD.* New York: Guilford Press.

Grieger, T. A., Cozza, S. J., Ursano, R. J., Hoge, C., Martinez, P. E., Engel, C. C., et al. (2006). Posttraumatic stress disorder and depression in battle-injured soldiers. *American Journal of Psychiatry, 163,* 1777–1783.

Ikin, J., Sim, M., McKenzie, D., Forbes, A., Creamer, M., McFarlane, A., et al. (2004). War-related psychological stressors and risk of psychological disorders in Australian veterans of the 1991 Gulf War. *British Journal of Psychiatry, 185,* 116–126.

Jacobsen, L. K., Southwick, S. M., & Kosten, T. R. (2001). Substance use disorders in clients with posttraumatic stress disorder: A review of the literature. *American Journal of Psychiatry, 158,* 1184–1190.

Jones, J. (1963). *The thin red line.* London: Sceptre.

McFarlane, A. C. (2000). Ethnocultural issues. In D. Nutt, J. R. T. Davidson, & J. Zohar (Eds.), *Post Traumatic Stress Disorder: Diagnosis, management and treatment* (pp. 187–198). London: Martin Dunitz, Ltd.

McFarlane, A. C., Yehuda, R., & Clark, C. R. (2002). Biologic models of traumatic memories and post-traumatic stress disorder: The role of neural networks. *Psychiatric Clinics of North America, 25,* 253–270.

National Institute for Health and Clinical Excellence. (2005). *The management of post traumatic stress disorder in primary and secondary care.* London: Author.

van der Kolk, B. A. (1997). The psychobiology of traumatic memory: Clinical implications of neuroimaging studies. *Annals of the New York Academy of Sciences, 821,* 98–113.

van der Kolk, B., A., McFarlane, A. C., & Weisaeth, L. (1996). *Traumatic stress: The effects of overwhelming experience on mind, body, and security.* New York: Guilford Press.

Case Incident 19

Pursuing International Humanitarian Aid Assignments

Sauli Puukari

Peter (a pseudonym) was born in 1958 to an ordinary working-class family and is the youngest of four children. He had a stable and safe childhood in a town in central Finland. He was an average student at school; his parents encouraged him to graduate from senior high school. Despite his preference for focusing on his social life, he managed the academic demands of senior high school and graduated in 1977. History and biology were his favorite subjects. He was also interested in languages but had some difficulty learning them, which he later understood was because of dyslexia. This discovery was a relief for him, and with hard work he was able to compensate for the difficulties in languages.

Six months of military service are required for men in Finland. After high school, Peter did his military service, and for a while he considered the possibility of having a military career. His sister's husband encouraged him to pursue paramedic training, and he became a paramedic/ambulance driver. Later on, he continued his education in the field of medicine, step-by-step studying to become a nurse, special nurse, and then physician and pursuing a specialization in occupational health. Today, he is working as an occupational health physician/rehabilitation physician.

Early Steps Toward International Transitions

During 1985, Peter was working as a nurse for the Finnish Red Cross and was asked if he was interested in participating in a 1-week intensive course for prospective participants of Red Cross international operations. The course had international participants and was given in English. The course was designed for participants to work long days to test their capacity to cope under stressful conditions and observe how they behave. Peter recalls he had always been interested in working abroad and testing his limits, so he liked the challenge. The following summer, after the course, he was invited to take part in a Red Cross operation in Kenya. This experience laid the foundation for pursuing his career path. It seems clear that Peter had a strong internal desire to do something challenging that involved working abroad. In 1991, Peter married Susan, who also had training in nursing and had considerable experience in the field.

The first time Peter was involved in United Nations (UN) peacekeeping operations was 1999–2000 in Kosovo during the crisis following the collapse of Yugoslavia. Before that, he had already been in a number of Red Cross operations in different parts of the world.

Gradual Steps Toward More Demanding Operations

Peter describes how he has had good opportunities to become prepared and grow for the more demanding Red Cross and UN peacekeeping operations. He acknowledges the Red Cross for the systematic work it has done to train personnel for its operations. For example, he says that his first operation in Kenya was in a reasonably stable environment and that a stable environment is often chosen as the first assignment for people interested in working for Red Cross international operations.

Critical Incident

In 1990–2000, during a Red Cross operation in Kosovo, Peter was establishing a field hospital in Albania and taking in refugees. In an interview at the end of this operation, Peter stated that he hoped that he did not have to come back to Kosovo and confront the faces of cruelty. Some of these hard experiences are described in the following paragraphs. It seems obvious that these experiences gave Peter a chance to see the more demanding side of these international operations and even consider not going back—a very understandable thought, given the experiences. Yet he did not quit: It was only a few months later he was contacted by UN peacekeeping forces who needed a physician for a Finnish battalion in Kosovo. That decision was a hard one for Peter because their fourth child was to be born soon; therefore, he first rejected the offer. However, soon after the child was born, the UN contacted him again and asked him to join the operation. After carefully considering the situation with his wife, he made the decision to participate. One can imagine the kind of dialogue that might occur in making this decision:

Peter: The man from the UN called me again asking to join their next operation.
Susan: Would you like to go?
Peter: Yes and no. I would really like to; the operations have been interesting and I have learned a lot though it is sometimes hard to be there. But we are having our baby soon.
Susan: I feel I need you here when we have the baby.
Peter: I will be here.
Susan: Well, perhaps after we have had the baby, perhaps you could go then?
Peter: Do you think so?
Susan: I think we could make some arrangements and get help from our relatives and friends.
Peter: Well, you know that . . . even it was hard in Kosovo, at the same time I feel that I can do my own part to be of help . . . and then . . . when the UN called me the second time, I must admit that I began to think about going again, but I thought it's not good given our situation at home.
Susan: I think we could do this if you can stay with me until we have the baby.
Peter: I could phone them and ask.
Susan: Good, do that.
Peter: OK, let's see how it goes.

On the basis of the available information, it seems quite clear that there were several important elements that gave Peter the motivation to continue. These include his strong original internal motivation and earlier positive experiences, contacts by the UN representatives, and the very important support from his wife. It is also noted that Peter's educational background was very suitable for international operations. According to Peter's own experiences, it was probably the second invitation from the UN that made the crucial difference and led him to reconsider continuing in the international operation. Right invitations at right times can change life paths!

The situation in Kosovo was chaotic. The first night they slept in an old factory, and for the first 6 weeks they were accommodated in a tent where they operated their field hospital during the day. During the second night in Kosovo, they received a message that a child had been wounded in a grenade explosion in a nearby village. These types of attacks usually happened at night, and they always had to go to the places in complete darkness with very little knowledge about the place where they were going. The place of the explosion, a flat, was crowded with people because a Finnish patrol was trying to keep order there. Some people shouted, "Don't come, there can be mines here!" Peter shouted from the vehicle to the patrol to order the people to leave the area in case of more grenades. As they entered the building, some Finnish soldiers warned about trip wires. Crying and shouting could be heard from the inside. Finally, it appeared that the "child" was a 58-year-old daughter of an elderly couple. A grenade had been thrown inside through a window as the family was sitting around a strong oak table, and it exploded under the table injuring them all; the daughter was the most seriously wounded one.

As Peter entered the room, there was a young soldier trying to bandage the wounds. Peter can still vividly remember the situation, which he thinks must have been a terrible experience for the young man. What was going on for him at this moment? Peter himself had already seen many serious injuries, but it was clearly a demanding situation even for him. After that night, he thought that if the situations continue to be as bad as this one, nobody can stay here longer than a month. However, Peter stayed for 6 months, in accordance with his original contract. After they had started their daily routines, these routines helped the medical personnel to "settle down." It is possible to speculate about the nature of Peter's reflections, about his dilemmas, and about how the critical incident challenged his ideas about what being a soldier was all about versus what really happened.

An Operation Aborted

The Persian Gulf Red Cross operation 1991 was in a certain sense the hardest one for Peter (and for Susan) in terms of how to readapt to normal life. The idea was that the Red Cross team would go to Baghdad to check where they could establish a hospital. All kinds of practical problems and political games made the task a difficult one. The team was stuck in Jordan and was not able to travel further. Saddam Hussein announced that the Red Cross did not want to come there even though the team was ready in Amman to move in. In the end, he did not give permission for the Red Cross to go to Baghdad. This political game continued. The team was a very good one and ready to get into action, but it was not allowed to enter Iraq. The team's members had to stay in Jordan 2 months, unable to do the job for which they were sent. When they finally returned to Finland, they all went directly to their homes. No debriefing or meeting was arranged to analyze the situation and the feelings the team members had to work through. This example illustrates how important it is to give an opportunity to express the frustrations, go through the events, and formally "close the files," even for an aborted operation.

The Demands of Peacekeeping Conditions

Peter describes how the UN peacekeeping forces serve under strict limitations regarding where they can go and who they can see. Security systems are tight. For example, when they move to certain places, they have check points where they must notify the base so that they can be looked for if something happens to them. Psychologically, the most demanding experiences have been the ones Peter has had in refugee camps where there are tens of thousands of people and only a very limited number of people taking care of them. The situations in which people have been seriously injured in explosions and the circumstances have been chaotic and uncertain have developed his capacity to focus on what can be done one step at a time.

As a doctor in the UN peacekeeping forces, Peter has mostly been responsible for the staff members of the forces. On the basis of his experiences, Peter said that the exceptional conditions require flexibility, composure, understanding and toleration of individual differences, professionalism (which means, for example, that one should not become too emotionally involved but should analyze the situation in order to make an action plan and then act accordingly), and the avoidance of risks. Yet, for some individuals, the hard conditions and circumstances can be too much. Peter remembers that some individuals, including members of the medical teams, have had psychological problems as a result of their traumatic experiences in the field operations. One of his colleagues even committed suicide. A very important aspect in tolerating the hard conditions is that one knows the contract has time limits. Peter said several times that it was easier for individuals to adapt to the field when they know that within a certain time (from some weeks to a few months) they can return home.

The Importance of the Home Front

Peter's wife Susan has given full support for his work and taken care of their children at home while Peter has been away from home in the operations. They now have six children. Susan's training and experience as a nurse provides her a good basis for understanding the nature of Peter's work. Susan also has a realistic understanding about the risks related to the Red Cross and UN peacekeeping operations. She recalls how it was easier for her to let her husband go when they had only one child, but as more children were born, she was more concerned about Peter's safety. Only once she opposed Peter's plan to take part in an operation that was supposed to take place in Afghanistan. She considered it too dangerous. Peter had already agreed to take part in the operation but canceled his participation.

Peter and Susan talked together about a possible operation beforehand and tried to weigh the positive and negative aspects, such as what could be the rewards of the participation professionally and as a human being and how demanding it might be for the family. As a father of six children, Peter also has to consider the financial aspects related to the possible operations. Sometimes the departures can be very sudden, and, therefore, they both see that it is important to discuss matters thoroughly enough so that when the time comes, it is possible to make the final decisions quickly. For Susan, the most challenging situation was when Peter went to Kosovo. Her friends' encouraging words meant a lot to her: "Of course you can manage well if you only remember to ask help when you need it." According to her experiences, the people who stay on "the home front" need good self-esteem and practical skills in organizing and prioritizing things and need not to demand too much from themselves and not to live according to others' expectations but to live their own life. During the operations, Peter and Susan were in contact through letters and, when phone connections worked, via telephone or by using text messages with mobile phones. Susan says that is important to trust that Peter is not foolhardy, but she understands that there are risks in these operations.

Coming back from field operations to work as a "normal" medical doctor in Finland is sometimes a big contrast to the extreme conditions in catastrophe or war zones, where people have often lost everything and may be seriously injured; in the regular job, people see a doctor primarily to complain about small aches and problems. Regarding adaptation, Peter has found that coming back is more difficult than going to the operations abroad. The Red Cross organized good debriefings (with only the one exception that has been previously described). However, according to Peter's experiences, the discussions with his wife Susan have been the most helpful for him. Now, he can usually readapt to Finland quite quickly, within 2 or 3 days. He just has to find the other "me" upon returning to the regular job as an occupational health physician. He has also realized that it is helpful for him to give presentations to schools and other organizations about his work in the international operations, and, of course, this is an excellent opportunity for other people to learn from him.

Key Issues

Peter is an excellent example of a person who has been acting according to the happenstance perspectives on career choices (see, for example, Krumboltz & Lewin, 2004; Mitchell, Levin, & Krumboltz, 1999). Peter has a very broad understanding of the field of nursing and medicine and an interest in working abroad and "testing his limits." According to Peter's experiences, the transitions to international Red Cross and UN peacekeeping operations have not been particularly difficult for him. This is probably due to his personal characteristics, his versatile work experiences that he obtained step-by-step, and his good relationship with and support from his wife.

Peter's story is a reminder that it is important to select the personnel participating in demanding international operations carefully and to screen the situation in the field. Particularly important is the role of leaders in these operations. Peter pointed out that good leadership was of great help in many difficult situations, and the lack of leadership caused uncertainty among the personnel. It is impossible to know whether a person is capable of participating in relief and peacekeeping operations before he or she has participated in the initial training and has had the first actual experiences. Therefore, career planning requires consideration of how to proceed step-by-step, gaining more experiences, and only then moving forward to more challenging operations.

Generally, Peter acknowledges the organizational support provided by the Red Cross for its way of organizing the operations and training and supporting the participating personnel before, during, and after the operations. Debriefing after field operations is critical. Although Peter's relationship with his wife provides considerable support for reviewing his experiences, not all personnel have this level of support. The aborted operation in Iraq, which ended without a meeting, underscores the importance of follow-up meetings to deal with the situation and the frustrating experiences of the people involved in the operation.

As can be seen from Peter's experiences as a nurse and a doctor in a number of international Red Cross and UN peacekeeping operations, the cultural differences are often not as important as the demanding field conditions, regardless of the country where the operation takes place. Therefore, it is important to point out to prospective staff members to be prepared to confront difficulties even though they may already have experience in international projects in more secure and "normal" environments.

The Role of Counseling

What could, then, be the role of counseling in an international case incident like Peter's? What type of counseling is needed and who should be providing it? It is obvious that guidance and counseling in a broad sense should be integrated into the activities of the organizations involved in international aid interventions and peacekeeping operations. In other words, a systemic approach is needed to provide peacekeeping personnel (either civil or military) with step-by-step education and the needed guidance and counseling services throughout the whole process. This is essential to help with cross-cultural adaptation and in facing sometimes very extreme circumstances and situations. Mentoring can be used to provide new personnel with the needed support in field conditions, where experiences in previous assignments are very valuable. Also, systematic use of peer support (which is emphasized during the initial training) is important.

Constant monitoring of the physical and mental state of the workers is also one of the key elements in taking care of personnel. On the basis of this monitoring, proper support and counseling can be provided according to the workers' personal needs. This systemic approach requires good leadership and a clear division of work in the organization and should be evaluated on a regular basis in order to identify possible deficiencies and new needs that require updating of organizational support and counseling services.

Given the special circumstances of field operations, too many formalities in guidance and counseling services would not work well, and the people who are responsible for providing counseling are more successful when they are regarded as members of the team rather than as distant professionals in their offices. Before and after the operations, counselors can be used, if requested, to help personnel in making decisions on whether to join an operation and to cope with adapting to the field and coming home. In the field conditions, guidance and counseling are also available upon request, but they should also be given on the basis of the constant monitoring, as described previously, and be a natural, informal part of the daily routines, along with peer support and mentoring.

Conclusion

The roles of counselors in international aid interventions and peacekeeping operations can be many, and counselors should be flexible in meeting the needs of workers. According to the ideas in Atkinson, Thompson, and Grant's (1993) article, at least the following roles can be identified: adviser, advocate, consultant, change agent, counselor, and psychotherapist. Given the complexity of the roles and field circumstances, all this calls for a systemic approach and team work, which is characteristic of all successful international operations whether in international aid or in peacekeeping.

Reader Reflection Questions

1. On the basis of Peter's story, how would you respond as a counselor if your client was interested in pursuing an international Red Cross or UN peacekeeping operation? What kinds of questions would you ask your client? What would you recommend if a client asked for your advice about participating in an international peacekeeping operation?
2. Suppose that your client has returned from an international operation and is requesting counseling for his or her future career options. How would you deal with your client's experiences in the operation and how would you start discussing his or her future options?
3. Close relationships ("the home front") are very important when people travel abroad to participate in demanding operations that carry risk. Suppose that a couple seeks counseling when they are considering whether or not one of them should join an international operation. How would you respond as a counselor when addressing the important aspects in making the decision?
4. Circumstances and conditions in the field operations can be very difficult, and the personnel may have to confront extreme situations. Suppose that you were counseling the staff members who were leaving and returning. What could you do to help them deal with difficult situations and circumstances? What hints are evident in Peter's story that might be useful for counseling?
5. Dealing with questions related to the demanding international field operations requires a great deal from a counselor. What kinds of networks are important for the counselor, and how could he or she use these networks (e.g., other professionals) as part of the counseling process?

References

Atkinson, D. R., Thompson, C. E., & Grant, S. K. (1993). A three-dimensional model for counseling racial/ethnic minorities. *The Counseling Psychologist, 21*, 257–277.

Krumboltz, J. D., & Lewin, A. S. (2004). *Luck is no accident: Making the most of happenstance in your life.* Atascadero, CA: Impact.

Mitchell, K. E., Levin, A. S., & Krumboltz, J. D. (1999). Planned happenstance: Constructing unexpected career opportunities. *Journal of Counseling & Development, 77*, 115–124.

Response 1

Claire O'Reilly and Julia Bürger

The world, as we know it, is changing and people are increasingly moving voluntarily and involuntarily across their familiar cultural and geographical territories. The need for humanitarian aid and related services is, at the beginning of the 21st century in many areas, still acute. One need only think of recent ongoing wars and feuds in Afghanistan and Iraq or the dramatic and violent situation in Darfur. Nongovernmental organizations provide critical humanitarian aid in war and politically unsafe environments. The case of Peter as nurse and later physician in international humanitarian assignments brings to light the demands on persons living and working in such environments. The well-known analogy that overseas business expatriates must function along the lines of superwomen and supermen is much more apt in the case of humanitarian aid workers who—apart from the "normal" stressful events that accompany an intercultural transition —work in perilous and hazardous environments, confronted with tragic human suffering and often making life-impacting decisions. The consequences to the individual are not only in terms of possible loss of life, but the experience can challenge and question the most sure-footed and stable of personalities. The need, therefore, for the management and counseling of humanitarian aid assignments and strategic thought behind each phase of the assignment is paramount, for the individual and family, the host country nationals, and the sending organization (a systemic approach, as the author of the case incident stated, is clearly needed).

Reflecting on the body of academic literature published to date in terms of work-related overseas assignments, we see that the vast amount of experiences documented has been for the business and expatriate community (notable examples in the last 10 years include Black & Gregersen, 1999; Black, Gregersen, & Mendenhall, 1992, on American expatriates; O'Reilly, 2004, on German expatriates; Stahl, 1998; Suutari & Brewster, 1999, 2003, on Finnish expatriates) and for students (Furnham & Bochner, 1982; Ward & Kennedy, 1993). One focus of increasing research attention has been the provision and appropriateness of health care (including the psychological health) of migrants and minority groups (Cheatham et al., 1997; Ponterotto, Casas, Suzuki, & Alexander, 1995). The case of foreign aid workers has in the past also received some attention (Kealey, 1989; Ward & Rana-Deuba, 2000), as have the case of defense forces and military personnel (e.g., Winslow, Kammhuber, & Soeters, 2004), although the case of medical personnel in the discourse of work-related foreign assignments in war zones has been largely neglected. A few isolated examples deal with aspects of physicians in the military and defense forces. The work of Thomas, Layes, and Kammhuber (1998), for example, examined the preparation and training of the German Defense Forces and the cultural differences and stress factors with which the soldiers have to deal while on assignment. Except for a book by Danieli (2002) relating observations and confessions by peacekeepers, humanitarian aid workers, and journalists in war zones, we do not know of an empirically grounded study in the English or German language that examines the nature of the adjustment of physicians in war zones. In our response, we therefore apply the literature on international sojourns to Peter's case where appropriate; this, in turn, will also be helpful to understand some of the counseling perspectives of physicians on humanitarian assignments.

Apart from culture-learning theories, which are important but in Peter's case not the dominant point of interest, we are adopting a stress and coping framework to understand the nature of cross-cultural transitions and adaptation (see, for example, Berry, 1997; Ward, Bochner, & Furnham, 2001), recognizing that the factors affecting cross-cultural adjustment are much the same as the factors involved in adapting to other transitional experiences—always involving loss and change for the individual and also presenting opportunities for personal and professional growth (Kim, 2001). The stress and coping framework for acculturation (see Berry, 1997) points at the significance of life changes and stressors during cross-cultural transitions (in Peter's case proving hugely significant) and the selection and implementation of coping strategies according to one's internal (i.e., personality characteristics) and external (i.e., social support, to this we will later return) resources (Ward et al., 2001).

This case incident of Peter touches on and resonates with all the topics found in the literature on overseas assignments and underlines the importance of careful consideration in the selection of personnel (the presence of certain personality traits over others), preparation and debriefing/training, coping resources for a successful assignment, proven professional expertise, and the gradual development of skills required for increasingly demanding tasks. Although each of these topics merits in its own way attention, there are three points we would like to examine further. We first turn our attention to the role of ongoing social support during a foreign operation: According to the case incident, "During the operations, Peter and Susan were in contact through letters and, when phone connections worked, via telephone or by using text messages with mobile phones." Second, the words "Regarding adaptation, Peter has found that coming back is more difficult than going to the operations abroad" is a reminder that the management of the operation on the part of the sending organization is not completed with the safe return of the worker to base. The third point is highlighted by these words from the case incident: "As can seen from Peter's experiences as a nurse and as a doctor in a number of international Red Cross and UN peacekeeping operations, the cultural differences are often not as important as the demanding field conditions, regardless of the country where the operation takes place." Using this statement, we raise the question of the fundamental role of culture in the humanitarian assignment.

The Role of Ongoing Social Support

Peter's case clearly points at the demanding conditions under which all members of Red Cross or UN peacekeeping operations have to operate. Particularly for humanitarian aid workers, high stress levels, correlated with danger, can be an unavoidable daily reality. Drawing parallels from a related study, Kammhuber (2000) described problem areas (*Belastungsfaktoren*) of military personnel on peacekeeping assignments: These included individual adjustment problems (e.g., lack of privacy, unstructured daily routine, which were apparent in Peter's case in Kosovo), separation from family (which applies in this case also), conditions in the country (e.g., climate change, language problems, hardship through suffering), conditions of operation (e.g., degree of danger, remaining neutral, working in multicultural groups, and questions of competence), and dealing with injuries and death. Although some of these problems were less pronounced in Peter's case than others, the nature of medical humanitarian assignments means that all of these problem areas are likely to arise at some stage or another of the operation. Social support is one very important moderating variable of adjustment before, during, and after a transition and has an emotional/affective, an instrumental, and an informative component (see Furnham & Bochner, 1986). As the most important external resource for coping, social support correlates with aspects of emotional well-being during transition (cf. Ward, 1996). Sources for social support can be many: the immediate partner and family, working peers, the sending organization, and host country nationals. The social support in Peter's case mainly comes from his wife Susan, but peers, good leadership, and preparation and debriefing units offered by the sending organization are also named in this case. What is not mentioned, but should not be forgotten, are host country nationals, who can also be an important source of social support (cf. Bennhold-Samaan, 2003). Even though under the circumstances described in Peter's case, it is the host nationals themselves who mainly need help, they, in fact, can prove to be a very helpful source of social support to the international aid workers, given not least their local and cultural knowledge of the country and their insights into the sources of cultural misunderstandings.

Support by the sending organization, in the form of counselors, leaders, and mentors (as suggested in the case incident), is very important when it comes to avoiding health problems or helping in the case of traumatic experiences. Because traumatic experiences in such situations are not only something with which the host country population has to contend but also face humanitarian personnel in operations, professional counseling concerning mental health should be provided ("constant monitoring" as suggested by the author of the case incident). In this respect, a study by Ehrenreich and Elliot (2004) points at the existing lack of stress management for humanitarian aid workers in U.S. nongovernmental organizations. They suggested that at least the opportunity to attend stress training or receive knowledge about posttraumatic stress disorder (PTSD) be given to people going to or returning from a foreign assignment. (Perhaps it is also part of the preparation Peter received, but this is not explicitly stated.) Peter related, for example, that some of his peers had to be sent home or could not cope with the situation and that one of his peers even committed suicide. What is important to underline here, in addition to what is said by the author of the case incident, is that reactions to the often traumatic environments are *not only* a matter of the personality of the individual but are also shaped by the dynamic within the person–situation context. Not being able to cope does not mean that the selection process failed but rather highlights the crucial nature of the counselor's role in accompanying the individual within the particular personality–context/environment constellation.

Another aspect, important for counseling, is that many members of military forces or humanitarian aid professionals do not report or admit to themselves that they might have been traumatized, especially if they have already experienced many very challenging situations without developing clinical symptoms. A case in point is that of German military physician R. Erös who, after many years in Afghanistan, described an incident of psychological collapse (traumatization) after having seen the most horrific war situations over a long time. His decision to seek counseling only came when his wife gave him an ultimatum to seek help, acknowledging that she did not know her husband anymore. In his autobiographical book, Erös (2002) tried to encourage those with such experiences to seek professional help immediately and not to wait for months as he did. Counselors in such a setting should be aware of the symptoms of acute stress disorder and PTSD and provide help as quickly as possible.

The primary source of social support comes from within a person's immediate family. Given the turbulent situation for the humanitarian aid workers during the assignment, a feeling of stability in this one important aspect of their lives is paramount to the outcome of the assignment. In Peter's case, emphasis is put on the supportive role his wife Susan plays. We learn that she provided support in the following ways.

- Was willing to accept her husband's career path
- Gave her full support to Peter's work—her background as a nurse being helpful in understanding his work

- Was in a position to voice her objections in one case to his returning to operations in Kosovo after their fourth baby was born

The shaping and the outcome of the assignment are closely connected to this support, echoing experience in the research literature time and again (i.e., expatriates with supportive partners are considered the most successful, personally and professionally, followed by singles; Harvey, 1985; O'Reilly, 2004). The least effective cases have been found to be expatriates whose partners opposed the foreign assignment in one way or another. The mutual discussion of Peter's plans and his consideration of his wife's objections to some of his assignments, as stated in the little conversation they had, is a very positive example of how the different needs and wishes of both sides are taken into account and the positive effect of this on the overall assignment.

Although the situation is clearly not an easy one for Susan, she has the personal resources to cope and gets support from her friends and relatives (for emotional as well as organizational problems that can occur while Peter is away). This situation is almost an ideal one, which cannot be expected of all people entering a comparable foreign assignment. It is therefore necessary to include the family of the sojourner in counseling, particularly in light of the fact that the family at home is left in a stressful situation (in terms of separation, not knowing exactly how the partner is doing, being reduced to a one-parent family during the operation), while at the same time conscious of providing support for the family member abroad. The establishing of self-help groups (*Selbsthilfegruppen*) or the like for these families, in addition to the possibility of receiving counseling by the sending organization, could be one way forward. This seems particularly relevant given a recent study on secondary traumatization in partners of Dutch peacekeeping soldiers (Dirkzwager, Bramsen, Adèr, & van der Ploeg, 2005). This study revealed that peacekeepers' stress reactions were related to various problems of their partners; therefore, a systemic approach to the treatment of persons with PTSD appears appropriate.

After the Assignment Is Over

According to the author of the case incident, "Regarding adaptation, Peter has found that coming back is more difficult than going to the operations abroad." This experience on reentry (defined as the process of reintegration into primary home contexts after an intercultural sojourn; Martin, 1984) is very similar to the experiences of other types of sojourners. Difficulties returning home are well documented and present challenges for sojourners and also for their families, friends, and colleagues (Black & Gregersen, 1999; Gaw, 2000). Most of the research on reentry is based on the idea of reentry as the endpoint in a linear process of leaving home, going overseas, and returning. The fact that an increasing number of individuals leave and return to their original "cultural contexts" multiple times, as in Peter's case, is often overlooked (Martin & Harrell, 2004). One can expect (and Peter himself says so) that having done the adaptation–readaptation process repeatedly, it becomes easier with time. On reentry, there are two key experiences that need to be reflected in counseling. First, it is important to acknowledge that a person does not return to home as it was, but instead that the once familiar environment has moved on and also changed. "The problem is this word home. It suggests a place and a life all set up and waiting for us" (Storti, 1990, p. 99). As returning individuals will find out, home is not "waiting" for them, and the fact that the family unit has in some way negotiated a life without the partner and parent can come as a shock to the individual. The second aspect refers to changes *within* individuals because of their experiences on assignment. Their returning state of mind can hardly grasp the simplicity of the normal daily routine, particularly if returning from hazardous war zones. As Peter related, "Coming back home from field operations to work as a 'normal' medical doctor in Finland was sometimes a big contrast to the extreme conditions in catastrophe or war zones; . . . in the regular job, people see a doctor to complain mostly about small aches and problems."

Another important aspect lamented by sojourners on returning home is the lack of application of their overseas experiences to their daily routines (Thomas, Kinast, & Schroll-Machl, 1999). As one sojourner related, "I felt a strange sense of displacement. . . . [The next moment I was back home], where no one was interested in hearing about the most incredible experience of my life" (Martin & Harrell, 2004, p. 312). The integration of experiences abroad, both in a professional and personal capacity, has been found to be an important aspect of personal growth and the sense-making process on reentry (see Bossard & Peterson, 2005). In this regard, one way Peter found helpful to integrate his experiences on returning home was his active step to give talks to schoolchildren and organizations. Alternatively, one possibility would be to use Peter's experiences by getting him involved as an adviser or speaker on the operations for people who are going out to similar humanitarian assignments. One last point we would like to underline is that reentry adaptation is most successful if facilitated by participation in reentry training before or after the sojourner's return home (in Peter's case, we know that a debriefing was forthcoming). Without reentry training covering both personal adaptation issues and professional reintegration issues, "the intercultural sojourn becomes encapsulated (J. M. Bennett, 1993), tucked away in the mind of the sojourner, and the opportunity is lost to integrate the personal growth and professional knowledge into the sojourner's current life" (Martin & Harrell, 2004, p. 311). The complex nature of the changes discussed above regarding reentry necessitates a reflected and informed take on the professional and personal challenges of the entire assignment from the counseling perspective.

The Fundamental Role of Culture

The author of the case incident makes the following point: "As can be seen from Peter's experiences as a nurse and as a doctor in a number of international Red Cross and UN peacekeeping operations, the cultural differences are often not as important as the demanding field conditions, regardless of the country where the operation takes place." Although the case of Peter shows that cultural differences and implicit cultural value systems did not seem to hinder his work, we would still like to emphasize that the importance of culture and cultural differences is often not realized by sojourners, because a person does not usually or consciously reflect on culture. In terms of counseling, we would therefore be cautious to assume that intercultural preparation might not be necessary in these cases. On the contrary, learning about cultural differences concerning medical care (which often has to do with the "worth of individual lives") can prove very worthwhile in preparation for the operation.

In their study on soldiers in the German Armed Forces in peacekeeping missions, Thomas et al. (1998) illustrated particularly well that brushing aside cultural aspects in the international deployment of physicians cannot be afforded. The authors related examples of physicians in Somalia who were stressed by several incidents. We learn of cases in which they were forced to see patients die because families objected to life-saving operations (namely the amputation of a limb to save lives). Another example was of a physician in Afghanistan who treated patients (men, women, and children) in order of the severity of their injuries—normal practice in Germany—which, in fact, left him without patients after a time. His decisions about who was to be treated when did not correspond with the value system of his patients and made his decisions suspect from their perspective (see Thomas et al., 1998).

Turning to the work environment of humanitarian assignments, we see that culture plays a role here too, particularly because the workforce on site is a diverse, multicultural one. Significant differences have been noted when forces from the North Atlantic Treaty

Organization (NATO) work with non-NATO countries (Winslow et al., 2004). Maillet (1998) conducted an ethics survey with Canadian Forces members and found that cultural tensions are prevalent in multinational deployments (e.g., differences on substantive ethical issues such as participating in the black market, gender integration).

Although there might not be ample time for extensive predeparture intercultural training, counseling and briefings with the individual must take a number of points into consideration: Some knowledge about the situational context; health and health provision; preferred communication styles and certain cultural taboos; and how to deal with problems arising from these issues on a cognitive, affective, and behavioral level should be included, and a mentor should be designated to provide information and help in such a situation. Apart from an informative exercise, ensuring that appropriate expectations are created is particularly important in light of findings by Rogers and Ward (1993) that discrepancies between expectations and actual experiences caused feelings of impaired psychological adjustment. Crossing cultures is a dynamic, complex process. Although there is no substitute for experience, understanding the context is crucial. Cross-cultural exposure is not cross-cultural knowledge or understanding (Bennhold-Samaan, 2003).

In this response, we have examined the case incident of Peter as a physician in humanitarian assignments and extrapolated three aspects that we believe are some of the cornerstones of counseling for this very specific group. This is not to be seen as an all-inclusive analysis of the complexities of the counseling tasks for this group; rather, we felt it important to highlight the aspects of social support and role of the "home front" in the final phase of the operation—namely, returning home—and, last but not least, the very question of the cultural trappings of humanitarian overseas endeavors. The counseling and mentoring of such individuals are complex, ongoing processes that demand continuous learning over time.

References

Bennhold-Samaan, L. (2003). The evolution of cross-cultural training in the Peace Corps. In D. Landis, J. M. Bennett, & M. J. Bennett (Eds.), *Handbook of intercultural training* (pp. 363–394). Thousand Oaks, CA: Sage.

Berry, J. W. (1997). Immigration, acculturation, adaptation. *Applied Psychology: An International Review, 46,* 5–34.

Black, J. S., & Gregersen, H. B. (1999). *So you're coming home.* San Diego, CA: Global Business.

Black, J. S., Gregersen, H. B., & Mendenhall, M. E. (1992). *Global assignments: Successfully expatriating and repatriating international managers.* San Francisco: Jossey-Bass.

Bossard, A. B., & Peterson, R. B. (2005). The repatriate experience as seen by American expatriates. *Journal of World Business, 40,* 9–28.

Cheatham, H. E., Ivey, A. E., Ivey, M. B., Pedersen, P. B., Rigazio-DiGilio, S. A., Simek-Morgan, L., et al. (1997). Multicultural counseling and therapy: The fourth force. In A. E. Ivey, M. B. Ivey, & L. Simek-Morgan (Eds.), *Counseling and psychotherapy: A multicultural perspective* (4th ed., pp. 131–206). Boston: Allyn & Bacon.

Danieli, Y. (Ed.). (2002). *Sharing the front line and the back hills. International protectors and providers: Peacekeepers, humanitarian aid workers and the media in the midst of crisis.* New York: United Nations.

Dirkzwager, A. J. E., Bramsen, I., Adèr, H., & van der Ploeg, H. M. (2005). Secondary traumatization in partners and parents of Dutch peacekeeping soldiers. *Journal of Family Psychology, 19,* 217–226.

Ehrenreich, J. H., & Elliott, T. L. (2004). Managing stress in humanitarian aid workers: A survey of humanitarian aid agencies' psychosocial training and support of staff. *Peace and Conflict: Journal of Peace Psychology, 10,* 53–66.

Erös, R. (2002). *Tee mit dem teufel: Als deutscher militärarzt in Afghanistan* [Tea with the devil: As a German military doctor in Afghanistan]. Hamburg, Germany: Hoffmann & Campe.

Furnham, A., & Bochner, S. (1982). Social difficulty in a foreign culture: An empirical analysis of culture shock. In S. Bochner (Ed.), *Cultures in contact: Studies in cross-cultural interaction* (pp. 161–198). Oxford, United Kingdom: Pergamon Press.

Furnham, A., & Bochner, S. (1986). *Culture shock: Psychological reactions to unfamiliar environments.* New York: Methuen.

Gaw, K. F. (2000). Reverse culture shock in students returning from overseas. *International Journal of Intercultural Relations, 24,* 83–104.

Harvey, M. G. (1985). The executive family: An overlooked variable in international assignments. *Columbia Journal of World Business, 20,* 84–92.

Kammhuber, S. (2000). *Interkulturelles lernen und lehren* [Intercultural learning and teaching]. Wiesbaden, Germany: Deutscher Universitätsverlag.

Kealey, D. J. (1989). A study of cross-cultural effectiveness: Theoretical issues, practical applications. *International Journal of Intercultural Relations, 13,* 387–428.

Kim, Y. Y. (2001). *Becoming intercultural: An integrative theory of communication and cross-cultural adaptation.* Thousand Oaks, CA: Sage.

Maillet, P. (Ed.). (1998). *Canadian Forces ethics and peacekeeping survey report.* Ottawa, Ontario, Canada: National Defence Headquarters, Defence Ethics Program.

Martin, J. N. (1984). The intercultural reentry: Conceptualizations and directions for future research. *International Journal of Intercultural Relations, 8,* 115–134.

Martin, J. N., & Harrell, T. (2004). Intercultural reentry of students and professionals: Theory and practice. In D. Landis, J. M. Bennett, & M. J. Bennett (Eds.), *Handbook of intercultural training* (pp. 309–336). Thousand Oaks, CA: Sage.

O'Reilly, C. (2004). *The expatriate life. A study of German expatriates and their spouses in Ireland.* Frankfurt, Germany: Lang.

Ponterotto, J. G., Casas, J. M., Suzuki, L. A., & Alexander, C. M. (Eds.). (1995). *Handbook of multicultural counseling.* Thousand Oaks, CA: Sage.

Rogers, J., & Ward, C. (1993). Expectation-experience discrepancies and psychological adjustment during cross-cultural reentry. *International Journal of Intercultural Relations, 17,* 185–196.

Stahl, G. K. (1998). *Internationaler einsatz von führungskräften* [The international assignment of managers]. Munich, Germany: Oldenbourg.

Storti, C. (1999). *The art of crossing cultures.* Yarmouth, ME: Intercultural Press.

Suutari, V., & Brewster, C. (1999). International assignments across European borders. In C. Brewster & H. Harris (Eds.), *International human resource management—Contemporary issues in Europe* (pp. 183–202). London: Routledge.

Suutari, V., & Brewster, C. (2003). Repatriation: Empirical evidence from a longitudinal study of careers and expectations among Finnish expatriates. *International Journal of Human Resource Management, 14,* 1132–1151.

Thomas, A., Kinast, E.-U., & Schroll-Machl, S. (1999). Entwicklung interkultureller handlungskompetenz von international tätigen fach- und führungskräften durch interkultureller trainings [The development of intercultural competence for international managers by means of intercultural training]. In K. Götz (Ed.), *Interkulturelles lernen—Interkulturelles training* [Intercultural learning–Intercultural training] (pp. 97–122). Munich, Germany: Mering, Hampp.

Thomas, A., Layes, G., & Kammhuber, S. (1998). *Sensibilisierungs- und orientierungstraining für die kulturallgemeine und die kulturspezifische vorbereitung von soldaten auf internationale einsätze* [Sensitivity and orientation training for the culture-general and culture-specific preparation of soldiers on international assignments]. Munich, Germany: Verlag für Wehrwissenschaft.

Ward, C. (1996). Acculturation. In D. Landis & R. S. Bhagat (Eds.), *Handbook of intercultural training* (2nd ed., pp. 124–147). Thousands Oaks, CA: Sage.

Ward, C., Bochner, S., & Furnham, A. (2001). *The psychology of culture shock* (2nd ed.). London: Routledge.

Ward, C., & Kennedy, A. (1993). Psychological and socio-cultural adjustment during cross-cultural transitions: A comparison of secondary students at home and abroad. *International Journal of Psychology, 28*, 129–147.

Ward, C., & Rana-Deuba, A. (2000). Home and host culture influences on sojourner adjustment. *International Journal of Intercultural Relations, 24*, 291–306.

Winslow, D., Kammhuber, S., & Soeters J. L. (2004). Diversity management and training in non-American forces. In D. Landis, J. M. Bennett, & M. J. Bennett (Eds.), *Handbook of intercultural training* (pp. 395–415). Thousand Oaks, CA: Sage.

Response 2

Karen Grant

This case offers an interesting complexity: The stress of spending the better part of 2 decades working internationally in humanitarian aid compounded with exposure to a critical incident seems to be less problematic for Peter than the psychological adjustment required upon returning home. Peter readily acknowledged the stress of providing aid to refugees throughout his 14 years with the International Red Cross (IRC) but emphasized the difficulty he had adapting to normal life after an aborted mission to Baghdad. In Kosovo, Peter found himself confronted by the "faces of cruelty" for the first time and was exposed to a critical incident involving a grenade bombing of civilians. Yet, despite these numerous international transitions under distressing circumstances and his exposure to civil war, Peter concluded that the worst difficulty he ever had was trying to "find the other me" when he returned periodically to his regular job. Obviously, the factors that sustained Peter psychologically during prolonged and acute periods of great stress did not equally mitigate his homecomings. The question, then, is to identify these psychological factors and find ways to evoke their reemergence through counseling.

The answer seems to lie in viewing the complexity of Peter's experience from the perspective of cultural identity transitions. His international transitions are far less disruptive than the shifting of values, beliefs, and actions among the various cultural identities within which he finds himself. Specifically, his various group memberships constitute many cultures, with intersecting similarities and differences. These cultures can be identified as Finnish military, medicine, International Red Cross, and family. This response considers the similarities and gaps among these intersecting cultural identities and their subsequent effects on Peter's responses to stressful events. Following this discussion are suggestions concerning therapeutic approaches that may aid Peter in reestablishing cultural identity coherence upon returning home.

Cultural Identity

The Social Self

The concept of identity as a static, self-referential presence has been revised by social constructivist theory. Embedded in the notion of cultural identity is the social constructionist argument for a dynamic "multiplicity of selves" that are formed and maintained by social relationships (Apker & Eggly, 2004; Shotter & Gergen, 1994). Thus, it is in the sense of "connectedness and belonging" (Brewer & Gardner, 1996, p. 83) and in the delineation of difference that the self is understood. Because an individual can belong to multiple social groups, different socially constructed identities can coexist and be in the foreground or background, depending on the context (Brewer & Gardner, 1996; Robinson, 2005). The interaction of these identities and the relative attributions of power they may have in a given context shape the process of meaning-making about events and experiences (Robinson, 2005).

Closely related is the concept of identity congruence, a proposition from social identity theory that relates psychological well-being to the level of internal and social identity consistency (Suh, 2002). Unlike social constructionist theory, social psychology maintains the notion of a personal, idiosyncratic self that interacts with social contexts. However, research in this area has indicated that group identification is in itself predictive of psychological health (Cameron, 1999). It has also shown that individuals incorporate the perspectives of these group identities and will interpret stressful events according to the group reaction (Tucker, Sinclair, & Thomas, 2005).

Culture

Most commonly, culture is defined as the ubiquitous, often invisible, patterns of deeply learned beliefs, behaviors, and values that are shared among members of a group, transmitted over time, and distinguish one group from another (Robinson, 2005). Culture shapes the way people see the world and maintains social consistency by providing the framework through which they know how to relate to other people, nature, time, and activities. Traditionally, the term has primarily applied to nationhood and ethnicity; however, other theorists (e.g., Chao & Moon, 2005) have proposed a multidimensional view that incorporates the intersecting layers of individual, group, societal, and universal values and behaviors. Cultural identities at the group level include race, gender, class, sexual orientation, and other dimensions of human difference that have socially constructed meaning and status (Hansen, Gama, & Harkins, 2002). The group level also includes organizational identities and their subsequent values and beliefs (Chao & Moon, 2005). Thus, culture can broadly mean the "socially shared aspects of experience and knowledge" (Fukuyama, as cited in Hansen et al., 2002, p. 164) and apply to any distinct and significant social group.

Cultural Transition

The transition process between cultures has been widely recognized as a stressful life event, which is made more so by vast differences in values, beliefs, behaviors, and communication processes (Berry, 1997). Integration into the new culture involves a process of personal and sociopolitical forces that shape which cultural beliefs and actions are kept, discarded, or added (cf. Robinson, 2005; Sue & Sue, 2003). A full discussion of acculturation and assimilation processes is beyond the scope of this response. It is important, however, to note that the incorporation of difference seems to contribute to psychological health (cf. "bicultural identity"; Trimble & Thurman, 2002).

The term *sojourner* is used to describe an individual who temporarily resides in different ethnic cultures, commonly for work reasons. Often, the experience of the sojourner remains that of the outsider because time is usually insufficient to allow for acculturation or assimilation processes to develop (Swaglert & Jome, 2005). In this situation, successful adjustment to the transition depends on both personal characteristics and social group parameters that guide cultural knowledge and degree of contact (Berry, 1997; Swaglert & Jome, 2005). It has been suggested that the adjustment by sojourners is best facilitated by belonging to groups that are structured and professional and least facilitated by less-defined roles such as those offered by Peace Corp or missionary positions (Church, 1982). However, in Peter's case, it can be argued that being a member of the medical personnel assigned to assist peacekeeping missions meant his transitions were supported by a structured, professional role even while being in the midst of more stressful situations. Moreover, Peter's international transitions as a sojourner are mediated by cohesive organizational cultures (military, International Red Cross, peacekeepers) that limit and define interaction with the new culture. More will be said about professional and organizational identities later in this response.

Peter's Cultural Identities

Regarding social group membership, Peter can be said to belong to multiple cultures and to hold different or similar concepts of his identity than do other members of these groups, depending on his sense of connectedness and belonging to the groups. In order to assess the similarities and gaps among these intersecting identities, a description of each value and belief system is necessary.

The overarching culture to which Peter belongs is Western European, which has often been described as promoting the values of individualism, competition, and direct action (e.g., Sue & Sue, 2003). Certainly, some of the values Peter acquired from his family fit within this paradigm: the virtue of hard work and persistence and the self-worth associated with overcoming a challenge. Embedded in this framework are his group identities, the values of which coincide with his earliest learning, but also expand to include a collectivistic perspective.

The first group identity the case introduces is Finnish military culture. Military culture is pervasive among Finnish people because of Finland's extensive conscription system. All male citizens at the age of 18 are assigned 6 months of military service, and the small percentage who are exempt are required to serve twice the amount of time in public service (Cordier, 2005; Silvonen, 2004). The military exerts tremendous socialization processes, both formal and informal, that create identification with the group (Tucker et al., 2005). Its culture has been described as one that embraces hierarchical relationships, collectivistic goals and actions, ritual and tradition, and enduring alliances (Krueger, 2000). An individual's adjustment to military life is influenced by the attitude of the home culture toward military activity (deVries, 1996). Since World War II, Finland has maintained a deep national commitment to security and peacekeeping on a global scale, while preserving the value of neutrality (Cordier, 2005). Thus, it seems safe to assume that Peter's transition into the military would have posed no real difficulties. In fact, its values would have been seamlessly entrenched in the larger Finnish cultural system.

Next, Peter entered what may be broadly called the medical culture, where he was predominately influenced by the perspectives of emergency medicine. The idea that professions can be social identities is supported by social psychology's research on organizational identity and occupational stress (Johnson, Morgeson, Ilgen, Meyer, & Lloyd, 2006). According to this theory, the values, beliefs, and behaviors of an organization, such as the military, or "extraorganizational" (Johnson et al., 2006, p. 498) groups, such as occupations or professions, can form the social context of a person's self-concept.

Peter's professional identity was first influenced by the paramedic culture. Linton (1995) has characterized emergency personnel as viewing "the opportunity to be socially responsible and help others as their primary reason for their choice of role" (p. 567). Furthermore, this group embraces the values of autonomy, action, dedication, conservatism, and self-control (Linton, 1995)—values easily integrated with Peter's early life and military experience.

Peter's switch to nursing for the Finnish Red Cross also incorporates a similar cultural perspective. Nursing culture is defined by a common group purpose based on an ethics of care (Suominen, Kovasin, & Ketola, 1997). Also, there is high value placed on group cohesion and interaction, and, like the military and paramedic culture, a dress code signifies belonging and status in the larger medical culture. The similarities continue in the reliance on ritualized actions and procedures, which create safety and trust, and the hierarchical relationships, which determine power and social interactions (Suominen et al., 1997).

The process through which medical students become acculturated to their profession has been well documented (Apker & Eggly, 2004). Specifically, physician culture is described as valuing objectivity, authority, hierarchical social order, autonomy, commitment, and motivation within an ethics of care. Here too, are found symbols of status, ritualized actions and procedures, and a high degree of professional group alliance. It is interesting, though, that the greatest emphasis in physician culture is placed on the qualities of emotional distance, objectivity, and authority (Broadhead, as cited in Apker & Eggly, 2004). As such, it seems possible that Peter's cultural identity as a physician provided him with additional values, beliefs, and actions to withstand the stress of treating combat injuries.

Before working directly with peacekeeping emergency medicine, Peter was involved in setting up hospital and medical care for the IRC. The IRC functions to mitigate the effects of war on civilian populations, while maintaining neutrality (Kellenberger, 2003). Help is offered within the principle of independence, with a focus on fostering the reemergence of autonomy and self-reliance among the population. The seven principles upon which all missions function are humanitarianism, impartiality, neutrality, independence, voluntary service, unity, and universality (International Red Cross and Red Crescent Movement, 2000). IRC culture, then, also provides congruence with Peter's other cultural identities.

Acting on a request from the United Nations, Peter next offered medical support for the Finnish peacekeepers in Kosovo. This switch from IRC to peacekeepers, Peter claimed, was not particularly difficult. Very likely it was easy because of the obvious similarities in goals and objectives and also possibly because of his earlier exposure to the Finnish military. The Finnish peacekeepers are a combination of civilian and military personnel whose primary goal is to coordinate postwar crisis management before international aid organizations arrive (Ryhänen, 2005). The value orientations of this peacekeeper culture include an ethics of care; justice; duty; efficiency; knowledge; and strong, supportive group attachments (Ryhänen, 2005). Again, this culture holds values, beliefs, and actions similar to Peter's other cultural identities.

Peter's transitions home to family are welcomed respites because there, too, his cultural identities remain coherent. His wife was trained as a nurse and, therefore, shares a medical-culture orientation. As well, Susan supports IRC missions and is familiar with the values and beliefs of military and peacekeeping cultures by virtue of being Finnish. As a couple, they value objectivity in their decision making, discussing positive and negative effects, professional and personal advantages, and financial aspects before taking action. Susan herself takes pride in being practical, organized, self-directed, and able to set priorities, qualities that she believes help her cope with Peter's absences. She also places high value on the support derived from interpersonal relationships.

As is apparent, the cohesiveness among Peter's various cultural identities is high. In each identity described so far, Peter is supported in maintaining the values, beliefs, and actions he holds to be most important. The case incident offers a summary of Peter's self-described value orientation: He values hard work, determination, challenge, duty, practicality, flexibility, tolerance of difference, composure, professionalism, emotional detachment, objectivity and analysis, prompt and efficient action, sensibility, good leadership, and the importance of family. In addition, his choice of professions indicates a strong orientation to justice, humanitarianism, and altruism. It remains, then, to look at his cultural identity as an occupational health physician to discover why that transition alone proves difficult.

Overall, the field of occupational health deals with the areas of industrial hygiene, fit-for-work assessments, physical safety hazards, ergonomics, and disease control (Macdonald, Ritchie, Murray, & Gilmour, 2000). In a study done on training needs for this profession, Macdonald et al. found that the preferred emphasis was on diagnosis and risk assessment, research, and law and ethics. The demands of the profession, however, also require skills in health promotion and management. Clearly, occupational health culture has some similarities with other medical cultures; however, it is in resolving the differences that Peter's transitional stress can be alleviated.

Therapeutic Considerations

As Peter's therapist, it would be important to pay attention to his experience of occupational stress, acute stress, and readjustment stress. The approach discussed here is derived from narrative therapy and social constructionist theory (cf. White & Epson, 1990). Briefly, such an approach considers reality as subjective and performative through social discourse. A client's problem is considered to be created by these contextual discourses, and the purpose of the therapeutic conversation is to coconstruct alternative discourses that may prove more helpful. The therapist listens for the meaning, or "narrative," the client gives to his or her actions and for the dominant discourses that created this narrative. Then through dialogue, therapist and client form an alternate story that emphasizes a preferred outcome. To begin in Peter's case, the therapist may want to deconstruct her or his idea that Peter's traumatic experiences are the problem.

Recognizing Resilience

Psychological resilience has numerous, although closely related, definitions. For the purpose of this discussion, resilience is described as "a general frame of reference or belief system that guides human beings in coping with environmental challenges" (Maluccio, 2002, p. 596). There is evidence that failure to recognize resiliency in clients can have a negative effect on therapy (Bonanno, 2004). Before approaching Peter's narrative of traumatic experiences, therefore, it would be more helpful to listen for his narrative of resilience.

Occupational stress is defined as chronic, work-related stress that is associated with symptoms of depression and reduced work performance (Revicki & Gershon, 1996). Research on emergency medical service workers and physicians has found that they are particularly vulnerable because of the "uncontrollable nature of their work, multiple practice settings, and potentially dangerous environments" (Revicki & Gershon, 1996, p. 391). However, if they experience role ambiguity and diminished or no support in their work environment, they are even more susceptible. Peter found the occupational stress of providing medical care to refugees psychologically demanding, but he was able to sustain himself in this work for more than 14 years. In his words, he attributes his ability to cope to flexibility, composure, understanding and toleration of difference, professionalism, emotional distance, reasonableness, and the ability to analyze and act accordingly. All of these attributes are sustained by the value and belief systems of most of his cultural identities. This cohesion of identities provides a sense of psychological well-being (MacNamee, 1992). Also, the dominant discourse among these cultural identities is that of positive meaning-making. Each group's interpretation of stressful events is that they exist in a context of purposeful, socially responsible, and time-limited action.

Therapeutically, Peter's apparent resilience to occupational stress could be explored by looking at how his lived experience was accommodated by the dominant discourses of those cultural identities. Evidence that these discourses were a necessary support for Peter in this context is that he found the aborted mission to Baghdad the most frustrating. As the case points out, it was the lack of a debriefing opportunity that made the situation difficult for all. Communal conversations, such as debriefings, produce a narrative of reintegration with the group and, thus, reconstitute identity (MacNamee, 1992). When this is not present, and the client is affected negatively as a result, the therapeutic conversation can deconstruct the narrative of marginalization and reconstruct the experience of inclusiveness. For example, the therapist could challenge the dominant, decentralized narrative by asking: What are you doing now that challenges the belief that you are "not yourself"?

Accordingly, Peter's experience of a critical incident could also first be explored for the narrative of resilience. Critical incidents, as originally defined, pertained to "any situation faced by emergency personnel that causes them to experience emotional reactions at such a level as to potentially interfere with their ability to function either during the event or after" (Mitchell, as cited by Linton, 1995, p. 567.) Again, this type of traumatic experience also creates a breach between self and others. Attachments are undermined, even ruined, resulting in a loss of an individual's self-concept as formed by the relational world (Herman, 1992). According to MacNamee (1992), individuals who locate themselves in their lived experience of being in crisis will describe their sense of marginalization with the imagery of being lost, unanchored, or different. For example, they might refer to themselves as "having no center," "not myself," or "flawed." Remember, this is the type of language Peter uses to describe his experience of returning home. In contrast, he simply refers to the critical incident as challenging his ideas of soldiers' experience.

A therapeutic concern here would be around creating a discourse that focuses on the belief that he was in crisis or that he needs to be identified with the crisis. As MacNamee (1992) pointed out, "someone is likely to think of herself as a 'person in crisis' as she engages in conversations and interactions with others who cooperatively construct such an identity for her" (p. 189). Clearly, the social discourses at the time of Peter's critical incident allowed him to construct a cohesive narrative about situations in which people were seriously injured from explosions as contributing to the development of his "capacity to focus on what one can do one step at a time," as the author of the case incident stated. This belief is consistent with the value and belief systems of his cultural identities and likely contributes to the resiliency he displays. Listening therapeutically for the emergence of this coherent narrative is crucial to the foregrounding of his resilience and to the creation of a new cultural identity narrative that incorporates his occupational health physician identity.

Mapping Identities

As introduced earlier, the discontinuity of self that Peter experiences in his civilian occupation can be viewed as arising from a narrative that privileges the gaps between this cultural identity and the others. It is in this culture that Peter experiences himself as decentered, lost, marginalized from his dominant identities; thus, the therapeutic process would be one of mapping the intersections among his cultural identities to construct an alternate story of cohesion.

To begin, the therapist might ask Peter how he views his situation. Listening to his description of his lived experience as an occupational health physician will allow both Peter and the therapist to hear the dominant story of difference. Arising from this narrative, the gaps between the value and belief system of occupational health physician culture and the other cultures will become apparent. Likely, Peter's narrative will draw attention to the predominance of lateral relationships (multidisciplinary teams) instead of hierarchical ones; less access to quick, decisive action; less sense of group cohesion and purpose; low-risk context; less challenging personal and situational demands for action; fewer direct results; less recognition; less autonomy; an emphasis on research and assessment; the goal of maintenance and prevention; and a focus on caring as opposed to emotional distance (especially in the areas of health promotion/prevention). The value and belief differences, then, seem to be the value of safety over risk, preparation over rescuing as a method of care, process over action, equality of knowledge over hierarchical, and lengthy consideration over quick decision.

Rather than focus on the "problem," the therapist could begin to coconstruct the preferred outcome of integration by being curious about Peter's lived experience as an occupational health physician in the following ways (adapted from suggestions in Parry & Doan, 1994).

- How is it that you have chosen to believe that this occupation has less meaning?
- What will make it hard for you to change your story?
- How are you supported and strengthened in your work as an occupational health physician?
- What would you want to bring with you from your career in humanitarian work to your experience of being an occupational health physician?
- How do you imagine accepting the belief that your experience of being an occupational health physician expands and includes your experience as an IRC physician?

Another method within the narrative framework would be to use circular questioning to introduce the perspective of "others" in characterizing this identity (MacNamee, 1992). Here, the therapist would ask how others might describe him as an occupational health physician. It might even be a good opportunity to bring Peter's wife in to integrate the narrative with her views of him in this profession. Ideas drawn from circular questioning create connections among relationships, crucial to the development and maintenance of social identity.

From these conversations, an alternate story of similarities among cultural identities will emerge that may emphasize the common beliefs and experiences of ritualized actions and procedures, reliance on authority, objectivity and neutrality in providing assessments, duty to report and protect, the goal of restoration to normal functioning, and the "capacity to focus on what one can do." In doing so, Peter will be able to transition permanently to occupational health physician culture with a sense of well-being.

Conclusion

This response has offered the idea of approaching Peter's experiences as cultural identity transitions, in which the cultural transition process was most difficult between his international humanitarian work and his home occupation. It has also offered the suggestion that Peter's seemingly not having as much difficulty with occupational stress and the trauma of a critical incident be viewed from the perspective of honoring and maintaining his narrative of resilience. Possibly, the similarity of values, beliefs, and actions among the various cultural identities that were present in Peter and that prepared him for humanitarian work, and the social discourses that arose from these cultural identities, sustained Peter's identity cohesion and connectedness. Finally, this response suggests a narrative approach to facilitate the integration of Peter's occupational health physician identity through social discourse. Overall, Peter's case is an example of disruption among the social discourses that form and sustain people's multiplicity of selves and that must, then, be resolved through reconnecting conversations.

Reader Reflection Questions

1. How would you, as Peter's therapist, elicit information about the value and belief systems of his various cultural identities? What questions would you ask? Would you introduce the idea of cultural identity?
2. If Peter and Susan were to have conflict about his occupational readjustment, how would you approach couple therapy? How would you facilitate a discussion in which Susan reveals her need to have Peter stay home permanently with

his family and Peter expresses his fear that he will not be able to tolerate being limited by civilian life?

3. Changes in family dynamics, such as Peter's transition to full-time parent, can produce tensions and difficulties among family members. How would you address parenting difficulties in couple or individual therapy? What would be your approach if you were the children's therapist?

4. Sociopolitical attitudes about the validity of a peacekeeping mission can change dramatically, depending on outcomes. As a therapist, how could you be of help to Peter if he felt discredited in his international work because of negative media portrayals of a mission?

References

Apker, J., & Eggly, S. (2004). Communicating professional identity in medical socialization: Considering the ideological discourse of morning report. *Qualitative Health Research, 14*, 411–429.

Berry, J. W. (1997) Immigration, acculturation, and adaptation. *Applied Psychology: An International Review, 46*, 5–34.

Bonanno, G. (2004). Loss, trauma, and human resilience: Have we underestimated the human capacity to thrive after extremely aversive events? *American Psychologist, 59*, 20–28.

Brewer, M., & Gardner, W. (1996). Who is this we? Levels of collective identity and self-representations. *Journal of Personality and Social Psychology, 71*, 83–93.

Cameron, J. T. (1999). Social identity and the pursuit of possible selves: Implications for the psychological well-being of university students. *Group Dynamics: Theory, Research, & Practice, 3*, 179–189.

Chao, G., & Moon, H. (2005). The cultural mosaic: A meta-theory for understanding the complexity of culture. *Journal of Applied Psychology, 90*, 1128–1140.

Church, A. T. (1982). Sojourner adjustment. *Psychological Bulletin, 91*, 540–542.

Cordier, S. (2005). Finland's armed forces: Continuity and change. *Scandinavian Review, 93*(1), 54–59.

deVries, M. (1996). Trauma in cultural perspective. In B. van der Kolk, A. McFarlane, & L. Weisaeth (Eds.), *Traumatic stress: The effects of overwhelming experience on mind, body, and society* (pp. 398–413). New York: Guilford.

Hansen, L., Gama, E., & Harkins, A. (2002). Revisiting gender issues in multicultural counseling. In P. Pedersen, J. Draguns, W. Lonner, & J. Trimble (Eds.), *Counseling across cultures* (5th ed., pp. 163–184). Thousand Oaks, CA: Sage.

Herman, J. (1992). *Trauma and recovery.* New York: Basic Books.

International Red Cross and Red Crescent Movement. (2000). *The fundamental principles.* Retrieved March 10, 2007, from http://www.redcross.int/en/default.asp

Johnson, M., Morgeson, F., Ilgen, D., Meyer, C., & Lloyd, J. (2006). Multiple professional identities: Examining differences in identification across work-related targets. *Journal of Applied Psychology, 91*, 498–506.

Kellenberger, J. (2003). Keynote speakers: The consequences of humanitarian crises. *Refugee Survey Quarterly, 22*(4), 19–26.

Krueger, G. P. (2000). Military culture. In A. E. Kazdin, *Encyclopedia of psychology* (Vol. 5., pp. 251–259), Washington, DC: American Psychological Association.

Linton, J. C. (1995). Acute stress management with public safety personnel: Opportunities for clinical training and pro bono community service. *Professional Psychology: Research and Practice, 26*, 566–575.

Macdonald, E. B., Ritchie, K. A., Murray, K. J., & Gilmour, W. H. (2000). Requirements for occupational medicine training in Europe: A Delphi study. *Occupational and Environmental Medicine, 57*(2), 98–105.

MacNamee, S. (1992). Reconstructing identity: The communal construction of crisis. In S. MacNamee & K. Gergen (Eds.), *Therapy as social construction* (pp. 187–199). London: Sage.

Maluccio, A. (2002). Resilience: A many-splendoured construct? [Review of the book *Resiliency: An integrated approach to practice, policy, and research*]. *American Journal of Orthopsychiatry, 72,* 596–599.

Parry, A., & Doan, R. (1994). *Story re-visions: Narrative therapy in the postmodern world.* New York: Guilford.

Revicki, D., & Gershon, R. (1996). Work-related stress and psychological distress in emergency medical technicians. *Journal of Occupational Psychology, 1,* 391–396.

Robinson, T. (2005). *The convergence of race, ethnicity, and gender: Multiple identities in counseling* (2nd ed.). Boston: Pearson Education.

Ryhänen, T. (2005). The moral orientations of Finnish peacekeepers. *Journal of Beliefs and Values, 26,* 17–28.

Shotter, J., & Gergen, K. (1994). Social construction: Knowledge, self, and others and continuing the conversation. *Communication Yearbook, 17,* 3–33.

Silvonen, K. (2004). Conscientious objection in Finland. *Peace Review, 16,* 207–209.

Sue, D. W., & Sue, D. (2003). *Counseling the culturally diverse: Theory and practice* (4th ed.). New York: Wiley.

Suh, E. (2002). Culture, identity consistency, and subjective well-being. *Journal of Personality and Social Psychology, 83,* 1378–1391.

Suominen, T., Kovasin, M., & Ketola, O. (1997). Nursing culture—Some viewpoints. *Journal of Advanced Nursing, 25,* 186–190.

Swaglert, M., & Jome, L. M. (2005). The effects of personality on the adjustment of North American sojourners in Taiwan. *Journal of Counseling Psychology, 52,* 527–536.

Tucker, J., Sinclair, R., & Thomas, J. (2005). The multilevel effects of occupational stressors on soldiers' well-being, organizational attachment, and readiness. *Journal of Occupational Health Psychology, 10,* 276–299.

Trimble, J., & Thurman, P. (2002). Ethnocultural considerations and strategies for providing counseling services to Native American Indians. In P. Pedersen, J. Draguns, W. Lonner, & J. Trimble (Eds.), *Counseling across cultures* (5th ed.). Thousand Oaks, CA: Sage.

White, M., & Epson, D. (1990). *Narrative means to therapeutic ends.* New York: Norton.